MOGG'S HANDBOOK

FOR

RAILWAY TRAVELLERS;

OR,

REAL IRON-ROAD BOOK:

BEING AN

ENTIRELY ORIGINAL AND ACCURATE DESCRIPTION OF

ALL THE TRAVELLABLE RAILWAYS

HITHERTO COMPLETED;

POINTING OUT

THE STATIONS, PRINCIPAL AND INTERMEDIATE,

ON ALL THE VARIOUS LINES.

TO WHICH ARE ADDED,

𝔗opographical 𝔖ketches

OF

THE SEVERAL CITIES, MARKET TOWNS, AND REMARKABLE VILLAGES;

AND DESCRIPTIVE ACCOUNTS OF THE PRINCIPAL SEATS OF THE NOBILITY AND GENTRY;

THE ANTIQUITIES, NATURAL CURIOSITIES, AND OTHER REMARKABLE OBJECTS IN THEIR VICINITY.

THE DETAILS

Deduced from Official Documents,

The Historical and Statistical portions from the best authorities, and the whole further enriched by many interesting particulars, the result of personal investigation.

𝔍llustrated by 𝔐aps.

BY EDWARD MOGG,

EDITOR OF "MOGG'S PATERSON'S ROADS,"

"MOGG'S POCKET ITINERARY," "MOGG'S PICTURE OF LONDON," ETC.

THIRD EDITION, WITH AN APPENDIX.

LONDON:

PRINTED FOR THE PROPRIETOR,

EDWARD MOGG,

14. GREAT RUSSELL STREET, COVENT GARDEN.

1846.

LONDON:
Printed by A. SPOTTISWOODE,
New-Street-Square.

ADVERTISEMENT

TO THE THIRD EDITION.

In presenting to the Public the Third Edition of his Hand-Book, rendered necessary by the entire sale of the former, and subsequent completion of several additional lines, the Proprietor begs to return his grateful thanks for the patronage with which he has been honoured, and favourable reception of his first effort at embodying in one general work the Railways of England, obviously required by the abandonment of Road and introduction of Railway travelling, now almost universal, to the principal places in the kingdom.

To the gentlemen generally connected with the different lines, from whom, in the course of its construction, he has derived assistance, but in particular to G. Stephenson and G. P. Bidder, Esqrs., J. Walker, Esq., J. K. Brunel, Esq., J. Braithwaite, Esq., F. Giles, Esq., J. Locke, Esq., and Captain Moorsom; and to F. Swanwick, Esq., T. Woodhouse, Esq., G. Dixon, Esq., J. Birkinshaw, Esq., S. Cabry, Esq., and J. Gibbs, Esq., he tenders the tribute of his humble thanks.

Aware that in entering on a subject of such absorbing interest he had ventured on an arduous task, and with an anxious desire to maintain his professional reputation, his best endeavours have been exerted to render the present volume worthy of the gigantic works it describes, that from their grandeur, magnitude, and extent, may with propriety be classed among the noblest efforts of British skill and enterprise.

Of these, among which are many that, abounding in scenery of the most grand and romantic character, alike fertile in subjects for the pen and pencil, are some that, well worthy of illustration, will doubtless assume the form of separate and more expensive publications; but as in that shape they would be of little service to the general traveller, the present for his purpose will prove the better plan. The principal features of them, to the Public the most important part, are here pointed out; no object of interest has been omitted; nothing has been exaggerated; on the contrary, faithfully to describe them has long occupied the attention of the Public's most obedient humble servant,

EDWARD MOGG.

Great Russell Street, Covent Garden,
    July 1846.

PREFACE.

If Itineraries that from their acknowledged utility have hitherto universally been held an indispensable accompaniment to travelling with pleasure upon turnpike-roads, a knowledge of which from their several details, could alone be gathered from such productions, it thence becomes obvious that a work descriptive of its railways must be equally a desideratum with all, but more particularly with that class of tourists who would enjoy, while exploring, the beauties of England.

Travelling with railway trains will be found very different to journeying by coaches, where a well-informed guard or intelligent driver was generally at hand ready to answer some few inquiries at least of the inquisitive passenger. On the contrary, the conductor of the railway train is too far removed from the majority of the company, consisting perhaps of 150 persons, to hold communication with any but the surrounding few; and as no intervening village inn is passed at which from some honest Boniface information might be occasionally derived, it follows as a matter of course, that from the pages of a work devoted thereto can alone be obtained anything satisfactory upon the subject.

To supply this deficiency, *Mogg's Handbook for Railway Travellers* is respectfully submitted to the public, in the hope that its pages, while conveying information, will prove not wholly uninteresting, and relieve the *ennui* occasionally experienced by tourists to whom a journey of 100 miles, even when performed at the rapid rate of railway travelling, may at times prove tedious.

The public will, it is not improbable, in the pages of the present work recognise — if the Editor may indulge in so great a liberty — an old friend with a new face. With his former works upon travelling,—his road-books in particular—the public have long been familiar; and to such as have hitherto honoured him with their preference, he trusts he may with confidence appeal in testimony of his capability for this undertaking.

In conclusion, he has only to remark that the same degree of accuracy by which his previous productions in a similar department have been hitherto distinguished will be clearly discernible throughout the pages of the present work, the details of which, as regards the line, have all been deduced from official documents, the topographical accounts drawn from the latest authorities, and the accuracy of names effectually ensured by an enlightened and extensive correspondence.

Great Russel Street, Covent Garden,
     July, 1816.

CAUTIONARY NOTE.

PRIOR to entering upon a description of the Railway, the Editor deems it his duty to throw out a few hints, attention to which will be amply repaid, and the pleasure of the journey be thereby increased, but, disregarded, will in all probability place persons inexperienced in this mode of conveyance in situations of great embarrassment, and, by possibility, personal danger. Travellers are therefore strictly enjoined to remember that *railway* is very unlike *road* travelling; that instead of journeying in a company of sixteen persons, the usual stage-coach complement, more than six times that number not unfrequently travel by one train, and that consequently the accumulation of luggage, being proportionate, requires more particular attention. In some of these establishments numbers are adopted, one of which is given to the traveller, the other attached to his trunk, that not unfrequently occupies a place on the top of the carriage in which he sits, — a mode of arrangement at all times desirable, but perhaps, from its quantity, not always attainable. The traveller whose equipment can be contained in a carpet bag, which may be placed under the seat he occupies, will find himself upon quitting the carriage in an enviable position compared with him who has to select his luggage from that of perhaps 150 persons.

To the arrangements of any company by whose carriages he proposes to travel the tourist will find it his interest rigidly to conform; they will, their extent considered, be generally found complete.

The ticket given to the passenger upon payment of his fare must be carefully preserved till demanded of him, as its loss would entail upon him a repayment of the money, which, though perhaps eventually recoverable, is an object attainable only at a great loss of time — a sacrifice to which travellers in haste can very rarely submit.

The Editor would strongly impress upon all persons intending to travel by railway trains, and who possess the leisure for early preparation, not to leave to the last moment application for a ticket, when from the confusion consequent upon a numerous assemblage, and anxious endeavour to keep the time, any mistake made in the receipt of change it may then be too late to rectify. Clerks in coach-offices have been known to profit largely by occasional errors thus committed, (unintentionally of course) and clerks at railway stations (the Editor speaks from experience) seem not a whit more honest. In these cases both coach proprietors and railway directors are alike blameless; and as the remedy for such losses may in many instances prove not worth the seeking, the public thus put upon their guard will doubtless in all possible cases by early application avoid the opportunity for their commission, and thereby considerably diminish the chances of such acts of delinquency.

Lastly, it is imperative upon every person intending to travel by railway to remember that the regularly appointed stations, all herein pointed out, and distinguished throughout in the itinerary line by an asterisk, thus (*) are the only places at which he can enter or quit the carriages; indeed the caution to retain his seat cannot be too often repeated, for though occasional stoppages at the stations might permit of his quitting, it is by no means desirable that he avail himself of the opportunity. In proof of this assertion it is only necessary to remind the reader of the fate of Mr. Huskisson, upon the opening of the Liverpool and Manchester Railway, in 1830, who lost his life from incautiously quitting the carriage, and standing unconsciously upon the line. The rapidity of the trains set at defiance the ordinary calculations of carriage speed, and subject all persons remaining on the rails to the chance of accidents that, when encountered, generally prove fatal. Not to create unnecessary alarm, however, it is due to truth to observe that the best possible means for their prevention have been provided in the shape of platforms, denominated, in accordance with their appropriation, arrival and departure parades: they are constructed on a level with the bottom of the carriage and between these platforms (which will be found at each end of the line, and at most, but not all, of the principal stations) the carriages draw up, and the transitions either to or from them are thereby rendered perfectly secure. But there are some stations, for instance, where the railway runs upon a level with the surrounding country, or occupies, as in a case of deep cutting, a narrow defile where passengers alight upon a level with the rail, and to these the Editor would particularly direct the attention. It needs therefore only to remark, that the public, thus cautioned, will of themselves be henceforth enabled to provide against the chance of accident.

Persons intending to travel by open carriage should select a seat with their backs to the engine, by which means they will avoid the ashes emitted therefrom, that in travelling generally, but particularly through the tunnels, prove a great annoyance; the carriage the farthest from the engine will in consequence be found the most desirable. Effectually, however, to guard against so great an evil, it may be found advisable perhaps to follow the practice recently introduced by the frequenters of Epsom, who in dusty weather have latterly adopted the use of the veil, the best possible protection to the face and eyes.

A TABLE OF DISTANCES ON THE LONDON AND BIRMINGHAM RAILWAY.

	LONDON	Harrow	Watford	Boxmoor	Berkhampstead	Tring	Leighton	Bletchley	Wolverton	Roade	Blisworth	Weedon	Crick	Rugby	Brandon	Coventry	Hampton
HARROW	11½																
WATFORD	17¾	6¼															
BOXMOOR	24½	13¼	7														
BERKHAMPSTEAD	27¾	16¼	10¼	3½													
TRING	31¾	20½	14¼	7¼	4												
LEIGHTON	40¾	29½	23¼	16½	13¼	9											
BLETCHLEY	46¾	35¼	29	22¼	19	11	6										
WOLVERTON	52½	41	34¾	28	24¾	20¾	11¾	5¾									
ROADE	60	48½	42¼	35½	32¾	28¼	19¼	13¼	7½								
BLISWORTH	62½	51	44¾	38	34¾	30¾	21¾	18¾	8½	2½							
WEEDON	69¾	58¼	52	45¼	42	38	29	23	17¼	9¾	7¼						
CRICK	75¼	63¾	57½	50¾	47½	43½	34½	28½	22¾	15¼	13	5½					
RUGBY	83¾	72¼	66	59¼	56	52	43	37	31¼	23¾	21¼	14	8½				
BRANDON	89¼	77¾	71½	64¾	61½	57½	48½	42½	36¾	29¼	26¾	19½	14	5½			
COVENTRY	94	82½	76¼	69½	66¼	62¼	53¼	47¼	41½	34	31½	24¼	18¾	10¼	4¾		
HAMPTON	102	90½	84¼	77½	74¼	70¼	61¼	55¼	47½	42	39½	32¼	26¾	18¼	12¼	8	
BIRMINGHAM	112¼	100¾	94½	87¾	84½	80½	71½	65½	59¾	52¼	49¾	42½	37	28½	23	18¼	10¼

Birmingham

EXPLANATION.

To find any required distance, as, for instance, between Weedon and Bletchley; seek Weedon in the left-hand column, and carrying your eye in the direction of Weedon on the right, stop under the column of squares headed Bletchley, when the angle formed by the line running under Weedon and that on right of Bletchley, enclosing the figures 23 at the bottom, shows the distance.

LONDON AND BIRMINGHAM RAILWAY.

General Description of the Line.

LONDON TO WATFORD.

The entrance to the Railway is through a portico of vast proportions, erected from designs by Hardwick; proceeding through which the traveller then enters the booking-office, where, having obtained a ticket for the class of carriage best suited to his circumstances, and which must be preserved with great care, he is then passed through a passage to the departure parade, alongside of which the train of carriages is ranged, and where persons are in attendance to point out that wherein he must take his seat. On quitting the Station at Euston Grove, you enter immediately upon a grand excavation, of width sufficient for the passage of four carriages; the walls of this sunken viaduct are conically shaped, and finished with a parapet that, surmounted by a palisade, ensures protection to the persons above passing in its vicinity. Through this stupendous artificial valley, of nearly a mile in length, the trains are drawn by two stationary engines, working an endless rope, at Camden Town, to the depôt there established, which, consisting of workshops, warehouses, and offices, covers a space of about thirty-three acres. The rapidity of the passage through this immensely elaborate and beautifully formed approach, which, shortly after quitting the Station, crosses the Hampstead road, not permitting an attentive examination, the curious in such works are recommended, at more leisure, to take a deliberate survey of the same, when its extraordinary merit, as a specimen of engineering excellence, will at once be made manifest to all, who, however imperfectly skilled therein, take interest in works of this description. Emerging from this at Park Street Bridge, to which point it is constructed upon a gradual ascent from the Station at Euston Grove, two chimneys of towering height present themselves, and point out the locality of the engine-houses, each containing an engine of sixty horse-power: these chimneys have a remarkable appearance, and are visible upon all sides save the north at some distance. From Park Street Bridge the Railway is carried by an embankment of about a quarter of a mile in length, to the cast-iron suspension bridge thrown over the Regent's Canal, in crossing which it reaches the before-mentioned depôt. At this point the endless rope is detached, and from hence the trains are drawn by locomotive engines. The reason for the adoption of the stationary engine for this distance is said to have originated in the refusal of Lord Southampton to permit the passage of locomotive engines through his estate, here perforated by the railway, from an apprehension of the injurious effect that, occasioned by noise and smoke, might result therefrom, and which, if not prevented, might have proved utterly destructive to the beautiful suburb known as Park Village and Mornington Crescent in its vicinity. If, however, his Lordship has by his refusal, which could excite no surprise, escaped from this dilemma, he has unfortunately fallen into another, seeing that the rapid revolution of the numerous wheels that carry the endless rope proves the tenour of its way to be any thing but noiseless. From hence, the New Church upon the brow of the hill at Highgate, and Hampstead Church, embosomed in trees, stand forth the prominent features of the surrounding landscape; the western extremity of which is closed by the swelling eminence universally known as Primrose Hill.

To those who, familiar with this locality, may consider the topographer as descending too deeply into detail, he begs permission to remark, that this work is intended alike for the information of the foreigner as for the English reader. Prolixity of description he is anxious to avoid, his aim being to enlighten, and, if possible, enliven the journey upon which the traveller is about to enter. From the depôt, the Railway is carried under Chalk Farm Lane with a gradual sweep through an excavation of considerable depth, to the mouth of the first (the Primrose Hill) tunnel, 1120 yards in length, emerging from which, a little to the west of the new road, by West End and Hampstead to Barnet, it proceeds with a southerly inclination to the Bell at Kilburn and Kilburn Bridge, a square-topped structure, two miles from Tyburn turnpike, or, to speak in more fashionable phraseology, the western extremity of Oxford Street, on the Watford road. From Kilburn Bridge, distant from London $3\frac{1}{4}$ miles, from Birmingham 109 miles, it proceeds between sloping banks, by a gently waving line, to Kensal Green, three miles and a half upon the Harrow road, under which it passes by a second short tunnel, slightly curved, of 320 yards in length. On left of Kensal Green tunnel, is the General Cemetery Emerging from the Kensal Green tunnel, it soon reaches the Mitre Bridge, at a distance of five miles from London, and $107\frac{1}{4}$ from Birmingham. The Mitre Bridge takes its name from a house of entertainment of some celebrity, that, upon the opening of the Paddington Canal, was established here upon its northern bank, but has long since been converted into a cottage ornée. On left of the Mitre Bridge lies Wormwood Scrubs, a beautiful open area, long used as a military exercise ground, and for reviews that, upon a small scale, occasionally take place there. From the Mitre Bridge, after a slight curve, it is carried in its course to Lower Place Gates, on left of Holsdon Green, and is continued in a direct line thence upon an embankment, to the Brent River Viaduct. Lower Place Gates, six miles from London, $106\frac{1}{4}$ from Birmingham, being the first occurrence of the Railway running on the level of the surrounding country, and crossing a public road, it may not be improper to remark that here, as in every similar instance, not on this line only, but upon Railways generally, gates have been erected, which, during the passage of the train, being closed on either side by the attendants in waiting, the possibility of accident is thereby prevented. Roads thus crossed are exceptions to the general rule of railway formation, as will appear upon an examination of their several Acts, by which it will be seen that railway companies are bound and compelled to construct their lines, either under, or over, every public thoroughfare, or private way. Shortly after passing the Mitre Bridge, the Birmingham, Bristol, and Thames Junction Railway branches forth upon the left; and, being carried under the Paddington Canal to the Great Western Railway, these two lines are thereby connected and enabled to communicate with the Thames. On left of the Brent Viaduct, seven miles from London, $105\frac{1}{4}$ miles from Birmingham, is Twyford Abbey, the seat of Mrs. Douglas. From the Brent River Viaduct the railway is carried through the valley, upon an embankment in a northerly direction, by a gentle sweep to the Harrow road, which it crosses near the seventh mile-stone from London, and in the vicinity of Wembly Green. The Harrow road is distant from London eight miles, from Birmingham $104\frac{1}{4}$. As far as the Mitre Bridge, and for some distance beyond it, the railway passing through two tunnels, and being lined by embankments more or less lofty, the ride is thereby rendered very monotonous; shortly after leaving Lower Place Gates, however, a change takes place, and it is carried upon an embankment which, rising in some instances to a height of between thirty and forty feet above the river and valley of the Brent, here exhibits a good but not extensive view of the country on either side, which being, like most of the land in the northern part of Middlesex, laid out in small farms, presents an agreeably diversified appearance, affording at the same time a glance at the Great Western Railway, and Paddington Canal, both of which, as we have already observed, pass in its immediate vicinity. At Wembly Green, on right, is Wembly Park, the seat of the Rev. John Gray. From the Harrow road, proceeding in a north-west direction, in a further distance of about $3\frac{1}{2}$ miles, the Railway reaches

THE HARROW STATION,

AN INTERMEDIATE ONE, DISTANT FROM LONDON $11\frac{1}{2}$ MILES, FROM BIRMINGHAM $100\frac{3}{4}$ MILES.

On left of Harrow station, about $1\frac{1}{2}$ mile distant, stands Harrow on the Hill. It is situated on the highest hill in the county of Middlesex, at a distance of ten miles north-west from London. This hill, insulated as it were, and rising out of a rich vale, affords a variety of beautiful prospects, while the church, with its lofty spire, forms a very conspicuous object for many miles round. Two miles distant, on right of Harrow station at Stanmore, is Bentley Priory, the beautiful seat of the Marquis of Abercorn. From Harrow station, the Railway proceeds in a north-west direction to the Stanmore and Pinner roads, and in another mile extends to Oxhey Lane, and enters Hertfordshire, at a distance of $14\frac{1}{2}$ miles from London, and $97\frac{3}{4}$ from Birmingham. Continuing its course over occasional cuttings and successive embankments, nearly due north from Oxhey Lane, for a mile and a half, it then, by a gradual inclination to east for half a mile, carried upon an embankment, reaches Watford, where, crossing the London road by a massive brick bridge, it makes a somewhat sudden turn to the left, and soon after, still continued upon a lofty embankment, crossing the river Colne in its course, by a beautiful viaduct, passes to the east of that town, and reaches

THE WATFORD STATION,

A PRINCIPAL ONE, DISTANT FROM LONDON $17\frac{3}{4}$ MILES, FROM BIRMINGHAM $94\frac{1}{2}$ MILES. — Journey resumed at page 16.

The view from Watford Bridge, crossing the London road, and indeed, from the bridge along the embankment (that here attains a height of forty feet), to the station, is extremely pleasing, the effect panoramic; looking down on both sides are beheld the summits of the houses, the latter intermingled with fields and gardens. On the left lies the town of Watford, watered by the river Colne, whose stream, seen hence on either side, increases the interest of this somewhat novel scene.

CASHIOBURY PARK.

On left of Watford is Cashiobury Park, the beautiful seat of the Earl of Essex; 2½ miles distant Moor Park, the fine seat of the Marquis of Westminster; and two miles beyond Watford, on left, the Grove, Earl of Clarendon. Of all these, as well as some other places merely noticed on the way hither, we shall, together with Watford, and the towns lying on either side of it, now proceed to give an account; this being done, the route will then be continued in regular stages from station to station, which plan will be pursued throughout the work. The traveller, therefore, who may be desirous of proceeding on his way uninterrupted by these remarks, will, by having recourse to the Index, refer to the page where the journey is again resumed, and in that way, if so disposed, continue to the end, resorting only, as occasion may require, to an account of any place hereafter to be described. With a view also to the convenience of travellers, some of whom long accustomed to itineraries, and who may prefer the mode of arrangement invariably adopted in the best road-books, the London and Birmingham line given in that form will be found at the end, thus rendering the present work the most complete of its kind, and enabling the tourist to trace his route in the form and manner best suited to his taste.

TWYFORD.

Twyford, one mile on left of the Brent River Viaduct, is remarkable for containing only three houses, the chief of which is Twyford Abbey, and for all the land (about two hundred and eighty acres) having been long in the possession of one owner, the late Mr. Willan, the celebrated stage-coach proprietor, who purchased it in the year 1806, of the Cholmeleys. He pulled down the old mansion, which was surrounded by a moat, now filled up, and erected a new one in imitation of the ancient Gothic, from designs by Mr. Atkinson. It is an irregular embattled building, with two octagonal turrets; the interior is conveniently disposed. The attached grounds are small, but pleasantly laid out. Immediately contiguous is a very small church of brick, now stuccoed over, and embellished in the style of the mansion. In it is a monument erected to the memory of Henry Bold, the poet, who died in 1683.

THE BRENT RIVER.

The Brent, a small stream, rises in the neighbourhood of Totteridge, in Hertfordshire, and, after taking an easterly direction for about two miles, turns suddenly to the south, and approaches the village of Whetstone, where it enters the county of Middlesex; it then takes a south-west inclination, and flowing a little to the north of Finchley, at a distance of about two miles from that village, crosses the Hendon road at Brent Street, a small hamlet to which it gives name; pursuing a western course, in a distance of about a mile and a half it reaches the Edgeware and Stanmore road, which it crosses a little beyond the five mile-stone from London, half a mile beyond which its waters are increased by a streamlet, that, rising a little to the right of Elstree, here fall into the Brent. Passing soon after the village of Kingsbury, and taking a more southerly inclination, it crosses the Harrow road near the sixth mile-stone, and in a further distance of half a mile reaches the Birmingham Railway at the Brent Viaduct. Its course from hence is nearly due west to Twyford Abbey, the grounds of which are adorned by its waters, that shortly after cross the Paddington Canal, and flow thence to Greenford. From Greenford it takes a southern direction, and, pursuing a meandering course, in a short distance reaches Hanwell, where, crossed by the beautiful Wharncliff Viaduct of the Great Western Railway, and Hanwell Bridge upon the Uxbridge road, it mingles its waters with the Grand Junction Canal, and finally falls into the Thames at Brentford.

WEMBLY PARK.

The manor, or manor farm, of Wembly, otherwise Wymbley, appears to have belonged formerly to the priory of Kilburn. On the dissolution of monastic houses, the manor was granted by King Henry VIII. to certain persons, who, in the same year in which they obtained the grant (1543), conveyed it to Richard Page, Esq. The family of Page long possessed very considerable property in the county of Middlesex; and this estate remained vested in that family till 1802, in which year it was purchased of Richard Page, Esq. by John Gray, Esq.

The mansion was rebuilt by Mr. Gray, about the year 1811, in a style of considerable elegance, and is surrounded by a park, comprising more than 250 acres of fine undulating land, well ornamented with wood.

THE HARROW STATION,

An intermediate one, is not a stopping place of the principal trains; a circumstance it has been deemed proper to notice, lest persons unaccustomed to this mode of conveyance might be led to imagine, that, desirous to return from Harrow, and resorting hither, they might obtain a seat in any of the carriages proceeding to London. Such is not the fact: all the trains of course pass it, but all do not call at the Harrow station. The hour of their departure for London varying with the season, can only be ascertained at the Harrow station, which is distant from the village about a mile and a half.

HARROW.

Harrow on the Hill, in Middlesex, ten miles N. W. from London, is situated on the highest hill in the county. This hill, insulated as it were, rising out of a rich vale, affords a variety of beautiful prospects. The view towards the east is terminated by the metropolis; to the south, by the Surrey hills. Toward the north it is the least extensive, being intercepted by the high ground about Stanmore and Harrow-weald; on this side, the village of Stanmore, and Bentley Priory (the seat of the Marquis of Abercorn), are the most conspicuous objects. The view toward the west and south-west, which is very extensive and beautiful, may be seen to the greatest advantage from the church-yard, whence the ground declines precipitately to Roxeth, where the scenery is very pleasing; the distant prospect includes Windsor Castle, with considerable portions of Berkshire and Buckinghamshire. The parish-church, with its lofty spire, forms a prominent feature in the prospect for many miles round; it was originally built by Archbishop Lanfranc, in the time of the conqueror; and some part of his church is yet standing. The celebrated physician and poet, Dr. Sir Samuel Garth, has a monument here. Harrow is chiefly celebrated for its free grammar-school, which now ranks among the first public seminaries in the kingdom. It was founded in the reign of Elizabeth, by John Lyon, a wealthy yeoman of Preston, in this parish. As regards Harrow, it only remains to remark, that whoever ventures upon a trip to that justly celebrated seminary, must keep strictly in view the time appointed for the departure of the trains from this station for London; the village of Harrow being lamentably deficient in accommodation for the tourist.

CANONS PARK.

This seat formerly belonged to Dennis O'Kelly, Esq. of sporting memory, and owner of the celebrated horse Eclipse, whose remains are interred in the paddock fronting the house. This spot is remarkable as being the site of a most splendid mansion, erected by the great Duke of Chandos, in which he resided in magnificent state. On the death of that nobleman, in 1744, it was pulled down, and the costly materials disposed of by auction. The present edifice is composed of some of the materials purchased at the demolition of the vast building above mentioned; it possesses a considerable degree of elegance, and is desirably situated on a gentle elevation. The church at Whitchurch or Little Stanmore, a small but elegant structure, contains all that now remains of the magnificence of Canons.

BENTLEY PRIORY.

Bentley Priory, Middlesex, $2\frac{1}{3}$ miles on right of the Harrow Station, the magnificent seat of the Marquis of Abercorn, is situated on the summit of Stanmore Hill, but in the parish of Harrow: it is supposed to occupy the site of an ancient priory, concerning which very little is known. The mansion has been much enlarged by the present noble owner, but is an irregular range of brick building, destitute of architectural beauty, and of rather a sombre character. The interior comprises a suite of very spacious apartments, but chiefly rests its claim for attraction on the works of art, which form a dignified portion of its embellishment. The mansion, from its elevated position, commands rich and extensive prospects. The attached grounds have been advantageously augmented, by enclosing a large portion of what was formerly common land, and now comprises more than 200 acres in the district appropriated to ornamental scenery.

BARNET.

Barnet, although at a considerable distance from, and entirely unconnected with, the Birmingham Railway, yet as appearing upon the map of the line, and being situate on the hitherto great road from London to Birmingham, its introduction here will, it is presumed, with a view to completeness of description, be deemed not inappropriate. Barnet, a market town of Hertfordshire and Middlesex, eleven miles north from London, is situated on the summit of a hill, whence it is called High Barnet, and also Chipping Barnet, from the privilege granted to the monks of St. Alban's of holding a market here; the word Chepe being the Saxon word for a market. The Church was built about the year 1400; combining with the old market-house, and other irregular buildings, it forms the foreground of a very pleasing street view. Queen Elizabeth founded a free school here, which is under the control of twenty-four governors, who elect the master and usher. Nine children are taught gratis, all the rest of the parish at five shillings per quarter. In this town is also a neat row of almshouses for widows, who are allowed the apartments with furniture. Here is also an hospital founded in the reign of Charles II. by Thomas Ravenscroft, Esq., who has an altar tomb in the church, "for six poor ancient women, being widows or maidens, inhabitants of the town."

The grant of a weekly market at Barnet was made to the Abbots of St. Alban's by Henry II. It is still held on Monday, and is noted for the sale of pigs; an annual fair is also held here in September, principally for the sale of cattle. Barnet is not a place of much trade, but lying on the great north road, and that denominated the parliamentary line from London to Birmingham and Holyhead, as also the high road to Liverpool and Manchester, Holyhead and Chester, it derived very considerable advantage from the expenditure of travellers. It contained many inns, and, from its favourable position, the first stage from London on these great lines, provided perhaps as many post horses as any town in England; this, and its connection with the numerous stage-coaches that travelled through Barnet, furnished the chief employ of its inhabitants, till within these few years, when steam navigation first interfered with its carrying trade, particularly to the north, the ruin of which has been finally accomplished by the formation of the London and Birmingham Railway; and thus this formerly flourishing town has been deprived of its chief source of revenue, a loss in which, in the shape of stage-coach and post-horse duty, the public have largely participated. On the common adjoining the town was a race-course; but an act of enclosure having passed some years since, the races have been discontinued. Barnet is remarkable for the decisive battle fought between the houses of York and Lancaster, in 1741, in which the great Earl of Warwick was slain. This was the man well known in history by the appellation of the King-maker. The field of battle was an open space of ground, called Gladsmore Heath, a little before the meeting of the Hatfield and old St. Alban's roads; and here, in 1740, an obelisk was erected by Sir Jeremy Sambrook, of Gobions, to commemorate this great event which Dugdale and others, though with little probability, think was at Friern Barnet, in Middlesex.

WATFORD

Previous to the conquest, Watford formed part of Caishoe, or Cashio; and, included under that appellation, was given by King Offa to the Abbey of St. Alban, to which it continued attached till the time of the dissolution, when the stewardship of this and other adjacent manors was given to John Lord Russel, of Chemies, in Buckinghamshire. James I., in the seventh of his reign, granted Watford to the Lord Chancellor Egerton, Baron of Ellesmere, in whose descendants, the Dukes of Bridgewater, it remained vested till about the year 1760, when it was sold to the then Earl of Essex, and is now the property of his descendant, the present Earl

The Abbots of St. Alban's had various privileges granted to them for this manor by different sovereigns: the charter of the market was bestowed by Henry I.; and Edward IV. gave them liberty to hold two fairs annually. The market-house is a long building, rough-cast above, and supported on wooden pillars beneath. The quantity of corn sold here is very great, and the number of sheep, cows, calves, hogs, &c., is proportionable. The police of the town is under the direction of resident and neighbouring magistrates.

The church is a very spacious building, dedicated to the Virgin Mary, and consists of a nave, aisles, and chancel, with a massive embattled tower at the west end, about eighty feet high, terminated by a small spire rising to the height of about twenty more. The nave is divided from the aisles by six pointed arches on each side, with plain mouldings, resting on octagonal columns; above the arches are the same number of obtuse-headed windows. The roof is of a circular form, the supporters rest on half figures, sustaining shields. The chancel, which appears of a more recent date than the nave, opens from the latter by a large pointed arch. The east window is divided by mullions into several compartments; but the light is obscured by a large altar-piece of oak, carved in the style of James II.'s time.

On the north side of the chancel is the chapel or cemetery of the Morisons, and now of the Essex family. This contains, among others of inferior execution, two very fine monuments by Nicholas Stone. At the south side of the churchyard is a good Free School, with convenient apartments for a master and mistress. This was founded and endowed by Mrs. Elizabeth Fuller, of Watford Place, which nearly adjoins the school, in the year 1704, for forty boys and twenty girls, who are partly clothed, and taught reading, writing, and arithmetic. The original endowments have been increased by some additional legacies. The government of the school is vested in nine trustees, who are chosen from the most respectable inhabitants of Watford, a preference being given to the kindred of the Foundress, a full-length portrait of whom is preserved in the school-room.

. The town of Watford is in Hertfordshire; it is 15 miles distant from London, and principally consists of one long well-built street, ranged on the sides of the high road, and nearly a mile in length: it is situated on the acclivity and summit of a gentle eminence, at the foot of which flows the river Colne, here crossed by a bridge. The chief employment of the labouring classes is derived from agriculture, while the silk and paper mills, of which there are several in the vicinity, furnish additional labour for many hands. Watford is environed by a very beautiful country, richly wooded, well watered, with good roads in all directions; and is further enlivened by some magnificent seats and numerous villas, many of which, though upon a minor scale, are nevertheless of first-rate respectability. Most of the drives in its neighbourhood present delightful specimens of sylvan scenery, and the society here is of the very best description. The Colne River, recently rendered navigable to St. Alban's, unites its waters with the Gade and the Grand Junction Canal, at about two miles distance from the town, which is thus enabled to maintain water communication not only with the metropolis, but also with the west and north-west parts of the kingdom.

ST. ALBAN'S.

St. Alban's, an ancient town in Hertfordshire, 21 miles north of London, and 7 from the Watford station, is seated on the Ver, which is a branch of the river Colne. This was once a chief city of Britain, and the residence of British princes before the invasion of Julius Cæsar; after which it was called Verulamium. When the Romans had achieved their conquest, they added walls to their ordinary British defence of earthern ramparts and ditches; and erected Verulam into a *municipium*, or city enjoying equal privileges with the Roman capital, which so attached the British citizens to the Roman government, that this place consequently felt the vengeance of Queen Boadicea, who here, and at London, destroyed 70,000 persons in the most cruel manner. Suetonius Paulinus, the then governor of Britain, in return for her barbarity, attacked her forces, gained a complete victory, and put 80,000 to the sword. Verulam was then rebuilt, and its inhabitants enjoyed their privileges till the Dioclesian persecution, A. D. 304; when the city was again rendered famous by the martyrdom of its citizen, St. Alban. When the Saxons gained footing in Britain, Verulam was among their first conquests, being by them denominated Werlameaster and Watlingceaster. Many vast fragments of the Roman masonry remain in the walls of the ancient station, the area of which, according to Dr. Stukeley's measurement, is 5200 feet in length, and 3000 in breadth. At present it is divided into several fields; but vestiges of the buildings are still to be traced, by the thinness of the turf over those parts where the streets ran; near the high road is an immense fragment of the wall, now called Gorhambury Block. After various revolutions, this vast city fell to decay; and, from its ruins, rose the present St. Alban's.

This town, which is situated on a more elevated spot of ground than the old city, was formerly a wood, named Holmhurst. It obtained its greatest prosperity from the stately abbey, erected in honour of St. Alban, whose relics were miraculously discovered by Offa, king of Mercia, after his unprovoked murder of St. Ethelbert, king of the East Angles, whom he had invited to his court to be his son-in-law. From Offa's subsequent compunction arose this magnificent abbey and monastery for Benedictine or black monks: and, after his time, it was greatly enlarged in successive ages. Its abbots were dignified with a mitre, and had precedency of all others in England: they were subject to no other power, but immediately to the Pope; and had episcopal jurisdiction over both clergy and laity, in all the possessions belonging to the monastery. Not a vestige, however, of this splendid foundation is now left, excepting the abbey church, and a large square gateway, opening with a spacious low-pointed arch. All the monastic buildings were pulled down in the reigns of Henry VIII. and Edward VI.; but the church, to the lasting honour of the corporation and inhabitants, was rescued from impending destruction, and purchased by them of the latter sovereign for 400*l*. This venerable fabric was then made parochial; and at the approach to the town, either from London, Dunstable, or Watford, it still arrests the traveller's attention, and forms a fine feature in the very beautiful country by which it is surrounded.

This structure is in the form of a cross: its entire length, including the chapel of the Virgin and west porch, is 539 feet; that of the transept 174 feet; the height of the tower 144 feet; of the body 65, and the breadth of the nave 74 feet 6 inches. The tower and central parts are in the Norman style of architecture, the whole fabric having been rebuilt soon after the conquest, chiefly with materials collected from ancient Verulam. The objects for the ingenuity of the artist in and about this place are many and various; and, had it not been for numerous devastations, the monuments and brasses would have been a fund of amusement for the antiquary; of the brass monuments, however, one only of particular value has escaped the general wreck. This noble specimen of monastic antiquity has been recently repaired by public subscription. Not a vestige remains of the abbey built by Offa, of whose munificence a murder was the true source: he invited Ethelbert, prince of the East Angles, to his court, on pretence of marrying him to his daughter, beheaded him, and seized his dominions. The pious Offa had recourse to the usual expiation of murder in those melancholy ages, the founding of a monastery. To the south of St. Stephen's Church are the remains of the church and house of St. Julian, founded for lazars by Gaufridus, Abbot of St. Alban's. Besides the Abbey Church, St. Alban's contains two others, respectively dedicated to

St. Michael and St. Peter, in the former of which is a fine monument to that renowned philosopher and statesman, Lord Chancellor Bacon.

In the centre of the town stood one of the magnificent crosses, erected by Edward I. in honour of his queen Eleanor: in 1703, this was taken down, and on its site was erected the present open octagonal building; this, though still retaining the name of "The Cross," has long been used as a butter and poultry market.

St. Alban's is famous for the victory obtained in 1455 over Henry VI. by Richard, Duke of York; the first battle fought in the famous quarrel, which lasted thirty years, and is computed to have cost the lives of eighty princes of the blood, and to have annihilated almost entirely the ancient nobility of England. In 1461, a second battle was fought here, in which Queen Margaret defeated the great Earl of Warwick. The rivers Ver and Colne have recently been rendered navigable from St. Alban's to Watford, at which place they unite their waters with the Grand Junction Canal. The town is governed by a mayor, high steward, recorder, twelve aldermen, &c., and sends two members to parliament. It gives the title of Duke to the family of Beauclerk, while its ancient name of Verulam gives the title of Earl to the Grimston family. There are several places of worship for dissenters in the town, to one of which belongs a charity school. Here also are various other charitable endowments.

St. Alban's, situated upon the great parliamentary road from London to Holyhead, of which it was the second stage from the metropolis, enjoyed, in consequence, no inconsiderable advantage from the expenditure of travellers, and its extensive connection with stage coach and posting establishments; and from the removal of these, occasioned by the formation of the London and Birmingham and London and Liverpool Railways, the town has experienced a great and irreparable injury.

RICKMANSWORTH.

Rickmansworth is a small market-town, occupying a low marshy situation near the confluence of the rivers Gade and Colne, and a small rivulet, which flows from Chesham and Flaunden, in Buckinghamshire. The manor was an ancient demesne of the Saxon kings, and was given by King Offa to the Abbey at St. Alban's, to which it was confirmed by succeeding monarchs, and had the charter of a weekly market, and two annual fairs, granted it by Henry III. After the dissolution, Edward VI. gave the manor to Ridley, Bishop of London: but Queen Mary bestowed it on the fell persecutor Bishop

Bonner. In Elizabeth's time it reverted to the Crown; and was finally sold by Charles I., to the Six Clerks in Chancery, to whom he had it conveyed as a security for borrowed money, to Sir Thomas Fotherley, whose son, John, was sheriff of Herts in the fourth year of Charles II. This family became extinct by the dreadful event of its possessor, son of the last-mentioned gentleman, being swallowed up, with his only daughter, in the great earthquake at Jamaica, in 1694. The church is a spacious building dedicated to the Virgin Mary, and consists of a nave, aisles, and chancel, with a handsome embattled tower of hewn flints; at the west end the upper part of the nave is also embattled; and the buttresses are very strong. On each side the nave are five plain pointed arches, rising from round columns, with square windows above, each divided into two trefoil-headed lights. Beyond these, extending across the space that appears to have originally been the chancel, is a large pointed arch; and at the sides, eastward, are two other arches, springing from octagonal columns, and reaching to the entrance of the present chancel. This edifice was repaired in the year 1677, and again in the years 1802 and 1803: the large gallery which is at the west end was probably erected about the former period. The interior contains many sepulchral memorials. The situation of Rickmansworth, in the vicinity of several streams, renders it very convenient for trades that require the aid of water; and several mills, for various purposes, have been erected in its neighbourhood.

This place has experienced considerable improvement within the last thirty years, from the formation of the Grand Junction Canal, which adjoins the town; and several manufactories have in consequence been here established, particularly a silk mill, in itself an object of great curiosity. On the rivulet that flows hither from Chesham, are also several paper mills; and all these, together with the manufacture of straw plait, in which the women and children are generally engaged, constitute the chief employment of the labouring classes. The market-house is a mean wooden fabric, supported on pillars, and open beneath. It was formerly celebrated for its trade in corn, but is now little frequented, though toll-free.

CASHIOBURY PARK.

Cashiobury Park, at Watford, in Hertfordshire, 15 miles from London, is the beautiful seat of the Earl of Essex. The family mansion at Cashiobury is a spacious edifice, pleasantly situated in an extensive and well-wooded park, through which flows the river Gade, and across which, by permission of the Earl, was carried the Grand Junction Canal. The house, originally begun in the time of Henry VIII. by Richard Morison, Esq., was completed in the style of that age by his son, Sir Charles Morison. It has since been greatly altered and improved by Wyatt. The apartments, which are spacious and elegant, are beautifully decorated. A kind of cloister, the windows of which are ornamented with stained glass, executed in a very superior manner, together with the castellated style here adopted, produces a very pleasing effect. The park, a splendid domain, is eminently beautiful, and affords some rich scenery and noble timber. The walks, said to have been originally laid out by the celebrated Le Notre, have been greatly improved and enlarged; and the pleasure-grounds, which are extensive, have undergone some judicious alterations, and are further adorned by a number of ornamental lodges, that, placed in different parts of the grounds, afford residences for the numerous keepers appointed to the preservation of this extensive and valuable property.

Adjoining Cashiobury is the Grove, the seat of the Earl of Clarendon. The mansion is an irregular structure of brick, standing on the west side of the river Gade, in a park about three miles in circumference, through which it flows in a divided stream; and the grounds are further enlivened by the Grand Junction Canal, that in its course also crosses the Park.

MOOR PARK.

Moor Park, Hertfordshire, $2\frac{1}{2}$ miles from the Watford station, on the left, is the splendid residence of the Marquis of Westminster. It is a magnificent building of the Corinthian order, standing in a finely wooded park about five miles in circumference, and having two fronts, facing respectively towards the North and South. The principal, or southern front, has a very elegant and grand portico, the pediment being supported on four noble columns. It was originally constructed of brick, at the expense of the Duke of Monmouth; but this nobleman had it entirely new-cased and fronted with Portland stone; and having built the magnificent portico, erected two wings for the chapel and offices, and connected them with the centre by colonnades of the Tuscan order. His architect was the celebrated Italian, Giacomo Leoni, assisted by Sir James Thornhill: the whole was erected, together wth judicious alterations in the park, at an expense of 150,000*l.*; but having subsequently become the property of Mr. Rous, a gentleman of narrowed circumstances, he pulled down the wings for the value of the materials, and thence in a great measure destroyed its imposing character. The central part of the building, however, was left untouched, and it now forms one of the most elegant residences in this part of the country. The internal parts of this mansion are uncommonly rich, and have an air of grandeur at once interesting and dignified. The apartments consist of a hall, splendidly ornamented; the saloon, a handsome room, the ceiling of which was painted by Sir James Thornhill, and is justly considered one of the finest works of that celebrated artist; the ball, or long drawing room, the ceiling of which is beautifully decorated, and the apartment otherwise embellished with numerous sculptured figures; which, together with the principal staircase, of noble proportions, painted with great ability, exhibits at one view the fine taste and judgment of the architect, together with the talent of the painter. The park, which owes its present improved state to Lord Anson, who here expended 80,000*l.*, was laid out by the celebrated Brown. It is extremely diversified, and adds considerably to the interest of the scenery by which it is surrounded.

GORHAMBURY.

Gorhambury, the delightful seat of Earl Verulam, on the left of St. Alban's, has derived an adventitious though brilliant lustre from its having been the property and residence of the great Lord Bacon and others of his family. The mansion is a spacious stone edifice, of the Corinthian order, connected with two wings of brick, stuccoed over. It was built between the years 1778 and 1783, by the late Lord Viscount Grimston, from the designs, and under the direction, of the late Sir Robert Taylor. A flight of steps leads to the grand entrance, which opens beneath a handsome pediment, supported by well-proportioned columns. The hall, library, and other principal apartments, are spacious: they contain a very rich collection of portraits, chiefly of the age of Elizabeth and her immediate successors. The park and grounds include about 600 acres, well stocked with fine timber, particularly with beech, oak, and elm. The scenery presents some beautiful landscapes, to which the contiguity of Pré Wood, and the many fine deer in the park, give additional interest.

WATFORD TO BERKHAMSTEAD.

From Watford the Railway proceeds in a very direct line under the St. Alban's road, through a cutting of considerable depth,—in some instances 60 feet,—to the Watford Tunnel, one mile in length. Emerging from the tunnel, in another mile it extends to Hunton Bridge. On left of Hunton Bridge is Langley Bury, agreeably situated upon an eminence overlooking the river Gade and the Grand Junction Canal: it was built by Lord Chief Justice Raymond, who took his title of Baron Langley from this place; his son bequeathed it to the Rev. Sir John Filmer, Bart.; and it is at present in the occupation of E. F. Whittingstall, Esq.

From Hunton Bridge, proceeding in a line with, and at a short distance from, the Grand Junction Canal, the river Gade, the London road, and rising grounds in their vicinity, that, viewed collectively, form the constituent features of a very beautiful landscape: in a mile and a half more it extends to Primrose Green, or King's Langley*; from whence, taking a north-west direction, and passing in front of Nash Mill, the very extensive paper manufactory and seat of John Dickinson, Esq., it soon reaches the Berkhampstead road, a viaduct over which conducts it in a short distance to Two Waters, and in another mile to

BOXMOOR STATION,

AN INTERMEDIATE ONE, DISTANT FROM LONDON 24¾ MILES, FROM BIRMINGHAM 87½ MILES.

On the left of Boxmoor, see Westbrook Hay, the seat of the Hon. G. D. Ryder. The scenery in the vicinity of Two Waters, and indeed, it may be added, nearly all the way from Hunton Bridge to Berkhampstead, is extremely beautiful; the former being enlivened by the Bulbourn Brook, the Grand Junction Canal, and the river Gade, that here unite their waters. Shortly after quitting Two Waters, the Railway recrosses the Berkhampstead road, and passing over Boxmoor, and the Grand Junction Canal, continues its course in a line parallel to that valuable aqueduct, of which, together with the London road, and beautiful country in the vicinity, a good view is beheld, and proceeds direct to

BERKHAMPSTEAD STATION,

A PRINCIPAL ONE, DISTANT FROM LONDON 27¾ MILES, FROM BIRMINGHAM 84¾ MILES.—Journey resumed at page 19.

In the close vicinity of Berkhampstead, on the left, are the following seats:—Haresfoot, T. Dorrien, Esq.; Ashlin's Hall, J. Smith, Esq.; and Bartlett's, late Mrs. Pechell; and about a quarter of a mile beyond the station, on the right, and close to the Railway, is Berkhampstead Place, Hon. Miss Grimston.

THE WATFORD TUNNEL.

The Watford Tunnel, 1 mile and 170 yards in length, passed of course in the dark, and at the rapid rate of railway speed, will nevertheless be deemed by most travellers a consignment to durance vile of much too long continuance; the best way to lessen the tedium of which will be, having first closed the windows, to consign himself, not to the anticipation of unpleasant consequences, but a state of composure as if for sleep, the only way

* Where has been established the King's Langley Station.

perhaps, in which these gloomy regions can be divested of their subterranean horrors. This was, as the reader may readily imagine, a work of immense labour; the vastness of which, a deliberate survey, not to be taken *en passant*, can alone convince him. In addition to its immense cost, and the danger incidental to mining operations, a loss of ten lives in one instance alone, was unfortunately experienced in the course of its construction.

TWO WATERS.

Two Waters, in Hertfordshire, 2 miles S.S.W. from Hemel Hempstead, and 22 miles N.W. from London, is an agreeable village pleasantly situated on the banks of the Bulbourn Brook and river Gade, and in the vicinity of the Grand Junction Canal. Two Waters has long been celebrated for its paper mills, the chief of which, Nash Mill, is the property of John Dickinson, Esq., at whose very extensive and complete establishment, well worthy of a visit, printing papers are produced in immense quantities, and of a texture so delicate, as closely to resemble the finest fabrics of China. This place, from its confluence of waters, whence it derives its name, was long the resort of lovers of the angle, but is not now, on that account, as formerly so well frequented; the prevailing opinion at present being that the introduction of chemical properties into the manufacture of paper have materially interfered with the purity of its streams.

BOXMOOR STATION.

Boxmoor Station, on Boxmoor, is the point to which the Railway at its first opening was completed: it is not now, however, much used, its utility having been in some measure superseded by that of Berkhampstead, $3\frac{1}{2}$ miles beyond it; and which, being one of the principal stations, is not only the resort of the residents of Berkhampstead and its vicinity, but, as supplying fuel and water, is one at which all the principal trains stop for their obtainment; while that at Boxmoor is merely a minor station of the company, appointed for the convenience of persons residing in the neighbourhood.

HEMEL HEMPSTEAD.

Hemel Hempstead, in Hertfordshire, 23 miles from London, is a small market-town, pleasantly situated on a gentle eminence, at a short distance from the river Gade. The church, which stands in a spacious churchyard adjoining the town, on the west side, appears to have been erected at the time of the Norman Conquest: it is built in the form of a cross, and consists of a nave, chancel, transept, and side aisles, with an embattled tower surmounted by a high octagonal spire, rising from the intersection. The market house is a plain edifice of wood, and the shambles form a neat range of brick building. The charitable donations consist of two free schools, and a small annuity to fifty poor widows. Large quantities of corn are annually sold at this market. Hemel Hempstead has derived considerable advantage from the formation of the Grand Junction Canal, which passes within a mile and a half of the town. This is, perhaps, one of the quietest market-towns in England, the place not lying upon any great line of communication, but about a mile and a half distant from the road from London to Berkhampstead, from which it is distant nearly four miles.

BERKHAMPSTEAD.

The kings of Mercia had a palace and castle here, which was afterwards enlarged and strengthened in the Norman times. Henry I. ordered it to be "razed to the ground" on account of the rebellion of its possessor, William, Earl of Mortaigne. It is probable that the demolition was only a partial one, or that the castle was soon after rebuilt; as Henry II. occasionally kept his court here, and granted great privileges to the inhabitants. The honours and castle of Berkhampstead are connected with the duchy of Cornwall, and consequently belong to the Crown, under whom the estates are held on lease. The ramparts of the castle are very bold, and the ditches still wide and deep; but the buildings are reduced to massive fragments of walls. The town of Berkhampstead is very ancient; it chiefly consists of one long street, irregularly built, with another branching out from the church towards the site of the castle; the buildings are chiefly of brick, interspersed with a few handsome erections. The church, a large and ornamented building, contains numerous sepulchral memorials, some of them curious and interesting. Berkhampstead is surrounded by a beautiful country, and in its vicinity are some fine seats.

BERKHAMPSTEAD TO TRING,

AND INCLINATION OF THE RAILWAY FROM EUSTON GROVE TO TRING SUMMIT DESCRIBED.

Here it may not be improper to remark that the inclination of the Railway, hitherto but partially noticed, may be thus briefly described.— From its departure, after a short descent, from Euston Grove, till its arrival at the *depôt*, it is a gradual rise, from which point it proceeds upon a level of a mile and a quarter in length; from thence, with a gradual descent, and almost imperceptible rise, it is carried to the vicinity of Kensall Green; from Kensall Green it is constructed upon a level to the viaduct over the Brent; from hence its inclination is that of an easy ascent to within a mile and a half of Watford: the former, a level — the latter, a declination — brings it to that town, to the farther end of which it continues with a gradual slope. Six miles beyond Watford it commences a steep acclivity (1 in 330), upon which it is continued, through deep cuttings (passing in its progress, about a mile beyond Berkhampstead, through Northchurch Tunnel, 360 yards in length), all the way to

TRING STATION
AND SUMMIT.

DISTANT FROM LONDON 31¾ MILES, FROM BIRMINGHAM 80½ MILES. — Journey resumed at page 24.

One mile distant from Northchurch Tunnel, on the right, is Northcote Court, —— Locksley, Esq.; and two miles distant is Ashridge Park, the magnificent seat of the Countess of Bridgewater, — both, of course, excluded from the view; but at a short distance beyond the tunnel, Ashridge Park becomes partially visible; the mansion, however, cannot be seen, but a monument erected to the memory of the late Earl, standing in the park, is clearly discernible from the Railway. On the left of Tring is Tring Park, Mrs. Kay; and one mile distant on the right is Stocks House.

TRING SUMMIT.

Tring Summit is, as its name implies, the most elevated part of the Railway, which here attains a height of 420 feet above the level of the sea.

The country in the vicinity of Tring, of which the traveller catches an occasional glance, is beautifully wooded; but the site of the station, and indeed the Railway itself for some distance before and for a considerable distance beyond it, is that of a deep ravine, the lofty sides of which exclude all objects from the view; it is literally a mountain pass. Those, however, who quit the Railway at Tring Station, and are admirers of the picturesque, will, by ascending to the summit of these hills, be highly gratified. Thence a very extensive and beautiful prospect is obtained, of which the town and vale of Aylesbury, — the latter enlivened by the winding of the Grand Junction Canal, with its Aylesbury and Wendover branches, — and the more direct line of the Railway itself, with the Aylesbury Railway branching therefrom, form the most prominent features.

TRING.

Tring, a small neat town situated in the north-west corner of the county of Herts, upon the high road to Aylesbury, at a distance of 7 miles from that place, and 31 from London, is of considerable antiquity. The church is a large and well-proportioned regular building, dedicated to St. Peter and St. Paul, and consists of a nave, side aisles, and chancel, with a massive tower at the west end; the walls are supported with strong buttresses and the whole is embattled. The tower has originallly opened into the church by a sharp-pointed arch with plain mouldings, and two small pillars on each side: the lower part is now used as a vestry. The nave is separated from the aisles by six pointed arches, rising from high clustered columns. The roof is of timber framework, with strong beams going across; the supporters on each side are terminated by a carved figure, each of which has a curious but well-sculptured design for a corbel base. The market-house is a mean edifice on wooden pillars; and the market held on Friday is chiefly for the sale of corn, in which the trade is considerable, meat, and straw plait; the manufacture of the latter article constituting the chief employment of the females in this part of the country. Various small donations, that have been given for the use of the poor, are enumerated on a table in the church; and a Sunday-school, for about eighty boys and girls, has been established here. The Roman road, called the Icknield Street, passes in the vicinity, and forms the communication (in winter a very bad one) between this place and Dunstable. The summit of the Grand Junction Canal is at Startops End, about a mile and a half from Tring, where have been formed three reservoirs that act as feeders to that valuable aqueduct. The country in the vicinity of Tring is finely wooded; and the views from the summit of the hills by which it is surrounded, are of great extent and beauty.

WENDOVER.

Wendover, a market-town of Buckinghamshire, 5 miles from Aylesbury, and 35½ from London, consisting principally of mean brick-built houses, lies in a bottom among the Chiltern Hills. The inhabitants, the women in particular, derive their chief support from lace-making; it experiences also no inconsiderable advantage from the canal, a branch of the Grand Junction, that some thirty-five years since was brought to the town, and by means of which a supply of coals is obtained from Staffordshire. A little more than a mile from hence, at Weston, is a large reservoir, that covers about seventy acres, and from which the canal obtains its supply of water. The market held on Thursday is but indifferently attended, and the market-house particularly mean. Wendover, which, till lately, sent two members to parliament, was first represented in the 28th of Edward I. It intermitted sending till the 21st of James I., when the privilege was restored upon petition. The right of election was vested in the housekeepers not receiving alms; the voters were not more than 130, most of whom were permitted to occupy the burgage houses rent-free; the conditions on which they enjoyed this privilege are easily comprehended. This corruption was, however, finally put an end to in 1832 by the Reform Bill, when Wendover was disfranchised. Hampden House, long the family seat of the Hampden family and of the patriot John Hampden, who represented Wendover in three successive parliaments, and about three miles distant, is now the seat of the Earl of Buckinghamshire. Wendover is situated in the southern division of Buckinghamshire, called the Chiltern, in the immediate vicinity of the ridge of hills that, extending from Dunstable in Bedfordshire, to Henly in Oxfordshire, from various points afford some very delightful prospects. The Chiltern division is exceedingly different from the other part in its external appearance, quality of soil, mode of agriculture, materials for building, and almost every other circumstance that can render two counties dissimilar. Many of the houses and walls are composed of flint, or flint and brick intermixed. The soil is thin, with a chalk bottom; and very extensive tracts are covered with beech trees. Many elegant mansions are also interspersed through this district, which is elevated, healthy, and pleasant.

AYLESBURY.

Aylesbury, a market-town of Buckinghamshire, $13\frac{1}{2}$ miles from Leighton Buzzard, 7 from Tring, 10 from Thame, and 38 from London, was formerly the Æglesbury of the Saxons. It was originally a strong British town, and maintained its independence till the year 571, when it was reduced by Cuthwolf, brother to Cealwin, King of the West Saxons. It is situated nearly in the middle of the county, on a gentle eminence that rises gradually on all sides, and is surrounded by that fertile tract of country called the Vale of Aylesbury, which contains some of the richest land in England, and feeds an incredible number of sheep. This town is described as being built with timber in the sixteenth century, but since then it has been greatly improved, and most of the houses are now of brick; for which it appears to be principally indebted to Sir John Baldwin, who erected several public buildings, procured the assizes to be transferred hither from Buckingham, and raised a causeway, three miles long, on one of the approaches to the town, where the road was both miry and dangerous. Aylesbury consists of several streets and lanes, lying round the market-place, in the middle of which is a handsome and convenient hall, where the quarter sessions and Lent assizes are held; but the Summer assizes have been restored to Buckingham, through the interest of Lord Cobham and the Grenville family. The county gaol still remains at Aylesbury, and an elegant market-house has been erected after the model of the Temple of the Winds at Athens. Much profit is derived by many of the inhabitants of Aylesbury and the villages in its vicinity, from their ingenious method of rearing young ducks in the winter, which obtain large prices in the metropolis; and lace-making is also carried on here to a very considerable extent. The church is an ancient and spacious structure, with a low tower rising at the intersection of the nave and transept; it is very suitably decorated, and has a curiously carved pulpit; besides which, the churchyard is large, disposed into several walks, and planted with double rows of trees: this religious structure becomes a conspicuous object for several miles round, owing to the elevated situation it occupies, in comparison with the surrounding flat tract of country. Aylesbury is an incorporated town governed by constables, and sends two members to parliament, who, by an act passed in 1804, are elected by the inhabitants of the borough that pay scot and lot, and those of the three hundreds of Aylesbury; to which have been added by the Reform Bill, the 10*l.* householders. The weekly market, which is held on Saturday, is well supplied with all kinds of provisions.

DUNSTABLE.

Dunstable, a market-town and parish, in Bedfordshire, at the distance of only 1 mile from the adjoining county of Hertford, $33\frac{1}{2}$ miles north-west from London, $12\frac{1}{2}$ from St. Alban's, 11 from Berkhampstead, 5 from Luton, and $9\frac{1}{2}$ from Tring, is seated near the entrance of the Chiltern Hills, at the junction of the Icknield with the Watling Street,—two Roman roads of that name that here intersect each other. The name of the former is still preserved in that of Hicknill, which issues from the town on the north side of the church, and is said to connect the city of Oxford with the town of Cambridge. Dunstable consists of four principal streets, intersecting each other at right angles, and running nearly in the direction of the cardinal points. The houses are mostly of brick, and some of them are of considerable antiquity. As the soil here is, in a great measure, destitute of water, the inhabitants, who heretofore obtained it from ponds, have, after great labour and expense, succeeded in sinking wells, that now supply the town with that essential article of human existence. The inhabitants of Dunstable were, till recently, principally supported by the passage of travellers; the town being situated on the great line of road from London to Birmingham and Holyhead, generally known as the great parliamentary line, from the sum hitherto annually voted for its improvement, and which, constructed from the plans and under the superintendence of the late Mr. Telford, was justly esteemed the finest in England. This source of advantage has, however, been completely cut off by the formation of the London and Birmingham, and Birmingham and Liverpool Railways; and its interest has thereby been seriously injured. Many of the inhabitants derive their chief sustenance from the manufacture of straw bonnets,—an article known throughout England by the appellation of the "Dunstable bonnet,"—and the conversion of straw into hats, baskets, and various other articles of elegant use; a pursuit in which the poorer classes of the surrounding villages are also principally engaged. A few of the females find employment in the manufacture of lace. The first representation of a play in England is said to have taken place here, under the direction of a priest. Dunstable was made a borough and market-town by Henry I., who had a royal palace near the church, called Kingsbury. He also built a priory here, of which there now remains only a part. The front of the church is singular; the great door is under a semi-oval arch, richly ornamented with various grotesque sculptures: the tower stands at the north end of the building. Several stone coffins have been discovered here; particularly one with an entire skeleton, in the year 1745. A number of tournaments, it appears, were held in this town at different times. The larks caught here are remarkable for their size, and are sent to the London markets in great numbers. The market is held on Wednesday. Maiden Bower, mentioned by Camden as a circular fortification, such as Strabo described the British towns, is about a mile and a half W.N.W. from Dunstable, near the edge of a low range of the Chiltern Hills: it consists of a vallum thrown up upon a level plain. About three quarters of a mile to the left of Maiden Bower, on the downs above Totternhoe, is a strong fortification towering on a promontory that projects into the lowlands, that lie, as it were, like a map at its foot. About a mile E. of the town, a high prominence of the Chiltern ridge, denominated the Five Knolls, from that number of barrows or Celtic tumuli that occupy the apex of the hill, at an elevation of nearly 800 feet above the level of the sea, presents a luxuriant prospect, and is itself visible for many miles: upon a clear day, this hill is distinguishable from Bardon Hill, in Leicestershire, a distance of nearly eighty miles.

TRING TO LEIGHTON BUZZARD.

From Tring Summit, about one mile beyond which it enters Buckinghamshire, the Railway proceeds with an easy sweep and somewhat sudden descent (1 in 330), for about $2\frac{3}{4}$ miles, to Seabrook Bridge, where, crossing the Grand Junction Canal, and carried upon an embankment from twenty-five to thirty feet high, it preserves the same inclination, passing through Horton, for a further distance of $4\frac{3}{4}$ miles, when it again changes its inclination to a descent so slight as to be scarcely perceptible; in this way it continues for about six miles, in three of which it reaches the

LEIGHTON BUZZARD STATION,

AT SOUTHCOTT, A PRINCIPAL ONE, 40¾ MILES FROM LONDON, 71½ MILES FROM BIRMINGHAM (Journey resumed page 29);

The town itself lying upon the opposite bank of the river Ouzle, (which here separates Buckinghamshire from Bedfordshire), and consequently in the latter county. The Leighton Buzzard Station, on a level with the surrounding country, is one of those where the traveller alights on the rail: he will therefore do well to remember the Editor's cautionary note at the commencement of this work, and remain there no longer than is necessary for the obtainment of his luggage.

Emerging from the gloomy confines of the Tring excavation, whose lofty sides, full sixty feet in height, exclude all objects from the view, the traveller surveys on either side a prospect of considerable extent and beauty; to the left it extends over the Vale of Aylesbury, that lies at the foot of the ridge of hills, recently passed, and generally known as the Chiltern ridge, a range of chalky hills that extend from the vicinity of Dunstable in Bedfordshire to Henley in Oxfordshire, overlooking the celebrated Chiltern Hundreds, well known as affording the easy means of escape from a seat in parliament, rendered by circumstances no longer desirable. The view to the right is considerably less extensive, being bounded by the western extremity of the Chiltern ridge, that here descends in beautiful slopes and graceful sweeps to the valley beneath, and the high ground between Dunstable and the Brickhills, three villages of that name, that in a further distance of a few miles rise into view; in this direction, also, the churches of Ivinghoe and Eddlesborough, — the last the most distant — stand forth the most prominent features of the surrounding landscape.

The chalky line that, seen in this direction marked upon the turf, points out the locality of the hill a mile beyond Dunstable, on the Birmingham road, that on a clear day is visible from Bardon Hill in Leicestershire, a distance of nearly eighty miles. A little before Seabrook Bridge, thrown over the Grand Junction Canal, that valuable aqueduct, whose summit is at Startop's End near Tring, again appears in sight upon the left; the curiously cut eminence known as West End, or Cheddington Hill[*], is also an attractive object here; half a mile beyond Horton, Slapton Church is seen upon the right, and the village of Mentmore, seen upon the left, situated upon an isolated hill, forms a conspicuous feature in the landscape, which here, the Railway running upon a lofty embankment of full thirty feet in height, is somewhat extensive, including the town of Leighton Buzzard, the Church, its

---

[*] Cheddington is distant from London 36¼ miles, and is the commencement of the Aylesbury Railway, that, in a distance of 7¼ miles from the Cheddington Station, reaches that town.

tower and spire, which lie as it were immediately in front of the spectator. From Broughton Brook Bridge (a mile and a half on the London side of the Leighton Buzzard Station), and a short distance beyond it, the Grand Junction Canal and River Ouzle are seen upon the right. Two miles distant from Leighton Buzzard on the right is Stockgrove, the seat of Colonel Hanmer; and about the same distance on the left is Liscombe House, Miss Lovett.

LISCOMBE HOUSE.

Liscombe House, the seat of Miss Lovett, is a quadrangular building: one side of it being occupied by a chapel, which, by the style of its architecture, appears to have been built about the middle or latter end of the fourteenth century; the house, however, is of much later date, no part of it appearing to be older than the reign of Queen Elizabeth; the windows have been modernised. Among the portraits at Liscombe, are several of the Lovett family; a half-length of Charles Brandon, Duke of Suffolk, with a pink in his hand; the first Earl of Bedford, a half-length on panel, dated 1555; Sir Nicholas Crispe, in armour; Sir Edmund Verney, standard-bearer to King Charles I. who was slain at Edgehill; Archbishop Sancroft, Titus Oates, &c. In the parish church are some monuments of the Lovetts. The impropriate rectory, which formerly belonged to Woburn Abbey, is now the property of Miss Lovett. The curacy, or donative, is in the gift of the Crown; but the Lovett family have been allowed to enjoy the patronage ever since the year 1642, when Sir Robert Lovett left the sum of 40*l.* per annum, as an augmentation of the curacy, to be paid by his heirs on condition that they should be allowed to nominate the curate, whose salary was before only 8*l.* per annum. A charity school for 24 children was here founded by the Lovett family in 1714.

LEIGHTON BUZZARD.

Leighton Buzzard, a considerable market-town of Bedfordshire, upon the confines of Buckinghamshire, and at a remove of only half a mile from that county, distant from Dunstable 7½ miles, Woburn 8 miles, Ampthill 14½, Aylesbury 12 miles, Bedford 23 miles, and by the Railway 40¼ from London, enjoys an advantageous position upon the banks of the Ouzle; the Grand Junction Canal, and line of the London and Birmingham Railway, the former there dividing the counties of Bedford and Bucks. The church is a large antique structure, and by the various grotesque carvings which are scattered about it, is supposed to have been built at the same time as the cross, it being constructed with the same sort of stone. At the intersection rises a square tower, surmounted with a spire; the whole being 193 feet in height, it forms a striking object when approached from London at a distance of about five miles, where the Railway running upon an embankment of considerable height, the descent from Tring summit, in a tolerably direct line, a good view of it is thereby obtained. Here are also a quakers' meeting, and other dissenting congregational establishments. The market on Tuesday is well supplied with cattle, corn, grocery, lace, and straw plait; the manufacture of the two latter forming the chief employment of the poorer classes of females both in the town and its vicinity, the Grand Junction Canal also furnishing the means of transport in conjunction with other canals, not only to the metropolis, but to most parts of the kingdom, is of considerable advantage to the town, in the coal, corn, and timber trades, which are here carried on to some extent. The principal antiquity of Leighton Buzzard, or Leighton Beaudesert, its ancient name, is a handsome pentangular cross, supposed to have been erected about 500 years ago; it is situated on an open area near the market-house. About half a mile from this place, are the remains of a Roman camp; and from this and other circumstances, Leighton Buzzard is supposed to be the Saxon Lygeanburg, taken with several more towns from the Britons by Cuthwolf.

WINSLOW.

Winslow, in Buckinghamshire, 5 miles from Aylesbury, $17\frac{1}{4}$ miles from Buckingham, and 51 from London, is a small market town, situated on the brow of a hill, and though of a very remote origin, — it having been given by King Offa to the Abbey of St. Alban's, in a council held at Verulam in the year 794, — it possesses no object that can interest the antiquary. It consists of three principal streets, neat and well built, the houses being mostly of brick; this is a place of very little trade, the men being chiefly engaged in husbandry, and the women in lace-making. The church is a large pile of building, consisting of a nave, two aisles, and a chancel, with a square embattled tower at the west end. Market on Tuesday.

WOBURN ABBEY.

The principal front of this extensive and magnificent quadrangular building faces the west, and is of the Ionic order, with a rusticated basement: the interior is fitted up in the most superb and costly style, and many of the apartments are enriched with scarce and valuable paintings by the old masters; the gallery also exhibits a large and highly interesting collection of portraits; the library is stored with a valuable selection of works by the best authors; and a small room at the end of it, fitted up in the Etruscan style, contains 13 fine antique Etruscan vases, brought by Lord Cawdor from the Vatican at Rome. The stables constitute the wings of an elegant building, whose centre is occupied by the riding-house and tennis-court; these are connected by a colonnade, a quarter of a mile long, with the Duke's private apartments. In the green house, a handsome building, 140 feet long, there is a great variety of valuable plants, besides some excellent statues, and a grand Bacchanalian vase six feet nine inches high, and six feet three inches in diameter; this superb antique monument was dug up some centuries since, from the ruins of Adrian's villa, and was brought into this country by Lord Cawdor about thirty-five years ago. The Park, surrounded by a wall 12 miles in circumference, is well stocked with deer; it contains several fine plantations, and abounds with wood; the grounds are beautifully diversified by inequality of surface, and the surrounding scenery partakes both of the grand and picturesque.

WOBURN.

Woburn, a market town of Bedfordshire, situate on the west side of the county, at a distance of 8 miles from Dunstable, 8 miles from Leighton Buzzard, $8\frac{1}{2}$ from Newport Pagnell, $7\frac{1}{2}$ from Ampthill, $15\frac{1}{2}$ from Bedford, $24\frac{1}{2}$ from Northampton, and $41\frac{1}{2}$ from London, derives its chief importance from the magnificent seat of the Duke of Bedford in its vicinity. Woburn, though small, is extremely neat and uniform in appearance, — advantages for which it is indebted to a conflagration, that in the year 1724 nearly destroyed the town, after which it was almost wholly rebuilt. The church was erected by Robert Hobbs, the last abbot of Woburn. It then belonged to the abbey, and is still of exempt jurisdiction, being in the exclusive possession of the Duke of Bedford. This structure furnishes a whimsical instance of capricious taste; the body being completely detached from the tower, which stands about six yards distant. The tower is a small square building with large buttresses at the corners, and four pinnacles; the top is embrasured; the dial about nine feet only from the ground. The church consists of three aisles, and a chancel; and the whole is embellished in a handsome manner. The market-house, rebuilt after the fire, and since considerably improved, consists of two floors; the basement appropriated to butchers' shambles, and the large room above to the corn market. The market on Friday is chiefly for butter and cheese. The munificence of the Russells has been of singular benefit to this town, where many monuments of their liberality exist. Here is a good free-school founded by Francis, the fifth Earl of Bedford, a charity school and alms-houses for twelve poor people. The chief employ of the poorer classes, the females in particular, consists in the manufacture of lace and straw plait, but the industrious have always a ready resource in the Abbey, where, among the many who make application, few ever encounter a refusal.

LEIGHTON BUZZARD TO THE WOLVERTON STATION.

From the Leighton Buzzard Station the Railway, preserving the same inclination, upon which, previous to reaching that point, it had for some time continued, viz. a gradual descent, passes with a slight curve under Linslade Tunnel, 290 yards in length, and from thence proceeds through successive cuttings and over occasional embankments, with an easy sweep to Stoke Hammond. Emancipated from the obscurity of Linslade Tunnel, the Grand Junction Canal, of which a good view is obtained, soon appears upon the right, and this is shortly after succeeded by another of Linslade House and grounds, the latter sanctified by the little village church that here embellishes the foreground of an interesting but not extensive landscape. In the opposite direction to Linslade House the seat of W. Pulsford, Esq., and about two miles distant, but obscured by the high grounds in its vicinity, lies Liscombe House, an ancient seat of the Lovett family, at present occupied by Miss Lovett. From Stoke Hammond the Railway takes a northern inclination, and continued by successive excavations and embankments, with very little variation of surface, in a further distance of three miles reaches

THE BLETCHLEY STATION,
AN INTERMEDIATE ONE, DISTANT FROM LONDON $46\frac{3}{4}$ MILES, FROM BIRMINGHAM $65\frac{1}{2}$ MILES.

Quitting the Bletchley Station, the Railway, continued upon the embankment, shortly after crosses the great Holyhead road, by a massive brick and iron bridge at Denbigh Hall, a wretched roadside public house $1\frac{1}{2}$ mile beyond Fenny Stratford. The bridge over the Holyhead road, denominated the Denbigh Hall Viaduct, is distant, by the Railway $47\frac{3}{4}$ miles from London, and from Birmingham $64\frac{1}{2}$ miles. On the left of the Stoke Hammond road see the village of Stewkley, and on the right the village of Great Brickhill, with Brickhill Manor House, the seat of P. P. Duncombe, Esq. From the Bletchley Station, one mile on the London side of Denbigh Hall, the Railway, carried on a lofty embankment, affords a good view on both sides, the village of Bletchley lying on the left; to the right, the view, though not extensive, is excellent, embracing the villages of Great Brickhill, and Little Brickhill, a well known stage upon the Birmingham and Holyhead road, and, lastly, the church of Bow Brickhill, that occupying the wood-crowned summit of the Brickhill

Hills, stands boldly conspicuous, the most striking object and distinguishing feature of the finely-wooded, and very beautiful country by which it is surrounded. The ground occupied by Bow Brickhill Church is the highest in the county of Bedford, being 683 feet above the level of the sea. The Bletchley Station recently formed has been rendered necessary by the removal of a similar pre-existing establishment at Denbigh Hall, the destruction of which proved to the inhabitants of Fenny Stratford and the villages in the vicinity a very great inconvenience. To obviate this the erection of a minor station at Bletchley was determined upon, and its completion, of vast advantage to the surrounding neighbourhood, has given great satisfaction. From Denbigh Hall Viaduct, carried with a sweep first an embankment, then through a cutting of considerable depth for $\frac{3}{4}$ of a mile, that crossed by a bridge carries the road from the Holyhead road on the left to Woughton, a village on the right, in a further distance of $1\frac{3}{4}$ mile, the Railway reaches Loughton, a village lying on the left of the line, in two more Bradwell, on the right, and in another

THE WOLVERTON STATION,

A PRINCIPAL ONE, DISTANT FROM LONDON $52\frac{1}{2}$ MILES, AND $59\frac{3}{4}$ FROM BIRMINGHAM. — Journey resumed at page 37.

To tourists disposed to divide the journey from London to Birmingham into two, and who may be desirous of domiciling for the night in the vicinity of the Railway, completing the journey upon the second day; to such as are anxious only for a trip, to sleep one night from home, returning by any of the next day-trains; to the keen sportsman with permission to amuse himself either over the manors or in the preserves of the neighbouring gentry; and, finally, to the heroes of the chase disposed to tallyho the hounds of any pack that seek the covers of this fine fox-hunting country;—to each and all of these the Inns at Stoney Stratford, distant only $1\frac{3}{4}$ mile from the Wolverton Station, will supply excellent accommodation.

THE WOLVERTON STATION,

The only one at which passengers are permitted to stop, and for whose accommodation means the most complete have been provided in the shape of refreshment and retiring rooms, replete with convenience, is altogether a vast establishment; it is, in fact, a central depôt, consisting of workshops, warehouses, founderies, factories, and furnaces, here erected for the construction of boilers, engines, carriages, and necessary repair of all the articles used in the carrying trade of this company; the necessity for which, for the information of travellers in general, will, by the following remarks, be rendered apparent. Stage-coaches, unless fitted with patent axletrees, were not always capable of performing long journeys without a change, and in case of accident, might in most towns be partially, if not wholly, repaired; not so the Railway carriage, or its conducting engine, which, in the absence of the means thus judiciously provided, must have been transported to Birmingham or London in every case of failure. It is a fact also, not generally known, that the immense power necessary to the propulsion of railway trains renders them incapable of very lengthened journeys, and a frequent and close inspection is consequently necessary;—in a word, steam engines, like horses, may be said to tire, and like horses to require rest. Their continuance too long in operation tends, from the immense heat and friction, to the destruction of the works, and they are consequently upon the performance of a certain distance, say fifty miles, invariably submitted to the examination of the engineer. The necessity for the erection of this establishment has been, it is presumed, rendered completely obvious, and it only remains to remark, that to all who take an interest in engineering operations, and who, possessing the leisure so to do, have been provided with a necessary passport, an attentive examination of this immense laboratory, that in addition to its other appliances possesses the advantage of water communication, will prove a real treat.

STONEY STRATFORD.

Stoney Stratford, a market-town of Buckinghamshire, situate, partly in the parish of Calverton, and partly in that of Wolverton, at a distance of 6 miles from Newport Pagnell, 8 miles from Buckingham, 14 from Northampton, and 52 from London, is built on the Watling Street, a Roman road of that name, which, entering the county near Brickhill, crosses it in a direct line. The houses are principally of freestone, and extend for about a mile in length on each side the road. Originally it appears to have consisted of a few Inns for the accommodation of travellers; but as the trade increased a stone bridge was thrown over the Ouse, and the road becoming more frequented, the place became in consequence considerably extended. Stoney Stratford had formerly two churches, or rather chapels of ease, but that on the east side of the road was nearly destroyed by fire in 1742, and has not since been rebuilt: the tower, however, is still standing; the other, dedicated to St. Giles, was rebuilt in a neat modern manner in 1777. It is supposed to have derived its name of Stoney, from the Watling Street Roman paved road, and the ford that there existed through the Ouse. Near St. Giles's Church is a neat market-place, but the principal business in the corn trade, here carried on to a considerable extent, is by means of samples displayed by the farmers in the public houses. In the days of

Camden the centre of the town was adorned with a cross, erected upon the spot where Queen Eleanor rested; but this was destroyed in the civil wars. The necessary regulations to preserve the peace are made by two of the neighbouring magistrates, who hold monthly meetings for that purpose. Situate on the great Parliamentary road (the finest in England) from London to Holyhead, Stoney Stratford enjoyed considerable advantage from the expenditure of travellers, a source of revenue that has, by the formation of the Birmingham Railway, been completely cut off, and the town has in consequence from this abstraction of numbers suffered severely. The only manufacture here is that of lace, in which the female population find their chief employ; the men are chiefly engaged in husbandry, Stoney Stratford being the centre of an extensive agricultural district. Here are meeting-houses for Baptists, and other dissenters. The town has many charity schools, and a society for apprenticing children. The Grand Junction Canal passes within a mile of this place, affording water communication not only with the metropolis but with most parts of the kingdom, and, by the establishment of the Railway, the resident gentry in its vicinity reach London in a three hours' ride, and Birmingham in three hours and a half. The market on Friday is well supplied with provisions and corn, the trade in the latter being the staple commodity and chief support of the place.

BUCKINGHAM.

Buckingham, the county town of Buckinghamshire, in the hundred of Buckingham, 18 miles from Banbury, 8 from Stoney Stratford, and $55\frac{1}{2}$ from London, is seated on the river Ouse, over which it has three stone bridges. It is supposed to derive its name from Bec, a beech, with which description of tree this county formerly abounded, and of which, the soil being favourable to its growth, the cultivation is still continued. It is a very ancient town, and was fortified with a rampart and turret by Edward I. the Elder, in the year 918, against the incursions of the Danes, against whom he shortly after advanced, and compelled them to sue for peace. In 941 the town was ravaged by the Danish soldiers, and again in 1010, when, having plundered the adjacent country, they retreated hither to secure their ill-gotten plunder. At the time of the Norman conquest, this is stated by Browne Willis to have been the only borough in the county, yet it was then but an inconsiderable place, and only taxed for one hide. In the reign of Edward III. its importance was increased by that prince making it a mart for wool; but the trade being removed to Calais, it again declined, and in the 27th of Henry VIII. was enumerated among the many decayed cities and towns, for whose relief an act of parliament was then passed. About this period the assizes, which had been generally held here, were removed to Aylesbury, through the interest of John Baldwin. The misfortunes of Buckingham were completed by a dreadful fire, which occurred in the year 1724, when, out of 327 houses, 138 were entirely consumed, besides several outhouses and manufactories, belonging to premises that escaped the conflagration. The damage on this occasion was estimated at 40,000*l.* Since this accident, its trade has, in a small degree, revived, and part of the county business has been brought back, an advantage for which the town is indebted to the influence of Lord Cobham. The most conspicuous and principal ornament of Buckingham is the Church, which stands proudly exalted on the summit of an artificial mount, anciently occupied by a castle. This stately fabric was begun in 1777, and completed in four years, at an expense of about 7000*l.*, the greater part of which was defrayed by the late Earl Temple, who was a great benefactor to the town. It is a spacious stone structure, with a handsome square tower at its south-west end, ornamented with pinnacles, embrasures, and a light tapering spire which rises to the height of 150 feet from the ground. The interior is constructed on the same plan as Portland chapel in London. The altar is embellished with a tolerable good copy of Raphael's celebrated picture of the Transfiguration, given to the parish by the Marquis of Buckingham. About 200 yards south-west of the church is the burial-ground, where a small chapel or room has been erected for the accommodation of the clergymen at funerals; no interment being permitted in or near the church, nor funeral ceremony allowed to be performed in it. The area surrounding the church is laid out in a pleasant walk, planted with trees, and further enlivened with a view of the serpentine course of the Ouse, which winds round three sides of the town. The Town Hall is a large brick building surmounted with a swan, the crest of the Temple family; the principal floor is reserved for the use of the magistrates, who here hold their parish court every three weeks, and sessions half yearly; and here is a court for the recovery of small debts. The town principally consists of one long straggling street, the houses of which are meanly built, and many of them thatched. Buckingham is not a place of much trade, but on the banks of the river are several corn and paper mills that furnish employment to such of the labouring classes as are not engaged in husbandry, while the women here, as in almost all the towns of this county, are wholly occupied in the manufacture of lace. Lace-making has, however, of late years much diminished in Buckinghamshire, a manufactory having been some years since established at Nottingham; the lace manufactured by machinery has proved, as affecting its price, a formidable rival to the poor lace-makers of this part of the kingdom, who, it is greatly to be feared, have sunk in the unequal contest. The Buckingham Canal, a branch from the Grand Junction, with which it unites near Stoney Stratford, affords the means of water communication, not only with the metropolis, but most parts of the kingdom. The corporation in the reign of Edward III. consisted of a mayor and three bailiffs; but the charter granted by Queen Mary vests the government of the town in a bailiff and twelve burgesses, whose titles were altered by Charles II. into those of mayor and aldermen; but the former charter was afterwards restored, and the magistrates are still entitled bailiff and burgesses, and in them the right of election was prior to the passing of the reform bill wholly vested by that act, however, the right of voting has been extended to 10*l*. householders. Buckingham has sent members to Parliament ever since the reign of Edward VI. The inhabitants are divided into several religious sects, and the presbyterians, quakers, and methodists have each a place of worship. Here is also a free grammar school, and several charitable foundations. Buckingham has given the title of Duke to several illustrious families, with whose character every reader of history must be familiar. The late nobleman, previously known as the Marquis of Buckingham, is generally believed to have attained his dukedom at the solicitation of Louis XVIII. who, previous to his return to France, entreated as a personal favour of George IV. that such distinction might be bestowed on his valued friend, whose mansion of Hartwell House, two miles from Aylesbury, was during that monarch's exile, generously devoted to his occupation and enjoyment. The market on Saturday is well attended.

STOWE.

Stowe, the magnificent seat of the Duke of Buckingham, and the greatest ornament of the county, appears, when viewed at a distance, like a vast grove, from amidst the luxuriant foliage of which a number of elegant towers, columns, obelisks, and temples, exhibit their various ornamental summits. The mansion is situated on a fine sloping lawn, with the principal front facing the south; this measures 916 feet from east to west, and consists of a centre, connected by elegant colonnades, to two pavilion wings, of the same height as the centre, a projecting pediment supported by six beautiful Corinthian columns, and two pilasters, forms the grand entrance; from hence, the descent to the lawn is by a flight of 31 steps, at the bottom of which, there is on each side a massive stone lion finely executed. The interior displays all that the power of art, added to an exquisite refinement of taste, could possibly produce; expense does not appear to have ever entered into the mind while forming and decorating this superb mansion. Its various apartments are of noble dimensions, and contain a vast collection of paintings of great merit and value, besides several curious specimens of the antique, all of which are judiciously disposed in appropriate situations: the library is suitably furnished; it contains about 10,000 volumes, besides a number of very valuable unpublished writings, including many Irish manuscripts, and the whole of the works of the celebrated Charles O'Connor; but notwithstanding the various claims to notice which almost all the apartments possess, the saloon appears to deserve most attention, on account of its antique grandeur; this is paved with the finest Carrara marble, in squares of 4 feet each; it contains a number of elegant scagliola columns, in imitation of Sicilian jasper, with white marble bases and capitals; twelve niches are occupied by large statues, and candelabra of exquisite workmanship, besides which here is a frieze and cornice in alto relievo, by that eminent artist Signor Valdre. This apartment, with all its combined decorations, is transcendently magnificent; but when lighted, and filled with the melodious strains that issue from a concealed music-gallery, the effect is considerably heightened. The grounds are very extensive, and contain all the varied features of the picturesque and beautiful; a profusion of ornamental buildings have here received suitable situations, and the delightful groves, and noble woods, are enlivened by the purling stream, which occasionally falls over artificial ruins, and then spreads its broad bosom over a fine lawn reflecting the surrounding variegated scenery.

BRACKLEY.

Brackley, a market town of Northamptonshire, on the confines of Buckinghamshire, $8\frac{1}{2}$ miles from Banbury, $7\frac{1}{4}$ miles from Buckingham, and 64 from London, is supposed to derive its name from the brakes or fern with which the adjacent country is said to have formerly abounded. It is situated upon a descent near a branch of the Ouse, and though at present but a small place, has been considerably larger, of much greater relative importance, and is considered one of the most ancient boroughs in the kingdom; many remains of its former greatness are still visible. Leland observes further that it was a flourishing town in the time of the Saxons, but was razed by the Danes; that after the Conquest it was again in a prosperous state; became one of the great staples for the sale of wool; and had the honour of being governed by a mayor. These privileges it received in the reign of Edward II.; and in the eleventh year of Edward III.'s reign, it was of such eminence, that it sent three representatives as merchant staplers, to a council, held respecting trade at Westminster.

The first notice on record of Brackley, as an incorporated town, is in a deed respecting the hospital, dated in the fifty-sixth year of Henry III., and in the seventh year of Edward II. the title of mayor was granted to its chief magistrate. The corporation consists of a mayor, six aldermen, and twenty-six capital burgesses. The mayor is chosen annually, by the burgesses, at the court leet of the lord of the manor. Here were anciently two churches dedicated to St. Peter and St. James, the former is still the parochial church, and the latter a chapel of ease to it. The present town of Brackley, rude in appearance, and mean in character, can only show its former extent by its ruins, and its pristine prosperity, by a reference to its records. As at present existing, it consists of one street extending from the bridge up the side of the hill, about a mile in length, the houses being chiefly constructed of stone. Here is an hospital kept in repair by the president and fellows of Magdalen College, Oxford; a free school, and handsome market hall, with a good market on Wednesday. In the vicinity of Brackley is a piece of land called Bayard's Green, where, in the days of chivalry, several tournaments were exhibited. Brackley, according to Oldfield, first sent members to parliament in the reign of Edward I., according to Brydges from the time of Henry VIII., and continued to send two from that time till the passing of the Reform Bill, when it was disfranchised.

NEWPORT PAGNELL.

Newport Pagnell, a market town of Buckinghamshire, $9\frac{1}{2}$ miles from Woburn, 6 from Stoney Stratford, 5 from Olney, and 50 from London, is situate at the junction of the small river Ouzle with the Ouse, the former dividing the town into two unequal parts. The Church is an ancient and stately building, and being situated on an eminence, commands an extensive and beautiful prospect, over the rich, fertile, and fine sporting country, by which it is surrounded. The presbyterians and baptists have each meeting-houses here, and Newport Pagnell is by no means deficient in charitable institutions. Over the Ouzle and Ouse are two good stone bridges, and from that river, whence it is raised by an hydraulic machine, the inhabitants derive an abundant supply of water. The manufacture of paper and lace furnish the chief sources of employment here; the latter for females, is much diminished, the lace-trade of Nottingham, where it is manufactured by machinery, having carried off that of Newport Pagnell, which has in consequence suffered severely: of the male population, among the labouring classes, many are engaged in husbandry. There are two markets held here weekly, the one on Saturday for corn and provisions, and a lace market much diminished on Wednesday. The residence of Cowper the poet, who died in April, 1800, was about four miles distant from this place near Olney, from whose contiguous scenery many descriptions in his elegant poem of the "Task" are known to have been derived.

WOLVERTON TO WEEDON.

From the Wolverton Viaduct, a handsome structure and happy combination of symmetry and solidity, 660 feet in length, the Railway is carried forward upon a lofty embankment full 40 feet in height — a work of immense labour — through the valley of the Ouse and Tave, the right side of which is lined with gently swelling hills that here descend in graceful slopes to its base, and continued upon a level of three miles in length with a curvilinear sweep; crossing in the way the turnpike-road from Stoney Stratford to Newport Pagnell, the Grand Junction Canal, and the Rivers Ouse and Tove, that here unite their waters, extends to Castle Thorpe. On left of Wolverton Viaduct, the Grand Junction Canal appears in sight, and beyond it are seen the churches of Stoney Stratford and Cosgrove. Wolverton Park, the seat of R. Harrison, Esq., and Wolverton House, Rev. H. Quartley, lie immediately on left of Wolverton Viaduct; and one mile beyond it is Cosgrove Priory, uninhabited; beyond Wolverton, on right, the steeple of Hanslope Church, occupying a commanding eminence, continues for some time the most conspicuous object in the surrounding landscape; in its vicinity is Hanslope Park, W. Watts, Esq. Two miles and a half beyond Castle Thorpe, on left, lies Grafton Regis, the church of which is occasionally visible. From Castle Thorpe, the Railway commences a gradual rise, and in a distance of three miles reaches Hartwell Park Farm, where, quitting the county of Buckingham, it enters Northamptonshire, in another mile extends to Ashton, and in a further distance of a mile and a quarter crosses the road from Stoney Stratford to Northampton, at the village of Roade, at a distance of $6\frac{1}{2}$ miles from the former, and $5\frac{1}{2}$ miles from the latter town. Here

THE ROADE STATION,

A PRINCIPAL ONE, HAS BEEN ESTABLISHED, BEARING THE NAME OF ThE VILLAGE, DISTANT BY THE RAILWAY FROM LONDON 60 MILES, FROM BIRMINGHAM $52\frac{1}{4}$ MILES.

One mile and a half on left of Ashton see Stoke Park, the seat of L. Vernon, Esq. Near Roade commences a deep cutting, which, from the substance to be removed, a species of rock, proved for some time a formidable obstacle to the progress of the Railway, as it had previously done to the Grand Junction Canal, in the construction of that work. The range of hills here passed is denominated the Blisworth Ridge, and through it, by a tunnel of 3080 yards in length, the Grand Junction Canal is carried; at about a mile distant from which, pursuing an almost parallel course, the Railway has been constructed by first blasting the rock, and subsequently "undersetting" it with masonry; in this way a smooth surface has been formed at an immense cost to the Railway proprietors. Two miles beyond Roade the Railway reaches

THE BLISWORTH STATION,*

AN INTERMEDIATE ONE, DISTANT FROM LONDON $62\frac{1}{2}$ MILES, FROM BIRMINGHAM $49\frac{3}{4}$.

Blisworth is situated on the cross road from Towcester to Northampton, at a distance of four miles from the former and five from the latter town. The viaduct that carries this road consists of one lofty arch, and, viewed from the valley beneath, strongly resembles the Highgate archway. Here crossing the turnpike-road and the Grand Junction Canal, the Railway is continued upon the rise it commenced at Castle Thorpe, for a mile and a half beyond Blisworth. Quitting the confines of the Blisworth cutting, the eye is regaled with the undulating surface of the Nen valley, through which its course is for some time continued. From the last-named point, viz., $1\frac{1}{2}$ mile beyond Blisworth, it commences a gradual descent, continued by alternate cuttings and embankments, for about three miles; and in a curvilinear direction, pursuing an almost parallel course with the Grand Junction Canal, when, after passing the Bugbrooke Suspension Bridge, leading to the village of that name, and shortly after through Stowe tunnel, 400 yards in length, it gradually rises for a mile and a quarter, after which it proceeds with an almost imperceptible descent to

WEEDON STATION,

A PRINCIPAL ONE, DISTANT FROM LONDON $69\frac{3}{4}$ MILES, BIRMINGHAM $42\frac{1}{2}$ MILES, DAVENTRY 4, AND NORTHAMPTON $8\frac{1}{4}$ MILES. — Journey resumed at page 49.

Emerging from Stowe tunnel, the tourist experiences as it were an emancipation; the eye reposes on a rich expanse of country, and the military depôt at Weedon and Church of Floore or Flower, both situate upon an eminence, rise into view. The Railway in a short distance further approaches very close to the Grand Junction Canal, and in that way, barely separated, both Railway and Canal reach Weedon; just previous to which a curious scene presents itself: both these great works are constructed upon embankments; the Railway, rather above the canal, affords a good view of its singular situation, which is immediately adjoining the churchyard, the surface of the canal being above the body of the church, and nearly upon a level with the bells. On the left of Weedon, the barracks, storehouses, laboratories, and magazine of this vast military establishment present an interesting and busy scene.

* Here commences the Northampton and Peterborough Railway, that taken within a short distance of Higham Ferrers, Wellingborough, Thrapston, Oundle and Stamford, reaches Peterborough in a total of $47\frac{1}{4}$ miles from Blisworth.

STOKE PARK.

Stoke Park is the seat of Levison Vernon, Esq. The mansion, which may vie with any other structure of the kind in the county, was erected by Francis Crane, Esq., to whom the estate on which it stands was given in consideration of money due to him from the crown in the time of Charles I. The design was obtained from Italy. The building was begun about the year 1630, and finished before 1636, during which interval he gave an entertainment to the king and queen. It consists of two wings, connected with the body by two corridors; the columns which support these, Bridges says, were formed of red stone, a colour different from the other parts of the house; but this defect was remedied by the whole front having been cased with handsome white stone, and it now exhibits a pleasing uniformity of colour, corresponding with the regularity of the structure.

EASTON NESTON.

Easton Neston, the almost deserted seat of the Countess Pomfret, formerly stood high in the estimation of connoisseurs and artists, for the splendid collection of ancient paintings and marbles it contained; but the Countess of Pomfret having, in 1755, given the statues, &c., to the University of Oxford, this seat has since lost much of its attraction. The mansion was partly erected by Sir Christopher Wren, and partly by Hawkesmoor, but has since undergone considerable alterations. The adjoining church contains several curious and highly interesting monuments well worthy the attention of the antiquary.

NORTHAMPTON.

Northampton, the county town of Northamptonshire, 14 miles from Kettering, 11 from Wellingborough, 9 from Towcester, 14 from Stoney Stratford, and 66 from London, is memorable in the annals of political and local history, for the number of councils and synods held here; for its formidable ancient castle, with its provincial earls; for numerous monastic foundations and military events; and finally for its modern improvements, its pleasantness, and agreeable situation, regarded either as a place of business or retirement. In narrating its history, it will be unnecessary to dwell on the legendary stories that have been related respecting the first settlement made here, and the inhabitants who formed it. It is stated, however, that a town was formed here during the Anglo-Saxon dynasty, and that the same was attacked, plundered, and burnt by the Danes, in their different predatory incursions into this part of the island. The Northumbrians, under Earl Morcar, took possession of this town in the year 1064· and in the genuine spirit of savage warriors, murdered many of the inhabitants, burnt the houses, and "carried away thousands of cattle, and multitudes of prisoners." According to records, there were then 60 burgesses in the king's lordships, and 60 houses; but at the era of the Norman Conquest, 14 of the latter were waste. By the Doomsday Survey, it appears that "there were only 40 burgesses in NorthHamtune then." William the Conqueror gave to Simon St. Liz, a noble Norman, the town of Northampton, and the whole Hundred of Falkeley (Fawsley,) then valued at forty pounds per annum, to provide shoes for his horses. In 1106, the Saxon Chronicle states, that Robert Duke of Normandy had an interview with his brother King Henry I., to accommodate the differences then subsisting between them. In his twenty-third year, that monarch and his court kept the festival of Easter at Northampton, with all the pomp and state peculiar to that age; and in the thirty-first year of the same reign, a parliament was held in this town, when the nobles swore fealty to the Empress Maud, on whom the king had settled the right of succession. In 1138, King Stephen, in order to attach the clergy to his interest,—a measure in those days so essentially necessary, — summoned a council to meet him at Northampton, at which all the bishops, abbots, and barons attended, for the purpose of making promotions in the church. In 1144, Stephen held his court here, when Ranulf Earl of Chester, who came to tender his services, was detained as a prisoner until he had surrendered the Castle of Lincoln and other fortresses as a security for his allegiance, he being suspected of conspiring with the Duke of Normandy against the king.

When the celebrated statutes of Clarendon were established, the 10th of Henry II., for the good order of the kingdom, and for the better defining the boundaries of ecclesiastical jurisdiction, and Archbishop Beckett alone refused his assent (a refusal attended with a train of evils vexatious to the king, and fatal to the prelate), a council of the states was convened at Northampton, before whom the archbishop was summoned to appear, and answer to the charges of contumacy, perjury, &c., which should then be exhibited against him. In the twentieth year of this reign, Antekil Mallore, who supported Prince Henry's unnatural rebellion, marched with a considerable force from Leicester to Northampton, where, having defeated the royalists, he plundered the town, and returned to Leicester with his booty, accompanied by nearly two hundred prisoners. In the twenty-sixth year of this monarch's reign, a convention of the barons and prelates was assembled here, to amend, confirm, and enforce the constitutions of Clarendon. By this council, the kingdom was divided into six circuits, and justices itinerant were assigned to each. From the formation of this convention, the advice of the knights and burgesses being required, as well as that of the nobles and prelates, it has been considered as the model by which parliaments have been constituted in succeeding times. The King of Scotland, with the bishops and abbots of that kingdom, attended this council, to acknowledge their subjection to the Church of England. In the tenth of Richard I., Geoffrey Fitzwalter paid 40s. to be discharged from the inspection of the coinage here: this is the first official mention of a mint at Northampton, though there are reasons to believe it of greater antiquity. How long it existed is uncertain, but mention is made of it in the two succeeding reigns. On the death of King Richard, John his successor being then in Normandy, a great council of nobles assembled in this town, and were prevailed on by the adherents of the new monarch, to take an oath of fealty to him, and support his claim to the crown.

King John, in the tenth year of his reign, having been displeased with the citizens of London, commanded the exchequer to be removed to Northampton. In his thirteenth year, in a council of lay nobles convened here, the king met the Pope's nuncios, Pandulph and Durand, in order to adjust those differences which had long subsisted between him and the Holy See. The king made large concessions, but as he would not, or could not, restore to the clergy their confiscated effects, the treaty was broken off, and the king was solemnly excommunicated by the legates. During the reign of Henry III., Northampton was frequently honoured with his residence, and particular marks of his favour; and in the war between that monarch and the confederate barons, it was alternately besieged and possessed by each of the contending parties. About this time an attempt was made to establish a *University* here, consisting of students, who at different times, and from various causes, had deserted Oxford. The new seminary was at first countenanced by the king; but the scholars having taken a decided part in favour of the barons were commanded to return to Oxford. A similar emigration took place from Cambridge, but was soon superseded by a royal mandate, which compelled the students to return to their old seminaries, and further provided that no university should ever be established here. It is, however, a manifest indication of the importance attached to Northampton, that both the universities should make choice of this place as their asylum and abode.

On Good Friday, in the seventh year of Edward I., the Jews residing in this town crucified a Christian boy, who fortunately survived their cruelty; for this atrocious act, fifty of them were drawn at horses' tails and publicly hanged. In the preceding year, three hundred had been hanged for clipping the coin. These and other enormities rendered the Jews so odious, that in the eighteenth year of this reign a statute was passed for their total expulsion from the kingdom, and for the confiscation of their property. Edward I. frequently resided at Northampton in great splendour; and on his death a parliament was held here to settle the ceremonial of his burial, and marriage and coronation of his successor. Another parliament met here in 1317, in which an impostor, John Paydras, the son of a tanner at Exeter, was brought to trial for affirming that he was the real son of Edward I., and that the king was a carter's son, and substituted at nurse in his stead; producing no evidence, however, in support of his assertions, he was condemned and executed. In the eleventh year of King Edward III., the mayor, bailiffs, and burgesses of Northampton, obtained the royal license to hold an annual fair (now discontinued) for 28 days. In this reign, several parliaments were held here. The last that assembled at Northampton was the fourth of Richard II., when the poll-tax was levied, which occasioned the rebellion wherein Wat Tyler was the chief. The next memorable event respecting this town was a *battle* fought in its vicinity between the Yorkists and Lancastrians, in which the latter were routed; this was in the 38th of Henry VI., when that unfortunate monarch was made prisoner by the Earl of Warwick, and thence conveyed to the Tower of London. Northampton was visited by Queen Elizabeth in 1563, and by King Charles I. in 1634; it was ravaged by the plague in 1637; and in 1642 was seized by the parliamentary forces, by whom it was fortified; the south and west bridges being converted into drawbridges, and additional works thrown up in defenceless places. In the north-east part of the town, parts of a fosse and a bastion of earth are still visible. The town suffered greatly by a flood, May 6th, 1663. The town of Northampton was formerly surrounded by *embattled walls*, and was defended by a large fortress or *castle*, and by bastion towers. In the walls were four gates, named from their relative situations, east gate, west gate, north gate, and south gate. By an inquisition taken in the time of King Edward I., it appears that those walls had at different places steps to ascend them. Like the walls round the city of Chester, these served for a public walk. They also constituted in winter the best footpath from one extremity of the town to another. This walk is reported to have been wide enough for six persons to walk abreast. A portion of the outer walls at the bottom of Gold Street is still kept up.

Northampton has sustained some severe losses by *fire;* but these, as is not unfrequently the case, eventually proved beneficial to the place; for to these calamities are to be attributed the increased width of the streets and general arrangement of the town. On Midsummer day, 1566, a fire destroyed several houses; but the most memorable occurrence of this nature was in the year 1675, when the greater part of the town was consumed, and many of the poorer families reduced to great distress. The general loss of property was estimated at 150,000*l*. Above 600 dwelling-houses were destroyed, and more than 700 families thereby deprived of their habitations and property. A noble subscription was immediately set on foot, and the town subsequently erected in a very superior manner.

Northampton enjoys an agreeable situation on an eminence, at the foot of which flows the river Nen. It formerly contained seven churches, but nearly the whole town having been destroyed by the fire in 1675, it now contains only four. The principal church, All Saints, stands nearly in the centre of the town, at the meeting of four spacious streets, having a stately portico of eight Ionic columns, with a statue of King Charles II. on the balustrade, erected in gratitude to him for his gift of 1000 tons of timber, and seven years' chimney-money, towards repairing and beautifying the church, which was done in 1712, and the inside completed in a very elegant manner; it contains a statue by Chantrey of the Hon. Spencer Perceval, has a good organ, and in the steeple a set of chimes. The church of St. Sepulchre is of a circular form, having a cupola in the centre, supported by eight Norman pillars. It is supposed to have been built by the Knights Templars, from a model erected over the Holy Temple in Jerusalem. St. Giles's church, in the skirts of the town, is nowise remarkable. St. Peter's is deserving attention, as a curious relic of our ancient architecture. Here are also places of worship for the different denominations of dissenters, and a Roman Catholic chapel.

The streets of this town are regular, and the houses, uniformly built of a kind of freestone, are mostly slated. The whole is well paved and lighted. The sessions-house is a handsome building in the Corinthian style. At the east end of the town is a noble infirmary, capable of receiving the afflicted poor on a very extensive scale. The street called the *Drapery*, though not the longest, is the finest in the town, for its breadth and the handsome appearance of its shops. At the east end of the Drapery is the *Woodhill*, a fine open square of about 600 feet, around which are neat private houses and handsome shops. This square forms one of the finest market places in Europe. The stalls and shambles are all temporary, and the horse market held here is deemed to excel all others in the kingdom for horses for the saddle and harness. It is the chief rendezvous of the horse-dealers of London and York. Here is an elegant shire hall, a theatre, a county gaol, erected on the principle of the late Mr. Howard, a town gaol, and numerous charitable institutions; there are also capacious barracks. Northampton gives title of Marquis to the family of Compton. It has sent two members to parliament ever since the reign of King Edward I. The town is governed by a mayor, two bailiffs, four aldermen, twelve magistrates, a recorder, town clerk, common council, and forty-eight burgesses. The recorder and town-clerk usually continue for life, though subject to annual election. The inhabitants are chiefly employed in trade and manufactures, principally in those of shoes, stockings, and lace; of the former great quantities are sent to the metropolis, as well as exported. Situate on the great line of road from London to Leicester, Nottingham, Sheffield, Leeds, Derby, Buxton, Stockport, and Manchester, Northampton has hitherto derived no inconsiderable advantage from the expenditure of travellers, and maintenance of coaching and posting establishments, a source of revenue that since the introduction of the railway system is not likely long to survive. At the eastern extremity of the town, a pleasant walk, its sides planted with shrubs and trees, and thus rendered an excellent promenade, was formed about thirty years ago at the expense of the corporation. By means of the river Nen, and numerous canals with which that river unites, Northampton possesses the advantage of a water communication that extends to the German Ocean, the metropolis, Liverpool, and Bristol. Two stations of the Birmingham Railway, one at Roade and the other at Blisworth, each five miles distant, have been established, by which means the distance between this place and London, 66 miles, is now reduced to little more than a three hours' ride. A race-course was formed on the north side of the town in 1778, on ground formerly an open field, and the races held there annually in the autumn are invariably well attended.

An establishment of Franciscans, or Grey Friars, another of Dominicans or Black Friars, another of Friars Eremites, a priory of Carmelites or White Friars, and a college of All Saints, formerly existed here. The justly celebrated Dr. Doddridge preached here for twenty-two years, and also superintended an academy, which by his learning and judicious management obtained considerable reputation. Weston Flavell, a pleasant village $2\frac{1}{2}$ miles distant, deserves notice as having been the residence of the Rev. James Hervey, the popular author of Meditations, &c., who possessed this rectory and preached here many years to overflowing congregations.

TOWCESTER.

Towcester, a market-town of Northamptonshire, 8 miles from Stoney Stratford, 12 from Daventry, 9 from Northampton, 11 from Brackley, and 60 from London, commonly called Towster, and in the Doomsday Book, Towcester, is situated in a valley upon the banks of the Tove, here crossed by three bridges. Numerous

Roman coins have been found here, particularly about Berrymount Hill, an artificial mount composed of earth and gravel, lying on the north-east side of the town; it is flat on the top, about twenty-four feet in height, and the diameter one hundred and two. This hill was surrounded by a moat, capable of being filled with water from the adjoining brook, and has every appearance of having been a Roman muniment. Horsley places here the station Lactodoro, with greater probability of correctness than at Stoney Stratford, as Gale and Stukeley have done, though both places have an equal claim as to their being on a great Roman road. The distance assigned between Benavenna and Lactodoro is xii millia, and the distance between Daventry and Towcester nearly accords with this, being twelve statute miles; for though the Roman was somewhat less than the English mile, yet the difference may be reconciled by the Watling Street proceeding straight, and the present road curving to the south. On the north-west side of the town are vestiges of a foss, and the ruins of a castle or tower, probably a Saxon work, for in that period this town appears to have been a place of considerable strength, and is said to have been so well fortified, that the Danes who besieged were unable to take it. However, at some time it must have suffered from these people, for in the year 921, King Edward, who was in possession of the whole kingdom, excepting a part occupied by the hostile Danes, issued his mandate for the rebuilding and fortifying Towcester. The Danes of Northampton and Leicester, who had previously made a truce with the Saxons, suddenly broke their engagement, and marching to this place, carried an assault for a whole day; but the inhabitants displayed their courage by a vigorous and successful resistance, and receiving additional succour, the Danes were obliged to retreat. In consequence of this, towards the close of the summer, Edward advancing with his army to Passenham, encamped there, till he had fortified Towcester, and encompassed it with a stone wall.

As at present existing, Towcester consists principally of one long and spacious street; and having been, till affected by the railway, one of the greatest thoroughfares in the kingdom, contains several good inns. The church, a neat structure, situate between the main street and the river, contains nothing remarkable, if we except a monument, there erected to the memory of William Sponne, who, in the reign of Henry VI., was a great benefactor to the town. Many of the inhabitants — the male portion in particular — found employment in the large coach establishments that previous to the completion of the Railway existed here. Silk and lace are the principal articles of manufacture — the latter in particular — of which a considerable quantity is made, not only in the town but in the villages in its vicinity. Market on Tuesday. Sir Richard Empson, of infamous memory, was the son of a sieve-maker in this place. He turned his attention to the law, by his skill in which, and consummate knavery, he became a favourite of King Henry VII., who made him chancellor of the Duchy of Lancaster, and, to serve the purposes of royal avarice, promoter-general for enforcing the penal statutes throughout the kingdom. This he, with his associate and coadjutor Edmund Dudley, executed with such extreme rigour and relentless cruelty, that they incensed the people to such a degree, that Henry VIII. was constrained to submit to popular remonstrance, and sign an order for their execution. Empson was tried at Northampton, and beheaded August 16th, 1510.

DAVENTRY.

Daventry, a market-town of Northamptonshire, 12 miles from Towcester, 17 from Banbury, $12\frac{1}{2}$ from Northampton, 5 from the Weedon Station, and 72 from London, occupies the slope and summit of a hill, and is encompassed with hills to the south and east. From the mode in which it is pronounced, "Danetree," the common people have imbibed a notion that the place originated with the Danes, and from this silly traditional conceit has been taken the device for the corporation seal, the figure of a Dane in the act of cutting down a tree. From such an etymology, however, the judicious antiquary appeals, and finds a better appellation in the British words, "Dwy-avon-tree," *i. e.* the town of two rivers, a name exactly descriptive of its situation, the town being situate near the sources of two rivers, that, rising in its vicinity, flow in different directions, and eventually fall into opposite seas. The one, the Nen, taking a north-eastern course, soon reaches Northampton, and, after passing in its way the towns of Wellingborough, Thrapston, through Oundle, and lastly the city of Peterborough, discharges itself into the ocean at Cross Keys Wash, in Lincolnshire. The other, the Leam, a tributary stream of the Avon, after pursuing a tortuous course, passing in its way the town of Leamington, to which it gives name, soon after unites with the Avon, about a mile from that town; the Avon increased by the Leam, pursues its course, passing in its way the walls of Warwick Castle, in a few miles further reaches Stratford, and flowing past the towns of Evesham and Pershore, in Worcestershire, unites its waters with the Severn, at Tewkesbury, in Gloucestershire, and is eventually lost in the Bristol Channel: it may therefore justly lay claim to singularity of situation.

A priory was founded at Daventry, in 1090, by Hugh de Leycester, for monks of the Cluniac order, which, by a long list of grants and benefactions, became richly endowed — a circumstance that did not escape the keen observation of Cardinal Wolsey; for it was one of the monasteries dissolved by the permission of Pope Clement VII., and King Henry VIII. in the seventh year of his reign; and granted to the cardinal for the purpose of erecting his intended new colleges at Ipswich, and Christ Church, in Oxford. Though Daventry sends no member to parliament, it is a borough, incorporated under a charter, said to have been originally granted by King John, and again renewed and confirmed in the reign of Elizabeth. By virtue of this, the town is governed by a bailiff, twelve burgesses, twenty common council men, one recorder, two sergeants at mace, and a town-clerk. The bailiff for the time being is a justice of the peace, of the quorum, and chief clerk of the market. The recorder and town-clerk are required to be barristers-at-law; the former must be approved by her Majesty, and is, by virtue of his office, continued a justice of the peace for life. The two sergeants-at-mace are empowered to arrest persons within the borough, attached for any debt under a hundred pounds, the bailiff, ex-bailiff, with the recorder, constituting a quorum, who may issue writs for the recovery of debts to that amount; they also possess the power of committal to the county gaol, no other justices having cognisance of causes within the borough. None but townsmen can serve on the local juries, and the inhabitants are exempt from serving on juries at the sessions and assizes for the county.

Daventry, pleasantly situated, and surrounded by a beautiful country, is a very narrow, mean-built town, dirty and ill-paved. The church, built of soft Kingston stone, is a tolerable piece of modern architecture, and here are meeting-houses for the different denominations of dissenters. Daventry, like all the towns situate on the Birmingham and Liverpool road, maintained coach establishments of considerable extent, attendance upon which furnished employment to many of the inhabitants, added to this, the expenditure of travellers on this, till recently, the greatest thoroughfare in the kingdom, was of great advantage; the completion of the railway has, as will be readily imagined, by the removal of this traffic, inflicted upon these classes an irreparable injury. The labouring population not employed in agriculture are engaged in the manufacture of shoes, stockings, and whips. Here is a well supplied market on Wednesday, and five annual great fairs for the sale of horses, horned cattle, sheep, and cheese; this being considered, though not equal to Northampton, a central place of horse-dealing for the kingdom. About a mile to the east of the town is the celebrated Borough Hill, a spot peculiarly interesting to the lovers of antiquarian research. On the top of this is a very large encampment, occupying nearly the whole of the summit. In extent, perhaps, it surpasses any similar work in the kingdom. The shape is oblong, inclining to the oval, or rather to the form of the human foot, and is said to be capable of containing an army of ninety-nine thousand men. Borough Hill overlooks an immense lake, the Daventry reservoir of the Grand Junction Canal, that passes within two miles of the town, through a tunnel of a mile and a quarter in length; and at the foot of the hill is Burnt Walls, where various walls, arched vaults, and foundations of buildings have been discovered, and whence large quantities of stone have been removed for building; upon the summit of Borough Hill, a beautiful flat race-course has been formed, but the annual races are now discontinued. Upon this eminence the army of King Charles was posted, previous to the battle of Naseby.

FAWSLEY PARK.

The mansion is a very irregular building, but some of its more ancient parts are calculated to display the manners and customs of our baronial ancestors; the kitchen contains two fire-places, one 15, and the other $12\frac{1}{3}$ feet wide, with double arched mantel-pieces of stone; these are placed back to back, that the operations of either may not be interrupted: the hall, a noble lofty room 52 feet long, has an abundance of carved work on its ceiling, and a grand bow-window forming a recess, which is richly ornamented with stone tracery; the windows are enriched with the armorial bearings of the numerous families connected by marriage with the ancient lords of this domain; and the chimney-piece, besides its elegant decorations, is curious, as having a large window over it, the smoke being conveyed by two funnels up into the collateral buttresses of the fire-place, by which means the uniformity of the hall, as to windows, is as well preserved as if there was no chimney. The apartments contain, among others, a number of family portraits; and the park, which is well stocked with deer, abounds with ornamental forest-wood, and is enlivened by some noble sheets of water, situated in finely-wooded dells in the valleys. Fawsley Park is the seat of Sir C. Knightley, Bart.

WEEDON BECK.

Weedon Beck, a village of Northamptonshire, and a principal station of the Birmingham Railway, about five miles from Daventry, derives its appellation from a small religious house that was founded here as a cell to the abbey of Bec in Normandy; it is also called Weedon-in-the-Street, from its being seated on the Watling Street Roman road. It is related, that Wulfere, one of the kings of Mercia, had a palace here; and that his daughter Werburgh, who was canonised as a saint, founded at this place a nunnery, which was endowed with singular privileges. This religious house, and most probably the royal mansion, were burnt by the Danes. Leland says, that a chapel, dedicated to St. Werburgh, was standing in his time, attached to the south side of the church. The church, incongruous in its architecture, presents from the singularity of its situation a curious appearance. The embankment of the Grand Junction Canal here, about thirty feet high, passing close to Weedon churchyard, the surface of the water is there seen above the body of the church, and nearly upon a level with the bells. Two public highways for carriages and one small river, pass under this embankment, and to the right of the Railway, the canal is carried under the turnpike road from London to Birmingham. This is altogether an extraordinary scene; but what most distinguishes Weedon is its immense Military Depôt, which for its magnitude is unsurpassed by any in the kingdom. This grand establishment, occupying an area of considerable extent, contains within its walls a vast accumulation of warlike implements. Every thing here is arranged upon a great scale. A house for the governor, a park of artillery magazines, a redoubt, laboratories, storehouses capable of containing 140,000 stand of small arms, capacious barracks, an exercising ground, and a military hospital. The amenity of the place and its healthy situation in a fine open country are circumstances alike conducive to health, and regiments returned from India, mostly impaired in constitution, are, for the purposes of restoration to convalescence and the service, generally sent to Weedon. A cut from the Grand Junction Canal communicates with the garrison, thereby carrying materials for its use by water into the heart of the establishment, and not only stores but troops have not unfrequently been transported hither from the metropolis by the canal. The establishment of the Birmingham Railway will, however, now be resorted to for the removal of the troops, who, in the course of four hours, may by its agency, as occasion requires, reach Weedon or London.

FROM WEEDON TO RUGBY.

At Weedon the Railway crosses the Birmingham and Holyhead road, at a distance of five miles east of Daventry, when first carried through a cutting of considerable depth, and commencing a gradual rise, it is continued upon an embankment, and pursuing a sidelong course for a distance of four miles with that great work, it is then carried over the Grand Junction Canal, by the Long Buckby Viaduct. Here a road on right, leads to Long Buckby, a considerable village, lying on right of the line, distant $1\frac{3}{4}$ mile; that on left to Daventry, 4 miles distant. A mile and a half beyond Weedon, the Railway reaches Brockhall Bridge, leading to Brockhall Park, the seat of T. R. Thornton, Esq., whose grounds here skirt the line, and in $1\frac{1}{4}$ mile further, gains Whilton Bridge; the road on right leading to Whilton, that on the left to Daventry, 3 miles distant. From a little beyond Brockhall Park, it proceeds in a straight line to Long Buckby Viaduct, distant from London $73\frac{1}{2}$ miles, from Birmingham $38\frac{3}{4}$ miles. From Long Bucky Viaduct still continuing to increase its elevation; its course is that of nearly a straight line crossing in its way that useful aqueduct, the Grand Union Canal to

CRICK STATION,

AN INTERMEDIATE ONE, DISTANT FROM LONDON $75\frac{1}{4}$ MILES, FROM BIRMINGHAM 37 MILES.

Crick Station is situate at some distance from the village — not an inconsiderable one — that lies on right of the line, a mile and a half to the east of Kilsby, a small village having its site near the tunnel, to which it gives name, on the cross turnpike road from Daventry to Lutterworth, at a distance of six miles from the former and ten from the latter town. Crossing the Watling Street Roman road, by a viaduct at Crick Station, its course thence after a slight curve is that of a straight line through a cutting of considerable depth to Kilsby Tunnel, one mile and 640 yards in length, and the longest upon the line. From the farther extremity of Kilsby Tunnel, in little more than a mile continued through deep cutting, the Railway quits the county of Northampton and enters Warwickshire, at Hill Moreton Viaduct, here carried over the turnpike road and Oxford Canal, continued upon the Hill Moreton embankment; in two miles beyond that village, it crosses the turnpike road from Rugby to Market Harborough at Clifton Viaduct, and in another mile reaches

THE RUGBY STATION,

A PRINCIPAL ONE, DISTANT FROM LONDON $83\frac{1}{4}$ MILES, FROM BIRMINGHAM 29 MILES.— Journey resumed at page 58.

In the vicinity of Rugby among the first-rate residences elsewhere noticed, will be found one that, from the recollection of its former occupier, possesses more than ordinary claim to the attention of the tourist; this is Bilton House, long the residence and property of Addison. The Midland Counties Railway commences at Rugby, where also the Manchester and Birmingham Extension Railway is intended to begin.

KILSBY TUNNEL.

Kilsby Tunnel, one mile and 640 yards in length, is the longest subterranean excavation on the line; it may justly be deemed work of herculean labour; and though tunneling common to min ing operations is in certain soils esteemed by the skilful engineer an object of easy accomplishment, the construction of Kilsby Tunnel, on the contrary, from the quality of the substratum, and quantity of water issuing from the springs with which it abounded, proved an operation of very considerable difficulty. The intervention of a quicksand also presented for a long time a formidable obstacle to its progress; the accumulation of waters from which could alone be subdued by the perpetual pumping of steam engines of great power. Every obstacle, however, was at length eventually overcome, at what cost (300,000 has been named) is to the proprietors most probably unknown. The passage thus formed through this tremendous hill cannot fail to excite astonishment in the mind of every ordinary observer: its situation and extent considered, added to the engineering difficulties here surmounted, it must be viewed by all persons conversant with such subjects as a magnificent, masterly, and surprising work of art.

RUGBY.

Rugby, a market town of Warwickshire, 13 miles from Coventry, 16 from Warwick, and 83 from London. The name of this town is written Rocheberie in Doomsday, and the place was so called according to Dugdale, from Roche a rock or quarry of stone, and Berie, a court, or habitation of note.

This town is seated on a healthful and pleasant eminence, and consists of various clean and cheerful streets. At the time of the Conqueror's survey, it appears to have been a place of little note, and it made few advances towards affluence and celebrity till a period not far remote from the present. A castle was constructed here, as is supposed in the reign of Stephen; but if conjecture be right in bestowing the date of the structure on that reign, it was erected only for a military purpose of a temporary description; and it seems evident that the pile was soon levelled with the ground, as no mention of it occurs in any page of historical record. the time of Henry III. Sir Henry Rokeby obtained from the cro. a charter for a weekly market, and for a yearly fair to last three 'ays. But although these grants were highly favourable to industry and speculation, the inhabitants failed to make any great progress in commercial importance. Few inland towns, not favoured with the neighbourhood of religious institutions, attained much note or wealth in the early stages of history. Rugby never witnessed the foundation of a monastic pile; but in the latter part of the sixteenth century, it was honoured with a benefaction still more propitious. At this period a school was founded, which has been attended with circumstances singularly felicitous and now ranks among the first classical seminaries in the country.

Rugby school was founded in the ninth year of Queen Elizabeth, by Lawrence Sheriff, Grocer of London, chiefly as a free grammar school for the children of the parishes of Rugby and Brownsover, " and next for such as were of other places thereto adjoining. For the accommodation of the master who was, " if it conveniently might be, to be ever a Master of Arts," he bequeathed a messuage, or mansion at Rugby, in which it is probable he had himself resided through the few last years of his life, and he directed that there should be built near this messuage a fair and convenient schoolhouse. To defray the expenses of this foundation, and of a contiguous almshouse, he bequeathed the revenue arising from the rectory of Brownsover, and a third portion of twenty-four acres of land, situate in Lamb's Conduit Fields, " near London," and termed the Conduit Close. These eight acres of land were then of trivial value; and in 1653, they produced so little, that the commissioners appointed in that year for charitable uses, under the great seal of England, were enabled on duly considering the annual income of this charity, to make only the following decree: —

" That the trustees should, out of the rents of the said trust-estate, pay quarterly to the schoolmaster his salary of three pounds, and to every of the almsmen his allowance of seven shillings and seven pence according to the founder's intent; and, out of the remainder of the said rents, should defray the necessary charges of repairing the school, the schoolmaster's house, and the almsmen's lodgings; and the overplus, after the charges of meeting were deducted, which were not to exceed twenty shillings per annum, should be distributed between the schoolmaster and the almsmen, according to the proportions of three pounds to the schoolmaster and seven shillings and sevenpence a quarter to every almsman."

In 1686, the Lamb's Conduit property was leased to Dr. Barbon of London, for fifty years at the annual rent of 50*l*.. At the instance probably of this lessee, a decree of Chancery was procured, making a partition of the land, and allotting to the charity its specific proportion. The expanding precincts of the metropolis now drew towards the hitherto neglected and obscure field, and the leaseholder began to apprehend the possibility of the golden harvest, that in fact ensued, though he did not live to share materially in its advantages. In 1702 (thirty-four years before the expiration of Barbon's term) the trustees granted a fresh lease to William Milman, Esq., afterwards Sir William Milman, of forty-three years; such new grant to commence at the termination of the former lease. At the early part of the last century, few persons viewed speculations of building as a probable mode of acquiring wealth, and Sir William Milman obtained his enlarged term of possession for the yearly consideration of sixty pounds. Thus until the year 1780 the annual produce of the estate belonging to the Rugby charity, was only 116*l*. 17*s*. 6*d*. But shortly after the grant of an extended term to Sir William Milman, extensive streets of commodious family houses were erected, and it was computed that a ground rent of at least 1600*l*. would accrue to the charity on the expiration of his lease. A much greater income has, in fact, arisen, and the funds of this charity amount at the present day to no less a sum than 5000*l*. per annum.

It is pleasing to observe, that the flourishing finances of this noble institution are conducted in a way calculated to spread wide the beneficent intentions of the founder, and to aid the enlarged scheme of education consequent on the improved manners of later eras. The trustees are twelve in number, and the chief nobility and gentry of the county discharge the duties of their office with honourable zeal and activity. By these distinguished persons regular meetings are held, and before them (in the month of August) an annual examination takes place. Fourteen exhibitions have been instituted, and the exhibitioners are allowed the sum of 40*l*. per annum, to assist in their support, for the term of seven years, at any college or hall they may select for residence, in either university. These are termed "the exhibitioners of Lawrence Sheriff," and the vacancies are filled up at the annual examination, a scholastic process conducted with exemplary strictness, and which is attended by a member of each of the two universities, appointed for that purpose by the vice-chancellor.

The ancient buildings of this great seminary were such as might fairly suit its limited condition, in the early part of the last century. They chiefly consisted of a humble tenement used by the head master for a residence, a principal schoolroom of a moderate size, and two or three additional schoolrooms, constructed at different times, as the finances would allow. The trustees had long meditated the erection of an entire new edifice; and at a meeting which took place at London in May, 1808, it was found that the funds would permit the execution of their purpose. Mr. Henry Hakewill was appointed architect, and by that gentleman designs were submitted to the annual meeting at Rugby, in the ensuing August, which were approved, and promptly acted on. The new structure is erected nearly on the same spot as the former humble building, at the southern extremity of the town of Rugby; for which choice of site there appear to have been sufficient reasons. It allowed of a front towards the principal street in the town, and was at such a distance from it as to permit the intervention of a quadrangle. The edifice is composed of white brick, and the angles, cornices, and dressings to the windows and openings are of Attleborough stone. The style of architecture is that which prevailed in the reign of Queen Elizabeth, the period at which the school was founded, — a grateful and elegant compliment to the memory of the founder. Independent of the tacit respect thus paid to the benificent person with whom the seminary originated, we are decidedly of opinion that Mr. Hakewill selected the character of building best adapted to scholastic purposes, and his design eminently unites the useful with the picturesque. The rooms appropriated to different objects of tuition are judiciously separated, while the scholars are divided with collegiate regularity. The building is massy, august, and interesting, from a graceful disposition of parts, rather than from plenitude of decoration. The principal front is that towards the south, which extends 220 feet.

The schools are entered by a gateway opposite the street, which leads to the principal court, a fine area 90 feet long by 75 feet wide, with a plain cloister on the east, west, and south sides. The buildings on the south of the court comprise the dining-hall belonging to the boys in the head master's house, and three schools for different classes; those on the west are occupied by the great school, and on the north are the French and writing schools. The east side adjoins the offices belonging to the head master's house; and, by the cloisters on that side, the scholars have access to the matron, &c., without interfering with the domestics of the masters' establishment. The head master's house is suited to the present high character of the institution. The apartments are sufficiently spacious; and from the bedroom floor there is a communication with a gallery extending to the length of the dormitories, which range over the schools, and consist of lofty and well ventilated rooms.

The whole of the buildings comprehended in the first intentions of the trustees are now completed; but the school has so much increased in numbers and reputation, that the trustees determined to give it the accommodation of a private chapel, and one in the pointed style has been in consequence erected.

The almshouses constructed according to the directions of Sheriff were for four poor men, two of whom had been inhabitants of Rugby, and two of Brownsover. The number of almsmen has been carefully augmented in proportion to the increased amount of the revenues.

Lawrence Sheriff, the benevolent founder of these institutions, moved in so humble a sphere that few circumstances can now be collected relating to his biography. He was born at Brownsover, a small village near Rugby, and removed to London where he kept a grocer's shop in the vicinity of Newgate market. Dr. Thomas styles him a haberdasher, a term which appears to signify a general dealer in small wares; and the word grocer, as used in the 16th century, probably implies no more. He was likewise a servant to Elizabeth, before that princess obtained sovereign power.

Besides this great scholastic foundation, there is a school in Rugby, built and endowed by Richard Elborow, gent. of Rugby, in the year 1707, for the instruction of thirty boys. Attached to the school are almshouses founded by the same person for six widows.

The church possesses no architectural interest. At the west end is a square tower, without buttresses, and devoid of ornament.

The town of Rugby has a weekly market, and eleven annual fairs. At these fairs are sold considerable numbers of cattle of every description; and the business of that which commences on the 22d of November is sometimes not concluded under a week. But the grammar school of Rugby is its great support; and the prosperity of the town has evidently kept pace with the progress in resources of that fortunate establishment. Here are no staple manufactures; and the increased facilities bestowed on trade by the improvements of inland navigation do not appear to have been cultivated with much advantage by the inhabitants. While dependent on its market and fairs, the town consisted of a few narrow streets of low-built incommodious houses. Under the auspices of its flourishing seminary, new buildings are continually rising, and many of these are of a solid and ornamental description.

LUTTERWORTH.

Lutterworth, a market town of Leicestershire, seven miles from Rugby, 12 from Leicester, and 89 from London, was formerly noted for a peculiar vassalage of its inhabitants, all of whom were compelled to grind their corn at one particular mill and their malt at another; these were denominated the Lodge Mills; and under a decree issued in 1631, upon the authority of King James, this tyranny continued in existence to the year 1758, when the inhabitants trying the question of right at the Leicester assizes, obtained a decision in their favour, empowering them to erect mills and grind where they pleased, with costs of suit amounting to 300*l*. In 1690 an act of parliament was passed for dividing and enclosing in this parish about 14,000 acres of land, in which act Basil Earl of Denbigh and Desmond is described as lord of the manor.

Lutterworth is situated on the banks of the small river Swift, which soon after leaving the town joins the Avon. Many of the modern houses are built of brick, but the more ancient ones are of an indifferent kind. The church, a large handsome building, consists of a fine tower, from which rise four beautiful turrets, a nave, two aisles, and a chancel, the last being separated from the nave, by a beautiful screen. By a storm which occurred 1703, the spire, which was fifty feet higher than the present turrets, was blown down, and, falling on the roof, did great damage to the building, the pews, &c. About the year 1740, the whole was repaired, and all the interior made new, except the fine old oak pulpit, which is preserved with much veneration in memory of the great reformer, Wickliff, who was rector of this place, and died suddenly in 1387, while hearing mass. His portrait by Fielding hangs over the gallery at the west end of the church. The chair in which he expired is also preserved with great care, as is another relic, the communion cloth of purple velvet trimmed with gold, which is shown as the very garment he wore. Wickliff was presented to the living of Lutterworth, by King Edward III. Being the first person who opposed the authority of the Pope, and the jurisdiction of the bishops, he was much persecuted, and after being buried forty-one years, his bones were, by order of the council of Sienna, taken from the grave, and after being burnt, the inveterate spirit of Catholicism, committed the ashes to the Swift. These desperate proceedings created much commotion, and many crafty tales were invented to justify the conduct of the priests. "The very names of Wickliff, Lord Cobham, Huss, &c." says Gilpin, "will not only awaken sentiments of gratitude and veneration in every ingenuous heart, but will likewise excite a laudable desire of being particularly acquainted with the lives and characters of those eminent worthies, who, in times of peculiar danger and difficulty, nobly dared to oppose the tyrannical usurpation and barbarous superstition of the Church of Rome, sacrificing every valuable consideration on earth to the cause of truth and liberty." Lutterworth has a Presbyterian meeting-house, and some charitable institutions. The cotton manufacture is carried on here to a considerable extent, as is also the stocking trade, in which many hands are employed. Market on Thursday.

BILTON HOUSE.

At the distance of about $1\frac{1}{2}$ mile from Rugby, on the southwest, is Bilton, a village which the lovers of genius will approach with respect, for it contains a mansion that was inhabited by Addison, during a period to which he had looked with the warmest anticipations of joy—that of his matrimonial connection with the fair Countess of Warwick. The manor of Bilton was procured by the Boughtons of Lawford, early in the reign of James I., and was purchased in the year 1711, of William Boughton, Esq. by Mr. Addison, for the sum of 10,000*l*.; in which purchase he was assisted by his brother, Gulstone Addison, governor of Fort St. George, at Madras. It would appear probable that Addison bought this estate with a view to his subsequent marriage; and he resided much here during the brief period of life which succeeded that event. The Countess Dowager of Warwick, his relict, was often at Bilton after his decease, and on her death, the estate devolved on her daughter by Mr. Addison, who lived here through the long remaining portion of her life, and here died in the year 1797.

Bilton House is a spacious but irregular mansion, evidently constructed at different periods. The largest division, and that which comprises the chief suite of rooms, bears marks of the style of architecture which prevailed in the time of the first James, and was probably erected by the Boughton family, soon after they acquired possession of the manorial rights. The remainder of the pile consists of a lower range of building, the windows of which look towards the gardens; and this part of the edifice would appear to have been constructed early in the eighteenth century, and was, perhaps, formed by Addison when preparing the seat for the reception of its dignified mistress. The house is entered by iron folding gates, which conduct to a venerable porch. The situation is desirably retired, and the windows of the principal rooms command a prospect, which, though limited, is far from being destitute of interest.

On entering the mansion a thrill of respect, even to veneration, unavoidably passes through the bosom of the examiner, when he finds that the furniture used by Addison still remains; and the pictures, partly selected by his judgment, or procured as a tribute to his feelings, yet ornament the walls, and occupy precisely the same stations as when he was wont to pause and admire them. Seldom has the residence of a poet had the fortune to be so preserved for the gratification of posterity!

Many of these pictures deserve notice from intrinsic merit of execution; and curiosity must needs be excited concerning the character of a collection that once belonged to such a man.

The gardens attached to this mansion are rather extensive, and are yet preserved in all the formality of the old taste. Straight lines, and long and massy hedges of yew prevail throughout. In the lower divisions are two ponds, by the side of which are seats with sombre coverings of yew, trained to screen them. On the north side of the grounds is a long walk, still termed Addison's walk, once the chosen seat of that writer, when intent on solitary reflection. In its original state, no spot could be better adapted for meditation, or more genial to his temper. The scenery around is closely bounded by soft ranges of hills, and the comely spire, and Gothic ornaments of the adjacent village church impart a soothing air of pensiveness to the neighbourhood. The seclusion of this walk was deepened by lines of trees, among which were some

Spanish oaks raised by Addison, from acorns given him by Secretary Craggs.

FROM RUGBY TO COVENTRY.

From Rugby, where the Railway crosses by a beautiful Gothic bridge of five arches, the road from that town to Lutterworth, in about a mile beyond Rugby, it reaches Newbold Bridge, the road on right leading to the village of that name, that on the left to Bilton; and in less than another mile extends to Long Lawford, a village lying on right of the line, as does Newbold Grange, the seat of T. Walker, Esq. From Long Lawford, in rather more than a mile, the Railway reaches Church Lawford, a village lying on right of the line, where, entering a cutting of considerable depth, that as a matter of course excludes all objects from the view, it is continued thence in a direct line to the Brandon embankment, of considerable elevation; that formed across the valley of the Avon exhibits its scenery to great advantage, unites it with Brandon Viaduct thrown over that river, and thus reaches the

BRANDON STATION,

AN INTERMEDIATE ONE, DISTANT FROM LONDON $89\frac{1}{4}$ MILES, FROM BIRMINGHAM 23 MILES.

On left of Brandon Station is Wolston, and Wolston House, and on right of it Brandon, a hamlet to Wolston, the ruins of Brandon Castle, and Brandon House, James Beech, Esq., two miles distant, but obscured by the high grounds is Combe Abbey, the beautiful seat of the Earl of Craven. The church of Binley, a village $2\frac{1}{2}$ miles from Coventry, on the Lutterworth road, at the western extremity of Lord Craven's park, situate upon an eminence, stands forth a prominent feature of the surrounding landscape.

From Brandon Station, continued through an excavation, with intervening embankments, the Railway proceeds in a direct line for about $1\frac{1}{4}$ mile, to Brandon Oblique Bridge, (over which is carried the road from Brandon to Baginton, and Stoneleigh), when, taking a northern inclination, it is continued thence with a curvilinear sweep for $1\frac{1}{3}$ mile, the latter half of which is a lofty embankment of nearly fifty feet in height. It then reaches the Sow Viaduct, here thrown over the river Sow, and enters the county of Coventry. From the last-named embankment, whence an excellent view is obtained, that proves an agreeable relief to the deep-cutting recently passed, the traveller catches the first glance of Coventry, the tall spires of its churches there rising into view. From the Sow Viaduct, the Railway, carried through a country revelling in rural beauty, in a distance rather more than a mile, crossing in its way the Sherborne brook, reaches the viaduct over the Coventry and Southam road, and entering an excavation, in three quarters of a mile more the

COVENTRY STATION,*

A PRINCIPAL ONE, DISTANT FROM LONDON 94 MILES, FROM BIRMINGHAM 18¼ MILES.—Journey resumed at page 105.

From about one mile beyond Kilsby Tunnel the inclination of the Railway is that of a very gradual descent for a distance of 11 miles to the vicinity of Coventry. The environs of Coventry are extremely beautiful, and abound in seats of the nobility and gentry, a notice of which will be found in the itinerary line, that following the descriptive one is placed at the end of the book.

BRANDON STATION.

Brandon, where an intermediate station, between Rugby and Coventry, has been established, is a hamlet to the parish of Wolston, in Warwickshire, lying on the south bank of the river Avon, on the north side of which lies Brandon, and the remains of Brandon Castle. The precise period at which this castellated edifice was erected cannot be ascertained; but it is known that military service was performed here in the reign of Henry I., at which time it was denominated Brandon, or Brandune Castle. The ruins consist of a few disjointed fragments of massy wall. The Brandon Viaduct, a beautiful structure of nine arches, viewed from the valley of the Avon, forms a fine feature, the chief constituent one, of a very beautiful landscape, the effect of which has been considerably increased by its erection.

COMBE ABBEY.

Combe Abbey is erected on the site of a religious house of the Cistercian Order, founded by Richard de Camvill, in the reign of King Stephen. This was the first settlement of the Cistercian monks in the county of Warwick, and various benefactors arose, whose pious gifts enabled the abbots and brethren to maintain a course of secluded dignity through the long term of nearly four centuries. When the dissolution of endowed religious houses took place in the time of Henry VIII., the revenues of this monastery were stated at 302*l*. 15*s*. 3*d*. per annum.

The property was granted by Edward VI. to John Earl of Warwick, and, after the attainder of that nobleman, was leased, at the rent of 196*l*. 8*s*. 1*d*. to Robert Kelway, surveyor of the court of wards and liveries, whose daughter Anne conveyed the possession, by marriage, to John Harrington, Esq., afterwards Lord Harrington. Lucy, the daughter of this lord, and wife to Edward Earl of Bedford, became heir on the death of a brother; but

* From whence a branch railway is now made through Kenilworth to Leamington, nine miles distant.

the profuse expenses in which she indulged caused the estate to be alienated to the ancestors of the Earl of Craven. In the latter noble family it is at present vested. The name by which this seat is distinguished, implies the flatness of its situation; but the adjacent country is of a pleasing character, and the attached park, which comprises 500 acres, is finely adorned with wood and water. The greater part of the present edifice was raised by Lord Harrington on the ruins of the monastic pile. The form of the structure is that so usual in the early part of the seventeenth century—the half of the Roman H; but in selecting this mode of architectural disposal, it would appear that his lordship attended in some measure to the shape of the original building. Considerable remains of two cloisters are still to be seen, which mark the course of the ancient structure. These fragments are in careful preservation, and consist chiefly of Norman arches and pillars, which are exhibited on the inner face of a fine corridor that ranges along the lower division of the mansion. The sides of this corridor are hung with antlers of every growth and size, and various emblems of baronial free warren.

Considerable enlargements have been made by different noble owners; but a laudable attention has been paid to architectural consistency in the great front view. On the west an additional pile has been raised, from a design, as it is said, of Inigo Jones. This division, though by no means allusive to the prevailing character of the edifice, is sufficiently distinct to avoid offending by incongruity of style, while it forms a fine and judicious augmentation to the interior.

Few ancient mansions contain ranges of apartments better suited to purposes of state and dignified hospitality than Combe Abbey. Many rooms are of noble proportions, and the avenues of communication are chiefly light and spacious. The walls are lined throughout with paintings of high interest, both from story and execution,—accumulated memorials of the taste and liberality of many noble proprietors. This collection is particularly rich in portraits of the ill-fated Stuart family,—a circumstance accounted for in the following manner:—

William Lord Craven, one of the heroic characters of the seventeenth century, was the most forward and the most entirely devoted, of the many champions produced by the charms and misfortunes of Elizabeth of Bohemia. This princess was the eldest daughter of James I., and was married to Frederic, the elector palatine, who was advanced to the regal honour as King of Bohemia, by the revolted states, when an attempt was made to shake off the yoke of the Emperor Ferdinand II. The battle of Prague deprived Frederic at once of regal dignity and hereditary right. On descending from the throne, he encountered fortune in her most adverse mood, and entered Holland a fugitive and a beggar. Many English cavaliers, the latest offspring of decayed chivalry, struggled without avail to reinstate him in power. The ardour of these knights was greatly stimulated by a romantic admiration of Elizabeth their queen. The votaries of this bright star of the Stuarts were numerous, and it is supposed that at an after-period, when Elizabeth resided in England, widowed in love as well as ruined in hopes, she found consolation in the tenderness of William Lord Craven, and was privately married to him, though political motives forbade the public avowal of her nuptials. By will she bequeathed to this nobleman her collection of pictures, including many original portraits of distinguished persons brought from Germany.

KENILWORTH.

Kenilworth, a small market-town of Warwickshire, 95 miles from London, is situate 5 miles south-west of the city of Coventry, and is nearly the same distance, on the north-east, from the town of Warwick. Sir William Dugdale observes that, previous to the conquest, Kenilworth was a member of the neighbouring parish of Stoneleigh, being an ancient demesne of the crown, " and had, within the precincts thereof, a castle situate upon the bank of Avon, in the woods opposite to Stonely Abbey, which castle stood upon a place called Hom (Holme) Hill; but was demolished in those turbulent times of warr betwixt King Edmund and Canutus the Dane."

At the time of the Norman survey, Kenilworth was divided into two parts, one of which was styled Optone, and was held of the king by Albertus Clericus, " in pure almes." The other portion was possessed by Richard the Forester. In the reign of Henry I., the manor was bestowed by the king on Geoffrey de Clinton, who founded here a potent castle and a monastery. But, though a fortified residence and a religious foundation were usually in the early ages the harbingers of wealth and consequence to a neighbouring town, Kenilworth does not appear to have ever attained much distinction for greatness of population or traffic. Henry III. bestowed the privileges of a weekly market on the Tuesday, and an annual fair to last three days; but it is likely that this market sunk into disuse, as, in the eighteenth of Queen Elizabeth, Robert Dudley Earl of Leicester obtained the grant of a weekly market on Wednesday, and a yearly fair on Midsummer day. The town now chiefly consists of an irregular street, nearly a mile in length, and has a manufacture of horn combs on a considerable scale. The castle which, when firm through all its battlements and courts, and peopled with the baronial pride of the land, formed so fine an ornament to this town, still imparts a melancholy grandeur to the neighbourhood by the unusual magnificence of its ruins. These remains, have indeed, powerful claims on the feelings of the examiner: they present one of the most splendid and picturesque wrecks of castellated strength to be found in any English county, and are united with various interesting passages of history.

Geoffery de Clinton, the founder of this structure, is believed to have been a man of mean origin, but his talents and acquirements were so conspicuous that he was made lord chamberlain and treasurer to King Henry I., and afterwards was appointed chief justice of England. The castle, however, shortly passed from his posterity. In the reign of Henry II. it was possessed by the king, who placed here a garrison when his eldest son rebelled against him. The account of the provisions taken up for the use of this garrison is curious, as showing the great value of money at the period. The following are the articles and the sums paid for them: — 100 quarters of bread corn, 8*l*. 8*s*. 2*d*., (little more than 2*d*. per bushel); 20 quarters of barley, 33*s*. 4*d*.; 100 hogs, 7*l*. 10*s*.; 40 cows, salted, 4*l*.; 120 cheeses, 40*s*.; 25 quarters of salt, 30*s*.

It is evident that the large fortified dwellings of the barons in those turbulent times not only afforded a retreat to the more defenceless, but were probably made on that account a source of profit to their owners; for we find that the sheriff, in accounting for the emoluments derived from the ward of this castle, mentions " certain money that he received in the nature of rent, from such as had their abode therein." In the reigns of Kings John and Henry III. large sums were expended on such buildings as assisted in rendering the fortress more defensible. The latter king in the 38th year of his reign granted the castle to Simon Montfort, Earl of Leicester, and Elinor his wife, but only for their respective lives. When this earl took arms against his sovereign, he appointed Sir John Gifford governor of the castle thus recently bestowed as a pledge of amity, and it was constituted for some time the great place of resort for the insurgent nobles. After the discomfiture and death of the Earl of Leicester, at Evesham, Simon Montfort, his son, continued to shelter himself in this fortress, where he was joined by those friends of the baronial faction that were able to effect an escape from the field of battle. Thus aided, he exercised his power with a ferocity usual in that barbarous age. He is said to have sent abroad his bailiffs and officers with an affectation of sovereign authority; and bands of soldiery frequently issued from the castle on predatory excursions, during which they spread the miseries of fire and sword with an unsparing hand.

These scenes of violence were interrupted by the approach of the king, who drew near, in much military pomp, at the head of an army of which the *posse comitatus* of Warwickshire formed a part. Simon Montfort, so arrogant when unopposed, now proved his cowardice to be equal to his cruelty, and secretly withdrew to France, naming Henry de Hastings governor of the castle. Conscious of the great strength of the place, and willing to prevent effusion of blood, the king sent a message of fair promise to the governor, demanding a surrender; but those within the walls not only rejected his clement overture, but basely insulted and maimed the messenger. The siege now commenced, and the garrison defended themselves with vigour. They were well provided with military engines, among which were some that cast stones to a considerable distance; and they occasionally ventured on desperate and destructive sallies; several large stones, supposed to be a part of those hurled during this siege, are yet shown in the vicinity of the ruins.

The royal forces were equally active, but the strength of the fortifications mocked their most resolute assaults. The king now had recourse to a commendable stroke of policy. An act had been passed, in a parliament lately held at Winchester, disinheriting all those in open rebellion; and Henry, at this juncture, caused a convention of the chief persons favourable to his interest to assemble at Kenilworth, by which twelve nobles and prelates were elected, with power to make such a farther determination concerning the confiscated property as immediate circumstances might render expedient. By these lords it was settled that all the disinterested persons (except the wife and children of the Earl of Leicester, and a few others), should have the privilege of redeeming their estates by a pecuniary fine apportioned to the degree of offence, which fine should not exceed five years' value, nor be less than two. This is the well-known decree termed the Dictum de Kenilworth. The persons elected met at Coventry, but the resolution was published by proclamation in the king's camp. The besieged, however, treated this overture with scorn; and Henry, quite convinced that no blandishments could afterwards avail, prepared to storm the castle. But famine and sickness, the inglorious but most profitable auxiliaries of a besieging army, so badly provided with means of assault as were the military of those ages, spread their horrible influence over the garrison, and arrested the progress of the sword. Although assured that the besieged were reduced to extremity, the king granted lenient terms, and took possession of the castle, after having lain before it six months. He shortly bestowed the fortress so tediously acquired on Edmund, his younger son, whom he created Earl of Leicester and Lancaster.

In the seventh year of Edward I., a costly and gallant tournament was held at Kenilworth. The knights were one hundred in number, and many were foreigners of distinction who entered England for the purpose of displaying their chivalry on this occasion. Roger Mortimer, Earl of March, was the promoter of the festival, and was the principal challenger of the tilt yard. The ladies were, likewise, 100 in number; and, as an instance of the splendour with which they were attired, it is recorded that they wore silken mantles. The exercises began on the eve of St. Matthew, and continued till the day after the feast of St. Michael. The dances were not less gallantly attended than the lists; and to avoid all painful distinctions that might arise from an attention to precedence, the whole party banquetted at a round table.

On the attainder of Thomas Earl of Lancaster, son of Earl Edmund, the castle returned to the crown; and was by Edward II. intended as a place of retirement, when he saw danger augmented on every side. But this ill-fated king was doomed to be brought hither as a prisoner. Henry Earl of Lancaster conveyed him to this place; and here he received intelligence of his formal deposition by the parliament held at Westminster. Shortly after his mournful reply to this information, he was hurried to Berkeley Castle, the theatre of his last wretched hours.

In the reign of Edward III., John of Gaunt, Duke of Lancaster, obtained possession of Kenilworth, by his marriage with Blanch, daughter of Henry Earl of Lincoln and Duke of Lancaster. The great aim of those who had hitherto conduced to the building of this strong castle was security: to elegance of domestic accommodation they were strangers. The reign of the third Edward produced a striking improvement in manners, and convenience and splendour of architectural arrangement were then first cultivated in England. By John of Gaunt large additions were made; and a great portion of the present ruins consists of the buildings raised by his munificence. In the person of King Henry IV., son of this duke, the castle again became the property of the crown; and so continued till Queen Elizabeth conferred it on Robert Dudley, Earl of Leicester. This earl expended great sums in adorning and enlarging the structure; and here he had the honour of entertaining Queen Elizabeth in a manner so magnificent, that a notice of the festivities has been justly said to form an almost necessary page of the national annals. Her Majesty arrived on the 9th of July, 1575, and the splendid revelry of the season has met with a curious and amusing chronicle in Laneham, an attendant on the court. From this writer we learn that the Queen, after dining at Long Itchington, and hunting by the way, "was met in the park, about a slight shoot from the Brayz, and first gate of the castl," by a person representing "one of the ten sibills, cumly clad in a pall of white silk, who pronounced a proper poezie in English rime and meeter." This her "Majestie benignly accepted, and passed foorth untoo the next gate of the Brayz, which for the length, largeness, and use, they call now the tylt-yard; whear a porter, tall of person, and wrapt also in sylke, with a club and keize of quantitee according, had a rough speech full of passions in meeter, aptly made to the purpose." When the porter had concluded his harangue, six trumpeters, "clad in long garments of sylk, who stood upon the wall of the gate, sounded a tune of welcum." This strain continued while, "her highness, all along this tylt-yard, rode unto the inner gate, where a person representing the Lady of the Lake (famous in King Arthurz book), with two nymphs waiting upon her, arrayed all in sylks, attended her highness coming." From the midst of the pool, where was a moveable island, "bright blazing with torches," the Lady of the Lake floated to land, and greeted her Majesty with a "well-penned meeter," expressive of "the auncientee of the castl," and the hereditary dignity of the earls of Leicester.

A burst of music closed this part of the ceremony. Over a dry valley leading to the castle gates "waz thear framed a fayr bridge, and upon the first pair of posts were set too cumly, square, wyre cages," containing "live bitters, curluz, shooverlarz, hearsheawiz, Godwitz, and such like deinty byrds. On the second payr were two great sylver'd bollz, featly adapted to the purpoze, filde with applz, pearz, oranges, poungarnets, lemmans," &c. "The third pair of posts, in too such sylver'd bollz, had (all in earz green and gold), wheat, barley, ootz," &c. The fourth post, "on the left hand, had grapes in clusters, whyte and red, and the match post against it, had a payre of great whyte, sylver lyvery pots for wyne." The fifth pair had each "a fair large trey, streaw'd with fresh grass," containing various specimens of sea fish,—a costly presentation, at that period, for a host in an inland situation. The sixth pair of posts sustained a more elevated burthen, and ascended from tokens of good cheer to the dignity of armorial bearings. On them "wear set two ragged stavez of sylver, as my lord givez them in armz, beautifully glittering of armour thereupon depending." On the seventh posts, the last and nearest to the castle, were placed various instruments, symbolical "of the gifts of Phœbus;" tropes of the arts which should be raised on the pomp of chivalric bearings, and which were thus justly hinted to form the last result of dignified effort.

Over the castle gate, on a "table beautifully garnisht aboove with her highness arms," was inscribed a Latin poem, descriptive of the various tributes paid to her arrival by the gods and goddesses. This was read to her by a poet, "in a long ceruleous garment, with a bay garland on his head, and a skro in his hand. So passing intoo the inner court, her Majestie (that never rides but alone,) thear set doun from her paifrey, was conveied up to chamber, when after did follo a great peal of gunz and lightning by fyrwork."

The festivities lasted seventeen days, and comprised nearly every pastime which the resources of the age could produce, The hart was hunted in the park, the dance was proclaimed in the gallery, and the tables were loaded from morn to midnight with sumptuous cheer. As a proof of the hospitable spirit of the earl, Laneham observes, that "the clock bell sang not a note all the while her highness was thear: the clock stood also still withall; the hands of both the tablz stood firm and fast, allweys pointing at two a'clock," the hour of banquet! The park was peopled with mimic gods and goddesses, to surprise the regal visitant with complimentary dialogues and poetical representations. More simple amusements were also studiously introduced; the men of Coventry performed their Hocktide play*; the rural neighbours were assembled to run at the quintin; and a marriage in strict consistency of country ceremonials was celebrated under the observance of the queen. Every hour had its peculiar sport. A famous Italian tumbler displayed feats of agility; morris-dancers went through their rude evolutions, by way of interlude; and thirteen bears were baited for the gratification of the courtiers. During the Queen's stay, five gentlemen were honoured with knighthood, "and nyne persons were cured of the peynfull and dangerous diseaz, called the king's evill."

Robert Dudley, Earl of Leicester, died without acknowledged legitimate issue, and bequeathed Kenilworth to his brother, Ambrose Earl of Warwick, for life; but he willed that the inheritance should descend to Sir Robert Dudley, his son. Sir Robert Dudley came into possession shortly after the decease of his father, but he quitted the kingdom, under the king's licence to travel for three years; and, not returning, his estates were seized for the use of the crown. At this period a survey of Kenilworth was taken by the king's officers, from which we extract a few particulars calculated to convey some idea of the building and dependencies, when perfected by the labour of many ages:—

---

* Founded on the massacre of the Danes, in 1002. The actors were led to the spot of performance by Captain Cox, a person of so much humorous notoriety in his day, that Ben Jonson names one of his masques printed in 1640, "A Masque of Owls at Kenelworth, presented by the Ghost of Captain Cox, mounted on his Hobby Horse."

"The circuit within the walls containeth 7 acres, upon which the walks are so spacious and fair that two or three persons together may walk upon most places thereof. The castle, with the four gate-houses, are all built of freestone, hewen and cut; the walls in many places of xv and x foot thickness, some more, some less, the least 4 foot in thickness square. There runneth through the grounds, by the walls of the castle, a fair pool, containing cxi acres, which at pleasure is to be let round about the castle. The circuit of the castle, mannours, parks, and chase, lying round together, containing at least xix or xx miles, in a pleasant countrey; the like both for strength, state, and pleasure, not being within the realm of England."

Prince Henry, to whom the estate was resigned by the king, avowed his readiness to pay to Sir Robert Dudley the sum of 14,500*l*. for his title to the castle and domains, notwithstanding the legal incapacity to which he had rendered himself subject; but owing to the death of the prince, not more than 3000*l*. were actually forwarded; and no part ever reached the fugitive Sir Robert. The estate was possessed by the king at the commencement of the last civil war, and it shared the disastrous fortunes of its regal owner. The castle of Kenilworth may figuratively be said to have died an inglorious death. A mighty building, like a mighty chieftain, seems to fall with consonant magnificence when it sinks beneath the pressure of conflict, amid the general havoc of a wide field of chivalry; but this castle crumbled into ruins under the petty assaults of sordid hands,—bannerless and without one contending hero to sigh over its destruction. Cromwell granted the whole manor to certain officers of his army, who demolished the splendid fabric in order to make a market of its materials. The turrets once dismantled, the relics were open to every spoliator. But the hand of depredation is now stopped, and the fragments, if left to the slow inroads of time, are likely to remain the memorials of baronial grandeur, for the melancholy gratification of many a succeeding age.

These ruins are very extensive, and present various combinations of the most romantic and picturesque description. They are in many parts screened and defended from the rain and winds by nestling shrubs and clinging ivy, which impart a lovely mellowness to the general display. Of the original fortress, it is believed that only one portion remains. This comprises three sides of a square tower, popularly termed Cæsar's tower, an appellation often bestowed on buildings of a similar construction. The walls of this structure are in some places 16 feet thick. The additions made by John Duke of Lancaster were large and massive. Considerable parts still remain in different stages of decay, and they are yet distinguished by the term of Lancaster buildings. That division of the pile that owes its foundation to the Earl of Leicester was of a magnificent character, and is likewise known by the name of its noble designer. In this part of the castle-ruins are to be seen the relics of the great hall of entertainment, a fine baronial room, 86 feet in length, and 45 feet in width.

The Leicester buildings were composed of a brown friable stone, not well calculated to stand the weather; and this part of the pile, though the last erected, is perhaps the most ancient in appearance. The great gate-house raised by the earl is in better preservation. The entrance was formerly through an arched way, now walled in; and the building is at present occupied by a farmer. In one apartment is a large and curious chimney-piece of alabaster, ornamented with the armorial bearings, crest, and motto of the Leicester family. This chimney-piece, together with the oaken wainscoating of the room in which it is placed, was removed to its present situation from one of the principal apartments of the Leicester buildings. The fine lake, which formerly ornamented three sides of the castle, and was the scene of much pageantry during Queen Elizabeth's visit, is now nearly dried up, and has long ceased to be an attractive object.

GUY'S CLIFF.

Guy's Cliff is about one mile and a half from Warwick, on the north-east. The river Avon here winds through most attractive meads, and, on its western bank, a combination of rock and wood, singularly picturesque, invited, at an early period, the reveries of superstitious seclusion and poetical fancy. It is supposed that there was here an oratory, and a cell for a hermit, in the Saxon times; and it is certain that a hermit dwelt in this lovely recess in the reigns of Edward III. and Henry IV. This is the spot to which the fantastical hero, Guy, is said to have retired after his duel with the Danish Colebrand; and here his neglected Countess, the fair Felicia, is reported to have interred his remains.

It appears that King Henry V. visited Guy's Cliff, and was so well pleased with its natural beauties, and, perhaps, so much interested by the wild legend connected with the place, that he determined to found a chantry for two priests. But warlike undertakings, and an early death, prevented the performance of this, among many other pious and benevolent intentions ascribed to the heroic Henry. Such a chantry was, however, founded in the first year of Henry VI., by Richard Beauchamp, Earl of Warwick; but the chapel (dedicated to St. Mary Magdalen), and some contiguous buildings, were not completed till after the earl's decease.

John Rous, the antiquary, resided in this delectable retreat, as a chantry priest. An asylum more desirable for a student can scarcely be imagined. Leland pronounced the dwelling at Guy's Cliff, "a house of pleasure — a place meet for the muses!"

The grounds attached to this residence are not extensive, but they abound in natural beauties, and are disposed with much taste. The rock on which the house and chapel are built presents towards the Avon a rugged and varied face, most fertile of the picturesque; and, perhaps, this portion of the cliff acquires a transient and mysterious charm from its connection with ancient poesy. Here is shown a cave, devoutly believed by neighbouring peasants to be that which Guy "hewed with his own hands," and in which he lived "like a palmer poore."

The chapel, founded by Richard Beauchamp, is a plain, substantial edifice in good repair, but otherwise treated with little ceremony. The founder caused to be carved from the solid rock, on which this chapel abuts, a rude statue of the famous Earl Guy, about eight feet in height. It would appear, from a print in Dugdale, that this figure was well preserved in the seventeenth century, but it is now much mutilated. The right hand formerly sustained a drawn sword, but both sword and arm have now disappeared. The hand of the shield-arm is also lost. The statue is likewise deficient in a leg; but a new one was bestowed a few years back, by a female statuary of rank and deserved celebrity, while on a visit to the Cliff.

The capacious stables, cellars, and out-offices of Guy's Cliff House are all formed by excavations from the solid rock.

About half a mile from Guy's Cliff is Blacklow Hill, rendered memorable by the summary execution of Piers Gaveston. This assuming favourite of Edward II. was arrested at Scarborough by a faction composed of many of the ancient nobles. It was intended to grant him an interview with the king, then at Wallingford; but on his way thither he was seized at Deddington, by Guy Beauchamp, Earl of Warwick, whom he had branded with the epithet of *the Black Hound of Arden*, and was hurried to Blacklow Hill, where his head was stricken off. On a part of the rocky hill near the top, is a monument with the following inscription:—

"In the hollow of this rock was beheaded Piers Gaveston, Earl of Cornwall, by barons as lawless as himself; a memorable instance of misrule. Anno 1311."

About the middle of the eighteenth century, this estate passed to Mr. Greathead, who built here a residence, but rather on a contracted scale, large and eligible additions to which were subsequently made by his son, the late Bertie Greathead, Esq. and the mansion is now respectable in size and character, as well as eminent for charms of situation.

STONELEIGH ABBEY.

The village of Stoneleigh is three miles from Kenilworth on the east. In this place was an abbey of Cistercian monks, which religious foundation was removed hither from Radmore, in Staffordshire, in 1154, the first year of Henry II. At this time there was in the manor, according to Dugdale, " sixty-eight villains, four boarders, and two priests; all which held 30 carucates of land."

At the time of the survey taken in the reign of Henry VIII., the revenue of this abbey was found to be 151l. 3s. 1d. On the dissolution, the property was bestowed by Henry, on Charles Brandon, Duke of Suffolk, and it afterwards passed to Sir Thomas Leigh, alderman of London. This gentleman shortly made large purchases of land in the neighbourhood; and, in the fourth year of queen Elizabeth, he obtained a patent of confirmation for the whole, together with the manor of Stoneleigh. By this Sir Thomas a spacious mansion was constructed on the site of the abbey, and here his descendants have resided to the present time. Sir Thomas Leigh, his great grandson, was a faithful adherent to Charles I., through the whole series of his troubles, and was created by that sovereign a baron of the realm, by the title of Lord Leigh, of Stoneleigh, in the nineteenth year of his reign. It is curious that a strong attachment to the Stuarts pervaded this family through the whole succession of its lords, even to the last, who died near the close of the eighteenth century. They never attended parliament, and resided entirely at Stoneleigh, in eccentric seclusion. Their house was ornamented with numerous portraits of that fallen family, whose calamities the liberal must commiserate, but whom the judicious had long perceived the propriety of discarding from political recollection. Here the Lords Leigh passed their existence, with rural sports for employment, quite indifferent to the public affairs of a world where their fanciful hereditary gratitude could not hope for efficient exercise. The last lord became subject to entire mental derangement previous to his decease; but his property passed, by a will made earlier in life, to his only sister, the late Hon. Mrs. Leigh, who died unmarried, and left the estate to the Rev. Thomas Leigh, of Addlestrop, Gloucestershire. At the demise of this gentleman, it descended to James Henry Leigh, Esq., his nephew, and eventually to the present proprietor, Lord Leigh.

The spacious residence, termed Stoneleigh Abbey, is situated in one of the most luxuriant and picturesque parts of the county of Warwick. The river Avon, here rendered wide even to a magnificence of amplitude, ornaments the grounds in the most attractive way with its classic waters; and woods, venerable and far spread, bestow an air of dignified quiet on the neighbourhood.

A considerable portion of the structure raised shortly after the expulsion of the religious from this choice spot, still remains; but the front and prime features of the edifice consist of a building of freestone, erected by Edward Lord Leigh, after designs by Smith, of Warwick. The church of Stoneleigh is a large but irregular Gothic building, containing monuments to several of the Leigh family, among which is that sacred to Alice Duchess Dudley, and her daughter.

LEAMINGTON.

Leamington, or Leamington Priors, is chiefly indebted to a circumstance of natural produce, and to the partiality of the gay, for flattering attentions that have long since caused it to disdain the name of village. This place, the spa of Warwickshire, is distant from the town of Warwick 2 miles; from Coventry, 8; and from Birmingham 22 miles. It is observed by Camden and by Dugdale, that Leamington possesses a salt spring; and Dr. Thomas, in his additions to the latter writer, says, that the inhabitants use it in making their bread. Other springs have been since discovered, and in the year 1797, Dr. Lambe chemically analysed the waters, and found that they contained medicinal properties of the most valuable description. An account of his discovery was inserted in the Manchester Memoirs, and the notice of the public was immediately attracted. Several medical persons of high respectability corroborated the statement of Dr. Lambe, and the afflicted on one hand, and the fashionable on the other, hastened to the spot of promise. But these ingenious writers met with a coadjutor in humble life, whose industry and merits should not be forgotten. This was Benjamin Satchwell, a laborious tradesman of the then obscure village, who successfully exerted himself in instituting a charity for the gratuitous relief of distressed invalids, to whom a use of the waters might be recommended.

Aided by the liberal contributions of the nobility and gentry, the establishment thus commenced has attained to an extent that enables it to administer annually the benefit of the waters to hundreds of poor applicants. These waters are used both internally and for the purpose of bathing; an analysis of them by Dr. Lambe will be found in the Manchester Memoirs, vol. iii. page 212. Leamington has from an obscure village rapidly advanced to a degree of opulence and elegance that justly entitle it to rank amongst the most regular and best built towns of the kingdom. It originally existed only on the south side of the river Leam, at a point 89 miles distant from London, on the road to Birmingham through Warwick, where a number of handsome buildings have been erected; this is denominated the old town;

in addition to which upon the opposite side of the river (here crossed by a handsome stone bridge) an entirely new town, consisting of houses and streets alike spacious and elegant has arisen. Leamington has now become the resort of rank, elegance, and fashion, for whose accommodation a number of very handsome buildings have been erected, besides pump and assembly-rooms, baths, libraries, a neat theatre, &c. Of these the new pump-room, and adjoining baths, claim particular notice, as being, perhaps, without exception, the most elegant in Europe; their erection cost an immense sum, and owing to the ingenious construction of the pipes, the engine is capable of supplying in a few hours, as many tons of the mineral fluid as would be required to float a man of war. The Regent Hotel is also an elegant structure, and one of the largest in England. The theatre, a very compact and eligible building situate in Bath Street, was the property of the late Mr. Elliston.

This place has also a picture gallery. Leamington enjoys a very delightful situation, the surrounding country is beautifully picturesque, and the walks and rides in the vicinity are well calculated to add to the celebrity of the place. It is the head-quarters of the Warwickshire hunt, and is on that account during the season much frequented by its members, their friends, and a host of visitors, who flocking to this centre of Nimrodian attraction, enliven by their presence the town and neighbourhood. The Warwick and Napton Canal passes close to the town, which uniting with the Oxford Canal by connecting it with the Grand Junction and other lines, gives to this place the advantage of a very extensive inland navigation.

WARWICK CASTLE.

Warwick Castle, one of the most magnificent samples of baronial grandeur of which this country can boast, is built on a rock, at the foot of which flows the river Avon. This stupendous structure is raised on the south-east of the town; from which, however, it is sufficiently detached for the purpose of dignified retirement. There is not any record concerning the precise era at which a fortified building was first founded on this spot. It is however clear, that the foundation took place prior to the Norman conquest; and it is probable that Ethelfrida, the daughter of King Alfred, first constructed here a stronghold, but of a gloomy and contracted character. Her melancholy though secure dungeon is believed to have occupied an artificial mount yet remaining on the west side, near the bank of the Avon. The fortress was constituted for some time the residence of the Vice-comites, or lieutenants of the earls of Mercia; and Turchill (styled by the Normans Turchill de Warwick) who was Vice-comites at the time of the Conquest, was directed by William I. to add considerably to the extent and strength of the fortifications. It appears that a church dedicated to the honour of All Saints was founded within the limits of the castle, at an early period; but this building was united to the collegiate church of St. Mary in 1125.

It is desirable to trace, as to outlines, the chief historical events immediately connected with the castle, during the union of its fortunes with those of the Earls of Warwick, through the lines of Newburgh, Beauchamp, Nevil, Plantagenet, and Dudley, to the family of the present noble earl. In the time of Roger de Newburgh, second Earl of Warwick, this castle appears to have been a place of much strength and consideration. Earl Roger died in 1153, and the castle was at that period garrisoned by soldiers on the side of King Stephen; but on the advance of Prince Henry, afterwards Henry II., the earl's widow delivered to him the fortress. William de Newburgh, the third earl, lived here in great splendour, and in the 20th of Henry II., procured an addition of two knights "to the five knights who before kept guard in Warwick Castle." In the reign of Henry III., the extraordinary strength of this building was alleged as a reason for particularly prohibiting the widowed Countess of Warwick from remarrying with any other than a person approved by the king.

In the furious contests which afflicted the latter years of the third Henry, Warwick Castle, almost impregnable to open assault, fell the victim of a want of caution. The rebels were stationed at Kenilworth in great power, and William Mauduit, the then earl neglected to keep due guard, though danger was so near and threatening; and, in consequence, his fortress was surprised, and all the building, except the towers, levelled with the ground, while himself and his countess were carried prisoners to Kenilworth. The family of Beauchamp shortly succeeded to the earldom, and by Thomas de Beauchamp, Earl of Warwick, in the reign of Edward III. the injuries sustained by the castle buildings in the time of Earl Mauduit were sufficiently repaired. He rebuilt the walls, added strong gates, and fortified the gateways with embattled towers. Thomas de Beauchamp, his son and successor, passed a great portion of his time in exile from the court; and we have already observed that he dedicated much of this calm season to architectural pursuits. By him was built a tower, shortly to be noticed, at the north-east corner of the castle, on which he bestowed the name of Guy's Tower.

The Nevil family succeeded to the earldom of Warwick, in consequence of a marriage between Richard Nevil, son and heir to the Earl of Salisbury, and Anne, daughter of Richard Beauchamp. This potent earl whose habitual splendour is recorded in the page of national history, maintained, in his Warwickshire Castle, a sumptuous style of living suited to his political consequence and the greatness of his resources.

George Duke of Clarence, who had married the daughter of this enterprising and restless noble, was created Earl of Warwick by his brother, King Edward IV. He chiefly resided at Warwick Castle after this creation; and added much to the strength and beauty of the works. The Dudley family succeeded to the Plantagenets; and on the failure of that line, the title was revived by James I. in the person of Robert Lord Rich, in whose posterity it continued till the year 1759. But the same king had previously granted the castle and attached grounds to Fulke Greville, afterwards Lord Brooke. When this accomplished person took possession of the castle it was in a ruinous condition, having been used for some time as a county gaol. But he expended a large sum in restoring the buildings, and arranging the dependent grounds. To his care and good taste it is evident that the structure is indebted for much of the excellent preservation in which even its most ancient parts are now seen. The unfortunate activity of Robert Lord Brooke, in the civil war of the 17th century, has already met with observation. By his direction the castle was placed in a state of garrison on the parliamentary side. Various scenes of calamity ensued, among which was a siege that commenced on the 7th of August, 1642, and terminated in the discomfiture of the assailants on the 23d of the same month. Francis Lord Brooke was created Earl Brooke of Warwick Castle, in 1746, and Earl of Warwick in 1759. In both these honours he was succeeded, in 1773, by George, his eldest son, the late earl, who dying in 1816, they devolved to the present noble owner.

The approach to Warwick Castle is calculated to produce the most striking effect. A broad and winding path, cut through the solid rock, confines the eye and exercises the fancy till a hundred long yards are trodden over with increasing expectation. A method of advance so quiet and serene prepares the mind for a spectacle of unusual character,—and unusually grand is, indeed, the object submitted to view. As we draw towards the extent of this rocky path, (by the way rendered smooth) three lofty and massive towers rise progressively to the view; and on proceeding a few steps further, they stand ranged in an embattled line unspeakably august and commanding. On the left is the tower termed Cæsar's, an elevation concerning the date of which no trace remains in published or private record. The mode of construction is somewhat rude, and possesses many singularities. Jutting from one side of this tower is an embattled turret of stone, where imagination may place a herald at arms, demanding in a long past century the name and purpose of those so hardy as to advance unbidden. To the right is the tower, named after the fanciful champion Guy. This part of the structure is upwards of 100 feet in height, and was built by Thomas Beauchamp, Earl of Warwick, in the latter part of the fourteenth century. The entrance is flanked by embattled walls, richly clothed with ivy; and the deep moat, now dry in security, its bottom converted into a velvetty path, is lined with various shrubs, and ornamented with some trees of a vigorous and noble growth. The disused moat is crossed by a stone bridge, and the entrance is by double machiolated towers, through a series of passages once big with multiplied dangers for the intruder. In the great court, to which the visitor passes, the display is truly magnificent. The area is now fertile in soft and well-cultivated green sward, but spread around are viewed the mighty remains of fortifications raised in turbulent ages by mingled ferocity and grandeur. The relics are perfect in outline, and no battlement exhibits the havoc of time, while the hand of tasteful domestic habit has spread a softness over the whole productive of most grateful relief. We behold with pleasure the ivy bestow pictorial mellowness on parapets and turrets which must have been only terrifically rugged when manned with warriors in steel, and fresh in early masonry; and broad Gothic windows supplant, with conspicuous felicity, the cheerless single-light, and fatal loophole.

The habitable part of this immense structure lies to the left of the great court; and in the progressive amelioration of feature effected in later ages every desirable attention has been paid to consistency of character. At the western, or more retired part of the area, is the artificial mount, a vast elevation, surmounted by a portion of ancient building. The walls which range round those divisions of the court not occupied by the residence are guarded by ramparts; and open flights of stone steps lead to various turrets, and form, with many passages, a ready line of communication through the whole of the fortress. A grand face of the building is displayed towards the river; and here the rock, which affords a foundation to the pile, rises perpendicularly to a considerable height before the stone-work of the superstructure commences. This front has all the regularity usual in buildings constructed with a view to security as well as baronial grandeur; but even this want of uniformity is estimable when considered as a characteristic of antiquity. The windows have experienced some alteration under the direction of the present earl, and much good taste has been evinced in every particular.

The interior of this august fabric surpasses the expectations raised by a view of its outward features; for with the ponderous towers and ramparts of stone we associate only ideas of chivalric hardihood and unpolished baronial pride. But domestic elegance and a warm love of the arts have combined in recent periods to arrange and decorate the halls; yet every effort at fresh and more gratifying modes of disposal has been carefully made allusive to the antique, castellated outlines of the edifice. The grand suite of apartments extend in a right line 333 feet, and are furnished in a chaste but munificent manner.

The Hall is a noble room, 62 feet long, and 37 feet wide, paved with black and white stone, and wainscotted. Various weapons and pieces of armour, interspersed with antlers, are attached to the sides. Piled round the wide fire-place are logs of wood, in attention to the usage of the ancient barons' household, in which establishment convenience was ever studied in preference to delicacy. But the hall is, properly, the only apartment devoted to so strict a *keeping* of manners. The sides of the *Antechamber* are panelled, and edged with gilt moulding; the floor is of polished oak.

The Cedar Drawing-room is of large proportions; the floor is of polished oak, the sides, lined with cedar, are well carved; the ceiling is highly ornamented, and the furniture superb. The *Gilt Room* is richly embellished. *The State Bedchamber* is hung with curious tapestry, worked at Brussels, in 1604. The costly bed-furniture belonged to Queen Anne, and was given to the late Earl of Warwick by King George III.

The *Dining* and *Breakfast Rooms* are also charming apartments. A valuable collection of family portraits, and other pictures of distinguished merit, are judiciously distributed throughout the different rooms, the gallery leading to the chapel, and principal passages.

The *Gallery of Armour* contains a fine collection of old English mail. The *Chapel*, approached by a gallery, though not large, is of a sedate and decorous character. The windows of each room in the grand suite command diversified and lovely prospects. To the right, the river Avon winds through a long expanse of decorated park scenery. On the left, various objects intercept the view, but all are consonant and picturesque.

The *Park*, attached to this noble castle, is very extensive, and finely adorned by wood and water. The garden grounds, or home domain, are arranged with the exquisite order of taste that has its basis in simplicity. A broad gravel walk, of devious progress, conducts through these grounds, and is embowered by a rich variety of evergreen foliage. Different vistas, designed with great judgment, afford fine views of the castle, the windings of the Avon and principal features of the surrounding country. In a conservatory, erected for the purpose, is deposited a very large *antique vase,* presented to the Earl of Warwick by the late Sir William Hamilton. This magnificent antique is composed of white marble, and is of a circular form. The decorations consist of Bacchanalian emblems, finely executed; and from the body of the vase proceed two handles, formed of interwoven vine-branches. This vessel is calculated to contain 163 gallons.

The lofty artificial mount, on the west of the castle, is now ascended by a spiral path, skirted by protecting trees and shrubs. At an advanced point of the ascent is a turret, approached by stone steps; but on the summit of the elevation, supposed to have been formerly crowned with the gloomy residence of the lady of the Mercians a large fir waves its broad branches in pensive but grateful triumph.

In one of the rooms attached to Cæsar's Tower are still preserved the sword, shield, helmet, &c. ascribed to the legendary champion Guy. The reader will scarcely need to be informed that this personage is reported to have been an earl of Warwick, who fought with and slew a gigantic Dane, by name Colebrand. After this duel, he is said to have retired to a hermitage, on the secluded and romantic spot since named "Guy's Cliff," where he died and was buried.

STRATFORD UPON AVON.

Stratford upon Avon, the birthplace of the immortal Shakspeare, appears, from authentic documents, to have been of some importance 300 years before the Norman Conquest; and it is said that a monastery was founded here shortly after the Saxons were converted to the Christian faith, that occupied the spot on which the church now stands. Ætheland, viceroy of the Wiccians, gave this town to the bishopric of Worcester, and it continued to belong to it for several ages subsequent to the Conquest. A considerable portion of the early consequence of this place must undoubtedly be attributed to the patronage it received from its mitred lords, who availed themselves of every opportunity of attending to its interests; but though it is now a neat town, consisting of twelve principal streets, yet it has lost much of its ancient appearance, owing to three severe fires which, at different times, committed great devastation. The house in which Shakspeare was born is situated in Henley Street, and was, some time since, divided into two distinct habitations, the one part is now, or was lately, used as a public-house or inn, and the other as a butcher's shop; opposite to this is a public-house bearing the sign of "The Falcon," where, according to Ireland, Shakspeare passed much of his time. The house where our great dramatic author spent the latter part of his life, after having gained for himself a comfortable independence, and named by him "New Place," was, in the year 1643, the temporary residence of Queen Henrietta Maria. After this the mansion passed through various hands till it unfortunately became the property of the Rev. Francis Gastrell, who, disliking the importunate questions of travellers, began by laying the axe to the root of a remarkably large mulberry tree, which had been planted by the hand of Shakspeare himself; afterwards levelled the buildings of New Place, on account of some trifling assessment he was compelled to pay towards the maintenance of the poor; and then left the town amidst the curses of the inhabitants.

The approach to the church, which is a very handsome structure, is by a long avenue of lime trees, whose intermingled branches impart considerable solemnity to the scene. The interior of this edifice is decorated in an elegant manner, and contains a number of monuments and inscriptions, but that chiefly sought by the curious traveller is to the memory of the renowned bard, whose ashes lie on the north side of the chancel, beneath a stone, bearing an inscription expressive of the abhorrence of the violations of sepulture. On the north wall, about five feet from the floor, is an elegant monument, representing the poet, with a pen in his right hand, and a scroll in his left, having on each side the figure of a boy, the one holding an inverted torch, and the other a spade; this is enclosed between two black marble pillars of the Corinthian order, and is surmounted by armorial bearings and other suitable embellishments.

The other public buildings most deserving of notice, are, the chapel formerly belonging to the Guild of the Holy Cross, adjoining which is the Guildhall, an ancient building, whose upper division is appropriated to the Grammar School, where it is said that Shakspeare received the rudiments of his education. The Town Hall also claims attention; it is a fine modern building of the Tuscan order, erected in 1768, and, in the next year, when the jubilee was celebrated, was dedicated to the memory of the immortal bard, by David Garrick, who honoured it with the name of "Shakspeare's Hall;" and presented a good statue of the poet, which now stands in a niche at the north end of the edifice. The chief room of this building is sixty feet long by thirty feet wide, and is adorned with portraits of John Frederick, Duke of Dorset, Garrick, and Shakspeare; the latter is represented as sitting in an antique chair, surrounded by books and manuscripts, and in the attitude of inspiration.

The town is approached by a stone bridge, erected at the expense of Sir Hugh Clopton, in the time of Henry VII.

It has a good market on Friday; and participated in the commotions which agitated this country in the seventeenth century, when it was alternately in the possession of the royalists and parliament forces. Stratford has not any staple manufacture of consequence, but has a respectable commercial interchange with the neighbouring places: it was incorporated in the seventh year of Edward VI. A fresh charter of incorporation was, however, granted in the sixteenth of Charles II., by which the municipal government is vested in a mayor, twelve aldermen (of whom the mayor is one), and twelve burgesses. In the year 1769, a festival, termed the Jubilee, was instituted at Stratford, in honour of Shakspeare, which consisted of various species of amusement; but the most classical of them was an ode and oration recited by Garrick in honour of the bard. Though the weather was wet and unfavourable for the occasion, yet the greatest good humour prevailed; and so great was the assemblage of exalted genius and high rank present at this national tribute, that many were unable to procure beds in the town, and are said to have been constrained to sleep in their carriages.

WARWICK.

Warwick is situate in the centre of the county to which it gives name, at a distance of 90 miles from London, 8 from Stratford upon Avon, 21 from Birmingham, 2½ from Leamington, 5 from Kenilworth, and 10¼ from Coventry. This very agreeable place, enriched by a castle of stupendous grandeur, adorned by a chapel of exquisite workmanship, and furnished with public buildings, decorous, substantial, and well suited, needs not the aid of monkish legend or flattering conjecture to render it attractive. But it has met, in Sir William Dugdale, with an historian whose partiality, as we must believe, rather than a defect of judgment, has induced him to lend the sanction of his name to strange tales and crude opinions, which the present age will certainly feel inclined to reject with a smile. We shall, therefore, only occasionally advert to such particulars as appear fantastical and imaginary, and do our best endeavour to trace as fully as our limits will allow, the history of the town and castle on solid ground. Differing with Camden, we can discover no reason for believing Warwick to have been a Roman station. No tangible vestiges of the Romans have been here discovered. Dugdale says, that "at any rate we cannot doubt but that this was one of the forts and garrisons raised on the banks of the river Avon by P. Ostorius." Considering that the Romans had a large camp so near as Chesterton, on the opposite side of the river, we, however, think even this far from probable.

It appears likely that this place was of Saxon origin, and according to some early writers, it gained a distinguished accession of consequence from the patronage of Ethelfrida, the celebrated daughter of King Alfred, and lady of the Mercians, who, in the year 915, constructed here a fortified dwelling, suited to the ferocious temper of the age, and termed the *Dungeon*. This building is believed to have been erected on the artificial mount still remaining on the west side of the castle, and, under such a protection, the town speedily advanced in population and repute.

In the Norman survey Warwick is deemed a borough, and is there stated to contain 261 houses, of which 130 were possessed by the king, 112 by certain of his barons, and 19 were the property of so many burgesses who enjoyed them with *Soc* and *Sac*, and all customs, as in the days of Edward the Confessor. The Norman Conquest appears to have been a propitious era for the town of Warwick. Previous to this epoch, the titular earls of Warwick were in reality no more than either fiduciary vice-comites, or substitutes to the Earl of Mercia, or immediate officers of the king; and did not, of their own right, possess the castle and town. When the Conqueror assumed the crown of England, Turchill, the son of Alwine, was vice-comites of Warwick; and, as he had refrained from giving assistance to Harold in opposition to the Normans, he was not only suffered to remain in quiet possession of his estates, but was for some time permitted to retain his local office, and was employed to enlarge and fortify the castle. He was likewise ordered to surround the town with a ditch, and strengthen it with gates. At a period shortly subsequent, the king advanced Henry de Newburgh to the dignity of Earl of Warwick; and thus commenced a long line of protecting nobles, under whose sway the town progressively attained much real consequence, and a flattering degree of celebrity. Its guardian castle now stretched forth new lines, so massive, as almost to deride assault; religious foundations (the certain harbingers of prosperity in early periods) were soon formed, while the fosse which encompassed the towers, and the gates constructed at the channels of approach, assisted in bestowing security on the efforts of the industrious.

In the reign of Edward I. the town was in a flourishing condition, and it now experienced considerable improvement. It appears that in the seventh year of this king, William de Beauchamp, Earl of Warwick, held a yearly fair lasting sixteen days, and a weekly market on the Wednesday. In the 18th of Edward I. the same earl obtained the king's charter, for another fair to last fifteen days. It may also be observed, that in this reign Warwick was the scene of various chivalric festivities, the principal actor in which was Roger de Mortimer, who conducted the knightly revels at Kenilworth Castle. Towards the latter end of this reign, the *paving* of the town was commenced; and at the same time the walls were begun. The expense of both these was defrayed by a toll on vendible commodities. But these two great works were far from being conducted with celerity; for in the 8th of Edward II. the same earl obtained permission to levy another toll for three years; and in the 6th of Edward III., Thomas de Beauchamp, the then earl, had a third patent granted, empowering him to take toll for the further charge of the paving and walls for a fresh term of seven years.

In the first of Philip and Mary the burgesses received the charter of incorporation; and, in the year 1572, Warwick was honoured with a visit from Queen Elizabeth. Of the proceedings that took place upon the occasion of this visit, and an account is preserved in a book called the *Black Book of Warwick*. This book, which also contains some interesting notices relating to the reigns of Elizabeth and James, is in the possession of the corporation.

During the civil war of the seventeenth century, this town suffered severely from the active part taken by Lord Brooke in public affairs. The castle was now rendered a depositary of arms, and placed in a regular state of garrison. This stronghold at one period of the war sustained a siege, and several skirmishes occured in the neighbourhood. Nor were the more ancient seasons of freedom from personal danger productive of entire tranquillity to the inhabitants, for when relieved from the appearance of professed foes, they were continually harrassed by the visits of armed throngs, who were only preferable to the enemy because they drained the householder's purse and board without holding a sword to his breast.

In the year 1694, Warwick experienced the calamity of a dreadful fire; when the greater part of the town, including the High Street, and nearly the whole of St. Mary's church was consumed. The loss sustained on this occasion has been variously estimated; it was computed at the time to amount to 96,000*l.*; but it is said that 120,000*l.* was employed in repairing the damage. The sum of 11,000*l.* was collected by brief, to which Queen Anne munificently added 1000*l.*, as a royal gift. This affliction, like all others of a similar nature, though bitterly severe to the inhabitants of the period, was productive of great local improvement; and we may safely assert, from the aspect of those parts of the town which escaped the conflagration, that the place is entirely indebted to its temporary misfortune for its chief domestic ornament.

But although the buildings were improved in size and character, when the town was thus restored, the principal streets were originally disposed with considerable regularity.

G

The town of Warwick stands upon a rock, at the foot of which flows the Avon. The acclivity, however, though somewhat abrupt, is not considerable; and the principal streets possess as much equality of site as is desirable for the purposes of traffic, while they are sufficiently remote from flatness to advance the great object of local cleanliness. The best approach in point of picturesque effect is that from the south-east, or Daventry and Banbury roads. The river Avon is here crossed by a neat stone bridge; and the castle towers, the spire of St. Nicholas, and the tower of St. Mary's, all stand displayed in captivating succession.

The principal street of the town, to which the traveller now passes, is conspicuous for neatness and real beauty. This street is of a good width, and of considerable length, and at the eastern extremity is an ancient gate, an architectural termination that considerably increases the perspective effect of the vista. At the western end is a second gateway, surmounted by a venerable chapel, of plain, but impressive features. The whole street between the two gates is formed in a direct line; the domestic buildings are sufficiently regular and generally substantial, and nearly in the centre, on the southern side stands the court-house or town hall, a respectable stone structure. The street which intersects this principal district, and passes nearly from north to south, contains in its northern division many capacious and ornamental buildings; but there are several other streets, independent of extensive suburbs. In the vicinity of the market-place, and in some other divisions of the town, are houses occupied by traders, so large and well-built, as satisfactorily to prove the commercial respectability of the place; but the majority of the domestic buildings unconnected with the precincts already noticed, are far from being of an estimable description. They present, with very few exceptions, no marks of striking antiquity, but are on a mean and contracted scale. Worked into a few houses, however, are to be found some very ancient fragments, perhaps the relics of religious foundations. The survey of this district is sufficient to prove the architectural benefits accruing to the town from the great fire.

John Rous, the historian of Warwickshire, mentions several *religious foundations* as having been formed at Warwick in Saxon eras; but his evidence is unsupported by earlier and more creditable record. The munificent patronage of the Earls of Warwick led to frequent pious and charitable foundations, in eras subsequent to the Conquest. Our limits only allow us to notice such as have left visible memorials in the now altered scene; but we must observe, as a proof of the splendour of the town during the sway of some of the more tyrannical and mighty of its earls, that Warwick formerly possessed several more *churches* than at present, of which little trace now remains except in the page of the historian.

The great buildings of early ages were all either of a castellated or devoted character. Warwick is fortunate in retaining a castle and a chapel which rank among the brightest specimens of those two classes of architecture; and it likewise possesses some public structures, calculated to ornament even the county town of an opulent district.

The principal *Church* is dedicated to St. Mary. A church so dedicated occupied the same spot before the Conquest. Henry de Newburgh, the first Earl of Warwick of the Norman line, formed the design of making this church collegiate, and of uniting the dean and secular canons, to be placed there with the priests belonging to the church of All Saints, a fabric that stood within the walls of the castle. The work of collegiate foundation was, however, completed by his son and successor, Earl Roger, in the year 1123 who bestowed on the associated canons, lands, advowsons, and tithes of considerable value. Succeeding earls of Warwick continued to protect these secular priests, and many benefactors of different ranks arose in after ages. At the time of the dissolution under Henry VIII. the yearly revenues were certified to be 334*l.* 2*s.* 3*d.*

The church of St. Mary, was rebuilt in the fourteenth century through the munificence of the earls of Warwick. The choir was commenced by Thomas de Beauchamp, the earl so much distinguished in the French wars of Edward III., and the whole structure was completed by his descendant, Thomas Beauchamp in the year 1394. This powerful family now fixed on the collegiate church for their place of burial; and they constructed towards the middle of the fifteenth century, a stately adjoining chapel for their peculiar cemetery. In the great fire of 1694, the larger portion of the church perished in the flames; but the choir, some rooms on the north, and the chapel, happily escaped. The plan of the new building is said to have been formed after a sketch of Sir Christopher Wren; but each feature denies the probable correctness of the assertion.

Although this building has no pretensions to beauty, it is still firm and capacious. At the west end is a square tower, the height of which, from the base to the top of the battlements, is 130 feet. Between the piers supporting the tower, a passage is wrought, allowing the transit of carriages. The church is of a cruciform description. The extreme length is about 186 feet; the breadth, 66 feet. The cross aisle, measures 100 feet 6 inches. The interior is rendered august by the remains of the ancient structure. We here view the choir, untouched by the ravage of the flames, and stand with reverence amid the memorials of a family, conspicuous in national history. On each side are ranges of stalls. The stone ceiling is finely designed and delicately worked. Among the chaste yet ample and elegant embellishments, are introduced the arms of the founder, and his arms quartered with those of his wife embosomed by seraphines. In the middle of the choir is the altar tomb of Thomas Beauchamp, Earl of Warwick, and his lady, Catherine, the daughter of Roger Mortimer, first Earl of March. On the tomb are the recumbent effigies of the persons interred. The earl's figure is in armour, and his right hand clasps the right hand of his countess, whose left is on her breast. On the sides and ends of the tomb are thirty-six figures representing the closest relatives of the deceased earl, with coats of arms beneath. These figures, usually termed *weepers*, curiously exhibit the peculiarities of dress prevailing at that period. Earl Thomas was a man of high consideration in the fourteenth century, and was much distinguished in the French and Scottish wars of Edward III. He was a munificent friend to the town of Warwick, and founded the choir in which his remains now lie interred. He died near Calais, on the 13th of November, 1370, being then in the sixty-third year of his age. His countess expired six weeks before him. The son and successor of this earl, likewise named Thomas, was chosen governor to Richard II. during the minority of that king. But he sank among the machinations of that era; and being dismissed from court, retired to his castle at Warwick, where he employed himself in various buildings, suited to the liberality of his temper and largeness of his revenue. He now completed the body of the collegiate church; and dying in 1401, was buried together with his countess, Margaret, daughter of Lord Ferrers of Groby, under a monument of white marble, in the south part of the church raised by his munificence. But in the destructive fire of 1694, this monument unfortunately fell a victim to the flames. A brass plate containing the effigies of himself and his lady, was found among the ruins and subsequently placed near the spot it formerly occupied, with an inscription explaining the calamity it has experienced.

There are numerous other monumental tributes in various parts of the church, but none of sufficient interest to demand notice here. We therefore proceed to observe, that on the north of the choir are three distinct substantial rooms. The first, termed the lobby, is now used as a receptacle for the fire engines belonging to the town; the central apartment is of an octagonal shape, and was originally the chapter-house of the dean and canons; but Sir Fulke Greville, Lord Brooke, selected this room for a monument to his own memory, which he caused to be erected in his lifetime.

The monument is of black and white marble, and of a heavy character. On the ledge of the table part is the following inscription:—" Fulke Greville, servant to Queen Elizabeth, councillor to King James, and friend to Sir Philip Sydney." The remains of his lordship lie in a vault beneath, embalmed and enclosed in a coffin of lead. The remarkable epitaph penned for himself by this great man has met with many critical observations; but we cannot readily perceive that he could deliver to posterity materials for an estimate of his character more modest yet more comprehensive. The man who faithfully obeyed a discreet princess, who had wisdom to give council to a weak sovereign, and whose qualifications were such as to render him the chosen friend of one of the most virtuous and accomplished cavaliers of the age, must needs be entitled to the respect of all who are reminded of these particulars. His lordship lamentably fell by the hand of a domestic assassin, in the seventy-fifth year of his age. A creature, pampered to insolence by the plenty of his lordship's table, felt offence at not being named in his will, (to which instrument he was one of the witnesses) as an object of his posthumous bounty, and stabbed him either with a sword or knife in an apartment of Brooke House, Holborn. Public justice was disappointed by the wretch likewise destroying himself before he could be taken. This proof of the insecurity of those surrounded by numerous domestics occurred in 1628. The third apartment is used as a library and vestry-room; beneath is a mausoleum for the noble family of Warwick.

The Chapel of Our Lady, usually termed the *Beauchamp Chapel*, adjoins the south chancel of St. Mary's church. This fabric was erected in obedience to the last will of Richard Beauchamp, Earl of Warwick. The building was begun in the twenty-first of Henry VI., and was completed in the third of Edward IV. The total expense of the structure, including the tomb of the founder, was 2481l. 4s. 7$\frac{1}{2}d$. at a time when bread corn was sold at 3s. 4d. the quarter. The exterior is a beautiful specimen of the decorated Gothic or English style, and is covered with tracery, panels, and other architectural enrichments. On the south are three large windows, divided by five upright mullions of delicate masonry. The buttresses display a variety of ornaments, and a highly finished open work parapet ranges round the south and east sides of the building. It appears that this beautiful specimen of the taste which prevailed in the time of Henry VI. experienced much injury in the seventeenth century. But Lady Catherine Leveson, a daughter of Sir Robert Dudley, gave, at the recommendation of William Dugdale, of Blythe Hall, Esq., (afterwards Sir William Dugdale,) the sum of 50l. towards its repairs, during her lifetime, and bequeathed 40*l.* per annum for the perpetual support and preservation of the monuments. The mayor of Warwick for the time being was appointed one of the trustees, and Sir William Dugdale himself was the first coadjutor of the mayor. The whole is composed of squared stones, and is in excellent preservation.

The interior is richly embellished in the style which the nobles of a former period were taught to believe acceptable demonstrations of pious zeal. The principal apartment is 58 feet long, 25 feet wide, and 32 feet high, and is furnished with monuments of a splendid character. The grand entrance to the chapel is from the southern part of the church, through a kind of porch or vestibule, highly ornamented with tracery panels and niches, the armorial bearings of the Beauchamps, &c. The floors, which are three in number, and composed of black and white marble, ascend by one step, each towards the altar screen. This spot is ornamented with a basso relievo, representing the Annunciation of the Virgin; and on each side is a shrine of delicate and elaborate workmanship. The east window is enriched with curious painted glass, containing, among other subjects, a portrait of the founder, kneeling before a desk and open book; and in the mouldings are introduced many wrought figures intended for angels and saints. The south side of the interior is highly worked. Beneath the three large and uniform windows, which constitute the upper portion, is a series of panels, tastefully designed, and finely executed.

In the central window are many paintings, containing various religious allusions, and family portraits. The western compartment is faced with a wooden screen, carved to correspond with the ornamented parts on the south. On different spots are fixed desks and seats, embellished with carvings of the bear and griffin.

Nearly in the centre of this principal apartment of the chapel stands the monument of the founder, which has been truly pronounced inferior to none in England, except that of Henry VII. in Westminster Abbey. This is an altar tomb of grey marble, and on the slab lies the figure of the earl, in the proportions of life, composed of brass, gilt. He is represented with the head uncovered, and resting on a helmet and crest: the hair is short, and the beard curled; the hands are lifted, but not united; the body is clad in plated armour, and at the feet are a griffin and a muzzled bear. Over the effigies is a hearse of brass hoops, gilt; and at the upper ends of four of the poles which strengthen the hoops of the hearse are enamelled shields, pendant from oak leaves in quatrefoils, with the arms of Beauchamp, and other armorial bearings. In very rich niches, on the sides and ends of the table part of the monument, are fourteen images of brass, gilt, representing male and female branches of the mourning family. Beneath are their arms, enamelled on shields in starred quatrefoils; and between the images are small whole-length figures of angels holding inscribed scrolls. On the monument is likewise a pious and historical inscription relating to the deceased; and it is remarkable that in various parts of this epitaph are inserted, without a due regard to propriety of punctuation, but it would seem as substitutes for the stops in ordinary use, the figure of a bear, and the representation of a ragged staff.

Richard de Beauchamp, Earl of Warwick, whose remains lie beneath this splendid monumental fabric, was one of the most distinguished characters of the fifteenth century. He took in open battle the standard of Owen Glendower, when that hardy chieftain rebelled against Henry IV. He likewise gained great honour in the battle of Shrewsbury against the Percys. He fought with eminent success in the French wars of Henry V., and was named to the tutelage of Henry VI., till that minor sovereign should attain his sixteenth year. He died at the castle of Roan, in 1349, and his remains were deposited, according to his own desire, in a chest of stone before the altar, on the right hand of his father's tomb, in the church of St. Mary, until the intended chapel and monument were completed. It is said by Gough "that, about the middle of the seventeenth century, the floor of Our Lady's chapel fell in, and discovered the body perfect and fresh, till on the letting in of the air it fell to decay. The ladies of Warwick made rings of the noble earl's hair."

On the north side of the chapel is the highly embellished monument of Robert Dudley, Earl of Leicester, who died in 1588, and his countess. The effigies of the deceased possess much merit of execution; but the redundant decorations of their very costly monument are rendered rather unpleasingly glaring by paints of various colours. Near the tomb is a wooden tablet, on which are inscribed, in gilt letters, some elegiac verses, written on the countess by Gervas Clifton. Not far distant is the monument of Ambrose Dudley, Earl of Warwick, who died in 1589. His figure is represented in plated armour, lying on a mat rolled up; at the feet is a muzzled bear. On an altar tomb, near the east end of the chapel, is a puerile effigy, in the coat and mantle of a child, with a double row of pearls on his head; at the feet is a bear chained. An epitaph of some length announces that here " resteth the body of the *noble Impe*, Robert of Duddeley, Baron of Denbigh, sonne of Robert Erle of Leicester, and nephew and heir unto Ambrose Erle of Warwicke." On a marble slab against the north wall is an inscription to the memory of Lady Catharine

Leveson, whose liberal benefaction towards the repair of this building has been already noticed.

Besides this principal division, there are other rooms connected with the chapel. Behind the altar is a narrow apartment, *called* the library of John Rous, the antiquary. On the north side are an oratory and a confessional, both elevated considerably above the level of the chapel flooring. The confessional is ascended by five steps, much worn, and contains some fine workmanship, and many features which allude, in an interesting manner, to the fanciful customs of the Roman Catholic religion. Separated from the chapel by an open screen are apartments probably designed for some of the numerous persons retained in support of the domestic dignity of former earls of Warwick.

The Church, a respectable stone structure, has a low spire springing from a square tower at its west end. The interior is plain, and of limited proportions. The County Hall is a spacious and ornamental structure, in which the assizes for the county, the quarter sessions, and county courts are held. The Market-house is a substantial stone building, for the accommodation of farmers and traders. The County Gaol adjoins the great hall, and is an extensive and well designed fabric. The Bridewell is a spacious structure, well adapted to its purposes. Over the west gate, which stands at one extremity of the principal street of Warwick, is a chapel dedicated to St. James. Connected with this is an establishment founded in the reign of Henry VIII. by Robert Dudley, Earl of Leicester, for twelve impotent men, each, not possessing means to the amount of 5*l.* per annum, and a master, a professor of divinity. By the vast increase in the value of property, the benefits of this foundation have been extended to twenty-two decayed gentlemen, who now receive 80*l.* per annum each, with a salary of 400*l.* per annum to the master; the intention of the founder being that one quarter of the profits of the estate should be appropriated to the use of that functionary. There are also meetinghouses for the different denominations of dissenters.

The principal streets of Warwick are well paved, and the town is lighted with gas. The weekly market on Saturday is well attended; it may also be added, that the attempt to establish a market at Leamington having failed, the vast increase in the population of that great resort of the fashionable world has added much to the business previously transacted on market days at Warwick.

Warwick is not of much manufacturing importance; it may however, and in all probability will experience a vast accession to the number of its visitors, by the formation of the Birmingham Railway, affording as it will to admiring thousands the easy means of access to its magnificent castle. Warwick sends two representatives to parliament, who are chosen by the inhabitants, paying scot and lot, to which have been added by the Reform Bill the 10*l*. householders. The mayor is the returning officer. The corporation consists of a mayor, recorder, twelve aldermen, twenty-four common councilmen, a town clerk, &c. Here is a small but neat theatre. Upon an excellent race-course, west of the town, whereon a grand stand has recently been erected, Warwick races annually take place in September; they last three days, when aided by the presence of the fashionables from Leamington. The course presents a brilliant assemblage of company. Race balls, held at Warwick and Leamington, alternately in the evening, terminate these sports.

By the Warwick and Napton Canal, which unites with the Oxford, and thereby communicates with the Grand Junction and other canals, the town possesses the advantage of a very extensive water communication.

COVENTRY.

The city of Coventry is supposed to have been founded at a very early period, as the final syllable of its appellation is evidently the British *Tre*, a town. The prefix to this simple and general term was added by the Saxons, and may rationally be concluded to express the circumstance of a covent or convent, being erected on the spot; and such a foundation we find to have taken place in a Saxon era. Camden observes that in early history, and in the pontifical decrees, the name of the city was often written *Conventria*, and he instances the expression thus translated, " Either the Bishop of Conventry is not in his right wits, or he seems wilfully to have quitted common sense." This, it is observed, must relate to Alexander de Savensby, who was consecrated in 1224, and, according to Godwin, was a very learned man, " but pretended to visions and apparitions scarce credible." Coventry was certainly not used by the Romans for military purposes, and few vestiges have been discovered to favour the idea of their entering largely on a domestic and tranquil association, with the original inhabitants.

The Warwickshire antiquary, *Rous*, is the first writer that mentions an early monastery of nuns in this city; and he informs us that when the traitor Edrick invaded Mercia, and destroyed many towns, in 1016, a house of nuns in Coventry, of which a holy virgin named St. Osburg, had been some time abbess, fell a prey to his ferocity. Leland says that King Canute first founded a monastery here.

In conducting the history of Coventry to the reign of King Edward the Confessor, we introduce it to an era, concerning which we are furnished with documents somewhat more satisfactory, though these are mingled with one of the most fantastical legends that ever met with a popular reception. In the early part of Edward's reign, Leofric, the fifth Earl of Mercia, and his countess, Godiva, (sometimes also called *Godifa, Godina,* and *Goditha*) founded a monastery on the ruins of St Osburg's nunnery. This Leofric was descended from Leofric Earl of Chester, in the time of Ethelbald King of Mercia, and appears to have been a man of eminent talents, as he stood high in the consideration of several successive monarchs, and is placed by historians at the head of various great state transactions. By King Canute he was made captain general of the royal forces. After the death of Canute he was chiefly instrumental in advancing to the crown Harold, the son of that king. Edward the Confessor was principally indebted to Leofric for his elevation to the throne, and was subsequently protected by his wisdom and power from many of the turbulent machinations of Earl Godwyn. The Countess Godiva was sister to Thorold sheriff of Lincolnshire, a man much imbued with the piety prevalent in that age, as appears by his founding the abbey of Spalding. She is said by Ingulphus to have been a most beautiful and devout lady.

The monastery founded by this illustrious pair was for an abbot and twenty-four monks of the Benedictine order, and it surpassed all others in the county for amplitude of revenue and splendour of ornaments. Among the reliques was an arm of St. Augustine, placed in a silver shrine, on which was an inscription, purporting that it was purchased of the Pope by Agelnethus Archbishop of Canterbury. Earl Leofric died of a good old age, in the thirteenth of Edward the Confessor, at his house at Bromley in Staffordshire, and was buried in a porch of the monastery church which he had founded. The Lady Godiva appears to have been actuated by zealous and habitual piety. Besides founding the monastery of Stow, near Lincoln, she conferred numerous benefactions on the foundations at Coventry. Her remains are interred in the other porch of the monastery church. With the foundation of its monastic structure commenced the prosperity of Coventry. While the means of commercial intercourse were difficult, no town that had not in its vicinity such mineral veins as were easy of access, and were essential to the homely needs of a people who had few wants besides those which the sword and ploughshare might supply, could hope to attract the tide of traffic without the aid of superstitious fascination. Tribes of devotees, saintly feasts, and monastic largesses, vaingloriously bestowed alike upon the helpless and the indolent, now increased the trade and population of the place, and rendered its tolls and services objects of consideration. From the general character of Earl Leofric as given by early historians, and from the bountiful and pious disposition he evinced in the foundation of his monastery, it might be supposed that he would not exact these tolls and services — for to him, as lord of the town, they were due — with too rigorous a hand. But it seems the citizens found them a grievance; and concerning the method in which they found relief from oppression is told a tale which we give in the words of Sir William Dugdale: — " The Countess Godiva, bearing an extraordinary affection to this place, often and earnestly besought her husband, that, for the love of God and the Blessed Virgin, he would free it from that grievous servitude whereunto it was subject; but he, rebuking her for importuning him in a manner so inconsistent with his profit, commanded that she should thenceforth forbear to move therein; yet she, out of her womanish pertinacity, continued to solicit him, insomuch that he told her if she would ride on horseback, naked, from one end of the town to the other, in the sight of all the people, he would grant her request: whereunto she returned — " *But will you give me leave so to do?*" and he replying, yes! the noble lady, upon an appointed day, got on horseback, naked, with her hair loose, so that it covered all her body but the legs; and thus performing the journey, returned with joy to her husband, who thereupon granted to the inhabitants a charter of freedom; in memory whereof, the picture of him and his said lady were set up in a south window of Trinity Church, in this city, about King Richard II.'s time, and his right hand holding a charter with these words written thereon: —

> I luriche for love of thee,
> Doe make Coventre toll free.

It is said by Rapin, "that the countess, previous to her riding, commanded all persons to keep within doors, and from their windows on pain of death; but notwithstanding this severe penalty, there was one person could not forbear giving a look, out of curiosity, but it cost him his life. This story appears legendary at the first and slightest glance. The females of the era at which Lady Godiva flourished accounted modesty of attire and scrupulous secretion of person virtues connected with religious merit; and we have evidence that the countess was habitually inclined to perform religious duty, to an extremity of attention, and was indeed one of the most zealous devotees of the age. Is it then likely that religious feelings would allow her to commit an act of such strange indecency for the mere exoneration from tolls and duties of a few hundreds of her husband's vassals? But if we can believe that pious habits were not sufficiently powerful to confirm this lady in the modest reserves which appear born with the sex, and which quit only in the last stages of depravity, shall we venture to imagine that a husband ever existed who would allow "the winds of heaven," to visit so freely a beloved wife's person? And that Leofric was a fond and approving husband, seems clear from the readiness with which he joined the name of Godiva with his own in the costly religious foundation at Coventry. The coarseness of his conduct, if we suppose him capable of so acting, cannot be attributed to the prevailing barbarity of the age; for female modesty and connubial strictness of conduct were dearly prized at this period, however deficient it might be in minor delicacies of sentiment and exterior polish. Leofric, then, must form an exception to the general feeling; but the man forming such an exception must be besotted, ignorant, and weak. Leofric, however, was neither: he was the councillor of kings, the defender of thrones, and the patron of the clergy.

The greatest impediment to an advance in mercantile consequence, during times so boisterous and unsteady, was the want of fortified barriers, to protect the trader in his speculations, and to insure the safety of the building in which he deposited his goods. In the second of Edward III.. the inhabitants received permission to collect a toll towards defraying the expense of *enclosing* their town. Perhaps the internal tranquillity which was produced by the wise government of Edward, rather than a want of means in the citizens, caused the building of the walls not to be commenced for 27 years after this grant was obtained. The city certainly wore a flourishing aspect during this bright reign. Several enactments of Edward evince the riches of the merchants; and it was now that the costly steeple of St. Michael's church, the admiration of succeeding ages, was designed and partly raised. A house for the reception of Carmelite Friars was, likewise, built on an extensive scale. By this king, the civil magistracy was constituted a body corporate.

In the time of Richard II., the walls, with the numerous gates and towers, were completed; and the king evinced his affection to this city by grants of various privileges to the corporation. Coventry was now pressing rapidly forward to the great era of its prosperity and magnificence. Its public buildings increased, and its traders fixed a staple manufacture in the city. The success with which the clothing business was cultivated appears from a grant of the king, "that the mayor and bailiffs should, for the space of five years, have his form of sealing woollen cloths here, to the value of xxiv pounds sterling." It was in the year 1397, that this rash sovereign chose the vicinity of Coventry for the scene of a tragic pageant, that involved in its consequences the loss of his crown and life. King Henry IV held a parliament here in the year 1404. This was the parliament since styled Parliamentum indoctorum, and from sitting in which all lawyers were prohibited. The meeting was held in a great chamber of the priory. The great favour conferred by the sixth Henry, in constituting the city and contiguous district a separate county was in the year 1451. Coventry, indeed, appears to have been at this period a city well deserving of regal partiality. Its religious buildings were numerous and splendid; its embattled walls were massy, and in high preservation; its merchants were spirited and enterprising, and we have proofs that they were affluent and generous. In the year 1459, a second parliament was held in this city, which like the former, was sufficiently memorable to gain an epithet in history, though one of an ungracious character. This was the violent meeting in which attainders were passed against Richard Duke of York, the Earl of March (afterwards Edward IV.), and the Earls of Salisbury and Warwick. This parliament was termed by the Yorkists, Parliamentum diabolicum, and all its acts were afterwards reversed.

In the year 1469, the Earl of Rivers and his son John were beheaded on Gosford Green, by order of Sir John Coniers, a commander in the army of northern insurgents, which had obtained some success in the neighbouring county of Oxford. King Edward IV., in whose reign this sanguinary act took place, was anxious to win the esteem of the city of Coventry: himself and the queen kept festival here during the Christmas of 1465; but his utmost blandishments had not power speedily to erase from the minds of the inhabitants an affectionate regard for the House of Lancaster.

In 1470, the Earl of Warwick, then intent on the destruction of the monarch whom he had enabled to reach the throne, entered Coventry with ordnance and other warlike stores. Edward shortly marched from Leicester; and, after resting at Combe Abbey, approached Coventry. He halted on Gosford Green, and demanded entrance, but finding the city hostile, he resumed his march, and lodged that night at Warwick. When reinstated in power by the victories of Barnet and Tewksbury, he revenged this insult by depriving the citizens of their liberties and franchises; or in other words by levying on them a fine of 500 marks, for that was the sum paid by Coventry for a restitution of its privileges. The goodwill of the inhabitants was, however, of too much consequence for Edward to treat them with continued harshness, or even with the indifference of neglect. He kept here the feast of St. George in 1474. His son, the ill-fated Prince Edward, in the same year, was one of the godfathers of a child of the mayor, and three years afterwards he was made a brother of the guilds of Corpus Christi and St. Trinity. This notice from the court sufficiently evinces the great political importance of the city at that period.

Richard III. visited Coventry, and was a spectator of the pageants during the festival of Corpus Christi. Immediately subsequent to the decisive battle of Bosworth Field, Henry VII. repaired hither, and lodged in the mayor's house.

Henry VIII. and Queen Katharine visited this place in 1510, "when there were three pageants set forth; one at Jordan Well, with the nine orders of angels; one at Broadgate, with divers beautiful damsels; and one at Cross Cheping; and so they passed on to the priory."

We have seen that Coventry was indebted for its early prosperity to the magnitude and importance of its monastic establishments; and much of its opulence and splendour through succeeding ages must unquestionably be attributed to the same source. A great priory at once protected the pauper and encouraged the merchant, and not only afforded a temporary palace to kings, but continually attracted throngs of all ranks from the most distant parts, intent either on the purposes of devotion, interchanges of religious amity, or speculations of traffic. It will readily, therefore, be apprehended that the city felt a great shock on the dissolution of monastic houses. But we find difficulty in believing, as was stated by John Hales, Esq., to the Protector Somerset, " that in consequence of the dissolution, trade grew so low, and there was such a dispersion of the people from this city, that there were not above 3000 inhabitants, whereas formerly there had been 15,000."

Queen Elizabeth visited Coventry during her progress through this part of the kingdom in 1565, and was received with a variety of splendid shows and pageants. The queen lodged, during her visit, at the White Friars (then a seat of the Hales family); but Coventry soon received within its walls a princess whom no blandishments awaited. In 1566, the unfortunate Mary Queen of Scots was conducted to this city, and was confined as a prisoner in the mayoress's parlour. Three years afterwards she was again brought hither, and kept in confinement at the Bull Inn (on the site of which the barracks now stand), under the care of the Earls of Shrewsbury and Huntingdon. During this mournful period the citizens kept watch and ward, night and day, at every gate, that none might pass without examination.

In the civil war which terminated fatally to Charles I., Coventry was well inclined to take an active part, though by a singular felicity, it escaped those miseries of siege and devastation to which so many other armed towns were subjected. When the king re paired to Leicester, in 1641, after having raised his standard at Nottingham, he demanded the attendance of the mayor and sheriffs of this city, but the popular party prevented their acceding to his desire. The Earl of Northampton (at that time the city recorder,) tried his influence, but was able to muster only 400. In the following year the city was garrisoned by the parliament, and the most vigorous measures were adopted for its defence; every precaution being taken to strengthen the place, and in this state it remained till the end of the year 1659.; but when the Restoration was voted by parliament, Charles II. was promptly proclaimed by the mayor and alderman amidst great acclamations of joy. On the day of coronation, too, the city conduits ran claret; and bonfires were lighted in the evening, in testimony of loyalty.

King James II. visited Coventry in 1687, and was presented with a gold cup and cover by the corporation.

The *Ecclesiastical History* of Coventry, as connected with the bishopric, requires a separate notice. Shortly after the Mercian kingdom was divided into five bishoprics, that of Lichfield was so far extended as to comprehend the chief part of the former possessions of the Carnavii. Peter, elected bishop of Lichfield in 1075, moved the see to Chester; and Robert de Limesie, in 1102, removed it again to Coventry, tempted, probably, by the riches and reputation of the monastery founded by Earl Leofric The five succeeding bishops likewise sat at Coventry; and the whole of these six prelates styled themselves Coventriæ Episcopi only. Hugh Novant, archdeacon of Oxford, consecrated bishop in 1188, restored the see to Lichfield, though not without opposition from the Benedictine monks of Coventry, who had gained an accession of repute from the bishop's residence, without forfeiting their particular influence; for although their superior lost the name of abbot, and became as prior, only substitute to the bishop, in whom the abbacy was really vested, he yet remained, like his predecessors the abbots, a baron of parliament. In consequence of disputes which now took place between the Chapter of Coventry and that of Lichfield respecting elections, both parties agreed, in the reign of Henry III., to the following regulations: — That the bishop should be elected both from Coventry and Lichfield; that the precedence in the episcopal title should be given to the former city; that the two chapters should alternately choose their bishop; and that they should form one body, in which the prior of Coventry should be the principal. From this time, until a period comparatively recent, the prelate was styled bishop of Coventry and Lichfield; and these regulations remained in force till that great era in ecclesiastical concerns, the dissolution of monastic houses. In the thirty-third of Henry VIII., an act was passed which ordained, " that the dean and chapter of Lichfield should be for ever the entire and sole chapter of the bishopric of Coventry and Lichfield; whereof the prior and convent of the dissolved priory of Coventry were heretofore the moiety or half part. " Such remains the constitution of the bishopric at the present day; but when, on the restoration, the truly excellent Hacket was appointed to this see, he gave the precedence in titular designation to Lichfield, and his example has been hitherto followed by succeeding prelates.

The city of Coventry is 91 miles N.N.W. from London, and is distant from Birmingham 18 miles, from Warwick 10, and from Kenilworth 5 miles. The chief parts of the city are seated on gently elevated ground, and the whole is watered by the Radford and Sherbourn brooks. The view of a town to the approaching traveller usually rests for interest upon some few prominent features; on a few public buildings which rise superior to the mass of habitations, and direct attention to eras of important history, by displaying the architecture of ages in which the place has conspicuously flourished. Coventry is fortunate in this particular. It has three spires, (one of pre-eminent beauty, and the others deficient in attraction only from a comparison with St. Michael's) which rise high in the air, and prepare the examiner for an entrance to a place of great population and striking architectural importance. The streets, which are narrow and badly paved, have in many instances been much improved, and are still improving, and the city is lighted with gas; many years must however elapse before the general aspect of Coventry can experience, in many instances, at least any very material change. This city has been singularly fortunate in escaping conflagration. There has not been a fire of any extent since the oldest house now standing was erected. In consequence, it presents for the most part the aspect of a city of the sixteenth century; the upper parts of the houses project, as was customary in ages when a free circulation of air formed no part of the builder's calculation; the streets are merely of the width that was judged necessary when the transit of carriages was slow and of rare occurrence; and the eye accustomed to modern amplitude of dimensions is not agreeably surprised at the view. But the circumstance that tends to the displeasure of the ordinary examiner, affords a harvest of high gratification to the lover of domestic architectural antiquities. Houses replete with the venerable traces of the fifteenth century are yet standing in several divisions; the freshness of complexion only injured by age, and the main works still firm in massy and almost impregnable oak. Persons imbued with such a taste must derive true pleasure from a perambulation of this city. The specimens of the style prevailing in different eras are strongly marked, and of the most gratifying description. To some are attached circumstances of local story which add to their interest; and others possess peculiarities of construction well worthy of the antiquary's notice. In many instances, where the front has experienced alteration, the interior still remains untouched; and the costly character of the carved embellishments here to be seen explain, without the trouble of appeal to record the prosperity of the place during the reign of the latter Henrys. From whatever side seen, Coventry presents an imposing appearance; the best view of it is, however, obtained from the N.E., from whence it is beheld to great advantage. The whole of its churches stand here disclosed with great pictorial effect. St. Michael's, beautiful and attractive, when seen from any point, forms the principal feature. Its sister spire (that of Trinity Church) rises modestly beyond, as if retiring in confessed inferiority of pretension. The tower of St. John's, and the steeple of the Grey Friars, ascend on either hand, and complete the display. The spot from which the two steeples that so eminently adorn Coventry are seen with the most striking effect, is in the neighbourhood of the now desolated priory, on the margin of Priory-mill Dam.

The length of the city of Coventry, from Hill Street Gate to Gosford Gate, is about three quarters of a mile, exclusive of the suburbs. The walls, no longer necessary to the preservation of civic security, are completely reduced; but traces of these, and of several of the gates are yet discernible. The former, which added so much to the importance of the city, were begun in 1355, and, together with the towers, were not completed in less than forty years. The walls were three miles in circumference, and in each division they were nine feet in thickness. At different points, skilfully suited to the purpose of defence, were thirty-two towers, and the twelve following gates:— New Gate; Gosford; Bastill (or Mill Lane) Priory, Cook Street; Bishop; Well Street; Hill Street; Spon; Grey Friars; Cheylesmore; and Little Park Street. The whole were kept in good repair for nearly three centuries, and the security they afforded to the city has been rendered evident by our notice of the confident readiness with which access was denied to Edward IV. and Charles I., when those monarchs appeared in arms before their gates. The active hostility of the citizens during the Cromwellian war convinced Charles II. of the propriety of throwing open the town; a measure to which the citizens in their transport of joy at the restoration readily consented; and, in consequence, the whole were destined to destruction. On July

22d, 1662, the Earl of Northampton, accompanied by many of the neighbouring gentry, and attended by the county troops made the first breach in the walls. The work of demolition employed nearly 500 men for three weeks and three days; at the end of which time the reduction was complete. But although the walls and towers were levelled, most of the gates were left untouched, and several have been taken down within the last half century. Traces of the wall may yet be discovered in several districts, and three of the gates of a subordinate character, viz. Bastill, Priory, and Cook Street, though in a dilapidated state, alone remain.

The religious and other public buildings of Coventry are well worthy of attention. The *Churches* are three in number: that of *St. Michael* is a beautiful specimen of the Gothic or English style. The more ancient part of the present structure is the steeple, which was begun in 1373, and finished in 1395. It was built at the charge of William and Adam Botoner, who were several times mayors of Coventry, and who are said to have expended on this work 100*l.* per annum till it was completed. An elevation more delicate in symmetry, or more striking in general character, was, perhaps, never designed by the great school of architects, who ranged without restraint of rule, over all the beauties which genius could combine for the purpose of effect or display. It commences in a square tower, no portion of which remains blank, though not any superfluous ornament is introduced. The windows are well-proportioned, and the buttresses eminently light. In various niches are introduced the figures of saints, and each division is enriched with a bold but not redundant spread of embroidery work and embossed carving. This tower is 136 feet 3 inches in height; and on it stands an octagonal prism 32 feet 6 inches high, which is supported by eight springing arches of graceful and easy character. The octagon is surmounted by a battlement, from within which proceeds a spire 130 feet 9 inches in height, adorned with fluting, and embossed pilasterwise. The beauties of this steeple are so evident to the common eye, that they need no aphorism of the scientific to impress them on the attention; but it may be observed that, according to local tradition, Sir Christopher Wren pronounced this structure a masterpiece of the architectural art. The body of the church is generally supposed to have been erected in the time of Henry VI.; and from the character of the architecture, it is probable the chief parts were constructed in the early part of that sovereign's reign. The whole is of the best character of Gothic, light, though august, and impressive from a felicitous arrangement of parts. The interior consists of a body and two side aisles, divided by lofty arches, with clustered pillars. The windows of the upper story, which range along the whole of the sides, are ornamented with ancient painted glass, expressive of various religious subjects. The ceiling is of oak, ribbed and carved. On each side of the nave is a gallery; and here is a good organ.

Trinity Church is in the immediate contiguity of St. Michael's, and loses much in estimation as a structure, from the comparison inevitably forced upon the spectator's mind, by this close neighbourhood of site. The building approaches to the cruciform character; and from the centre rises a square tower, out of which directly issues a lofty spire; but from the want of that octagonal prism, which adds so much to the beauty of St. Michael's, the steeple is subject to a comparative deficiency in lightness, injurious to the effect that must otherwise be produced by its really fine proportions. The original spire of this church was blown down in the year 1664; the new building was completed in 1667, and is composed of stone taken from a quarry without the New Gate; its entire height from the ground to the apex is 237 feet. The faces of the tower have been highly worked, though with much less delicacy than the building of St. Michael's; but it is to be lamented, that both churches are formed of a friable stone found in the neighbourhood, which perishes rapidly under the vicissitudes of the weather; a circumstance destructive of the more elaborate touches of the chisel so patiently bestowed on the decorations of both. The east end of the church was taken down in 1786, and rebuilt in a style tolerably consonant to the general character of the structure. The interior is marked by that studious cultivation of twilight gloom generally found in the works of Gothic designers; but is in no other way remarkable. The monuments are few and uninteresting, with the exception of one to the memory of Dr. Holland, the well-known translator.

St. John's Church is a respectable stone structure of the cruciform character, with a low and weighty tower rising from the centre. The interior is plain, and much encumbered by the four massy pillars that support the tower. Behind St. John's church, is Bablake Hospital, an old building with a court in the middle of it. In one part of it is Bond's alms-houses, for ten poor men and one poor woman; and in the other is a foundation for clothing and educating thirty-eight poor boys. The town has also a good free grammar-school (formerly an hospital), founded by John Hales, who purchased the plunder of the hospital at a very cheap rate: part of the chapel forms the present school, which has a library belonging to it. Here are also places of religious worship for dissenters of different denominations.

The most important of the buildings connected with civic business or ceremonials is *St. Mary's Hall*. This structure has attracted the notice of many eminent antiquaries, and is well calculated to convey to the living age a just idea of the magnificence of Coventry, when the city was the resort of devotees, and the favourite *chamber of princes*. This building, now used for the purposes of civic dignity, stands a short distance on the south from St. Michael's Church. The exterior chiefly rests for attraction on a fine and spacious window, which occupies the larger portion of the front; the masonry of the upper division is extremely good, and the spaces between the mullions of the lower half are filled with rich and well finished niches. The building is entered by a porch, with an arched roofing. Beyond the porch is a court-yard, on the right of which is seen the east side of the hall, and on the left a flight of stairs communicating with an open gallery, that leads directly to the great room of entertainment.

In the other buildings connected with the court, we view, untouched by innovation, the arrangement of ages, in which the whole business of a festival was conducted within the walls of one establishment. A door under the gallery opens to the kitchen, a spacious room replete with testimonials of the good cheer enjoyed by the associated guilds. On the north side are lofty arches supported by octangular columns. " At each extremity of a large arch, over the coppers, is an angel holding a shield containing a mark or monogram, probably the builders; the letters J. B. are quite distinct." On the side towards the east are four chimneys, with communicating arches, and the window over each is in a style of architecture corresponding in excellence to that prevailing in the more important parts of the structure; the basement story, or cellar, of the hall is likewise fertile in proofs of the zeal and perseverance of the builders of the fifteenth century. The great hall, where have sat in dignified wassailry, so many historic characters, dear to the fancy from the gathering crust of antiquity that now obscures their features, is a noble room of entertainment, 21 yards long and 10 yards wide. At the north is a splendid semicircular window divided into nine parts, and painted with figures of several monarchs, and with armorial bearings, and other ornaments. Three or the west windows, formerly ornamented with paints, were re-glazed within the last half century with plain glass. The windows on the east side are extremely fine, though now much damaged. Beneath the north window, and filling the space from the seat of communication to its commencement, is a spread of tapestry of the highest local interest, and which cannot fail to excite the admiration of the examiner. The dimensions of this valuable performance are 30 feet in length, and 10 feet in height. King Henry, his queen, and attendants, are represented thereon in figures as large as life. Here is also a superb painting of George III. which was presented to the corporation by Lord Eardly.

The County Hall, erected in 1785, is a structure well

adapted to public business. The front is of stone, and has a rustic basement, with a range of columns supporting a pediment in the centre. *The Mayor's Parlour* is a place of official resort, suited only to the limited notions of magisterial dignity, or accommodation, which prevailed in the early centuries of civic importance. The period at which it was first constructed does not appear. In 1775, it was in part taken down, and rebuilt at the expense of nearly 600*l.*; but the exterior of the building, and the internal arrangement, are at present equally unworthy of the magistracy of so respectable a city. The mayor, or one of the aldermen attends every day, except Fridays and Sundays, to preside over public business. *The Draper's Hall*, a chaste elevation of stone, ornamented with Tuscan pillars, was erected in 1775; it is 49 feet 6 inches in length, and 25 feet in width. *The Barracks*, which occupy the site of the Bull Inn, an ancient hostel already described as connected with some interesting incidents in local history, were erected in the year 1793. They are handsome, as a building; the front towards the high street is faced with stone, and though not very extensive, are conveniently arranged.

The Cathedral of Coventry occupied a place called Hill Close, on a slight declivity from the north side of St. Michael's, and Trinity churchyards. This was assuredly a splendid edifice, and is said to have been built on the model of the cathedral at Lichfield. All who have written concerning the ancient state of this city remark upon the grandeur of effect that must have been produced by the assemblage of fine churches there exhibited, when the cathedral was standing. Three such structures, viewed from the area in which they were raised, without the slightest interruption, and quite free from the alloy of contiguous mean objects, must, indeed, have presented a display rarely exceeded in any district famed for ecclesiastical splendour. With a wantonness of barbarity that cannot now be explained, King Henry VIII. caused this cathedral to be levelled to the ground when he destroyed the neighbouring monastery.

The Grey Friars, or Friars Minors, are believed to have settled in Coventry, about the year 1234, and had, at first, only an oratory which was covered with shingles delivered for that purpose from the woods of Kenilworth, by order of King Henry III. These friars were most rigid and austere in manners, and disclaimed all endowment of lands, voluntarily living on charity, for the sake of mortification. But they were especially fortunate in procuring liberal alms; and the contributions of the devout enabled them to raise a monastery and church more splendid than would seem suited to the wishes of such humbler religionists on the south side of the city. Of the habitable parts of the building not any traces exist. The remains of the church consist of a fine steeple, with a spire springing from an octagon. This spire, which is lofty and well-proportioned, adds much to the imposing effect of the city in regard to public structures; it long stood a solitary monument of the former greatness of this once splendid monastery, and until recently, when under the authority of the parliamentary commissioners, a beautiful new church, correspondent in style, was erected on the adjacent ground, and annexed thereto. It is in the parish of St. Michael.

The White Friars, or Carmelites, another order of mendicants, first settled in Coventry about the year 1342, the 16th of Edward III. A house for their reception was built by Sir John Poultney, four times lord mayor of London; whose arms in Dugdale's time were still extant over the gates. Although these friars, like the Franciscans, disclaimed the pomp and vanity of landed endowments, they never closed their hands when alms were offered, or declined a charitable legacy, however large the amount. They shared the general fate of monastic institutions in 1538, and surrendered their house by an instrument dated the 30th of October. The monastery, with its possessions, passed into the hands of John Hales, Esq. who converted the building into a residence, and here had the honour of entertaining Queen Elizabeth. The building is now used as a house of industry for the united parishes of St. Michael, and the Holy Trinity. The present fabric combines parts of the ancient monastery, and of the domestic structure raised by the Hales family; to which have been made considerable additions by the directors of the poor. The monastic edifice appears to have been extensive, and well-arranged, and its remains will, upon examination, amply gratify the antiquarian.

The Cross of Coventry, a fabric of extensive celebrity, though not of a very ancient date, stood near the centre of the corn market, but was removed in 1771.

It has been already said that the Earls of Chester raised a castle within the manor of Cheylesmore, on the south side of the city; and after the ruin of the castle, a manor-house was constructed in the same situation. Of this building there chiefly remain some pieces of stone-work, connected with mean tenements raised on the site, which indicate the massy character of the structure.

Coventry acquired affluence and reputation at a very early period from the success with which it cultivated manufactures. The cloth caps and bonnets made in this city, became articles of important traffic at the commencement of the fifteenth century, and woollen broad cloths remained the staple manufacture until the war of 1694, between England and France, when the Turkey trade was destroyed. In the early part of the sixteenth century

Coventry became famous for a manufacture of blue thread, but the art was lost before the year 1581. The manufacture of striped and mixed tammies, and of camlets, shalloons, and calimancoes, flourished through the greater part of the eighteenth century, but is now almost entirely lost. The principal manufactures at present are those of ribands and watches.

The manufacture of ribands was introduced about a century back, and for some years, was confined to the hands of a few. It has since spread to a great extent, and is now supposed to afford employment to 16,000 persons in the city, and surrounding villages. The manufacture of watches was not pursued to any great extent till within the last fifty years; but the trade has latterly experienced so considerable an increase, that it is by some considered more watches are now made in Coventry than in the metropolis, — an opinion in which the writer cannot coincide.

Coventry, although situate in the centre of England, possesses through the Oxford and Coventry canal, and various others with which it unites, the advantage of an extensive water communication, by which means it is enabled to transmit heavy merchandise not only to the metropolis, but also to the ports of Liverpool, Bristol, and Hull. It was till recently a principal stage upon the great parliamentary line of road from London to Holyhead, and in consequence derived no inconsiderable advantage from the maintenance of extensive coach etablishments, and the expenditure of travellers. With some of these, but particularly the coach establishments, and it may also be added the posting houses, the formation of the Birmingham Railway has materially interfered, some having sustained irreparable injury, while others have been involved in ruin. Coventry may, however, upon the whole, be deemed extremely fortunate, in not having been like many other places, excluded from the line to their great detriment if not total destruction; as in all probability the arrival ot visitors to this ancient city will be very considerably increased, the distance from London (94 miles) being accomplished by the railway trains in about five hours. With such advantages of manufacture and interchange, although the city may not appear so captivating to the traveller as when enriched by all its structures, fresh in aspect and flourishing in character, it may still with confidence rely on its own efforts for attaining at least an equality, if not an intrinsic superiority to the proud height which it gained in the days of the third Edward and the sixth Henry.

Coventry gives the title of Earl to a family descended from John Coventry (son of William Coventry of this city), who was lord mayor of London in 1425. The city is divided into ten wards, and is internally governed by a mayor, ten aldermen, and twenty common council: the recorder is usually a nobleman; the mayor and aldermen are justices of the peace for the city and county.

Coventry returns two members to parliament, who are chosen by the freemen and 10*l.* householders; the latter were added by the Reform Bill, the sheriffs being the returning officers. The privilege of sending representatives was enjoyed by this city during the four first parliaments of Edward I. Occasional interruptions afterwards occurred, but since the year 1453 the privilege has remained undisturbed.

There are four annual *fairs*, at which much business is transacted. The most important of these was granted by Henry III., and according to the charter is permitted to continue eight days. There is a procession connected with this fair, which has attracted much notice, and is allusive to the story of Lady Godiva. "To this day," says Pennant, "the regard of Godiva towards this city is remembered by a procession on the Friday in Trinity week; and a charming fair one still graces the procession — not literally like the good countess, with her own dishevelled hair, &c., but in linen, closely fitted to her limbs, and of a colour emulating their complexion." This *show* was a matter of annual occurrence till within the last thirty years; but it is now only occasionally presented. While mentioning the representative of Lady Godiva a personage of almost equal notoriety with the countess, it is in connection with this story, deemed proper to add, that a figure commemorative of Peeping Tom, who is said for his presumption to have been stricken blind, is now to be seen at a house communicating with the High street. This figure is kept in repair at the expense of the corporation, and is upon every repetition of the show re-embellished.

NUNEATON.

The town of Nuneaton appears entirely indebted for its early prosperity to the foundation of a monastery in the time of King Stephen. This religious house was founded by Robert Earl of Leicester, and was of the order of Fontevrault, in Poictiers; which order possessed the peculiarity of comprehending both monks and nuns within the pale of one establishment. It is certain that there was at one period a prior, resident at Nuneaton, but it is not ascertained that he had any monks in his train. The priors had superior rule in the house.

This monastery was well endowed, and the nuns obtained in the 10th of Henry III. the grant of a weekly market. In the 23d of the same reign, they procured a charter for a yearly fair. On the dissolution of religious houses, in the reign of Henry VIII., the revenues were stated at 290*l.* 15*s.* 0½*d.* The priors and the whole of the nuns were favoured with pensions for life. A portion of the building, comprehending one entire arch and fragments of walls, yet remain, as a melancholy memorial at the northwest extremity of the town, in the adjacency of the road leading towards Atherstone.

The church of Nuneaton is a respectable Gothic building. Here is a free-school, founded in the 6th of Edward VI. towards the establishment of which that king gave three closes of ground lying within the liberties of Coventry, and formerly belonging to the Trinity Guild. This town derives considerable benefit from the weaving of ribands, has a weekly market on Saturday (which is, however, not largely attended), and three annual fairs.

COVENTRY TO BIRMINGHAM.

From the Coventry Station where it crosses the Kenilworth road, the Railway continued through a cutting for a mile and a quarter runs upon a level, and quitting the county of Coventry, re-enters Warwickshire. A mile and a half distant on the right is Allesley Park, James Beck, Esq. From 1¼ mile beyond Coventry carried on an embankment that affords a good view of the surrounding country, it commences a very gradual rise, which it maintains for a distance of seven miles. In rather more than a mile it reaches Fletchamstead Hall, anciently a seat, now a farm-house, lying on the right; in 3 miles more Beechwood Tunnel, 160 yards in length, in another mile Berkswell Bridge, and in a further distance of half a mile, extends to Wooton Green Viaduct. On the right of Wooton Green is Berkswell Hall, the beautiful seat of Sir John Eardley Wilmot, Bart. From Wooton Green Viaduct, where it crosses the Kenilworth and Coleshill road, carried on an embankment, in 2 miles more it extends to the Blythe River Viaduct, a quarter of a mile beyond which it reaches

THE HAMPTON STATION,

AN INTERMEDIATE ONE, DISTANT FROM LONDON 102½, FROM BIRMINGHAM 9¾ MILES.

Here the Birmingham and Derby Junction Railway branches off, a line recently completed from hence to Derby, a distance of about 38½ miles. From a mile and a quarter beyond Coventry, the Railway, constructed upon an embankment along which with little interruption it is continued for nearly 3 miles, then reaches the Beechwood excavation, a rocky pass, more than 50 feet in depth; that crossed by Beechwood Bridge, one of the most beautiful on the line, leads to Beechwood Tunnel, the entrance to which, constructed in costly masonry in the Egyptian style and manner, is in its effect most imposing. From Wooton Green, the Railway in another mile attains a short level, when, commencing a descent, it in that way reaches Hampton Station. Two miles distant from the Hampton Station on right, at Meriden, a well-known stage upon the Birmingham road, is Meriden Hall, Lady Sykes, near which is Packington Hall, the beautiful seat of the Earl of Aylesford. From the Hampton Station, the inclination of the Railway is that of a gradual ascent, for about 7 miles, in one and a half of which it reaches the London and Birmingham road, here carried over the Railway, and in two more extends to Marston Green Viaduct. Soon after quitting the excavation under the London road, the town of Solihull is seen on left. One mile beyond the London road on the left is Marston Hall C. Thornley, Esq., two miles distant on left of Marston Green Viaduct is Elmdon Hall, unoccupied; and three miles on right is the town of Coleshill, distinguishable by its spire, that continues for some distance the most striking feature of the landscape. Near Coleshill is Maxstoke Castle, T. Dilke, Esq. A little beyond Marston Green Viaduct, the Railway, continued on a rise, enters upon an embankment that affords a good view, and crossing a branch of the Cole by Easthall Viaduct, is in that way carried across the valley, a distance of about a mile and a quarter to the vicinity of Kit's Green, where crossing a tributary stream of the Sow, by the Sheldon Viaduct, it quits the county of Warwick and enters Worcestershire, at a distance from London of $107\frac{1}{2}$ miles, and $4\frac{3}{4}$ miles from Birmingham. A little beyond the Sheldon Viaduct on left, but obscured from the view, is Lea Hall, —— Brown, Esq. An excavation of considerable depth commences here, and is continued for about a mile and a quarter, when succeeded by an embankment, in half a mile more it reaches the Stichford Viaduct, that here crosses the river Cole, when, quitting the county of Worcester, the Railway re-enters Warwickshire. The road here crossed leads on left to Yardley, and on right to Castle Bromwich. An excavation of considerable depth and of a mile and a half in length ensues, crossed by various bridges, among them one of great beauty. The rise commenced a little beyond Hampton Station, soon terminates, and is succeeded by an embankment which, constructed on a level from its elevated position, exhibits an excellent view of the surrounding very beautiful country, terminated in the distance by the tall spires and towering chimneys of the great *Toy-shop* of the world. The Railway on a nearer approach exhibits to great advantage the viaduct of the Grand Junction Railway, and crossing the Lawley Street Viaduct, a massive and masterly erection, enters the Birmingham Station, at a distance of $112\frac{1}{4}$ miles from London

At the station omnibuses are in attendance ready to convey persons to all parts of the town at the charge of sixpence each;

but for the convenience of others preferring that mode of conveyance hackney coaches, and what here are called cars, may be obtained, for which the following are the rates of charge:—

HACKNEY COACHES OR CARS DRAWN BY ONE HORSE.

	s. d.		s. d.
Not exceeding one mile	1 0	Two miles and a half	2 6
One mile and a half	1 6	Three miles	3 0
Two miles	2 0	Three miles and a half	3 6

returning with the same fares with an addition of one half of the charge for the original distance.

The following is a list of the principal hotels, all of which are within a mile of the Station:— Albion Hotel, High Street; Castle, High Street, George Digbeth; Hen and Chickens, New Street; Royal Hotel, Temple Row; New Royal Hotel, New Street; Stork Hotel, in the Square; Swan, High Street; and White Hart, Digbeth. In addition to which it may be briefly remarked that Birmingham abounds in houses of entertainment suited to the taste of travellers of every class.

PACKINGTON HALL

Is the seat of the Earl of Aylesford. The manor of Packington came to the ancestor of the present noble proprietor, in the early part of the eighteenth century, in consequence of a marriage with the daughter of Sir Clement Fisher.

The neighbourhood of Packington is said to contain the highest ground in England, and many points command prospects as beautiful and various as they are extensive. The spacious mansion was much improved by the late earl and his father, and is now a commodious residence of the first class, though not of an ornamental character. The grounds possess a natural inequality favourable to the picturesque effect; and are well-wooded and finely adorned with water. The parish church of Packington, a small neat structure standing in the Park, was rebuilt in the latter part of the eighteenth century, from a design by Bonomi.

HAMPTON IN ARDEN,

A station of the London and Birmingham, and Birmingham and Derby Junction Railways, distant 6 miles from Coleshill, 3 from Solihull, $9\frac{3}{4}$ from Birmingham, and $102\frac{1}{2}$ from London, is a very large parish of Hemlingford Hundred, Warwickshire, embracing in extent an area of many miles. It includes within its circuit, the chapelry of Balsall, together with the hamlets of Knowle, Nuthurst, and Kinwalsey. Of these, two are deserving of particular notice — Knowle and Balsall. Knowle or Knoll, the nearest of these to the mother church, is a pleasing village, situate, as the name implies, on elevated ground. This lordship was possessed by Eleanor, the consort of Edward I., and on the death of that queen, it was given with many others to the monks of Westminster, on condition of their performing certain pious ceremonies on the eve of St. Andrew, the day on which the amiable Queen Eleanor's anniversary had usually been kept. About the latter end of the reign of Richard II., Walter Cooke, a churchman of high preferment and repute, erected at his own expense, a chapel in the village of Knowle; and in the fourth year of Henry IV. he founded a chantry here of either one or two priests. Retaining his friendly inclinations towards this spot, he procured in the fourteenth of the same king, a licence to institute, in conjunction with some other persons, a guild within the chapel, of which fraternity many noble and celebrated men became members. With the concurrence of Elizabeth, the widow of Lord Clinton, he afterwards obtained permission for himself and that lady to found here a college of ten chantry priests. But at the dissolution of such institutions in the reign of Henry VIII., there were only two chantry priests on this foundation, and the revenues were stated at no more than 22l. 3s. 3d. The income of the guild, supporting three chantry priests, was returned at 29l. 14s. 7d. The chapel is a building of much beauty, consisting of a nave, two aisles, and a chancel. In the south wall are four stone seats in recesses, beneath embellished arches, and further towards the east is a handsome piscina. On the north side are seven stalls, and on the south side six; these are ornamented with various satirical allusions, among which may be noticed an ape holding a bag, and a bear looking at it; a fox holding an open book, &c. In the south wall of the south aisle occur a piscina and a locker. Over the rood-loft are some remains of paintings, comprising whole-lengths of the Virgin Mary, another saint, and an angel. Several of the pews are embellished with carving; and in the windows are still preserved some painted glass. In ploughing a field near Knowle, an urn of a dark brown colour was discovered, containing coins of the lower empire, to the weight of fifteen pounds.

BALSALL.

The hamlet of Balsall, generally denominated Temple Balsall, was given to the Knights Templars by Roger de Mowbray; which religious knights erected a church in this place, and constructed here a house as a preceptory or cell, to their principal mansion, the Temple in London. Besides the manor of Balsall, the Knights Templars had various other landed possessions in Warwickshire; and their preceptory at Balsall was supported with much splendour until the termination of the order of Templars in England, in the reign of Edward II. The Knights Hospitallers briefly succeeded to the possessions of the Templars at Balsall, but it does not appear that they had any preceptory or residence at this place. On the dissolution of monasteries, this manor came, after various transmissions, to Lady Catherine Leveson, the daughter of Sir Robert Dudley, and this lady bequeathed the whole lordship for the founding of an hospital for the reception and maintenance of indigent females, either widows or unmarried women, of fair character, to be chosen from the inhabitants of certain specified parishes, that of Balsall having the preference. A minister was appointed to " instruct the pensioners for the good of their souls," and it was directed that he should likewise " teach and instruct 20 of the poorest boys of Balsall parish, until fit to be apprentices."

The church of Balsall will be viewed with considerable interest, as it has experienced scarcely any alteration since its erection by the Knights Templars. This building is in the form of an oblong square; and is, according to an admeasurement stated by Dr. Thomas, 104 feet in length, 39 in breadth, and 57 in height. The interior is not subject to any division. The walls are three feet in thickness, and the roofing is composed of timber, formed partly into squares, at the angles of which were shields of arms, now removed into the great hall. At the east end is a lofty painted window of five lights, and on each side are three windows, consisting alternately of three and four lights, the heads beautifully ramified, and all dissimilar. At the east end is likewise a window of five lights; and over it a circular window of twelve compartments. The doors are four in number, and very small. Over that at the south-west corner is a turret, rising no higher than the centre of the roof. The buttresses are light, and not graduated. The ornamental sculpture, consisting of imposts to the arches, and a row of ten heads on a cornice, or moulding, at the west end, is of excellent workmanship. It may be observed that the chancel is not distinguished from the nave by any other circumstance than the floor in that part rising one step. In the south wall, at the east end of the church, are three stone stalls or recesses.

The ancient hall of the Templars is still existing, though now surrounded with brickwork, and disfigured by square-headed windows. This spacious apartment appears to have been wholly framed of timber, and divided into three aisles by massive wooden pillars.

The bequest of Lady Leveson has proved of the most propitious character, and the number of alms-people has been augmented at several periods, in consequence of the affluent state of the finances. The various buildings connected with this charity are substantial and extensive, and the whole institution ranks among the most advantageous and pleasing possessions of the county.

SOLIHULL.

Solihull formerly ranked as one of the market-towns of Warwickshire, but its market has long since fallen into disuse. It principally consists of one street, and the whole wears the tranquil appearance of a village in which there is little to attract notice, except the church, a large handsome cruciform structure. Here was formerly the chief seat of the barony of Limesie, and from the ruins of this baronial residence, and its dependent habitations, sprung the town of Solihull, in the reign of Henry III. Grants for a weekly market and annual fair were speedily procured; but the town was never distinguished either by commercial enterprise or manufacturing industry; and the population now, as formerly, are principally engaged in agricultural pursuits.

COLESHILL.

The town of Coleshill is built upon an eminence, at the foot of which flows the river Cole, and to these circumstances of site it probably owes its appellation. The town principally consists of one street, with a smaller one branching from the middle to the churchyard. The domestic buildings, like those of most country towns, are of a mixed description; the major part respectable, with the occasional intervention of some of a superior class. The church, an ancient structure, is a fine attractive specimen of the decorated Gothic, or English style of architecture, with an ornamental square tower at its west end, from which springs a lofty octagonal spire; occupying the summit of the hill, it commands extensive prospects, and forms in itself a very conspicuous object in the surrounding landscape. The interior is spacious and contains some well executed monuments, the most conspicuous among which are those of the Digby family. The inhabitants are chiefly engaged in agricultural pursuits. The town, prior to the introduction of railways, derived no inconsiderable advantage from the expenditure of travellers, Coleshill being situate on the great line of road from London to Liverpool, through Coventry and Lichfield. The channel of communication, however, having been cut off by their introduction, this place, in common with many others on the line, has suffered severely. Coleshill has a weekly market on Wednesday, and three annual fairs. Coleshill

Park is situate to the west of the town, but the mansion has been long taken down. The seat formerly on this spot was for many years the residence of the Digby family, created Earls of Bristol in the reign of James I. The title of Earl of Bristol became extinct in the Digby family on the death of John, the third earl, in 1698. The present Earl Digby takes the title of Viscount from the town of Coleshill.

BLYTHE HALL.

Blythe Hall, the former residence of Sir William Dugdale, (of whom W. S. Dugdale, Esq., its owner, is the lineal descendant) was purchased by that eminent writer of Sir Walter Aston, in 1625. This is a spacious and respectable seat, but placed in a low situation, on the border of the river Blythe, at the distance of one mile from the town of Coleshill.

MAXSTOKE CASTLE.

This fine structure was chiefly erected by William de Clinton, Earl of Huntingdon, in the reign of Edward III., and continued to be the chief seat of the ancient family of Clinton until the reign of Henry IV., when it was passed in exchange for certain manors in Northamptonshire, to Humphrey Earl of Stafford, afterwards Duke of Buckingham. On the attainder of Henry, the grandson of this duke, the castle was committed to the care of an officer appointed by the crown; and it may be observed that King Richard III. visited this stronghold, when on his march towards Nottingham preparatory to the fatal battle of Bosworth. From the Staffords, the estate, after remaining some time with the crown, passed to the Comptons; and of them it was purchased, in the reign of Elizabeth, by the Lord-Keeper Egerton; by whom it was again sold to Thomas Dilke, Esq. In this family it remains at the present day, and is now the residence of his descendant, T. Dilke, Esq.

The castle is built in the form of a parallelogram, and is encompassed by a moat. At each corner is an hexagonal tower, with embattled parapets. The entrance is by an august and machiolated gateway, strengthened on each side by a tower of hexagonal form. The gates are covered with plates of iron; and the marks of the discarded portcullis are yet visible. These gates were erected by Humphrey Duke of Buckingham; and they are adorned with his arms, his own coat being impaled with the bearings of his wife, a daughter of the house of Nevil, and supported by two antelopes, assumed in right of his mother, who was one of the co-heirs of Thomas of Woodstock, Duke of Gloucester. To these are added the burning *nave*, and the *knot*, the badges of his own ancestry. A portion of the interior of this edifice was accidentally destroyed by fire, but the greater part of the ancient building still remains, and is an interesting specimen of the architectural arrangements of the fourteenth and fifteenth centuries. Among these apartments are the spacious hall; a large dining-room, with a door and chimney ornamented with curious carving; and the venerable chapel. In the walls of the great court are yet remaining the *caserns*, or lodgments for soldiers.

BIRMINGHAM.

This important manufacturing town, which is distinguished in the commercial annals of Great Britain for a spirit of enterprise united with habits of perseverance — for the rare association of a genius to invent and a hand to execute, is situate in the northwest extremity of the county of Warwick, in a kind of peninsula which is bordered by parts of Staffordshire and Worcestershire. The name of this place is often pronounced Brummicham, a popular mode of pronunciation that may be in some measure defended by an appeal to old writings, where the word is frequently spelled Brumwychcham or Brumwycham. It has been supposed that the original name of the town was partly formed in allusion to the natural growth of the shrub termed broom on its site, and in its vicinity; and in confirmation of this opinion it may be observed that three other places in this neighbourhood bear the name of Bromwich, as Castle Bromwich, West Bromwich, Little Bromwich.

The first writers who notice Birmingham mention the success with which the inhabitants cultivate the manufacture of articles of an iron fabric; and Mr. Hutton, the historian of this populous and most industrious town, labours to establish the belief of such a trade existing here as early as the times of the ancient Britons. The chief arguments in favour of this conjectural opinion are comprised in the following observation: — "Upon the borders of the parish stands Aston furnace, appropriated for melting ironstone, and reducing it into pigs; this has the appearance of great antiquity. From the melted ore in this subterranean region of infernal aspect, is produced a calx, or cinder, of which there is an enormous mountain. From an attentive survey the observer would suppose so prodigious a heap could not accumulate in a hundred generations; however, it shows no perceptible addition in the age of man." — " There is also a common of vast extent, called Wednesbury Old Field, in which are the vestiges of hundreds of coal pits, long in disuse, which the curious antiquarian would deem as long in sinking, as the mountain of cinders in rising." Birmingham, from its situation between Wall (Etocetum,) and Alcester (Alauna,) is thought to have been a station on the Roman Ickneild Street; and traces of the way are discernible, but no vestiges of Roman fortification are to be discovered.

It appears that Birmingham was a place of some consideration in the time of the Saxons, as William de Birmingham, lord of the manor, proved, in the year 1309, that his ancestors had the privilege of a market here before the Conquest. But in the Norman survey, this place is merely rated for four hides of land, and woods of half a mile in length, and four furlongs in width; the whole being valued at 20s. At a very early period, the lordship became vested in a family who assumed a surname from this possession, and who appear to have liberally protected the interests of the town. Peter de Birmingham obtained a grant for a weekly market on the Thursday, in the reign of Henry II.; and William de Birmingham procured, in the time of Henry III., charters for two yearly fairs. A license to take toll, for the term of three years, on every article sold in the market, towards the expense *of paving the streets* of Birmingham, was obtained, through the influence of Audomore de Valance, Earl of Pembroke, in 1319; but it would seem that the town was not then in a very flourishing condition, as on this toll proving insufficient, the work was suffered to lie dormant for eighteen years. A second license for the term of three years was afterwards obtained, and the work was then completed. The De Birmingham family remained possessed of the manorial rights till the reign of Henry VIII., and resided in a moated house about 60 yards south of St. Martin's church; of the house or the moat, however, not a vestige now remains.

Through the centuries occurring between the period of the Norman conquest and the civil war in the time of Charles I., the inhabitants appear to have steadily attended to the labours of the anvil, without interfering in either of the great political questions which divided so many parts of the island; except that, in the reign of Henry III., William de Birmingham led some few of the tenants of his lordship to the field of Evesham, where they fought unsuccessfully on the side of the barons. But, notwithstanding the indefatigable industry of the inhabitants, Birmingham made but few advances, during these ages, to high commercial consequence, or greatness of population. The aspect and character of the place in the reign of Henry VIII. are thus noticed by Leland:—

"The beauty of Birmingham, a good market-town in the extreme parts of Warwickshire, is one streete, going up alonge, almost from the left ripe of the brooke, up a meane hill by the length of a quarter of a mile. There be many smithes in the town, that use to make knives and all manner of cutting tools; and many loriners that make bittes; and a great many naylers; so that a great part of the town is maintained by smithes, who have their iron and sea-coal out of Staffordshire."

In the disastrous civil wars of the seventeenth century, Birmingham sided with the parliament. King Charles was here in 1642; but so active was the dislike entertained towards him by the inhabitants, that when his majesty quitted the town, they seized the carriages containing the royal plate, and conveyed them to Warwick Castle. In the ensuing year Prince Rupert, with a detachment of 2000 men, was ordered to open a communication between Oxford and York. At Birmingham a single company of foot, aided by a troop of horse from Lichfield, denied him entrance, and hastily threw up slight works for the defence of the place. The barriers were soon broken, but the prince still found some difficulty in advancing, as the inhabitants had filled with carriages the deep and narrow road by which he wished to gain access. He therefore entered by another avenue. The inhabitants and their military assistants opposed him on each occasion with great bravery; but their numbers were too small for efficient resistance; and, after a running fight maintained with great spirit through the streets, the parliamentarian party left the town to the mercy of their assailants. In the course of this series of tumultuous conflicts, William Fielding, Earl of Denbigh, a volunteer under the prince, was killed by a random shot. On the other side a clergyman, who acted as governor, was slain in the Red Lion Inn, having refused quarter from those who seized him. Prince Rupert, incensed by the vigorous but hopeless resistance he had experienced, set fire to several houses, and levied a heavy fine on the townspeople.

In the year 1665 this place experienced, in a dreadful degree, the disease emphatically termed the plague. The bodies of the numerous victims to its virulence were conveyed for interment to Lady Wood Green, an acre of waste land then denominated the pest ground. We have hitherto seen Birmingham respectable for industry, but limited in extent. Her laborious habits, unaccompanied by striking genius or activity of speculation, had not yet lifted her above the level of such a society of mere smiths as were seen working at the forge by the observant Leland. The restoration of monarchy in the person of Charles II., is the period from which Birmingham dates her great rise in commercial prosperity. Implements of husbandry, tools used in carpentry, and such coarse articles of iron manufacture, had till now chiefly engrossed the attention of the artisan. The reign of the second Charles, a long holiday after the troubles of civil contest, produced a relaxation in public manners, and a demand for those embellishments of luxury which may be termed the playthings of elegant habit. In this reign, the *toy trade* was first cultivated in Birmingham. Industry, the great basis of successful effort, was already the possession of the natives. Encouragement stimulated genius, and the trade has since been carried on to an extent unprecedented in the annals of manufacture, and productive not only of local wealth but of national pride.

From the Restoration to the present time, the history of Birmingham is happily comprised in a view of its progress in arts, buildings, population, and commercial opulence, with the exception of a lamentable instance of a turbulent and most dangerous spirit in the lower classes. On Thursday, July 14th, 1791, about eighty persons of various denominations assembled at an hotel in this town to celebrate the anniversary of the French Revolution. A mob collected, and the party assembled for the celebration prudently retired; but the populace, not content with this moderate triumph, broke the windows of the hotel, and their numbers increasing, they proceeded to acts of more serious violence, encouraging each other in the work of devastation by clamours fantastically expressive of a love of church, king, and good order! The horrors of a popular ferment in a place containing such numerous throngs of artisans, to whom riot was as a festival when once it was set on foot, may be readily imagined. The idle and the vicious issued from every alley of the town, and joining the cry of " No false rights of man!" stimulated the inflamed and thoughtless congregation of labourers to such undertakings as promised most plunder. As the mob professed themselves peculiar friends to the Church of England, they commenced their operations by setting fire to the meeting-house belonging to the celebrated Dr. Priestly. This they soon reduced to ashes; and a second conventicle shared the same fate. They then proceeded to the dwelling of the philosophic and amiable preacher, which was about a mile distant from the town. Dr. Priestly himself happily escaped their rage; but they burned his extensive premises; and we lament to say that his philosophical apparatus and valuable manuscripts (the fruits of many years' labour, and observation) perished in the flames! The mob remained in possession of power for the three following days, though judicious steps were taken by the magistrates to appease the tumult. These horrible days will long be remembered in Birmingham! All business was necessarily at a stand; the principal shops were shut, and no inhabitant deemed himself secure from the visitation of a throng so perniciously compounded of the capricious and the designing. The firebrand of discord spread its ravages throughout the town, and many of the rioters, reduced to a state of brutal intoxication by the liquors of which they had previously plundered the proprietors, perished in the flames themselves had raised. On the evening of Sunday the 17th, military assistance arrived; but the rumour of such an approach was sufficient. This mob had too much ferocity to possess genuine courage; and the despicable concourse so formidable to the unarmed, slunk quietly away on the slightest appearance of opposition. Among the ravages committed in this disastrous season must be noticed the following: — On Friday, the 15th of July, were burned the mansion of John Ryland, Esq. at Easy Hill; Bordesley Hall, the elegant residence of Mr. Taylor; and Mr. Hutton's house and stock in the paper trade, books, furniture, &c. At Birmingham, on Saturday the 16th, were destroyed the house and furniture of Mr. Hutton, at Saltley, the residences of G. Humphreys, Esq. and W. Russell, Esq. at Show Hill Green; and Mosely Hall, a seat occupied by the venerable Lady Carhampton, who was enfeebled and blind through age. Five other houses were also burned in the course of this day. Sunday the 17th was ushered in by the destruction of King's Wood meeting-house; and on the same day, besides other devastations, the mob plundered Edgbaston Hall, the residence of Dr. Withering. The damage arising from these outrages was moderately estimated at 60,000*l*. Public justice was satisfied by the execution of two of the principal offenders, and an act was obtained. in 1793 to reimburse the persons who had sustained injury.

The buildings of Birmingham, like those of most English towns, were originally commenced in the vicinity of the river. The chief street of the ancient town is that termed Digbeth, a tract naturally well sheltered, and containing, in addition to the Reay, some excellent springs that still form the best resource of that part of the town in point of water. At the time of the Restoration it is supposed that Birmingham consisted of about fifteen streets though not all finished; and about 900 houses. The increase of buildings since that period has exceeded the calculations of the most sanguine; and the town no longer crouches in humility of site, but boldly solicits the ingress of the winds from every point of the compass. Modern Birmingham is approached on every side, save the north-west, by an ascent; and, as scarcely any of the streets lie on a level, every shower conduces to cleanliness and health. The general appearance of the town to a stranger upon his first entrance is by no means prepossessing; the ancient part in particular is very irregular, and disfigured by many streets and lanes that, considered as public thoroughfares, can be viewed in no other light than intricate, narrow, and bad; an observation from which, however, must be exempted New Street, High Street, a portion of Dale End, Bull Street, Edgbaston Street, the Bull Ring, ornamented with a statue of Lord Nelson, and Digbeth. These may be pronounced the principal seat of trade and commerce, and abound in shops that for elegance and show, splendour of decoration, and costly display of articles exhibited for sale, in endless variety, may safely challenge a comparison with any in the metropolis. The Bull Ring, and Digbeth, however, are on market days, viz. Monday, Thursday, and Saturday, much inconvenienced by the traffic there carried on, greatly to the obstruction of these leading thoroughfares, and annoyance of the surrounding inhabitants, notwithstanding a market hall and other conveniences, have, with a view to the removal of so great a nuisance been recently erected in their immediate vicinity. St. Philip's churchyard, a sort of square, and the streets by which it is surrounded and approached, viz. Colmore Row, Temple Row, Waterloo Street and Bennett's Hill, are, together with Paradise Street, and Newhall Street (the latter a noble avenue), all lying as it were nearly in the centre of the town, and furnishing striking evidence of its internal improvement, are for the most part spacious and handsome erections. As the chief parts of this immense place are of comparatively modern erection, the examiner will be induced to expect that the great errors of antiquity in respect to formation of streets, and character of domestic architecture have been avoided; and, generally speaking, his anticipations will prove correct. Travelling from its centre in every direction, broad, spacious, and well-built streets meet the eye; the avenues branching forth from the sides of which are lined, in many instances, either with extensive manufactories or dwellings of minor importance. The parish of Aston, now joined to Birmingham, and forming part of the borough, is very extensive, principally consisting of small streets thickly populated. Edgbaston parish, connected with Birmingham by continuous lines of streets, is a district of considerable size, chiefly consisting of buildings erected in the villa style. The generality of these being constructed on a scale of considerable magnificence, and encompassed with tastefully disposed grounds, the whole wears an agreeable and cheerful aspect, and is further characterised by features that, strongly indicative of prosperity, stamp it as the abode of the wealthy manufacturer or retired merchant. Birmingham is well paved throughout, is lighted with gas, and, although situate for the most part upon an eminence, is nevertheless abundantly supplied with water, the upper part of the town, from water-works, which, with a large reservoir, have been constructed at Gravelly Hill, near Erdington, the lower from the Reay, and a variety of springs in the vicinity of that river.

CHURCHES AND CHAPELS.

There are altogether sixteen churches and chapels of ease in Birmingham, these will be hereafter described, but as a proof of their utter insufficiency to furnish adequate accommodation to the numerous inhabitants of this populous borough, it may be sufficient to state that, at a public meeting held at the town hall on Tuesday, November 27th, 1838, the Lord Bishop of Worcester in the chair; and at which were present Lord Calthorpe, the Hon. G. F. Calthorpe, the Rev. Archdeacon Spooner, the Rev. J. P. Lee, Richard Spooner, Esq. J. Taylor, Esq. &c. &c. &c., and the most influential and leading members of the community. The following among many other resolutions, for which we have not room, were carried: —" That the church accommodation in the borough of Birmingham, having been shown not to exceed 24,000 sittings in all, while its rapidly increasing population is already little, if at all, short of 180,000 souls, an irresistible claim is established for enlarged means of instruction, through the instrumentality of the established church; and that all her members in this community are bound by the most sacred obligations to exert themselves for the diminution of the lamentable disproportion that exists between the numbers of our people and the supply of the means of grace. That with the view of supplying in some degree this appalling deficiency of church accommodation, a society to be called "The Birmingham Church-building Society" be now formed, and among other rules and regulations the following, for which we can alone find room, established. That the object of this society shall be, to provide (within the next five years) ten additional churches within the parishes and hamlets composing the borough of Birmingham, for which the sum of 12,000*l*. was immediately subscribed. Of the sixteen edifices to which we have above alluded, the following summary account will, it is presumed, suffice. St. Martin's church, situate at the upper end of Digbeth, may be deemed the mother church of Birmingham. It is an ancient structure, with a tower and spire, and supposed to have been erected in the thirteenth century. This building was originally formed of stone but in the year 1690 the whole of the edifice, except the spire, was cased with brick. It underwent a thorough repair in 1786, when the interior was entirely renovated, — a circumstance that unfortunately led those entrusted with the care of the works to treat with too little respect some monuments intended to perpetuate the memory of the Lords de Birmingham. These monuments sustain recumbent effigies, but have not any inscription. The interior of the church is neat and appropriate, and the steeple is provided with a set of twelve musical bells.

Until the early part of the eighteenth century, Birmingham remained one parish. A triangular portion of the town covering about 100 acres was then divided from the rest, and constituted a separate parish by the name of St. Philips. The church for the new parish was begun in 1711, and completed in 1719. The building is of an embellished, but chaste and elegant character. The steeple on the west side is surmounted by a cupola; for many hints in the design of which the architect was evidently indebted to the splendid fabric of St. Paul, in London. This structure stands on elevated ground, and is judiciously placed in an open area calculated to display to great advantage its claims to architectural beauty; the surrounding cemetery, forming the centre of a handsome square, occupies four acres, and is planted with numerous trees. St. Philip's church stands nearly in the middle of the town, a little to the east of Bull Street. The triennial musical festivals in aid of the general hospital were long prior to the erection of the town hall held in St. Philip's church. Christchurch, situate at the junction of New Street, and Ann Street, completed in 1805, a stone structure with a tower and spire, and generally denominated the Free Church, is suitably plain both in its external and interior features; it was erected at a cost somewhat exceeding 20,000*l.* the whole of the lower portion of Christchurch consists of free seats. St. George's church, a handsome Gothic structure, erected in the style of the time of Edward III., with a lofty tower, and spire, stands in the north-west part of the town at the corner of Great Hampton Row, and Tower Street. St. Peter's, Dale End, erected in the Grecian style, was completed in 1827. St. Thomas's church, at Holloway Head, a splendid specimen of Grecian architecture and capable of containing 2000 persons, was completed in 1829. All Saints' Church, a large and handsome brick building, erected at the north-west extremity of the town, near Grosvenor Row, Birmingham Heath, was completed in 1833. A handsome church commemorative of Dr. Ryder, late bishop of the diocese, and thence denominated Bishop Ryder's church, has also been erected at Gosta Green. To these may be added the old parish church of Edgbaston at the west end of Wellington Road, and the new church of St. George, recently completed, situate in Calthorpe Street, Edgbaston. The ground on which this edifice has been erected is the liberal gift of Lord Calthorpe, the noble proprietor of nearly the whole of the valuable property by which it is surrounded, who has endowed the church, and contributed the greater portion of the funds, between 5000*l.* and 6000*l.* required for its erection. The parish of Aston, forming part of Birmingham, a notice of its church, though somewhat remote, is consequently necessary to complete the account of its ecclesiastical buildings. Aston church, though wearing an appearance of considerable antiquity is, notwithstanding, in good preservation; it is a handsome building with a lofty tower and spire and occupies a beautifully retired situation at a distance of about a mile and a half from the centre of the town. In addition to these, Birmingham contains six chapels of ease, of which we now proceed to give a brief account. St. John's Chapel Deritend, near Deritend Bridge, thrown over the river Reay, is situate on the south side of the town, at a short distance from its entrance, by the London and Coventry road. This commodious and respectable building was erected on the site of a more ancient one, in 1735, and the square tower at the west end, added in 1762. St. Bartholomew's Chapel, situate near Dale End, and calculated to contain about 800 persons was erected in 1749. St. Mary's Chapel, situate between Whittall Street, and Loveday Street, was erected in 1774; it is of the octagonal form, but destitute of all pretension to architectural beauty. St. James's Chapel, Ashted, is situate on the south side of Great Brooke Street, near the Cavalry Barracks. It is formed of part of a mansion erected some years since by Dr. Ash, an eminent physician of Birmingham. This intended residence was not completed, but, having by suitable alteration, been converted to its present purpose, was consecrated in 1810. St. Paul's Chapel, situate in the centre of St. Paul's Square, a short remove from the north end of Newhall Street, is a handsome structure, with a lofty tower, and steeple of considerable architectural beauty; it was commenced in 1773, and the body of the building, finished in 1776, and remained in an unfinished state till the year 1823, when it was finally completed. The interior is extremely neat, and the whole is finished in a style of great simplicity, with the exception of an oriel window over the communion table, which is filled with painted glass, illustrative of different passages in the epistle of St. Paul. Trinity Chapel, situate, opposite the south end of Bradford Street, Bordesley, a small but elegant Gothic structure, of great architectural beauty, was erected from designs by Mr. Goodwin. The interior is ornamented with a Catharine wheel window, beautifully painted, and an altar-piece by Foggo, representing Christ healing the sick at the pool of Bethseda. To the foregoing list, may be added a Scotch church, two Roman Catholic chapels, a quaker's meeting, a Jew's synagogue, and chapels and meeting houses for all denominations of dissenters.

PUBLIC BUILDINGS, OFFICES, SCHOOLS, AND CHARITABLE INSTITUTIONS.

The Town Hall, a magnificent building of brick, faced with Anglesea marble, may be deemed one of the chief ornaments of the town; it is situate at the corner of Congreve Street, and Paradise Street, immediately opposite the north end of New Street, from which point the best view of this colossal structure is obtained. It is built after the model of a Roman temple. A massive rusticated basement, 23 feet in height, supports the building which is ornamented on its eastern and western sides with twelve, and on its southern by eight Corinthian columns of Anglesea marble that sustain an entablature, pediment, and cornice. The upper part of the building, which is of oblong form, is 160 feet long, 100 feet broad, and the whole 83 feet high; an arcade, formed into a double piazza in front, lengthens the base. The principal apartment of the interior is a saloon of noble proportions, 145 feet long, 65 feet wide, and 65 feet high. This splendid room contains a large orchestra, capable of holding 400 performers, and an immense organ (deemed one of the finest in the world) that fills a deep recess. A spacious gallery, capable of containing 1200 persons, is erected in front, while two galleries that will hold 300, each, line the sides. This vast area is lighted by twenty-seven windows; the spaces between which are lined with Corinthian pilasters, and further adorned with massive and elegant candelabra. The ceiling is richly ornamented. The lower portion of the building contains, in addition to various committee rooms, a large room under the organ, and a complete residence for the hall-keeper. The organ is publicly exhibited on Thursdays, upon payment of one shilling for admittance.

The Free School, situate on the south side of New Street, an elegant structure in the style of the time of Edward VI., erected from designs by Mr. Barry, is justly considered one of the chief ornaments of the town. The Free School is an extensive and noble foundation, for which the inhabitants are indebted to the piety of Edward VI. The history of this establishment is connected with that of a guild, founded at Birmingham in the year 1389, and termed the Guild of the *Holy Cross*. On the dissolution of such fraternities in the reign of Henry VIII., the revenues of this association were valued at 31*l*. 2*s*. 10*d*. The lands continued vested in the crown till 1532, when King Edward VI. assigned them to certain inhabitants of Birmingham, for the foundation of a free grammar-school; and so great has been the increase in the value of landed property in the neighbourhood, that the annual produce is now more than 5000*l*. Seven exhibitioners are sent to the University of Oxford, and several inferior schools, in different parts of the town, are supported by this establishment. The Blue-coat School, a handsome brick edifice erected in 1724, but enlarged at a very considerable expense in 1794, is situate at the north-east corner of St. Philip's churchyard. This establishment, an humble imitation of Christ's Hospital in London, is also denominated the Charity School: it is entirely supported by voluntary contributions; and 150 orphan boys, and about 50 girls, are here maintained and educated. The remaining charitable establishments for the instruction of youth may be thus briefly summed up:—they consist of two national schools, conducted upon the principle established by Dr. Bell, two upon the plan of Lancaster, a Protestant Dissenters' Grammar School, numerous Sunday and infant schools, and though last, not least, an institution for the deaf and dumb.

The General Hospital, a noble edifice of brick, situate in Summer Lane, was commenced in 1766, when the centre portion of the building was erected, but did not experience its final completion till 1790, at which time it was further augmented by the addition of two wings, and now ranks among the most distinguished ornamental fabrics of the town. It is maintained chiefly by annual subscriptions, legacies, the dividends arising from some funded property, and the profits accruing from the triennial musical festivals heretofore held in St. Philip's Church, but since the erection of that magnificent structure, in the splendid saloon of the Town Hall.

The Market Hall, recently erected from a design by Mr. Edge, and situate opposite the Nelson statue in High Street, with entrances from Bell Street and Philip Street, is a plain Grecian structure, that, admirably adapted to the purpose for which it was designed, may justly be deemed an additional ornament to the town. It has, however, not altogether attained the chief object sought by the commissioners in its erection, viz. a clearance of the public thoroughfares, — a measure the establishment of Smithfield in its proximity has alike failed to effect. The dealers in corn and hay still cling to and crowd the vicinity of the Bull Ring, and confining their transactions to the old spot, not only render all but impassable that spacious area, but establish a nuisance, intolerable to all the respectable inhabitants, the proprietors of public-houses alone excepted, in its immediate neighbourhood.

The Theatre Royal in New Street is a building correspondent in size and character to the opulence, respectability, and population of this flourishing town. The front in New Street is much admired for its simply elegant and uniform appearance. The interior, arranged in the best taste, is decorated in the style and manner of the London Theatres, and is brilliantly illuminated with gas; it has two tiers of boxes, a gallery and pit, and is calculated to contain 2000 persons.

The News Room, situate on Bennett's Hill, is a handsome building of the Ionic order. The principal room, a spacious apartment, is amply supplied with newspapers foreign and English, reviews, magazines, the higher class of periodicals, prices current, &c. &c. A society of arts was established here in 1821. It is held in a neat classic building, of the Corinthian style of architecture, erected in New Street. The chief objects of the society are the encouragement of native talent in painting, and establishment of a school of design, in aid of the more elegant branches of manufacture. A School of Medicine and

Surgery, a Museum of Natural History, and a Mechanics' Institution have also been established here. A Botanical and Horticultural Society was formed here in 1829; to an examination of whose beautiful gardens and splendid conservatories, stored with every variety of fruit and flower, whether of foreign origin or British growth, we cordially recommend all visitors of Birmingham. They are situate on the western side of Calthorpe Street, Edgbaston. A very complete and commodious set of baths, denominated the Lady Well, from the spring of that name, celebrated as having long supplied the lower part of the town with water, has been established in Smallbrook Street.

Birmingham boasts also its Vauxhall — a very humble imitation, it must be admitted, of the far-famed gardens of that name near London, that although somewhat fallen from their high estate, are nevertheless, as a place of public amusement, excelled by nothing of the kind in Europe.

Every facility has been afforded to this vast manufacturing town for the conduct of its business; in furtherance of which, and for ensuring justice to the public in the sterling worth of articles here produced in gold and silver, an Assay Office has been some time established, where, previous to exposure for sale, their value being first ascertained, they are then regularly stamped. The Assay Office is in Cannon Street. The Stamp Office is in Colmore Row, and the Post Office, much enlarged, on Bennett's Hill. The public office, a large and handsome building, is in Moor Street. Cavalry barracks, capable of containing 160 men, were erected here in 1793. They are situate in Brooke Street.

ARTS, MANUFACTURES, AND COMMERCE.

Situated nearly in the centre of England, and remote from any navigable river, its pristine position was consequently unfavourable to commercial intercourse upon a large scale; but industry and art have supplied this deficiency; and by the introduction of canal navigation, heavy merchandise is now conveyed not only from Birmingham to the metropolis, the eastern and western seas, but to most of the principal manufacturing and commercial towns in the kingdom. We next proceed to notice the manufactures of this grand emporium of the mechanical arts, to do justice to which a volume might well be devoted. Discarding, as we are compelled to do, from the limited space to which these remarks are necessarily confined, their several details, and which, if entered into, would to the public generally — the mechanical portion alone excepted — prove utterly uninteresting, we proceed to give, in a condensed form, an account of the various articles for which Birmingham is justly and deservedly celebrated.

Near the north-west extremity of the town stands Soho, esteemed the first manufactory of the kind in Europe, whether as regards the value of its productions or the extent and grandeur of the buildings in which it is carried on; these cover a space of many acres, and consist of various ranges of buildings sufficiently capacious for the employment of a thousand workmen. Of this vast establishment Messrs. Boulton and Watt are the proprietors, the latter a descendant of the great James Watt, whose services rendered to his country by his improvement of the steam-engine are recorded on a statue erected to his memory in Glasgow, of which city he was a native. Although not the first article here fabricated, yet as a machine, the powers of which, though not hitherto fully developed, have, nevertheless, attained a degree of perfection, and have been applied to purposes that till within these few years were treated as completely chimerical, its importance, in a national point of view, duly considered, demands the first notice in this place. Without further preface then, steam-engines, manufactured here in great numbers, may literally be said to be a staple of Soho, and adapted to every purpose to which mechanical power can possibly be applied, are hence transported to all parts of the world. Buckles, buttons, watch chains, trinkets of all descriptions, gilt toys, and articles of a similar description were the early productions of the Soho establishment; the manufacture of plated goods on a large scale was then introduced, and was succeeded by articles of elegance and splendour in stone bronze, and or molu. These consisted of all kinds of vases, candelabra, clock cases, watch stands, ice pails, and many others equally valuable. The manufacture of wrought plate was subsequently introduced, in the formation of which the chaser's art was, by the aid of machinery, in a great measure superseded. But among the multiplicity of articles here manufactured, all of which more or less excite admiration, the steam-engine is the greatest prodigy. This may with truth be pronounced at the present day the *primum mobile* of this vast establishment, which, it should be added, is, as a measure of necessity, closed to the public. The articles made at Soho may be taken, generally speaking, as samples of the produce of the Birmingham manufactories; to which, however, the following must be added. The manufacture of leather was at one time a successful pursuit, and saddlery and harness — the latter in particular — was sent hence not only to London but to all parts of the kingdom. This trade now no longer flourishes. At the present day iron and steel are, by the ingenious artisans of this busy place, converted into every possible form of which they are susceptible. Conservatories, the most elegant, and of enormous size, are here constructed of the former material. Ship and register stoves, kitchen-ranges, and articles the most ponderous, are produced, gradually descending from such as are in daily use for domestic purposes, down to the diminutive needle. The manufacture of guns gives great employment; its capability of production in this line will be learned from the fact, that during the late war, between 6000 and 7000 muskets were for some time forwarded weekly to government; their qualification for the service having been previously ascertained at the Proof-house here erected in 1813. Button-making has long been a principal pursuit of the Birmingham manufacturer, and though not carried on so extensively since the abandonment of bright and adoption of covered buttons, still gives employment to very many hands. The manufacture of brass was introduced here about the year 1740, and numerous brass founderies have since been established. The brass work of Birmingham of superior excellence is wrought, in many instances, with an effect that, in the shape of cornices, curtain rods, and a variety of articles, appears with a brilliancy little inferior to gold. Many of these, struck with dies of good design, stand out in bold relief, such as hat and cloak pins, curtain clasps, &c.; and the fittings and finishings of first-rate carpentry are the produce of what is denominated the stamping press. This is an engine of very extensive power, and produces ornaments of the smaller kind, such as articles of jewellery, and what are generally termed gilt toys, in great perfection, and endless variety.

It is a fact not generally known, that the steel pen of the present day, struck from a die, and thus produced, is the work of an instant, and although greatly inferior to the specimens which upon its first introduction obtained, as they deserved, superior prices, a grinding competition at present existing in that line has led to the manufacture of articles, many of which are rudely formed, and most imperfectly finished. In the casting department of the iron foundery light and elegant articles of good design, slightly tinged, are made to represent the best specimens of bronze. Glass-making, both plate and crown, glass-bending, cutting, and polishing, and the manufacture of glass shades and beads are advantageously pursued.

To Baskerville, the printer, Birmingham is indebted for the introduction of *papier mâché* or paper-board work, that in its present improved mode of manufacture (from milled boards) is produced in every variety of form of which it is susceptible. To the exertions of the late Mr. James Taylor, a spirited individual, who died in 1775, the manufacturers of Birmingham are indebted for the introduction of the gilt button, the painted, japanned, and gilt snuff-boxes, and a variety of enamelled articles. Many of these are ornamented with designs, the work of superior artists, constantly engaged in their production, and are wrought with such excellence of effect, and at a price so extremely moderate, as to render certain, in addition to an extensive sale for home consumption, a considerable demand for exportation. Japanning is here executed to perfection, and combining elegance of design with excellence of execution, produces in all branches to which that art is applicable, articles alike distinguished for brilliancy, beauty, and durability. Die-sinking, modelling and engine turning, employ many hands; and the manufacture of screws, nails, and cut brads is here carried on to a great extent, as are also those for the making of tubes used either for the conveyance of gas, water, vinous or spirituous liquors.

Birmingham has recently received a charter of incorporation, by which the government of the town is vested in a mayor, recorder, sixteen aldermen, and forty-eight common councilmen. The town is divided into sixteen wards; and the corporate body is by the charter constituted a court of record for the borough, to be held on Wednesday in each week for the recovery of debts under 20*l*. The rapid increase in the population of this important borough will be proved by the following extract from the parliamentary returns, by which it appears it contained in 1811 a population of 85,753, showing an increase of 24 per cent. on that of 1801; in 1821, 106,721, showing an increase of 33 per cent.; and in 1831, 142,251, which upon a very moderate calculation can at the present day amount to little short of 180,000 souls. Birmingham, its wealth, population, and manufacturing importance considered, (the metropolis apart) ranks as the fourth town in the kingdom. It has sent two members to parliament since the passing of the Reform Bill, and is distant from London 109 miles, Liverpool 85¾, Bristol 85½, Hull 131¾, Carlisle 204, Glasgow 299¾, and Edinburgh 295¾.

BIRMINGHAM TO LIVERPOOL AND MANCHESTER
BY THE
GRAND JUNCTION RAILWAY.

BIRMINGHAM TO WARRINGTON.

The station of this great work, an elegant structure, erected from designs by Mr. Franklin, is situate in Curzon Street, Birmingham, adjoining that of the London and Birmingham Railway Company. It is altogether one of the chief ornaments of the town, and, furnished with waiting, refreshment and retiring rooms, is replete with convenience for the accommodation of travellers. Premising that in pursuance of the plan upon which the London and Birmingham Railway has been given in the former part of this work, by dividing it into journeys of as many miles as intervene between each of the principal stations, and then returning to a review of the various objects, whether towns, seats, or villages, passed in the progress, we shall proceed to observe that the Grand Junction Railway, shortly after quitting the station, reaches the Lawley Street Viaduct, a massive structure of ten arches, that, first thrown over that spacious avenue, and subsequently the river Reay, forms the means of communication between both lines with Birmingham. The Birmingham Railway then branches off to the right, and the Grand Junction Railway, continued with an easy sweep in a short distance, carried on an embankment, reaches a lofty viaduct of rather more than 300 yards in length. By means of this beautifully formed bridge, built in the form of a crescent, and consisting of twenty-eight arches, the Railway is carried across the river and valley of the Reay.

A short embankment carries it to Duddeston Bridge, here thrown over the road leading from Birmingham to Duddeston, lying on right of the line, where a lunatic asylum, hidden by an excavation, has been established. On left of Duddeston is an establishment of the Company, consisting of workshops, warehouses, and wharfs, for the reception, landing, and embarkation of heavy merchandise. From Duddeston Bridge, continued by alternate cutting and embankment, the Railway reaches the viaduct over the Castle Bromwich and Coleshill road (one mile from Birmingham), the former $3\frac{1}{4}$ miles, the latter $7\frac{1}{2}$ miles on right, Birmingham being 2 miles distant on the left. At Castle Bromwich is an ancient seat of the Earl of Bradford, whose more magnificent mansion and seat is at Weston-under-Lizard, in Staffordshire. On right of the viaduct over the Castle Bromwich road, see the village and chapel of Saltley. From the viaduct near Saltley, continued through a short cutting, the Railway then enters on a lofty embankment, full thirty feet high, and in three quarters of a mile more is carried by the Aston viaduct, (a beautiful structure of ten arches, that conveys it over the Birmingham and Fazely canal and the Sutton Coldfield road) to Aston, and in about another mile to

PERRY BAR STATION,

AN INTERMEDIATE ONE, DISTANT FROM BIRMINGHAM $3\frac{1}{4}$ MILES, FROM LONDON $115\frac{1}{2}$ MILES, FROM LIVERPOOL 94 MILES, FROM MANCHESTER 95 MILES.

Here a road on left branches off to Birmingham, $4\frac{1}{4}$ miles distant; on right, to Walsall, 5 miles distant. The inclination of the Railway from Birmingham almost to Perry Bar is that of a gradual descent from the Aston viaduct. Here, on left, a momentary glance is obtained of Aston Hall, the seat of J. Watt, Esq., a fine old baronial mansion, that, approached by a noble avenue of trees, presents a striking appearance. The view in this direction being heightened by the beautiful village church of Aston, with "its heaven-directed spire," that, embosomed in trees, adds considerably to the interest of this delightful scene. At the farther extremity of Aston Park, where the Railway quits Warwickshire and enters the county of Stafford, the view changes, and, no longer confined, opens upon a beautifully variegated country. On right of Aston Viaduct the eye ranges over the valley of the Tame and its tributary streams. Here the Birmingham Water Works, with their tall chimneys and beautiful reservoir, form the foreground of the landscape, that, overlooked by Gravelly Hill, is terminated by the high ground, and hills of Sutton Coldfield. About a mile from the further extremity of Aston Park, on right, lies Wilton Hall, the seat of N. Boddington, Esq., and Holdford J. Willmore, Esq.; and about a mile north of the village of Perry Bar, boldly conspicuous, is beheld the magnificent Roman Catholic College of Oscott. From Perry Bar Station, continued in a gently waving line, through occasional cuttings, and carried by a castiron bridge across the Tame, the Railway enters an excavation, crossed by the old Walsall road, at a distance from Perry Bar of bout $1\frac{3}{4}$ mile. From the bridge over the old Walsall road, continued by a succession of cuttings and embankments, the Railway at length enters the Newton excavation, a portion of which, from its tremendous depth, full sixty feet below the level of the land above, may, with truth, be deemed a deep abyss, gradually approaching the natural surface, at the extremity of which stands the

NEWTON ROAD STATION,

AN INTERMEDIATE ONE, DISTANT FROM BIRMINGHAM $6\frac{1}{2}$ MILES, FROM LONDON $118\frac{3}{4}$ MILES, FROM LIVERPOOL $90\frac{3}{4}$ MILES, FROM MANCHESTER $91\frac{3}{4}$ MILES.

Here a beautiful bridge of three arches carries the road from Great Bar to West Bromwich. On right of Perry Bar Station is Perry Hall, the seat of J. Gough, Esq. On left of the bridge over the old Walsall road, stands the noble old mansion of Hampstead Hall, the most distinguished feature of the agreeable village of Handsworth, and seat of J. L. Moilliet, Esq. On left of Newton Road Station is Charlemont, the seat of J. Halford, Esq.; and one mile distant is Sandwell Park, the magnificent seat of the Earl of Dartmouth. Sandwell Hall, a noble mansion, the interior of which is fitted up in a style of great elegance, and decorated with valuable paintings, stands in the centre of a beautiful park, that, begirt with trees, ornamented with a fine sheet of water, and studded with noble timber, from its inequality of surface exhibits, from many points, views that, rich in sylvan scenery form a striking contrast to the blackened town of West Bromwich, in its vicinity. Two miles distant, on right of Newton Road Station, is Great Bar Hall, the beautiful seat of Sir E. D. Scott, Bart. From Newton Road Station, where crossed by a bridge of three arches that carries the road from Great Bar to West Bromwich, the Railway running in a direct line through meadows fertilised by the Tame, that, serpentising by its side, enriches the scene, a good view is obtained both from the bridge above and Station House below; about half a mile beyond which the Railway crosses the Tame by a cast-iron bridge; and in another half mile arrives at Bescott Bridge.

On right of Bescott Bridge is Bescott Hall, W. Marshall, Esq. From Bescott Bridge, a road crosses the Railway that on left conducts to Wednesbury, $1\frac{1}{2}$ mile distant, to Dudley $5\frac{1}{2}$ miles distant, and on right to Walsall $1\frac{1}{2}$ mile distant. In a quarter of a mile beyond this, crossing the Tame in its way, by a cast-iron bridge, the Railway reaches

THE WALSALL STATION,

A PRINCIPAL ONE, DISTANT FROM BIRMINGHAM $9\frac{1}{2}$ MILES, LONDON 122 MILES, LIVERPOOL $86\frac{3}{4}$ MILES, MANCHESTER $87\frac{3}{4}$ MILES.

A little beyond the Walsall Station a road carried over the Railway conducts on left to Darlaston, $\frac{3}{4}$ of a mile distant, Bilston, $2\frac{1}{2}$ miles distant; and on right to Walsall 2 miles distant. One mile distant from the Walsall Station, on right, is Bentley Hall, the seat of E. Anson, Esq. This place is remarkable as having been the property of Colonel Lane, who, together with his sister, so much distinguished themselves in concealing and effecting the escape of King Charles, after his defeat at the decisive battle of Worcester. In this vicinity also is the beautiful viaduct of the Darlaston, Walsall, and Bentley branches of the Birmingham Canal, and here may be witnessed the extraordinary sight of the canal crossing the brook, the road the canal, and the canal crossing the road. From near Perry Bar, the inclination, which to Walsall Station is a rise of 1 in 532, now changes to 1 in 330 (an acclivity that considerably diminishes the speed of the trains), upon which it is continued nearly to Wolverhampton, when a short level succeeds. From the Walsall Station the Railway enters a cutting of very considerable depth, through which it is conducted in conjunction with a viaduct of two arches, the Darlaston and Walsall branches of the Birmingham Canal, above mentioned, and succeeded by an embankment, that from its elevation affords a good view) in that way reaches the

WILLENHALL STATION,

AN INTERMEDIATE ONE, DISTANT FROM BIRMINGHAM $11\frac{3}{4}$ MILES, FROM LONDON 124 MILES, FROM LIVERPOOL $85\frac{1}{2}$ MILES, FROM MANCHESTER $86\frac{1}{2}$ MILES.

A little before Willenhall Station, a road that crosses the Railway leads on left to Bilston, and on right to Walsall. From Willenhall Station, where the Railway is crossed by a bridge that, carried over a road, leading on left to Bilston, $1\frac{1}{2}$ mile distant, and on right to Walsall, $3\frac{1}{4}$ mile distant, the train enters a rocky excavation, whose rude, rugged, and unsightly sides excluding all objects from the view, present a formidable, imposing, and altogether unpleasant aspect. This rocky pass is spanned by a bridge that conducts the turnpike-road from Willenhall, just passed, to Wolverhampton, where commences an excavation so slight as to permit a communication between the fields on each side, a formation fraught with extreme danger, of which it has been not altogether unproductive. Carried in a direct line hence for a distance of about $1\frac{1}{2}$ mile, it reaches a tunnel that, 380 yards in length, carries the Wyrley and Essington Canal, and in a short distance further gains the

WOLVERHAMPTON STATION,

A PRINCIPAL ONE, DISTANT FROM BIRMINGHAM 14 MILES, FROM LONDON $126\frac{1}{4}$ MILES, FROM LIVERPOOL $83\frac{1}{4}$ MILES, FROM MANCHESTER $84\frac{1}{4}$ MILES. — Journey resumed at page 141.

Four miles distant from Wolverhampton is Wrottesley Park, the beautiful seat of Sir John Wrottesley, Bart.

SUTTON COLDFIELD.

Sutton Coldfield, situate near the north-west border of Warwickshire, at its junction with the county of Stafford, is placed, as its name implies, in a bleak and cheerless district, but is fertile in the opinion of the antiquary. Two Roman roads, the Ickneild Street and the Ridgway, pursue their course at a short distance from the town. A portion of the former has long been and still is the road from this place to Birmingham.

The town of Sutton Coldfield, which chiefly consists of one principal street, is neat in appearance, and contains some few dwellings of an ornamental character. The church is a handsome structure, comprising a nave, chancel, and side aisles. The aisles were built by Bishop Vesey in the latter part of the reign of Henry VIII.

The nave, which was ancient, was taken down and rebuilt in its present form about the middle of the last century. The inhabitants are chiefly engaged in the production of articles connected with the Birmingham manufactures, which, during the last century, were introduced here to the great advantage of the town. The municipal power, according to the constitution procured by Bishop Vesey (who here founded a free grammar-school,) consists of a warden, twenty-four assistants, a town clerk, steward, &c. The warden for the time being is coroner. This is a royal town, and has a separate jurisdiction. It has a weekly market on Monday, and two annual fairs.

WALSALL.

Walsall, a market town of Staffordshire, distant 6½ miles from Wolverhampton, 9¼ from Lichfield, and 118 from London, stands on an agreeable eminence, is approached on all sides by spacious roads, and chiefly consists of 12 principal streets. The manor, which is of considerable extent, was formerly the property of the great Earl of Warwick. The Earl of Bradford, the present lord, is the munificent patron of the place. The church dedicated to St. Matthew occupies the summit of the hill; it is a handsome Gothic structure, with a tower and lofty spire; the original portion of the building is of great antiquity, but the whole was repaired, it may almost be deemed rebuilt, in 1821. St. Paul's Chapel, a Grecian structure, and chapel of ease to the mother church, was erected in 1826. A subscription in aid of the necessary fund for providing an extensive increase of church and school accommodation in the parish of Walsall, has been nobly headed by the Earl of Bradford, the donor of the living, who has munificently placed the sum of 1000*l.* at the disposal of the vicar, and the committee acting with him; and Lord Hatherton has also most liberally granted an eligible site for the intended new church at the Birchills. Besides these, there are in this town places of public worship for the different denominations of dissenters, and a Roman Catholic chapel. Here is an excellent free grammar-school, founded either by Queen Elizabeth or Queen Mary, the funds of which being in a flourishing state, the trustees have thereby been not only enabled to extend the benefits of the original institution, but also to form additional establishments upon a minor but more extensive scale; in addition to these, Walsall abounds in charitable institutions, some of them exhibiting striking instances of benevolence in the various founders. The inhabitants of the town and its vicinity are chiefly engaged in the manufacture of saddlers' and coach and harness makers' ironmongery, in the manufacture of saddlery, harness and the articles generally denominated horse millinery, of all which this place is the grand emporium. The town is incorporated under a mayor, recorder, twenty-four aldermen, a town-clerk, and two serjeants at mace. A court of quarter-sessions is regularly held at stated periods. Walsall has sent one member to parliament since the passing of the Reform Bill, the right of voting being enjoyed by the 10*l.* householders. The mayor is the returning officer.

Here is a small but neat theatre, a handsome public library and news-room, and the George Hotel, one of the best looking buildings of the town, is an excellent and spacious establishment. A race-course lies on the west side of the town, on which has been erected a grand stand, and the races are generally well attended.

LICHFIELD.

Lichfield, a city of Staffordshire, is supposed to be indebted to the Saxons for its origin, and to have risen from the ruins of the Roman Etocetum, or wall; it is very pleasantly situated in a fine valley, surrounded by gentle eminences; the majority of the houses are handsome erections, and many of them are occupied by families of independent fortune.

Here was formerly a castle, where Richard II. was confined when a prisoner, on his way to London; but no vestiges of it are now in existence. The town is divided by a large sheet of water into two portions—the city, and the close: the latter district occupies much higher ground than the rest of the town; it was fortified for the king in the time of the civil wars, and during that period withstood several sieges; the first of which was against Lord Brook and Sir John Gell, in March 1643, when the former was shot through the eye by a gentlemen of the Dyot family, and the spot where he fell is now distinguished by a pavement of white pebbles, and a marble tablet, bearing an inscription commemorating the event. During these unhappy disputes the cathedral suffered very considerable damage, not only from the fire of the batteries and musketry but also from the rapacity of the republican soldiery. Immediately after the Restoration, Dr. Hackett was appointed to this see; and he, the very morning after his arrival, set about cleansing and repairing his episcopal church; and, by his own large contributions, and the subscriptions he obtained from the neighbouring gentry, was soon enabled to restore this noble pile to its former splendour. In 1788, it again underwent a thorough repair by subscription, under the superintendence of James Wyatt, Esq., of London. The extent of the whole building from east to west is 411 feet in length, and from north to south 67 feet in breadth. It is a spacious and very elegant structure, surmounted by three beautiful steeples, and displaying on its portico, and north and south entrances, such exquisite workmanship as is hardly to be equalled in England. The interior of this noble edifice is fully equal in splendour and magnificence to the exterior: it contains a fine organ — which is composed of twenty-five different stops, and is highly esteemed for the fulness and beauty of its tones — a number of elegant monuments; and has, on many accounts, an imperative claim on the attention of the traveller. It is walled in like a castle, and stands so high as to be seen at the distance of many miles. In the north-east corner of the close, stands the bishop's palace, to the west of which is the deanery house, and near it several other handsome buildings.

The city is divided into three parishes, each possessed of an elegant church; it contains a guildhall, anciently appropriated to the meetings of the religious fraternity of St. Mary, and St. John the Baptist, and which the corporation now use for public purposes. It is a neat stone edifice, adorned with the city arms, &c.

Lichfield contains several good charitable institutions, and has a neat theatre; it sends two members to parliament, has a market on Tuesday and Friday, and is famous for its ale, the sale of which is considerable and lucrative.

Lichfield is a county of itself, containing a jurisdiction extending about 12 miles in compass; it has the power of holding assizes, and determining cases of life and death. It is governed by two bailiffs, chosen yearly out of twenty-four burgesses, a recorder, a sheriff, a steward, and other officers. It has a good free-school, founded by Edward VI., at which many eminent literary characters received the first rudiments of their education; among which were, Addison, Ashmole, Woolaston, Garrick, and that celebrated Hercules of literature, Dr. Samuel Johnson.

WEDNESBURY.

Wednesbury, in Staffordshire, 8 miles from Birmingham, and 117½ from London, standing at a short distance from the source of the Tame, is a market-town of great antiquity.

In the time of the Mercians this place was distinguished by a noble castle fortified by Adelfleda, who was for some time governess of this extensive kingdom. No part of this work of antiquity now remains, except perhaps, a few traces of its foundation.

This town is distinguished for its numerous and valuable manufactures, the principal of which are guns, coach harness, iron axletrees, saws, trowels, edge-tools, bridle-bits, stirrups, nails, hinges, wood-screws, and cast-iron works of every description. Enamel paintings, in the highest style of execution, are likewise among its more prominent productions.

For their proficiency in these different branches, the inhabitants are principally indebted to the abundance and excellence of the coal wrought in their immediate neighbourhood. This coal is beyond all doubt the best in the kingdom for the smith's forge, on account of the intense heat which it produces. It extends in separate veins from 3 to 14 feet in thickness, and affords to its various proprietors a princely revenue

Here is also found that peculiar species of iron ore denominated blond metal, used chiefly in the manufacture of nails, horse-shoes, hammers, axes, and other heavy tools of a similar description. Some spots, likewise abound with a sort of reddish earth employed in painting or glazing vessels of different kinds. This earth is known by the appellation of *hip*.

The church, recently repaired at a very considerable expense, is an elegant building in the pointed style of architecture, and adorns the summit of the hill on which the castle already mentioned was situated. At one end rises a handsome tower, supporting a lofty spire of unusual beauty. The interior is divided into a chancel, nave, and north and south aisles. These last are separated from the nave by a range of very neat arches, which rest upon octagonal pillars. One arch being intersected by another pillar, produces a singular and awkward effect. In the chancel are several prebendal stalls, ornamented with most exquisite carved work. The prospect from hence is among the most extensive in the county. The market-day here is on Wednesday, when supplies of all kinds of provision are plentiful. One of the collateral branches of the Birmingham Canal, entering this parish, affords to the inhabitants the most perfect facility of commercial communication.

Darlaston, celebrated for the manufacture of gun-locks, lies immediately on the south of Wednesbury. The church, which is a brick edifice of an oblong shape, was erected by Thomas Page, a celebrated author of the sixteenth century. There are here meeting-houses for quakers, dissenters, one appropriated to the methodists, who are numerous, and the other to a small body of independents.

WEST BROMWICH.

West Bromwich, formerly a village, but now a considerable market-town of Staffordshire, is distant from Birmingham 5 miles, 3 miles from Wednesbury, and from London $114\frac{1}{2}$ miles. West Bromwich lies on the high road from London to Liverpool and Holyhead; and, as at present existing, occupies, in addition to the ancient village, the tract till these few years known as West Bromwich Heath.

The main street, nearly a mile in length, contains some good houses, with a few of a superior character interspersed; but by much the larger portion of the place is extremely irregular, and altogether very inelegant; and the whole from its proximity to the coal pits, and glass, gas, and iron-works, wears a blackened appearance.

The old church, dedicated to All Saints, an ancient building surmounted by a tower, was some years ago repaired, and the interior much enlarged, when the side aisles were thrown into the body, so as to present one entire space; this occupies an elevated position at the northern extremity of the town. Christchurch, a beautiful and elegant Gothic structure, was erected by the Parliamentary commissioners in 1822. Here is a splendid Roman Catholic chapel, of which the Hon. and Rev. George Spencer was the priest, and chapels and meeting-houses for the different denominations of dissenters. A national school, and Sunday and charity schools, both in connection with the established church, and the dissenting establishments.

The neighbourhood abounds with coal-pits; and to this circumstance is mainly attributable its rapid increase. The pits are principally the property of the Earl of Dartmouth, the munificent patron of the place, whose beautiful seat, Sandwell Park, lies to the eastward of the town.

West Bromwich is celebrated for its gas-works, well worthy of a visit. These works, the largest in the world, are situate upon the Dudley road, and approached by a handsome Grecian portico, the visitor enters at once into the heart of this stupendous establishment. Its capabilities are vast, its powers enormous, and its effects surprising. Three hundred common, and eighty patent retorts, distribute daily to twelve gas-holders,—viz. six in the works at Swan village, five in Birmingham, and one in Bilston—350,000 cubic feet of gas, the appendant apparatus to which is in like proportion. Its powers of distribution in opposite and different directions, including eight towns independent of Birmingham, and the various hamlets and villages in the vicinity of West Bromwich, embrace an extent of full 16 miles. The lineal admeasurement of the great mains are about 100 miles, the largest 6 inches, the smaller 2 in diameter. Extraordinary as it may appear, the Staffordshire and Birmingham gas company, in whom the property of this vast establishment is vested, are possessed of powers sufficient to supply double the amount of their present daily demand; and as it is in contemplation to light not only the principal roads, but the heretofore great Holyhead line, they are fully prepared whenever called upon for that purpose, to enter not only into that, but still more extensive contracts. Here are also crown glass-works conducted upon a most extensive scale; and these, with the manufacture of gas, iron, the mining operations of the coal-pits, such as sinking, working, and raising the coal, constitute the chief employment of the labouring classes.

A population so employed, it will be readily imagined, are rough, rude, and uncouth in appearance; their manners coarse, and we add with regret, notwithstanding the advantages of gratuitous instruction abundantly supplied, are altogether uneducated.

The market on Saturday is well supplied, and presents altogether, from the noisy and incongruous multitude then assembled, a very extraordinary but by no means exhilarating scene. The Birmingham and Dudley canals, deserving of a visit pass in the vicinity, and give it, in conjunction with other canals, the benefit of a very extensive water communication.

BILSTON.

Bilston, a market town of Staffordshire, 2¾ miles from Wolverhampton 10¼ miles from Birmingham, and 102 from London, lying to the east of Wolverhampton, and comprehended within the boundaries of that parish, to which it was formerly a chapelry, has rapidly risen to its present eminence, and now ranks as one of the most flourishing places in the county. It stands upon rising ground, at a short distance from the bank of the Birmingham Canal, that in conjunction with other canals gives it the advantage of an inland navigation that extends to the ports of London, Liverpool, Bristol, and Hull, the principal mining and manufacturing districts in the kingdom. This place, above a mile in length, is altogether very irregular and ill-built, with the exception of the principal street (the once great road from London to Holyhead) in which there are many substantial buildings. Furnaces for smelting ore, forges, founderies, and slitting mills, worked by steam, are frequent in this neighbourhood which abounds with vast mines of coal, ironstone, quarry stone, and clay. Here is also found a particular species of sand much used in casting metals. Bilston has two churches. St. Leonard's erected in the grecian style, on the site of the old chapel in 1825: the living is a perpetual curacy, within the exempt jurisdiction of the Dean of Wolverhampton, but the right of nomination and presentation is vested in the inhabitants at large, by whom the curate is elected. St. Mary's is a fine Gothic building. The living is a curacy in the gift of the Bishop of the diocese. Here is a handsome Roman Catholic chapel, and chapels, and meeting-houses for the different denominations of dissenters, and schools for the gratuitous education of the juvenile classes. At Bradley, a hamlet immediately adjoining this place, is a very extraordinary phenomenon. A fire on the earth has now continued burning for sixty years, defeating every attempt hitherto made to extinguish it. It arises from a burning stratum of coal, about four feet thick, and eight or ten yards deep, to which the air has free access in consequence of the main coal having been dug out from under it. The calx affords a very excellent material for the repair of the roads, and the workmen in collecting it frequently find large quantities of alum of an excellent quality. What is likewise curious is, the surface is occasionally covered with sulphur, for many yards in such quantities as to be easily gathered.

The environs of Bilston, from its soil, coal-pits, climate, and noxious vapours by which it is surrounded, is perhaps one of the least inviting spots that can well be imagined, the earth upturned in every direction, exhibits on all sides the proofs of disembowelment; the whole face of the country, disorganised and disfigured, presents heaps of cinders, fragments of stone, clay and coals; and the groups of miners, athletic in form and half-savage in appearance that surround the pits, complete a *coup d'œil* of a most repulsive character; the only reconciliation to which will perhaps be found in the recollection of its almost inestimable wealth.

DUDLEY.

Dudley, a market town of Worcestershire, standing in a detached and isolated part of that county, and surrounded on all sides by Staffordshire, is distant 10 miles from Birmingham, and 119½ from London. This town, which of late years, has very considerably increased, has one principal street, the approach from the towns of Birmingham and Stourbridge; parallel with this run some smaller ones, and these are intersected by others of inferior note, the major portion of which consist of manufactories or dwellings of minor importance. The principal church, that of St. Thomas, near the entrance of the town from Stourbridge, being greatly dilapidated, was taken down in 1817, and an elegant new Gothic structure erected in its stead, which, standing on an eminence, and having a lofty spire, is a great ornament to the town and surrounding country. The other, dedicated to St. Edmund, a plain brick edifice, stands at the opposite end of the town, near the entrance from Birmingham. Here is also a Roman Catholic chapel, a quaker's meeting, and chapels and meeting-houses for different denominations of dissenters. Dudley has also an excellent free grammar-school, and various charity and Sunday-schools. The neighbourhood abounds in extensive coal mines, and quarries of iron and limestone, the great source of its wealth and prosperity; in the working of which, and manufactory of iron and glass, the population are principally engaged. It is a busy bustling place, the resort of persons connected with the iron trade, and though somewhat irregular is by no means inconvenient. The whole is well paved, and lighted with gas; but from the numerous smelting-houses and forges by which it is surrounded, the place is much blackened. The staple productions of Dudley are iron, coal, limestone, and glass. The former smelted here, is subsequently reduced into almost every form of which it is susceptible. By means of steam-machinery of manifold power, iron first rendered into plates, with surprising rapidity, is subsequently slit into bars of every required substance. Articles the most ponderous are here produced, in addition to chains and nails of all descriptions. The manufacture of glass is also here extensively pursued. Its mining operations, however, greatly surpass its manufacturing importance. The quantity of coal and iron here raised, and hence transported is immense.

This place enjoys the benefit of an extensive inland navigation, embracing the principal ports and places in the kingdom. The title of Viscount Dudley was renewed in 1763, in the person of Lord Ward, by the title of Viscount Dudley and Ward, but was altered to that of Earl Dudley, in 1827. Dudley was created a borough by the Reform Bill, and sends one member to parliament, the right of voting being vested in the 10*l.* householders.

The most distinguished ornament of Dudley is its Castle, supposed to have been built about the year 760 by Dodo or Dudo a distinguished Saxon, from whom it likewise derived its name; it is a noble work of antiquity, situate on the summit of a hill at the northern extremity of the town. During the civil wars this castle was twice besieged: first in 1644, when after holding out for three weeks it was relieved by a corps of the king's forces from Worcester, and again in 1646, at which time it was surrendered to Sir William Brereton commander of the parliamentary troops, by Colonel Levison governor for the king. From the lofty site of this castle, the view from its ruins is noble and extensive, comprehending five counties of England and a great part of Wales, varied by ridges of mountains, rich fertile vales, and populous towns, the spires of different churches, and many elegant habitations.

The sides of the hill on which it stands display a beautiful and varied covering of trees, the mansion itself consists of a number of buildings surrounding a court, and encompassed by an exterior wall flanked with towers. Of these buildings the keep appears evidently to be the most ancient part. Next to it, in point of age, is the chapel, in which there are two very noble Gothic windows. The great gateway, with the apartment over it, may have been erected about the same time; none of the other buildings seem to be older than the time of Henry VIII. A nocturnal view from this eminence, from the numerous furnaces by which it is surrounded, exhibits a very extraordinary and impressive scene. The recesses of this limestone rock will to the examiner possessed of nerve sufficient for the undertaking, and interested in such scenes prove a real treat. A descent into the coal mines to those who have the courage for so hazardous an experiment, not altogether unattended with danger, arising from fire damp, a serious visitation too common in these regions, and other causes, will nevertheless amply repay by the wonders here to be witnessed, the perilous ordeal to which in its exploration he must necessarily submit. Not "full fathom five" but full 500 feet, perhaps will be the depth he must reach previous to entering on an examination of its recesses.

Removed from the earth's surface, he enters at once into its very bowels, and an immense region of gloom; the inner sides of which shaped into arches, supported on vast and massy pillars purposely left in working for the support of the superincumbent mass, diverge from its centre in various directions, branching into caverns of different heights, that lined with irregular masses are seen on either side, while shagged arches, and overhanging rocks that seem to threaten instant annihilation perpetually present themselves; multitudes of men, moving like unearthly spectres, seen indistinctly wandering in light but just sufficient to render the "darkness visible;" the noise of the different miners in active operation reducing the already detached portions with pickaxes preparatory to their removal, or the process of blasting; and lastly, the reverberating thunders of the explosion when effected, are objects calculated to excite the most sublime ideas, not unintermingled however, with sensations of terror. The boats moving on canals into which if desirous of exploring its inmost recesses, he must trust himself, increase the terrors of this somewhat infernal scene; which may not inaptly be deemed a perfect counterpart to Virgil's entrance into Tartarus.

It is scarcely necessary to remark, that to the young, the active, and the enterprising alone, are such scenes accessible: the more experienced, infirm, and female portion of society will, it is most probable, not venture on so perilous an encounter.

WOLVERHAMPTON.

Wolverhampton, a principal station of the Grand Junction Railway, and market town of Staffordshire, distant from Birmingham 13¼ miles, and from London 122¾, is a place of great antiquity; but nothing is recorded concerning its history, till the year 996; when the pious Wulfruna, relict of Aldhem, Duke of Northampton, built and endowed a monastery here. Previous to this period its name was simply Hampton; but it now began to be distinguished by the appellation of Wulfrunes Hampton, since modified or corrupted into Wolverhampton.

Wolverhampton, by far the most extensive and populous town in Staffordshire, is very extensive, well built, and healthy, notwithstanding its proximity to numerous coal mines, — a circumstance which is mainly attributable to its elevated position. The buildings of brick and tile are tolerably good, but have a sombre appearance, and the streets in the older parts of the town, chiefly filled with manufactories and workshops, are narrow and dirty; the environs, however, particularly the principal lines of approach from the surrounding towns, exhibit some very superior specimens of domestic architecture, and enlivened by gardens, present altogether a very agreeable appearance. The collegiate church dedicated to St. Peter is pleasantly situated on elevated ground, towards the eastern side of the town. It is a stone building consisting of a lofty nave, two aisles and a chancel, a very fine Gothic tower, embattled at the top, and richly ornamented, rises from the centre. Five pointed arches, resting on octagonal pillars support the nave. The interior is fitted up in the cathedral style, with the stalls for the dean, prebends, canons, &c., and the pulpit composed of stone, placed against one of the south pillars, and adorned with beautifully sculptured niche-work, is esteemed an object of great interest and curiosity. The views from the surrounding cemetery are extensive and beautiful. St. John's Church erected in 1776, a handsome stone structure, occupies the centre of a spacious square cemetery planted with trees on the south side of the town. St. George's Church, standing on the eastern side of the town is a noble stone structure in the Grecian style of architecture; and St. Paul's, a handsome but unfinished Gothic building stands on its western side. Here is a superb Roman Catholic chapel, and chapels and meeting-houses for different denominations of dissenters, and in connection with them, various charity and Sunday-schools. The free grammar-school, founded by Sir Stephen Jennyns, a native of this town, and lord mayor of London, in the year 1688, a handsome brick building, enriched by the improvement of its funds, is now a noble institution, and in addition there is a blue-coat school and a national school. Wolverhampton diffuses its charity in great abundance, in aid of which a dispensary is here established. The neighbourhood abounds in valuable coal mines, in iron-works and forges, lead is also found in the vicinity; and in addition to the articles fabricated here, including the manufacture of japanned ware, those described as works for which Birmingham is celebrated (the steam-engine excepted), are all more or less the products of

Wolverhampton. For the manufacture of locks, keys, &c. of every variety, gradually descending from such as are of size enormous to those of form the most diminutive, and of surpassing excellence. Wolverhampton has long been justly and deservedly celebrated. The farmers in the vicinity have not unfrequently their smithies, at which, in the absence of other employment, they work, and men and even women in many instances labour with equal zeal, and are alike expert at file and forge. A public news-room and mechanics' institute have been established here.

Wolverhampton has a neat theatre, and on the west side of the town a beautiful race-course with a grand stand, and the races in the season are fully and fashionably attended. The Staffordshire and Worcestershire Canal, the Liverpool and Birmingham Junction Canal, the Wyrley and Essington Canal, and the Birmingham Canal pass in the immediate vicinity of Wolverhampton, that by means of these and others with which they unite, maintains a water communication that extends to the Thames, the Severn, the Mersey, and the Humber, and principal manufacturing districts of Yorkshire and Lancashire. The markets on Wednesday and Saturday are abundantly supplied. The Lion and Swan are the principal hotels; but accommodation the most ample will be found in the numerous inns, though not posting-houses, with which the town abounds, suited to the taste of travellers of every description. Wolverhampton, created a borough by the Reform Bill, returns, in conjunction with the towns of Bilston, and Wednesfield, the townships of Willenhall and Sedgely, two members to parliament, the right of voting being vested in the 10*l*. householders. The constable of the deanery of Wolverhampton is the returning officer.

WOLVERHAMPTON TO STAFFORD.

The Wolverhampton Station is a large establishment; it is one mile distant from the town, and here warehouses for goods, workshops, smithies and sheds, the latter for the reception and reparation of engines have been erected, and refreshment and retiring rooms, with every requisite, have been provided for the accommodation of passengers. Here the carriages undergo an inspection; wheels are greased; water and coke are supplied; and, the engine invigorated, starts like a giant refreshed, with increased rapidity. The summit of the Grand Junction Railway (440 feet above the level of the sea) has been attained, and from Wolverhampton station it is constructed upon an embankment that, from its elevation, affords a good view of the country on either side. Its inclination has now changed to that of a rapid descent, down which the trains rush with accelerated speed. Passing under a bridge that carries the road from Wolverhampton to Cannock, a town distant 8 miles from the line on the right; in about a mile further, Dunstal Hall, the seat of H. Hordern Esq., and Oxley Hall, A. Hordern Esq.; the latter the birthplace of the late Mr. Huskisson, who lost his life on the opening of the Liverpool and Manchester Railway, are beheld on the left of the line; about the same distance on right, lies Show Hill, W. Manning Esq., and a little beyond it Low Hill, J. S. Pountney Esq. In a short distance further, a bridge crossing the Railway conducts to Bushbury, a village lying on right of the line that, situated on an eminence, here rises into view. Bushbury Hall or Old Fallings is the seat of G. Briscoe, Esq. The manor of Bushbury was long the property of the Goughs, ancestors to the celebrated antiquary of that name. The church, an ancient building in the pointed style, surmounted by a massy embattled tower, is worthy of a visit.

Bushbury Hall, afforded, during the unhappy period of the Protectorate, an asylum to Charles II., who was here for some time concealed by the kindness of Thomas Whitgreave, Esq., its then proprietor, a tomb to whose memory has been erected in Bushbury Church. The chair in which the king sat is preserved with great care at Bushbury Hall. In rather less than two miles from the Wolverhampton Station, the Railway reaches Wetstone Green Bridge, where a road on right leads to Bushbury, three quarters of a mile distant, and on left to Pendeford Hall the seat of T. Fowler, Esq.

One mile and a half distant on left of Wetstone Green Bridge, is the village of Ford Houses, and on right Moseley Court, G. Whitgreave Esq., and Moseley Hall, Capt. T. Holyoake, continued by successive cuttings and embankments, in a tolerably direct line; the Railway in another mile reaches a bridge that carries a road leading on left to Coven Heath half a mile distant, and on right to Hilton Hall, the beautiful seat of Colonel Graham, two miles distant. Half a mile beyond the last mentioned bridge, the Railway carried on an embankment, that from its elevation affords a good view of the surrounding very beautiful country, gains Paradise Bridge, carrying the road, that on left conducts to Cross Green, a quarter of a mile distant, and on right to Shareshill, a village 2 miles distant, the latter, the site of two Roman encampments. In less than half a mile beyond Paradise Bridge, the Railway reaches Slade Heath, where it crosses, by an iron bridge, the Staffordshire and Worcestershire canal, of which a good view is obtained, and carried thence (at its commencement close to the turnpike-road from Wolverhampton to Stafford) in a direct line, in little more than a mile, crossing in its way the Sharedon Brook, arrives at the

FOUR ASHES STATION,

AN INTERMEDIATE ONE, DISTANT FROM BIRMINGHAM $19\frac{3}{4}$ MILES, FROM LONDON 132 MILES, FROM LIVERPOOL $77\frac{1}{2}$ MILES, FROM MANCHESTER $78\frac{1}{2}$ MILES.

The Four Ashes Station is so named, from its proximity to a road-side public-house of that sign, where in the bygone days of posting prosperity, many an hour was whiled away by the returning loiterers on that no longer frequented line. On left of Four Ashes Station lies Somerford Hall, its grounds enlivened by the waters of the Penk and beautifully timbered, the seat of the Hon. Edward Monckton, and 3 miles distant approached by a noble avenue of trees Chillington, Park, the elegant seat of T. W. Giffard, Esq. Two miles distant from Four Ashes Station on left is the little town of Brewood. The embankment upon which the Railway has been for some distance carried affords a good view of the surrounding country, and after passing the Four Ashes Station, the Wrekin Hill in Shropshire rises into view. To the embankment at Four Ashes, an excavation of considerable depth succeeds, carried through which the Railway in a further distance of a mile and a half reaches the

SPREAD-EAGLE STATION,

AN INTERMEDIATE ONE, DISTANT FROM BIRMINGHAM $21\frac{1}{4}$ MILES, FROM LONDON $133\frac{1}{2}$ MILES, FROM LIVERPOOL 76 MILES, FROM MANCHESTER 77 MILES.

Three miles distant on right is Hatherton Hall, the seat of Mrs. Walhouse; 2 miles distant on left is Stretton Hall. This was formerly the property of the Congreve family, ancestors to the dramatic writer of that name, and is now the seat of G. Monckton, Esq. whose family have long been resident here. The great Roman road here crossed conducts on left to Shifnall, 12 miles distant, and to Shrewsbury $27\frac{1}{4}$ miles distant, on right to Cannock $4\frac{3}{4}$ miles distant, and to Lichfield 14 miles distant.

The Railway continuing through the excavation, the Roman road is carried over it by a bridge, as is also the turnpike-road from Wolverhampton to Stafford, a short distance beyond it to the

PENKRIDGE STATION,

AN INTERMEDIATE ONE, DISTANT FROM BIRMINGHAM $23\frac{3}{4}$ MILES, FROM LONDON 136 MILES, FROM LIVERPOOL $73\frac{1}{2}$ MILES, FROM MANCHESTER $74\frac{1}{2}$ MILES.

The line now approaches close to the turnpike-road, and continues so for a mile, along which a mound of earth has been erected for the prevention of accidents to persons travelling that, till recently, much frequented thoroughfare. For some distance, both before and beyond the Spread-Eagle Station, the Railway has been formed through an excavation, which, succeeded by intervening embankments and short cuttings, terminates in a lofty mound, a noble causeway, varying from 15 to 40 feet in height, upon which it is carried across the valley of the Penk. The last-named embankment from its elevation, commands a good view of the delightful scenery that adorns its banks. The country expands on either side, and hence is beheld the main stream of the Penk flowing on left of the Railway, a tributary stream of that river running on the right, closely approached by the Staffordshire and Worcestershire canal; but a little before arriving at Penkridge, the pinnacled tower of its curious old church climbs into notice, and upon a nearer approach, a good view of the town, (that from its stillness wears an air of village tranquillity), is obtained, upon quitting which, by the viaduct that here crosses the river is beheld a burst of considerable beauty. To the right the Penk, increased in size by its confluence of waters, is seen pursuing its placid course through the arches of the beautiful bridge, that, carrying the turnpike-road from this town to Stafford, forms altogether the foreground of a very delightful landscape; to this succeeds a finely-wooded country, from which the mansion of Lord Hatherton, embosomed in trees, peeps forth, terminated in the distance by the extensive wilds of Cannock Chase, that, clothed with heather, close the distance.

Cannock Chase was a celebrated forest during the period of the Mercians, being the favourite chase of their monarchs; it was then and for succeeding centuries covered with a profusion of majestic oaks. Many years, however, have passed away since it was wholly stripped of its foliage, and converted into a bleak and dreary waste. This sad change is well described by Drayton in his Poly-olbion, but much more beautifully by Mr. Master, in his *Iter Boreale*, of 1675, of which elegant composition, the Rev. R. Williams, of Fron, in Flintshire, has given the following beautiful translation:—

> "A vast, a naked plain confines the view,
> Where trees unnumbered in past ages grew;
> The green retreat of wood-nymphs; once the boast —
> The pride — the guardians — of their native coast.
> Alas, how changed! each venerable oak
> Long since has yielded to the woodman's stroke;
> Where'er the cheerless prospect meets the eye,
> No shrub, no plant, except the heath, is nigh.
> The solitary heath alone is there,
> And wafts its sweetness in the desert air,
> So sweet its scent, so sweet its purple hue,
> We half forget that here a forest grew."

At Penkridge, a road branches on right to Cannock, distant 4¼ miles, 2½ miles on right of which is Beaudesert, the beautiful seat of the Marquis of Anglesea. The inclination of the Railway for eight miles beyond Wolverhampton is that of a rapid descent, 1 in 330; this is for the next two miles diminished to 1 in 440, and in that way it reaches Penkridge; to this succeeds a level of rather more than a mile in length, from whence, carried on a descent 1 in 400, it reaches Stafford. Quitting Penkridge, by a beautiful viaduct, here thrown over the Penk, and carried in a line nearly direct, the Railway enters an excavation which, succeeded by an embankment, carries it to Dunston, a distance of about two miles, the turnpike-road from Penkridge to Stafford, and beyond it the river Penk running on its right side. On left of Dunston lies the village of Acton Trussell. About a mile beyond Dunston, the turnpike-road from Penkridge to Stafford crosses the line by an oblique bridge, and taking an eastern direction, with an easy sweep carried through successive cuttings and embankments, crossing in its way the Hawksmoor Brook, in rather more than 1½ mile it spans by an arch the Spital Brook, shortly after which it recrosses the turnpike-road from Penkridge to Stafford, under which it passes, and in rather more than ¼ of a mile reaches the turnpike-road from Stafford to Newport, and the

STAFFORD STATION,

A PRINCIPAL ONE, DISTANT FROM BIRMINGHAM 29 MILES, FROM LONDON 141¼ MILES, FROM LIVERPOOL 68¼ MILES, FROM MANCHESTER 69¼ MILES.—Journey resumed at page 149.

About a mile beyond Dunston, on left, lies the village of Coppenhall. On left of the Spital Brook is Rowley House, G. Reen, Esq.

The environs of Stafford abounds in seats. Three miles distant on right is Tixall Hall, the fine old seat of Sir T. C. Constable, Bart. Ingestrie Hall, the splendid domain of Earl Talbot, 5 miles distant, Shugborough, the magnificent seat of the Earl of Lichfield, and Sandon Hall, the beautiful seat of the Earl of Harrowby. On left of Stafford is Stafford Castle, the seat of Lord Stafford, Castle Church hill, and Billington Camp, these being in view nearly all the way from Penkridge to Stafford, stand forth from their elevated position the most striking objects of the surrounding country.

HILTON HALL.

Hilton Hall, the seat of Colonel Graham, a spacious structure stands on the northern side of a small but well-wooded park. The grounds tastefully disposed, and beautifully diversified by inequality of surface, exhibit from many points a varied succession of sylvan scenery. A lofty Norman tower erected upon the highest ground in the park, dignifies this small domain, and affords from its summit a panoramic view alike rich, varied, and extensive. Here was formerly an abbey of Benedictine monks, founded by Henry de Audeley, in the year 1223, which was valued at the time of the dissolution at 89*l*. 10*s*. 1*d*. per annum. No vestiges of this fabric can now be discovered. The service enjoined to be performed by the lord of the neighbouring manor of Essington to the lord of Hilton is so peculiar, that it seems to deserve particular notice. By his charter the former was bound to bring a goose to the hall here every New Year's-day, and drive it at least three times round the fire, while Jack of Hilton was blowing the fire.* This part of the ceremony being finished, then the lord of the manor of Essington, or his bailiff, carried it to the table, and received a dish from the lord of Hilton for his own mess. This service was actually performed for upwards of 140 years, but nothing has been heard of it since, nor is the origin of the custom known.

BREWOOD.

A small market-town of Staffordshire, 4½ miles south of Penkridge, 10 miles from Stafford, and 132 from London, is situated nearly two miles west of the Four Ashes Station (a minor one) of the Grand Junction Railway. A small priory of Cistercian or Benedictine nuns dedicated to the Virgin Mary, was founded here in the reign of Richard I., and continued to flourish till the general dissolution, when its revenue was valued at 11*l*. 1*s*. 6*d*. per annum.

Brewood situated on a branch of the river Penk, is a small neat town, which, from the stillness there prevailing, wears more the appearance of a large village; detached, and at a distance of two miles from the turnpike-road from Wolverhampton to Stafford, and equidistant from the Lichfield and Shrewsbury road, and placed out of the line of travelling, it has long been, and still is, distinguished by the air of tranquillity generally pervading places destitute of trade. The church, a fine old structure, with a lofty spire, stands near the centre of the town. The free grammar-school founded here is a fine institution. A national school has also been established here. The Birmingham and Liverpool Junction Canal recently formed, passes in its immediate vicinity, and thereby gives it the advantage of a very extensive inland navi-

---

* This Jack of Hilton is a little hollow image of brass, which leans upon its left knee, and has its right hand placed on its breast. In its mouth is a little hole just sufficient to admit the head of a large pin; and water is poured into it by a hole in its back, which is afterwards stopped up. This image being set on a strong fire, the air evaporates through a hole at the mouth with a continued blast, which blows the fire very strongly.

gation, — a work from which, perhaps, although at present unproductive, it may at no distant period derive very great benefit.

PENKRIDGE.

Penkridge, a small town of Staffordshire, 5¾ miles from Stafford, 10¼ from Wolverhampton, and 131½ miles from London, is a minor station for the Grand Junction Railway. This place is supposed to derive its name from the river Penk, here crossed by a stone bridge, which flows at its foot; the Staffordshire and Worcestershire canal also passes on its eastern side.

Penkridge, a small neat town, situate in the centre of an agricultural district, bordering on Cannock Chase, is undoubtedly a place of very great antiquity; according to some, it is the Pennocrucium of the Romans, mentioned in the itinerary of Antoninus. On this point, however, there is considerable diversity of opinion among antiquaries. Camden regarded it as having been that of a Roman station, while Plott, Stukely, and Horsley, transfer it to Stretton, a village about 3 miles south of the town. The church, an old building with a square tower, was formerly collegiate.

Penkridge, for many years a market town, is now a place of little business. Situate on the Wolverhampton and Stafford road, it derived no inconsiderable advantage from the expenditure of travellers on that hitherto much frequented thoroughfare. To this traffic, however, the establishment of the Grand Junction Railway has by its annihilation of posting and stage-coach travelling, proved detrimental to an extent it is impossible to describe, and its prosperity in that line is thereby altogether destroyed.

STAFFORD.

Stafford, the county town of Staffordshire, 16 miles distant from Lichfield, and 141 miles from London, is a principal station of the Grand Junction Railway.

The origin of this place is involved in obscurity, but there seems reason to suppose it was a town of some importance prior to the Norman conquest. In Doomsday Book it is termed a *city*, and was then governed by two bailiffs; but the first charter now extant was not granted till the reign of King John; this charter was confirmed by Edward VI., and many new privileges added to those it already possessed. Queen Elizabeth established the assizes here (previously removed to Lichfield,) and appointed the sessions to be held here by act of parliament in the first year of her reign. Though placed low, the situation of Stafford is extremely pleasant: it is seated amidst meadows watered by the Sow, by which, with its tributary streams, it is nearly surrounded. The Sow, about a mile distant from the town, barely separated from, and pursuing a sidelong course with the Penk, both rivers fall into the Trent at Great Haywood, a village about 5 miles distant on the right.

The form of this borough is that of an irregular ellipsis, the greatest diameter of which extends from north-east to south-west. The streets are well paved, and the houses, chiefly constructed of stone, are built in a regular and compact manner; and in the centre of the town, a large and spacious market-place lying on right of the high street, considerably enlivens its appearance.

In ancient times it was defended, except on the side next the Sow, by a wall and ditch supplied with water from that river. It was never, however, capable of withstanding a regular siege. Sir William Brereton, general of the republican army, took it by surprise in May 1643, with the loss only of a single man. The walls were then destroyed, and the ditches filled up. According to Pennant, it had formerly four gates; other authorities maintain, no more than three: that formerly standing at the entrance of the town from London, near the bridge over the Sow, called Green Gate, was taken down in 1780. Goal Gate occupied a situation at its northern extremity, and Broad Eye a position on its western side. These gates have all been removed; their names, however, are still retained in two of the principal streets of the town, viz. Green Gate and Goal Gate, which with High Street, form the great thoroughfare and constitute a line of respectable buildings, with some few of a superior order, and the best shops. The other parts of the town present a poverty of appearance, and the whole place, except on the arrival of the railway trains, wears an air of great dulness.

Stafford, though forming one parish, has two churches; the principal one, that of St. Mary, formerly collegiate, is a large ancient building, in the form of a cross, with a low octagonal tower rising from its centre. The style of its architecture in general is the early pointed; the period of its original erection is not exactly known. The interior contains an elegant altar-piece, a curious font, a singular relic of antiquity, and a noble organ. A number of ancient and modern monuments occupy different portions of this noble structure. The church of St. Chad is an old and decayed building of brick. Here is an elegant Roman Catholic Chapel, a quaker's meeting, and chapels and meeting-houses for different denominations of dissenters. The free-school is an ancient building; it was founded by Edward VI.; and in addition to this, a national school, and charity and Sunday schools, in connection with the established church and dissenting congregations, diffuse to the juvenile poor the advantages of gratuitous instruction. An alms-house for the reception and relief of the aged and necessitous is among its advantages.

The County Hall, situate near the centre of the town, is a large and spacious structure, 100 feet long: the interior contains, in addition to the civil and criminal courts where the assizes are held, and various rooms appropriated to town and county business, an elegant assembly room, which extends nearly the whole length of the building.

The County Gaol is an extensive edifice of modern erection. Here is a large and extensive county infirmary, and a lunatic asylum, the latter a noble institution, surrounded by beautiful grounds, and conducted upon the principles recently considered as most conducive to the restoration of the mental faculties, and practised at Hanwell in Middlesex, is at once an ornament to the town and an honour to the county. Stafford has also a small but neat theatre. The inhabitants are principally engaged in the manufacture of shoes, and the business of tanning; it is also celebrated for the excellence of its ale.

Situate on the great line of road from London, through Birmingham to Liverpool and Manchester, Stafford maintained no less than three posting-houses; and from its extensive connection with stage-coach establishments, added to the expenditure of travellers, its engagements in mail-coach contracts, and numerous advantages attendant thereon, the business in these branches was very beneficial. It is scarcely necessary to observe that to all this the introduction of railways has given a death-blow; and although more fortunate than many places similarly circumstanced, in having retained its position, instead of being entirely excluded from the line; yet, taking into consideration the circumstances, that not only human beings but horses, carriages, and cattle, are all transported by the Railway trains, its losses from this abstraction of business must have been enormous.

In virtue of a charter granted by George IV., the former one having expired, Stafford is governed by a mayor, recorder, 10 aldermen, 20 common council men, and 2 serjeants-at-mace. It sends 2 members to parliament, and was formerly deemed a close borough,—a condition from which recent contests have completely removed it. By means of the Sow, rendered navigable to Great Haywood, where it unites with the Grand Trunk Canal, Stafford enjoys the advantage of an inland navigation that extends to the Thames, the Severn, the Mersey, and the Humber, the manufacturing and mining districts of the kingdom.

STAFFORD TO WHITMORE.

The Stafford Station is very complete in its arrangements for the accommodation of passengers, and equipment of the engines, that here furnished with an additional supply of coke and water, the train again starts on its journey.

From Stafford Station, carried with an easy sweep, in about 1½ mile it crosses the Clanford Brook, and enters upon an embankment that carries it across the valley of the Sow, the channel of which, from its tortuous course, it was deemed necessary to divert; and, in consequence, that river pursues here, and for about 1½ mile further, a parallel course with the Railway. About half a mile beyond Clanford Brook, on left, lies Seighford, a village one mile distant from the line, whence the tower of its church is discernible; beyond it is Seighford Hall, the seat of F. Eld, Esq.; on right of Clanford Brook is Cresswell Hall, Rev. E. Whitby, and 1½ mile distant Tillington House, W. Locker, Esq.

The marshy course of the Sow is mostly flooded in wet seasons. From the last embankment in the vicinity of Clanford Brook, the Railway, constructed by alternate excavation and embankment soon reaches the

GREAT BRIDGEFORD STATION,

AN INTERMEDIATE ONE, DISTANT FROM BIRMINGHAM 32½ MILES, FROM LONDON 144¾ MILES, FROM LIVERPOOL 64¾ MILES, FROM MANCHESTER 65¾ MILES.

The road that crosses the line at Great Bridgeford by a lofty arch leads on left to Eccleshall, 3¾ miles distant, that on right to Stafford, both situate upon the high road, now nearly deserted, from London to Chester. Three miles and a half distant, on left, is Ranton Abbey, the seat of the Earl of Lichfield.

Ranton Abbey, used as an occasional residence only during the hunting season, is chiefly remarkable as exhibiting the ruins of a religious house founded by Robert Fitz-Noel, in the reign of Henry II. for canons regular of the order of St. Augustine, and which was subsequently converted by the founder himself into a cell to the abbey of Hughman. Considerable remains of the monastery are still standing; they consist principally of a lofty, well-built tower, and the outer walls of the church, which are extremely low, with a small portion of the cloisters. From Great Bridgeford, where a mill, always a favourite feature of the artist, forms the foreground of a landscape of limited extent, the Railway, pursuing a course parallel with the Sow, in less than a mile crosses it, and continuing its course by the side of the Moss Brook, a tributary stream of the Sow, in rather more than half a mile reaches the romantic little village of Shallowford, that, revelling in a luxuriance of rural beauties, may be visited with advantage by all in search of the picturesque: here the Railway, running on a level with the land, gates for the prevention of accidents during the passage of the trains have been provided.

From Shallowford, crossing the Meese Brook, and commencing a rise, it pursues for a short distance, a course parallel with that streamlet, and entering an excavation that strongly contrasts with the charming situation of Shallowford, in another mile reaches the

NORTON BRIDGE STATION,

AN INTERMEDIATE ONE, DISTANT FROM BIRMINGHAM $34\frac{3}{4}$ MILES, FROM LONDON 147 MILES, FROM LIVERPOOL $62\frac{1}{4}$ MILES, FROM MANCHESTER $63\frac{1}{2}$ MILES.

Here a road on left leads to Eccleshall, $2\frac{1}{4}$ miles distant, on right to Stone $3\frac{1}{4}$ miles distant. At Eccleshall is Eccleshall Castle, the seat of the Bishop of Lichfield and Coventry.

At Norton Bridge the Manchester and Birmingham Railway is intended to unite with the Grand Junction Railway, and at Stone $3\frac{1}{4}$ miles distant on right of Norton Bridge, will commence the Manchester and Birmingham Extension Railway, the course of which may be traced upon the maps accompanying this work. It is intended to proceed from Stone by Rugely, Lichfield, Tamworth, and Nuneaton, and unite with the London and Birmingham Railway, at Rugby, a line that, shortening the distance to Liverpool, Manchester, and Chester, will altogether avoid Birmingham. From Norton Bridge Station, where the Railway, crossed by an arch that carries the turnpike-road from that place to Stone and Eccleshall, it proceeds in a north-west direction, by an embankment to the Meese Brook, over which, in a short distance, it is conveyed by a cast-iron bridge; in a distance of less than half a mile it again spans that stream, and, in another mile, pursuing a course nearly parallel with the Meese Brook, reaches a lofty bridge that carries the road through Cold Meese to the village of Swinnerton and Swinnerton Park, 2 miles distant, both visible from the Railway.

The manor-house of Swinnerton, situate amidst delightful grounds, that afford, from many points, extensive prospects, has been the property of the Fitzherbert family (of whom its present owner, T. Fitzherbert, Esq. is a lineal descendant), from the Norman conquest. The road on left leads to Eccleshall, 4 miles distant. From the road to Swinnerton, carried with an easy sweep through a fine open country, in another mile, in the course of which it twice crosses the Meese Brook, the Railway reaches the village of Mill Meese that lies immediately on right of the line; round this it sweeps, and carried in a direct line, the Meese Brook running on its left, the road from Mill Meese to Standon on its right, in rather more than a mile it extends to Standon, a village half a mile distant on the left, that here forming the chief constituent feature and foreground of a very beautiful landscape, will be viewed with rapture by all admirers of the picturesque. From Standon Bridge in rather less than half a mile, it reaches Bower's Bent, about a mile beyond which it enters a short excavation, from whence it emerges to a fine open country passing in its way Hatton Mill, lying on a right of the line, and the village of Chapel Chorlton on the left, and in a distance of 2 miles from Bower's Bent, reaches Stableford Bridge. At Stableford Bridge the Railway is spanned by an arch, over which is carried a turnpike-road, that on left leads to Market Drayton $10\frac{1}{4}$ miles distant, on right to Lane End 7 miles distant.

Stableford Bridge is situate in a delightful valley, amidst an amphitheatre of hills, that, clothed with wood, present, from their lofty summits, luxuriance of form, and babbling streams that lave their base, a rich, varied, and romantic landscape. In the heart of this delightful scenery, surrounded by beautiful grounds, and ornamented with a noble sheet of water ($1\frac{1}{2}$ mile distant from Stableford Bridge on left) lies Maer Hall, the seat of Josiah Wedgwood, Esq.; 4 miles distant on right of Stableford Bridge is Trentham Hall and Park, the noble seat of the Duke of Sutherland. Shortly after quitting Stableford Bridge the Railway enters a rocky excavation, of a depth varying from 15 to 50 feet, whose lofty sides involve in gloom the fleeting trains, that in a distance of rather more than $1\frac{1}{2}$ mile from Stableford Bridge reaches the

WHITMORE STATION,

A PRINCIPAL ONE, DISTANT FROM BIRMINGHAM 43 MILES, FROM LONDON $155\frac{1}{4}$ MILES, FROM LIVERPOOL $54\frac{1}{4}$ MILES, FROM MANCHESTER $55\frac{1}{4}$ — Journey resumed at page 164.

ECCLESHALL,

A small market town of Staffordshire, is distant $3\frac{3}{4}$ miles from the Great Bridgeford Station, a minor one, of the Grand Junction Railway, 7 miles from Stafford, $5\frac{1}{2}$ miles from Stone, and $147\frac{3}{4}$ from London. It is pleasantly situated on the margin of a small stream that flows into the river Sow.

The appearance of this place is extremely neat, the houses being in general well built, and disposed with considerable regularity; it chiefly consists of one principal street, the high road to Chester, that runs through it. Eccleshall is distinguished principally for its castle, which was founded at a very early period, but by whom history does not inform us; it was completely rebuilt in 1310 by Walter de Langton, Bishop of Lichfield, and lord high treasurer of England, who established it as the principal palace of the bishops of Lichfield; his successors, however, for some time rarely resided here.

At the time of the civil wars between the house of Stuart and the parliament, it was garrisoned for the king, and stood a severe siege against the republican forces, but was ultimately compelled to surrender; it was thereby rendered uninhabitable, and so remained till 1695, when the whole south front having been renewed by Bishop Lloyd, it afterwards became, and still continues, their occasional residence. The church is chiefly remarkable as having been the place in which Bishop Halse concealed Queen Margaret when she flew hither from Maccleston. The inhabitants are principally engaged in agricultural pursuits.

STONE,

A market town of Staffordshire, 7 miles from Stafford, 9 miles from Newcastle, 141 miles from London, is a place of considerable antiquity, and was formerly remarkable for its religious foundations. It occupies a pleasant situation on the margin of the Trent, at its confluence with the Filly Brook, whose united streams here enrich by their accession of waters that valuable aqueduct the Grand Trunk Canal, a navigation 139 miles in length, that in its progress from the Mersey to the Severn passes close to the town.

Stone chiefly consists of one principal street, in the middle of which is an extensive market-place. The church, dedicated to St. Wulfad, a noble structure, is considerably disfigured by the diminutive height of its tower. Here is a free-school, a charity-school, and an excellent endowment for poor widows, the gift of the Gower family. The inhabitants are principally employed in the manufacture of shoes, and the Grand Trunk Canal, connecting it with the Thames, the Severn, the Mersey, the Humber, and principal manufacturing and mining districts, has proved greatly advantageous to the place.

Stone, situate on the great line of road from London to Liverpool, has suffered a considerable diminution in the advantage it derived from the expenditure of travellers on that till recently much frequented thoroughfare, with the traffic on which the formation of railways has most materially interfered. The inhabitants of Stone, however, appear anxiously to desire an extension of the system and a railway, already in progress, viz. the Manchester and Birmingham, intended to connect the former with Stockport, Congleton, and this place, and unite with the Grand Junction Railway, at Norton Bridge Station, is already in progress.

It is also intended to connect Stone with Rugby and Manchester, by the Manchester and Birmingham Extension Railway, which branching from the London and Birmingham line at Rugby, will, by proceeding through the valley of the Trent, passing Stone in its way, avoiding Birmingham, considerably abridge the distance between the metropolis and Manchester.

NEWCASTLE-UNDER-LYME,

A market-town of Staffordshire, $4\frac{1}{2}$ miles from the Whitmore Station of the Grand Junction Railway, and 150 miles from London, is a place of considerable antiquity. Newcastle is said to be indebted for its name to a castle erected here by Edmund Earl of Lancaster, the younger son of Henry III., in lieu of a former one existing at Chesterton, in the vicinity, and thence the term Newcastle; the adjunct "under Lyme," alluding to a forest of that name, was annexed to distinguish it from Newcastle-upon-Tyne, in Northumberland.

The situation of Newcastle on a branch of the Trent is extremely pleasant: it is a large and spacious place, and the streets exhibit uniformity of arrangement; but the buildings, though neat, are for the most part ancient; and altogether destitute of architectural display, it may be deemed a fine old town. The streets in general are broad, well paved, and lighted with gas, and the principal one, the chief thoroughfare, a fine avenue, is enlivened by an excellent market-place, in the centre of which stands the market-house.

Newcastle had formerly four churches, of which only one now remains; this is a chapelry to Stoke. The new church of St. George, a modern Gothic structure, stands at the northern extremity of the town. Here is a handsome Roman Catholic chapel, and chapels and meeting-houses for dissenters of different denominations. A free-school, national school, and Sunday schools in connection with the church and dissenting congregations have also been formed here. An alms-house for 20 poor women was founded here by the Stafford and Grenville families.

The neighbourhood abounds in coal mines, the chief source of its wealth and prosperity. The inhabitants are principally engaged in the clothing trade, the manufacture of hats, and in stone pottery, of which a greater quantity is made in this place than in any other part of England, 100,000*l*. worth being sometimes exported in a single year; the coal mines employ great numbers, and the Grand Trunk Canal, with its Newcastle branch, affords the means of cheap and easy transport to its manufactures, the produce of the great coal works at Harecastle, and pits of the surrounding country, which are by its agency conveyed to the principal ports, manufacturing and mining districts of the kingdom. Of the Potteries we shall speak hereafter.

The town was incorporated by Henry I. and afterwards by Elizabeth and Charles II., and is governed by a mayor, two justices, two bailiffs, and 24 common councilmen. The corporation have the power of holding a court for the recovery of debts under 40s.

Newcastle sends two members to parliament, and has done so since the reign of Edward III. The right of voting is vested in the freemen and 10l. householders. The mayor is the returning officer. The markets on Monday, Wednesday, and Saturday are well supplied. Horse-racing is a favourite recreation of the inhabitants, and the races held annually on a spacious course about a mile west of the town, are fully and fashionably attended. Situate on the great line of road from London to Liverpool, through the Potteries, Newcastle till recently derived considerable advantage from the expenditure of travellers, and its connection with stage-coach, and posting establishments. To all this railway travelling has given a death blow, but there is good reason to believe that the Birmingham and Manchester, and Chester and Crewe Railways now forming, and intended to unite at Harecastle, in the vicinity, will, when completed, more than compensate for the loss that in that line it has lately sustained.

STOKE UPON TRENT,

A market-town of Staffordshire, is distant two miles from Newcastle-under-Lyme, and 156 from London.

Stoke, as its name implies, derives its appellation from its situation on the banks of the Trent, one of the noblest rivers in England, among which it ranks as third, whether we regard its size, or the extent of its course. It stream, bold and clear, bearing a strong resemblance to the Thames, but exceeding that noble river in rapidity.

Stoke, though low, is pleasantly situated, and the town, though giving title to the borough, is the smallest in size of any in the Potteries; it chiefly consists of one principal street. The whole is well paved, and lighted with gas. The church, recently erected by public subscription, aided by a grant from the parliamentary commissioners, is a noble structure, and here are a quakers' meeting, and a few chapels belonging to the different dissenting congregations. A national school, and Sunday schools, in connection with the established church, and the methodist and dissenting chapels, have been established here.

The inhabitants are principally employed in the manufacture of pottery ware. Stoke is advantageously situated at the junction of the Newcastle and Grand Trunk Canals. The Caldon Canal also unites with the Grand Trunk about a mile north of the town, and gives it the benefit of an inland navigation that extends to the principal ports and manufacturing districts of the kingdom. Stoke returns two members to parliament, in conjunction with the towns of Tunstall, Burslem, Hanley, Lane End, the townships of Longton and Penkhull, with Boothen, Fenton Vivian, Fenton Culvert; the hamlet of Sneyd, and Vill of Rushton Grange that collectively form the borough of Stoke upon Trent and the Potteries.

BURSLEM.

Burslem, a market-town of Staffordshire, 3 miles north-east of Newcastle-under-Lyme, and $159\frac{1}{2}$ from London, is seated on a gentle eminence on the margin of the Grand Trent Canal about a mile and a half distant from the mouth of the Harecastle tunnel, 1888 yards in length; it is one of the principal towns of the Potteries, is a large and well-built place, with spacious streets and excellent approaches, and abounding in extensive manufactories altogether presents an appearance indicative of wealth and prosperity.

The neighbourhood abounds in coal, iron-stone, and clay, and consequently affords every facility for working at the least possible cost the articles for which it has long been celebrated. The old parish church of St. John, an ancient structure, with a massive square tower, formerly a chapelry to Stoke, but now a distinct rectory, stands on the south side of the town. The new church of St. Paul occupies an elevated position upon its western side; it is a large and handsome stone structure in the Gothic style, was built by the liberal contributions of the inhabitants, assisted by the parliamentary commissioners, and is capable of accommodating 2000 persons; its interior well-proportioned, is much admired. It contains a noble organ, 27 feet high. A third church is in a course of erection at Cobridge, and efforts are now making throughout the Potteries to provide a large increase of church accommodation.

The town-hall and market-house, a neat edifice, stands in the centre of the market-place. The inhabitants are chiefly engaged in the manufacture of stone pottery, delf ware, and porcelain china. Glass works upon an extensive scale are also established here, and of all these the quantities transmitted hence for home consumption and transportation are immense.

The coal mines give great employment, and for the transit of its manufacturing and mining produce, not only to all parts of the country but to every port of the kingdom. The Grand Trent Canal affords the utmost facility. Here is a Roman Catholic chapel, and chapels for different dissenting congregations, a free-school, a national, and Sunday schools.

HANLEY.

Hanley, a market-town of Staffordshire, is distant about 2 miles from Newcastle-under-Lyme, and 147 miles from London. Hanley, a chapelry to Stoke upon Trent, in conjunction with Shelton, a township of Stoke, constitutes one of the largest, most spacious and best built towns of the county; it is the principal one of the Potteries, is unquestionably a very handsome place, and consisting of ranges of well-built streets, conveniently and judiciously disposed, and manufactories, constructed upon an immense scale, holds pre-eminent rank in the wealthy district of which it is the centre. Hanley church is a noble edifice of brick, surmounted by a square tower 100 feet high, and was erected in 1788, at an expense of 5000*l*. The church of Shelton, an elegant stone structure, is believed to have cost about double that sum. In addition to these are chapels and meeting-houses for dissenters of different denominations. Here are established national schools, upon the principle of Bell and Lancaster, and Sunday schools connected with the church establishment and dissenting chapels. Water-works and gas-works, that supply not only Hanley and Shelton but Burslem, have been established here. The inhabitants are principally engaged in the manufacture of pottery ware, which produced in every possible form, varying from the plain delf plate to the most elegant and brilliant specimens of decorated china, are hence transported in immense quantities to all parts of the world. A race-course occupies an elevated position at the eastern extremity of the town, where the races are annually held, and which, from the dense population of the Potteries district, are generally fully attended.

THE POTTERIES.

The Potteries is a district of Staffordshire, that, embracing a cluster of towns, surrounded by villages, the inhabitants of which are principally engaged in the manufacture of pottery ware, extending in a direct line from Bradley, near Cheadle, its eastern extremity, to Whitmore (its western boundary) a village lying on left of Newcastle-under-Lyme, forming the southern side; and on its northern extending from Winkhill Bridge, 6 miles from Leek, its eastern side, to Audley, a village 5 miles north-east of Newcastle on the west, gives an area of rather more than 100 square miles, over which are spread the pottery towns and villages. Of the towns an account will be found under the heads of " Newcastle-under-Lyme," " Burslem," " Hanley," " Lane-End," and " Stoke-upon-Trent;" but the manufactures being there merely alluded to, their importance considered, it has been deemed expedient, under one general head, more fully to explain; and the following, derived from the best sources, will, it is believed, give as accurate an account of the introduction, rise, and progress of pottery, as for the purposes of general information can be deemed necessary.

Premising that the major part of the articles necessary to its production abound in this part of Staffordshire, it will excite no surprise that here originating, pursued with unremitting zeal and industry, aided by the resources of chemistry, and conducted by gentlemen of first-rate ability, the manufactures of this district should have attained to a celebrity so extensive as to create a demand for them in every part of the civilised world. The following, chiefly from the pen of a popular writer, will explain the articles used, the sources whence they are obtained, and the general process and plan upon which is conducted the manufacture of pottery ware.

The measures or strata by which the beds of coal are divided, consist most commonly of clays of different kinds, some of which make excellent fire bricks for building the potters' kilns and *saggars* (a corruption of the German *schrugers*, which signifies cases or supporters) in which the ware is burnt. Finer clays of various colours and textures are likewise plentiful in many places, most of them near the surface of the earth; and of these the bodies of the wares themselves were formerly manufactured. It is impossible now to ascertain the exact length of time since this manufacture was first established here. It can be traced with certainty for more than two centuries back, but no document or tradition remains of its first introduction. Its principal seat was formerly the town of Burslem, and it was then called a butter pottery, that is a manufactory of pots for keeping butter. It is so denominated in some old maps. Camden, who died in 1623, does not appear to have heard of the existence of this trade, nor is any mention made of butter pottery in Speed's map of 1610. One of the earliest authors who notices it is Dr. Plott, who died in 1696, and published his Natural History of this county in 1686. As a proof, however, of the antiquity of the manufacture in this neighbourhood, it may be proper to mention that about 120 years ago, below the foundation of a building then taken down, and supposed to have been not less than 100 years old, the bottom of a potter's kiln was discovered, with some of the saggars upon it, and pieces of the ware in them; and that about the same time a road which had long before been made across a field, being worn down into a hollow way, the hearth of a potter's kiln was found to be cut through by the hollow part of the road; and it was not among the then existing or then remembered potteries, that these old works were discovered, but at a considerable distance in places where no tradition remained among the oldest inhabitants of the neighbouring villages, that any pot-works had ever been. It may be added that pieces of ware, of the rudest workmanship, and without any glaze or varnish, are frequently met with, in digging for the foundations of new erections. Though these old remains are, doubtless, the productions of distant periods, they give little or no light into the successive improvements made in the art; nor, indeed, could any good purpose be answered by any inquiry of that kind; for though the manufacture has, within memory, advanced with amazing rapidity to its present magnitude, it seems to have continued for a long series of years almost uniformly rude and uninteresting. Even so late as the time when Plot wrote, the quantity of goods manufactured was so inconsiderable, that "the chief sale of them was to the poor crate-men, who carried them at their backs all over the country." All the ware was then of the coarse yellow, red, black, and mottled kind, made from clays found in the neighbourhood; the body of the ware being formed of the inferior kinds of clay, and afterwards painted or mottled with the finer or coloured ones, mixed with water, separately or blended together, much in the same manner as paper is marbled. The common glaze was produced by lead ore finely powdered, and sprinkled on the pieces of ware before firing; sometimes with the addition of a little manganese, for the sake of the brown colour it communicates; and where the potters wished to show the utmost of their skill in giving the ware a higher gloss than ordinary, they employed, instead of lead ore, calcined lead itself; but still sprinkled it on the pieces in the same rude manner. A few years after the publication of Plot's work, a new species of glaze was introduced, produced by throwing into the kiln, when brought to its greatest heat, a quantity of common salt, the fumes of which occasioned a superficial vitrification of the clay. How long this practice might have existed in other countries is unknown; but it was first brought hither about the year 1690, by two ingenious foreigners, of the name of Elers, of whom a descendant was, some years since, a respectable magistrate in the county of Oxford. These foreigners established a small pot-work at this place — Bradley — not, we believe, Bradwell, as Dr. Aikin's correspondent writes. It is said that the inhabitants of Burslem, and the other adjacent places, flocked with astonishment to see the immense volumes of smoke which rose "from the Dutchmen's ovens," on casting in the salt, — a circumstance which sufficiently shows the novelty of this practice in the Staffordshire potteries. The same persons introduced likewise another species of ware, in imitation of the unglazed red china from the east; and the clays in this country being suitable for their purpose, they succeeded wonderfully for a first attempt, insomuch that some of their teapots are said to have been sold as high as a guinea a-piece; and some of the specimens which still remain in the country are very perfect of their kind. We have seen several of them at different places south of Leek, in the farm-houses. Both the texture and quality of the ware itself, and the form and workmanship, are by no means contemptible, though much inferior to those of more recent manufacture. The Elers, however, did not long continue in this situation; finding the manufacturers about them very inquisitive, and not choosing to have their labours so narrowly inspected, they quitted Staffordshire, and set up a manufactory near London.

This practice of the new glaze with salt, was succeeded in a short time, by a capital improvement in the body of the ware itself, which the tradition of the country attributes to the following incident. Mr. Artbury, one of the potters, in a journey to London, happened to have powdered flint recommended to him, by the ostler of his inn at Dunstable, for curing some disorder in one of his horse's eyes; and for that purpose a flint stone was thrown into the fire, to render it more easily pulverizable. The potter observing the flint to be changed by the fire to a pure white, was immediately struck with the idea that his ware might be improved by an addition of this material to the whitest clays he could procure. Accordingly he sent home a quantity of the flint stones, which are plentiful among the chalk in that part of the country; and on trial of them with tobacco-pipe clay, the event proved fully answerable to his expectations. Thus originated the white stone ware, which soon supplanted the coloured ones, and continued for many years the staple branch of pottery. It was natural that this discovery should be kept as secret as possible; hence they had the flints pounded in mortars, by manual labour, in cellars or in private rooms; but the operation proved pernicious to many of the workmen, the fine dust getting into the lungs, and producing dreadful coughs and consumptions; and these alarming complaints of the men may be presumed to have hastened the discovery of the source from which they had arisen. The secret becoming generally known, the consequent increase of demand for the flint powder, occasioned trials to be made of mills, of various constructions, for stamping and for grinding it; and the ill effects of the dust, which could not be entirely guarded against when the stones were either pounded or ground dry, pointed out an addition of water in the grinding. This method being found effectual, as well as safe, is still continued: the ground flint comes from the mill in a liquid state, about the consistence of cream; and the tobacco-pipe clay being mixed up with water, about the same consistence, the two liquors are proportioned to one another by measure instead of weight.

The use of flint had not been long introduced when an improvement was made by an ingenious mechanic in the neighbourhood, Mr. Alsager, in the potter's wheel, by which its motion was greatly accelerated. This enabled the potters to form their ware not only with greater expedition and facility but likewise with more neatness and precision than they had done before. The manufacture was by those means so far improved, in the beginning of the last century, as to furnish various articles for tea and coffee services, and soon after for the dinner table also. Before the middle of the century, these articles were manufactured in great quantity as well for exportation as home consumption. The salt glaze, however, the only one then in use for these purposes, is in its own nature so imperfect, and the potters, from an injudicious competition among themselves, for cheapness rather than for excellence, had been so inattentive to elegance of form, and neatness of workmanship, that this ware began to be rejected from genteel tables, and supplanted by a white ware of finer form, and more beautiful glaze, which, about the year 1760, was imported in considerable quantities from France.

The introduction of a foreign manufacture, so much superior to our own, must have had very bad effects on the potteries of this kingdom, if a new one still more to the public taste had not happily soon after been produced here. In the year 1763, Mr. Josiah Wedgwood, who had already introduced several improvements into this art, as well with respect to the forms and colours of the wares as the composition of which they were made, invented a species of earthenware for the table, of a firm and durable body, and covered with a rich and brilliant glaze, and bearing sudden vicissitudes of cold and heat without injury. It was accompanied also with the advantages of being manufactured with ease and expedition, was sold cheap; and as it possessed, with the novelty of its appearance, every requisite quality for the purpose intended, it came quickly into general estimation and use. To this manufacture the queen was pleased to give her name and patronage, commanding it to be called Queen's Ware, and honouring the inventor by appointing him her majesty's potter. It is composed of the whitest clays from Derbyshire, Dorsetshire, and other places, mixed with a due proportion of ground flint. The pieces are fired twice, and the glaze applied after the first firing in the same manner as porcelain. The glaze is a vitreous composition of flint and other white earthy bodies, with additions of white lead for the flux, analogous to common flint glass; so that, when prepared in perfection, the ware may be considered as coated over with real flint glass. This compound being mixed with water to a proper consistence, the pieces, after the first firing, are separately dipped in it: being somewhat bibulous, they drink in a quantity of the mere water, and the glaze, which was united with that portion of the water, remains adherent, uniformly all over their surface, so as to become, by the second firing, a coat of perfect glass.

To Mr. Wedgwood's continued experiments we are indebted for the invention of several other species of earthenware and porcelain adapted to various purposes of ornament and use. The principal are the following:—1. A Terra Cotta, resembling porphyry, granite, Egyptian pebble, and other beautiful stones of the siliceous or crystalline order. 2. Basaltes, or black ware; a black porcelain biscuit of nearly the same properties with the natural stone; striking fire with steel, receiving a high polish, serving as a touchstone for metals; resisting all the acids, and bearing, without injury, a strong fire, stronger, indeed, than the basaltes itself. 3. White Porcelain Biscuit, of a smooth wax-like surface, of the same properties with the preceding, except in what depends upon colour. 4. Jasper, a white Porcelain Biscuit of exquisite beauty and delicacy, possessing the general properties of the basaltes, together with the singular one of receiving through its whole substance, from the admixture of metallic calces, with the other materials, the same colours which those calces communicate to glass or enamels in fusion, — a property which no other porcelain or other earthenware body of ancient or modern composition has been found to possess. This renders it peculiarly fit for making cameos, portraits, and all subjects in basso relievo, as the ground may be of any particular colour, while the raised figures are of pure white. 5. Bamboo, or cane-coloured Biscuit Porcelain. This possesses the same properties as the white porcelain biscuit, mentioned above. 6. A Porcelain Biscuit, remarkable for great hardness, little inferior to that of agate. This property, together with its resistance to the strongest acids and corrosives, and its impenetrability by every known liquid, adapts it for mortars and many different kinds of chemical vessels.

These six distinct species, with the queen's ware already mentioned, expanded by the industry and ingenuity of the different manufacturers, into an infinity of forms, for ornament and use, variously painted and embellished, constitute nearly the whole of the present fine English earthenwares and porcelain which are now become the source of a very extensive trade, and which, considered as an object of national art, industry, and commerce, may be ranked among the most important manufactures of the United Kingdom.

The following description of the process used in the manufacturing the earthenware was communicated to Dr. Aikin by a person on the spot. The practice has varied in but a trifling manner since that time. A piece of prepared mixture of clay and ground flint, dried and prepared to a proper consistence, is taken to be formed into any required shape and fashion, by a man who sits over a machine called a wheel, on the going round of which he continues forming the ware. This branch is called *throwing*, and, as water is required to prevent the clay sticking to the hand, it is necessary to place it for a short time in a warm situation. It then undergoes the operation of being turned, and is made much smoother than it was before, by a person called a turner, when it is ready for the handle and spout to be joined to it, by the branch called *handling*. Dishes, plates, tureens, and many other articles are made from moulds of ground plaster; and when finished, the whole are placed carefully (being then in a much more brittle state than when fired) in saggars, which, in shape and form, pretty much resemble a lady's band-box, without its cover, but much thicker, and are made from the marl or clay of this neighbourhood. The larger ovens, or kilns, are placed full of saggars so filled with ware; surrounded by a fire, which consumes from twelve to fifteen tons of coal. When the oven has become cool again the saggars are taken out, and their contents removed, often exceeding 30,000 various pieces; but this depends upon the general sizes of the ware. In this state the ware is called *biscuit*, and the body of it has much the appearance of a new tobacco-pipe, not having the least gloss upon it. It is then immersed or dipped into a fluid generally consisting of sixty pounds of white lead, ten pounds of ground flint, and twenty pounds of stone from Cornwall, burned and ground, all mixed together, and as much water put to it as reduces it to the thickness of cream, which it resembles.

Each piece of ware being separately dipped into this fluid, so much of it adheres all over the piece, that when put into other saggars, and exposed to another operation of fire, performed in the glossing kiln, or oven, the ware becomes finished by acquiring its glossy covering, which is given it by the vitrification of the above ingredients. Enamelled ware undergoes a third fire after its being painted, in order to bind the colour on. A single piece of ware, such as a common enamelled teapot, a mug, jug, &c., passes through at least fourteen different hands before it is finished, viz., the slipmaker, who makes the clay; the temperer, or beater of clay; the thrower, who forms the ware; the ball-maker, and carrier; the attender upon the drying of it; the turner, who removes its roughness; the spout maker; the handler, who applies the handle and spout; the first, or biscuit fireman; the person who dips it into the lead fluid; the second, or glass fireman; the dresser, or sorter in the warehouse; the enameller, or painter; the muffler, or enamel fireman. Several more are required to the completion of such pieces of ware, but are in inferior capacities, such as turners of the wheel, turners of the lathe, &c. &c. The transference of designs from the common blue ware to the more definite delineations is effected much after the manner in which engravers lay down their drawings, — with this difference only : in china it is an impression from an engraved plate, which multiplying prints at pleasure as a less expensive method is the practice here followed. The pattern applied to the transfer paper when fixed is then removed by immersion in water, and the article glazed after the usual method.

WHITMORE TO CREWE.

Whitmore Station, though situate in a deep defile, is nevertheless, from its elevated position, one of the loftiest on the line; the inclination of the Railway, from the neighbourhood of Norton Bridge, a distance of about 10 miles, being that of a continued rise it here attains a height of 390 feet above the level of the sea. Surrounded, however, by hills, its situation as regards the country in its immediate vicinity is that of a valley, here traversed by the Mill Meese stream, that occasionally enlivens by its presence this somewhat solitary scene.

The Whitmore Station is in a situation well chosen for convenience, from its proximity to the Potteries. It is furnished with waiting and retiring rooms for the passengers, and workshops for the occasional repair of the engines. Many people assemble at this station to meet the trains; and the carrying trade of the company from hence is of considerable extent.

The Whitmore Station, except on these occasions, wears, from its secluded situation, an air of great stillness; and the view of it for some distance previous to arriving there, terminated by the bridge, that at that point crosses this rudely-formed ravine, is extremely picturesque, and one upon which the pencil of the artist, if successfully employed, would produce a very beautiful effect.

The bridge above mentioned carries the turnpike-road, that on left leads to Market Drayton, 10 miles distant, on right to Newcastle-under-Lyme $4\frac{1}{4}$ miles distant. One mile distant from Whitmore Station on right, is Whitmore village and Whitmore Hall the seat of Capt. Mainwaring, and 3 miles distant is Butterton, Hall, Sir W. Pilkington, Bart.

From Whitmore Station, after a short level, the Railway continued on a considerable declivity 1 in 350, soon emerges from the rocky cutting into a valley called Madeley Moss, bounded on both sides by hills romantically wild, and in a further distance of $2\frac{3}{4}$ miles reaches

THE MADELEY STATION,

AN INTERMEDIATE ONE, DISTANT FROM BIRMINGHAM 45¾ MILES, FROM LONDON 158 MILES, FROM LIVERPOOL 51¼ MILES, FROM MANCHESTER 52½ MILES.

At Madeley Station, a bridge thrown over the Railway carries the turnpike-road that leads on left to Woore, 3¼ miles distant, and Audlem, 8 miles distant; on right to Newcastle-under-Lyme 5½ miles distant, and the Potteries 7 miles distant.

On right of Madeley station 1 mile distant, seated on an eminence, overlooking delightful grounds ornamented with a beautiful sheet of water, and backed by noble woods, stands Madeley Manor House, the seat of the Hon. Mrs. Cunliffe Offley. Three miles and a half distant is Keel Hall, the seat of Ralph Sneyd, Esq. On left of Madeley the eye reposes with pleasure on the rich woods of Weston, rising in majestic grandeur on the slopes of Bar Hill, that overlooks the village, and from whose summit (653 feet above the level of the sea) may be seen a prospect of vast extent, variety and beauty. Thence the eye ranges over the well-wooded county of Stafford, and fertile vale of Cheshire, bounded on the west by the mountains of Wales. Added to which, the Railway itself from Madeley, crossed by various bridges in its course, and continued in a direct line, presents a lengthened and beautiful perspective view. In a word, artists will find in the environs of Madeley a field fertile in subjects for the employment of the pencil.

From Madeley Station, continued through an excavation of full 40 feet in depth, overhung with wood, the train rushes down a rapid descent 1 in 180 for a distance of 3⅓ miles, at which point it may almost be said to dash down a declivity, 1 in 160, for a further distance of three miles, when the descent decreases to 1 in 330. To the last-named excavation, an embankment of 40 feet in height succeeds; this affords a good view particularly in the vicinity of Wrinehill. Two miles beyond Madeley, on left, close to the Railway, lies Wrinehill Mill, distinguished by its dam, and Wrinehill Hall, backed by the wide spreading woods of Wrinehill, well known as one of the best covers in Staffordshire. A stream a little beyond Wrinehill divides Staffordshire from Cheshire, soon after entering which, on right, is beheld Betley Mere, sheltered by the high grounds of Betley (a village on the turnpike-road from London to Chester), which, with Betley Court and Betley Hall, backed by an amphitheatre of woods, here rise into view. Betley Court is the seat of F. Twemlow, Esq. — Betley Hall, the seat of G. Pollett, Esq. Half a mile beyond Wrinehill Mill a road crosses the line, leading on left to Doddington Hall, the beautiful seat of Sir John Delves

Broughton, Bart., and on right to the villages of Wrinehill and Betley. The Railway, continued on a descent, and carried on an embankment of considerable elevation, now affords a charming view of the rich pastures of Cheshire, in another mile arrived at Den crosses the road (not turnpike), that leads from Wrinehill and Betley, to Wybunbury and Nantwich; 1½ mile beyond Den, crossed by two bridges, it reaches Chorlton, and in three quarters of a mile more Basford.* Here the high road from London to Chester crosses the line at a distance of 5 miles from Nantwich on left, and 10 miles from Newcastle-under-Lyme on right. From Basford it is carried on a level by alternate excavation and embankment, one of which of considerable elevation affords a good view, and this, succeeded by a cutting of considerable depth, conducts to

CREWE STATION,

A PRINCIPAL ONE, DISTANT FROM BIRMINGHAM 53¾ MILES, FROM LIVERPOOL 43½ MILES, FROM MANCHESTER 44½ MILES. — Journey resumed at page 168.

CREWE HALL.

This very elegant mansion appears to have been formerly surrounded with offices, square courts, and gardens, corresponding in character with the house, and laid out according to the then prevailing fashion of formality. The grounds are now disposed in the modern style, and in the immediate vicinity of the house have a fine undulating surface, the general effect being considerably heightened by the formation of a lake; but the mansion remains nearly in its original taste, though it has been made to harmonise with the modern landscape: indeed few buildings in the kingdom could have exhibited at any time finer specimens than this, of the singular style that prevailed at the revival of Grecian architecture in England.

Crewe Hall is a large quadrangular edifice of red brick with others of a darker colour disposed in diamonds throughout; its door-cases, cornices, &c., are of stone, and all the fronts are broken by large bay-windows, which give it an unusual boldness and relief, that is much increased by the open-worked battlements. In the south and east fronts are the entrances,—the former opening to an old staircase of singular curiosity and beauty, that leads to the apartments on the first floor; at the foot of this staircase, in the south-east angle, is the great dining-room, a very noble apart-

---

* Here an intermediate station has been established, the continuance of which being considered doubtful, it has been deemed on that account not worthy of notice.

ment, which, as well as that on the right, is highly ornamented in the mixed style, and deserves the particular attention of the tourist: the drawing-room, with its enormous marble chimney-piece, also demands notice, and the gallery extending along the whole south front is decorated with numerous valuable portraits, while the domestic chapel exhibits a fine large painting of the Last Supper, besides two beautiful specimens of ancient stained glass.

NANTWICH.

Nantwich, a market town of Cheshire, is distant 6 miles from the Crewe station, a principal one of the Grand Junction Railway, 9 from Tarporley, 19¼ from Chester, and 164 from London.

Nantwich is situated near the borders of Staffordshire and Shropshire, in a luxuriant vale on the banks of the Weaver, which divides it into two unequal parts. The Birmingham and Liverpool canal, crossed by a noble iron bridge, passes its western extremity, and this is joined by the Ellesmere and Chester Canal about two miles from the town. This vale consists of some of the finest dairy land in the county, and produces in considerable quantity the fine cheese distinguished by its name for which Cheshire is celebrated.

Nantwich consists chiefly of three principal streets, and though of considerable antiquity, is one of the largest and best-built towns of the county; the eastern is the oldest portion of the town, but the western extremity exhibits many modern and well-built houses.

The church is an ancient structure built in the form of a cross, with an octagonal tower rising from the centre, surmounted with battlements and pinnacles. The east and west windows of the church are large, and are filled with elegant tracery; and in the chancel are several neat stalls, said to have been brought from Vale Royal Abbey, at the dissolution, and also the remains of a tessellated floor. This, though formerly considered as the second town in the county, is now considerably reduced by the removal of the salt trade and much of its business to other towns more conveniently situated. Exclusive of its trade in salt, Nantwich is noted for the quantity of excellent cheese made in the town and its vicinity, and the manufacture of shoes for the London market forms a considerable branch of its trade. The silk and cotton trades are also carried on here.

Nantwich gives title of baron to the Marquis of Cholmondeley, who, as lord of the manor, holds a court baron in the town for the recovery of debts under 10*l*. The town is governed by constables, has a free-school, Sunday schools, and charity schools, several alms-houses, a quakers' meeting, and a few dissenting chapels.

CREWE STATION.

Crewe Station is replete with accommodation for the tourist, and here in case of necessity an additional engine has been provided. Crewe, an insignificant village, that till the establishment of the Railway was remarkable only for the noble seat of Lord Crewe, Crewe Hall, about a mile distant from the station on right, has risen into an importance which from its favourable position will shortly experience a considerable increase.

Here commences the Chester and Crewe Railway, a line that in a distance of 22¾ miles from this station reaches the city of Chester, from whence the Chester and Birkenhead Railway, a line of 15 miles in length, is nearly completed, which, forming a total of 37¾ miles between Crewe and Birkenhead, a village on the western shore of the Mersey immediately opposite Liverpool, will in the distance between London and Liverpool effect a saving of about 5 miles.

It was also proposed to extend a branch Railway* from Crewe by Stockport to Manchester; but this will most probably be superseded by the Manchester and Birmingham Railway at present in progress, and already noticed under the head of Norton Bridge. All these upon the accompanying map are rendered fully apparent, and if referred to will probably reconcile the reader to the opinion here delivered.

The turnpike-road, carried over the Railway at Crewe, conducts on left to Nantwich, 5 miles distant, and on right to Sandbach, 5 miles distant, to both which places there are conveyances. Carried in a direct line for some miles upon a level, a lengthened perspective of the Railway is here obtained. Shortly after quitting Crewe, emerging from the excavation, it is constructed nearly upon a level with the surrounding country, and in a distance of two miles reaches the

COPPENHALL STATION,

AN INTERMEDIATE ONE, DISTANT FROM BIRMINGHAM 55¾ MILES, FROM LONDON 168 MILES, FROM LIVERPOOL 41½ MILES, FROM MANCHESTER 42½ MILES.

Soon after quitting the excavation at Crewe the country expands, and an extensive prospect of the surrounding scenery unfolds itself to view, terminated on the west by the blue mountains of Wales. Looking eastward, the lofty eminence of Bound Hill, near Audley, in Staffordshire, and Mow Copt, a range of hills dividing that county from Cheshire (whose summit ascends to a height of 1091 feet above the level of the sea,) rising in majestic grandeur, terminate the view.

Coppenhall is an insignificant village, the church of which lies

* The proposed lines above-mentioned, and since executed, will be found under their respective heads of Manchester and Birmingham, Chester and Crewe, and Chester and Birkenhead Railways.

immediately on left of the line; it abounds, as does the whole neighbourhood, with beds of peat. An alternation of cutting and embankment carries the Railway in a further distance of $2\frac{3}{4}$ miles, through a succession of rich pastures, passing in its way the villages of Warmingham on right, and Church Minshull on the left to the

MINSHULL VERNON STATION,

AN INTERMEDIATE ONE, DISTANT FROM BIRMINGHAM $58\frac{1}{2}$ MILES, FROM LONDON $170\frac{3}{4}$ MILES, FROM LIVERPOOL $38\frac{1}{2}$ MILES, FROM MANCHESTER $39\frac{1}{2}$ MILES.

Pursuing its way through a delightful country, by an excavation of nearly a mile in length, it then enters on an embankment,—an agreeable contrast, as unfolding to the view the lovely fields that line its sides,—and in a distance of $1\frac{1}{2}$ mile from Minshull Vernon, reaches the Middlewich Branch Canal, over which it is carried by a neat bridge. From this embankment a fine view is obtained of the fertile plains of Cheshire, here enlivened by the windings of the Weaver running on the Railway's western side, in which direction the wood-crowned summit of the Peckforton Hills, the rock and castle of Beeston, the latter rising suddenly from the plain at a distance of 10 miles, stand forth the most prominent features of the surrounding landscape. On right the eye ranges over a rich expanse of country, terminated in the distance by the lofty hills of Derbyshire and Staffordshire. On right of the bridge over the canal lies Lea Hall, formerly a seat, now a farm.

To the last named embankment succeeds an excavation, through which, in a distance of a mile from the canal bridge, the Railway reaches

THE WINSFORD STATION,

AN INTERMEDIATE ONE, DISTANT FROM BIRMINGHAM 61 MILES, FROM LONDON $173\frac{1}{4}$ MILES, FROM LIVERPOOL $36\frac{1}{4}$ MILES, FROM MANCHESTER $37\frac{1}{4}$ MILES.

Here a turnpike-road crosses the line, that on left leads to Chester 18 miles distant, and on right to Middlewich $2\frac{1}{2}$ miles distant. On left of Winsford Station 1 mile distant, is the village of Winsford, celebrated for its salt-works, as is Over, a mile further to the left.

Wharton, a village in this vicinity, also participates in the salt, trade, in the manufacture of which the major part of the inhabitants of Middlewich are more or less engaged. One mile distant on left of Winsford Station is Winsford Lodge, J. Dudley, Esq., and Wharton Lodge, J. Dudley, jun., Esq.; and 5 miles distant,

Oulton Park, the beautiful seat of Sir P. Egerton, Bart. Two miles distant, on right, is Manor Hall, W. Court, Esq., and 1 mile beyond Winsford on right is Bostock Hall, J. France France, Esq. From Winsford Station the Railway, carried on a descent, with very little variation, through a series of cuttings, in a distance of about 3 miles reaches Vale Royal Viaduct, that, continued by a lofty embankment, full 60 feet high, carries the Railway across the channel and valley of the Weaver. The river Weaver rises near Cholmondeley Castle, in Cheshire, and taking a direction nearly due west, passes in its progress Nantwich, Minshull, Weaver, and Winsford, where it becomes navigable, proceeds thence through Vale Royal to Northwich, where, increased by the waters of the Dane and Croke, after pursuing a tortuous course it finally falls into the Mersey near Frodsham. Its way at first lies principally through level pastures, till its arrival at Winsford Bridge, where it enters one of the most delightful valleys in England. From this point it proceeds through banks that, abruptly rising in majestic grandeur, clothed with woods, cast their dark shadows in its passing stream; in this way it continues to Vale Royal, where, enriched by the umbrageous foliage of Vale Royal Abbey, that there reposes in the lap of luxury, it passes in its course as above described to the Mersey.

The view from Vale Royal Viaduct of Lord Delamere's noble domain, where the frail bark floating on its bosom bearing its burthen under easy sail, increases the interest of this lovely scene, is altogether of the most enchanting character; it is one to do justice to which the powers of the pen and pencil are alike inadequate. Vale Royal Viaduct, 456 feet in length, is a handsome structure; it consists of five arches of 63 feet span, rising to a height of 60 feet, is constructed of Runcorn stone; and, viewed from the valley beneath, where it bestrides the stream, presents a light and elegant appearance.

To the Vale Royal embankment succeeds an excavation of considerable depth, in some instances 30 feet, along which, continued in a direct line that from its rise affords a lengthened perspective view of the line crossed by various bridges, the Railway reaches in a distance of $1\frac{1}{2}$ mile the

HARTFORD STATION,

A PRINCIPAL ONE, DISTANT FROM BIRMINGHAM $65\frac{1}{2}$ MILES, FROM LONDON $177\frac{3}{4}$ MILES, FROM LIVERPOOL $31\frac{3}{4}$ MILES, FROM MANCHESTER $32\frac{3}{4}$ MILES. — Journey resumed at page 174.

VALE ROYAL ABBEY.

Vale Royal Abbey is the seat of Lord Delamere. Little now

VALE ROYAL ABBEY.

remains of the ancient building, which was not as described by Warton in his elegy, when speaking of the illuminated windows, "high o'er the trackless heath at midnight seen;" but in fact seated in a deep valley, on the banks of the river Weaver, which formerly spread itself over a wide surface, that now exhibits a range of luxuriant meadows. The present mansion consists of a centre with two projecting wings of red stone, the right one being continued behind the centre. The stone basement appears by the doors and windows to be a fragment of the old abbey, but every other semblance of the monastic edifice has been destroyed by alterations; notwithstanding which, and the lowness of the elevation, the building (being approached by well-wooded grounds,) bursts at once upon the eye in a very striking manner, and its extensive front assumes considerable dignity. A large porch in the centre of the front is the present entrance, from whence a long corridor leads to a flight of stairs that conducts the visitor to an anteroom, hung round with the antlers of various animals, and a number of ancient weapons: the windows of this apartment and the corridor below are decorated with a profusion of stained glass in the ancient style. A door opens hence to the eating-room, and a corresponding one leads over the old wing, through a long gallery, to the different bed-chambers. The drawing-rooms and library are situated beyond the great hall, which is on the other side, and is a magnificent apartment, now used as the principal sitting-room; it is of very spacious dimensions, and has a coved roof richly carved in the style of the seventeenth century; it is altogether far superior to most college halls, and is also decorated with a large and valuable collection of family portraits and other paintings.

NORTHWICH,

A market town of Cheshire, is 2 miles distant from the Hartford Station, a principal one of the Grand Junction Railway, 11¾ miles from Warrington, 18 miles from Chester, and 173 miles from London. Northwich, a small but very ancient town, occupies the sides and summit of a hill on the banks of the Weaver, near its confluence with the Dane, which unites with the former a little above Northwich. The Weaver thus increased, after pursuing a tortuous course falls into the Mersey at a distance of about 10 miles north-east of the town. The streets are irregular, and the buildings in general of considerable antiquity, and the appearance of the place is rendered somewhat remarkable by the extensive but mean-looking erections in which the process of evaporation from the produce of the brine pits is conducted, that more or less surround the town; but its elevated position, overlooking the reaches of the river, and surrounding country, renders it altogether extremely pleasant.

The church, a spacious structure, is remarkable for the peculiarity of its choir, which is semicircular; the roof of the nave is adorned with the figures of wicker baskets of a shape similar to those used in the manufacture of salt; the surrounding cemetery affords from its elevated position an excellent view. There are also a few dissenting chapels here. Northwich has a well-endowed free grammar-school, founded by Mr. John Daynes, of St. Bartholomew's, London. This place is distinguished as the chief of the salt towns, and is the only one which, in addition to its brine springs, possesses mines of rock salt. It has since been discovered in the adjoining townships of Wilton, Marston, Wincham, and Winnington. Salt is manufactured on an extensive scale at several places in Cheshire, but the principal part of the trade is now concentrated in the neighbourhood of Northwich: Here the salt is made from the brine pits and from the natural rock. The latter peculiarity, and the advantageous situation of the town on the banks of the Weaver, and its contiguity to the Grand Trunk Canal, by which a communication has been opened with so many parts of England, have all concurred to render Northwich pre-eminent for its salt trade. Rock-salt is found at from 28 to 40 yards below the surface. Rock-salt pits are opened at a great expense. In their formation a shaft is sunk similar to that of a coal-pit, but more extensive. Having penetrated to a sufficient depth, they hew out pillars generally about seven yards in thickness to sustain the roof, and then employ gunpowder to separate what they mean to raise. This is conveyed to the surface of the earth in baskets made for the purpose. The pits at the greatest depth are dry, and of an agreeable temperature, and a descent thereto, rendered perfectly safe and easy of accomplishment, not unfrequently made by well-dressed persons of both sexes, in considerable numbers, will amply repay, by the wonders there to be witnessed, the trouble of a visit.

When illumined by candles, the mine, from its enormous columns, lofty roof, and retiring arched recesses, that, formed of the crystalline rock, diverges in different directions, from the brilliant coruscations thereby produced, shines with a resplendent and dazzling brilliancy of effect that rarely fails to leave a lasting impression upon the mind. The inhabitants are principally engaged in the manufacture of salt, and boat-building and the cotton trade are carried on here.

Northwich was not long since the scene of a serious disaster; this was the sudden sinking of the earth immediately over one of the pits, that had by injudicious working been left wholly without support for the superincumbent earth, and a convulsion involving loss of life was the consequence.

The mine, long deemed insecure, had from the noise of falling masses fortunately forewarned the people employed in the works of its dangerous state; the shock experienced, however, was not anticipated. This in its effect resembled an earthquake, the ground subsiding carrying in its fall the engine-house, stables, and cottages of the workmen. Eight men and a boy, together with four horses in the stable, were carried to a depth of nearly fifty feet, and were buried in the ruins. Of the former, three men and the boy were saved, the remainder perished, and of the horses three were killed. The alarm occasioned by this dreadful catastrophe spread consternation in Northwich (its effect being there felt) and the surrounding neighbourhood, where it will long be remembered; and seriously as it is to be regretted, its consequences will, it is to be hoped, prove productive of measures calculated to prevent the recurrence of so serious a calamity.

MIDDLEWICH,

A market town of Cheshire, distant $2\frac{1}{2}$ miles from the Winsford Station, an intermediate one of the Grand Junction Railway, 7 miles from Northwich, 21 from Chester, and 167 from London, is pleasantly situate near the confluence of the small rivers Wheelock and Croco with the Dane that falls into the Weaver near Northwich. The Grand Trunk Canal also passes through the town, between which and the Chester Canal a junction has been formed by the Middlewich branch canal; by means of these united aqueducts and the various canals with which they communicate, Middlewich enjoys a water communication that extends to the Thames, the Severn, the Mersey, the Dee, and the Humber, and principal manufacturing and mining districts. Middlewich is a small neat town, but the parish, which is extensive, embraces 14 townships. The church is spacious, and on the south side of it is a college founded by Thomas Savage, Archbishop of York, and an oratory founded by the Leighs of Lyme. Here are meeting-houses for different denominations of dissenters and a free-school. This town, the origin of which is supposed to be as remote as the time of the Romans, derives its name from its central situation between the salt towns. Middlewich, as well as most of the towns in this county whose names terminate with *wich*, has long been celebrated for the great quantities of salt manufactured from the salt springs in its vicinity, the waters of which are said to yield one fourth of their weight in salt. The manufacture of salt is the chief employment of the inhabitants, a portion of whom are engaged in the cotton trade, which was introduced here about thirty years since.

HARTFORD TO WARRINGTON.

The Hartford Station is provided with waiting and retiring rooms, and is altogether very complete; it stands close to the bridge that carries the turnpike-road from Northwich, 2 miles distant on right, to Tarporley, 8 miles, and to Chester, 16 miles distant on left.

The summit of this bridge affords an excellent view of the line. Two miles before Hartford Station on right is Davenham Hall, J. Hoskin Harper, Esq., 1 mile on right of which is Whatcroft Hall, G. J. Shackerley, Esq. One mile distant from Hartford on right is Winnington Hall, unoccupied; and farther to the right, Marbury Hall, J. H. Smith Barry, Esq., and the celebrated salt-works of Marston. Four miles distant is Wincham Hall, E. V. Townshend, Esq., Belmont Hall, J. H. Leigh, Esq., and farther to the right Arley Hall, R. E. E. Warburton, Esq.

From Hartford Station the Railway continued through the excavation in a direct line, for a short distance on a level, then on a descent in $1\frac{3}{4}$ mile reaches Weaverham, where a bridge carries the turnpike-road that leads on left to Chester, $15\frac{1}{2}$ miles distant on right to Warrington, $9\frac{1}{2}$ miles distant to

ACTON STATION,

AN INTERMEDIATE ONE, DISTANT FROM BIRMINGHAM 68 MILES, FROM LONDON $180\frac{1}{4}$ MILES, FROM LIVERPOOL $29\frac{1}{4}$ MILES, FROM MANCHESTER $30\frac{1}{4}$ MILES.

On left of Acton Station is Grange Hall, Lady Brooke. From Acton Station the Railway carried on a descent, through an excavation of about $1\frac{1}{2}$ mile in length, enters on a lofty embankment that, carried across Dutton Bottom, enriched by the sylvan scenery of Dutton Wood, unites it with the Dutton Viaduct. This vast structure consists of 20 arches of 63 feet span; its total length is rather more than a quarter of a mile, and its rise from the level of the river to the crown of the arch 60 feet, it loses much in effect from its position, which if crossing water only would be considerably increased: on the contrary the arches of the Dutton Viaduct, being many of them dry, the beauty of the structure is thereby greatly diminished; and in consequence it falls short in that picturesqueness of appearance which under other circumstances it could not fail to produce. From the summit is beheld the winding course of the Weaver, and more direct channel of the canal here cut to shorten the navigation.

The valley of the Weaver has been so fully described under the head of Vale Royal as to render unnecessary a repetition of its beauties; it will therefore suffice if, in the view here witnessed, we point attention to the principal features of the delightful scenery that surrounds the Dutton Viaduct. All but enveloped in woods of every hue, it appears, when calmly contemplated, the abode of solitude, a spot which Cicero might well have chosen for his villa — its tranquillity disturbed only by the falls of the Weaver. An opening to the west alone gives proof of its proximity to the haunts of men, in which direction is beheld a house of entertainment, known as Pickerings' Boat; westward of this the Weaver, its windings expanding into an amplitude of breadth, perchance enlivened by a passing sail, bares its broad bosom to the view: rich pastures line its shores. Delamere House may be distinguished, with Delamere Forest beyond it, the distance being terminated by the lofty hills that rise in the vicinity of Frodsham. Two miles distant from Dutton Viaduct, on left is Aston Hall, A. W. Hervey Aston, Esq. To this beautiful scenery Birdswood succeeds, and a cutting that contrasts strongly with the scenery at Dutton Viaduct.

The Trent and Mersey Canal now runs parallel to the Railway, that soon reaches the Frodsham and Northwich road, here carried over the line by a bridge (Frodsham being $3\frac{1}{2}$ miles distant on left, Northwich 8 miles on right,) from which, in a direct line passing through a short tunnel, the train arrives at

PRESTON BROOK STATION,

AN INTERMEDIATE ONE, DISTANT FROM BIRMINGHAM $72\frac{1}{4}$ MILES, FROM LONDON $184\frac{1}{2}$ MILES, FROM LIVERPOOL 25 MILES, FROM MANCHESTER 26 MILES.

Here a road branches on left to Frodsham, 4 miles distant, on right Warrington $5\frac{1}{2}$ miles distant.

Preston Brook and Preston on the Hill conjointly constitute a township of Daresbury parish; it is a small place, but being situated at the junction of the Trent and Mersey with the Duke of Bridgewater's canal, derives some little advantage from the traffic on those lines. Preston Brook is not wholly destitute of accommodation for the tourist, a house of entertainment having been erected adjoining the line.

From Preston Brook continued on a descent through a cutting of considerable depth, in a short distance it reaches the Duke of Bridgewater's canal, which crosses the Railway by an aqueduct of two arches. To the cutting an embankment succeeds, followed by the Moore excavation, in which is situated the

MOORE STATION,

AN INTERMEDIATE ONE, DISTANT FROM BIRMINGHAM $74\frac{3}{4}$ MILES, FROM LONDON 187 MILES, FROM LIVERPOOL $22\frac{1}{2}$ MILES, FROM MANCHESTER $23\frac{1}{2}$ MILES.

Two miles beyond Preston Brook on right is Newton Bank, J. Jackson, Esq., and Daresbury Hall, S. Chadwick, Esq.

On left of Moore is Norton Priory, the beautiful seat of Sir R. Brooke, Bart., and 3 miles distant the village of Runcorn; on right of Moore is Moore Hall, General Heron, and the Elms, W. Stubbs, Esq.

NORTON PRIORY.

Norton Priory is the seat of Sir Richard Brooke, Bart. The present mansion occupies the site of the former religious edifice: it is a spacious and very handsome quadrangular building, situated near the Mersey, the estuary of which forms a fine object on the right, while the castle and rocks of Halton constitute very striking features in the prospect to the left of the front view. Some of the ancient walls of the priory, and the ornamental doorway, leading to them are preserved in the present edifice. This doorway consists of semicircular arches, resting on pillars with sculptured capitals, and enriched with foliage, chevronals, and other ornaments. The vaults have been latterly much altered and subdivided, but they originally consisted of groined arches, sprung from short octagonal columns with capitals.

Norton Priory was besieged by a party of royalists in the year 1643, but they were beaten off by the family with considerable loss.

The grounds have been laid out with great taste; they contain a fine old gigantic figure of St. Christopher, and are intersected by the Duke of Bridgewater's canal, the windings of which in some parts add greatly to their natural beauty, though from the traffic thereon not to their seclusion. This canal forms the grand communication by inland navigation between Manchester and Liverpool; it may be considered as the first modern public work of the kind executed in England, although completed at the expense of a private individual, and was finished in the short space of five years from its commencement by the celebrated Duke of Bridgewater, assisted by that uncommon genius for mechanical inventions, Mr. James Brindley. Of the former it would be unpardonable not to praise his attention to public works at an age too often spent in dissipation; and of the latter it may be truly said, that in all his undertakings he was never at a loss, for whenever a difficulty arose he removed it with a facility that appeared like inspiration, and that without the least appearance of vanity or ostentation,

The canal in question extends more than 29 miles, and the water is kept on a level till its termination at Runcorn, where it is precipitately lowered 95 feet, by a series of 19 locks, of admirable construction.

The Moore excavation is followed by a lofty embankment, which connects the Railway with the Warrington Viaduct, a bridge of 200 yards in length, that consisting of arches of different dimensions crosses the Mersey and Irwell canal, and the Mersey river, that here pursue a parallel course. The last-named embankment and the viaduct afford a delightful view; on left is beheld a beautiful expanse of meadow, through which the Mersey increased in breadth, and more contracted channel of the Mersey and Irwell canal, proceed in their course to Liverpool; a similar scene is seen on right, with this difference, that viewed in that direction, the Mersey is of diminished width. Continued upon an embankment from Warrington Viaduct the Railway reaches

WARRINGTON STATION,

A PRINCIPAL ONE, DISTANT FROM BIRMINGHAM $77\frac{3}{4}$ MILES, FROM LONDON 190 MILES, FROM LIVERPOOL $19\frac{1}{2}$ MILES, FROM MANCHESTER $20\frac{1}{3}$ MILES.—Journey resumed at page 179.

WARRINGTON.

Warrington, a market town of Lancashire, and principal station of the Grand Junction Railway, is distant $17\frac{3}{4}$ miles from Liverpool, 18 miles from Manchester, and 184 from London. The town situate on the banks of the Mersey over which is a handsome stone bridge, is of considerable size, with four principal streets running nearly in the direction of the cardinal points of the compass; from these principal streets branch smaller ones for the most part filled with warehouses or manufactories. The streets generally with the exception of the principal ones are narrow and inconvenient, and are chiefly filled with shops, and small houses, with a few handsome modern buildings interspersed. "The entrance into the town," says Mr. Pennant, "is unpromising, the streets long, narrow, ill built, and crowded with carts and passengers, but farther on, are airy, and of a good width, yet afford a striking mixture of mean buildings with modern houses," a description from which, at the present day, it differs only in extension of size; in the environs, however, are some superior buildings. The whole is paved and lighted with gas. Here are three churches. The parish church of Warrington, dedicated to St. Helen, a massive structure with a square tower is of different periods. The chancel is the most ancient part of the building, the flamboyant style of the windows fixing it to about the middle of the fourteenth century. There are on the south side of the altar a Piscina and three Sedilia; the nave was rebuilt in the year 1770, but has no pretensions to architectural beauty. The interior is much disfigured by a flat plaster ceiling. On the north side is a chapel now belonging to Lord Lilford, in the pointed style, in which is a handsome tomb containing the remains of Sir Thomas and Lady Boteler, who were murdered at Bewsey Hall, in 1526. On the south side is the Patten Chapel, in which are several handsome monuments. This was rebuilt about the same time as the nave.

Trinity Church, in the Grecian style, was erected in the year 1760. St. Paul's, a modern structure, in the early English style, erected in 1831, from designs by Mr. Blore, with a tower curtailed of its fair proportions by considerations of expense, was built partly by private subscription and partly by a government grant. The Church at Padgate, erected in 1838, is a plain brick edifice, and St. James's in Latchford, a small but elegant building, was erected in 1829. In addition to these there is a large Roman Catholic chapel capable of containing about 1000 persons, and chapels and meeting-houses for different denominations of dissenters. Here is a large and well endowed free-school, a national school, an infant school, and schools in connection with the dissenting congregations. Here is a neat theatre, and a set of assembly rooms. Warrington may in some measure be considered a seaport town, the Mersey admitting, by the help of the tide vessels, from seventy to eighty tons burthen to Bank Quay, about a mile from the town where warehouses, cranes, and other conveniences for the landing and embarkation of goods are erected. The spring tides rise at the bridge to the height of nine feet. Upwards, the river communication, shortened by cuts, and continued by canal, extends to Manchester. The inhabitants are principally engaged in the manufacture of sailcloth, in glass-making, iron-founding and pin-making; and it has long been celebrated for the excellence of its malt, in which it carries on a considerable traffic.

Prior to the introduction of railways, Warrington, lying on the high road to Liverpool, Preston, Lancaster, Carlisle, Edinburgh and Glasgow, derived very considerable advantage from the expenditure of travellers, and its connection with stage-coach and posting establishments; of the former no less a number than seventy are said to have daily passed through this place. All these advantages, by the substitution of mechanical for animal power, have of course been swept away, and the innkeepers, ruined by the change, are left, like Othello, to exclaim their " occupation's gone : " men, horses, carriages, and baggage being transported by these trains, — a measure probably not contemplated by the legislature when passing the act, and who, it would appear, if not altogether outwitted, have at least overlooked the loss sustained by the revenue in the shape of post-horse duty, and injury inflicted on the agricultural interest. Warrington, however, more fortunate than many towns that have been altogether excluded from the line in having been appointed a principal station, has in consequence suffered much less than many others from the loss of its carrying trade.

WARRINGTON TO LIVERPOOL AND MANCHESTER.

The Warrington Station is, perhaps, from its proximity to Liverpool and Manchester, one of the most important on the line; it is altogether upon a great scale, is complete and perfect in its arrangements, this being a central point at which many trains meet, and from whence an equal number depart.

A road on right conducts from the station to Warrington half a mile distant, and here the almost deserted turnpike-road to Liverpool branches off to the left.

On left of Warrington is Bank Hall, J. W. Patten, Esq., and on right embosomed in wood, Orford Hall, —— Hornby, Esq.

Quitting Warrington Station, the Railway, continued upon a gentle descent through an excavation, shortly after enters upon an embankment which affords a good view, and soon reaches the

WINWICK STATION,

AN INTERMEDIATE ONE, DISTANT FROM BIRMINGHAM $80\frac{1}{4}$ MILES, FROM LONDON $192\frac{3}{4}$ MILES, FROM LIVERPOOL 17 MILES, FROM MANCHESTER 18 MILES.

On right of Winwick, is Winwick Hall, Rev. I. J. Hornby. From Winwick Station, in a distance of $2\frac{1}{4}$ miles, the Railway reaches the

NEWTON JUNCTION STATION

AN INTERMEDIATE ONE, DISTANT FROM BIRMINGHAM $82\frac{1}{2}$ MILES, FROM LONDON $194\frac{3}{4}$ MILES, FROM LIVERPOOL $14\frac{3}{4}$ MILES, FROM MANCHESTER $15\frac{3}{4}$ MILES.

Persons proceeding from London to Manchester are referred for the continuance of the journey from Newton Junction to that town to page 194, where it is continued.

Newton Junction Station is situated near the centre of the Liverpool and Manchester Railway where the line on left extends to Liverpool, on right to Manchester. Here the trains from both these great towns meet on their way to London, and here arriving separate for their different destinations. It only remains to remark that the inclination of the Grand Junction Railway, which, from Warrington for some distance, is that of a gentle descent, at about three miles from Newton commences an acclivity, the last mile of which, a rise of 1 in 85, is a steep ascent. The Grand Junction Railway terminates at Newton Junction, and the journey from thence is continued, without any change of carriage, on the Liverpool and Manchester line, now the property of the Grand Junction Railway company. First class carriages for London do not take up passengers at any station on the Liverpool and Manchester Railway, but set them down at any station on that line for which they have been booked. For the convenience of the tourist, therefore, who having started from London or Birmingham may be desirous of continuing the route as if it were upon the same line, the journey from Newton Station will now be continued as it began, with this difference, the distance from Manchester from whence the train departs, after its arriving at Newton Junction, its distance, instead of diminishing, will now increase. Resuming the journey then upon the plan it commenced, with the slight difference above mentioned, we proceed to observe, that shortly after quitting Newton Junction station, the Railway commences a gradual ascent, and, carried on a lofty embankment, in some places elevated to a height of 70 feet above the level of the valley, it crosses the Sankey Viaduct, a bridge of nine arches, carried over the Sankey Navigation (a canal of considerable traffic, that commencing at St. Helen's, after a circuitous course, falls into the Mersey at Runcorn Gap), in a distance of $1\frac{3}{4}$ mile from Newton Junction, reaches the

COLLINS GREEN STATION,

AN INTERMEDIATE ONE, DISTANT FROM BIRMINGHAM $84\frac{1}{4}$ MILES, FROM LONDON $196\frac{3}{4}$ MILES, FROM LIVERPOOL 13 MILES, FROM MANCHESTER $17\frac{1}{2}$ MILES.

The Sankey Viaduct and embankment afford a good view: on left is beheld the Sankey Navigation, with its show of moving objects, winding its way through the Sankey valley, along which, as far as Warrington, it keeps company with the Grand Junction Railway. On right of the Sankey Viaduct the Sankey Navigation and Newton race-course, with its grand stand, form striking features in the landscape. From Collins Green Station it crosses Parr Moss, a sort of morass, which from the soft and saponaceous nature of its soil, proved a source of great expense in the formation of the Railway, which in another mile reaches

ST. HELEN'S JUNCTION STATION,

AN INTERMEDIATE ONE, DISTANT FROM BIRMINGHAM 85 MILES, FROM LONDON $197\frac{1}{4}$ MILES, FROM LIVERPOOL 12 MILES, FROM MANCHESTER $18\frac{1}{2}$ MILES.

On left of Parr Moss is Bold Hall, the beautiful seat of Sir H. Bold Hoghton, Bart.; two miles distant on right of St. Helen's Junction is the town of St. Helen's, where commences the St. Helen's and Runcorn Railway, that crossing the Liverpool and Manchester line at St. Helen's Junction, extends to Runcorn Gap, upon the river Mersey, five miles distant. Its chief employ is the transportation of the produce of St. Helen's coal-pits to Runcorn Gap, the conveyance of passengers being with its proprietors a secondary object. From St. Helen's Junction, the Railway, carried through an excavation, ascends a steep acclivity, the Sutton Incline, 1 in 96 a rise, so sudden as to render necessary an additional engine, which, being placed in the rear, forces the train to the summit, upon attaining which it arrives at

LEA GREEN GATE STATION,

AN INTERMEDIATE ONE, DISTANT FROM BIRMINGHAM $96\frac{1}{4}$ MILES, FROM LONDON $208\frac{1}{2}$ MILES, FROM LIVERPOOL 10 MILES, FROM MANCHESTER, $20\frac{1}{2}$ MILES.

On right of the Sutton Incline is Shirley Hall, the seat of M. Hughes, Esq. Here the Rainhill Level, the summit of the line two miles in length, is passed rapidly, in one of which it attains the train, and reaches

KENDRICK'S CROSS STATION, RAINHILL,

AN INTERMEDIATE ONE, DISTANT FROM BIRMINGHAM $88\frac{1}{4}$ MILES, FROM LONDON $200\frac{1}{2}$ MILES, FROM LIVERPOOL 9 MILES, AND FROM MANCHESTER $21\frac{1}{2}$ MILES.

Here the Railway is spanned by an oblique arch carrying the turnpike-road on left to Warrington, on right through Prescot two miles distant to Liverpool; the village of Rainhill lying on the left. An excavation follows, through which the Railway reaches the end of Rainhill Level. To this succeeds the Whiston Incline, a steep declivity, down which the train rushes, moderated occasionally by the use of the break, and soon carried on an embankment, arrives at the

HUYTON QUARRY STATION,

AN INTERMEDIATE ONE, DISTANT FROM BIRMINGHAM $90\frac{3}{4}$ MILES, FROM LONDON 203 MILES, FROM LIVERPOOL $6\frac{1}{2}$ MILES, FROM MANCHESTER 24 MILES.

Three quarters of a mile beyond Huyton Quarry Station, is

HUYTON GATE STATION,

AN INTERMEDIATE ONE, DISTANT FROM BIRMINGHAM $91\frac{1}{2}$ MILES, FROM LONDON $203\frac{3}{4}$ MILES, FROM LIVERPOOL $5\frac{3}{4}$ MILES, FROM MANCHESTER $24\frac{3}{4}$ MILES.

On right is the village of Huyton, one mile distant is the Hazels, and farther to the right is Knowsley Park, the magnificent seat of the Earl of Derby. One mile beyond Huyton Gate on left is Halsnead Hall, R. Willis, Esq. In a short run of half a mile the Railway reaches

ROBY LANE STATION,

AN INTERMEDIATE ONE, DISTANT FROM BIRMINGHAM 92 MILES, FROM LONDON $204\frac{1}{4}$ MILES, FROM LIVERPOOL $5\frac{1}{4}$ MILES, FROM MANCHESTER $25\frac{1}{4}$ MILES.

Two miles distant on right of Roby Lane, is Croxleth Park, Earl of Sefton. The Railway running now on a lofty embankment that from its elevation affords a delightful view in a distance of $2\frac{1}{4}$ miles arrives at

BROAD GREEN STATION,

AN INTERMEDIATE ONE, DISTANT FROM BIRMINGHAM $93\frac{1}{4}$ MILES, FROM LONDON 206 MILES, FROM LIVERPOOL $3\frac{1}{2}$ MILES, FROM MANCHESTER 27 MILES.

Between Roby Lane and Broad Green on left is Summer Hill House, T. Case, Esq. One mile distant on left of Broad Green Station is Childwall Hall, the charming seat of the Marquis of Salisbury, on right of Broad Green is Wavertree Hall, C. Lawrence, Esq. The Railway from this vicinity resembles the approaches to London and Birmingham. Villas of every order of architecture, many of them erected at great cost, contrast with cottages, that, built in the Elizabethan, Gothic, Swiss, and Italian styles, characterised by simple elegance, and surrounded by gardens more or less extensive, stand forth the striking proofs of wealth and prosperity. From Broad Green Gate to the embankment last passed a rocky excavation of considerable depth (in some instances nearly 70 feet) succeeds. This deep defile, two miles in length, from which all tourists are anxious to escape, is succeeded by an embankment, an agreeable relief, and upon which the Railway is carried to

EDGEHILL STATION,

At which point a separation of the trains takes place, the luggage trains descend through a tunnel on left to the docks and wharfs of the company, and the carriage-trains, carried forward by their own weight, proceed through another on right to the principal station of the company in Lime Street, Liverpool, distant from Birmingham $97\frac{1}{4}$ miles, from London $209\frac{1}{2}$ miles, and from Manchester $30\frac{1}{3}$ miles. Here omnibuses are in attendance ready to convey persons to all parts of the town, at the charge of sixpence each, but for the convenience of others preferring that mode of conveyance, hackney coaches, and what are here denominated cars, may be obtained, the charges for which are as follows:—

Coach fares, under 1000 yards, 1s.; under 1700 yards 1s. 6d.; and sixpence for every additional 700 yards.

Cars under 1000 yards 8d.; under 1700 yards 1s.; and for every additional 700 yards four-pence.

Returning with the same fare, half the foregoing charges.

Time, between twelve at night, and six in the morning, double the foregoing fares.

The following are the principal hotels in Liverpool:—

The Adelphi Hotel and the Waterloo Hotel in Ranelagh Street, and the Queen's Arms in Castle Street, are the three first-rate hotels; to these may be added the King's Arms, the Grecian, The George, The Saracen's Head, The Angel, and The Wellington, all of which are in Dale Street. The Union, The Neptune, and The Bull, are in Clayton Square, and The Brunswick is in Hanover Street. The character of The Commercial in Dale Street may be gathered from its name: a longer list the limits of this work forbid, but it must in fairness be added, that Liverpool, like London, abounds in houses of entertainment suited to the taste of travellers of every class.

THE LIVERPOOL TUNNEL.

The Liverpool Tunnel, a stupendous subterranean excavation, one mile and a quarter in length, passing immediately under the town, is a work that cannot fail to excite astonishment in all beholders, but to those imbued with a taste for engineering holds out the strongest temptation to examination — an adventure not to be entered upon without an official attendant. For a description of the Liverpool Station, the reader is referred to the account of Liverpool.

PRESCOT.

Prescot, a market town of Lancashire, 198 miles from London, occupies an elevated position on the high road from Warrington to Liverpool, at a distance of 10 miles from the former, and 8 from the latter town. It chiefly consists of one principal street. The church, a large and spacious building, from its situation on an eminence, and lofty steeple 156 feet high, forms a conspicuous object to the surrounding country for many miles. Here are, besides meeting-houses for dissenters, a free-school and several alms-houses. The parish, abounding in collieries, supplies coals not only to the town of Liverpool but numerous adjacent villages at a very cheap rate. Among the manufactures of Prescot those of watch tools, watch movements, and fine files are more particularly celebrated, to which may be added engravers' tools of all descriptions. The former of these have been long established here, and in consequence of the many and various improvements that have originated in this town, the business in that line is now carried on to a considerable extent. The inhabitants are principally employed in the manufacture of watch movements, springs, chains, wheels, wires, cases, and the various component parts of watches, here produced in great perfection, and in the drawing of pinion wire, which is said to have originated here. The small files are also much valued for their fineness of steel and cutting. Coarse earthenware, sail-cloth, and cottons, are also manufactured in this town and the vicinity, and the trade in coals is very considerable. The markets on Tuesday and Saturday are well supplied.

ST. HELEN'S.

St. Helen's, formerly a small place, from its advantageous situation on the Sankey Canal, and from its natural characteristics, has gradually increased to a town of considerable size and importance. What has been observed of Prescot may with propriety be applied to St. Helen's, with this difference chiefly, that the manufactory of plate glass at Ravenhead in the vicinity has long been esteemed the most extensive in the kingdom. Cast plate glass with concave and convex mirrors are manufactured here of a size and quality quite equal to any thing imported from the Continent. Of the latter some have been made thirty-six inches in diameter, and of the former, plates brilliant and beautiful are produced of a size 143 feet in height by 72 inches wide. In these extensive works nearly 300 persons are sometimes employed in the processes of melting, casting, blowing and polishing, in addition to two steam-engines employed in grinding and polishing the plates. The hall in which the glasses are cast is a vast room 200 feet long by 70 feet wide, and the works altogether upon a great scale are well worthy of a visit.

Here are also very extensive copper works. The chief source

of advantage to St. Helen's is undoubtedly its coal, with which the country in the vicinity literally abounds, and which by means of the Sankey Navigation, the first canal cut in England, are transmitted to the Mersey for the supply of Liverpool and the surrounding towns and villages on the banks of that river, a more rapid and direct communication with which is maintained by the St. Helen's and Runcorn Railway, some time since completed. This work, principally employed for the transportation of merchandise, is nevertheless regularly traversed by railway trains engaged in the conveyance of passengers from Liverpool and St. Helen's to Runcorn Ferry.

KNOWSLEY PARK.

Knowsley Park is the seat of the Earl of Derby. The mansion stands on an elevation in the park, and has evidently been erected at various periods. Its most ancient part is of stone, and has two round towers; this is said to have been raised by the first earl of Derby, for the reception of his son-in-law King Henry VII., on whose head the crown, taken from the tyrant Richard III. after the battle of Bosworth Field was placed by this nobleman, who had been one of the main instruments of Richmond's victory. In consequence of this royal visit, not only were various grand preparations made in enlarging and decorating the mansion, but a road was purchased leading from Sankey and Winwick to the river, and the handsome stone bridge that now crosses the Mersey at Warrington was erected, and a causeway thrown up across the marshes to the rising ground on the Cheshire side, all of which were kept in a state of repair by him and his successors till the time of William, sixth earl of Derby. James, the tenth earl, retired to this seat some time previous to his decease, and made great additions to the house, though some say he rebuilt it. This interesting mansion is decorated with a large and very valuable collection of paintings, by the old masters, besides which here are a number of portraits of the ancient and honourable family of the Stanleys, earls of Derby, many of them not only curious as works of art, but rendered particularly interesting, as serving to perpetuate the likenesses, costumes, &c. of individuals who eminently distinguished themselves for their bravery, magnanimity, loyalty and sufferings. The surrounding park is extensive and beautiful; it enjoys many charming views, and is abundantly wooded, though many of the finest trees lean towards the north-east, and are almost stripped of their foliage and smaller branches.

LIVERPOOL.

Liverpool, a seaport and market-town of Lancashire, is $17\frac{1}{4}$ miles north of Chester, $36\frac{1}{4}$ miles west of Manchester, 95 miles north of Birmingham, 77 from the Isle of Man, 137 from Dublin, 215 from Glasgow, and 206 north-west of London.

To enter largely on a description of this important place, in the limited space to which our remarks must necessarily be confined, is altogether impossible; to do justice to which a volume might well be devoted; an arrangement so diffuse, however, would, from its voluminous size, evidently defeat its object, and as, for the purpose of taking a passing glance at its principal features, the objects of tourists generally, it is altogether unnecessary to descend deeply into detail, we shall endeavour to submit, as briefly as may be, in a condensed form, a summary of its most remarkable objects, accompanied with such remarks as will enable him, during a short stay, to leave nothing unobserved, that to the intelligent traveller can be deemed a matter of interest.

Seated on the margin of the Mersey, which, narrow at its entrance, here expands into an estuary varying from half a mile to three miles in breadth, its situation is eminently beautiful. Looking southward the eye reposes on the Cheshire shore, that, rich in fertility, forms the opposite bank of the river; this at all times wears an animated appearance from the continual crossing of the ferry-boats, but at about an hour before and after high water, presents a perpetual and varied succession of panoramic beauties. Steam-vessels of a size stupendous, about to cross the great Atlantic, are then seen quitting the port, while others that have recently performed that till hitherto perilous passage, are beheld gallantly entering the harbour; the gladdened hearts of the passengers welcomed by the cheers of the assembled multitudes that throng the quays. Lesser, but nevertheless large steam-ships destined to different, some to distant ports, some for Ireland, some coastwise bound, others for the Continent, the Channel, or the Thames, are now in motion.

Covered with vessels of a different class, whose whitened sails now fully bosomed to the wind, now eddying to the breeze, are hastening to their destination; the Mersey at these periods presents a *coup d'œil* of the most imposing and enchanting character; westward a vast expanse of ocean meets the eye, terminated on its southern side by the mountains of Wales, that rising in majestic grandeur skirt the line.

Viewed from the Cheshire shore its appearance is most imposing. Seen in this direction, the Mersey, with its multitude of moving objects, a long line of quays, and docks that display a forest of masts, form the foreground, immediately in the rear of which rises a line of large and lofty warehouses, and these backed by the town itself, stretching far and wide, enlivened by lofty domes, its glittering vanes and towering steeples; its grandeur, magnitude, extent, and commercial importance considered, it may safely be averred that no place in England, save the metropolis, no maritime or mercantile town on the Continent can produce a parallel.

The present prosperity of Liverpool has evidently arisen from a combination of causes, among which may be chiefly noticed its natural situation, its free water carriage maintained by means of canals, with the manufacturing towns and mines of the surrounding country, the enlightened policy of its civil government, and moderate harbour dues.

An account of its early history must be sought elsewhere; no room for remarks thereon can be found in works of this description, the pages of which can only point attention to its most distinguished and principal features.

Liverpool, with its suburb of Toxteth Park, consists of only one parish, but has several churches and chapels of ease to the mother church.

Until the reign of William III. this town had but one church, and that only a chapelry to Walton, a village about two miles distant; but about the year 1698 an act of parliament was obtained empowering the inhabitants to erect a new church; and from about that time may be traced the rapid progress of its population and commerce, which has advanced to a degree, that Liverpool has at length become second only in importance to the metropolis of the empire.

The town extends three miles in length along the river, and is about a mile and a half in breadth. All the new streets and leading thoroughfares are well built, spacious, and airy, but the lesser lines, the older portions in particular, are intricate and narrow, and are principally filled with warehouses, workshops, and manufactories; the whole is well paved and lighted with gas.

At the south end of the town is St. James's Walk and the Mount, commanding a beautiful prospect of the town, the harbour, the ocean, and the Welsh mountains.

The marine parade, a spacious, pleasant, and lengthened promenade, occupying a beautiful position in front of the river and the Prince's dock, is also a favourite and fashionable resort.

On the west side of the town lie the docks, which, with the quays, wharfs, and warehouses, comprise an immense range of buildings; the tobacco warehouse alone, belonging to government, being capable of containing 7000 hogsheads of tobacco. Liverpool has 24 churches, one of which only is parochial. The most remarkable of these are the following:—

The Church of St. Paul, a miniature imitation of the great cathedral of London, situate a short distance from the Exchange, is chiefly remarkable for the style of its architecture: its interior, singular in appearance, is more imposing than its exterior, from the disposition and character of the pillars that support the dome. The Church of St. George at Everton is an object of considerable architectural interest, as being nearly the first cast-iron church erected in the kingdom; the whole of the framework, doors, pillars, groins, roof, pulpit, and ornamental enrichments being formed of cast iron; the length of this extraordinary building is 119 feet, its breadth 47. It is ornamented with a splendid window of stained glass; and the tower, 96 feet high, standing on a hill, the site of an ancient beacon, is 340 feet above high water mark. St. John's, near the east end of Dale Street, is a spacious stone structure in the Gothic style with a lofty tower. St. Thomas's Church of the Ionic order is very handsome in appearance; it is near the Custom-house. St. Mark's, a spacious structure capable of containing 2500 persons, is situate at the top of Duke Street, near the Cemetery. St. Michael's occupies the centre of Kent Square; Christchurch, situate in Hunter Street, and St. Luke's, the latter a beautiful specimen of pure Gothic, situate at the upper end of Bold Street, are those more immediately entitled to particular notice. Exclusive of five Roman Catholic chapels and a Jews' synagogue, there are about twenty-six chapels belonging to the dissenters of different denominations. In connection with the church establishment, national and Sunday schools are here established, as are also others in conjunction with the dissenting congregation. The public structures connected with the trade and commerce of the town are erected in a style of costly elegance, alike creditable to the taste and opulence of the inhabitants, and admirably adapted to the purposes of their appropriation, are characterised by excellence of arrangement, utility, convenience, and facility for the enjoyment of the more elegant accomplishments. Of these the new Custom-house, occupying a spacious area (the site of the Old Dock) at the south end of Pool Lane, may from its magnitude be deemed, perhaps, the most distinguished feature. This is a magnificent edifice of freestone of the Ionic order, erected from designs by Mr. Foster at an expense of 200,000*l.*, of which 150,000*l.* was a grant from government, the corporation supplying the remainder; it consists of a centre and two wings, but is not, as its name implies, wholly confined to custom-house business, the centre portion of the building and west side only being appropriated to that branch of the public service. The eastern wing contains the Excise Office, Dock Trust Office, and Post Office.

Next to the Custom-house, the Liverpool Exchange is the most spacious in plan, and ornamental in architectural elevation;

it was erected by a subscription of 100,000*l.* The building occupies three sides of a quadrangle, having the north front of the town hall erected at an expense of 100,000*l.* for the fourth side, and altogether includes an area of 194 feet by 180; the centre of which is adorned by a superb group of bronze statuary by Westmacott, erected at an expense of 9000*l.*, to commemorate the victories of the immortal Nelson. The Exchange buildings may be esteemed among the finest specimens of Grecian architecture in this country, and perhaps the most splendid structure ever raised in modern times for commercial purposes. The Lime Street Station of the Grand Junction, and Liverpool and Manchester Railway company in Lime Street, is one of the chief ornaments of Liverpool, to do justice to which could alone be effected by entering into a detail not only of its splendid front with its elegant architectural embellishments, but also of the well arranged offices, arrival and departure parades, warehouses, &c. &c. of this vast carrying company. For an account of all these well worthy of a deliberate survey, the Editor refers to works of local interest, his duty ending with recommending to general attention its leading features, and for which in the pages of this work room only could be found. The Corn Exchange, upon the plan of that in Mark Lane, London, in the Grecian style, a handsome structure, is in Brunswick Street. The Theatre Royal in Williamson Square is a large and commodious building, the interior of which is elegantly decorated; and in addition to which there are the Royal Amphitheatre and Sans Pareil in Great Charlotte Street, the Liver Theatre in Church Street, the Queen's Theatre or Circus in Christian Street, the Wellington rooms at the corner of Great Oxford Street, and Mount pleasant, a large and elegant building fronted with stone, and decorated with sculpture, containing a splendid suite of apartments, are appropriated to concerts, balls, and assemblies. Here are also various literary and scientific institutions; they chiefly consist of the Royal Institution in Colquit Street, where also are held the meetings of the Literary and Philosophical Society. The Lyceum in Bold Street; the Athenæum in Church Street; a Law Library in Clarendon Buildings, and Mechanics' Institute in Mount Street. Here also have been established Zoological Gardens, and Botanical Gardens, admission to which may be obtained by tickets only, easily procurable at any of the principal hotels. St. James's Cemetery (formerly a stone quarry) beautifully and tastefully disposed, deserves a visit; here in a vault are deposited the remains of that celebrated but unfortunate and ill-fated statesman, the late Mr. Huskisson, who lost his life upon the opening of the Liverpool and Manchester Railway. A Cemetery called the Necropolis, has also been formed by the dissenters.

The more wealthy inhabitants are engaged in mercantile pursuits, in the West India trade, the African trade, the South American trade, more recently the East India trade, the Irish trade, and the American trade. The trade with Ireland in corn, cattle, and provisions, is of very great extent, and was for many years that by which Liverpool most benefited; but this is now surpassed by the American trade, which consists of more than three fourths of the whole commerce of this kingdom with that vast empire. Of the importations thence, cotton wool forms the chief article, which subsequently re-exported in the form of cotton twist, may be termed the staple trade of Liverpool. The trade in cheese is also considerable. Its merchants, an opulent, active, and intelligent class, are distinguished by a spirit of enterprise: they were the originators of the Railway system, of which that between Liverpool and Manchester was the first completed; and independent of the railways already in operation, in all of which they are more or less shareholders, it is a fact not generally known, that of the principal lines at present in progress, in which also they are extensively engaged, some must have sunk into ruin but for the powerful aid of the people of Liverpool.

Ship-building here forms a principal pursuit, it being computed that 3000 shipwrights are employed in the dockyards alone; sail-making, boat-building, and rope-walks, with the manufacture of cordage, chain, and other cables, and anchors, employ many hands. Among the principal articles of manufacture here, independent of such as are connected with shipping, are those of china, porcelain, earthenware, watch movements of all kinds, and the manufacture of fine files. Here are also brass founderies, iron founderies, salt-works, copperas-works, soap-works, sugar-houses, breweries, distilleries, and chemical works.

The estuary of the river Mersey may not improperly be called an arm of the sea, opening to this point a ready access to the western ocean; its breadth from Seacombe Point to the opposite shore is 1200 yards; from Otter's Pool to the opposite coast 2 miles: at spring tides it rises from 20 to 30 feet. Thus ships of any burden may come up fully laden to the town, while vessels of less draught find water sufficient to carry them nearly to Warrington. The river wall, about $2\frac{1}{2}$ miles long, forms a fine frontage, and is disposed into quays that, conducting to different docks, extend the whole length. These, 20 in number, include wet and dry docks, with graving docks, for the repairing of vessels, thus rendering it one of the most commodious seaports in the world.

The charitable institutions of Liverpool are upon a great scale, and the bounty of its inhabitants to the unfortunate, distributed unsparingly, will be evident from the following account. The blue-coat school, erected in 1710, for the maintenance and education of 200 boys and girls. The infirmary, a noble institution, not only receives distressed objects of Liverpool, but is open to all, who, coming from a distance under any dangerous calamity, are instantly admitted. Upwards of 1500 patients are annually admitted here; but a far greater number of out-patients receive medical assistance. This forms one edifice with the hospital for seamen's widows, the building being connected by two handsome colonnades, with a turret on the top of each, and a clock in the middle of the pediment. The hospital for seamen forms one of the wings of the infirmary. This charity extends likewise to the widows and children of mariners; it is aided by a monthly collection of 6d. from the wages of every sailor going from the port of Liverpool. An asylum for the blind in which they are taught music and many useful trades; a fever hospital, the ladies' charity for the relief of women in child-bed; a penitentiary for unfortunate women; a strangers' friend society for the relief of travellers, and a society for the relief of small debtors, form prominent features of its benevolent spirit. Other charitable institutions adapted to the relief of every species of distress are numerous; and charity and Sunday schools for youth of both sexes literally abound.

The borough gaol, erected according to the Howardian plan, for solitary confinement, with every possible convenience, and another for county prisoners at Kirkdale are both upon an extensive plan. Great improvements have been made, and are still making in Liverpool. A complete set of salt-water baths, in which the water flows from the sea, have been formed here, and machines similar in construction to those at Brighton and Margate are provided for the use of those who give preference to immersion in the ocean. There is also a floating-bath. The high grounds on the east side of the town defend the place from the piercing winds that blow in that direction; but it is open to the genial breezes of the south and west that thus render it in general very temperate and healthy. Epidemical disorders rarely show themselves here.

Liverpool, from its distance, formerly deemed remote, is, by the establishment of railways, now placed within easy reach, in fact, within a day's ride of the metropolis; and as it will in all probability experience a vast accession of visitors, of which, presuming that a large proportion will consist of pleasure tourists, it has been deemed advisable to direct attention to the facilities which here exist for visiting the beauteous scenery of North Wales, the Menai Bridge, and other interesting objects in that part of the principality, the Isle of Man, the west and north coast of Ireland, the southern coast of Scotland, and perchance its capital. Steam-vessels of the best construction, and replete with accommodation, are constantly crossing the Irish sea; and to all these the tracks, with their several distances, may be traced upon Mogg's "Map of Steam Navigation," a work to which we have deemed it a duty to refer our readers; it will be found as containing a body of valuable information that will in vain be sought elsewhere, of great utility.

The first charters granted to Liverpool appear to have been by Henry I. and Henry II.; several additional charters were afterwards granted, but it was not remarkable in history till besieged by Prince Rupert in the civil war of Charles I.

Liverpool is governed by a mayor, chosen annually on St. Luke's day, a recorder, and common-council, consisting of forty-one members, including the mayor, recorder, and town-clerk; those who have served the office of mayor, are afterwards styled aldermen, and the three junior aldermen are coroners. The income of the corporation is about 60,000$l.$ a-year. It sends two members to parliament, the right of election being in the mayor, bailiffs, freemen, and 10$l.$ householders. The returning officers are the mayor and two bailiffs.

This town is celebrated for its markets, of which St. John's in great Charlotte Street, the largest in the kingdom, was erected at an expense of more than 35,000$l.$ St. James's market, in Great George Street, less than half the size of St. John's, cost about 14,000$l.$ St. Martin's market, in Scotland Road, cost about 13,000$l.$ The Islington Market faces the end of Lime Street, the fish market is in Great Charlotte Street, and the cattle market about three miles from the town on the London road.

The markets for provisions on Wednesday and Saturday are amply supplied with necessaries and luxuries. The corn-market is held on Tuesday and Saturday.

There are two companies for the supplying the town with water, and two gas companies. It has already been remarked that the town is well lighted, and the supply of water, it may be added, is abundant.

FOREIGN PACKETS.

The following is a list of the foreign packets that leave Liverpool at different periods, the particulars of which will be most correctly ascertained from the Liverpool papers and placards that are posted on the quays, and in different parts of the town, duly announcing the day and hour of their departure:—

Bahia, a regular line of packets.
Boston, a regular line of packets.
Calcutta, monthly.
Genoa and Leghorn, every fortnight.
Havannah, monthly.

Lima, every three months.
Lisbon, three times a month.
Messina and Palermo, monthly.
Monte Video and Buenos Ayres, irregularly.
New York, every fortnight.
Oporto, every three weeks.
Philadelphia, monthly, and occasional intervening periods.
Pernambuco, a line of packets at irregular periods.
Rio de Janeiro, every fortnight.
St. Thomas, a regular line of packets.
Valparaiso, every six weeks.

Steam-packets start every half-hour from St. George's Dock, and the Prince's Parade for Birkenhead, Seacombe, Monks' Ferry, New Brighton, and Woodside; to Eastham five times a-day, to Runcorn and Manchester daily.

COASTWISE.

Steam-packets start for Carlisle and Annan in the summer daily, for Lancaster three times a-week, for Whitehaven three times a-week, in the summer. Workington and Maryport in summer twice a-week, for Dumfries weekly, and Glasgow during the summer daily.

ISLE OF MAN.

To Douglas in the summer daily.

NORTH WALES.

For Aberconway, three times a-week in the summer. For Beaumaris, Bangor, and Caernarvon, three times a-week in the summer; for Rhyl, Rhydlan, and Abergeley, three times a-week in the summer.

₊ Of these coasting steamers it should be observed that the number is during the summer occasionally increased—diminishes with the decline of the season, and in the depth of winter, if not wholly discontinued, their employment rarely exceeds a weekly occupation, rendered necessary by the traffic existing between Liverpool and these towns. As in stage-coach travelling the trouble of previous inquiry at the principal hotels will be amply repaid, by a reference to the most commodious and best appointed vessels, and the prevention of disappointment and best accommodation be thereby secured.

IRELAND.

For Ardglass and Strangford Lough, weekly.
Belfast, three times a-week.
Cork, twice a-week.
Drogheda, four times a-week.
Dublin, daily.
Dundalk, weekly.
Londonderry, twice a-week.
Newry, weekly.
Portrush and Larn, weekly.

WARRINGTON TO MANCHESTER.

For the convenience of tourists travelling to Manchester, it will now be necessary to return to the Newton Junction Station, where the line, diverging on the right to that town, will be continued on the Liverpool and Manchester Railway, upon the plan adopted in describing the Grand Junction line. Of the difference of the latter, however, from the former, the diminished width of the Liverpool and Manchester line will at a glance convince him. In pursuance, therefore, of our plan we proceed to observe, that from Newton Junction carried forward on a gradual descent upon an embankment, in a distance of one mile from Newton Junction Station, the Railway reaches the

NEWTON BRIDGE STATION,

AN INTERMEDIATE ONE, DISTANT FROM BIRMINGHAM $83\frac{1}{2}$ MILES, FROM LONDON $194\frac{3}{4}$ MILES, FROM MANCHESTER $14\frac{3}{4}$ MILES, FROM LIVERPOOL $15\frac{3}{4}$ MILES.

The embankment from Newton Junction Station to Newton Bridge affords on either side a good view of the country, which is here beautifully variegated. On right the eye ranges over the valley of the Mersey, interspersed with villages and hamlets, the distance being closed by the high grounds of Cheshire and Staffordshire, that in that direction bound the view, the foreground being enlivened by the spire of Winwick church. Ample accommodation for tourists will be found at Newton, where a house of entertainment has been established on right of the line.

On left of Newton Bridge Station the embankment, which here rises to the height of 40 feet, affords a panoramic view of the town of Newton. Here a mill, the painter's favourite object, lends additional interest to the scene. On left of Newton Bridge is Golborne Park, Miss Scarisbrick; one mile distant the Heyes, H. Crichley, Esq., and two miles distant New Hall, Sir John Gerard, Bart. On left of the line, Rivington Pike, a lofty hill, near Wigan, whose summit rises 1545 feet above the level of the sea, is visible for some distance. Here a turnpike-road, carried by a lofty viaduct, crosses the line that leads on left to Wigan, $7\frac{1}{2}$ miles distant, to Leigh, 5 miles distant, and on right to Warrington, 5 miles distant. From Newton Bridge Station, the Railway reaches in a distance of three quarters of a mile the

PARKSIDE STATION,

AN INTERMEDIATE ONE, DISTANT FROM BIRMINGHAM $84\frac{1}{4}$ MILES, FROM LONDON $196\frac{1}{2}$ MILES, FROM MANCHESTER 14 MILES, FROM LIVERPOOL $16\frac{1}{2}$ MILES.

At Parkide Station the trains stop to take in an additional

supply of fuel and water,—a circumstance that, upon the opening of the line September 15, 1830, led to the death of the late Mr. Huskisson who, as has already been observed in the course of this work, lost his life from incautiously quitting the carriage, and unconsciously standing upon the line. The consequence was, the unfortunate gentleman was struck down by the engine, that passing over his legs, they were literally crushed; the unhappy sufferer was then removed with all possible speed to the house of the Rev. Mr. Blackburn at Eccles, where after a few hours' suffering under extreme torture he expired. A tablet at Parkside records the melancholy event.

Here the North Union Railway branches off through Wigan to Preston, an account of which will be found under its proper head.

To the Parkside Station an excavation succeeds, through which the Railway is constructed to the

BOLTON JUNCTION STATION,
AT KENYON STOCKS.

AN INTERMEDIATE ONE, DISTANT FROM BIRMINGHAM 86½ MILES, FROM LONDON 198¾ MILES, FROM MANCHESTER 11¾ MILES, FROM LIVERPOOL 18¾ MILES.

Here the Bolton and Leigh Railway branches forth on left, for an account of which the reader is referred to that work, of which, under its proper head, a full account will be found.

From Bolton Junction the Railway soon reaches an embankment, carried on which, in a distance of two miles, it reaches the

BURY LANE STATION,

AN INTERMEDIATE ONE, DISTANT FROM BIRMINGHAM 88½ MILES, FROM LONDON 200¾ MILES, FROM MANCHESTER 9¾ MILES, FROM LIVERPOOL 20¾ MILES.

One mile before Bury Lane see on right the village of Culcheth and Culcheth Hall, the seat of ——.

From Bury Lane Station, after crossing the Glazebrook Stream, the Railway enters on Chat Moss, and in a distance of 1¾ miles reaches the

FLOW MOSS STATION,

AN INTERMEDIATE ONE, DISTANT FROM BIRMINGHAM 90¼ MILES. FROM LONDON 202¼ MILES, FROM MANCHESTER 8 MILES, FROM LIVERPOOL 22¼ MILES.

Chat Moss, an extensive triangular-shaped morass, is about 3 miles in length from east to west, and about 4 miles in width from north to south. This dreary waste, long deemed irredeemable, was at great cost to the railway proprietors rendered for the purposes of the Railway firm and secure. It abounds in peat that furnishes fuel to the poor inhabitants residing in its vicinity, in addition to which some few patches of it have been reclaimed, and partially converted to agricultural purposes. The moss itself, monotonous in appearance, affords no object upon which the eye can repose with pleasure, but upon the left is enlivened by the villages of Astley and Tildesley, that at no great distance rise into view. The prospect on right, the foreground of which is filled with this dreary swamp, extends into Cheshire, the lofty hills of which county and those on the confines of Derbyshire close the view.

Half a mile from Flow Moss Station the train arrives at

LAMB'S COTTAGE STATION,

AN INTERMEDIATE ONE, DISTANT FROM BIRMINGHAM $90\frac{3}{4}$ MILES, FROM LONDON 203 MILES, FROM MANCHESTER $7\frac{1}{2}$ MILES, FROM LIVERPOOL 23 MILES.

From Lamb's Cottage Station, in a distance of three quarters of a mile, the trains reach

BARTON MOSS STATION,

AN INTERMEDIATE ONE, DISTANT FROM BIRMINGHAM $91\frac{1}{2}$ MILES, FROM LONDON $203\frac{3}{4}$ MILES, FROM MANCHESTER $6\frac{3}{4}$ MILES, FROM LIVERPOOL $23\frac{3}{4}$ MILES.

One mile distant from Barton Moss Station on left see the village of Worsley and Worsley Hall, R. H. Bradshaw, Esq. To the Barton Moss Station, in a distance of $2\frac{3}{4}$ miles succeeds the

PATRICROFT STATION,

AN INTERMEDIATE ONE, DISTANT FROM BIRMINGHAM $94\frac{1}{4}$ MILES, FROM LONDON $206\frac{1}{2}$ MILES, FROM MANCHESTER 4 MILES, FROM LIVERPOOL $26\frac{1}{2}$ MILES.

At Patricroft a road crosses the line leading on left to Bolton, $4\frac{1}{2}$ miles distant, on right to Warrington, 13 miles distant. A mile beyond Patricroft the train reaches the

ECCLES STATION,

AN INTERMEDIATE ONE, DISTANT FROM BIRMINGHAM $95\frac{1}{4}$ MILES, FROM LONDON $207\frac{1}{2}$ MILES, FROM MANCHESTER 3 MILES, FROM LIVERPOOL $27\frac{1}{2}$ MILES.

Eccles, an extensive and populous parish with a large and ancient church, is rendered remarkable by the death of Mr. Huskisson, who in a few hours after the fatal accident that befel him at Parkside, here breathed his last, in the house of the Rev. Mr. Blackburn. Two miles and a quarter beyond Eccles the train arrives at

WEAST LANE STATION,

AN INTERMEDIATE ONE, DISTANT FROM BIRMINGHAM $96\frac{1}{2}$ MILES, FROM LONDON $208\frac{3}{4}$ MILES, FROM MANCHESTER $1\frac{3}{4}$ MILES, FROM LIVERPOOL $28\frac{3}{4}$ MILES,

And in another mile reaches

CROSS LANE STATION,

AN INTERMEDIATE ONE, DISTANT FROM BIRMINGHAM $97\frac{1}{2}$ MILES, FROM LONDON $209\frac{3}{4}$ MILES, AND FROM MANCHESTER $\frac{3}{4}$ OF A MILE,

In which last distance it enters the

MANCHESTER STATION,

A PRINCIPAL ONE, DISTANT FROM BIRMINGHAM $98\frac{1}{4}$ MILES, FROM LONDON $210\frac{1}{2}$ MILES, FROM LIVERPOOL $30\frac{1}{2}$ MILES.

Here omnibuses are in attendance ready to convey persons to all parts of the town at the charge of sixpence each, but for the convenience of others preferring that mode of conveyance, hackney coaches, and what are called cars may be obtained, the charges for which are as follows:— Any distance, not exceeding 1172 yards, 1s.; any distance exceeding 1172 yards, and not exceeding one mile, 1s. 6d., and for every succeeding third of a mile 6d.; for a carriage drawn by two horses. Any distance not exceeding one mile, 1s., and for every additional third of a mile, 4d., for a carriage drawn by one horse. Charges for time not exceeding a quarter of an hour, 1s.; and for every additional quarter of an hour, 6d., for a carriage drawn by two horses; for one-horse carriages not exceeding a quarter of an hour 1s., and for every succeeding quarter of an hour, 4d. The above fares to be taken either for time or distance at the option of the driver. The following are some of the principal hotels:—

The Bush Inn, Dean's Gate; the Golden Lion, Dean's Gate; the Mosley Arms, Piccadilly; the Palace Inn, Market Street; the Peacock Inn, Market Street; the Royal Hotel, Mosley Street; the Railway and Commercial Hotel, Liverpool Road; the Swan Inn, Market Street; Talbot Inn, Market Street; Commercial Inn, Market Street.

The characters of the Commercials in Market Street and Liverpool Road may be learned from their name: a longer list would be of little use, but it must in candour be admitted that Manchester, like London, abounds in houses of entertainment suited to the taste of travellers of every class.

MANCHESTER.

Manchester is a market-town of Lancashire, $36\frac{1}{4}$ miles from Liverpool, and 182 from London.

Manchester, the grand centre of the cotton trade, is the largest and most populous manufacturing town in the kingdom, the metropolis alone excepted. Characterised by great industry, it is exceeded only in wealth by London, and, perhaps, Liverpool. It is a place of great antiquity and supposed to have been a station (Mancunium) long before the Roman conquest, when it became a town.

It is situated at the confluence of the Irk and Medlock with the Irwell, which here expands to a breadth of 150 feet, and has been rendered navigable to Liverpool, between which and Manchester, independent of the roads and railway, there is a daily intercourse by steam-boats; and by means of an extensive system of canal navigation, a water communication is maintained not only with the metropolis but every part of the kingdom.

The town extends about two miles in length and about a mile and a half in breadth, but its dimensions are continually increasing by the erection of new houses and additional streets, and Portland Place, Mosley Street, Grosvenor Square, Ardwick Green, and Salford Crescent in particular, have a very fine appearance.

On the west side of the Irwell is a distinct township called Salford; it is under a separate jurisdiction, but divided only by the river; it is thereby as it were incorporated with the town, as is the Borough with London, and may therefore be deemed the Southwark of Manchester.

Manchester has of late years experienced great improvement, the entrances in almost every direction, characterised by an appearance of great wealth, are broad, spacious, and elegant, and the whole is well paved and lighted with gas. The central parts of the town consist of narrow streets, lanes, and courts, all crowded with workshops, warehouses, and manufactories; but towards the extremities of the town, as at London, Bristol, and Birmingham, among the more modern buildings are many very handsome and elegant houses, either standing alone, or formed into rows, terraces, places, and parades; and the environs generally, the residence of the merchants, manufacturers, and more wealthy classes, abound in beautiful buildings embracing every style of architecture, interspersed with villas in the Italian style, and Swiss and Gothic cottages of considerable beauty.

The public buildings of Manchester are numerous, handsome, and many of them elegant. Of the various religious edifices, whether belonging to the established church or dissenting classes, many of them are remarkable for their architecture.

There are twenty-three churches, and (including four Roman Catholic) about double that number of dissenting chapels. The collegiate church is a handsome Gothic structure, ornamented with beautiful scultpure, a finely-carved roof, the relics of painted windows, and contains numerous chapels and chantries, with a powerful organ. From the south porch to the north door, the length of the cross aisle is 100 feet; the whole breadth of the church, including Brown's chapel, 120 feet; the whole length of the building from east to west is 216 feet; the tower has a very handsome appearance, and the whole was some few years s nce repaired. The collegiate body consists of a warden, four fellows, two chaplains, two clerks, four singing men, and four chorister boys.

The College Church, St. Mary's, built by the clergy of the collegiate church, is a very elegant structure, with a beautiful spire, and clock which shows the age of the moon. The lantern has a very striking appearance, and is surmounted by a large globe, on the top of which is a cross. The interior, of great elegance, contains several excellent paintings and a curiously carved choir.

St. Peter's church is a remarkably elegant building of Doric architecture, and much resembles a Grecian temple.

The remaining churches we have not room to describe, but they are nevertheless all more or less deserving attention, and are well adapted to their several situations: the dissenting chapels we have already alluded to.

No town in England is more distinguished for the number of its charitable institutions. The seminaries of education are also numerous, and a liberal spirit is diffused in the town for the promotion of knowledge, literature, and science.

Of the charitable institutions, Cheetham Hospital, commonly called the College, is intended for the maintenance and education of 80 boys, from the age of 6 to 14, at which period they are furnished with a new suit of clothes, and with a small premium are put apprentice to some useful trade. The buildings of the college or hospital comprise a refectory, kitchen, dormitory, coffee-room, and various other domestic apartments, besides a large collegiate library, amounting to upwards of 15,000 volumes, including many scarce and valuable manuscripts. Most of the rooms and the whole building resemble the college structures of the universities. To this establishment, worthy of a visit, and to its library, gratuitous admission may be obtained from 8 in the morning till 12 at noon, and from 1 in the afternoon till 5 in the evening.

The grammar-school was founded by Hugh Oldham, Bishop of Exeter, who died in 1519, and endowed it with certain lands, and some corn-mills which he had purchased in Manchester, the whole of which is vested in trustees for the accomplishing the testators' and donors' intentions. Amongst other provisions it is directed, that no male infant of whatever county in the kingdom, shall be refused admission. The master and usher are to be appointed by the president of Corpus Christi College in Oxford, and in default of nomination within a reasonable time, to devolve on the warden of Manchester College. The principal master, besides a dwelling-house, &c., has 240*l.* per annum, and the second master 120*l.*, besides three others who have 80*l.* a-year each. This school has eight exhibitions for Oxford University, each of 25*l.* a-year, and those who are entered at Brazen Nose College, have a fair chance of some valuable exhibitions from lands in Manchester, bequeathed by the late Mr. Hulme.

The infirmary is a fine pile of building opposite Piccadilly, it includes a large general hospital, a dispensary, and a lunatic hospital and asylum. In the front is an area, enclosed with iron palisades, within which is a large piece of water, the public baths, and some fine walks.

The lying-in hospital, a commodious building, stands on the margin of the Irwell in Stanley Street.

The Ladies' Auxiliary Society is an institution of a similar kind, by which poor women are during their confinement accommodated with various necessary articles, both for themselves and their infants. The House of Recovery or Fever Ward is an appendage to the infirmary, and was established in 1796; it contains 21 wards, has accomodation for 100 patients, with proper offices, and is appropriated to the reception of persons suffering under contagious fevers, those afflicted with typhus and scarlatina being entirely separated from the rest, the apartments being ventilated in the best possible manner to prevent the spread of the predominant effluvia, and circumscribe the circulation of the morbid matter. The Strangers' Friend Society, instituted in 1791, distributes clothes, beds and blankets, and whatever may be found necessary for the comfort of poor strangers, who have been industriously sought out, when sinking under the presence of poverty and disease. An Infirmary for Diseases of the Eye, a Lock Hospital, a Humane Society, and a Penitentiary, have also been established here. The Boroughreeves Charity arises from lands and money left for distribution to poor aged and impotent inhabitants in Manchester. These are provided with linen cloth, coats, gowns, and money at discretion, according to their respective wants. The lands having been sold for building, the value of that part of the property has been thereby increased to fourfold its former value, and its benefits in consequence considerably extended. There is also a Commercial Clerks' Society for the relief of the sick, and families of decayed members; a Philanthropic and Commercial Travellers' Society, and several institutions of a similar kind. The Manchester Poorhouse, a handsome and commodious building, stands in Strangeways, and a similar institution in Green-gate, Salford. The Royal Lancastrian school upon the plan of Joseph Lancaster, founded on the twenty-fifth of October, 1809 educates 1000 children, and two schools, upon the plan of Bell, afford instruction to about 600 more, in addition to which, there are numerous charity and Sunday schools. Of the associations for promoting literature and science, the principal is the Literary and Philosophical Society established in 1781. It has published several volumes of its memoirs, some of which have been translated into the French and German languages. The Philological Society was instituted in 1803, on the model of a similar society in Liverpool. The Manchester Agricultural Society, instituted for the purpose of promoting and encouraging the useful arts and sciences of life, was established in 1767, and since that period has distributed many premiums for valuable discoveries, it also grants gratuities to cottagers who support their families without parochial aid; and honest and good servants are also rewarded by honorary presents. Of the institutions connected with the public business of the town, the Exchange, for the resort of the merchants, manufacturers, and tradesmen, is a very fine and spacious building. It is situated in Exchange Street fronting the market-place, and was erected by subscription in 1808. It is built in the Doric style. On the lower floor is the news-room, a magnificent hall comprising an area of 460 feet; and the upper rooms appropriated to public dinners, meetings, &c. &c. are on a corresponding scale.

The Town Hall, a fine building of the Ionic order, admirably adapted to municipal business, is in King Street; the Post Office is in Exchange Street. The portico, a beautiful building in the Ionic style, erected by subscription in 1803, is situated in Mosley Street; it contains a good library and a very commodious newsroom, amply supplied with newspapers, reviews, magazines, &c; and is much frequented by professional gentlemen; above is a handsome gallery used as a library. The Manchester Royal Institution, upon the plan of that in London, a very handsome building, is in Mosley Street where is also the Club-house; the Mechanics' Institute is in Cooper Street. The Theatre Royal, a spacious structure, the interior of which is handsomely decorated, is in Fountain Street, and the Circus or Royal Amphitheatre is in Great Charlotte Street.

The Public Baths, already noticed, are near the Infirmary, in addition to which there are the Adelphi Swimming Baths in Salford. The New Bailey Prison, founded in 1787, but since enlarged to nearly double its original size, has two elegant entrances, and wears on the whole the appearance of great strength. It contains a commodious court-house, a grand jury room, apartments for the magistrates, counsel, &c. The rivers that run through the town, are crossed by several bridges: there are three over the Irwell, nine over the Medlock, a still wider stream, of which that at Oxford Street in particular, claims attention. Shuter's Brook has three, and Shude Hill Pits, one. Not to mention more than twenty over the different canals, the grand aqueduct of Ashton Canal over Shuter's Brook, in a diagonal direction, is of singular construction, and is truly picturesque on the approach from Piccadilly. The town is abundantly supplied with water from a large reservoir, about two miles from the market-place, considerably above the level of the town, containing when full upwards of 212,000 tons of water.

Manchester is supported and has risen to its present consequence entirely by its manufactures, and the various trades and occupations which these, with the demands of a rising town, necessarily draw along with them. Of these manufactures by far the principal and the source of most of the rest is that of cotton. The greater part of the cotton trade of Great Britain, which besides its own consumption, supplies that of all Europe, America, and the West Indies; of Africa, and even partly of India; this trade of which the raw material is transported hither, upwards of 2000 miles, most of it to be returned, in a finished state to the very place of its production, which to facilitate these exports and imports, has given rise to Liverpool, the emporium of the west. To perform its various operations, has given birth to the greatest system of machinery that ever existed, and which besides employs next to agriculture itself, more people than any other trade in the kingdom. The greater part of this immense business centres in Manchester, extending around it in all directions to Furness and Derby on the north and south, and to Leeds and Liverpool on the east and west. The various branches of these manufactures are carried on, more or less, through all this district, but by far the most extensive, especially the spinning, in Manchester. Manchester is besides the general depôt from which the raw material is distributed through all parts of the district, and in which all this scattered merchandise is again collected, when finished, into a centre, to be again expanded over a wider circle to be sent to Hull, Liverpool, and London, and thence all over the world. The principal articles manufactured at Manchester at present are velvets, which though of cotton are brilliant in colour, and closely resemble those made of silk, fustians, dimities, calicoes, checks, tickings, jeans, shirtings, ginghams, quiltings, handkerchiefs, nankeens, diapers, muslins, muslinets, cambrics, and almost every kind of fancy cotton, and cotton and silk goods. The weaving of silk and manufacture of lace are also extensively pursued. The spinning trade is daily becoming more extensive, and considerable quantities of yarn are annually exported. The spinning is almost entirely performed by means of machinery aided by a number of boys and girls; and however we may lament the effects of these great manufacturing establishments on the morals of the people, they unquestionably display in a striking manner all the complicated powers of machinery. The cotton being carried to the mill in its rudest state, is made to pass through a succession of rollers, spindles, &c., and to undergo the various operations of cleaning, carding, drawing, stretching, and twisting, until the mass of unconnected fibres comes out from this process a continuous thread of the utmost fineness, of very great strength and with its value augmented one thousandfold. In 1818 several new factories were built in the neighbourhood, and at present the whole number of spining mills, and factories in the town amounts to about sixty. The weaving is also carried on to a great extent, and the invention of power-looms, or looms worked by machinery, have been recently introduced, and have extended considerably. These, however, supersede manual labour in a small degree, when compared with the spinning-machines. When all the people employed about power-looms are taken into account, three people can weave nearly as much cloth in the common way as two can do by power-looms. The cloth, however, which is made in power-looms is generally better than that made by hand. Various other operations are performed by machinery, and nearly the whole of these machines, which were formerly driven by water, are now wrought by the steam-engine, by far the most ingenious and refined contrivance of all, and which is here carried on at little expense on account of the abundance of coal. But the erection and keeping up of this various and complicated machinery is itself a source of very great business in and around Manchester. This gives rise to great iron founderies, and other works of a similar kind, and to the invention even of new machines to facilitate its operations. Of these the wire card manufactory is one of the most curious. The leather in which a great number of wires is to be fixed, in order to form the card being set before it, the machine cuts the wire, bends it, fixes it in the leather by first piercing a hole, and repeats all these and many other operations 150 times in a minute; sixty of these machines also only requiring the attendance of three men, four boys, and one girl. Besides the weaving and spinning, the printing, dyeing, and bleaching business are carried on to a very great extent in and around Manchester. The hat manufacture is also very extensive, and several well managed sulphuric acid, or oil of vitriol works, besides a great number of other manufactories are in operation.

Manchester has recently received a charter of incorporation, by which the borough is divided into fifteen wards, which include the townships of Manchester, Chorlton upon Medlock, Hulme, Ardwick, Beswick, and Cheetham. The municipal body consists of a mayor, recorder, sixteen aldermen, and forty-eight councillors. The corporation are authorised by the charter to hold a court of record for the trial of civil actions, where the damage sought to be recovered shall not exceed 20*l.* This place has, by the Reform Bill, been constituted a borough, and returns two members to parliament, the right of voting being vested in the 10*l.* householders; but it should be added that Salford, which is to Manchester what Southwark is to London, but altogether under a separate jurisdiction, has also, by that act, been constituted a borough, with the right of returning one member to parliament: collectively, therefore, Manchester may be said to send three representatives to the national council.

THE NORTH UNION RAILWAY.

FROM PARKSIDE ON THE LIVERPOOL AND MANCHESTER RAILWAY TO PRESTON.

The North Union Railway commences at the Parkside Station of the Liverpool and Manchester Railway, a spot rendered memorable by the accident which there happening to the late Mr. Huskisson proved fatal to that eminent but unfortunate statesman. From Parkside constructed upon a gradual rise, taking an easy sweep in an easterly direction, in a distance of rather more than a mile and a quarter, it crosses the turnpike-road from Newton to Leigh and Bolton, and in a rather less distance gains the Golborne Brook which it crosses. From its commencement it is carried through Golborne Dale, the scenery of which is enriched by the grounds of Golborne Park lying on left of the line, the waters of the Golborne Brook, enlivening its western side; and in a distance of a little more than $1\frac{3}{4}$ mile from Parkside, extends to the village of Golborne, the mill there turned by the brook forming a prominent feature in the foreground of the landscape. From Golborne, proceeding with an easy sweep, and taking a western inclination, in rather less than a quarter of a mile it reaches

GOLBORNE STATION,

AN INTERMEDIATE ONE, AT GOLBORNE SMITHY, DISTANT FROM PARKSIDE RATHER LESS THAN $2\frac{1}{4}$ MILES.

A viaduct here carries it over the road, that on right leads to the village of Rowton, on left to Edge Green. From Golborne Station its course is that of a straight line to Bamfurlong, a distance of $1\frac{3}{4}$ mile, the first half mile of which is a gradual rise, the remainder a descent so slight as to be in travelling imperceptible. At Bamfurlong it is carried over a road that on right leads to Hindley, on left to Ashton. From Bamfurlong it proceeds with an easy sweep upon the same gentle descent for one quarter of a mile to the Wigan and Manchester Canal, over which it is carried by a viaduct, and continuing upon the same descent for about half a mile, is thence constructed on a level of half a mile in length, when it commences a gradual rise; and in another mile reaches the Leeds and Liverpool Canal; this it crosses, and soon after carried over the Douglas river, by a line nearly direct, with a short but steep ascent, reaches Chapel Lane, in Wigan, over which it is borne by a viaduct, and in a short distance continued upon a level gains

WALL GATE STATION, WIGAN,

A PRINCIPAL ONE, LYING ON THE WEST SIDE OF THE TOWN, DISTANT FROM PARKSIDE 7 MILES, FROM MANCHESTER $20\frac{1}{4}$ MILES, FROM LIVERPOOL $21\frac{1}{2}$ MILES.

The elevated situation of Wall Gate Station affords a panoramic view of the western part of Wigan, from whence with a gradual sweep, it proceeds upon a considerable acclivity for 2 miles to the Boar's Head, upon the turnpike-road from Wigan to Preston, which it crosses by a viaduct at a distance of about $1\frac{1}{4}$ mile from Standish, lying on right of the line; in a further distance of 60 yards it crosses the road from Wigan to Chorley, 6 miles distant on the right. From the turnpike-road to Chorley and Standish, still rising, pursuing an almost parallel course with the river Douglas running on its western side, it proceeds with an easy sweep for $1\frac{1}{4}$ mile to the

STANDISH STATION,

AN INTERMEDIATE ONE, AT PARSONAGE LANE, STANDISH, DISTANT FROM PARKSIDE 10 MILES, FROM PRESTON 12 MILES.

At Standish Station, on left of which lies the parsonage, it crosses Parsonage Lane by a viaduct, from whence, continued on an ascent, and carried forward in a direct line to Hichbibi Brook, which it crosses at a distance of $1\frac{1}{4}$ mile, the last $\frac{1}{4}$ of which is of increased steepness, in another $\frac{1}{4}$ of a mile it attains the summit, that from its elevation, 285 feet above the level of the sea, commands a good view of the surrounding country. From the summit it commences a descent, in half a mile reaches Coppul Chapel, and in another half mile the

COPPUL STATION,

AN INTERMEDIATE ONE, DISTANT FROM PRESTON $9\frac{1}{2}$ MILES, FROM WIGAN $5\frac{1}{2}$ MILES, FROM PARKSIDE $12\frac{1}{2}$ MILES.

From Coppul Station where it crosses the turnpike-road from Chorley to Standish it is continued on a descent, and carried forward in a direct line; in rather more than half a mile reaches the Clankatt Brook, which it crosses; a little more than a $\frac{1}{4}$ of a mile beyond which, it passes over the turnpike-road from Wigan to Chorley, at a distance of $2\frac{1}{2}$ miles from the latter town. Continued upon a descent, it is carried with an easy sweep in another mile, to the river Yarrow, here crossed by a viaduct, when, changing its inclination, and commencing a rise, it proceeds in a line nearly direct for a mile to

EUXTON STATION,

A PRINCIPAL ONE, DISTANT FROM CHORLEY ABOUT $1\frac{1}{2}$ MILE, FROM PRESTON $5\frac{3}{4}$ MILES, FROM PARKSIDE $16\frac{1}{4}$ MILES, FROM LIVERPOOL $32\frac{3}{4}$ MILES, FROM MANCHESTER $30\frac{1}{4}$ MILES, FROM LONDON $212\frac{3}{4}$ MILES.

Quitting Euxton Station after a short curve continued on a rise, it proceeds in a direct line to the Chorley and Eccleston road, which in half a mile it reaches; and crossing it by a viaduct, changes its inclination to a gradual descent, upon which, continued for about half a mile, it reaches the road to Rose Whittle, in another $\frac{1}{4}$ of a mile the road from Leyland to Chorley, and in a further distance of $\frac{3}{4}$ of a mile gains

GOLDEN HILL STATION,

AN INTERMEDIATE ONE, DISTANT FROM PRESTON $4\frac{1}{4}$ MILES, FROM PARKSIDE $17\frac{3}{4}$ MILES.

Here it crosses the road from Leyland to Blackburn, and continued upon a descent in a direct line for rather more than $1\frac{1}{2}$ mile reaches the

FARRINGTON GATE STATION,

AN INTERMEDIATE ONE, DISTANT FROM PARKSIDE $12\frac{1}{2}$ MILES, FROM PRESTON $2\frac{1}{2}$ MILES,

A little before which it crosses the river Lostock. From Farrington Gate Station, where it crosses the road from Eccleston to Walton le Dale, continued upon a gradual descent for about $\frac{1}{4}$ of a mile, it then proceeds with increased declivity, and an easy sweep to Penwortham, which in $\frac{3}{4}$ of a mile more it reaches, and, carried over the turnpike-road by a viaduct, in rather more than half a mile, commences a gradual ascent, upon which it is carried to the bridge over the Ribble; from whence, continued on a rise, in less than half a mile, it reaches the Preston Station in Fishergate, Preston, a principal one, distant by Railway 22 miles from Parkside, 36 from Manchester, 38¼ from Liverpool, from London 218½ miles.

WIGAN.

Wigan, a market town of Lancashire, and principal station of the North Union Railway, is 19 miles from Manchester, 21¾ from Preston, 22 from Liverpool, and 200 from London. Wigan is situate near the source of the small river Douglas, whose banks are celebrated as the scene of the memorable defeat of the Saxons by King Arthur.

As far back as Leland's time, it was at that period as large as Warrington, but better built and well inhabited. As at present existing it covers a considerable space, and is neat though irregular in appearance. The original edifices are ancient, but of late years it has much increased in trade, buildings, and population, (the latter being double the amount of 1801); several new streets containing many handsome houses have been erected, the approaches improved, and the whole widely extended. It is now well paved and lighted with gas.

The church is a stately edifice, with a lofty tower. Wigan has besides a chapel of ease; and here are also two Roman Catholic chapels, and meeting-houses for different denominations of dissenters.

The Town Hall was erected in 1720, at the joint expense of the Earl of Barrymore and Sir Roger Bradshaw. A free-school and a blue-coat school have been founded here, and a dispensary upon an extensive scale. The inhabitants were formerly principally engaged in the manufacture of coarse linen, checks, and fustians, and in large brass and pewter works, but at present the cotton trade furnishes the chief employ. The coal trade is here also a profitable pursuit.

Wigan is a borough by prescription with the right of returning two members to parliament; it is incorporated under a mayor, recorder, twelve aldermen, and two bailiffs. In a field near Schole's Bridge a sulphurate spring has been discovered, the water of which resembles that at Harrowgate, in Yorkshire.

CHORLEY.

Chorley, a market town of Lancashire, is two miles on right of the Euxton Station of the North Union Railway, and 208¼ from London. It stands on the high road from Manchester to Preston, at a distance of 31½ miles from the former, and 9¼ from the latter town; and is situate near the source of a small rivulet called the Chor, which gives name to the place.

The river Yarrow, a valuable stream rising in the moors to the east, flows near the town, enriches the township, and gives motion to numerous mills that are erected on its banks; these, with the printing and bleaching grounds for many miles round, intermixed with cotton manufactories, communicate to the whole district an aspect of great activity and industry.

The church is an ancient pile of building, the walls of which are studded with coats of arms and old inscriptions, and the windows are decorated with various paintings. Here are also several dissenting chapels, a free grammar-school, several Sunday schools, and six alms-houses. A prison has also been erected here.

The vicinity of Chorley abounds in coal mines, and also with lead and alum, together with quarries of slate, flag, ashler, and mill-stones; the working of which, as well as the many machines erected of late years in the calico, muslin, and fustian branches, in conjunction with the print works and bleaching grounds, in all of which the inhabitants are more or less employed, have within a few years more than doubled its still increasing population.

The town is governed by one magistrate, who with other justices, hold a petty sessions here and at Rivington, in the neighbourhood, once a month alternately.

The Liverpool and Leeds deviation, and the Lancaster canal pass here, and by means of these and others with which they unite, and junction of the latter with the river Ribble at Preston, heavy merchandise is with ease transported to the eastern and western seas, the Trent, the Severn, and the Thames. The markets are on Wednesday and Saturday.

RIVINGTON.

Rivington, a large village, distant about 5 miles from Chorley, and where is a free grammar-school founded by Queen Elizabeth, is remarkable for a lofty hill on which is erected a high peak or beacon, that served in the civil wars as a watch-tower or signal-post: this is denominated Rivington Pike. From its commanding situation (1545 feet above the level of the sea,) and the beautiful and extensive views obtained from it, many parties frequent this elevated spot in the summer evenings. Rivington Pike is visible from many points of the North Union Railway.

PRESTON.

Preston, a market town of Lancashire, is distant $21\frac{1}{2}$ miles from Liverpool, $31\frac{1}{2}$ from Manchester, and $217\frac{1}{4}$ from London.

Preston is pleasantly situated on an agreeable eminence on the northern bank of the river Ribble, which here crossed by two handsome stone bridges, in a distance of about two miles from the town expands into a broad estuary, and soon falls into the Irish sea.

Respecting the antiquity of this town very little is recorded; though Camden remarks that it rose out of the ruins of *Ribchester*, a celebrated Roman station, which was situated farther up the river. It is said to have derived its name from the number of religious houses formerly existing here, and hence called Priest's town, afterwards contracted to Preston. As at present existing, Preston is a large, handsome, and well-built town, with broad, spacious, and irregular streets, chiefly formed of substantial houses; the whole is well paved and lighted with gas; manufactories and warehouses line the lesser thoroughfares, but within its boundaries and in its immediate vicinity are many large and elegant mansions, and surrounded by excellent roads whichever way approached, is characterised by features strongly indicative of wealth and prosperity. Near the town are also many fine walks, but the most favourite one is that of Enim, from which the Pretender is said to have viewed the town and country below it in 1745 with extraordinary emotion.

During the greater part of the last century the town was much resorted to as an agreeable retirement by old and respectable families of slender income; but having during the last forty years become the seat of very extensive manufacturing establishments, the character of the inhabitants has experienced a very great alteration. This change was in a great measure effected through the spirited exertions of a single individual, the late Mr. John Horrocks, who in the year 1791, commenced nearly without capital a small manufacture of muslin, and taking advantage of the vast improvement then introduced into cotton spinning, he formed several establishments in this branch of business, and in the course of a very few years became the master of no less than six large factories, and obtained influence sufficient to secure his return to parliament, without opposition, at the general election in 1802.

The population of the town had been nearly stationary for a full century previous to the year 1790, and generally estimated at 6000 persons, since which its rapid increase will be rendered apparent from the fact of its having attained in 1801 to 11,887, in 1819 to 21,958, in 1821 to 22,811, and in 1831 to 33,112, and it is now supposed to contain 40,000 persons.

The parish church is a large building, and the parish, which is large, has three chapels of ease,—Broughton, St. Lawrence, and the New Chapel.

The proportion of Roman Catholics is perhaps greater here than in any other town in England. This body of Christians (who have a magnificent college at Stoneyhurst, thirteen miles distant,) possess two large chapels; one of which, if not the finest, is the largest, in the kingdom, and both of them are generally well filled; the methodists have also a large meeting-house here, and in addition to these there are a quakers' meeting-house, and chapels and meeting-houses for the different denominations of dissenters.

Here is a free grammar-school, together with charity and Sunday schools in connection with the established church and dissenting congregations. A dispensary is also established here. The prison or penitentiary house, near the entrance of the town from Chorley by Walton Bridge, is constructed upon the plan of the late Mr. Howard. Here is a handsome town hall, with a suite of assembly rooms, and a good theatre; and the races held annually in the autumn on a beautiful race-course north of the town, are fully and fashionably attended.

The bridge over the Ribble by which the Railway reaches Preston is a beautiful stone structure; it consists of five arches of 120 feet span, and is altogether a great ornament to the town. The view from its summit, of vast extent, is justly esteemed one of the finest in England.

The inhabitants are principally engaged in the cotton trade, here carried on to a great extent; the coasting trade also employs many hands; the Ribble is only navigable for coasting vessels, but by means of the Lancaster canal, the Douglas navigation, the Leeds and Liverpool Canal, and others with which they unite, Preston possesses a water communication that extends to the Thames, the Severn, the Mersey, the Trent, the Ouse, the Humber, and the Dee.

It is governed by a mayor, recorder, seven aldermen, and seventeen capital burgesses, (who together form the common council of the borough,) and a town-clerk.

County courts and quarter sessions are held in this borough. The markets on Wednesday, Friday, and Saturday, are well supplied.

A sort of *carnival* or *jubilee*, denominated *Preston Guild*, is held every twenty years in confirmation of the charter granted to the burgesses of Preston by Henry II. This begins about the latter end of August. It lasts twenty-eight days, and invariably attracts a vast assemblage of company. Upon these occasions, the gentlemen at the head of the different manufacturing and trading establishments, preceded by bands of music, and displaying symbolical representations of their respective branches of manufacture and commerce, walk in procession through the principal streets of the town followed by their several workmen. The mayor and corporation, with the wardens of the different companies at the head of their incorporated bodies, each in their official dresses, and bearing their usual insignia, join the procession and proceed to church. The workmen upon these occasions are showily and characteristically habited; and the factory girls, elegantly and fancifully attired, add considerably to the interest of this imposing scene. The whole presents an extremely brilliant appearance, and forms altogether a grand spectacle. Public dinners are given, entertainments for the lower classes are provided, and races, plays, balls, and concerts are frequent during the continuance of this interesting festival.

THE PRESTON AND WYRE RAILWAY.

FROM PRESTON TO KIRKHAM, LYTHAM, BLACKPOOL, POULTON AND FLEETWOOD.

Of the Preston and Wyre Railway, with its branches, the following are the particulars, and distances:— From Preston to Lea road 3 miles; Salwick 6 miles; and Kirkham 9 miles; a little beyond which commences the branch to Lytham, distant from Preston 15 miles. In about 3 miles beyond Kirkham the Blackpool branch commences, completing in a total of 11 miles the distance between that town and Preston. Passing the Blackpool branch it is continued in a northern direction, to Poulton 15 miles, and in 5 miles more reaches Fleetwood, 20 miles from Preston. Fleetwood, not long since an insignificant village, principally owing to the exertions of Sir Peter Hesketh Fleetwood, Bart., whose seat, Rossal Hall, is in the vicinity, has rapidly risen in importance, and now ranks as a market town, and, for its size, may be deemed one of the busiest places in Lancashire. The church, dedicated to St. Peter, though small, is a neat structure; in addition to which there is a Roman Catholic chapel, with meeting-houses for the Independents, Wesleyans, and Quakers. The inhabitants are principally employed in commercial pursuits, and the carrying trade, both of which increase daily; it has also a small import and export trade with the East and West Indies. Steam vessels, second to none, run regularly between this place, Scotland, Ireland, and the Isle of Man; while by smaller ones daily communication is maintained with that portion of Lancashire denominated Furness, and the district of the lakes. Market day, Monday. Population, 2833.

Blackpool, as a bathing place, although not of much greater antiquity than Fleetwood, from the beauty and salubrity of its situation, the purity of the water, and the excellence of the beach, which, when the tide is out, is more than half a mile wide, has become one of the most attractive points in Lancashire. Here are excellent accommodations, good and extensive rides, rational amusements, and an infinite diversity of highly interesting prospects.

LONDON and BIRMINGHAM RAILWAY, ITINERARY LINE.

LONDON to BIRMINGHAM.

From *Euston Grove, Middlesex, to	
Camden Town, Park Street Bridge	1
Chalk Farm Lane	1¼
Primrose Hill Tunnel	1½
Kilburn Bridge	3¼
L.—*To London* 3 m.	
To Watford 11¾ m.—R.	
Kensal Green Tunnel	4¾
L.—*To London* 3½ m.	
To Harrow 6½ m.—R.	
The Mitre Bridge	5
Lower Place Gates	6
L.—*To Acton* 2¼ m.	
To London 5 m.—R.	
Brent River Viaduct	7
Harrow Road, Viaduct over	8
L.—*To Harrow* 3 m.	
To London 7 m.—R.	
Kenton Lane Viaduct	10¼
L.—*To Harrow* 1¼ m.	
To London 9½ m.—R.	
*Harrow Station	11½
L.—*To Harrow* 1¼ m.	
To Stanmore 2½ m.—R.	
Hatchend Bridge	12¾
L.—*To Pinner* 1 m.	
To Stanmore 2½ m.—R	
Dove House Bridge	13¼
L.—*To Pinner* 1½ m.	
To Stanmore 2½ m.—R.	
Weald Bridge	13¾
L.—*To Rickmansworth* 6 m.	
To Stanmore 3½ m.—R.	
Oxhey Lane Bridge	14½
L.—*To Pinner* 2 m.	
To Stanmore 3 m.—R.	
Watford Heath, *Herts*	15¼

PRIMROSE HILL TUNNEL, the formation of which occupied 2 years, is 1120 yards in length.

KENSAL GREEN TUNNEL is 320 yards in length, on left of it is the General Cemetery, where upon a beautiful enclosure tastefully disposed, and secure from depredation, a public company have established the first mortuary of its kind in the vicinity of the metropolis.

BRENT RIVER VIADUCT, on left, Twyford Abbey, *Mrs. Douglas.*

HARROW ROAD VIADUCT, on right, Wembly Park, *Rev. J. Gray*, and 1½ m. distant, the village of Kingsbury; its name denotes it to have been a royal residence, probably some of the Saxon monarchs. The church is supposed to occupy the site of a Roman encampment, and is partly built with Roman tiles. In this village Dr. Goldsmith had a temporary residence whilst preparing his " History of Animated Nature," and here is believed to have written his Vicar of Wakefield.

HARROW STATION, 2 m. distant, on right, Bentley Priory, *Marquis of Abercorn.*

Watford Heath Bridge....	15½	
Cross the London Road L.—*To Berkhampstead* 11½ *m.* *To London* 15 *m.*—R.		
Colne River Viaduct......	16¾	**WATFORD**, on left, Cashiobury Park, *Earl of Essex*, and 2 m. beyond Watford, The Grove, *Earl of Clarendon*.
**WATFORD* Station and Bridge, over the St. Albans and Rickmansworth Road..................	17¾	
L. {*To Watford* ½ *m.* *To Rickmansworth* 3¾ *m.*} *To St. Albans* 7 *m.*—R.		**WATFORD TUNNEL** is 1 mile in length.
Watford Tunnel	18½	
Hunton Bridge and Leavesden Green Road, Viaduct	20	
*King's Langley Station..	21	
L.—*To King's Langley* ½ *m.* *To St. Albans* 5 *m.*—R.		**HUNTON BRIDGE**, upon the hill, on left, Langley Bury, *E. F. Whittingstall*, Esq.
The Iron Bridge	22	
Cross the Grand Junction Canal and River Gade		
London Road, Viaduct over	22½	
L.—*To London* 21 *m.* {*To Hemel Hempstead* 2 *m.* *To Berkhampstead* 4½ *m.*} R.		**TWO WATERS**, on right, Nash Mill, the seat of *John Dickinson*, whose vast manufactory of paper here, worked by machinery, of astonishing capability, will amply gratify by a visit all who have the good fortune to obtain access thereto.
Two Waters, Hemel Hempstead, and Bovingdon Road Viaduct over	23	
L.—*To Bovingdon* 2¾ *m.* *To Hemel Hempstead* 1½ *m.*—R.		
*Boxmoor Station and London Road, Viaduct over	24¾	
L.—*To Berkhampstead* 3 *m.* *To London* 23 *m.*—R. *To Hemel Hempstead* 1½ *m.*—R.		**BOXMOOR**, on left, Westbrook Hay, *Hon. G. D. Ryder*.
Grand Junction Canal, Viaduct over	25¼	
Berkhampstead and Hemel Hempstead Road, Viaduct over	27½	

Itinerary Line. 214

L.—To Berkhampstead ¼ m.	BERKHAMPSTEAD, on left, Bartletts, late *Mrs. Pechell;* Ashlins Hall, *T. Smith*, Esq.; and Haresfoot, *T. Dorrien*, Esq.; on right of Berkhampstead, is Berkhampstead Place, *The Hon. Miss Grimston*, and at Hemel Hempstead, Gadesbridge, *Sir Astley Paston Cooper*, Bart.
To Hemel Hempstead 2 m.	
*BERKHAMPSTEAD 27¾	
To Hemel Hempstead 4½ m. ⎫ R.	
To Dunstable 11 m. ⎭	
Northchurch Tunnel...... 28½	NORTHCHURCH TUNNEL, is 360 yards in length; over it the Road from Northchurch to Dunstable, executed at the expense of the late Earl of Bridgewater, is carried: this Road conducts also to Ashridge Park, the magnificent seat of the *Countess of Bridgewater*, 1 m. distant, on right; the column in the Park, erected to the memory of the late Earl by his Countess, is visible from the Railway, a little before Tring Station.
Northcote Court Viaduct.. 30¼	
Wiggington and Aldbury Viaduct 31	
*PENDLY OR TRING STATION at Tring Summit,	
And Tring and Albury Viaduct 31¾	
L. ⎧ To Tring 2 m.	
⎨ To Wendover 6 m.	NORTHCOTE COURT VIADUCT, leads to Northcote Court, on right, the seat of — *Locksley*, Esq.
⎩ To Aylesbury 8¾ m.	
To Ivinghoe 3¼ m.—R.	
Pitstone Green, Bucks 34¼	TRING STATION, 1½ m. distant, on right, Stocks House, —— *Gordon*, Esq., 2 m. distant, on left, is Tring Park, *Mrs. Kay*.
Seabrook Bridge 34¾	
Cross the Grand Junction Canal	
Aylesbury Railway 35¼	
L.—To Aylesbury m. 7½	LEIGHTON BUZZARD STATION, 3½ m. distant, on right, Stockgrove, *Col. Hammer*.
Cheddington 36¾	
Horton 37	
Broughton Brook Bridge 39¼	
Southcott or	LINSLADE TUNNEL, is 290 yards in length; a little beyond it, on right, see Grand Junction Canal, and shortly after Linslade House, the seat of *W. Pulsford*, Esq., and the Village Church. About 2 m. distant, on left, is Liscombe House, *Miss Lovett*.
*LEIGHTON BUZZARD Station 40¾	
L.—To Aylesbury 10 m.	
To Leighton Buzzard ½ m. ⎫	
To Woburn 8 m. ⎬ R.	
To Bedford 23 m. ⎭	
Linslade Tunnel 41¼	STOKE HAMMOND ROAD, see on right, upon an eminence, Great Brickhill, and Great Brickhill Manor House, the seat of *P. P. Duncombe*, Esq.
Stoke Hammond Viaduct.. 44¼	
Fenny Stratford and Winslow Road, Viaduct over 45¼	
L.—To Winslow 8 m.	
To Fenny Stratford 2¼ m. —R.	STOKE HAMMOND ROAD, see on left, the village of Stewkley.
*Bletchley Station 46¾	BLETCHLEY STATION, 4½ m. distant, on left, Whaddon Hall, *W. S. Lowndes*, Esq.
L.—To Buckingham 11¼ m.	

To Fenny Stratford 1 m. —R.		
Denbigh Hall Viaduct	47¾	LOUGHTON, 1 m. distant, on left, Shenley House, *W. Bailey*, Esq.
Cross the London and Birmingham Road		
L.{ To Stoney Stratford 6¼ m. To Birmingham 63½ m.		WOLVERTON STATION, 3½ m. distant, on right, Linford House, *H Uthwatt*, Esq.; on left of Wolverton is Wolverton House, *Rev. H. R. Quartley*, Wolverton Park, *R. Harrison*, Esq., Cosgrove Hall, *Major Mansell*, Cosgrove Priory, *unoccupied*, and 3½ m. distant, Wakefield Lodge, *Duke of Grafton*, 5½ m. distant, Thornton Hall, *Sir T C. Sheppard*, Bart., and Wicken Park, *Lord Dungannon*.
To Fenny Stratford 1¼ m. and to London 46 m. }R.		
Woughton Road Viaduct	49	
Loughton..............	50¼	
Bradwell	51¼	
*Wolverton Station and Viaduct	52½	
L.—To Stoney Stratford 1¾ m.		
To Newport Pagnell 4¼ m. To Oundle 9¼ m. }R.		CASTLETHORPE, 1 m. distant, on right, Hanslope Park, *W. Watts*, Esq., 3 m. distant, Gayhurst, *Lord Carrington*, and Tyringham, *J. B. Praed*, Esq.
Cross the Grand Junction Canal and Rivers Ouse and Tove		
Castlethorpe	54½	
Ashton	58¾	
*Roade Station, Northamptonshire	60	
L.—To Towcester 6½ m. To Northampton 5½ m. —R.		ROADE, on right, Courteenhall House, *Sir W. Wake*, Bart., 3 m. distant, Preston Deanery, *L. Christie*, Esq., and 4 m. distant, Delapré Abbey, *E. Bouverie*, Esq., 2 m. distant, on left, is Stoke Park, *L. Vernon*, Esq.
*Blisworth Station	62½	
L.—To Towcester 4 m. To Northampton 5 m.— R.		
Grand Junction Canal Viaduct	63	
Bugbrook Viaduct	66½	
Stowe Tunnel, under the London and Birmingham Road.................	68¼	WEEDON STATION, 2⅔ m. distant, on left, Everdon Hall, *Mrs. Philpot*, and 4 m. distant, Fawsley Park, *Sir Charles Knightley*, Bart., on left of Weedon is Flower House, late *R. Pack*, Esq.
L.{ To Towcester 6¾ m. To London 66¾ m.		
To Daventry 5½ m.—R.		
*Weedon Station	69¾	
Cross the London and Birmingham Road		

Itinerary Line.

L.—To Daventry 4 m.	
To Northampton 8¼ m.	
To Towcester 8 m.	R.
To London 68 m.	
Brockhall Bridge	71¼
Whilton Bridge	72½
Long Buckby Viaduct	73½
L.—To Daventry 3 m.	
To Long Buckby, 1¾ m.—R.	
Cross Grand Junction Canal	
Grand Union Canal, Viaduct	74¼
*Crick Station	75¼
Kilsby Tunnel	76¾
Hill Moreton Viaduct, Warwickshire	79¼
Cross the Oxford Canal and London Road	
L.—To Rugby 3 m.	
To Northampton 16½ m.	R.
To London 82½ m.	
Clifton Viaduct	82¼
L.—To Rugby 1 m.	
To Lutterworth 7½ m.—R.	
*Rugby Station	83¼
L. { To Rugby ½ m. To Southam 12 m. To Leamington 14 m. To Warwick 16 m.	
To Lutterworth 7 m.	R.
To Leicester 20 m.	
Long Lawford	85
Church Lawford	86¼
*Brandon Station and Viaduct	89¼
Cross the River Avon	
Brandon oblique Bridge	89¾
Sow Viaduct	90¼
Cross the River Sow, and enter the County of Coventry	
Sherborne Bridge	92
Cross the River Sherborne	
Coventry and Southam Road Viaduct over	92¼
L.—To Southam 13 m.	

BROCKHALL BRIDGE, on right, Brockhall Park, *T. R. Thornton*, Esq.

WHILTON BRIDGE, on left, Norton Hall, *B. Botfield*, Esq.

LONG BUCKBY VIADUCT, 2 m. distant, on left, Welton House, *G. Weildon*, Esq., and 1½ m. further to the left, Bragborough House, *R. H. Lamb*, Esq.

CRICK STATION, 2 m. distant, on left, Ashby Lodge, *G. H. Arnold*, Esq., and on right, Watford Park,

KILSBY TUNNEL, is 1 m. and 640 yards in length. From the summit of the hill through which it passes, in the vicinity of Kilsby, a beautiful view is obtained, of which the railway forms a very interesting feature.

HILL MORETON VIADUCT, on right, Hill Moreton Manor House, *T. Townsend*, Esq.

RUGBY, on left, Rugby Lodge, *T. Caldecott*, Esq., 2 m. distant is Bilton House, *Hon. J. B. Simpson*, Cawston House, *Lord John Scott*, and 3 m. distant, Bilton Grange, *Capt. Hibbert;* on right of Rugby is Newbold Grange, *T. Walker*, Esq., 1 m. distant is Newbold Vicarage, *Rev. J. T. Parker*, Brownsover House, *J. W. Boughton Leigh*, Esq., 2 m. distant, Coton House, *Marchioness of Queensberry*, 4 m. distant, Newbold Hall, *Sir Grey Skipwith*, Bart., and 5 m. distant, Newnham Padox, *Earl of Denbigh*.

LONG LAWFORD, on right, Holbrook Grange, *J. Caldecott*, Esq.

BRANDON STATION, on right, Brandon House, *J. Beech*, Esq., 2 m. distant, Combe Abbey, *Earl of Craven*, and on left, the ruins of Brandon Castle.

*P 5

To Coventry ½ m.—R.
*COVENTRY Station .. 94
L. { *To Kenilworth 5 m.* / *To Leamington 9½.* / *To Warwick 10 m.* }
{ *To Lutterworth 15½ m.* / *To Nuneaton 8¼ m.* / *To Tamworth 18½ m.* } R.
One mile and a quarter beyond the Coventry Station cross a branch of the river Avon and re-enter Warwickshire
Fletchamstead 95¾
Beechwood Bridge 98¼
Beechwood Tunnel, end of 98½
Dockers Lane Bridge 99¼
Berkswell Bridge 99¾
Wooton Green Viaduct .. 100¼
Cross the Kenilworth and Coleshill Road
L.—*To Kenilworth 5¼ m.*
To Coleshill 7½ m.—R.
Blythe Viaduct 102¼
Cross the river Blythe
*Hampton Station, and Birmingham and Derby Junction Railway
{ *To Derby by Railway 38½ m.* } R.
London and Birmingham Road.................. 104
L.—*To Birmingham 8½ m.*
To London 101 m.—R.
Marston Green Viaduct .. 105
Easthall Viaduct 105½
Cross a branch of the Cole
Sheldon Viaduct 106½
Cross a branch of the Cole, and enter Worcestershire
Stichford Bridge 109
Cross the River Cole, and re-enter Warwickshire
**BIRMINGHAM* 112¼

COVENTRY, 2 m. before on left, Whitley Abbey, *Dowager Lady Hood.* On left of Coventry is the Charter House, *unoccupied,* 1½ m. distant, Stivichall Hall, *Capt. Gregory,* 3 m. distant, Baginton Hall, *Samuel Clark Jervoise,* Esq., 4 m. distant, Stoneleigh Abbey, *Lord Leigh,* and 5½ m. distant, the ruins of Kenilworth Castle, on right of Coventry is Hawkesbury Hall, *F. Parrot,* Esq., and 2 m. distant, Allesley Park, *James Beck,* Esq.

BERKSWELL BRIDGE, on right, is Berkswell Hall, *Sir John Eardley Wilmot,* Bart.

HAMPTON STATION, 1½ m. distant, on right, is Packington Hall, *Earl of Aylesford,* 2 m. distant, Meriden Hall, *Lady Sykes,* and 5 m. distant, Maxstoke Castle, *T. Dilke,* Esq.

LONDON AND BIRMINGHAM ROAD, 1½ m. distant, Elmdon Hall, *unoccupied.*

MARSTON GREEN VIADUCT, ½ m. before on left, Marston Hall, *C. Thornley,* Esq.

SHELDON VIADUCT, 1 m. distant, on right, Sheldon Hall, *G. Chilwell,* Esq. and ½ m. beyond it Lea Hall, —— *Brown,* Esq.

Grand Junction Railway.

BIRMINGHAM to LIVERPOOL by the GRAND JUNCTION RAILWAY.

*BIRMINGHAM, Warw., to
The Coleshill Road 1
  To Coleshill 8 m.—R.
Birmingham and Fazeley
  Canal and Sutton Cold-
  field Road.............. 1¼
    To Sutton Coldfield 5½ m. ⎫
    To Tamworth 13 m.   ⎬ R.
*Perry Bar, *Staffordshire*.. 3¼
  To Walsall 5½ m.—R.
  L.—*To Birmingham* 4¼ m.
The Walsall Road........ 5
  To Walsall 4¼ m.—R.
*Newton Road 6½
*Bescot Bridge 9¼
  L. ⎰ *To Wednesbury* 1¼ m.
     ⎱ *To Dudley* 5½ m.
  To Walsall 1½ m.—R.
*James Bridge 10
  L.—*To Darlaston* ¾ m.
  To Walsall 2 m.—R.
Cross the Dudley extension Canal
*Willenhall 11¾
  L. ⎰ *To Bilston* 1½ m.
     ⎱ *To Wolverhampton* 3 m.
  To Walsall 3¼ m.—R.
Tunnel 13¾
WOLVERHAMPTON
  STATION 14
    ⎧ *To Wolverhampton* 1 m.
    ⎪ *To Stourbridge* 10 m.
  L.⎨ *To Shifnall* 13½ m.
    ⎪ *To Bridgenorth* 14 m.
    ⎩ *To Kidderminster* 15½ m.
  To Walsall 7 m.—R.
Staffordsh. and Worcestersh.
Canal Viaduct at Slade Heath 18½
  L.—*To Wolverhampton* 6½ m.
*Four Ashes 19¾
  L.—*To Brewood* 2 m.
*The Spread Eagle 21¼
  L. ⎰ *To Shiffnal* 12 m.
     ⎱ *To Shrewsbury* 27½ m.

THE GRAND JUNCTION RAILWAY.—This great work commences in Curzon Street, Birmingham, in the county of Warwick, at an elevation of 365 feet above the level of low water at Liverpool, and skirting the eastern extremity of the town, is carried thence with an easy sweep and gradual descent across the Coleshill Road, the Birmingham and Fazely Canal, and the Sutton Coldfield Road. At this point it passes Aston Park, where, approached by an avenue of trees, stands Aston Hall, a noble and commanding edifice, erected by Sir Thomas Holt, bart. in the reign of James the first and his successor; it is now the property of *James Watt*, Esq. whose father, by his improvement of the steam engine, and successful application of its herculean power, has erected an imperishable monument to his memory. From the Sutton Coldfield Road the Railway is continued in a direction nearly northwest on the confines of Aston Park, which with the county of Warwick it quits, and enters Staffordshire about three quarters of a mile before arriving at Perry Bar, the first station from Birmingham. From Perry Bar, crossing the valley of the Tame, and passing Perry Hall on the right, the seat of *John Gough*, Esq. it soon reaches the Walsall Road. Here upon the left stands the noble old mansion of Hamstead Hall, the residence of *J. L. Moilliet*, Esq. and the most distinguished feature of the agreeable village of Handsworth. The grounds of this seat winding along the banks of the Tame are pleasing and romantic, being covered with a profusion of stately trees; here a lime placed on a rocky eminence is particularly remarkable for its uncommon size, its height being 70 feet, and the shadow which it throws extending to 160. 2 miles distant from the Walsall Road on right is Great Barr Hall, the seat of *Sir E. D. Scott*, Bart. From the Walsall Road, the Railway continuing its course along the valley of Tame, soon gains the Newton Road, the second

To Cannock 4¾ m. To Lichfield 14 m. } R.	
*PENKRIDGE	23¾
Cross the river Penk	
To Cannock 4½ m.—R.	
*STAFFORD	29
To Sandon 4½ m. To Rugeley 9¾ m. To Uttoxeter 13½ m. To Lichfield 17 m. } R.	
L.—To Newport 13 m.	
*Great Bridgeford	32½
To Stafford 3¼ m.—R.	
L.—To Eccleshall 3¾ m.	
*Norton Bridge	34¾
L.—To Eccleshall 2¼ m.	
To Stone 3¼ m. To Cheadle 13¼ m. } R.	
Stableford Bridge	41½
To Trentham 5 m. To Lane End 7 m. } R.	
L.—To Market Drayton 10¼ m.	
*Whitmore	43
To Newcastle-under-Lyme 4¼ m. To Trentham 5 m. To Leek 16m. } R.	
L.—To Market Drayton 10 m.	
*Great Madely	45¾
To Newcastle-under-Lyme 5½ m. To the Potteries 7 m. } R.	
L.—To Audlem 7¾ m.	
Wrine Hill, Cheshire	47¾
L.—To Nantwich 6½ m.	
To Newcastle-under-Lyme 6¼ m.—R.	
Basford	51½
L.—To Nantwich 4½ m.	
To Newcastle-under-Lyme 4½ m.—R.	
*Crewe	53¾
L.—To Nantwich 5 m.	

station from Birmingham, 2¾ m. beyond which it reaches Bescot Bridge, the third station—on right of Bescot Bridge stands Bescot Hall, the residence of *W. Marshall*, Esq. This seat and the surrounding inclosures are finely decked with luxuriant foliage, and from their general elevation above the level of the surrounding country, display a very extensive and interesting view. From Bescot Bridge, where it crosses the road from Wednesbury to Walsall, the Railway continues its course along the left bank of the Tame to James Bridge, this is the fourth station from Birmingham; 1 m. distant, on right of James Bridge, is Bentley Hall, the seat of *E. Anson*, Esq. This place is remarkable as having been the property of Col. Lane, who, together with his sister, so much distinguished themselves in concealing and effecting the escape of King Charles the Second after his defeat at the decisive battle of Worcester. From Bescot Bridge the Railway takes a north-west direction to Willenhall, the fifth station, 4 m. on right of which is Hilton Hall, the property of *Col. Vernon Graham*. 2¼ m. from Willenhall, by a viaduct thrown over the Essington and Wyrley canal, and in its immediate vicinity it reaches the Wolverhampton station, the sixth from Birmingham; 3 m. distant from Wolverhampton on left is Wrottesley Hall, the seat of *Sir J. Wrottesley*, Bart. The inclination of the Railway from Birmingham is that of a gradual descent for 2½ m. after which, proceeding upon a level for ½ a m., it is then altered to a very gentle rise from that point all the way to Wolverhampton, where it attains a height of 440 feet above the level of low water at Liverpool. From the Wolverhampton station the Railway is carried with an easy sweep to the northward, and passing the confines of that busy town, crosses the Staffordshire and Worcestershire canal, at a distance of 4½ m. from Wolverhampton, in 1¼ m. further it reaches Four Ashes, the

To Sandbach 5 *m.*
To Congleton $11\frac{1}{2}$ *m.* } R.
To Macclesfield 19 *m.*
*Church Coppenhall ...... $55\frac{3}{4}$
*Minshull Vernon .... $58\frac{1}{2}$
Middlewich Canal Viaduct. $59\frac{1}{2}$
*Winsford 61
L.—*To Chester* 18 *m.*
To Middlewich $2\frac{1}{2}$ *m.*—R.
Vale Royal Viaduct 64
Cross the River Weaver
*Hartford................ $65\frac{1}{2}$
To Northwich 2 *m.*
To Knutsford 9 *m.* } R.
L. { *To Tarporley* 8 *m.*
To Chester 16 *m.*
Weaverham .... $66\frac{1}{2}$
L.—*To Chester* $15\frac{1}{2}$ *m.*
To Warrington $9\frac{1}{2}$ *m.*—R.
*Acton 68
Dutton Viaduct .... $69\frac{1}{2}$
Cross the River Weaver
Frodsham and Northwich Road................ $71\frac{3}{4}$
L.—*To Frodsham* $3\frac{1}{2}$ *m.*
To Northwich 8 *m.*—R.
*Preston Brook .... $72\frac{1}{4}$
L.—*To Frodsham* 4 *m.*
To Warrington $5\frac{1}{2}$ *m.*—R.
*Moore................... $74\frac{3}{4}$
Warrington Viaduct ...... $76\frac{3}{4}$
Cross the Mersey and Irwell Canal and River Mersey
**WARRINGTON*
Lancashire .... $77\frac{3}{4}$
L.—*To Liverpool* $17\frac{3}{4}$ *m.*
To Manchester $18\frac{1}{2}$ *m.*—R.
*Liverpool and Manchester Railway, Newton Junction $82\frac{1}{2}$
**LIVERPOOL*......... $97\frac{1}{4}$

Or

*Newton Junction as above $82\frac{1}{2}$
**MANCHESTER*....... $98\frac{1}{4}$

N. B.—The particulars of the road from Newton Junction to

seventh station. On left of Four Ashes is Somerford Hall, *Edward Monckton*, Esq. beyond which is Chillington Park, *T. W. Giffard*, Esq. From Four Ashes it extends in $1\frac{1}{4}$ m. more to the Spread Eagle, the eighth station from Birmingham. At the Spread Eagle, the Railway crosses the high road from Lichfield to Shrewsbury, and from Birmingham through Walsall to the latter town, and $2\frac{1}{2}$ m. further passes close to the town of Penkridge, the ninth station from Birmingham, $2\frac{1}{4}$ m. on right of Penkridge is Teddesley Hall, *Lord Hathertom.* At Penkridge the Railway crosses the river Penk, and is thence carried forward to Stafford, the tenth station. The environs of Stafford, but more particularly the vicinity of Trentham, present a succession of sylvan scenery unrivalled in beauty, and of a most enchanting character; to the west of the town, Castle Church, hill, and Billington camp, from their elevated position stand forth the most prominent objects of the surrounding country. From Stafford the Railway traversing the valley of the Sow for $3\frac{1}{2}$ m. reaches Great Bridgeford, the eleventh station, where crossing that river, to which it runs parallel in a further distance of $2\frac{1}{4}$ m. it extends to Norton Bridge, the twelfth station from Birmingham. From hence, still traversing its valley, and occasionally crossing the Sow, to which river it continues to run parallel for a distance of $6\frac{3}{4}$ m., it at length reaches Stableford Bridge, $1\frac{1}{2}$ m. from whence it gains Whitmore, the thirteenth station from Birmingham. From Whitmore, proceeding in a direct line for a distance of $2\frac{3}{4}$ m. it passes close to Great Madely, the fourteenth station from Birmingham. From Great Madely it proceeds to the left of Wrine Hill, just previous to reaching which it quits Staffordshire, after traversing that county for upwards of forty-four miles, and enters Cheshire. Leaving Wrine Hill, it proceeds in a line

Liverpool, and from Newton Junction to Manchester, are given in the following road, which is the line of the Liverpool and Manchester Railway. The total distance from London to Liverpool by the London and Birmingham, and Grand Junction Railways, is 209½ m. and from London to Manchester 210½ m.

nearly direct, and with a gradual descent, which it has done all the way from Great Madely to the village of Basford, where crossing the road from Nantwich to Newcastle at 1¾ m. distance from Basford it reaches Crewe, the fifteenth station from Birmingham. On right of Crewe is Crewe Hall, the magnificent mansion of *Lord Crewe*. Two miles beyond Crewe it reaches Church Coppenhall, the sixteenth station, and in two miles and a quarter farther extends to Minshull Vernon, the seventeenth station from Birmingham. From Minshull Vernon its course is, with the exception of a short level, by a gradual descent, crossing in its way the Middlewich canal, to Winsford, a further distance of two miles and a half, this is the eighteenth station; here the Railway crosses the road from Chester to Middlewich, which latter place it leaves two miles distant on the right. After reaching Winsford, it gradually descends to Vale Royal Viaduct, a distance of three miles, where crossing the river Weaver, in a farther distance of a mile and a half, it arrives at Hartford, the nineteenth station from Birmingham. On left of Vale Royal Viaduct, surrounded by its beautiful grounds, stands Vale Royal Abbey, the noble seat of *Lord Delamere*. Here it may not be improper to remark that the Railway, from its entrance into Cheshire till its arrival at this spot, traverses a most beautiful valley, crossing in its course some of the richest grazing land in the kingdom, and whence is transmitted to the metropolis among many other valuable productions, the well known article of Cheshire cheese. The character of Vale Royal may be gathered from its name, which in common candour it must be admitted is most appropriate. From Vale Royal Viaduct the Railway proceeds on a level to Hartford, a distance of four miles and a half from Winsford, and there reaches the nineteenth station from Birmingham. At Hartford the Railway crosses the high road from Chester to Northwich, passing the latter place at a distance of two miles on the right; from Hartford it proceeds to Weaverham, where crossing the road from Tarporley to Warrington, it shortly afterwards reaches Acton, a distance of three miles and a half from Hartford, and the twentieth station from Birmingham. From Hartford its course runs parallel to the Weaver, which river it reaches by a gradual descent, and then crosses at Dutton Viaduct, from whence it proceeds first with a gradual declination and subsequently an easy ascent to Preston Brook, the twenty-first station from Birmingham. From Preston Brook, where it crosses the road from Frodsham to Warrington, the Railway continuing its course at no great distance from the Duke of Bridgewater's canal, proceeds with a gentle descent and easy sweep to Moore, the twenty-second station from Birmingham; two miles beyond Moore is Warrington Viaduct, thrown over the Mersey and Irwell canal, and the river Mersey, at a distance of one mile from whence it reaches Warrington, the twenty-third station, round which it sweeps, and by a gradual rise of about three miles, but somewhat sudden ascent in the fourth, reaches Newton Junction upon the Liverpool and Manchester Railway, the twenty-fourth station from Birmingham, at a distance of eighty-two miles and a quarter from that town, and where terminates the line of the Grand Junction Railway.

LIVERPOOL and MANCHESTER RAILWAY.

*LIVERPOOL, Lancas., to Broad Green Gate	3½
*Huyton Lane Gate	5¾
*Kendrick's Cross	9
St. Helens and Runcorn Railway	12
*Grand Junction Railway	14¾
*Newton Bridge	15¾
L. { To Newton ¼ m. To Wigan 7½ m. To Leigh 5 m.	
To Warrington 5 m.—R.	
*Parkside	
*North Union Railway	16½
*Bolton and Leigh Railway	18¾
*Bury Lane	20¾
*Lamb's Cottage	23
*Patricroft	26½
L.—To Bolton 7 m. To Warrington 10 m.—R.	
*Eccles	27½
L.—To Manchester 3¾ m. To Warrington 14¾ m.—R.	
*MANCHESTER	30½

LIVERPOOL, 2 m. beyond, on right, Childwall Hall, *Marquis of Salisbury.*

HUYTON, 1 m. distant, on left, The Hazles, *Sir T. Birch*, Bart. and 2 m distant, Knowsley Park, *Earl of Derby*, 1 m. beyond, Huyton on right, Halsnead Hall, *R. Willis*, Esq.

KENDRICK'S CROSS, 2. m. beyond, on left, Shirley Hall, *M. Hughes*, Esq. and on right, Bold Hall, *Sir H. Bold Hoghton*, Bart.

NEWTON BRIDGE, on left, Golborne Park, *Miss Scarisbrick*, and 2 m. distant, New Hall, *Sir John Gerard*, Bart.

PATRICROFT, 1 m. distant, on left, Worsley Hall, *R. H. Bradshaw*, Esq. and on right, Trafford Park, *T. J. Trafford*, Esq.

The LIVERPOOL and MANCHESTER RAILWAY commences by an ascent through a tunnel of above a mile in length, to the farther extremity of which the trains are drawn by a stationary engine erected for the purpose; here the locomotive engines commence running, first upon a level of about ¾ of a mile, when an almost imperceptible descent is commenced, upon which it is continued for a further distance of 5 miles; from this point it ascends a rapid rise of 1½ m. and thereby attains an elevation of 200 feet above the level of low water at Liverpool; upon that level it is continued for a distance of 2 m. when it commences a descent equalling in degree its previous sudden elevation, and down which the carriages need not the propelling power of steam, to conduct them with great rapidity. In a farther distance of 3 m. constructed upon a very gradual elevation, it reaches the point of union with the Grand Junction Railway. From this point the inclination of the Railway is that of a slight descent for a distance of rather more than 6 m., it is then continued upon a very gradual rise for a distance of about 5¼ m. when it attains a level of rather more than 4 m. upon which it is continued to Manchester.

PICKERING and WHITBY RAILWAY.

*PICKERING, Yorks., to The Newton Road	¾
Leavisham Brook	4¼
Newton and Leavisham Road	6

THE PICKERING and WHITBY RAILWAY commences at Bakehouse Lane, in Pickering, and following the course of Pickering Beck, a small stream, in a distance of 4¼ m. reaches Leavisham Brook, here passing the villages of Newton on the left,

Raindale Mill	7
Saltersgate Brook	10
Fen Steps Summit	12¼
Goadland and Pickering Rd.	13¼
Goadland and Whitby Road	14½
Beck Hole	15½
Road from Growmond Brdg.	17¾
Growmond Abbey	18
Esk Hall	21
Whitby and Pickering Road	21¼
Suspension Bridge	22½
WHITBY	24

and Leavisham and Lockton on the right, and following the windings of the Pickering Beck through Newton Valley, and occasionally crossing that stream in a further distance of 2¾ m. it reaches Raindale Mill, in about 3 m. more extends to Saltersgate Brook, 2¼ m. from which it attains the summit at Fen Steps. The inclination of the Railway from its commencement to the Newton and Leavisham Road, a distance of six miles, is that of a very gradual rise, from that point the acclivity increases, and in that way with very little variation it is continued to Fen Steps, the Summit, where it attains an elevation of 535 feet above the level of low water at Whitby. From Fen Steps the Railway takes a north-eastern direction, and in a nearly direct line continues with a very gradual declination to the Goadland and Whitby Roads, from whence it proceeds in a straight line with a somewhat sudden descent to Beck Hole. From Beck Hole it follows the course of the Eske, through Goadland Dale, in its way, crossing the Eske three times, two of which occur in the immediate vicinity of Growmond Abbey, reaching that place in a total distance of eighteen miles from Whitby. From Growmond Abbey it is carried through Eskdale, occasionally coursing, and seven times crossing the river Esk to the garden of Esk Hall, the seat of *J. C. Coates*, Esq. in a farther distance of 1½ m. it gains the Suspension Bridge over the Esk, and in 1¼ m. farther reaches Whitby, to which place it is continued upon a very gradual descent all the way from Beck Hole. The Whitby and Pickering Railway belongs not to the class that may be literally said to "annihilate both time and space," locomotive engines not being employed thereon, its inclination being unfavourable to the propelling power of that valuable machine, which, notwithstanding its astonishing capability, in cases of sudden elevation utterly fails; stationary engines are consequently made available in ascending the steeper acclivities, while upon the more gradual rise, the moderate descent and level portions of the line horses are employed; the visitors to the Whitby and Pickering Railway will nevertheless have no reason to regret the absence of a rapidity that would most assuredly detract from and very considerably diminish the interest of this delightful ride, the Railway passing as it does through a country unrivalled for the beauty and diversified nature of its scenery; upon this subject, however, the contracted space to which these remarks are necessarily confined, leave the Editor no room for enlargement, to those, therefore, who may feel inclined to doubt this assertion, he confidently refers for confirmation to a very beautiful work with plates, descriptive and illustrative of the very interesting country by which it is environed. As a further proof of its attraction, it may not be improper to remark, that in one month during the summer of 1836, nearly 5000 persons were conveyed upon it, an immense number, taking into consideration its vast distance from the metropolis, the places whence it starts and where terminates.

⁎ An alteration has taken place in the arrangements of the Whitby and Pickering Railway, which is now wholly worked by locomotive power.

LEEDS and SELBY RAILWAY.

*LEEDS, Yorkshire, to	
*Garforth	6½
*Micklefield	9
*Milford	12
*Hambleton	16
*SELBY	20

right, Gateforth Hall, *H. Osbaldeston,* Esq. This seat being situate upon an eminence, commands a beautiful and very extensive prospect. Hambleton Haugh, on right of Hambleton, and Brayton Barfe, 1½ m. beyond that place, the latter measuring nearly 100 acres, are two insulated round hills, that form interesting objects in a country, otherwise remarkable for its flatness. N. B. All the places named on this line are Stations, and Passengers can consequently be taken up or set down at any of them. In connexion with the Leeds and Selby Railway, there are two first-rate steam packets which ply between Selby and Hull, the distance by water being 43 m. and by the road 34½ m.; it may also be added, that Railroads from Selby to Hull, and from Selby to Manchester, are at present in progress, which, when perfected, will complete a line of 140 m. in length, thereby uniting the ports of Liverpool and Hull.

LEEDS, 3½ m. beyond, on right, Temple Newsham, *Marquis of Hertford.*

GARFORTH, 2 m. distant, on right, Kippax Park, *T. D. Bland,* Esq.

MICKLEFIELD, 2 m. distant, on left, Parlington House, *R. O. Gascoigne,* Esq. 2 m. distant, on right, is Ledstone Hall, *C. Wilson,* Esq.

HAMBLETON, 1 m. distant, on

BOLTON and LEIGH and KENYON JUNCTION RAILWAY.

*Kenyon Stocks, *Lancas.*, to	
The Newton and Leigh Road	1½
L.—*To Newton* 4¼ *m.*	
To Leigh 1 *m.*—R.	
Wigan and Manchester canal	2
*LEIGH	2¾
Manchester and Chorley Road	6¼
L.—*To Chorley* 9¾ *m.*	
To Manchester 10 *m.*—R.	
Leigh and Bolton Road	8¼
To Leigh 6 *m.*—R.	
L.—*To Bolton* 1¼ *m.*	
*BOLTON	9¾

for a further distance of rather more than 1½ m.; for the next ½ m. the ascent is moderate, after which it enters upon an acclivity so steep as to render necessary the assistance of a stationary engine erected for the purpose, and by which the trains are drawn from the bottom to the top, and on their return lowered. From hence its course is that of a gradual rise for 2¼ m. and for the next ¼ m. nearly upon a level, in ¾ m. farther it enters upon a rapid descent of ¾ m. where another stationary engine is employed to raise and lower the trains, and in another ½ m. of more moderate descent it reaches Bolton.

MANCHESTER and CHORLEY ROAD, on right, Hulton Hall, *W. Hulton,* Esq.

The BOLTON and LEIGH and KENYON JUNCTION RAILWAY commences at Kenyon Stocks, upon the Liverpool and Manchester Railway, by a very gradual descent of rather more than one eighth of a mile, when it attains a level of 1242½ yards, not quite ¾ of a mile in length; here it commences a rise of 737½ yards, about three eighths of a mile, this is succeeded by a level of 44 yards, after which it descends for 150 yards, and thus reaches a short level of 100 yards in length. From this point the Railway is constructed upon a very gradual rise for rather more than ¾ of a mile, when the acclivity very considerably increases, and so continues

NEWCASTLE and CARLISLE RAILWAY.

NEWCASTLE-upon-Tyne, Northumberland, to
The Tyne river Viaduct	2¾
*Blaydon, or Scotswood	3½
*Wylam	7½
*Stocksfield, or Bywell	12
*Corbridge	16¾
Famley Tunnel	17
*HEXHAM	20

To Bellingham 16 m.—R.
South Tyne Viaduct	22½
*Four Stones	24¼
*Haydon Bridge	27¾

L.—To Aldstone Moor 15¼ m.
*Bardon Mill	31
*HALTWHISTLE	37¾
Haltwhistle Tunnel	38¼
Greenhead	40¾
*Rose Hill	43

To Gilsland Spa 2½ m.—R.
Low Row, *Cumberland*	46
*Milton, or Brampton Station	48¾

To Brampton 1½ m.—R.
How Mill	52¼
*Corby and Wetherall Viaduct	55¼

Cross the river Eden
*CARLISLE town station	60
*CARLISLE canal station at the Basin	61¼

LOW ROW, on right, Naworth Castle, *Earl of Carlisle*, and beyond it the ruins of Lanercost Priory, both well worthy of a visit.

CORBY, on left, Corby Castle, the very beautiful seat of *H. Howard*, Esq. and 2 m. distant, on right, Warwick Hall, *T. Parker*, Esq.

The NEWCASTLE and CARLISLE RAILWAY, commences at Newcastle, and following the course of the Tyne, upon its northern bank for a distance of 2¾ m. then crosses that river, and in 1¾ m. farther reaches Blaydon; from Blaydon its course

BLAYDON, 1 m. distant, on left, Axwell Park, *Sir T. J. Clavering,* Bart.

BYWELL, on right, Bywell Hall, *T. W. Beaumont,* Esq.

CORBRIDGE, 1½ m. distant, on right, Beaufront, *J. Errington,* Esq.

HEXHAM, at Hexham Abbey, *T. W. Beaumont,* Esq. and on right, The Hermitage, *S. Brooksbank,* Esq.

HALTWHISTLE, 2 m. before, on left, Unthank Hall, *R. Pearson,* Esq. and 2 m. beyond Haltwhistle, Blenkinsop Hall, *J. B. Coulson,* Esq.

GREENHEAD, on left, the ruins of Blenkinsop Castle.

ROSE HILL, 2½ m. distant, on right, is Gilsland Spa, a beautiful watering place much frequented during the season by persons of fashion from both sides of the Tweed. Here are three houses for the accommodation of company, all extremely commodious, and upon a plan similar to those at Harrongate; these are called The Shaws, Wardrew House, and the Orchard House; the whole are delightfully situate in the midst of a wild romantic valley, called the Vale of Irthing, which here contracts itself into a deep glen; on both sides of the river are some very beautiful walks; the Roman wall passes about 1 m. south of the village; and about 2 m. distant is a fine natural cascade, almost equal to the celebrated fall of the Clyde.

lies through the valley of the Tyne, at no great distance from its southern bank, and passing the villages of Wylam, Stocksfield, and Corbridge, at a short distance from the latter place, it enters Famley tunnel, 170 yards in length, and in 3 m. more reaches Hexham; from Hexham it takes a north-west direction, and in a farther distance of 2½ m. crosses the South Tyne; continuing its course on the north bank of that river it soon reaches Four Stones, and in 3½ m. more extends to Haydon Bridge. About 1½ m. beyond Haydon Bridge, the Railway again crosses the South Tyne, and continuing upon its southern bank for a distance of about 2½ m. re-crosses that river, a little beyond Bardon Mill; after re-crossing the South Tyne, it continues at no great distance from its northern bank, nearly all the way to Haltwhistle, ½ m. beyond which it enters Haltwhistle tunnel, 200 yards in length, and shortly after pursuing the course of Tipple Burn, a small stream, that in the vicinity of Haltwhistle falls into the South Tyne, in a farther distance of 3 m. is by a viaduct carried over that rivulet at Greenhead. From Greenhead it crosses the Carlisle road to Rose Hill, from whence its course lies between the Irthing river and the turnpike road to Low Row, where it re-crosses the Carlisle road to the southward of which it is constructed in a direct line to Milton; from Milton it takes a south-west direction to Corby, on the Eden, over which it is carried by a bridge or viaduct of 100 feet in height to Wetherall, upon the opposite bank of that river, and from thence its course is in a direct line nearly north-west to Carlisle. The inclinations of the Newcastle and Carlisle Railway are extremely favourable to expedition, a fact that the following statement will fully substantiate. From Newcastle the Railway proceeds upon a gradual rise for about 42 m. where it attains a height of about 400 feet above Newcastle; this is the summit, and at this height it is continued upon a level for about 6 m.; it then commences a descent of 396 feet, which being divided over a space of 12 m. the remaining distance to Carlisle, it follows, as a matter of course, is of easy accomplishment.

It may not be improper to add, that there is no stationary engine employed upon this line, that the whole is worked throughout by locomotive power, and that the entire distance 61 m. is performed by first class trains in three hours.

From the Canal basin, Steam boats take passengers to Annan and Liverpool.

STOCKTON and DARLINGTON RAILWAY.

*STOCKTON, Durham, to Middlesborough extension Railway	1
L.—To Middlesborough by the Railway 4½ m.	
Little Preston	2¼
*Bowesfield Lane	2¾
L.—To Yarm 1¼ m.	
To Stockton 3 m.—R.	
*Yarm Branch	3¾
*YARM	4¾

Or

Yarm branch as above	3¾
Urley Nook	4
*The fighting Cocks	8¼
Throstle Nest	11¾

LITTLE PRESTON, 2 m. distant, on right, Elton Hall, W. *Sutton*, Esq.

BOROUGHBRIDGE and DURHAM ROAD, 2 m. distant, on right, Windleston Hall, *Sir R. J. Eden*, Bart. and 2 m. distant, on left, Redworth House, *R. Surtees*, Esq.

WEST AUCKLAND, 1 m. before on left, see Brusselton tower, a pleasure-house commanding most delightful views over the surrounding country.

BISHOP AUCKLAND, here is a splendid Palace of the *Bishop of Durham*.

The STOCKTON and DARLINGTON RAILWAY commences at Cottage Row, Stockton Quay, and is from that place constructed upon a gradual rise which with very little variation it maintains for a distance of 21¾ m. at which point it attains an elevation of 400 feet above the level

To Stockton $10\frac{1}{4}$ *m.*—R.
L.—*To Darlington* 1 *m.*

Croft branch	12
L.—*To Croft by the Railway* $3\frac{1}{2}$ *m.*	
*DARLINGTON	$12\frac{1}{4}$
Whessoe	14
Boroughbridge and Durham road	$20\frac{1}{2}$
To Durham $11\frac{3}{4}$ *m.*—R.	
L. { *To Boroughbridge* $40\frac{3}{4}$ *m.* / *To Richmond* $19\frac{1}{2}$ *m.*	
Bishop Auckland	$23\frac{1}{2}$

Or

Boroughbridge and Durham Road as above	$20\frac{1}{2}$
*Shildon	$21\frac{1}{4}$
*West Auckland	$24\frac{1}{4}$
Witton le-Wear	27

The Stockton Steam vessels disembark their passengers at Middlesborough, a small village at the mouth of the Tees, to which place the Railway has been extended, and from thence, upon their arrival, locomotive carriages depart for Stockton, Yarm, and Darlington. The distance from Middlesborough to Stockton by the Railway is $5\frac{1}{2}$ *m.*

of Stockton Quay; it then ascends a short but steep acclivity of about half a mile, in which its elevation is increased about 75 feet: here it commences a rapid descent, upon which it is continued for rather more than a mile; from this point it enters upon a gradual rise of about one and one third of a mile, when it ascends rapidly for a farther distance of 1 m. thereby attaining the summit at an elevation of 550 feet above the level of Stockton Quay; from the summit it descends suddenly for $\frac{1}{2}$ a m. and from this last point it is continued upon an almost imperceptible rise to Witton-le-Wear.

N. B. Locomotive Engines do not run to either Bishop Auckland or West Auckland, but the coaches are conveyed regularly to the latter place several times during the day; over the inclines by fixed steam engines, and along the level about a mile in length by horses.

THE GREENWICH RAILWAY.

From *Duke Street Station London Bridge, to Bermondsey Street	$\frac{1}{4}$
Church Street, Horsleydown	$\frac{1}{2}$
Wellington Street	$\frac{3}{4}$
Spa Road Bermondsey, or Bermondsey New Church	1
Blue Anchor Lane	$1\frac{1}{4}$
Corbet's Lane, commencement of the Croydon Railway	$1\frac{1}{2}$
Surrey Canal	$2\frac{1}{4}$
Deptford High Street	$3\frac{1}{4}$
Ravensbourne River	$3\frac{1}{2}$
*Greenwich, Church Row	$3\frac{3}{4}$

The GREENWICH RAILWAY wholly constructed on arches, affords from its summit a good view; the first part of it passing through a crowded neighbourhood, singular in appearance, is of course confined, but arrived at Bermondsey Church, the prospect brightens, the country expands on either side, and though by no means extensive is extremely pleasing. Of this the Croydon Railway, here seen to great advantage, forms, perhaps, the most prominent feature.

THE NORTH UNION RAILWAY.

From Park Side on the Liverpool and Manchester Railway to Preston.

*Park Side Station to Newton and Leigh Road	1¼
Golborne	1¾
*Golborne Station	2¼
L.—To Edge Green	
To Lowton 1 m.—R.	
Bamfurlong	4
To Hindley 2 m.—R.	
L.—To Ashton 2 m.	
Wigan and Manchester Canal	4¼
Leeds and Liverpool Canal	6¼
*WIGAN, Wall Gate Station	7
Wigan and Preston Road, Boar's Head	9¼
To Standish 1¼ m.—R.	
Wigan and Chorley Road	9½
To Chorley 6 m.—R.	
*Standish Station	10
*Coppul Station	12½
To Chorley 2 m—R.	
L.—To Standish 3 m.	
Euxton, Chorley Road	15¾
To Chorley 2 m.—R.	
*Euxton Station	16¼
To Chorley 2 m.—R.	
*Golden Hill Station	17¾
To Bamber Bridge 1¼ m.—R.	
L.—To Leyland ¾ m.	
*Farrington Gate Station	19½
*PRESTON Station in Fishergate Street	22

GOLBORNE, on left, Golborne Park, and farther to the left, New Hall, *Sir J. Gerard*, Bart,

WIGAN, before on left, Westwood House, *C. Walmsley*, Esq., and 2½ m. distant, Winstanley Hall, *M. Banks*, Esq., 2 m. distant from Wigan, on right, is Hindley Hall, *Sir Robert Holt Leigh*, Bart. 1 m. beyond Wigan, on right, Bank House, *T. Woodcock*, Esq., and Haigh Hall, *Earl of Balcarras.*

STANDISH STATION, on left, Standish Hall, *C. Standish*, Esq., and 2 m. distant, Wrightington Hall, *C. Scarisbrick*, Esq.

COPPUL STATION, 2 m. distant, on right, Adlington Hall, *Gen. Brown Clayton*, and Duxbury Hall, *F. H. Standish*, Esq.

EUXTON STATION, on right, Astley Hall, *Lady Hoghton*, and Gillibrand Hall, *J. N. Fazakerly*, Esq.

GOLDEN HILL STATION, on left, Shaw Hall, *J. A. Farrington*, Esq.

PRESTON, on left, Penwortham Priory, *Col. Rawstorne*, Penwortham Lodge, *W. Marshall*, Esq., on right, Walton Lodge, *W. Calrow*, Esq., Darwen Bank, —— *Hodgett*, Esq.; Frenchwood, —— *Starkie*, Esq., and Cuerdale Hall, *J. Parker*, Esq.

Birmingham and Derby Junction Railway.

From HAMPTON STATION on the LONDON and BIRMINGHAM RAILWAY to DERBY.	
From *Hampton Station to The London and Birmingham Road	1
L.—*To Birmingham* 8½ m. *To Coventry* 9¼ m. *To London* 100½ m. } R.	
Coventry and Coleshill Road	1½
L.—*To Coleshill* 3½ m. *To Coventry* 9¼ m.—R.	
Packington Park	1¾
Cross the river Blythe	
Coleshill and Packington Road	2½
Tods Wood Bridge	3¼
Cross the river Blythe	
Hawkswell Bridge	3¾
Cross the river Blythe	
L.—*To Coleshill* 2 m. *To Maxstoke* 1½ m.—R.	
Cross the river Blythe twice	
*Coleshill Station	4¾
L.—*To Coleshill* ¾ m. *To Maxstoke Castle* ¼ m.—R.	
Cross the river Blythe	
Coleshill and Atherstone Road	6
L.—*To Coleshill* 1½ m. *To Atherstone* 10¾ m.—R.	
Bourne river Viaduct	6¼
Cross the river Bourne	
Nether Whitacre and Lea Marston Road	7¼
*Kingsbury Station	9¾
L. { *To Tamworth* 6 m. *To Birmingham* 11¼ m. *To Coventry* 13¼ m.—R.	
Kingsbury and Wheatley Road	10½
Thistlewood Brook Viaduct	11
Cliff and Wheatley Road..	11½
Dosthill and Wilnecote Road	12¼

PACKINGTON PARK, is the seat of the *Earl of Aylesford*.

COLESHILL STATION, 1½ m. distant, on left, Coleshill Park, the deserted seat of *Earl Digby*, on right, Maxstoke Castle, *T. Dilke*, Esq.

COLESHILL AND ATHERSTONE ROAD, on left, Blythe Hall, *William Stratford Dugdale*, Esq.

BOURNE RIVER VIADUCT, 1 m. distant, on left, Hams Hall, *Charles Bowyer Adderley*, Esq.

KINGSBURY STATION, 2 m. distant, on left, Moxhull Hall, *Hon. Mrs. Berkeley Noel.*

THISTLEWOOD BROOK VIADUCT, on left, Cliff Hall, *R. Willoughby*, Esq., and 1½ m. distant, Middleton Hall, *Sir Francis Lawley*, Bart.

FAZELEY and ATHERSTONE ROAD, 1 m. distant, on left, Drayton Manor, *Rt. Hon. Sir Robert Peel*, Bart., and Bonehill, *Rt. Hon. W. Yates Peel.*

ANKER VIADUCT. The Anker Viaduct, near Tamworth, that carries the Railway over the Tamworth and Atherstone roads and the river Anker, is a beautiful stone structure. It consists of nineteen segmental arches, viz. eighteen of thirty feet square span with a rise of seven feet six inches, and an oblique arch sixty feet on the face, with a rise of twelve feet, the total length being 807 feet.

TAMWORTH and ASHBY ROAD, 1 m. distant, on right, Amington Hall, *Cap. A'Court.*

Birmingham and Derby Junction Railway.

Fazeley and Atherstone Road	12¾
L.—*To Fazeley 1 m*	
To Atherstone 6 m.—R.	
Coventry Canal	13½
Anker Viaduct over the Tamworth and Atherstone Roads, and the river Anker	14
*TAMWORTH STATION	14½
L. { *To Tamworth ½ m.* *To Lichfield 7¼ m.* *To Sutton Coldfield 7½ m.*	
Tamworth and Ashby de la Zouch Road	15¼
L.—*To Tamworth 1 m.*	
To Ashby de la Zouch 12¼ m.—R.	
Wiggington and Syrescote Road	15¾
Wiggington and Harleston Road	17
Salters Street Highway	17¼
*Elford Station	18¼
L.—*To Tamworth 5 m.*	
To Harleston 1½ m.—R.	
Tamworth and Burton Road	18¾
L.—*To Tamworth 4¾ m.*	
To Burton 10 m.—R.	
*Alrewas Station	20¾
L.—*To Lichfield 6¼ m.*	
Croxall Viaduct	21¼
Cross the rivers Tame, and Trent	
Barton Mill	22¾
*Barton Station	23¼
Branston	25¾
Burton Branch Canal Viaduct	27¼
*BURTON UPON TRENT STATION	27½
L. { *To Tutbury 4½ m.* *To Uttoxeter 13¾ m.* *To Lichfield 11 m.*	
To Ashby de la Zouch 8¼ m.—R.	
Tutbury and Burton Road	28

ELFORD STATION, on left, Elford Hall, **Rt. Hon. Fulke Greville Howard**.

ALREWAS STATION, 2½ m distant, on left, Wichnor Park, *Theophilus Levett*, Esq., 1 m distant, on right, Croxall Hall, *J. Levett Prinsep*, Esq., and 1 m. distant, Catton Hall, **Rt. Hon. Sir Robert Wilmot Horton**, Bart.

CROXALL VIADUCT. The Croxall Viaduct, built of wood, carries the Railway over the rivers Tame and Trent near their junction; its total length is 1310 feet, having 52 bays of 20 feet span each.

BARTON STATION, on right, Walton Hall, *M. Gisborne*, Esq.

BRANSTON, on right, Drakelow, *Lady Sophia Gresley*, and 2 m. distant, on left, Dunstall Hall, *C. Arkwright*, Esq.

BURTON UPON TRENT, 2½ m. distant, on right, Bretby Park, *Earl of Chesterfield*.

TUTBURY and BURTON ROAD, 2¼ m. distant, on left, Rolleston, *Sir Oswald Mosley*, Bart.

NEWTON SOLNEY and EGGINTON ROAD, on left, Egginton Hall, *Sir H. Every*, Bart., and Dovecliff, *T. Thornewill*, Esq., on right, Newton Park, *W. Worthington*, Esq.

WILLINGTON STATION, 1½ m. distant, on left, Burnaston House, *A. N. E. Mosley*, Esq., on right, Willington Hall, *Rev. F. W. Spilsbury*, 2½ m. distant, Foremark, the beautiful seat of **Sir Francis Burdett**, Bart., and 4½ m. distant, Caulk Abbey, **Sir George Crewe**, Bart.

Birmingham and Derby Junction Railway.

Wetmoor Hall	29
Dove River Viaduct	30¼
Newton Solney and Eggington Road	30½
*Willington Station	32
Grand Trunk Canal Viaduct	33¼
Twyford and Derby Road	35¼
Normanton and Barrow Road................	36½
Derby and Ashby Road ..	38
L.—To Derby 1 m.	
To Ashby de la Zouch 12½	
London and Derby Road	
L.—To Derby 1 m.	
To London 125 m.—R.	
Derby Canal Viaduct over	38½
River Derwent Viaduct over	
*DERBY STATION ...	38¾

TWYFORD and DERBY ROAD, 1½ m. distant, on left, The Pastures, B. Heathcote, Esq., and 4 m. distant, Radbourne Hall, E. S. Chandos Pole, Esq.

DERBY and ASHBY ROAD, on right, Osmaston Hall, — Fox, Esq.

LONDON and DERBY ROAD, 2½ m. distant, on right, Elvaston Hall, Earl of Harrington.

DERBY STATION, 1½ m. distant, on left, Markeaton Hall, F. Mundy, Esq., and 1½ m. distant, on right, Chaddesden Hall, Sir Robert Wilmot, Bart.

GREAT WESTERN RAILWAY.

LONDON to BATH and BRISTOL.

From the *Paddington Station to Wormwood Scrubs	2¼
Old Oak Common	3
Acton	4
*Ealing	5½
*Hanwell	6¾
Wharncliffe Viaduct ..,..	7
Cross the river Brent	
Metropolis Bridge over the Uxbridge Road......	7½
L.—To London 8¾ m.	
To Uxbridge 6¼ m.—R.	
*Southall Park	8
Southall Green	8¾
Paddington Canal Viaduct	10
Cross the Paddington Canal	
Grand Junction Canal Viaduct	10½
Cross the Grand Junction Canal	
Dawley	11¼
*West Drayton.	13

EALING, ½ m. distant, on right, Twyford Abbey, Mrs. Douglas.
HANWELL, 1½ m. distant, on left, Boston House, Col. Clitherow. On right of Hanwell is Hanwell Park, Charles Turner, Esq.
THE WHARNCLIFFE VIADUCT, an elegant stone structure, carries the Railway across the Brent river and valley; the course of the former is described at page 5. It is so named in compliment to Lord Wharncliffe, to whose powerful advocacy of their bill, in its progress through parliament, the Great Western Railway Company, considering themselves highly indebted, as expediting its enactment, have, as a lasting proof of their gratitude, named this bridge the Warncliffe Viaduct; the summit affords a good view of the Hanwell Lunatic Asylum, on left of the line, and beyond it the rich woods of Osterley Park, the beautiful seat of the Earl of Jersey.
SOUTHALL PARK, and mansion is the privare lunatic asylum of the late Sir W. Ellis.
GRAND JUNCTION CANAL VIADUCT, ½ m. distant, on left, Cranford Park, Countess of Berkeley.

Great Western Railway. 232

L.—*To Colnbrook 4 m.*	
Colne River Viaduct	13¾
Cross the River Colne	
Iver Road, Buckinghamshire	14¼
Langley Marsh	16
Upton and Westmoor Green Road	17½
*Slough Station	18¼
L. { *To Windsor* 2½ *m.* { *To Ascot Race Course* 8¼ *m.*	
Farnham Royal and Salt Hill Road	19
Burnham Road	21
Hitcham Road	21¾
*MAIDENHEAD STATION, at the Dumb Bell, on the Bath Road	22½
Note. To the centre of the town of Maidenhead is 1½ mile.	
River Thames Viaduct	23
Maidenhead, Braywick and Windsor Road	24
L.—*To Windsor* 6¼ *m.*	
Shoppenhanger Lane	25
White Waltham Road	26¾
Waltham St. Lawrence Road	28
Ruscombe	29¾
*Twyford Station	30¼
To Henley 4½ *m.*—R.	
River Slade Viaduct	30¾
River Loddon Viaduct	31
Sonning Road Viaduct	32
River Kennet Viaduct	34¾
*READING STATION	36
L. { *To Basingstoke* 16 *m.* { *To Newbury* 18 *m.*	
To Henley 8 *m.*—R.	
Purley	39½
*Pangbourne Station	40¾
L.—*To Basingstoke* 18 *m.*	
Reading and Wallingford Road	42¾
L.—*To Wallingford* 7½ *m.*	
To Reading 7½ *m.*—R.	

WEST DRAYTON, 1 m. distant, on right, Huntsmoor Lodge, *Hon. Charles Tollemache.*

IVER ROAD, 1 m. distant, on right, Delaford Park, *C. Clowes,* Esq., 1 m. beyond the Iver Road, on right, *M. Swabey,* Esq., and Iver Grove, *Lady Gambier,* on left, Richings Lodge, late *Rt. Hon. John Sullivan.*

LANGLEY MARSH, 1 m. distant, on left, Ditton Park, *Lord Montague;* on right, Love Hill, *Sir G. W. Tapps Gervis,* Bart., and Langley Park, *Robert Harvey,* Esq.

SLOUGH STATION, 2½ m. distant, on left, Windsor Castle, the magnificent palace of the Queen, on right, Stoke Park, *Grenville Penn,* Esq., Stoke Place, *Col. Vyse,* Stoke House, *J. Evans,* Esq., Wexham Lodge, *Major Bent,* and Wexham Rectory, *Rev. H. Dyson.*

MAIDENHEAD STATION, on right, at Taplow, Taplow Court, *Lord Kirkwall,* Taplow House, *Pascoe Grenfell,* Esq., 2 m. distant, Cliefden, *Rt. Hon. Sir George Warrender,* Bart., Dropmore, *Lady Grenville,* and Hedsor Lodge, *Lord Boston.*

WHITE WALTHAM ROAD, ½ m. before, on left, Heywood Lodge, *J. Sawyer,* Esq., and on left of the White Waltham Road, Shottesbrook Park, *Hon. Mrs. Vansittart.*

RUSCOMBE, 1 m. distant, on left, Stanlake House, *L. Currie,* Esq., 2 m. distant, on right, Scarletts, *Rev. J. A. Austen Leigh,* and Bear Place, *Col. Hanmer.*

TWYFORD STATION, 1 m. distant, on left, Hurst House, *Sir J. Conroy,* Bart., Hurst Lodge, *G. H. Elliot,* Esq., Hurst Grove, *Capt. Boldero,* and 3 m. distant, Billingsbear Park, *Lord Braybrooke,* 1½ m. distant, on right, Shiplake House, *Joseph Phillimore,* LL.D., and 3 m. distant, Park Place, *E. Fuller Maitland,* Esq.

SONNING ROAD VIADUCT, ½ m. distant, on left, Woodley Lodge, *J. Wheble,* Esq., 1½ m. distant, Early Court, *Lady Sidmouth,* and Maiden

Bassildon	$43\frac{1}{4}$
River Thames Viaduct	$43\frac{1}{2}$
*Goring Station	$44\frac{1}{8}$
Cleeve Mill	$44\frac{5}{8}$
South Stoke	46
River Thames Viaduct	$46\frac{3}{4}$
*Moulsford or Wallingford Station, at the Wallingford and Oxford Road	$47\frac{1}{8}$
To Wallingford $2\frac{3}{4}$ *m.* / *To Oxford* $15\frac{3}{4}$ *m.* } R.	
West End, Cholsey	$48\frac{1}{4}$
South Moreton	50
Wantage and Wallingford Road at	
Hagborne Marsh	$51\frac{3}{4}$
L.—*To Wantage* $8\frac{3}{4}$ *m.*	
To Wallingford $5\frac{1}{4}$ *m.*—R.	
Dudcot, Vauxhall Farm	53
Milton	$55\frac{1}{4}$
*Steventon Station	56
L.—*To East Ilsley* $6\frac{1}{2}$ *m.*	
To Abingdon 4 *m.* / *To Oxford* 10 *m.* } R.	
West Hendred Wood	58
Wilts and Berks Canal	$58\frac{3}{4}$
Wantage and Abingdon Road	$59\frac{1}{2}$
L.—*To Wantage* 2 *m.*	
To Abingdon $7\frac{1}{4}$ *m.*—R.	
River Ock Viaduct	60
*Farringdon Station, at the Farringdon and Wantage Road	63
L.—*To Wantage* $3\frac{3}{4}$ *m.*	
To Farringdon $5\frac{1}{4}$ *m.*—R.	
Baulking and Wantage Road	65
Baulking and Uffington Road	$65\frac{3}{4}$
Uffington Road	66
Uffington and Farringdon Road	67
Longcott and Compton Beauchamp Road	$68\frac{3}{4}$
Becket Park and Compton Beauchamp Road	$69\frac{1}{2}$

Early, *E. Golding*, Esq., on right, Holme Park, *R. Palmer*, Esq.

READING STATION, on left, Coley Park, *Mrs. Monk*, and Southcott House, *J. Lutyens*, Esq.

PURLEY, on right, Purley Park, *B. Peel*, Esq., and across the Thames, Mapledurham, *Mrs. Smith*, 1 m. beyond Purley, on left, Purley Hall, *Rev. J. Cooke*.

PANGBOURNE STATION, 1 m. distant, on left, De La Bere, *J. S. Bredon*, Esq., on right, across the Thames, Walliscote, *Capt. Fowler*, and Coombe Lodge, *W. Alfrey*, Esq.

BASSILDON, $\frac{3}{4}$ m. before, on left, Bassildon Park, the beautiful seat of *J. Morrison*, Esq.

MOULSFORD or WALLINGFORD STATION, 2 m. distant, on right, Mongewell, *Mrs. Palmer*.

HAGBORNE MARSH. In the vicinity of this place is obtained the first view of Farringdon High Trees, near Farringdon, 15 m. distant in a right line.

DUDCOT, $1\frac{1}{4}$ m. beyond, and $1\frac{1}{2}$ m. distant, on right, at Sutton Courtenay, The Abbey Manor House, *F. Justice*, Esq., and across the Thames, Culham House, *J. S. Phillips*, Esq.

STEVENTON STATION, 1 m. distant, on left, Milton Hill, *Mrs. Bowles*, on right, Milton House, *J. R. Borret*, Esq., $2\frac{1}{2}$ m. distant, Hendred House, *C. Eyston*; $2\frac{1}{2}$ m. beyond Steventon Station, and $2\frac{1}{4}$ m. distant, on left, Lockinge Park, *Sir H. W. Martin*, Bart.

BAULKING and WANTAGE ROAD, 2 m. distant, on left, at Kingston Lisle, is the seat of *E. Martin Atkins*, Esq.

FARRINGDON STATION, $4\frac{1}{2}$ m. distant, on right, Pusey House, *P. Pusey*, Esq., Wadley House, *T. M. Goodlake*, Esq., 5 m. distant, Buckland House, *R. G. Throckmorton*, Esq., and Carswell House, *T. H. Southby*, Esq.; at Farringdon, Farringdon House, *W. Bennet*, Esq., and 2 m. distant from Farringdon, Buscot Park, *Pryse Pryse*, Esq.

Great Western Railway.

*Shrivenham Station	70¾
Bourton	71½
Cross the Wilts and Berks Canal and river Cole, Viaduct	72¼
Enter Wiltshire	
Stratton Green, *Wilts*	75¼
L.—*To Swindon* 2 *m.*	
To Highworth 4½ *m.*—R.	
Swindon and Cricklade Road	76¼
L.—*To Swindon* 1½ *m.*	
To Cricklade 6½ *m.* R.	
Cross the North Wilts Canal to the Cheltenham and Great Western Union Railway and *SWINDON STATION*	77
L.—*To Swindon* 1½ *m.*	
To Highworth 6 *m.*	
To Cricklade 7 *m.*	
To Cirencester Station by Railway 18 *m. and Cheltenham by Railway* 42¼ *m.* ⎬ R.	
Note.—Cirencester Station is distant 3½ m. from Cirencester, from whence to Cheltenham by Road is 15 miles.	
Swindon and Wotton Basset Road	78
L.—*To Swindon* 1½ *m.*	
To Wotton Basset 5 *m.*—R.	
Lydiard Tregoze Road	79¾
Wilts and Berks Canal	80¾
*WOTTON BASSET STATION at the Wotton Basset and Marlborough Road	82¼
L.—*To Marlborough* 11 *m.*	
To Wotton Basset 1¼ *m.*—R.	
Wotton Basset and Calne Road	83½
L.—*To Calne* 11½ *m.*	
To Wotton Basset, 1 *m.*—R.	
Trow Lane Farm	85¼
Calne and Malmesbury Road	87

UFFINGTON ROAD, ¾ m. distant, on left, see the village of Uffington, and 1¾ m. beyond it, the celebrated White Horse, formed by order of Alfred, as a token of the signal victory he obtained over the Danes at Ashdown, in this neighbourhood. Near the White Horse, is Uffington Castle, the supposed site of the Danish encampment.

LONGCOTT and COMPTON BEAUCHAMP ROAD, 1½ m. distant, on left, Compton House, *Mrs. Rodes.*

SHRIVENHAM STATION, 2½ m. distant, on left, is a mutilated Druidical remain, denominated Waylane Smith's Forge, the supposed residence of the invisible blacksmith, mentioned in Scott's beautiful novel, Kenilworth; on right of Shrivenham Station, is Becket Park, the fine seat of *Viscount Barrington,* Watchfield House, *Col. Blagrave,* 3 m. distant, Warneford Place, *Mrs. Warneford,* and 4 m. distant, Coleshill House, *Earl of Radnor.*

STRATTON GREEN, 1¾ m. distant, on right, Stanton House, *Rev. Dr. Trenchard.*

SWINDON STATION, on left, at Swindon, is Swindon House, *A. Goddard,* Esq. 2½ m. distant from Swindon, on left, is Wroughton House, *W. Codrington,* Esq., and Burdrop Park, *J. J. Calley,* Esq.

LYDIARD TREGOZE ROAD, 2 m. distant, on right, is Lydiard Park, *Lord Bolingbroke.*

ROAD to BRADENSTOKE ABBEY, 1¼ m. distant, on left, the remains of Bradenstoke Abbey, that converted to a farm belongs to *Lord Methuen.*

CALNE AND MALMESBURY ROAD, 3 m. distant, on right, is Dauntsey House, — *Fenwick,* Esq.

L.—To Calne 7 m.	
To Malmesbury 7 m. R.	
Road to Bradenstoke Abbey	88
Friday Street	88¾
Christian Malford	89¼
River Avon Viaduct	90
Langley Burrell Road	91¾
*CHIPPENHAM STATION	93½
L. { To Calne 5½ m. / To Devizes 10 m.	
To Malmesbury 9½ m. } R. / To Marshfield 9½ m. }	
London and Bath Road ...	94½
Notton Road	95
Thingley	96¼
L.—To Devizes 11½ m.	
To Corsham 1½ m.—R.	
*Corsham Station	97½
L. { To Melksham 4½ m. / To Trowbridge 10 m.	
Box Tunnel, entrance of...	98½
Chippenham Road	100
*Box Station	100¼
Middle Hill Tunnel	100¾
Bathford	102¾
L. { To Bradford 5 m. / To Trowbridge 8 m.	
To Bath 3¼ m.—R.	
River Avon Viaduct	103½
Bathampton	103¾
Kennet and Avon Canal....	105
*BATH STATION	106¼
L. { To Frome 13 m. / To Wells 19½ m.	
*Twiverton Station	107¾
Twiverton Tunnel entrance	108¼
Bristol and Bath Road	108¾
Corston Brook............	109½
*Salford Station and Tunnel	111
River Chew Viaduct......	112¾
*KEYNSHAM STATION	113
Keynsham First Tunnel ..	114
Brislington Tunnels, entrance of, ...	115
River Avon..............	116½
*BRISTOL STATION ..	118

CHIPPENHAM STATION, on left, is Monckton House, *Mrs. Michell*, and Ivy House, *Mrs. Humphreys*, 3 m. distant, is Bow Wood, the beautiful seat of the *Marquis of Lansdowne*, and Bremhill Vicarage, *Rev. W. L. Bowles*; on right of Chippenham Station, is Harden Huish Park, *T. Clutterbuck*, Esq., 3¼ m. distant, Draycot Park, *W. T. Long Wellesley*, Esq., and 6 m. distant, Grittleton House, the beautifully wooded seat of *Joseph Neeld*, Esq.

CORSHAM STATION, on right is Corsham House, *Lord Methuen*, and 2 m. distant, Hartham Park.

THINGLEY, 1 m. distant, on left, is Notton House, *J. Anstey*, Esq. near which is Lackham House, *Captain Rooke*.

BOX STATION, 4 m. distant, on right, is Lucknam, *C. Boode*, Esq.

RIVER AVON VIADUCT, on right, is Shockerwick, *J. Wiltshire*, Esq.

CORSTON BROOK, 1 m. distant, on left, is Newton Park, *Colonel Gore Langton*; on right, is Kelston House, *Joseph Neeld*, Esq.

A TABLE OF DISTANCES

EXPLANATION.

To find any required distance, as, for instance, between Wolverhampton and Crewe; seek Crewe in the left-hand column, and carrying your eye in the direction of Crewe on the right, stop under the column of squares headed Wolverhampton, when the angle formed by the line running under Crewe and that on right of Wolverhampton, enclosing the figures 30¾ at the bottom, shows the distance.

```
BIRMINGHAM
 3¼  Perry Bar
 6½  3¼  Newton Road
 9¼  6   2¾  Bescot Bridge
10   6¾  3½  ¾   James Bridge
11¾  8½  5¼  2½  1¾  Willenhall
14  10¾  7½  4¾  4   2¼  Wolverhampton
19¾ 16¼ 13¼ 10¼  9¾  8   5¾  Four Ashes
21¼ 18  14¾ 12  11¼  9½  7¼  1½  Spread-Eagle
23¾ 20¼ 17¼ 14½ 13¾ 12   9¾  4   2½  Penkridge
29  25¾ 22½ 19¾ 19  17¼ 15   9¼  7¾  5¼  Stafford
32¼ 29¼ 26  23¼ 22½ 20½ 18¼ 12½ 11¼  8¾  3½  Bridgeford
34¾ 31½ 28¼ 25¼ 24¾ 23  20¾ 15  13½ 11   5¾  2¼  Norton Bridge
43  39¾ 36½ 33¾ 33  31½ 29  23¼ 21¾ 19¼ 14  10½  8¼  Whitmore
45¾ 42½ 39¼ 36½ 35¾ 34  31¾ 26  24½ 22  16¾ 13¼ 11   2¾  Madeley
53¼ 50¼ 47¼ 44¼ 43¾ 42  39¾ 34  32½ 30  24¾ 21¼ 19  10¾  8   Crewe
55¼ 52½ 49¼ 46½ 45¾ 44  41¾ 36  34½ 32  26¾ 23¼ 21  12¾ 10   2   Coppenhall
58¼ 55¼ 52  49¼ 48½ 46½ 44¼ 38¾ 37¼ 34¾ 29½ 26  23¾ 15½ 12¾  4¾  2¾  Minshull Vernon
61  57¾ 54½ 51¾ 51  49¼ 47  41¼ 39¾ 37¼ 32  28½ 26¼ 18  15¼  7¼  5¼  2½  Winsford
65¼ 62¼ 59  56¼ 55½ 53¾ 51½ 45¾ 44¼ 41¾ 36¼ 32¾ 30½ 22¼ 19¾ 11½  9¾  7   4¼  Hartford
68  64¾ 61½ 58¾ 58  56¼ 54  48¼ 46¾ 44¼ 39  35½ 33¼ 25  22½ 14¼ 12½  9½  7   2½  Acton
72¼ 69  65¾ 63  62¼ 60½ 58¼ 52½ 51  48½ 43¼ 39¾ 37½ 29¼ 26¾ 18½ 16½ 13¾ 11¼  6¾  4¼  Preston Brook
74¾ 71½ 68¼ 65¼ 64¾ 63  60¾ 55  53¼ 51  45¾ 42¼ 40  31¼ 29  21  19  16¼ 13¾  9¼  6¾  2½  Moore
77¼ 74¼ 71¼ 68¼ 67¾ 66  63¾ 58  56¼ 54  48¾ 45¼ 43  34¾ 32  24  22  19¼ 16¾ 12¼  9¾  5¼  2   Warrington
82¾ 79¼ 76  73¼ 72¾ 70½ 68¼ 62¾ 61¼ 58¾ 53½ 50  47¾ 39¾ 36¾ 28¾ 26¾ 24  21¼ 17  14½ 10¼  7¾  4¾  Newton Junc.
97¼ 94  90½ 89  87¼ 85¾ 83½ 77¾ 76  73¾ 68¼ 64½ 62¼ 54¼ 51¾ 43¼ 41¼ 38½ 36¼ 31½ 29¼ 25  22½ 19¼ 14½  Liverpool
```

PERRY BAR — NEWTON ROAD — BESCOT BRIDGE — JAMES BRIDGE — WILLENHALL — WOLVERHAMPTON — FOUR ASHES — SPREAD-EAGLE — PENKRIDGE — STAFFORD — BRIDGEFORD — NORTON BRIDGE — WHITMORE — MADELEY — CREWE — COPPENHALL — MINSHULL VERNON — WINSFORD — HARTFORD — ACTON — PRESTON BROOK — MOORE — WARRINGTON — NEWTON JUNCTION — LIVERPOOL

INDEX.

ABERCORN, Marquis of, 7.
Acton, 220.
—— Station, 174.
——, Trussell, 145.
Adderley, C. B., 229.
Addison, his seat, 50.
Adlington Hall, 228.
Advice to travellers, v.
Alban, St., 11.
Alban's, St., account of, 11.
Allesley Park, 105. 217.
Alrewas Station, 230.
Amington Hall, 229.
Anglesea, Marquis of, 144.
Anker Viaduct, 229.
Anson, E., 129. 219.
Arkwright, C., 229.
Arley Hall, 174.
Arnold, G. H., 216.
Ashby Lodge, 216.
Ashridge Park, 20. 214.
Ashlin's Hall, 17. 214.
Ashton, 37.
Astley Hall, 228.
Aston, 127.
—— Hall, Cheshire, 175.
——————, Warwickshire, 128. 218.
—— Park, 128. 218.
—— Viaduct, 127, 128.
Avon, River, 46.
Axwell Park, 225.
Aylesbury, account of, 22. 25.
—————— Railway, 20. 214.
——————, Vale of, 20.
Aylesford, Earl of, 106, 107. 217. 229.

Bacon, Lord, 16.
Baginton Hall, 217.
Bailey, W., 215.
Balcarras, Earl of, 228.
Balsall, account of, 108.
Bamfurlong, 228.
Bank Hall, 179.
—— House, 228.
Banks, M., 228.
Bardon Hill, 24, 25.
Barnett, account of, 8.
Barry, Mr., 121.
Bartletts, 17. 214.
Barton Moss Station, 196.
———— Station, 230.
Basford, 166. 219.
Battle of Naseby, 48.
Beaudesert, 144.
Beaufront, 225.
Beaumont, T. W., 225.
Beck, J., 105. 217.
Beech, J., 58. 216.
Beechwood Tunnel, 105.
—————— Bridge, 105.
—————— Excavation, 105.
Beeston Castle, 169.
Belmont Hall, 174.
Bent, Major, 232.
Bentley Hall, 129. 219.
———— Priory, 4, 5. 7. 212.
Account of, 8.
Berkhampstead, 214. Account of, 19.
—————— Castle, 19.
—————— Place, 17. 214.
—————— Station 17.
Berkswell Bridge, 105.

INDEX.

Berkswell Hall, 105. 217.
Bescot Bridge Station, 129. 218.
———— Hall, 129. 219.
Betley Court, 165.
———— Hall, 165.
———— Mere, 165.
Billington Camp, 145.
Bilston, account of, 136.
Bilton, 56.
———— Grange, 216.
———— House, 50. 216.
Birch, Sir T., 222.
Birds Wood, 175.
Birmingham, 217. Account of, 112. Arts, manufactures, and commerce, 123. Charitable Institutions, 120. Churches and Chapels, 117. Church building Society, 118. Early history, 112. Present state, 116. Hackney coaches, 107. Hotels, 107. Public buildings, 120. Railway Station at Birmingham, 126. Railway Station in London, 1. Riots, 115. Schools and charitable institutions, 120. Town Hall, 120. Water-works, 128.
Birmingham, Bristol, and Thames Junction Railway, 3.
Birmingham Canal. Curious view of the Darlaston, Walsall, and Bentley branches, 129.
Birmingham and Derby Junction Railway, 105. 217.
Birmingham and Fazely Canal, 127.
Birmingham and Liverpool Junction Canal, 146. 167.
Birmingham and Manchester Railway, 155.
Birmingham Railway, itinerary line, 212.

Bishop Auckland, 227.
Blacklow Hill, 69.
Blaydon, 225.
Blenkinsop Hall, 225.
Bletchley Station, 29. 214.
Blisworth Excavation, 38.
———— Ridge, 37.
———— Station, 38. 215.
———— Tunnel, 37.
Blythe Hall, 111.
———— River, 111.
———————— Viaduct, 105.
Boadicea, Queen, 11.
Boddington, N., 128.
Bold Hall, 181. 222.
———, Henry, his monument, 5.
Bolton Junction Station, 195.
———— and Leigh Railway, 195. 222. Itinerary line, 224.
Bonehill, 229.
Borough Hill, 48.
Bostock Hall, 170.
Boston House, 231.
————, Lord, 232.
Botfield, B., 216.
Bound Hill, 168.
Bouverie, E., 215.
Bowers Bent, 152.
Boxmoor Station, 17, 18. 213.
Brackley, account of, 35.
Bradford, Earl of, 127. 131.
Bradshaw, R. H., 196.
Bradwell, 30.
Bragborough House, 216.
Brampton Station, 225.
Brandon, 58. 59.
———— Castle, 58. Account of, 59.
———— embankment, 58.
———— House, 58. 216.
———— Oblique Bridge, 58.
———— Station, 58. 216. Account of, 59.
———— Viaduct, 58, 59.
Brent River, account of, 5.

Brent Street, 6.
—— Viaduct, 3.
Bretby Park, 230.
Brewood, 143. Account of, 146.
Brickhill, Bow, 29.
——, Great, 29.
——, Little, 29.
—— Manor House, 29. 214.
Bridgeford, Great, 219.
—————— Station, 150.
Bridgewater, Countess of, 20. 214.
Bridgewater's, Duke of, canal, 175.
Briscoe, G., 142.
Broad Green Station, 182.
Brockhall Bridge, 49. 216.
—— Park, 50. 216.
Brooke, Sir R. 176.
——, Lady, 174.
Broughton Brook Bridge, 25.
——, Sir J. D., 165.
Brown, Mr., 106. 217.
Brownsover House, 216.
Buckingham, account of, 32.
—— Canal, 33.
Buckinghamshire, Earl of, 21.
Bugbrook, 38.
—— Suspension Bridge, 38.
Bulbourne Brook, 17, 18.
Burdett, Sir Francis, 230.
Burnaston House, 230.
Burslem, account of, 156.
Burton-upon-Trent Station, 230.
Bury Lane Station, 195.
Bushbury and Bushbury Hall, 142.
Butterton Hall, 164.
Bywell Hall, 225.
Caldecott, J., 216.
——, T., 216.
Caldon Canal, 155.

Calrow, W., 228
Calthorpe, Lord, 118, 119.
——, Hon. G. F., 118.
Camden Town depôt, 1.
Cannock Chace, account of, 144.
Canon's Park, account of, 7.
Carlisle, 225.
——, Earl of, 225.
Carrington, Lord, 215.
Case, T., 182.
Cashiobury Park, 5. 213. Account of, 14.
Castle Bromwich, 106. 127.
—— Church Hill, 145.
—— Thorpe, 37, 38.
Catton Hall, 230.
Cautionary note, v.
Caulk Abbey, 230.
Cawston House, 216.
Chadwick, S., 176.
Chalk Farm Lane, 2.
Chandos, Duke of, 7.
—— Pole, E. S., 231.
Chapel Chorlton, 152.
Charlemont, 128.
Charles I., 39. 42.
Chat Moss, 195.
Cheddington Hill, 25.
Chesterfield, Earl of, 230.
Chester and Crewe Railway, 155.
Childwall Hall, 182. 222.
Chillington Park, 143. 220.
Chiltern Hills, 21. 23, 24, 25.
—— Hundreds, 25.
Chitwell, G., 217.
Chorley, account of, 207.
Chorlton, 166.
Christie, L., 215.
Church, Coppenhall, 220.
——, Lawford, 58.
Clanford Brook, 150.
Clarendon, Earl of, 5. 15. 213.
Clavering, Sir T. J., 225.
Clayton, General Brown, 228.

Cliefden, 232.
Cliff Hall, 229.
Clifton Viaduct, 50.
Clitherow, Col., 231.
Clowes, C., 232.
Cold Meese, 151.
Cole, River, 106.
Coleshill, 106. Account of, 110.
——— Station, 229.
Collins Green Station, 180.
Colne River, 4. 10. 11.
——— and Viaduct, 4.
Combe Abbey, 58. 216. Account of, 59.
Constable, Sir T. C., 145.
Cooper, Sir A. P., 214.
Coppenhall, 145.
——— Station, 168.
Coppul Station, 206. 228.
Corbridge, 225.
Corby Castle, 225.
Cosgrove Hall, 37. 214.
——— Priory, 37. 214.
Coton House, 216.
Court, W. 170.
Courteenhall House, 215.
Coven Heath, 142.
Coventry, account of, 89.
——— and Oxford Canal, 103.
——— Station, 59. 217.
Cowper, the poet, 36.
Craven, Earl of, 58. 216.
Creswell Hall, 150.
Crewe, 219.
——— Hall, 166. 221.
———, Lord, 221.
———, Sir George, 230.
——— Station, 166. Account of, 168.
Crichley, H., 194.
Crick Station, 50. 216.
Cross Green, 142.
——— Lane Station, 196.
Croxall Hall, 230.

Croxteth Park, 182.
Cuerdale Hall, 228.
Culcheth Hall, 195.
Dane River, 170, 171.
Daresbury Hall, 176.
Darlaston, 129.
Darlington, 227.
Dartmouth, Earl of, 128.
Darwen Bank, 228.
Davenham Hall, 174.
Daventry, Account of, 46.
Delaford Park, 232.
Delamere Forest, 175.
——— House, 175.
———, Lord, 170. 221.
Delapré Abbey, 215.
Den, 166.
Denbigh, Earl of, 216.
——— Hall and Viaduct, 29.
Derby, Earl of, 182. 222.
——— Station, 231.
Dickinson, J., 17. 18. 213.
Digby, Earl, 111. 220.
Dilke, T., 106. 111. 217. 229.
Distances, Table of, Birmingham Railway, vii.
Distances, Table of, Grand Junction Railway, 235.
Ditton Park, 232.
Doddington Hall, 165.
Dorrien, T., 17. 214.
Dovecliff, 230.
Drakelow, 230.
Drayton Manor, 229.
Dropmore, 232.
Ducks, curious method of rearing, 22.
Duddeston Bridge, 127.
Dudley, 129. Account of, 137.
——— Castle, Account of, 138.
———, Earl, 138.
———, Edmund, 46.
———, J., 169.
Dugdale, Sir W., 111.
———, W. S., 111. 229.

Duncombe, P. P., 29. 214.
Dungannon, Lord, 215.
Dunstable, account of, 23.
Dunstal Hall, near Wolverhampton, 142.
Dunstall Hall, near Burton-upon-Trent, 230.
Dunston, 145.
Durham, Bishop of, 226.
Dutton Viaduct, 220.; and view from, 174, 175.
Duxbury Hall, 228.
Dyson, Rev. H., 232.
Easton Neston, account of, 39.
Easthall Viaduct, 106.
Eaton Hall, 183.
Eccleshall, account of, 152.
———— Castle, 151.
Eddlesborough, 25.
Eden, Sir R. I., 226.
Edgehill Station, 183.
Edward I., 41, 42.
——— II., 42.
——— III., 42.
——— VI., 34.
Egerton, Lord Chancellor, 9.
Eggington Hall, 230.
Eld, F., 150.
Elford Hall, 230.
Elford Station, 230.
Elizabeth, Queen, 8. 42.
Ellesmere and Chester canal, 167.
Elmdon Hall, 106. 217.
Elms, The, 176.
Elton Hall, 226.
Elvaston Hall, 231.
Empson, Sir R., 46.
Esk Hall, 223.
Essex, Earl of, 5. 9. 213.
Ethelbert, St., 12.
Euston Grove Station, 1.
Euxton Station, 206. 228.
Evans, I., 232.
Everdon Hall, 215

Every, Sir H., 230.
Farrington, J. A., 228.
Farrington Gate Station, 206. 228.
Fawsley Park, 215. Account of, 48.
Fazakerley, J. N., 228.
Fenny Stratford, 29.
Finchley, 6.
Fitzherbert, T., 151.
Flow Moss Station, 195.
Flower Church, 38.
————, village and house, 215.
Ford Houses, 142.
Foremark, 230.
Four Ashes Station, 143. 146. 218.
Fowler, T., 142.
France France, J., 170.
Frenchwood, 228.
Gade River, 11. 18.
Gadesbridge, 214.
Gambier, Lady, 232.
Garth, Dr. Sir Samuel, his monument, 7.
Gateforth Hall, 224.
Gaveston, Piers, 69.
Gayhurst, 215.
General Cemetery, the, 3. 212.
George IV., 211, 212.
Gerard, Sir J., 194. 222. 228.
Giffard, T. W., 143. 220.
Gillibrand Hall, 228.
Gilsland Spa, 225.
Gisborne, M., 230.
Godiva, Lady, 90.
Golborne, 204.
———— Park, 194. 204. 222. 228.
———— Station, 204. 228.
Golden Hill Station, 206. 228.
Goldsmith, Dr., 212.
Gordon, 214.
Gorhambury, account of, 16.
Gough, J., 128. 218.

Grafton, Duke of, 215.
Grafton Regis, 37.
Graham, Colonel, 142. 145. 219.
Grand Junction Canal, 6. 11. 18. 20. 24, 25, 26. 32. 37, 38. 48, 49. 89. Aylesbury and Wendover branches of, 20. Summit of, 21.
Grand Junction Railway Itinerary line, 218. Station in Birmingham, 126. Station in Liverpool, 183. Station in Manchester, 197. Summit, 141. Viaduct, 106.
Grand Trunk Canal, 153, 154, 155. 172. 173.
Grand Union Canal, 50.
Grange Hall, 174.
Gravelly Hill, 128.
Gray, Rev. J., 4.
Great Bar Hall, 129. 218.
Greathead, B., 69.
Great Western Railway, 4. Itinerary line, 231.
Gregory, Captain, 217.
Grenfell, P., 232.
Grenville, Lady, 232.
Gresley, Lady Sophia, 230.
Grimston, Hon. Miss, 17.
Grove, The, 5. 213. Account of, 15.
Guy, Earl of Warwick, 77.
Guy's Cliff, account of, 68.
Haigh Hall, 228.
Halford, J., 128.
Halsnead Hall, 182. 222.
Haltwhistle, 225.
Hampden, John, and Hampden House, 21.
Hampstead Hall, 128. 218.
Hampton Station, 105. Account of, 107.
Ham's Hall, 229.
Hanley, account of, 157.

Hanmer, Colonel, 25, 214.
Hanslope Church, 37.
———— Park, 37. 215.
Hanwell Bridge, 6.
———— Park, 231.
Harecastle, 154, 155.
———— Tunnel, 156.
Haresfoot, 17. 214.
Harper, J. H., 174.
Harrington, Earl of, 231.
Harrison, R., 37. 215.
Harrow, 4. Account of, 7.
———— School, 7.
———— Road, 3.
———— Station, 4. 212. Account of, 6.
————, view from, 7.
Harrowby, Earl of, 145.
Hartford, 220. Station, 170.
Hartwell House, 34.
———— Park Farm, 37.
Harvey, R., 232.
Hatherton Hall, 143.
————, Lord, 131. 144. 220.
Hatton Mill, 152.
Hawkesbury Hall, 217.
Hawkesmoor, 39.
Hawksmoor Brook, 145.
Haydon Bridge, 225.
Hazles, The, 182. 222.
Heathcote, B. 231.
Hedsor, Lodge, 232.
Hemel Hempstead, account of, 18.
Henley, Lord, 216.
Henry I., 40.
———— II., 40.
———— III., 41.
———— VIII., 6. 12. 46, 47.
Hermitage, The, 225.
Heron, General, 176.
Hertford, Marquis of, 224.
Hervey Aston, A. W., 175.
———— Rev. J., 44.
Hexham, 225.

Hexham Abbey, 225.
Heyes, The, 194.
Heywood Lodge, 232.
Hibbert, Captain, 216.
Hill Moreton, embankment and Viaduct, 50.
Hill Moreton Manor-house, 216.
Hilton Hall, 142. 219. Account of, 145.
———, Jack of, account of, 146.
Hindley Hall, 228.
Hodgett, Mr., 228.
Hoghton, Sir H. B., 181. 222.
Holbrook Grange, 216.
Holdford, 128.
Holyoake, Captain, 142.
Hood, Dowager Lady, 217.
Hordern, A., 142.
———, H., 142.
Hornby, 179.
———, Rev. I. J., 179.
Horton, 24, 25.
Howard, Fulke Greville, 230.
Howard, H., 225.
Hughes, M., 181. 222.
Hulton Hall, 224.
Hunton Bridge, 16.
Huntsmoor Lodge, 232.
Huskisson, Mr., 142. 195, 196. 204.
Huyton Gate Station, 182.
——— Quarry Station, 182.
Icknield Street, 21. 23. 130.
Ingestrie Hall, 145.
Iver Grove, 232.
Ivinghoe, 25.
James Bridge Station, 129. 218.
Jersey, Earl of, 231.
Jervoise, S. C., 217.
Kay, Mrs., 20. 214.
Keele Hall, 165.
Kendrick's Cross Station, 181.
Kenilworth, account of, 61.

Kenilworth Castle, 217. account of, 61.
Kensal Green, 2. 19.
——————— Tunnel, 3.
Kilburn and Kilburn Bridge, 2.
——— Priory, 6.
Kilsby, 50. 59.
——— Tunnel, account of, and view from, 50. 216.
King, John, 41.
Kingsbury, Middlesex, 212.
——————— Station, Warwickshire, 229.
King's Langley, 17.
Kippax Park, 224.
Kirkwall, Lord, 232.
Kit's Green, 106.
Knightley, Sir C., 48. 215.
Knowle, account of, 108.
Knowsley Park, 182. 222. Account of, 185.
Lamb, R. H., 216.
Lamb's Cottage Station, 196.
Lane, Colonel, 129.
Lane End, 152. 156.
Lanercost Priory, 225.
Lanfranc, Archbishop, 7.
Langley Bury, 16. 213.
Langley Park, 232.
Lawley, Sir F., 229.
Lawley Street Viaduct, 106. 127.
Lawrence, C., 182.
Lea Green Gate Station, 181.
Lea Hall, 106. 217.
Leamington, account of, 71.
Leam River, 46.
Lee, Rev. J. P., 118.
Leeds and Liverpool Canal, 228.
Leeds and Selby Railway, 224.
Leigh, Lord, 70, 217.
———, Sir R. H., 228.
———, J. H., 174.
———, J. W. Boughton, 216.
Leighton Buzzard, 28, 29. 214. Account of, 26.

Leighton Buzzard, Station, 25.
Levett, T., 230.
Lichfield, account of, 132.
———, Earl of, 145. 150.
——— and Coventry, Bishop of, 151.
Linford House, 215.
Linslade House, 29. 214.
——— Tunnel, 28. 214.
Liscombe House, 25. 29. 214. Account of, 25.
Liverpool, 220. 222. Account of, 185. Churches, 187. Custom House, 188. Exchange, 188. Hackney Coach Fares, 183. Hotels, 183. Station, 183. Tunnels, 183. Views of and from, 186. Steam Packet, 193.
Liverpool and Manchester Railway, 179 to 183. Itinerary line, 222.
Liverpool and Birmingham Junction Canal, 141.
Locksley, Esq., 20. 214.
Locker, W., 150.
Long Buckby, 49.
——— Viaduct, 49, 50.
Loughton, 30.
Louis XVIII., 34.
Love Hill, 232.
Lovett, Miss, 25, 26. 29. 214.
Low Hill, 142.
Lower Place Gates, 3.
Lowndes, W. S., 214.
Lutterworth, account of, 55.
Lyon, John, 7.
Madeley, Great, 219.
——— Moss, 164.
——— Station, 165.
——— Manor House, 165.
Maer Hall, 152.
Maiden Bower, 24.
Mainwaring, Captain, 164.
Manchester, 220. 222. Account of, 197. Charitable Institutions, 199. Hotels, 197. Public Buildings, 198. Station, 197.
Manchester and Birmingham Railway, 153.
Manchester and Birmingham Extension Railway, 50. 151. 154.
Manning, W., 142.
Manor Hall, 170.
Mansell, Major, 215.
Marbury Hall, 174.
Market Drayton, 152.
Marshall, W., 129. 228. 219.
Marston Hall, 106. 217.
——— Green, 106.
——— Viaduct, 106.
——— Salt Works, 174.
Maxstoke, Castle, 106. 217. 229. account of, 111.
Meese Brook, 151.
Mentmore, 25.
Meriden Hall, 106. 217.
Mersey, River, 170, 171. 177.
——— and Irwell Canal, 177.
Middlewich, account of, 173.
——— Branch Canal, 169.
Middleton Hall, 229.
Midland Counties Railway, 50.
Mill Meese, 151.
——— Stream, 164.
Minshull Vernon, 220.
——— Station, 169.
Mitre Bridge, 3.
Moilliet, J. L., 128. 218.
Monckton, Hon. E., 143.
———, G., 143.
Montague, Lord, 132.
Moor Park, 5. Account of, 15.
Moore, 220.
——— Excavation, 176.
——— Hall, 176.
——— Station, 176.
Mosely Court, 142.

Mosely Hall, 142.
Mosley, Sir Oswald, 230.
———, A. N. E., 230.
Moss Brook, 150.
Mow, Copt, 168.
Moxhull Hall, 229.
Nantwich, 168. Account of, 167.
Nash Mill, 17. 213.
Naworth Castle, 225.
New Hall, 194. 222. 228.
Newbold Bridge, 58.
——— Grange, 58. 216.
——— Hall, 216.
——— Vicarage, 216.
Newcastle and Carlisle Railway, 225.
——— under Lyme, account of, 154.
Newnham Padox, 216.
Newport Pagnell, account, 36.
Newton Excavation, 128.
——— Bridge Station, 194.
——— Junction Station, account of, 179.
——— Park, 230.
——— Road Station, 128, 129. 218.
Noel, Hon. Mrs. Berkely, 229.
Normandy, Duke of, 40.
Northampton, 37. Account of, 39.
Northchurch Tunnel, 20. 214.
Northcote Court, 20. 214.
North Union Railway, 195. 22. Account of, 204.
——————— itinerary line, 228.
Northwich, account of, 171.
Norton Bridge Station, 151. 219.
——— Hall, 216.
——— Priory, account of, 176.
Nuneaton, account of, 104.
Offa, King, 9.
Offley, Hon. Mrs. Cunliffe, 165.
O'Kelly, Dennis, 7.

Orford Hall, 179.
Oscott Roman Catholic College, 128.
Osterley Park, 231.
Oulton Park, 170.
Ouse River, 32, 33, 36, 37.
Ouzle, River, 24, 25, 26. 36.
Oxford Canal, 50. 72. 89.
Oxhey Lane, 4.
Oxley Hall, 142.
Paradise Bridge, 142.
Packington Hall, 106. 217. Account of, 107. Park, 229.
Paddington Canal, 6.
Park Street Bridge, 2.
Park Village, 2.
Parker, J. T., 216.
Parker, J., 228.
Parkside Station, 194. 228.
Parlington House, 224.
Parr Moss, 180, 181.
Parrot, F., 217.
Pastures, The, 231.
Patricroft Station, 196.
Patten, J. W. W., 179.
Peel, Sir Robert, 229.
———, W. Yates, 229.
Pendeford Hall, 142.
Penk River, 146.
——— and Valley, 144.
——— and Viaduct, 145.
Penkridge, 219. Account of, 147.
——— Station, 143.
Penn, G., 232.
Penwortham Lodge and Priory, 228.
Perceval, Hon. Spencer, 43.
Perry Bar Station, 127, 128 218.
Perry Hall, 128. 218.
Philpot, Mrs., 215.
Pickering and Whitby Railway, 222.
Pilkington, Sir W., 164.

Pollet, G., 165.
Pomfret, Countess, 39.
Potteries, The, account of, 157.
Pountney, J. S., 142.
Praed, J. B., 215.,
Prescot, account of, 183.
Preston, Lancashire, account of, 208. 228.
———, Middlesex, 7.
——— Brook, 220.
——————— Station, 175.
——— on the Hill, 175.
Preston and Wyre Railway, 211.
Primrose Hill, 2.
——————— Tunnel, 2.
Prinsep, I. L., 230.
Pulsford, W., 29. 214.
Quartley, Rev. H. R., 37. 215.
Queen, the, 232.
Queensberry, Marchioness of, 216.
Radbourne Hall, 231.
Rainhill, 181.
Ranton Abbey, account of, 150.
Rawstorne, Colonel, 228.
Reay River, 127.
Redworth House, 226.
Reen, G., 145.
Richard I., 41.
——— II., 42.
——— III., 94.
Richings Lodge, 232.
Rickmansworth, account of, 13.
Ridgway, the, 130.
Rivington, account of, 208.
Rivington Pike, 194. 208.
Roade Station, 37. 215.
Roby Lane Station, 182.
Rolleston, 230.
Rose Hill, 225.
Rowley House, 145.
Roxeth, 7.
Rugby, account of, 51. 55.
——— Lodge, 216.
——— School, 52.

Rugby Station, 50. 216.
Runcorn Gap, 181.
Russell, Lord John, 9.
Ryder, Hon. G. D., 17. 213.
Salford, 198, 204.
Salisbury, Marquis of, 182. 222.
Saltley, 127.
Salt Mines, 172.
Sandbach, 168.
Sandon Hall, 145.
Sandwell Park, 128
Sankey Navigation, 180.
——— Viaduct, 180.
Sawyer, I., 232.
Scarisbrick, Miss, 194. 222. 228.
Scott, Lord J., 216.
———, Sir E. D., 129. 218.
Seabrook Bridge, 24, 25.
Sefton, Earl of, 182.
Seighford, 150.
——— Hall, 150.
Shackerley, G. J., 174.
Shallowford, 150, 151.
Sharedon Brook, 142.
Shareshill, 142.
Shaw Hall, 228.
Sheldon Hall, 217.
——— Viaduct, 106.
Shenley House, 215.
Sheppard, Sir T. C., 215.
Sherburne Brook, 58.
Sherriffe, Lawrence, 52. 54.
Shirley Hall, 181. 222.
Shottesbrook Park, 232.
Show Hill, 142.
Shugborough, 145.
Simpson, Hon. J. B., 216.
Skipwith, Sir G., 216.
Slade Heath, 142.
Slapton, 25.
Smith, J., 214.
———, Barry, J. H. 174.
Sneyd, R., 165.
Solihull, 106. Account of, 110.
Somerford Hall, 143. 220.

INDEX.

Southcott, 24.
Sow River, 58. 106. 148, 149, 150. 152.
—— Viaduct, 58.
Spilsbury, Rev. F. W., 230.
Spital Brook, 145.
Spooner, Rev. Archdeacon, 118.
——, R., 118.
Spread-Eagle Station, 143. 218.
Stableford Bridge, 152. 219.
Stafford, 219. Account of, 147.
—— Castle, 145.
—— Station, 145.
——, Lord, 145.
Staffordshire and Worcestershire Canal, 141, 142. 144.
Standish, F. H., 228.
——, C., 228.
—— Hall, 228.
—— Station, 205. 228.
Standon, 151.
—— Bridge, 152.
Stanmore, 7.
—— Little, 8.
Starkie, Mr., 228.
Startops End, 21. 25.
Stephen, King, 40.
Stewkley, 29.
Stitchford Brook and Viaduct, 106.
Stivichall Hall, 217.
Stock's House, 20. 214.
Stockgrove, 25. 214.
Stockton and Darlington Railway, 226.
Stoke Hammond, 28, 29.
—— House, 232.
—— Park, Buckinghamshire, 232.
——————, Northamptonshire, 37. 215. account of, 38.
—— Place, 232.
Stoke-upon-Trent, account of, 155.
Stone, account of, 153.

Stoneleigh Abbey, account of, 70. 217.
Stoney Stratford, 37. Account of, 31.
Stowe, account of, 34.
—— Tunnel, 38. 215.
Stratford-upon-Avon, account of, 77.
Stretton Hall, 143.
Stubbs, W., 176.
Sullivan, Rt. Hon. I., 232.
Summer Hill House, 182.
Sutherland, Duke of, 152.
Sutton Coldfield, 128. Account of, 130.
—— Incline, 181.
Swabey, M., 232.
Swinnerton Manor House and Park, 151.
—————— Village 151.
Sykes, Lady, 106. 217.
Taff Vale Railway, 37.
Tamworth Station, 230.
Tapps Gervis, Sir G. W., 232.
Taplow Court, 232.
—— House, 232.
Taylor, J., 118.
Teddesley Hall, 220.
Temple Newsham, 224.
Thornewill, T., 230.
Thornley, C., 106. 217.
Thornton, T. R., 50. 216.
Thornton Hall, 215.
Tillington House, 150.
Tixall Hall, 145.
Tollemache, Hon. C., 232.
Tove, River, 37.
Towcester, account of, 44.
Townsend, T., 216.
Townshend, E. V., 174.
Trafford, T. J., 222.
Trafford Park, 222.
Trentham Hall and Park, 152.
Tring, account of, 20.
—— Excavation, 25.

Tring Park, 20. 214. View near, 20.
——— Station and summit, 20.
Turner, C., 231.
Twemlow, F., 165.
Two Waters, 17. Account of, 18.
Twyford Abbey, 3. 212. Account of, 5.
Tyringham, 215.
Unthank Hall, 225.
Uthwatt, H., 215.
Vale Royal, 170.
——— Abbey, 221. Account of, 170.
——— Viaduct, 170. 220.
Vansittart, Hon. Mrs., 232.
Ver River, 11.
Vernon, L., 37, 38. 215.
Verulam, 11.
———, Earl, 16.
Vesey, Bishop, 131, 132.
Vyse, Col., 223.
Wakefield Lodge, 215.
Walhouse, Mrs., 143.
Walker, T., 58. 216.
Wall Gate Station, 205.
Walmesley, C., 228.
Walsall, 127. 129, 130. Account of, 131.
——— Hall, 230.
Walton Lodge, 228.
Warburton, R. E. E., 174.
Warrender, Sir G., 232.
Warrington, 220. Account of, 179.
——— Station, 177.
——— Viaduct, 177. 220.
Warwick, Earls of, 74. 131. Account of, 79.
——— Castle, account of, 72.
——— Hall, 225.
——— Vase, account of, 77.
——— and Napton Canal, 72. 89.
Wat Tyler, 42.

Watford, 4. 19. 213. Account of, 9.
——— Bridge, 4. View from, 4.
——— Park, 216.
——— Station, 4.
——— Tunnel, 16. 213. Account of, 17.
——— Viaduct and View, 4.
Watling Street, 23. 31. 48. 50.
Watt, J., 128. 218.
Watts, W., 37. 215.
Wavertree Hall, 182.
Weast Lane Station, 197.
Weaver, River, account of, 170, 171. 172.
——— Valley and Falls of the, 174, 175.
Weaverham, 174.
Wedgwood, J., 152. 161.
Wednesbury, 129. Account of, 133.
Weedon, 38. View near, described, 38. 49.
——— Beck, account of, 48.
——— Military depôt, 38. 49.
——— Station, 38. 215.
Weildon, G., 216.
Welton House, 216.
Wembly Green, 2. 4.
——— Park, 4. 212. Account of, 6.
Wendover, account of, 21.
West Auckland, 227.
Westbrook Hay, 17. 213.
West Bromwich, 129. Account of, 134.
Westminster, Marquis of, 5.
Weston Flavell, 44.
Westwood House, 228.
Wetstone Green Bridge, 142.
Wexham Lodge, 232.
——— Rectory, 232.
Whaddon Hall, 214.
Wharncliffe Viaduct, 231.
Wharton, 169.

INDEX.

Wharton Lodge, 169.
Whatcroft Hall, 174.
Whetstone, 6.
Whilton, 50.
——— Bridge, 50.
Whitby, Rev. E., 150.
Whitchurch, 8.
Whitgreave, G., 142.
——————— T., 142.
Whitley Abbey, 217.
Whitmore, 219. 164.
——— Hall, 174.
——— Station, 152. 154.
Whittingstall, E. F., 16. 213.
Wichnor Park, 230.
Wigan, 228. Account of, 207.
——— and Manchester Canal, 228.
Willan, late Mr., 5.
Willenhall Station, 130. 218.
William the Conqueror, 40.
Willington Station, 231
——— Hall, 230.
Willmore, J., 128.
Willis, R., 182. 222.
Willoughby, R., 229.
Wilmot, Sir J. E., 105. 217.
———, Horton, Sir R., 230.
———, Sir R., 231.
Wilton Hall, 128.
Wincham Hall, 174.
Windleston Hall, 226.
Windsor Castle, 232. Account of, 211.
Winnington Hall, 174.
Winsford, 169. 220.
——— Bridge, 170.
——— Lodge, 169.

Winsford Station, 169.
Winslow, account of, 27.
Winstanley Hall, 228.
Winwick Hall and Station, 179.
Woburn, account of, 27.
——— Abbey, account of, 28.
Wolston House, 58.
Wolverhampton, account of, 139.
——————— Station, 130. 218.
Wolverton House, 37. 215.
——— Park, 37. 215.
——— Station, 30. 215. account of, 30.
——— Viaduct, 36, 37. 215.
Woodcock, T., 228.
Wooton Green, 105.
——————— Viaduct, 105.
Worcester, Battle of, 129.
———, Bishop of, 118.
Wormwood Scrubs, 3.
Worsley Hall, 196. 222.
Worthington, W., 230.
Woughton, 30.
Wrekin, The, 143.
Wren, Sir Christopher, 39.
Wrightington Hall, 228.
Wrinehill, 165. 219.
——— Wood, 165.
Wrottesley, Sir J., 130.
——— Hall, 219.
——— Park, 130.
Wyrley and Essington Canal, 130. 141.
Yardley, 106.
Yarm, 226.

THE END.

LONDON:
Printed by A. SPOTTISWOODE,
New-Street-Square.

AN APPENDIX

TO

MOGG'S HAND BOOK

𝔉or 𝔑ailway 𝔗ravellers;

BEING A DESCRIPTION

OF THE

RAIL ROADS,

AT PRESENT IN OPERATION FOR THE CONVEYANCE
OF PASSENGERS IN VARIOUS PARTS
OF THE KINGDOM.

BY EDWARD MOGG,

EDITOR OF MOGG'S PATERSON'S ROADS.

LONDON:

PUBLISHED AND SOLD BY THE PROPRIETOR,

EDWARD MOGG,

14, GREAT RUSSELL STREET, COVENT GARDEN.

1846.

The following Railways form the subject of this Appendix, and the pages herein named refer solely to that part of the work. They are arranged as follows:—

1. *South Western, or London and Southampton Railway.* The description of commences at page 1. The Itinerary line at page 1 of that division.

2. *Midland Counties Railway.* The description of commences at page 28. The Itinerary line at page 6 of that division.

3. *Birmingham and Gloucester Railway.* The description of commences at page 46. The Itinerary line at page 32 of that division.

4. *Chester and Crewe Railway.* The description of commences at page 60. The Itinerary line at page 17 of that division.

5. *Chester and Birkenhead Railway.* The description of commences at page 68. The Itinerary line at page 18 of that division.

6. *North Midland Railway.* The description of commences at page 71. The Itinerary line at page 9 of that division.

7. *Lancaster and Preston Railway.* The description of commences at page 90. The Itinerary line at page 20 of that division.

8. *York and North Midland Railway.* The description of commences at page 95. The Itinerary line at page 15 of that division.

9. *Croydon Railway*, an Itinerary line only, will be found at page 19 of that division.

10. *Manchester and Leeds Railway*, an Itinerary line only, will be found at page 24 of that division.

11. *Eastern Counties Railway*, an Itinerary line only, will be found at page 26 of that division.

12. *Hull and Selby Railway*, an Itinerary line only, will be found at page 21 of that division.

13. *Northern and Eastern Railway*, an Itinerary line only, will be found at page 28 of that division.

14. *Bristol and Gloucester Railway.* The description of commences at page 102.

15. *Manchester and Bolton Railway.* The description of commences at page 106.

16. *Bolton and Preston Railway.* The description of commences at page 108.

17. *Manchester and Birmingham Railway.* The description of commences at page 109.

18. *Cheltenham and Great Western Union Railway.* The description of commences at page 114.

19. *York and Scarborough, and York and Pickering Railways.* The description of commences at page 101.

20. *Great North of England and the Durham Branches* follow page 36. *Great North of England,* the last of the Itinerary lines.

21. *Great Western Railway, with the Bristol and Exeter Railway* separately paged, follow the *Durham Branches* that commence at page 36 of the Itinerary lines, and are followed by

22. *The Dover Railway,* that succeeded by the *Brighton Railway,* also separately paged, complete the volume.

SOUTH-WESTERN, OR

LONDON AND SOUTHAMPTON RAILWAY.

LONDON TO KINGSTON.

QUITTING the station at Nine Elms, near Vauxhall, the Railway, constructed on a gradual rise, in less than ⅓ a mile reaches a level of rather more than a mile in length, at the termination of which, the embankment on which it is formed, gradually increasing in elevation, affords, if not an extensive, a very excellent view, the foreground of which is filled by the open space known as Battersea Fields, situate on the south bank of the Thames, that, at the time of high water, forms a fine feature of the landscape. Upon the northern bank of the river is beheld that noble monument of British munificence, Chelsea Hospital, the country to the north of it gradually rising into an amphitheatre of hills, being backed by the eminences of Hampstead and Highgate, that terminate the view. Eastward is seen, rising in lofty majesty, the magnificent cathedral of St. Paul, that, pointing out the site, dignifies by its presence the centre of the great Metropolis. On left of the Railway, almost as far as Battersea Lane, rich meadows line its side, from which, suddenly ascending, the eminence known as Battersea Rise, upon the Wandsworth road, bordered by a detached line of suburban villas, commanding a delightful prospect, bounds the view. In a distance of rather more than 2 miles, the Railway, carried over the road from Clapham to Battersea by a massive brick bridge of oblique form, turns suddenly to the south, and passing under the Wandsworth road, in a short distance further reaches

THE WANDSWORTH STATION,

AN INTERMEDIATE ONE, DISTANT FROM LONDON 2½ MILES, FROM SOUTHAMPTON 74 MILES. — Journey resumed at next page.

WANDSWORTH,

So called from its situation on the banks of the river Wandle, that here falls into the Thames, is a considerable village of Surrey, situate 6 miles from London, on the Kingston road. It has long been distinguished for its manufactures, for all which it is indebted to the Wandle, that, although a small stream, turns, in its course to the Thames, flour, oil, iron, white-lead, and paper mills, in addition to which the businesses of bleaching, dyeing, the printing of silks and cottons, all requiring the aid of water, are here carried

B

on to a considerable extent, as are breweries and distilleries, the latter, in particular, upon an extensive scale. Here are two churches, and meeting houses for the different denominations of dissenters, with charity schools in connection with the established church and dissenting congregations. The houses in the High Street, though very irregular, are in general of a respectable character, but those upon East and West Hill consist chiefly of detached villas, that, from their elevated situation, command some very delightful prospects. In Garrat Lane was formerly held, upon the dissolution of Parliament, a mock election of a Mayor of Garrat, to which Foote's farce of that name gave no small celebrity.

From Wandsworth Station, the train is carried forward between sloping banks, upon a considerable rise, for about ½ a mile, in which distance it arrives at the road from Tooting to Wandsworth, here borne over the Railway by an oblique bridge. Shortly after reaching this point, the line attains a level of about 1¼ mile in length, in less than ½ a mile of which, emerging from the cutting, it enters on an embankment that affords a good view of the country on either side. At a distance of 4 miles from Nine Elms, it crosses Garrat Lane, and very shortly after the river Wandle, over both of which it is borne by oblique bridges, that over the Wandle being of 65 feet span. 1½ mile distant from Garrat Lane, on the hill upon the right, see West Hill House; it is situate about ⅓ a mile beyond Wandsworth, upon the Portsmouth road, and immediately adjoining Wimbledon Park. The prospect on left of the embankment, though not extensive, is pleasant, being terminated in that direction by the rising grounds about Norwood, that, studded with villas, stand forth the most striking object in the distance. In rather more than ⅓ a mile from Garrat Lane, the Railway reaches the road from Merton to Wandsworth, which it crosses on the level of the surrounding country, and where, for the prevention of accidents, gates have been erected, that, during the passing of the trains, are closed against all who may happen to be then travelling thereon. From a little before the Wandsworth and Merton road, the Railway commences a considerable rise, 1 in 330, and carried through a cutting, passing in its way under an oblique bridge, bearing the road from Garrat to Wimbledon, in a short distance further gains the road from Wimbledon to Merton and

THE WIMBLEDON STATION,

AN INTERMEDIATE ONE, DISTANT FROM LONDON 5¾ MILES, FROM SOUTHAMPTON 70¾ MILES.—Journey resumed at next page.

On right of Wimbledon Station is Wimbledon Park, the property of Earl Spencer. This is esteemed one of the finest parks in England. It contains twelve hundred acres, is adorned with fine plantations, beautiful declivities, and a sheet of water, containing fifty acres. The eminences in this park present many varied and delightful points of view:— Harrow-on-the-Hill, Highgate, the Metropolis, Norwood, and Epsom Downs. The house was burnt down in 1785, but a new mansion was afterwards built, in a better situation, from designs by the late Mr. Holland: it was completed in 1801.

WIMBLEDON,

A pleasant village, seated on the border of the common to which it gives name (the scene of many a fatal duel), enjoys, from its elevated position, some very delightful prospects. It is irregularly built, the better class of houses chiefly consisting of gentlemen's seats (for an account of which the reader is referred to the Itinerary line, at the end of the work). The church was rebuilt, the chancel excepted, in 1788, by private subscription of the inhabitants; it is in the Grecian style. In the churchyard is the tomb of the rich miser, John Hopkins, celebrated by Pope as *Vulture Hopkins*, who died in 1732.

From the last-named rise (1 in 330) which terminates a little beyond the Garrat and Wimbledon road, continued through cutting, the Railway enters on a level, upon which it is continued for nearly 3 miles. Emerging from the last-named excavation about $\frac{1}{3}$ a mile beyond the Wimbledon Station, it enters on an embankment, the country expands on either side, and the Railway near the 7th mile-stone reaches Combe Lane. On left of Combe Lane is Cannon Hill, and beyond it, bordering the Epsom and Ewell road, Morden Park. Carried over Combe Lane, by an oblique bridge, and continuing its course upon a level embankment of considerable elevation, the view on the right is bounded by the rich foliage of Combe Wood, and Kingston Hill, that, suddenly rising beyond it, terminate the view. In rather more than a mile beyond Combe Lane, the Railway, changing its inclination, quits the level, just previous to which it passes by Wittles Farm, upon the right, through another cutting, and commencing a short but rather steep ascent, 1 in 330, in that way reaches the road from Malden to Richmond Park, an avenue remarkable for its straightness, at the farther extremity of which Combe House, long the residence of the late Earl of Liverpool, rises into view. From the road to Combe House, the line, constructed upon a level embankment of $1\frac{1}{2}$ mile in length, runs through fertile fields, and first crossing the Hog's Mill river, reaches the farther extremity of the last-named level and embankment. From this point, viz. $9\frac{1}{4}$ miles from London, it enters a cutting of considerable depth, and of nearly 1 mile in length; the first ½ mile of which is a rather sharp ascent, 1 in 330, the latter a descent of the same ratio. Upper Marsh Lane, leading to Kingston, crosses the first part of this excavation, by a bridge thrown over it, and in the latter part, a little beyond the bridge that carries the turnpike road from Kingston to Ewell, Epsom, and Leatherhead, lies

KINGSTON STATION,

A PRINCIPAL ONE, DISTANT FROM LONDON 10¼ MILES, FROM SOUTHAMPTON 66¼ MILES. — Journey resumed at next page.

KINGSTON,

A market town of Surrey, 10 miles from London, is situate on the south bank of the Thames, over which has been erected a new stone bridge, and consists of two principal streets and several smaller ones, with a spacious market-place in the centre. The erection of modern houses, intermixed with those of a more ancient date, gives an appearance of picturesque irregularity to the town. The church is a spacious structure. A new court-house was built some few years since, where the Lent assizes for the county are held. This place formerly sent members to Parliament, till, by petition, the inhabitants prayed to be relieved from the burden. The corporation consists of bailiffs, a high steward, recorder, town clerk, justices, &c., who are authorised to hold a court every week for the decision of all kinds of pleas and actions. The hamlet of Norbiton, the principal approach from London, consists of first-rate residences; but that of Surbiton, upon the Guildford road, of some delightful villas, that command fine views of the Thames, backed by the rich woods of Hampton Court Palace, that rise from the margin of that noble river. The chief trade of the place consists of corn, meal, and malt, which are here sold in large quantities. Situate on the great line of road from London to Portsmouth, the carrying trade of Kingston was considerable, and its connection with stage coaches and maintenance of posting establishments, proved at all times, but particularly during the late war, of great advantage to the town, that, from its abstraction of business in this way, occasioned by the formation of the South Western Railway, has suffered severely. Kingston was occupied by the Romans, and numerous remains of that people have been discovered in and near it. Some of our Saxon kings were also crowned here; and close to the north side of the church is a large stone, on which, according to tradition, they were placed during the ceremony. Here is a free-school, founded by Queen Elizabeth, the school-room of which is an ancient chapel, that belonged to the demolished hospital of St. Mary Magdalen. Here also is an almshouse, built in 1668, by Alderman Cleave, for six men and as many women.

KINGSTON TO WOKING.

Emerging from the excavation about ¼ mile beyond the Kingston Station, the Railway enters on an embankment of considerable elevation, by which it arrives, in ¾ mile more, at the pleasant village of Long Ditton, the ornamental cottages of which present a very picturesque appearance, and exhibit altogether one of those agreeable contrasts rarely to be met with in railway travelling. Continuing to descend for about ½ mile beyond Long Ditton, the line then commences an ascent of 1 in 330, and carried by embankment, with an easy sweep, passing Thames Ditton on the right to the Portsmouth road at Ditton Marsh, crosses that once great thoroughfare by an expansive arch of oblique form, at a distance of 12¼ miles from London. The embankment here being of considerable elevation, affords a good view of the country on either side. Here the verdure of Ditton Marsh contrasts beautifully with the variegated scenery by which it is surrounded. On left of the line, the high grounds and rich woods of Esher and Claremont rise into view, and these blending their beauties with those of Esher Place on the opposite side of the village, present altogether one of the richest bits of landscape to be seen throughout the journey. Viewed either way, the Portsmouth road, on which occasionally may still be seen a four-horse team or fashionable barouche, enlivens the scene, which to the right, unfolds the umbrageous woods of Hampton Court, that, with those of Ember Court in the immediate vicinity of the Railway, line its northern side. For ¼ mile beyond the Portsmouth road, the Railway is constructed upon a descent of 1 in 330, at the termination of which it crosses the road from Weston Green to Hare Lane, from whence it is continued on a level for ¾ of a mile, in one of which it reaches the road from Hampton Court to East Moulsey and Esher, and the

ESHER AND HAMPTON COURT STATION,

AN INTERMEDIATE ONE, DISTANT FROM LONDON 12¾ MILES, FROM SOUTHAMPTON 63¾ MILES.—Journey resumed at page 8.

The Esher Station, a neat structure, situate in the centre of delightful scenery, from its proximity to points of great attraction, may, with great propriety, be selected as the spot for which the tourist should make, who, bent upon a day's pleasure, may be desirous of exploring the beauties of the surrounding country, or of entering on an examination of any of the various objects of absorbing interest, with which the vicinity abounds. ½ mile distant from the Esher Station on right, is Ember Court; this (which was once the seat of the celebrated Speaker of the House of Commons, Arthur Onslow) skirts the road leading from the Station to Hampton Court, that, after passing through East Moulsey, is reached in a distance of 2 miles from the Station. 1 mile west of Hampton Court, is the beautiful village of Hampton, and opposite to it, at a distance of 1 mile from Hampton Court Bridge upon the left, Moulsey Hurst, formerly the scene of pugilistic contest, but now somewhat more refined, is, at the races annual here, the resort of no small portion of the fashionable world. About 1 mile distant from Esher Station on right at Thames Ditton is Boyle Farm, and last, not least, from Thames Ditton to the town of Kingston, one of the most beautiful walks that can well be imagined. The Thames, here expanded to an amplitude of breadth, bares its broad bosom to the view, backed by the noble woods of Hampton Court; while upon the right an unconnected range of rustic villas skirts the line. Parties who may be desirous of participating in the pleasure of this delightful walk, need not return to the Esher Station; but dining at Kingston may, if so disposed, reach London by any of the trains that call at the Kingston Station. To complete our description of the objects in its neighbourhood, it will now be necessary to return to the Esher Station, 1 mile on left of which, upon the Portsmouth road, lies Esher, the village of which, with Claremont and Esher Place, well worthy of a visit, exhibit a combination of sylvan scenery of surpassing excellence.

HAMPTON COURT.

Hampton Court, a royal palace, was originally built by Cardinal Wolsey, in a style of superior magnificence to any thing then existing: such was the magnitude, and so various and costly were the decorations bestowed on this mansion (it contained 280 silk beds for visiters), that it far exceeded all the royal palaces, and thence created much envy against the Cardinal, who, to screen himself from its effects, presented the palace, with all its costly furniture, to Henry VIII.; and it has continued a royal demesne ever since. The palace consists of three quadrangles; the first and second are ancient, but the third, comprising the royal apartments, was built by King William, under the direction of Sir Christopher Wren. The grand façade towards the garden extends 330 feet, and that facing the Thames, 328 feet. The portico and colonnade of the grand entrance, and indeed the general design of these elevations, are in a style of stately grandeur.

The paintings in the various apartments of this palace are extremely numerous, and it is also decorated with very rich tapestry. Among the former, are the celebrated *Cartoons of Raphael*, which have been removed from Windsor Castle. The Park and gardens, with the ground on which the palace stands, are about 3 miles in circumference. The gardens afford a complete specimen of the old style of arrangement, in which mathematical figures were preferred to the forms of natural beauty. The Privy Garden is ornamented with terraces and a fountain. On this side is an extensive grape-house, measuring seventy feet in length, and fourteen in breadth. The interior is wholly occupied by one vine of the black Hamburgh kind, which was planted in the year 1769, and has, in a single year, produced 2200 bunches of grapes, weighing, on an average, one pound each. Adjoining the palace-garden is Hampton Court Park, which extends to Hampton-Wick, and is bounded on the south by the river Thames, and on the north by the high road to Kingston. It is well stocked with deer, and has several avenues of trees, with other fine timber disposed in a less formal manner.

CLAREMONT.

This seat is the property of the King of Belgium; it was purchased by government in 1816, for the country residence of the late Princess Charlotte, and her illustrious consort, then Prince of Saxe Coburg: the sum paid for it was 69,000*l.*, full 30,000*l.* less than it cost the famous Lord Clive for the erection of the mansion, and the improvement of the grounds, both of which were executed by Brown. The present structure forms an oblong square of 44 yards by 34; it occupies a well-chosen situation, commanding many fine views, and on the principal front, a flight of thirteen steps leads to the grand entrance, under a pediment resting on Corinthian columns: there are eight spacious rooms on the ground floor, besides the entrance hall and great staircase. The home demesne contains about 420 acres; the park and other parts of the estate, about 1600 acres, in several farms. A small Gothic building that was erected in the garden for the Princess, has, since her demise, been converted into a mausoleum, dedicated to her memory; it contains a fine bust of her Royal Highness, and the windows are ornamented with beautifully painted glass, by Backler.

ESHER PLACE.

This was anciently a palace of the prelates of Winchester, being built by Bishop Wainfleete, and greatly improved by Cardinal

Wolsey, when he held that see in conjunction with those of York and Durham. A second mansion from a design by Kent, in the same style as the original, was afterwards built: to this succeeded an elegant house, erected by Mr. Spicer. The grounds, beautifully picturesque, are thickly planted, finely diversified, and watered by the Mole, and command from many parts a variety of rich and pleasant prospects. From an eminence in the park, are beheld Richmond Hill, Hampton Court, Harrow-on-the-Hill, the windings of the Thames, and Windsor Castle. These enchanting scenes are immortalised in the charming poetry of Thomson:

> "Esher's groves,
> Where, in the sweetest solitude, embrac'd
> By the soft windings of the silent Mole,
> From courts and senates, Pelham finds repose!"

And the unassuming Dodsley has seated the Genius of Gardens

> "In the lovely vale
> Of Esher, where the Mole glides lingering; oth
> To leave such scenes of sweet simplicity!"

The philosopher, too, will here find subjects of meditation, especially when he is disposed to reflect on the instability and vanity of all earthly grandeur. To this place (then called Asher) was the magnificent Wolsey commanded to retire, just after he had perceived, for the first time, that he had for ever lost the favour of his Sovereign.

From the Esher Station, continued for a short distance on a level, and constructed with an easy sweep, the Railway soon crosses the road leading direct from the old Iron Mill on right to Esher, and shortly after the river Mole, when, commencing a gradual rise, it passes in the rear of Esher Place, that, suddenly rising on left of the line, exhibits the wood-crowned summits of its gently swelling eminences, and beautifully disposed grounds to great advantage. From the bridge over the Mole, the Railway, carried on a gradual rise and embankment, arrives in ¾ of a mile at Broad Lane (leading on left to Hersham, on right to West Moulsey), over which being carried by an oblique bridge, it enters on a short level, at the termination of which it is continued upon a rather sharp ascent (1 in 330) to the road leading from Hersham to Walton, from whence it is continued upon a more gentle rise (1 in 446) to the road to Walton and

THE WALTON STATION.

AN INTERMEDIATE ONE, DISTANT FROM LONDON 15½ MILES, FROM SOUTHAMPTON 61 MILES.—Journey resumed at next page.

OATLANDS.

Oatlands, near Weybridge, in Surrey, was formerly the seat of the Duke of York, of whose executors it was purchased by Lord Francis Egerton. The park and the surrounding grounds, beautifully disposed, are nearly six miles in circumference, in the centre of which stands the mansion, a magnificent edifice that, elevated upon a noble terrace, enjoys prospects of great extent, variety, and beauty. The grotto, which consists of two superb rooms, incrusted with shells and minerals, and a winding passage in which is a bath, is uncommonly beautiful and romantic; it was erected at an expense of 10,000l. to the Duke of Newcastle, its former proprietor. The Southampton Railway has, by consent of the noble owner, been permitted to intersect the grounds.

PAINSHILL PARK. *

The beautiful grounds at Painshill were formed by the Honourable Charles Hamilton, who took a considerable part of them, on the north side, from the barren heath: the south side is a bank above the river Mole, which runs at the foot of it. Availing himself of the inequalities or the land, his plantations were made and buildings placed with the utmost judgment; a spacious piece of water was also formed, which, though considerably above the level of the river, is supplied from it by an ingenious though simple contrivance. The present edifice is a handsome white building; the front, which is facing the river, is adorned in the centre with a pediment, supported by four columns, and bowed sides. The beauty and unexpected variety of the scene; the happy situation, elegant structure, and judicious form of the buildings; the flourishing state, uncommon diversity, and contrasted grouping of the trees, and the contrivance of the water, will not fail to excite the most agreeable sensations.

From the Walton Station, where a bridge thrown over the line carries the road from Walton, 1 mile distant on right, to Cobham, 3¼ miles distant on left, passing in the immediate vicinity of Burwood Park, that lies unseen upon the left, the Railway, constructed on a rise of 1 in 330, is carried by deep cutting through the splendid domain of Oatlands, the delightful scenery of which is of course excluded from the view. Emerging from the park, at a point where a bridge that carries the road from Walton to Weybridge marks its termination, the Railway, entering on a descent of 1 in 330, a little before the 17th milestone, in that way reaches —

---

* 3 miles on left of Walton Station.

THE WEYBRIDGE STATION,

AN INTERMEDIATE ONE, DISTANT FROM LONDON $17\frac{1}{4}$ MILES, FROM SOUTHAMPTON $59\frac{1}{4}$ MILES.— Journey resumed below.

The Weybridge Station is situate in a cutting of considerable depth, and is here crossed by a bridge that carries the road from Weybridge, about $\frac{3}{4}$ mile distant on right, to Cobham, 3 miles distant on left. Shortly after emerging from Oatlands Park, an avenue of firs, severed by the Railway seen on each side the line, at the summit of the cutting, presents a curious appearance. About $\frac{1}{2}$ a mile beyond the Weybridge Station, the Railway, quitting the confines of the cutting, enters on an embankment, and crosses by a bridge of seven arches the old river Wey, here an insignificant stream. The eye is now regaled with the sight of fertile fields on the right, that contrast beautifully with the swelling eminences known as St. George's Hills upon the left, whose finely wooded sides descend in graceful slopes to the valley, through which the silent Mole pursues its sluggish course. $\frac{1}{2}$ a mile beyond the old river Wey, a short level succeeds to the descent, commenced at the Walton and Weybridge road, at the farther extremity of which the Railway crosses the road from Byfleet to Chertsey. At this point it commences a rise of 1 in 338, upon which it continues for about 3 miles, affording a view of the lands lying on each side of the line. Soon after quitting the Byfleet and Chertsey road, it crosses Ham Haw Common, and the Wey Navigation, that commences at Godalming and terminates at Weybridge, where it unites with the Thames; in a short distance further, the road, leading to Sheer Water Farm on the right, and passing a plantation that, formed on its southern bank, obscures the Basingstoke Canal, arrives at Woking Heath, where it crosses the road from Chertsey to Woking, and in a further distance of $\frac{3}{4}$ of a mile arrives at the

WOKING STATION,

A PRINCIPAL ONE, DISTANT FROM LONDON $22\frac{1}{2}$ MILES, FROM SOUTHAMPTON 54 MILES.— Journey resumed at page 12.

The Woking Station is provided with waiting rooms for the accommodation of passengers, is furnished with additional engines for a change, a store of fuel, force-pumps, and all the necessary appliances for putting in motion the carriages of the company. Here commences the Guildford Branch Railway, that in a distance of 6 miles from Woking gains the

GUILDFORD STATION,

A PRINCIPAL ONE, DISTANT FROM LONDON $28\frac{1}{2}$ MILES.

1 mile distant on left of Woking Station is Hoebridge Place, once a noble seat, at which its then possessor, Sir Edward Zouch, is said to have frequently entertained King James I., on his excursions

hither from the palace of Oatlands; and a tradition prevails that the tower still remaining a little to the northward of the house, was erected for the sole purpose of pointing out the way across the heath, by means of a light placed at the top of it, to messengers and others who had occasion to repair hither to the king by night. At Ripley is Ockham Park, Earl of Lovelace.

GUILDFORD,

The county town of Surrey, and the most singular and romantic, perhaps, throughout its whole extent, is 29½ miles south-west from London. This place was one of the residences of the West Saxon kings, the ruins of whose castle (the out-works of which included above five acres) still remain, about 300 yards southward of the High Street. Of these, the principal is the Keep, which stands on an artificial mount, and forms a quadrangle 47 feet by 45½, and 70 feet high. The lower part, to the height of eight or nine feet, is of chalk, above which the walls are carried up with flint, ragstone, and Roman tile, disposed in the herring-bone fashion. In the chalky cliff, about 200 yards to the south-west, are several caverns of considerable depth, of which many idle tales are reported by tradition. This town is situated on the declivity of a chalk-hill, principally on the east bank of the river Wey. It is spacious and well built, consisting of one long street, intersected by nine smaller ones, and having many commodious inns. It returns two members to parliament. The town-hall, in which the assizes are held, is a spacious building, erected in the year 1683: it contains whole-length portraits of James I., Charles II., and James II. (the two latter by Sir Peter Lely), William III., and his Queen, and a picture of Vice-Admiral Sir R. Onslow receiving the Dutch flag after the victory in 1797; the latter was painted by John Russell, Esq., R.A., a native of Guildford, whose father was several times mayor here. The building in which the judges now sit (an elegant room), 40 feet by 30, and 20 feet high, was built at the joint expense of Lords Onslow and Grantley, in the years 1789 and 1790. The town contains three churches, respectively dedicated to the Holy Trinity, St. Mary, and St. Nicholas. The former is a new edifice of brick, erected on site of the old one, which fell down in April, 1740: in it is a costly monument of Archbishop Abbot; with an elaborately wrought cenotaph, in memory of the Right Honourable Arthur Onslow, who was thirty-three years Speaker of the House of Commons, and died in 1768. The churches of St. Mary and St. Nicholas are both ancient buildings; some part of the latter is of Norman architecture. On the north side of the High Street, nearly opposite to Trinity Church, is an hospital, founded by Archbishop

Abbot, in the year 1619, for a master, twelve brethren, and eight sisters; to the latter were added four more poor women, by an order of the Court of Chancery, in 1785. The original endowments have been much increased by subsequent donations. This building is of brick, and encloses a quadrangular area, 66 feet by 63, having a noble tower-gateway, surmounted by four turrets at its entrance. In the north and east windows of the chapel are various compartments, enriched with stained glass, representing the history of the Patriarch Jacob, &c. In the master's dining-room, is a portrait of the Archbishop, together with those of Wickliffe, Fox, and other reformers. In the record-room, at the top of the spiral staircase, which occupies one of the turrets, the Duke of Monmouth was confined, in 1685, when on his way from the west of England to London. Here is a free grammar-school, founded in the reign of Edward VI., in which many eminent persons have received their education; together with a charity and other schools, as well as meeting-houses of Baptists, Presbyterians, Quakers, and Roman Catholics. A small theatre has been built here. The race ground is a fine circular course, about 2 miles eastward of the town, where a plate, of 100 guineas value, given by William III., and three subscription-plates, exclusive of matches, are run for annually, in the Whitsun week.

WOKING TO FARNBOROUGH.

From the Wey Navigation to the Woking Station, the Railway is constructed in a line nearly direct, ¾ of a mile on the London side of which, continued upon embankment, it is carried forward with an increased, it may be termed a steep, acclivity, 1 in 330, for a distance of nearly 6 miles, at which point, viz. the vicinity of Frimley Wall, distant from London 28 miles, it attains a height of 200 feet above the level of Trinity high-water mark at London. Woking Heath, an open barren spot, presents a very wild appearance, and is altogether destitute of any distinguishing feature on the left, but upon the right the tower of Horsell Church, the only one that greets the traveller from London to Basingstoke, is, with the village, visible about 1 mile distant. About ½ a mile beyond the Woking Station, a road runs under the line that leads on left to Guildford; on right through Horsell and Chobham to Sunninghill and Windsor, and in ¼ a mile further another that on left leads to Guildford, and uniting with the Horsell road immediately on right of the line, there branches off through Bisley to Bagshot. The Basingstoke Canal, first seen in the vicinity of the Woking Station, now becomes the companion of the Railway, and pursuing a serpentine course from Horsell to the Hermitage, an ancient seat lying on its northern bank, approaches very close to the line near the 25th milestone; it then takes a somewhat sudden turn to the north, and as suddenly returns to its side very near the 26th milestone, where the Railway crosses by a bridge the road from Bagshot (5½ miles distant on right) to Guildford (6 miles on left of the line). The view from the vicinity of the Woking Station to near the Hermitage on left is circumscribed by the high ground that rising rapidly in that direction is devoid of interest; its increasing elevation, however, presents upon the right a pleasing prospect, that extends to the range of hills running along Bagshot Heath, where the eminence denominated King's Beech Hill, a point well known to all followers of her Majesty's stag hounds, and distinguishable by its trees (situate about a mile from Sunninghill and Ascot race-course), rises into view. Immediately on right of the line, near the 25 milestone, the beautifully wooded eminence known as Knapp Hill, the site of the Hermitage, an ancient seat, ascends as it were, from the banks of the Basingstoke Canal, and for a time shuts out the distant prospect. Continued upon a lofty embankment, and upon a considerable acclivity (1 in 330), the elevation commands a view of the country, particularly upon the right, for some distance; but it is altogether a dull and uninteresting scene, consisting chiefly of open heath, its only enlivening feature being the Basingstoke Canal, that, crossed by insignificant bridges, is beheld for some time serpentizing by its side. About a mile beyond Knapp Hill, the Railway crosses the road from Bagshot on right, to Guildford on left, at a distance of 5¼ miles from the former, and 5½ miles from the latter town; in another mile, the road from Cowshot to Pirbright, and continuing on the rise of 1 in 330, in that way reaches the 28 milestone. At the Cowshot and Pirbright road the Basingstoke Canal again approaches the Railway, and although only occasionally visible, pursues a parallel course with it for about 2⅔ miles. A little beyond the 28 milestone, changing its inclination, it is carried forward through a cutting of considerable depth, upon a still steeper acclivity (1 in 300), for about 1¼ mile, at which point, viz. about ¼ of a mile beyond the 29 milestone, a bridge of five arches crosses the line. Here the Railway (which has continued upon the rise for the last 9¼ miles) attains an elevation of 220 feet, but affords no view. It now enters on a rapid descent, 1 in 330, upon which it is carried through the cutting to a little beyond the 30 milestone, where the Basingstoke Canal borne by an aqueduct of two arches, crosses the line, as does the road from Frimley to Guildford, the former being carried over, the latter under the Railway. At this point the descent terminates, as does the deep cutting through which it has been carried for the last two miles, and to which a short embankment succeeds. From a little beyond the 30 milestone, the line is constructed upon a level of 4 miles in length; the road from Frimley to Ash passes under it at 30¼ miles, as does the Blackwater river at 30½ miles, there dividing the counties of Surrey and Hants, the former of which, at that point, it quits, and enters the latter. At the 31 milestone, the Railway enters an excavation, and in another ½ mile reaches the Farnham and Gosport road (here carried over the line by an oblique bridge) and the

FARNBOROUGH STATION,

A PRINCIPAL ONE, DISTANT FROM LONDON 31½ MILES, FROM SOUTHAMPTON 45 MILES. — Journey resumed at next page.

The Farnborough Station is situate in the last-named excavation, at a distance of 2¾ miles from Blackwater, and the military college at Sandhurst on the right, and 6¾ miles from Farnham on the left: it is furnished with waiting-rooms for passengers, extra engines for a change, a store of fuel, force pumps for replenishing the boilers, and all the requisite appurtenances of an efficient engineering establishment, and is consequently capable of affording, in a case of emergency, the most powerful assistance.

FARNHAM.

Farnham stands at a short distance from the north bank of the river Wey; it consists of one principal street, running nearly east and west, and some smaller ones branching off to the north and south, and contains many excellent houses. The church lies a little to the south of the High Street, and is an extensive fabric, apparently erected at the latter end of the fifteenth century. It consists of a nave, which is continued to form the chancel, a north and south aisle, and has a remarkably substantial tower. The interior contains several handsome monuments, and has a good painting of the twelve apostles for an altar piece. The manor of Farnham was given to Ethelbald, King of the West Saxons, to the see of Winchester, to which it has ever since belonged. The town sent members to Parliament in the 4th and 5th of Edward II., but was probably one of the places which voluntarily relinquished this privilege, in those days considered as a burden. The castle was built by Henry, brother of King Stephen, bishop of Winchester, and has been the summer residence of the bishops of that diocese ever since. It was once a magnificent building, but is now much decayed. During the civil war, it was a place of great strength, having a deep moat and strong walls, defended by several towers, and was garrisoned for the king; but being taken by the parliamentary army the works were blown up, and the whole dismantled. On the Restoration, this castle was repaired at great expense by bishop Morley. Adjoining the park is Jay's tower, the ascent to which is by 63 stone steps. This was partly beaten down by Cromwell's cannon. Though not a corporation, the town is governed by twelve masters or burgesses, out of whose number two bailiffs are annually chosen. Here is a free-school, a good charity-school, and market-house. Farnham is remarkable as being surrounded with plantations which produce the most esteemed hops in the kingdom. Market on Thursday.

FARNBOROUGH TO WINCHFIELD.

Emerging from the confines of the cutting a little beyond the Farnborough Station, the Railway, continuing its level course upon an embankment, enters on a wide expanse of heath, that presents altogether a monotonous appearance. The traveller is now pursuing a parallel course with that part of the great western road leading from Blackwater to Hartford Bridge, well known as Hartford Bridge Flat, which runs along the ridge of hills, that at about 2 miles distant on right, rising suddenly from the lowlands, there terminates the view. The land on left of the line is little better than a barren wide-spreading waste, that extends from the Railway side nearly to Farnham. In less than $\frac{1}{2}$ a mile from the Farnborough Station, the line crosses the road from Blackwater to Cove, a small village lying on left of it, shortly after Cove Brook, a tributary stream of the Blackwater river, at $32\frac{1}{4}$ miles; at $33\frac{1}{4}$ miles, the road from Farnham to Blackwater; and at the 34 milestone, an occupation road leading to Bramshot Farm. Here the Railway commences a gradual rise of 1 in 528, upon which it is continued for about $\frac{3}{4}$ of a mile, crossing the road from Cove to East Everley and Yateley, and in less than $34\frac{3}{4}$ miles reaches the Fleet Pond, an insulated lake of many acres, that enlivens by its presence this scene of seclusion. The Fleet Pond is crossed on its northern side by a bridge, at the western extremity of which another spans the line, bearing a road that leads on left to Farnham, and on right passing in its way Brook Farm, a *ferme ornée*, distant about $\frac{1}{2}$ a mile to Hartford Bridge. At the farther end of Fleet Pond, the Railway enters upon a level of 2 miles in length, in $1\frac{1}{2}$ of which, carried through cutting, it reaches, near the 36 milestone, the road from Farnham (6 miles distant on left) to Hartford Bridge ($2\frac{1}{2}$ miles distant on right), in which direction, $\frac{3}{4}$ of a mile distant, is Elvetham, a seat of Lord Calthorpe. In another $\frac{1}{2}$ mile an occupation road leading to his Lordship's domain runs under the line. Here the Railway commences the somewhat steep ascent of 1 in 330, upon which it is continued for two miles: at the commencement of which the scene entirely changes, and the embankment upon which it is constructed, in some places full 50 feet in height, affords an excellent view of the beautiful woodlands that line its sides, which, chiefly consisting of fertile meadows finely timbered, present a luxuriant appearance, particularly the last mile and a half, where the Winchfield road is seen descending the hill, from the London and Odiham road, on right of which, crowning the eminence, is beheld Winchfield House, immediately as it were in front, but in fact a little beyond

THE WINCHFIELD STATION,

AN INTERMEDIATE ONE, DISTANT FROM LONDON 38 MILES, FROM SOUTHAMPTON $38\frac{1}{2}$ MILES. — Journey resumed below.

Three and a half miles distant from Winchfield Station on right is Bramshill Park, Sir John Cope, Bart., and $5\frac{1}{2}$ miles distant Strathfieldsaye, the fine seat of the Duke of Wellington. One mile distant on left of Winchfield Station is Dogmersfield Park, the noble seat of Lady Mildmay. The mansion is a very extensive building, situated on an eminence, in a park containing about 700 acres, which includes a great diversity of ground, is beautifully wooded, adorned with a fine lake, and commands some good views over the adjacent country. The house has two fronts, and several spacious and elegant apartments decorated with paintings by eminent masters; and the library is enriched by a valuable collection of books.

WINCHFIELD TO BASINGSTOKE.

Still continuing its upward inclination, 1 in 330 for $\frac{1}{2}$ mile beyond the Winchfield Station, the Railway reaches, through deep cutting, a short tunnel (80 yards in length), that carries it under the London and Odiham road, and entering on a level of a mile and a half arrives near the 39 milestone at Murrell Lane, here carried over the line, leading to Murrell Green, a well-known stage upon the Salisbury road, 1 mile distant on right, and to Odiham, 2 miles distant on the left. A little beyond Murrell Lane Bridge, the Railway enters on a lofty embankment, nearly 60 feet in height; upon this it is carried across the valley of the Whitewater river, a small stream that, pursuing its silent course, enlivens by its presence the delightful meadows that adorn its margin: the view of this valley beheld from the summit of the embankment, seen at such a depth, is singularly romantic, and may be said to present one of the richest bits of landscape on the line. The Railway carried in its course across the valley, over Holt Lane, a little before the 40th milestone commences a gradual rise, 1 in 469; and in rather less than $\frac{1}{3}$ a mile, where it is carried upon the level of the land, passes under an oblique bridge that bears the road from Hook to Odiham; in fact the turnpike road from Odiham to Reading, the former lying 2¾ mile on left, the latter 10 miles distant on right. Shortly after passing this oblique bridge, the Railway enters a deep cutting of nearly a mile and a half in length, through which it is constructed, and whose lofty sides temporarily exclude all objects from the view : the traveller's continuance therein is however very short. Near the 41 milestone, the road from London to Basingstoke is carried over the line, a little beyond which the Railway commences a rapid descent (1 in 330), upon which it is continued for 1¼ mile; in something less than 41½ miles passes under another bridge, that carries the road from Newnham to Odiham, and at 41¾ miles, quits the deep cutting for a delightful valley, over which it is carried upon an embankment, crossing in its way the road from Nately Scures to Newnham near the 42 milestone; at 42¼ a tributary stream of the Loddon river, a little beyond which terminates the descent of 1 in 330: to this succeeds a rise of a similar ratio. At 42¾ miles, the road from Nately Scures to Basing Mill passes under the line, ¼ mile beyond which the embankment terminates, and to it succeeds a cutting of about ¾ mile in length. At the commencement of this, very near the 43 milestone, the old road from London to Basingstoke is carried over the line. About ½ mile beyond the 43 milestone, the Railway enters on a short level, when, emerging from the confines of the last-mentioned cutting, it comes out upon the natural level of the land, and at the 44 milestone, where it is carried over the lane leading from Old Basing to Hackwood Park, commences crossing the valley of the Loddon, over which it is carried upon an embankment of from 40 to 50 feet in height, that affords a good view. At 44¼ miles, it crosses the village of Old Basing, and (commencing shortly after a sudden rise, 1 in 254) at 44½ miles, the deepest part of the valley. About a ¼ mile beyond the Loddon, the turnpike road from Old Basing to Chinham runs under the line, when the land suddenly rising, the Railway reaches the termination of the embankment and rise of 1 in 254. In something less than 45 miles, commencing a rise of 1 in 250 it enters an excavation of about a mile in length; at the farther extremity of this the turnpike road from Basingstoke to Reading runs over the line, a little beyond which the Railway reaches the

BASINGSTOKE STATION,

A PRINCIPAL ONE, DISTANT FROM LONDON 46 MILES, FROM SOUTHAMPTON 30½ MILES.—Journey resumed at page 19.

The Basingstoke Station occupies an elevated position on the north side of the town, being situate on the summit of an eminence that rises suddenly from the Loddon river, the source of which is in the vicinity; it is a neat erection, furnished with a waiting-room and other conveniences, and here is a depôt for a small number of engines. Nearly adjoining it a new inn has been erected.

One mile distant on left of Basingstoke is Hackwood Park, the beautiful seat of Lord Bolton, and 3 miles distant Herriard Park, G. P. Jervoise, Esq.

HACKWOOD PARK

is very extensive, with a surface boldly irregular, partaking of the beautiful character of the neighbouring chalk downs. The scenery is picturesque, the views being diversified by large groves of the finest forest-trees, particularly oak, ash, and beech, interspersed with thorns, beautifully luxuriant and large. The house, which is situated towards the eastern boundary of the park, is encompassed by about a hundred acres of pleasure-grounds, disposed into lawn, terrace, shrubbery, and a noble wood. The mansion was orignally a lodge, built in Queen Elizabeth's time, and used as a place of meeting for the company assembled for the purpose of hawking, and as a banquetting-room after the sport was over. This lodge now forms the centre part of the building, which, after a variety of additions and alterations, has arrived at its present excellence.

OLD BASING,

a small village, about 2 miles north-east from Basingstoke, is memorable for a bloody battle fought here between the Danes and Saxons, commanded by King Ethelred and his brother Alfred, in the year 871, in which the latter were defeated. It became still more famous, however, from the gallant stand made against the forces of the Parliament in the reign of Charles I., by John fifth marquis of Winchester, the brave nobleman who rendered his name immortal by his gallant defence of Basing House, during a tedious siege and blockade, or rather a succession of them, which, with short intermissions, continued upwards of two years. The journal of the siege was printed at Oxford in 1645, and is said by Granger to be one of the most eventful pieces of history during the civil war.

BASINGSTOKE

is a large, ancient, and populous town, occupying a pleasant situation, in a well-wooded part of the county of Hants, and enjoying a tolerable trade in corn and malt; by means of the Basingstoke Canal (one of the bubbles of the year 1778), and the rivers Wey and Thames, a line of navigation is opened between Basingstoke and the metropolis. The church is a spacious and handsome structure, consisting of a nave, chancel, and side-aisles, with a low square tower. Near it stands a free-school; it has also three charity-schools, one of which is supported by the Skinners' Company of London. The government of the town is vested in a mayor, recorder, seven aldermen, seven capital burgesses, and other officers. There is a good market-house, and town-hall over it, where the sessions are held twice a year, and where the magistrates meet weekly. Situate on the line of road from London to Southampton, Winchester, and Poole, and also at the point of division, on the road to Salisbury, Exeter, Plymouth, and the Land's End, Bridgewater, Barnstaple, and the northern part of Devonshire, Basingstoke was consequently a very great thoroughfare, and participated not only in the advantages resulting from the expenditure of travellers, but also from large establishments of horses and men in the employ of the several coach proprietors, engaged in working the western mails and other stages, and whose several concerns in this town were conducted upon an extensive scale. To all this the formation of the South-Western Railway has, as a matter of course, given a death-blow, and Basingstoke, in common with many other towns, has, from the consequent abstraction of business, and loss of its carrying trade, suffered severely. On an eminence at the northern extremity of the town, a beautiful object is observable in the ruins of the Holy Ghost Chapel. Market on Wednesday.

BASINGSTOKE TO WINCHESTER.

Continued upon the sudden rise it commenced of 1 in 250 at the 45 mile-stone, the Railway is carried forward from Basingstoke, by an alternation of cutting and embankment, with a gradual sweep, a little to the north of the Salisbury road, crossing immediately upon its departure the turnpike road from Basingstoke to Newbury, that runs under the line. At $47\frac{1}{4}$ miles it reaches the road to Winklebury Farm, immediately in front of Winklebury Hill, an ancient encampment. From this road carried upon an embankment of about 30 feet in height, taking a southerly inclination, the line crosses first the road leading from Kempshot Park ($2\frac{1}{2}$ miles distant on left) to Rooks Down (1 mile distant on right), and very shortly after the Salisbury road at the village of Worting, a well known stage upon the Great Western line. The traveller, on crossing the Salisbury road, catches a glance at the village, that agreeably situated and partly surrounded by woods presents a pleasing appearance. On right of Worting is Worting House: 1 mile distant is Manydown and Tangier, and $1\frac{1}{4}$ mile distant Malshanger House. From Worting, where it reaches the 48 milestone, the Railway, constructed by alternate cutting and embankment, still upon the rise of 1 in 250, reaches at about 48½ mile the road to Oakley, on right of which is Oakley Park. Here it enters the Oakley cutting, an excavation of nearly a mile in length. An occupation road at 49¼ mile and the road to Church Oakley at 49¾ mile cross this cutting, which (in some instances full 50 feet deep) terminates near the 50 milestone, as does the rise of 1 in 250, upon which the Railway has been continued for the last 7 miles. From a little before the 50 milestone, the line, carried forward on a level of alternate excavation and embankment for about a mile and three quarters, with a gradual sweep, crosses the road from Oakley to Bull's Bushes, that here passes under the line, as does the road from Dean to Bull's Bushes, near the 51 milestone. In rather less than 51¾ miles, emerging from an excavation, it enters on an embankment of about 1¼ mile in length, crossing at Steventon the road to Dean, a village situate upon the Salisbury road, 1 mile distant on right, near which is Ash Park. From Steventon it is carried forward with a gradual bend, and at 52½ miles crosses the road from North Waltham to Overton, formerly a market town, at present a considerable village, and well known stage upon the Salisbury road. The railway continued from Steventon upon an imperceptible rise, affords from the Steventon embankment, of considerable height, a good view of the village of Steventon, its church, the valley, and beautifully wooded country, by which it is surrounded: it is however of short continuance, for entering about 52¾ mile a cutting of considerable depth, that leads to Lichfield Tunnel, 200 yards in length, the view then terminates, till emerging therefrom, in another mile, a momentary glance of it is again obtained. The road leading from Stratton Park, upon the Winchester road to Overton above mentioned upon the Salisbury road, here crosses the line. The Railway at Lichfield Tunnel reaches its summit at an elevation of 400 feet above Trinity high water mark at London, the datum level of the line: it now commences a descent of 1 in 250, upon which it is continued for a distance of nearly 17 miles. Near the 54 milestone it enters a cutting, rough which it is carried to Popham Hill. About 54½ miles, the road from Popham Beacon to Overton crosses the line, which, in a distance of rather less than 55 miles, reaches the Popham Tunnels, in the vicinity of Popham Beacon. The Popham Tunnels, of which there are two, of 200 yards in length, are approached through an excavation of great depth, and are separated by an open cutting of 96 feet deep, and 200 yards long; over the second runs the road from Basingstoke to Stockbridge and Salisbury. Popham Beacon, although rising to a height of 460 feet above the datum level, is no wise remarkable in appearance, there being scarcely any perceptible difference between that eminence and the various hills by which it is surrounded; its summit, however, commands a good view of the finely wooded country by which it is environed, and from its vicinity, prior to the fall of Fonthill Abbey in Wiltshire, that beautiful but fragile structure was clearly discernible at the distance of 40 miles. It is scarcely necessary to remark, that the view from this Hill is entirely lost to all travellers of the Railway, save such as proceed no farther than the Andover Road Station; but as the seats in this part of Hampshire are frequented in the season by the first families, the editor has felt it his duty to point attention to whatever is worth visiting in the vicinity. In rather less than a mile beyond the centre of Popham Tunnels, lies

THE ANDOVER ROAD STATION,

A PRINCIPAL ONE, DISTANT FROM LONDON 56 MILES, FROM SOUTHAMPTON $20\frac{1}{2}$ MILES.

Two miles distant from the Andover Road Station, on right, is Stratton Park, Sir Thomas Baring, Bart., and 4 miles distant, the Grange, Lord Ashburton.

The Andover Road Station* is the most important between London and Southampton; it is provided with retiring rooms, and additional engines, and here a large warehouse has been erected for the reception of goods arriving by carriage from Salisbury, Exeter, and the west of England, or waiting their transmission thence to the intervening towns or the metropolis. It is situate in the cutting, near the termination of the Tunnel, from which the Railway soon emerging enters on an embankment (with the exception of a short cutting) of $2\frac{3}{4}$ mile in length, upon which it continues its downward course of 1 in 250, through open fields, that within a few years known as Northbrook and Stratton Downs have since been successfully converted to cultivation. This lengthened causeway, that derives its name from the village to which it conducts, is called the Mitcheldever embankment; it is the highest on the line, and most probably in the kingdom, being upwards of 100 feet above the surface of the meadows below. The village of Mitcheldever, seen on left, with its old church, and well wooded country in its vicinity, form the constituent features of a beautifully picturesque landscape. Three occupation roads run under it, as does the road from Stratton Park, upon the Southampton road, through Mitcheldever upon the left, and a continuous line of villages, Weston, Stoke Charity, Hutton, and Wonston, on right, all

* A new road is now made from this station to Andover.

seated on a tributary stream of the Test, to Sutton, an intermediate stage, upon the Basingstoke and Stockbridge road. These form pleasing objects, and are seen to great advantage from the Mitcheldever embankment on right. Near the 59 milestone, the Railway enters an excavation of two miles in length, in the centre of which lies Lunway's Inn Tunnel, and the 60 milestone; the excavation leading therefrom, terminating 1 mile beyond this, it enters on the Hook Pit embankment, that forms, with the intervention of two short cuttings only, an artificial terrace of 2 miles in length. The Winchester Race Course is upon Worthy Down, that rising immediately on right of this embankment, the view from it is consequently confined. Hook Pit Farm, lying on left of the line, is passed at about 61 miles from the metropolis. This long embankment terminates at Headbourne Worthy, a little before the 63 milestone, where the road from Headbourne Worthy to King's Worthy, Abbot's Worthy, Easton, and Martyr's Worthy (a cluster of small villages, on the margin of the Itchen river), runs under the line. Here occurs a short cutting crossed by an occupation bridge, a little beyond which the 63 milestone is attained. The last remaining $1\frac{1}{2}$ mile to Winchester is divided into two nearly equal proportions, viz. the Hyde embankment and excavation, so named from the village they approach in the vicinity of Winchester; from the former the traveller gets a distant view on left of the beautiful valley through which runs the river Itchen, and here the city of Winchester with its venerable cathedral first rises into view; near the latter the turnpike-road to Andover is carried over the Railway which here reaches

THE WINCHESTER STATION

A PRINCIPAL ONE, DISTANT FROM LONDON $64\frac{1}{2}$ MILES, FROM SOUTHAMPTON 12 MILES.—Journey resumed at next page.

On the top of the deep cutting, adjoining this Station, stand the Winchester Barracks.

WINCHESTER,

A city of high antiquity, enjoyed all the advantages, and experienced all the vicissitudes, incidental to the seat of government and principal royal residence, from the union of the Saxon kingdom, under Egbert, till during the reign of Edward I., when, the increasing importance of London occasioning the removal of the court, it began to decline. The city is agreeably situated on the declivity of a hill, gradually sloping to the river Itchin: it is not a place of much trade, but the principal business of the county (Hampshire) is transacted here, which occasions a considerable in flux of strangers; and it is the residence of many respectable families: it possesses also the advantage of an immediate communication with the sea, by means of a navigable canal. Among the public buildings which embellish the city of Winchester, its ancient and venerable cathedral stands pre-eminently conspicuous. This edifice exhibits an excellent school for the study of our ancient architecture, in its progress through the styles respectively denominated Saxon, Norman, and English. It also obtains an imperative influence, from the importance of the scenes that have been transacted within its walls, and the monuments to distinguished characters with which it is enriched. The college at Winchester was founded by Bishop Wykeham, between the years 1387 and 1393: its buildings occupy a considerable space of ground, and retain the venerable aspect of the date at which the foundation was completed. Of the more modern erections, the town-hall, the infirmary, and the county gaol (the latter upon the plan of Howard), are the most considerable. The churches and chapels were formerly not less than ninety in number, of which there are now remaining scarcely twelve. Here is a neat theatre, and occasional music meetings are held at Winchester, which has also its winter assemblies, concerts, balls, races, and every other fashionable amusement. This city sends two members to parliament, and has a market on Wednesday and Saturday. Situate at the junction of the two roads from London through this city to Southampton Poole, the Isle of Wight, and coast of Hampshire, the carrying trade of Winchester was of course considerable, an advantage of which it has been deprived, by the establishment of the South Western Railway; it is, however, fortunate in having been made a principal station of the line, and, considering the frequent intercourse maintained between this city and Southampton by railway trains, the probability is, that as regards the expenditure of travellers, the proprietors of inns may reasonably calculate upon an increase of business.

WINCHESTER TO SOUTHAMPTON.

Immediately upon leaving the Station the Railway enters a cutting of considerable depth, in some instances 40 feet deep, passing under the Stockbridge road and Romsey road, both of which are thrown over the line. To this excavation, of rather more than half a mile in length, succeeds an embankment of 30 feet in height, that at the 65 milestone brings it to the level of the land. Thence is obtained a good view of Winchester, in the valley on the left, with its cathedral and college chapel; a little farther the village and ancient hospital of St. Cross, the landscape beautifully wooded, St. Catherine's Hill crowned with a clump of firs forming the background. From this point, which it reaches by a line nearly direct from Winchester, it is carried through the valley of the Itchin to Southampton. Continued by embankment and excavation for about ½ a mile, it is then carried through a cutting of nearly 40 feet deep, a little to the westward of St. Cross (celebrated for its hospital and remains of its ancient church), and thence with an easy sweep to the Southampton road, which near the 66 milestone runs over the line. St. Catherine's Hill, or College Hill, immediately opposite St. Cross, is only separated from that establishment by its meadows, the Southampton road, and branches of the river Itchin. On its summit are the remains of an ancient entrenchment, supposed to have been formed by the Romans. On this eminence also near the top, on the north-east side, is the form of a labyrinth, impressed on the turf by the continued coursings of the students of Winchester College, who frequently thread its mazes in the full spirit of diversion and exercise. To the last-named cutting of rather more than ½ mile in length a short embankment succeeds, and the Railway carried forward in a direct line, principally through excavation, a little to the left of Compton to the margin of the Itchin, is carried thence with a gradual bend to the

TWYFORD STATION,

AN INTERMEDIATE ONE, DISTANT FROM LONDON 67¾ MILES, FROM SOUTHAMPTON 8¾ MILES. — Journey resumed below.

From the 67 milestone, the village of Twyford forms a pleasing object. On the left of Twyford Station is Twyford House, Twyford Lodge, and Shawford Lodge, and 4 miles distant Rose Hill Park (Earl of Northesk). In the church of Twyford is a fine mural monument by Nollekens, to the memory of the late Jonathan Shipley, bishop of St. Asaph, who died in the year 1788, in his 74th year, an excellent bust of whom is here displayed. At a Roman Catholic seminary in this parish, Pope is said to have been partly educated. Emerging from a deep cutting, and passing the 67 milestone, a little before the Twyford Station, the Railway enters on an embankment of ½ mile in length, pursuing a parallel course with the Itchin at the foot of Compton Down: it then enters an excavation (of 60 feet in depth at the centre), through which it gains the 68 milestone; ¾ mile beyond which, carried in a direct line, it reaches by the Otterbourne embankment Brambridge Lane (that runs under the line), where it crosses an arm of the Itchin. ½ mile distant on right of Brambridge Lane, is the village of Otterbourne, containing a very pretty new church, erected from designs by Mr. Carter of Winchester, architect. 1 mile distant, on right, is Cranbury Park, and 4 miles distant Hursley Park, the beautiful seat of Sir W. Heathcote, Bart. On left of Brambridge Lane is Brambridge House, and 2½ mile distant Marwell Hall. Upon the embankment (two miles in length, which commenced about ½ a mile before Brambridge Lane, and upon which it is constructed through the valley of the Itchin), the Railway upon its arrival there is carried forward in a direct line to Aldbrook, where it crosses the road leading from that village to the turnpike road from Winchester to Southampton, and a branch of the Itchin at a distance of 69¾ miles from London. A little before reaching the 70 milestone, its downward inclination of 1 in 250, upon which it entered at Litchfield Tunnel, for a time terminates, and a level of less than a ¼ of a mile succeeds, which commencing near the 70 milestone, carries it again across the Itchin, from whence it is constructed on a descent of 1 in 250 for a ¼ of a mile, and then through a shallow cutting in a line tolerably direct, on a descent of 1 in 528, to the road to Bishopstoke, a village ½ a mile distant on left of the line, of which a pleasing view is obtained. At the Bishopstoke road, the Railway reaches the 71st milestone and at 71¾ miles the Gosport and Portsmouth branch Railway *, from whence continued through shallow cutting, in a line parallel with the road from Southampton to Winchester, through South Stoneham and Twyford, it crosses that thoroughfare at 72½ miles, and proceeding on its western side shortly after enters on an embankment, upon which continued for ¼ a mile it arrives at Swathling, 73¼ miles from London. Here it crosses the turnpike road from Romsey, 7¼ miles distant on right, to Botley, 5¼ miles distant on left, and also to Gosport, 15½ miles distant, whence there is a floating bridge across the harbour to Portsmouth. Botley, an agreeable village, seated on the Hamble river (navigable for boats to the Southampton water), in a finely-wooded country, was long the residence of Cobbett the political writer, to whom the public are indebted for a turnpike road from Winchester through Botley to Gosport, at that time considered by the inhabitants of both a great boon: here also, after retiring from the stage, fell a victim to filial affection that justly celebrated actor, the late John Fawcett, Esq. At Swathling, the Railway crosses a tributary of the Itchin, and changing its downward inclination from 1 in 528 to 1 in 400 enters an excavation of rather more than ½ a mile in length, that carries it in a direct line through the grounds of South Stoneham House to an embankment of diminished declination (1 in 440), but of nearly equal length, by which it arrives at the Portswood cutting, that, crossing the grounds of Portswood House, conducts to the viaduct over the Itchin water at Northam and the 75 milestone. In the Portswood excavation, the descent of 1 in 440 terminates, and continued on a level after

* Where has been established the Bishopstoke Station, 4¾ miles from Southampton.

crossing the Itchin water, whither it is carried with a gradual bend, it is thence continued in a direct line, first through an excavation of nearly ⅓ a mile in length to the Portsmouth road, and a canal, and carried across the eastern extremity of the town arrives at

THE SOUTHAMPTON STATION,

A PRINCIPAL ONE, DISTANT FROM LONDON 76½ MILES, SALISBURY 21¾ MILES, POOLE 34 MILES, LYMINGTON 20¼ MILES, GOSPORT 16¾ MILES, PORTSMOUTH 17¾ MILES.

Southampton is a borough town, consisting of seven parishes (including Stoneham), situated at the union of the rivers Test and Itchin, which form Southampton bay: many of the streets are handsome and well built. The High Street terminating at the quay much resembles, in width and beauty, the High Street of Oxford, and has a charming view of the river and the New Forest. The town is well paved and lighted, and supplied with excellent water. The approach to this place from the London road is exceedingly striking, from the beautiful view of Southampton bay, the Isle of Wight, and the scenery of the New Forest; elegant seats and rows of trees line the road on both sides; and this entrance is still farther heightened by that venerable remain of antiquity, the Bargate. The walls with which the town was anciently surrounded are, in many places, quite destroyed, but in others still present a venerable appearance. Although consisting of six parishes exclusive of North Stoneham, Southampton contains but five churches, viz. Holy-Rood, St. Michael's, All-Saints', St. Mary's, and the united parish church of St. Lawrence and St. John. That of Holy-Rood is remarkable for its elegant organ, and several handsome monuments. It is a vicarage, value 12*l*. 1*s*. 10*d*., in the patronage of Queen's College, Oxford, of the real value of about 250*l*. per annum. St. Michael's has a high slender octagonal tower, which serves as a landmark for vessels entering the harbour; it is a vicarage, value 12*l*. 11*s*. 10*d*.; patroness, the Queen. All-Saints' is an elegant modern structure, fronting the High Street. The whole length is 95 feet, breadth 61 feet, and height to the ceiling 47 feet; it is a rectory, value 8*l*. 1*s*. 10*d*.; patroness, the Queen. St. Lawrence's is a small church, situate in the High Street; it is a rectory, value 7*l*. 10*s*., united with that of St. John, value 6*l*. 13*s*. 4*d*., in 1736, when its church was pulled down. St. Mary's is a rectory, value 37*l*. 5*s*., but it is a precentorship in the gift of the Bishop of Winchester, worth at least 1400*l*. per annum. There are several meeting-houses for dissenters of different denominations. Near the town is an asylum for soldiers' orphans, on the plan of the asylum at Chelsea. A grammar-school, founded here in the reign of Edward VI., is in high repute. Among the principal charities are Thorner's Almshouses, for the relief of poor widows; a charity-school founded by Alderman Taunton, for educating and apprenticing poor boys, besides several of less consequence. About ½ a mile from the Bargate stand the barracks, enclosing an area of two acres. On an eminence at a small distance from the town, stands the Polygon, an elegant pile of buildings, commanding extensive sea and land views. The inhabitants carry on a considerable trade with the northern parts of Europe, in timber, hemp, tallow, &c.; with Portugal, in wine and fruit; and with Wales and Newcastle, in iron, coals, lead, and glass. It has likewise a good trade with the islands of Jersey and Guernsey, to which they send large quantities of wool, which is principally returned in knit hose, and other manufactured goods. Ship-building is carried on in the docks near the town. Southampton was incorporated by Charles I., under a mayor, aldermen, recorder, sheriff, two bailiffs, common council, &c. There are for the town 11 justices of the peace; viz. the bishop of Winchester, the recorder, the present and former mayor, 5 aldermen, and 2 burgesses; all who have passed the chair are aldermen. The mayor is admiral of the liberties. This borough was chartered by Henry II., and by King John was made a county of itself; it returns two members to Parliament. Near the west quay is a range of convenient baths, in which the water is changed every tide; here is also a commodious warm bath: further towards the channel is another suit of convenient and well-frequented baths, and several bathing-machines have been established at the Crosshouse near Itchin Ferry. At the bottom of Orchard Street, without the Bargate, is a spring of the nature of Tunbridge Wells, and used with effect for the same complaints. The public rooms are situated near the baths, and command a delightful prospect. Here is also a good theatre, at which that celebrated son of song, the late Charles Incledon, made his first public appearance; several well furnished libraries, and three respectable banks.

A vast increase in the trade of Southampton has of late taken place, and the town has acquired additional importance, from the recent formation of its spacious docks, and its establishment as the Steam Packet Station for the East and West India mails, and of those for Corunna, Lisbon, Gibraltar, Malta, and other places on the south-east corner of Europe. To India, in particular, it may now be termed the high road, the time between this port and Bombay, through the exertions of that great benefactor to his country, Lieut. Waghorn, R.N., by the overland route, now occupying little more than thirty days, and which that gentleman confidently anticipates he shall ere long be able to accomplish in three weeks!!!

Hotels: Castle, Dolphin, Radley's, Royal Hotel, Royal George, Royal York, Star, Sun, Vine, Windsor.

MIDLAND COUNTIES RAILWAY,
RUGBY TO DERBY AND NOTTINGHAM.

The Midland Counties Railway commences at Rugby in Warwickshire, at a point distant from the Metropolis by the London and Birmingham Railway $83\frac{1}{4}$ miles, from whence it proceeds with an easy sweep, being carried by a viaduct consisting of 11 arches of 50 feet span, and an embankment across the valley of the Avon, the river, and Lutterworth road, to the Oxford Canal, distant from Rugby 1 mile, on right of which is Brownsover House. Brownsover, a small but pleasant village, derives some celebrity, from having been the birthplace of Lawrence Sheriff, the founder of Rugby School. From the Oxford Canal it is carried in a gently waving line, by successive excavation and embankment, to the Lutterworth and Coventry road. $1\frac{1}{2}$ mile beyond the Oxford Canal on right is Coton House; 1 mile on left of the Lutterworth road is Newnham Paddox, the beautiful seat of the Earl of Denbigh. The inclination of the Midland Counties Railway, for about $\frac{1}{2}$ a mile beyond Rugby, to which point it is a perfect level, is a somewhat steep ascent, 1 in 330, upon which it is continued for 4 miles, viz. a mile beyond the Coal-pit Lane, where having attained the summit 400 feet above the level of the sea, it changes to a moderate descent (1 in 440), and so continues to

THE ULLESTHORPE STATION,
A PRINCIPAL ONE, DISTANT FROM RUGBY $7\frac{7}{8}$ MILES, FROM DERBY $41\frac{1}{4}$ MILES, FROM NOTTINGHAM $39\frac{1}{2}$ MILES, FROM LONDON $91\frac{1}{8}$ MILES.

The Coal-pit Lane leads from Lutterworth $2\frac{1}{2}$ miles distant on right to Cloudesly Bushes, about the same distance on left. A little beyond Coal-pit Lane, passing the village of Willey on the left, the line crosses Watling Street Roman Road, and is thence carried, as above described, to the Ullesthorpe Station.

At Ullesthorpe Station, the Railway crosses the Lutterworth and Hinckley Road, Lutterworth lying 3 miles on right, and Hinckley 7 miles on left of the line. Half a mile distant on left of the Ullesthorpe Station, is Claybrook Hall (T. E. Dicey, Esq.). From Ullesthorpe, taking a N. E. direction in a further distance of $1\frac{3}{4}$ mile, it reaches Leir immediately on right of the line. Leir is a hamlet to the parish of Lutterworth, and a source of the Soar, a stream that, after pursuing a tortuous course, passes by the north and west sides of Leicester, where it becomes navigable. Thence it continues almost due north, whence, after passing close by Mount Sorrel, and receiving an accession of water from two or three small rivers, it finally falls into the river Trent, in the vicinity of Thrumpton and the Nottingham branch of the Midland Counties

Railway. From Leir the Railway, passing in its way Stanborough Mill, is carried forward in a line nearly direct to

THE BROUGHTON ASTLEY STATION,

AN INTERMEDIATE ONE, DISTANT FROM RUGBY 11⅛ MILES, FROM DERBY 38⅛ MILES, FROM NOTTINGHAM 36¼ MILES, FROM LONDON 94⅜ MILES.

From the Broughton Astley Station, the course of the Railway is nearly in a direct line to the Lutterworth and Leicester road, which it crosses, and, in something like ¾ of a mile beyond it, the Whetstone Brook, over which it is borne, when, changing its direction, it then diverges to the north-west, and, continued with a gradual sweep, is in that way constructed to the Milldam of the Union Mill and Union Canal, which it crosses by a viaduct of 11 arches of 20 feet span, and in half a mile more reaches the

WIGSTON STATION,

AN INTERMEDIATE ONE, DISTANT FROM RUGBY 16½ MILES, FROM DERBY 32¾ MILES, FROM NOTTINGHAM 30⅞ MILES, FROM LONDON 99¾ MILES.

The Wigston Station is situate on the cross road from Wigston Magna, a considerable village on the London and Leicester road through Welford, 1½ mile on right of the line; the village of Blaby on the Rugby and Leicester road being about the same distance on the left. The inclination of the Railway from Ullesthorpe to the Wigston Station, is a continued descent of 1 in 400, with the exception of a short level at the Wigston end. Shortly after quitting the Wigston Station, an excavation through which it is carried conducts to an embankment, both being about 1 mile in length, carrying it on in a northern direction, with an easy sweep to Knighton Tunnel, 100 yards long, a little beyond which the road from Welford to Leicester crosses the line, and the train arrives in another mile at the

LEICESTER STATION,

A PRINCIPAL ONE, DISTANT FROM RUGBY 20 MILES, FROM DERBY 29⅛ MILES, FROM NOTTINGHAM 27¼ MILES, FROM LONDON 103⅜ MILES. — Journey resumed at page 32.

Two miles on left of Leicester is Remptone Hall, and Leicester Frith House, one mile beyond which is Frith House: the proprietors' names will be found in the Itinerary line.

LEICESTER.

Leicester, the county-town of Leicestershire, 14¼ miles N. W. from Market Harborough, and 96 N. W. from London, by Railway 103¼, stands on the river Soar. This town is fabulously said to have been built by King Lear; it is however of great antiquity, and at the time of the Roman invasion was a place of strength belonging to the Britons, and the capital of the Coritani. It afterwards became a Roman station, and is the Ratæ of Antoninus. It stands on the Foss-way, and great numbers of Roman coins and other antiquities have been found here. In Doomsday Book, this town is styled a city, and is said to have been very populous. Before the castle was dismantled, it was a prodigious building, and was the court of the great duke of Lancaster. Its hall and kitchen are still entire, the former of which is lofty and spacious. This, during the reign of several of the Lancastrian princes, was the scene of frequent parliaments, in one of which a law was enacted for the burning of heretics; and here the assizes, the sessions for the town, the elections for members of parliament, and assemblies of the corporation are held. Leicester contains six parishes, and eight churches. St. Mary's adjoins the castle, and was rebuilt after having been destroyed in the time of the Conqueror. St. Martin's is esteemed the principal church in the county. St. Nicholas' Church is supposed to be the oldest in Leicester; it formerly consisted of three aisles, but at present has only a nave and south aisle, with a square tower at the west end. All-Saints' is a good structure, having three aisles and a chancel; St. Margaret's is a neat building, in the tower of which is a set of 10 bells; in addition to which the church of St. George, an elegant structure in the English style, with a tower and spire, erected in a district of St. Margaret's parish, was opened in 1827. St. Leonard's Church was taken down when Leicester was garrisoned, in 1642, because its situation commanded the north bridge. In this parish formerly stood a mint, in which, during the early periods of the history of Leicester, money was coined, and coins from Athelstan to Henry II. are still preserved. Leland writes that King Richard III. was buried here. Trinity Church, a diminutive building, the architecture of which is of doubtful character, erected at the sole expense of Frewin Turner, Esq., was opened in 1838. Christ Church, a cruciform structure, built by subscription, in the early English or Lancet style, with a short bell tower, was opened in 1839. An elegant Roman Catholic chapel was erected in the gothic style about 1830, adjoining which, and correspondent in character, is a residence for the priest. The places for religious worship besides the churches of the established religion, are those for the Presbyterians, Quakers, and Baptists. The abbey stood about a mile from the town: there cardinal Wolsey died, in 1530. During the civil war, in the reign of Charles I., this abbey was burned by a party from

Ashby-de-la-Zouch, and has ever since been in ruins. The corporation of Leicester consists of a mayor, recorder, steward, bailiff, twenty-four aldermen, forty-eight common-councilmen, a town clerk, &c. Leicester sends two members to parliament; the right of election is in the freemen and inhabitants, paying scot and lot, to which have been added, by the Reform Bill, the ten pound householders. Like most provincial towns, the area of the market-place, which at Leicester is particularly handsome and spacious, forms the grand centre of attraction, and chief seat of business, and is, generally speaking, the best built part of the town. Many of the streets of this place are narrow, and in Leland's time, the whole town was built of timber; but its general appearance has lately improved with its increased opulence, and the houses in general are modern: the whole is well paved and lighted with gas. It is noted for the number and excellence of its inns. The Town-hall nearly adjoins St. Martin's Church, and was, before the reformation, the Corpus-Christi guild: this hall, in point of magnitude, is considerable, but it is not elegant. The Exchange is a plain building, situate in the market-place. The Hotel is a handsome edifice occasionally appropriated as assembly-rooms, lodgings for the judges, and for the sittings of the county magistrates. The Theatre, a handsome building, in the Grecian style, with a portico in front, is situate in the market-place; the interior modelled upon the plan, and decorated in the style, of the St. James's Theatre* in London, is extremely elegant. It was erected in 1837, and is capable of containing 1500 persons. There are several hospitals in this town; that called the Holy Trinity was founded in 1352, by Henry, earl of Lancaster. St. John's Hospital was given by Queen Elizabeth to the corporation, and was afterwards used as a wool-hall, but at the latter end of the reign of James I. six poor widows were placed in it; Bent's Hospital supports four widows; Wigstone's Hospital is a regular building, founded in the reign of Henry VI., and consists of a master, confrater, twelve men and twelve women. The Infirmary at the south end of the town will contain 54 patients; near it is an asylum for lunatics. A building was erected in 1792 by John Johnson, Esq., a native of Leicester, which he called the Consanguinitarium, the rooms of which are neat and convenient, and the windows glazed with stained glass; besides these there are Simond's and Countess's hospitals and Spital House. The Free School was augmented in the reign of Queen Elizabeth; besides which there is a Green-coat school, St. Mary's school, and St. Martin's school. The prisons are the county gaol, and the county and town bridewells. In 1787, a mineral spring was discovered

* This, in compliment to Prince Albert, is now called the Prince's Theatre.

near this town, the beneficial effects of which have been repeatedly proved in diseases of the skin, in glandular obstructions, and in several complaints of the stomach and bowels. Leicester is situated in the midst of the finest wool district in this kingdom, and its principal trade is in the manufacture of stockings, of which, several years ago, the annual value amounted to 60,000*l.*

Leicester is supplied, by canal navigation, with coal, deals, dry goods, and groceries; and communicates by this means with all the principal towns in England. This town, from the introduction of railway travelling, and consequent abstraction of its carrying trade, for which, from its position on the great north road, it was finely situated, must, as a matter of course, suffer severely. The New Walk is an agreeable promenade of three quarters of a mile in length, by twenty feet in width. The ground was given by the corporation, and the expense of laying it out, planting, &c. was defrayed by a public subscription. It extends in a south-east direction from the town, and from different parts of it many pleasing views are obtained of the town, meadows, and the surrounding country. The races held annually in the autumn are run on a fine course, situated at the south-east end of the town, at its entrance from London by the Market Harborough road. Market on Saturday.

LEICESTER TO LOUGHBOROUGH.

The inclination of the Railway from Wigston Station, to very near to Leicester, is a continued descent of 1 in 400. From the Leicester Station, situate at the entrance to the town, upon the great London road, the Railway constructed on a level of $\frac{1}{2}$ a mile in length then enters on a descent of 1 in 500, and on an embankment of $2\frac{1}{4}$ miles in length, crossing about a mile from the town the Uppingham road. From this point it is carried forward in a line nearly direct, and for some time parallel with the turnpike road from Leicester to Loughborough, through a deep cutting, on a level of $1\frac{1}{2}$ mile in length, when it commences a descent of 1 in 500, in rather more than $\frac{1}{2}$ a mile, passing the village of Barkby and Barkby Hall on the right, and Thurmaston on the left, from whence both lines converging, unite at

THE SYSTON STATION,

AN INTERMEDIATE ONE, DISTANT FROM RUGBY $24\frac{3}{4}$ MILES, FROM DERBY $24\frac{1}{2}$ MILES, FROM NOTTINGHAM $22\frac{5}{8}$ MILES, FROM LONDON $107\frac{3}{4}$ MILES.

One mile distant from Thurmaston on left is Birstall House; on left of Syston, 1 mile distant, is Wanlip Hall. The Syston Station is situate on the turnpike road from Leicester to Melton

Mowbray, at a distance of 10½ miles from the latter town, and ½ a mile from Syston, one of the most considerable villages of Leicestershire. It is situate almost in the heart of the finest fox-hunting country in England, Melton Mowbray, forming the grand centre of Nimrodian attraction, to which, during the season. the nobility and gentry flock from all parts of the kingdom. This, though not a place of much trade, derives considerable advantage from the expenditure of the gentlemen connected with the Melton hunt. The season commences on the first Monday in November, by the Quorndon hounds meeting at Kirby Park, the hunting residence of Sir Francis Burdett, 2 miles from the town, and terminates the first or second week in April with Croxton Park races.

From the Syston Station, carried on an embankment with a gradual sweep, crossing in its course the Roman Foss-way ½ a mile beyond Syston, and in another ½ mile the river Wreak, it is thence continued, by successive excavation and embankment, a distance altogether of 2½ miles all on a level, passing the village of Cossington on the left, to

SILEBY STATION,

AN INTERMEDIATE ONE, DISTANT FROM RUGBY 27¾ MILES, FROM DERBY 21⅝ MILES, FROM NOTTINGHAM 19¾ MILES, FROM LONDON 111 MILES.— Journey resumed at next page.

One mile and a quarter on left of Sileby Station, is Mount Sorrel. 2 miles distant from Mount Sorrel on left, is Rothley Temple, and Swithland Hall.

MOUNTSORREL.

This place was originally called Mount Soar Hill, from its situation on a steep craggy hill on the banks of the river Soar. The natural features of this place are singularly romantic and beautiful: a ridge of high hills extending hence through the midst of Charnwood forest into Derbyshire, terminate immediately on the west side of the town, which extremity is lofty and steep, presenting a variegated face of grass and rock; and on the highest point, called Castle Hill, almost overhanging the town, there formerly stood a fortress, supposed by Mr. Nichols, the historian of Leicestershire, to have been built by Hugh Lupus, Earl of Chester: the garrison of this castle stood a severe siege against King Henry III.; but at last it surrendered to the sovereign, and was shortly afterwards demolished. Mountsorrel Hill is a rock of reddish granite, of which many of the houses are built, and the streets paved: this stone is of great durability, and after exposure to the air resists all kinds of tools; it is often dug up in imperfect cones, and being too hard to be cut or broken, its smoothest face is laid outwards in beds of the excellent lime of Barrow. Here were formerly two chapels, but only one now remains; this is a very neat building, and is subordinate to the church of Barrow: the different denominations of dissenters have also meeting-houses for the accommodation of their several congregations. The parishes of Rothley and Barrow are separated by Barn Lane, at the end of which there formerly stood a curiously decorated cross, but this was, in 1793, removed into the grounds belonging to Sir John Danvers, Bart., who erected in its place a small market house in imitation of a pavilion. Market on Monday.

Quitting Sileby Station, the Railway commences a descent of 1 in 500, upon which it is continued for a distance of 6 miles, in two and three quarters of which, carried chiefly on an embankment, and crossing in its course three tributaries of the Soar, it reaches the village of Barrow-upon-Soar, and the

BARROW STATION,

AN INTERMEDIATE ONE, DISTANT FROM RUGBY 29⅞ MILES, FROM DERBY 19⅜ MILES, FROM NOTTINGHAM 17½ MILES, FROM LONDON 113⅛ MILES.

Shortly after quiting Sileby Station, the beautifully woody eminence of Baddon Wood is beheld upon the left. On left of Barrow, lies the village of Quorndon, Quorndon Hall, and Quorndon House, and 2½ mile distant, Beaumanor Park. Quitting the Barrow Station, formed in a cutting of considerable depth, the Railway carried on an embankment, traversing the valley of the Soar, and pursuing a course parallel to that river, which it crosses about ¾ mile beyond Barrow, in 1¾ more reaches the

LOUGHBOROUGH STATION,

A PRINCIPAL ONE, DISTANT FROM RUGBY 32¾ MILES, FROM DERBY 16¾ MILES, FROM NOTTINGHAM 14⅞ MILES, FROM LONDON 116 MILES. — Journey resumed at p. 36.

One mile distant from Loughborough on left, is Burley Hall, and 1½ mile distant Garendon Park. 3 miles distant on right of Loughborough is Prestwold Hall, 3½ miles distant, Stanford Hall, visible from the Railway, and further to the right Rempstone Hall.

LOUGHBOROUGH,

A market town of Leicestershire, its extent and population considered, may be deemed the second town in the county, having in the course of the last 40 years attained to double its former size, its population being increased during that period in like proportion. It formerly consisted of one parish, to which belonged the two hamlets of Knight Thorpe and Woodthorpe, both about 1 mile distant. Great part of the town was the property of the late Marquis of Hastings when Earl of Moira, to whom it descended from his uncle the earl of Huntingdon, in whose family it had been since the time of Queen Mary. In an act of enclosure passed in 1759, his late lordship, then Lord Moira, was acknowledged as lord of the manor, and the masters, fellows, &c. of Emanuel College, Cambridge, as patrons of the rectory. The Moira estate and manor in Loughborough were purchased in 1810 by Thomas Denning, Esq., who since his accession thereto has effected many improvements in the town; in particular the market, much improved in size by the removal of the old Butter Cross and other buildings, is now a large and spacious area, surrounded by good houses and handsome shops. Here, on the coronation of Queen Victoria, the poorer classes were regaled to the number of 4000 with a good dinner of roast beef and plum-pudding. Here is a free grammar school, endowed by Thomas Burton about the year 1650, with the rents arising from certain lands left by him for that purpose, and for the maintenance of a chantry within the church. The estates, by a decree of the Court of Chancery, became vested in the hands of 12 feoffees, who, in 1825, erected a large building, which contains several rooms, one appropriated to classical education; a second to reading, writing, and arithmetic; a third to girls only; and the fourth, the principal room, in which 250 are taught on the plan of the national schools, in addition to which there are Sunday schools in connection with the church establishment and dissenting congregations. Storer's charity also supplies plain clothing to poor boys and girls, and bread weekly to aged men and women. The mother-church, dedicated to All-Saints, which is a large pile of building, consists of a nave, side aisles, chancel, transept, and a handsome tower, the latter having been built by subscription near the end of the sixteenth century: it stands at the northeast end of the town, at its entrance from the Nottingham road. A division of the parish has lately been made, allotting about one-third of the whole to the new parish, which is called Emanuel, after Emanuel College, Cambridge; to whom belongs, as in the case of the old church, the right of presentation. Emanuel Church is erected in the modern gothic style, and stands at the south-west extremity of the town: it was opened for divine service in 1837. A new Roman Catholic chapel was erected about 1834; it is a very handsome building, constructed much after the manner of a public hall, and comprises a commodious residence for the priest: in addition to which there are meeting-houses for Baptists, Presbyterians, Wesleyans, and Quakers.

The inhabitants are chiefly engaged in the manufacture of hosiery, lace, and in wool-combing, in addition to which Loughborough, from its situation on the great north road, derived considerable advantage from the expenditure of travellers and its connection with coaching and maintenance of posting establishments, from the loss of which occasioned by the introduction of the railway system, it has, in common with all towns similarly circumstanced, suffered severely. The Loughborough canal, a short cut, forming a chain of connection with the river Trent, and thence with most of the canals in the kingdom, gives it the advantage of a very extensive water communication, by which Loughborough has been greatly benefited.

LOUGHBOROUGH TO DERBY.

The Loughborough Station is situate $\frac{1}{2}$ a mile distant from the town, on the London road through Loughborough to Nottingham. From the Loughborough Station, the Railway carried through the valley of the Soar, upon an embankment in a line nearly direct, in a further distance of $1\frac{1}{2}$ mile, crosses that river, and quitting the county of Leicester enters Nottinghamshire, and in $\frac{3}{4}$ mile more, chiefly excavation, reaches Normanton, in another $\frac{1}{2}$ mile the Ashby-de-la-Zouch and Nottingham road, and in 2 miles more, chiefly carried through excavation, extends to

THE KEGWORTH STATION,

AN INTERMEDIATE ONE, DISTANT FROM RUGBY $37\frac{1}{4}$ MILES, FROM DERBY 12 MILES, FROM NOTTINGHAM $10\frac{1}{4}$ MILES, FROM LONDON $120\frac{1}{2}$ MILES. — Journey resumed at next page.

The inclinations of the Railway from the Loughborough to the Kegworth Station are as follows:— The long descent of nearly 6 miles, commenced at Sileby, terminates at Loughborough Station, from whence a level of $\frac{1}{2}$ a mile, a rise of 1 in 1320 for $1\frac{1}{4}$ mile, a level of $1\frac{1}{4}$ mile, a rise of 1 in 850 for not quite $\frac{1}{2}$ a mile, and a level of $\frac{3}{4}$ of a mile carry it to the 36 milestone, $\frac{3}{4}$ of a mile on the London side of it, where it commences a descent of 1 in 500, that carries it to the Kegworth Station. One mile on left of the Kegworth Station lies the town, or, more properly speaking, the village, of Kegworth, $1\frac{1}{2}$ mile distant from which is Lockington Hall, and, 5 miles distant, Donington Park, the magnificent seat of the Marquis of Hastings.

KEGWORTH,

Formerly a market town, but now a village of Leicestershire, is situate on the great north road from London through Derby, at a distance of 115 miles by road from the former, and 11 from the latter. It is pleasantly situate upon a fine eminence, overlooking the Soar that flows at its foot, and is crossed by a handsome stone bridge built at the expense of the Duke of Devonshire. Here is a fine old church, not to be excelled by any in the county; it is a handsome light building, consisting of a nave, aisles, transept, and chancel, with a tower and spire; most of the windows are large, with two mullions and tracery, and some of them have pieces and complete figures of painted glass. On the south side of the chancel are three stone seats or stalls, with the seat on one plane, and ornamented with purfled pinnacles, foliated pediments, &c. Its inhabitants are engaged in various trades and agricultural pursuits.

From the Kegworth Station, continuing its course through the valley of the Soar, in a curvilinear direction, the Railway carried forward, chiefly on an embankment for $1\frac{3}{4}$ mile, crosses in $\frac{3}{4}$ of a mile the road from Kegworth to Kingston-on-Soar, a small village immediately on right of the line, and in another mile reaches Ratcliffe, a small village on the left, which brings it to the 39 milestone, when, entering on a level of $1\frac{1}{4}$ mile, in about half that distance it gains the Red Hill tunnel, 130 yards long, emerging from which it arrives at the viaduct over the river Trent, and Cranfleet cut, that conveys it to the Nottingham Branch. On right of the Nottingham Branch is Thrumpton Hall.

At the Nottingham Branch the Railway diverges; the line on right leading to Nottingham is elsewhere described; the line to Derby here continued branches off to the left, and carried with a graceful sweep and gradual ascent, crossing in its way the Erewash canal, in another mile unites with the line to Nottingham at the turnpike road from Nottingham to Ashby-de-la-Zouch, from which point it is carried with an easy sweep, a gradual ascent, and short level, passing the villages of Sawley on the left and Long Eaton on the right, to

THE SAWLEY STATION,

AN INTERMEDIATE ONE, DISTANT FROM RUGBY $42\frac{3}{8}$ MILES, FROM DERBY $6\frac{3}{4}$ MILES, FROM NOTTINGHAM $8\frac{7}{8}$ MILES, FROM LONDON $125\frac{5}{8}$ MILES.

Two miles and a half distant from Sawley Station on left is Shardlow House, 2 miles beyond which is Aston Hall; $\frac{1}{2}$ mile on right of Sawley Station is Breaston village; and $1\frac{1}{2}$ mile distant, Risley Hall. A little before reaching Sawley Station the Railway commencing a rise, upon which it is continued for $3\frac{1}{2}$ miles, carried in a gently waving line, with the exception of the first $\frac{1}{2}$

mile, chiefly through cutting, the last mile of which the Derby and Sandiacre canal becomes its companion: on the right it reaches

THE BORROWASH STATION,

AN INTERMEDIATE ONE, DISTANT FROM RUGBY 45½ MILES, FROM DERBY 3⅞ MILES, FROM NOTTINGHAM 11⅞ MILES, FROM LONDON 128¾ MILES.

One mile beyond the Sawley Station, ¼ mile distant on left, is the village of Draycott; 1½ mile distant on right is Draycott House; and farther to the right, Hopwell Hall. Half a mile distant from Borrowash Station on left is Elvaston, the fine old seat of the Earl of Harrington, in whose family it has been vested from the time of Henry VIII. From the Borrowash Station the Railway is carried forward in a course tolerably direct upon a rise of 1 in 528 for a mile beyond it, the first ⅔ of which it has the Derby and Sandiacre canal upon its northern, and the river Derwent on its southern side, the latter then deserting it to pursue its tortuous course to Derby, the canal communicating with that town by, although a devious, a more direct line. A mile beyond the Borrowash Station the Railway enters on a level of ½ a mile in length, a little beyond which it gains

THE SPONDON STATION,

AN INTERMEDIATE ONE, DISTANT FROM RUGBY 46¾ MILES, FROM DERBY 2½ MILES, FROM NOTTINGHAM 13 MILES, FROM LONDON 130 MILES.

On right of Spondon Station is Spondon, a very considerable village, and Spondon Hall, and 1¼ mile distant, Locko Park. From the Spondon Station, carried forward in a direct line, the Derby and Sandiacre canal, continuing on its right, constructed on an embankment with a rise of 1 in 528 in a ¼ mile, it reaches Chaddesdon Mill, on right of which is Chaddesdon Hall. From Chaddesdon Mill its course is that of a direct line, till within a short distance of its termination, when turning to the left it reaches

THE DERBY STATION,

A PRINCIPAL ONE, DISTANT FROM RUGBY 49¼ MILES, FROM NOTTINGHAM 15½ MILES, FROM LONDON 132½ MILES.

Two miles distant from Derby, on left, is Osmaston Hall. Arrived at the Derby Station, the main line of the Midland Counties Railway, viz., from Rugby to Derby, has been described. To complete the details, however, and render available in every way the resources of this noble work, the reader is requested to accompany us in first concluding the journey to Nottingham, and, subsequently, in another along the direct line from Derby to that town, the latter of which having described, we must for this purpose return to the continuation of the line from the Nottingham branch, from whence the Railway is described to Nottingham at page 40.

DERBY

Is of great antiquity, and was a royal borough in the reign of Edward the Confessor; it is situated in a fertile district, on the banks of the river Derwent, which is navigable hence to the Trent, and is here crossed by a handsome stone bridge. The houses in general are well built, particularly the leading thoroughfares, in which are many handsome erections; the streets are broad, spacious, well paved, and lighted. The Market Place, a fine area, 300 feet square, is surrounded with very handsome shops and houses, and is further enlivened by the town hall, that, standing on its western side, gives dignity to the whole. It contains, among other public buildings, a county and town hall, a gaol, an assembly room, and a theatre, which are all handsome buildings. Here were till lately 5 churches, belonging to the established religion, to which a sixth, Trinity Church, in memory of the late Bishop Rider, with a tower and spire of mixed architecture, was added in 1839. Of these, All Saints Church alone requires particular notice; this is a very handsome structure, though far from being of a uniform style of architecture; the tower rises to the height of 170 feet, and its upper part is richly ornamented with tracery, crockets, high pinnacles, and battlements, and the interior is particularly light, elegant, and spacious; it contains several monuments well worthy of examination. Besides the parish churches, here is an elegant Roman Catholic chapel, and meeting houses for the different denominations of dissenters of almost every class. A county infirmary on a large scale, considered one of the most complete establishments of its kind in Europe, was erected in 1810. Here is a military depôt, capable of containing 15,000 stand of arms, with detached magazines for gunpowder and other warlike stores. The contiguity of the river has rendered Derby an extremely favourable spot for the institution and carrying on of manufactures requiring the aid of water; and, accordingly, here are extensive silk, cotton, and other works, to which machinery has been adapted with astonishing success; one of these, called the Silk Mill, is situated on an island in the river Derwent; it is the first and one of the largest of its kind that ever was erected in England, and is composed of full 14,000 wheels, all set in motion by a single water-wheel, 23 feet in diameter; words are incapable of conveying a just idea of this very curious machine; it requires to be seen to be understood, and that for a longer period than is usually allowed to the casual visiter; suffice it then to say, that here all the operations are performed which are necessary, for preparing the silk for the weavers. Derby also contains manufactories where all kinds of ornaments are made with the marble, spar, and petrifactions that abound in this neighbourhood; besides which here are large porcelain works, that produce an article capable of vying with that of China, both for fineness of texture and brilliancy of colours. The inhabitants also derived considerable advantage from the carrying trade, of which, from its favourable position on the great north road, it enjoyed a large share; and the stage-coach and posting establishments, here very extensive by the employment of many hands, proved extremely beneficial. Of all this Derby, in common with many other places similarly circumstanced, has been deprived by the introduction of Railway travelling, and by its consequent loss of business in both branches has sustained an irreparable injury. The corporation consists of a mayor, high steward, nine aldermen, a recorder, fourteen burgesses, town clerk, &c. The recorder, removable at pleasure, is chosen by the corporation, as is the town clerk, who is coroner and clerk of the peace, both of whom when appointed are submitted for the approval of the crown. This town sends two members to parliament, and has well supplied markets on Tuesday, Wednesday, and Friday. The Race Course, with its grand Stand, beautifully situated between the banks of the Derwent river and Derby canal, is in the racing season fully and fashionably attended.

THE NOTTINGHAM BRANCH.

From the Nottingham Branch, carried upon an embankment, with an easy sweep on a gradual ascent, the Railway in $1\frac{1}{4}$ mile reaches the line from Derby to Nottingham, and

THE LONG EATON STATION,

AN INTERMEDIATE ONE, DISTANT FROM RUGBY $41\frac{3}{8}$ MILES, FROM DERBY $9\frac{1}{2}$ MILES, FROM NOTTINGHAM 6 MILES, FROM LONDON $124\frac{5}{8}$ MILES.

At the Long Eaton Station, a road leads to the village of Long Eaton, $\frac{1}{2}$ a mile distant on the left, on right to the Trent, over which there is a ferry, to the fine old seat of Thrumpton Hall. From the Long Eaton Station, the Railway is continued in a gently waving line, through the valley of the Trent, when in rather more than $\frac{1}{2}$ a mile, carried on a level, crossing the Erewash river, and passing the Coniry Farm on right, in $\frac{3}{4}$ mile, it reaches

Attenborough (where a road on left leads to Chilwell), and in another ¾ mile,

THE BEESTON STATION,

AN INTERMEDIATE ONE, DISTANT FROM RUGBY 44 MILES, FROM DERBY 12½ MILES, FROM NOTTINGHAM 3 MILES, FROM LONDON 127¼ MILES.

From the Erewash river the Railway is continued for a mile, on a rise of 1 in 1060, when it enters on a level of two miles in length, upon which it is constructed, to a mile beyond the Beeston Station. On left of Attenborough lies the village of Chilwell; on right are beheld the rich woods of Clifton Hall, that rising majestically from the margin of the Trent form the most prominent object and distinguished feature of a very delightful landscape. About ¾ mile beyond Attenborough, the Railway approaches the Trent, whose devious course is deserted by the navigator at Clifton, from whence to Nottingham the distance is considerably abridged by a canal, that, denominated the Beeston Cut, carries it in a more direct line to the southern side of that town. From a mile beyond the Beeston Station, carried on a rise of 1 in 880, in rather less than ¾ mile, it reaches Beeston Cut, which it crosses, when its inclination changing to a descent of 1 in 528 in ⅜ mile more brings it to a level, upon which in less than ½ mile it is carried to

THE NOTTINGHAM STATION,

A PRINCIPAL ONE, DISTANT FROM RUGBY 47½ MILES, FROM DERBY 15½ MILES, FROM LONDON 130⅝ MILES.

On left of Beeston Station is the village of Beeston, ¼ mile beyond it on left are the following, that literally form a cluster of seats, Lenton Grove, Highfield House, Lenton House, Lenton Firs, and across the Nottingham road, Wollaton Hall, the magnificent seat of Lord Middleton. The Nottingham Station terminates the second section of the Midland Counties Railway, to render the account of which complete, it will now be necessary to return to Derby.

FROM DERBY TO NOTTINGHAM.

For the route from Derby to Nottingham, the reader is referred to the Itinerary Line at the end of the book, where that portion of the Midland Counties Railway is given continuously.

NOTTINGHAM

Is a large and populous place, the county town of Nottinghamshire, and long distinguished as one of the chief seats of the stocking manufacture. It is one of the most pleasant and beautiful towns in England, from its picturesque situation, and the striking appearance of its buildings. It is situated on a rocky eminence, which runs in a line parallel with the course of the Trent, at the distance of ¾ of a mile north of that noble river, the intervening space being occupied by a fine range of extensive meadows, the little river Lene running close to the town, and bounding the meadows on the north, as the Trent does on the south. The Trent here is nearly 200 feet wide, and forms a very considerable navigable stream, into which, at no great distance above the town, enter the Derwent, the Soar, and the Erewash. It is crossed opposite the town by a bridge of 19 arches. Nottingham is built on the ascent of the hill, on the top of which, overlooking the precipice below, stand the ruins of the castle, a very conspicuous object, and formerly a fine ornament to the place. The approach to the town is extremely striking, from whatever quarter it is entered. The hill on which it stands is so steep, that the ground-floors of the houses towards the top of it are considerably elevated above the roofs of those at the bottom, so that several streets may be observed rising above each other. The streets in the town are very numerous: in general they are narrow, and not formed on any regular plan; but several improvements have been made in widening, repairing, and hollow draining some of them, and further alterations are in contemplation. The rock under the houses is of so soft and sandy a nature, and so easily excavated, that all the cellars are cut out of it; furnishing capacious stores for malt liquor, for which the town is celebrated, particularly for its ale. Great caves and caverns are also found in this rock, many of them modern, but others very ancient, and of unknown origin. The ancient walls and gates of the town are now entirely destroyed. Of the public buildings in Nottingham, the castle, at present in ruins, is the most conspicuous. It was a large and handsome building, erected after the demolition, and near the site, of the ancient fortress by the duke of Newcastle, during the short reign of James II. It stands on a rustic basement, which supports an ornamental front of the Corinthian order, with a grand double flight of steps leading to the apartments. The whole building is surrounded by a handsome terrace, which commands a very fine prospect along the Trent, and has long been a favourite promenade. The apartments were originally very fine. It was long a deserted domain of the Duke of Newcastle, whose more magnificent seat of Clumber, a princely residence, is in this county. Nottingham Castle fell a sacrifice to the folly of a riotous and infuriated mob, by whom its destruction by fire was completed on the

10th of October, 1831, and nothing now remains of this once noble fabric but bare walls. The ancient fortress was founded by William the Conqueror, and was then thought impregnable. Here David, king of Scots, was confined a prisoner, and also the celebrated Roger Mortimer, Earl of March, who was seized here by Edward III. and his friends entering through a secret passage, still called Mortimer's Hole. During the civil wars the standard of Charles I. was first hoisted on an eminence in the vicinity, north of the castle walls; but the fortress was afterwards demolished by order of Charles II. In 1807 this spot, containing about two acres, was sold in building lots at a very high price, under the appropriate appellation of Standard Hill. It is intersected by four streets, Standard, King, Charles, and Hill Streets, making King Charles's Standard Hill. It is now occupied by some very excellent buildings, and the extra-parochial church of St. James. The extra-parochial rights of Standard Hill have been twice disputed, but are now confirmed to the proprietors by the decision of the Court of Queen's Bench. Behind the castle is the park, of 130 acres, used for pasture and gardens: from various parts of it the prospects are rich, beautiful, and picturesque. It contains some curious caves, and at the upper end of it, adjoining the Derby road, are the barracks, a spacious range of brick buildings erected by Government in 1793, in an open and airy situation. Nottingham contains five parish churches, St. Mary's, St. Peter's, and St. Nicholas, besides the aforesaid extra-parochial church of St. James. St. Mary's, the principal church, standing on a bold eminence about 170 feet above the level of the adjacent meadows, presents a very striking object from every part of the town. It is built in the form of a cross, with a very august tower in the centre, in the Gothic style of architecture prevalent in Henry VII.'s reign, and the whole appearance of the structure is venerable and impressive. It has recently been completely restored, at an expense of 3000*l*. St. Peter's stands near the market-place, and is a handsome building, with a lofty spire. It retains some memorials of Saxon and a good deal of Gothic architecture, and has received various modern additions during a recent repair. St. Nicholas church was pulled down during the civil wars by order of Colonel Hutchison, on account of the advantage its lofty tower gave to the royal army then besieging the castle. The present building was erected in 1678; it is of brick, ornamented with stone corners, window frames, &c. and has a light and airy appearance. The interior is well lighted, and fitted up with great attention to the comfort of the congregation. St. James's church was erected in 1808, for the accommodation of the Calvinistic party in the Church of England. It is a neat, light, and elegant building, in imitation of the Gothic style, and very tastefully executed both within and without. To these a fifth, St. Paul's, has since been added; and a sixth, All Saints, is now erecting. A handsome Roman Catholic chapel with a Doric front was erected in 1827. Nottingham has, besides these, a number of places of worship for Dissenters.

The public charities of Nottingham are numerous, and many of them on a very extensive scale. The principal are, Plumtre's Hospital, Collins's Hospital, the Lumbley Hospital, and a variety of others. The workhouses are very clean and commodious. Of the other benevolent institutions the most important is the General Infirmary, a very excellent establishment, which was founded in 1781, and has proved of the greatest benefit in relieving the distresses of the people. It is a spacious and elegant building, consisting of a centre, two advanced wings, and two ends, to which considerable additions have been made through the benevolence of an unknown donor, who gave 20,000*l*. three per cent. consols, for this praiseworthy purpose. It stands in an airy situation, surrounded with pleasant walks and gardens; and its internal arrangements are on a very judicious and excellent plan. It is liberally supported by benefactions, legacies, and annual subscriptions. The lunatic asylum, both for paupers and those who can pay for admission, is on a considerable scale. It is among the first completed under the act of parliament, and was opened in 1812. The building is in an airy situation, at a short distance east of the town, and in its management and arrangements for the accommodation of patients is said to be not inferior to any other building of the kind yet established. The public and charity-schools of Nottingham are commensurate with the size and opulence of the town. Of the buildings and establishments connected with public business, the market-place has long been admired; it is one of the largest and handsomest in the kingdom, surrounded with excellent houses, and having every accommodation for its various purposes. At the east end of it stands the new exchange, a very fine building of four stories in height, erected by the corporation in the early part of the last century, and since then considerably improved and beautified: it is 123 feet in length, and about the same in width: under it are spacious and convenient shambles. The county-hall is a handsome building, erected by the county in 1770 on the high pavement, and in the immediate vicinity of St. Mary's church. The town-hall for the town and county of Nottingham is a large building three stories high, with the town prison on the ground-floor, and a lofty flight of steps leading to the first floor, which is commodiously and handsomely fitted up for its various purposes. The county prison, formerly under the ancient county-hall, is now behind it, and being on the southern slope of the rock, is both airy, and commands extensive views. The town and county jail is as commodious as circumstances will admit, though much is wanted to render it complete. The regulations of these prisons, which were complained of by Howard, are now greatly improved, according to the spirit of the present day. The town bridewell stands in St. John's Street, and is now on an excellent footing. The public amusements of Nottingham principally consist in the winter season of concerts and balls, and here is a neat theatre. Annual races are also held in July or August. The walks in the vicinity are numerous, and the scenery and prospects very pleasing. The town is supplied with water, not however in the best manner, from deep wells and from water-works on the river Lene. The supply of coal is ample, though the increased facilities of water-carriage, by extending the market, have greatly increased, instead of lowering, the price of this necessary. The trade and manufactures of Nottingham have long been very extensive, for which indeed it is well adapted by its situation near the centre of the kingdom, in the line of the great Trent and Mersey navigation, which in conjunction with other canals afford it an easy access both to the eastern and western seas, the Severn, and the Thames. The staple manufacture is that of stockings, chiefly the finer kinds, as those of silk and cotton. These are all wrought on the stocking frame, a simple and ingenious contrivance, invented in the reign of Queen Elizabeth by William Lee, a native of this vicinity. In consequence of the demand for silk and cotton in the stocking manufactures, the spinning of these articles has been introduced into the town and neighbourhood, and several mills have been erected, which give employment to an immense number of people. Much cotton, however, is still obtained from the mills in Derbyshire. For the last 20 years also a great number of hands have been employed in the manufacture of lace for veils, shawls, gloves, &c. which has greatly increased the business of the town. The bone lace trade was also at one time a source of profitable industry to many females, but has since declined. These finer manufactures being easily carried are chiefly conveyed by land. A very large share is exported to different parts of Europe, America, and the West Indies. The malting trade was formerly considerable here, but has greatly declined; and this has also been the case with several others, which have been removed to more favourable situations. Nottingham, however, has become a great depôt for supplying the adjacent country with provisions, grocery goods, and all the other articles in daily demand; and in this respect it has derived great benefit from the extension of inland navigation. Situate on the great north road, the carrying trade of Nottingham was of course considerable, which added to the expenditure of travellers, its maintenance of posting, and connection with coaching establishments, formed altogether a fruitful source of revenue to the town. Of all these, however, the establishment of the Railway system has effected the ruin; and, in consequence, its losses from this abstraction of business have proved extremely detrimental to the place. It is a town and county of itself. The corporation consists of a mayor, six aldermen, a recorder, two sheriffs, two coroners, two chamberlains, and a common council of twenty-four burgesses. It sends two members to parliament, and has exercised this right for 500 years. The right of election belongs to the burgesses and freeholders, to which, by the Reform Bill, have been added the 10*l*. householders. Nottingham is a place of great antiquity, and of some note in history, but its origin is hid in obscurity. It has markets on Wednesday and Saturday, and three annual fairs, for cattle and horses, in March, April, and October.

BIRMINGHAM AND GLOUCESTER RAILWAY.

BIRMINGHAM TO BROMSGROVE.

The Birmingham and Gloucester Railway commences at the principal station of that company in Birmingham, from whence, constructed on a steep ascent of 1 in 84, it reaches the road to Bordesley Green, and carried forward in a line nearly direct, crossing in its way the Coventry road, the Birmingham and Warwick Canal, and Stratford-upon-Avon road, it extends in $1\frac{1}{4}$ mile to Camphill, where has been formed a depôt of the company for locomotive engines, and for the convenience of persons residing at that end of the town of Birmingham, denominated

THE CAMPHILL STATION,

A PRINCIPAL ONE, DISTANT FROM BIRMINGHAM $1\frac{1}{4}$ MILE, FROM CHELTENHAM $44\frac{1}{2}$ MILES, FROM GLOUCESTER $51\frac{1}{4}$ MILES.

From the Camphill Station, a little beyond which the Railway enters Worcestershire, it is carried upon an embankment of diminished steepness, 1 in 305, for another mile, across Balsall Heath, when it enters an excavation, through which, passing Moseley in its way, it is taken to the Alcester road at

THE KINGSHEATH STATION,

AN INTERMEDIATE ONE, DISTANT FROM BIRMINGHAM $3\frac{1}{4}$ MILES, FROM CHELTENHAM $42\frac{1}{2}$ MILES, FROM GLOUCESTER $49\frac{1}{4}$ MILES.

Half a mile before reaching Moseley, on right of which is Moseley Hall, the train toils up a steep ascent of 1 in 100, which, upon its arrival there, changes to 1 in 400; upon this it is carried to the Kingsheath Station, Selly Hall lying 1 mile distant on the right. On emerging from the deep cutting of the Hazelwell excavation, a little beyond Kingsheath Station, the traveller obtains the first glance of the Lickey, a wild and lofty range of mountains that rise a little to the northward of Bromsgrove. From Kingsheath Station, carried forward in a curvilinear line by successive excavation and embankment, the Railway reaches, by a rise of 1 in 300, a level upon which it is constructed, to the Worcester and Birmingham Canal at Bredon Cross. About $\frac{1}{2}$ a mile beyond Bredon Cross, where it commences a rise of 1 in 300, taking a south-west direction, the line crosses the Birmingham and Redditch road, and carried, with the exception of the last mile, through successive excavations, reaches in a distance of 7 miles from Birmingham the Redditch road at Northfield, from whence it proceeds in a southern direction upon an embankment of 1 mile in length, when it enters an excavation, through which it is continued to Grovely Lane Tunnel, 440 yards long, $\frac{1}{4}$ of a mile beyond which it emerges from the excavation leading therefrom, and there terminates the ascent of 1 in 300, upon which, from this point, viz. $9\frac{1}{2}$ miles from Birmingham, it has been continued. Carried forward in a southern direction with an easy sweep upon an embankment, and descent of 1 in 300, to the vicinity of Cofton Wood, it then commences a rise of 1 in 300, upon which it reaches Barnt Green: $2\frac{1}{2}$ miles distant from Barnt Green on left is Bordesley Hall. From Barnt Green it is continued on the rise of 1 in 300, in nearly a direct line, chiefly through the Lickey excavation, in the centre of which the last named rise ceases, and there changes to a descent of the same proportion. At a distance of $12\frac{1}{4}$ miles from Birmingham, the Railway attains the summit of the inclined plane, 511 feet 1 inch above the level of Bristol Float. Arrived at the summit of the incline, the eye is regaled with a very delightful prospect: on right rises the lofty Lickey, a range of hills that, 900 feet in height, extend towards Hagley. Southward is seen the vast plain of Worcester, which lies spread out like a map in front of the spectator, where the town of Bromsgrove, with its church and lofty steeple, lying apparently at his feet, form a prominent feature of the landscape, and fill the foreground, the view being terminated by the Malvern Hills that meet the clouds. Eastward the richly wooded eminence, known as the Ridgeway, bounds the prospect, and on the south-east seemingly unites with the lofty chain of the Cotswold Hills, that converging towards the Malverns close the view. Down this incline, which is constructed in a direct line upon the steep descent of 1 in 37 for two miles, crossing in its way the Burcot and Redditch road, the Alcester and Birmingham road, and passing Finstall House upon the left, the train rushes with extreme rapidity to the

BROMSGROVE STATION,

A PRINCIPAL ONE, DISTANT FROM BIRMINGHAM $14\frac{1}{4}$ MILES, FROM CHELTENHAM $31\frac{1}{2}$ MILES, FROM GLOUCESTER $38\frac{1}{4}$ MILES. — Journey resumed at next page.

One mile and a half distant on left of Burcot, on the road to Alcester, is Hewell Grange, the fine seat of the Honourable R. H. Clive.

BROMSGROVE,

A market-town of Worcestershire, situate in a valley on the banks of the Salwarp, 12 miles N. E. of Worcester, $13\frac{1}{4}$ N. W. of Alcester, 6 N. E. of Droitwich, and 116 from London, is a long straggling town. it chiefly consists of one principal street, that contains some very good houses, while many of the more ancient ones are framed of wood, and curiously decorated with black stripes and cross pieces, scallops, flowers, leaves, and other ornaments, that from their glaring contrast of colours produce a most inharmonious effect. The church, which occupies a knoll on the N. W. side of the town, stands so high as to be ascended by fifty steps; it is a pleasing Gothic structure, dedicated to St. John the Baptist. The tower and spire, the height of which is 189 feet, form a most commanding object, and cannot perhaps be surpassed for antique elegance by any other in the county: it consists of three aisles; the windows contain some very good painted glass, and here are some handsome monuments of the Talbots of Grafton, ancestors of the Earls of Shrewsbury. In addition to this a chapel of ease, erected at Catshill, called Christchurch, was opened for public worship in 1838. The lord of the manor holds a court-baron in the town-hall every three weeks, for the recovery of small debts; and the town, which formerly sent members to Parliament, is governed by a mayor, recorder, and aldermen. The inhabitants are chiefly employed in the manufacture of household linen, small articles of iron-ware, nails, needles, and tenterhooks. There is a grammar school here founded by Edward VI., with an additional endowment by Sir Thomas Cookes, who gave exhibitions from the school to Worcester College, in Oxford, of his own foundation. The market is on Tuesday, and here are two fairs for cloth cheese, horses, and cattle, on the 24th of June and 1st of October

DROITWICH. 49

From the Bromsgrove Station, which is distant from the centre of the town about 1½ mile, the Railway is carried forward in a direct line, passing close to Newton Farm upon the right, to Sugar Brook, a distance of a mile, upon the following inclinations: the first eighth is a descent of 1 in 300, the last three eighths of increased steepness, 1 in 100, when it commences a rise of 1 in 300, upon which it is continued for 1¾ miles with an easy sweep, crossing in its way the road from Bromsgrove to Alcester, ¾ of a mile beyond which it arrives at

THE STOKE PRIOR STATION,

AN INTERMEDIATE ONE, DISTANT FROM BIRMINGHAM 16¾ MILES, FROM CHELTENHAM 29 MILES, FROM GLOUCESTER 35¾ MILES.

From the Stoke Prior Station, pursuing a course nearly parallel with the Worcester and Birmingham canal, the Railway is carried with an easy sweep, in a distance of 2 miles (in the first of which it passes Astwood on the right), to the viaduct over that navigation, ½ a mile beyond which it reaches

THE DROITWICH STATION,

A PRINCIPAL ONE, DISTANT FROM BIRMINGHAM 19¼ MILES, FROM CHELTENHAM 26½ MILES, FROM GLOUCESTER 33¼ MILES. — Journey resumed at next page.

DROITWICH

Comprises three parishes, exclusive of the Liberty of Dodderhill, and derives its name from its wet situation, and dirty appearance. It is a place of very considerable antiquity, and is famous for its salt springs, which constitute the chief business and wealth of its inhabitants. It was a very populous place in the time of William the Conqueror, and celebrated for the production of salt, mention of which is made in *Doomsday Book*; it had, however, very much declined in population and importance, till within these few years, when again it began to increase in size, and now contains about 450 houses, exclusive of Dodderhill. It has three parish churches, St. Andrew's, St. Mary Whitton, and St. Peter's; and a neat chapel. This borough is governed by a recorder, town-clerk, two bailiffs, and inferior officers, and returns one member to parliament. The brine springs are said to be much stronger than those of Nantwich in Cheshire, are continually overflowing, and the salt they produce is esteemed the best in Europe. The brine is pumped up out of pits by horses into reservoirs, whence it is conveyed by pipes to the salt-works, and

E

discharged into the boilers, which are of wrought iron, of various dimensions, but all about two feet and a half deep. It takes about twenty hours boiling, when the salt is deposited at the bottom; it is then carried in oval wooden baskets to the stove, where it remains forty hours to dry, and is then fit for use. A canal about 7 miles long, navigable for vessels of sixty tons burden, conveys the salt into the river Severn, at Hawford, about 3½ miles from Worcester; and supplies the neighbourhood with coal, of which there is a very considerable consumption. Market on Friday.

DROITWICH TO SPETCHLEY.

From the Stoke Prior to the Droitwich Station, carried chiefly on an embankment, the inclinations are as follows: the first ½ mile is a descent of 1 in 100, which then changes to 1 in 300, upon which it continues for a mile, when it enters on a level that carries it to the viaduct over the Worcester and Birmingham canal, in a mile beyond which, the first half being a descent of 1 in 100, the last a level, it reaches the Droitwich Station, upon the road from Droitwich to Alcester, at a distance of 1½ mile from the former, and 11¼ from the latter town. The embankment upon which the Railway is continued from the Stoke Prior to the Droitwich Station, affords occasionally, though not an extensive, a good view of the country, of which the church of Hanbury, seated on an eminence upon the left, the high grounds about Dodderhill Common, in its vicinity, the woods of Hanbury Hall, and the canal form the chief features. From the Droitwich Station, situate in an excavation, 1½ mile on right of which is Hadsor House, the Railway, passing Huntingtrap Farm on the left, carried forward upon a level, in a line nearly direct reaches, in 1¼ mile, Dean Farm, and in rather more than ¼ mile beyond it, Dunhamstead, where it approaches very near a short tunnel of the Worcester and Birmingham canal that passes in the vicinity. To the last named level, a rise of 1 in 681 succeeds, upon which inclination it continues for rather more than ¼ of a mile further, which brings it to nearly 21¼ miles from Birmingham. Here it enters on an embankment, constructed on a level 1¾ mile in length, upon which, passing Oddingley on the right, and Netherwood Farm on the left, where it approaches very near the Worcester and Birmingham canal, it proceeds with an easy sweep to Evelench, about ¼ mile beyond which the level terminates, when it enters on a descent of 1 in 397, upon which, continued through a cutting of rather more than ½ a mile in length, it reaches the Worcester and Crowle road at Ravenshill. A little beyond Ravenshill, the Railway, emerging from the excavation, enters on an embankment, and a level of rather more than ½ a mile in length, when it commences a rise, by which, carried chiefly through cutting, it reaches Bredicot, from whence continued on a descent of 1 in 300, principally through excavation, it is carried to the Worcester, Alcester, and Evesham roads, at

THE SPETCHLEY STATION,

A PRINCIPAL ONE, DISTANT FROM WORCESTER 3½ MILES, FROM BIRMINGHAM 25¼ MILES, FROM CHELTENHAM 20½ MILES, FROM GLOUCESTER 27¼ MILES. — Journey resumed at next page.

On left of the Spetchley Station is Spetchley Park.

WORCESTER,

The capital of the county, has the general reputation of being one of the best-built and most agreeable cities in the kingdom; its situation is greatly favourable to the display of its buildings and the comfort of the inhabitants. Seated on the banks of the Severn, its spacious streets rise gradually from the margin of that river, whilst they are sheltered from the chill and injurious blasts of the east, by a well-wooded hill. The circumference of the city is about 4 miles: the streets are in general broad and well paved, and continual improvements are taking place. The cathedral is of Anglo-Saxon origin, but the cathedral buildings have twice experienced the desolating effects of fire, and now present few relics of architecture more ancient than the early part of the thirteenth century. The existing fabric was dedicated in the presence of King Henry III. and many of the principal nobility in the year 1218, but was considerably augmented and improved in various succeeding ages; the last alteration of importance taking place about the year 1380. In regard to the exterior, this edifice displays little ornament, but constitutes an object of great beauty, on account of its dignified proportions, and the elegant lightness of its architecture. The interior presents an august architectural display, in which the pointed style almost universally prevails. The choir is extremely magnificent, and affords in its different parts many instructive examples of the progressive modes adopted in English architecture. The monuments are very numerous, and many of them of great interest; among these must be noticed the tomb of king John, which is the most ancient royal monument now remaining in England. On the south side of the cathedral is a capacious cloister, constructed about the year 1372. The adjacent chapter-house is a beautiful structure, erected nearly at the same time with the cloister. This building, which is worthy of minute inspection, now serves the double purpose of a council-room and library. The palace of the bishop stands near the cathedral, on a commanding site upon the east bank of the river Severn. It has ten churches, and several of them are highly respectable as architectural objects. The Guildhall is a spacious and handsome structure, finished in 1723, from a design of White, a native architect; and the bridge over the Severn, in 1781, is an erection of considerable elegance. The commerce of this city is considerable, arising not only from the surplus products of the county and its own manufactures, but from the great conveniences resulting from its very extended water-carriage. The principal manufactures are those of a beautiful species of porcelain, and of gloves, which are much approved, and were formerly exported in large quantities. Worcester contains various almshouses, charity-schools, a neat theatre, new county-gaol, and a public infirmary; it sends two members to parliament; has an excellent market on Wednesday, Friday, and Saturday; and the hop-market, in the season, is one of the most considerable in the kingdom.

SPETCHLEY STATION TO THE ASHCHURCH OR TEWKESBURY STATION.

From Oddingley to Bredicot, the eastern side of the valley is lined with finely swelling eminences, that, rising in amphitheatric form, clothed with rich woods, present a very beautiful appearance.

The Railway, carried forward in a line nearly direct from the Spetchley Station, upon an embankment for rather more than a mile, reaches a short cutting, through which upon a level it is carried to near the 26 milestone from Birmingham, when it enters on an embankment of about $\frac{1}{2}$ a mile in length, that, by a descent of 1 in 300, takes it to a level of rather more than $\frac{1}{2}$ a mile, by which, passing Pitchmoor Hill in its way, it reaches the Worcester and Pershore road, at a distance of 5 miles from the former, and 7 miles from the latter town. From the Worcester and Pershore road, the Railway, carried with an easy sweep, by successive excavation and embankment, reaches in $1\frac{1}{4}$ mile Abbots Wood, upon the inclinations, first of a rise of 1 in 833 for rather less than a mile, then on a descent of 1 in 300. From Abbots Wood, carried forward in a direct line, chiefly upon an embankment, on a descent of 1 in 300, in rather less than a mile, it reaches Narrow Wood Lane, in rather more than $\frac{1}{4}$ a mile, the Pirton Road, a little beyond which the descent diminishes to 1 in 1000, upon which, carried through excavation to Perry Wood, it reaches the Pershore and Severn Stoke road, the village of Besford, lying on left, and Croome Park, the beautiful seat of the

Earl of Coventry, on right of the line. A short distance beyond the Pershore and Severn Stoke road, the Railway reaches Defford Common, at the Pershore and Croome road, and in 1 mile more the Pershore and Upton road, at a distance of 3 miles from the former, and 6 miles from the latter town and site of

THE DEFFORD STATION,

AN INTERMEDIATE ONE, DISTANT FROM BIRMINGHAM 32½ MILES, FROM CHELTENHAM 13¼ MILES, FROM GLOUCESTER 20 MILES.

From the Defford Station, the Railway in a short distance reaches the river Severn, which it crosses by an iron bridge of three arches, each of 57 feet span, and two land arches of stone, in plain Grecian style, and soon arrives at the village of Eckington and

THE ECKINGTON STATION,

AN INTERMEDIATE ONE, DISTANT FROM BIRMINGHAM 32½ MILES, FROM CHELTENHAM 12¼ MILES, FROM GLOUCESTER 20 MILES.

At Defford Station, Bredon Hill, an immense mountainous mass, rises as it were in front of the spectator; from its summit, 1100 feet in height, is beheld a most magnificent prospect. On left of Eckington is Wollashill, the grounds of which, rising on the side of Bredon Hill, participate in the delightful views obtained from that lofty eminence. On left of Eckington, across the Severn, lies Strensham, celebrated as the birthplace of Samuel Butler, the author of Hudibras. This inimitable writer shared the fate too commonly experienced by men of genius, for though he received many promises, and some few civilities from the great men of his day, more particularly the Duke of Buckingham, the Earls of Dorset, Clarendon, and others, who admired his genius, and courted his company, yet he never could obtain any establishment that might render him independent; and after living in obscurity to the age of 68, he died in want, on 25th of September 1680, and was interred, at the expense of a friend, in the churchyard of St. Paul, Covent Garden, London, where a tablet, erected by private subscription, under the porch of that church, records his death.* A monument was afterwards erected to his memory in Westminster Abbey, by Alderman Barber. A little beyond Eckington, the Railway, entering on a level of less than ½ a mile in length, carried with an easy sweep, in a distance of 1¼ mile, reaches the Bredons Norton road, the village lying on left of the line. From the Bredons Norton road, the Railway is carried forward in a direct line, upon the last named level, when it commences a rise of 1 in 300, upon which it is carried to the Tewkesbury and Pershore road at

* This was some years since removed, and the Editor regrets to add, that every effort hitherto made for that purpose has proved fruitless, in the apparently vain endeavour to effect its restoration.

BREDON STATION,

AN INTERMEDIATE ONE, DISTANT FROM BIRMINGHAM 36¼ MILES, FROM CHELTENHAM, 9½ MILES, FROM GLOUCESTER 16¼ MILES.

The Bredon Station is formed in a cutting, a little beyond which, the Railway, carried forward in a direct line, chiefly on an embankment, reaches in 1¼ mile the Carrant brook, where quitting Worcestershire, and the vale of Evesham, it enters the vale and county of Gloucester. Here it commences a rise of 1 in 5782, upon which it continues to Northway, when it enters on a descent of 1 in 300, and in that way reaches the Tewkesbury and Stow road (the London line), and

THE ASHCHURCH OR TEWKESBURY STATION,

A PRINCIPAL ONE, DISTANT FROM BIRMINGHAM 38½ MILES, FROM CHELTENHAM 7¼ MILES, FROM GLOUCESTER 14 MILES.— Journey resumed at next page.

TEWKESBURY

Is a large and handsome town of Gloucestershire, 9 miles north-west of Cheltenham, and 103 west-north-west of London. It occupies a beautiful situation on the east bank of the Avon, near its confluence with the Severn, and between the Carrant brook and Swilgate river, which flow into the Avon, the former above and the latter a little below the town, its western side being enlivened by the Severn Ham, a delightful spot, the site of the race-course, that, surrounded by these streams, there forms an island, and is a great ornament to the town. It contains many good houses, and consists of three principal streets, from which branch others of minor importance, with lanes and courts, the latter of which, mostly leading to the river, are favourable to cleanliness, that characterises the town throughout, the whole of which is well paved and lighted. The old church is a venerable structure, and one of the largest and most magnificent in England; it formerly belonged to the Mitred Abbey founded here in the eighth century. It is cruciform, built in the Norman style and manner of a cathedral, and consists of a nave, choir, transept, and massive square central tower (from the angles of which rise crocketed pinnacles), with the addition of several chapels, that have been erected at different periods. It is 300 feet long, and the cross aisle is 120 feet; the effect of the choir is singularly grand and beautiful, and is in other respects well calculated to arrest the attention of the historian, particularly from the rich monuments that have been raised over its patrons, or of the unfortunate nobles that were slain at the battle of Tewkesbury. Here lie Edward Prince of Wales, son of Henry VI., and George Duke of Clarence, brother of Edward IV. Besides this, Trinity church, a neat structure, capable of containing 900 persons, and erected by private subscription, was opened August 30th, 1839; and here are numerous places of worship for dissenters, a town-hall, a free school, hospital, several almshouses, numerous charity schools, and other benevolent institutions. Here is also a neat and commodious gaol. The principal bridge built over the Severn in 1824, consists of one arch of 179 feet span, and is esteemed one of the best county bridges in the kingdom; there are others of minor importance across the smaller streams. The inhabitants are principally engaged in stocking-knitting, frame-work, and manufacture of nails, mustard, and malt. The government of the town is vested in two bailiffs, who are justices of the peace, chosen annually out of 24 burgesses; it sends two members to parliament, and the markets on Wednesday and Saturday are well supplied. The memorable battle of Tewkesbury (familiar to most readers of English history) took place in the vicinity of the town; the field on which it was fought, still called the Bloody Meadow, is situated about $\frac{1}{4}$ a mile distant. This battle, the last that took place between the Yorkists and Lancastrians, was fiercely contested, and terminated fatally for the latter, who were totally defeated, Queen Margaret taken prisoner, and sent to the Tower, and her son Edward Prince of Wales was inhumanly murdered by the Duke of Gloucester, after the battle, in cold blood.

FROM THE ASHCHURCH OR TEWKESBURY STATION TO CHELTENHAM.

From the Ashchurch Station the Railway is carried forward in a direct line, for a short distance, upon the descent of 1 in 300, when it attains a short level, upon which, continued for rather more than a $\frac{1}{4}$ of a mile, it then commences a rise of 1 in 300, upon which it reaches Piddington, from whence it descends at the rate of 1 in 94,930 to Treddington Lane. From the embankment at Treddington Lane, the lofty range of the Cotswold Hills is seen to great advantage on left of the line, where they form the chief feature of a very delightful landscape, their sides being occasionally enriched with thick and wide-spreading woods; on left of the Bishop's Cleeve and Stoke Orchard road, Cleeve Down rises to the height of 1134 feet above the level of the sea. Cleeve Clouds, as they are called, command a most magnificent prospect, and contain many vestiges of military transactions, and in addition, what to the multitude will be considered a far more fertile field of amusement, the Cheltenham race-course. From Treddington Lane it takes a south-west direction, and carried by embankment on a rise of 1 in 300, reaches in a further distance of 1¼ mile the Stoke Orchard and Bishop's Cleeve road, from whence it is carried with an easy sweep, passing Wingmore Farm on the left, chiefly on a rise of 1 in 300 to Brockhampton. From Brockhampton it is carried upon embankment, on a rise of 1 in 300, to the Swindon and Bishop's Cleeve road, passing the village of Swindon on the right, a little beyond which it enters an excavation, through which it reaches Maule's Elm, on the Gloucester and Tewkesbury road at Cheltenham, the last ¼ of a mile upon a rise of 1 in 100 and in ⅛ mile more.

THE CHELTENHAM STATION,

A PRINCIPAL ONE, DISTANT FROM BIRMINGHAM 45¾ MILES, FROM GLOUCESTER 6¾ MILES.—Journey resumed at next page.

CHELTENHAM

Is a parish and market town in Cheltenham hundred, Gloucestershire, 8 miles south-east from Tewkesbury, and 94 north-west from London. It takes its name from the river Chelt, which passes through the town and falls into the Severn. The parish is 10 miles in circumference, and consists of five hamlets besides the town, viz. Alston, Westal, Naunton, Asle, and Sandford. The town is about a mile in length, and consists of one long principal street, from which there are branches leading to the numerous new buildings that have of late been erected here. It stands in a fine fertile vale near the foot of the Cotswold Hills. The improvements in Cheltenham, from the celebrity of its medicinal waters, have, within a few years, been very great, and it is now a large, handsome, and well-built town, annually increasing in size and importance. The mother church, dedicated to St. Mary, is a venerable Gothic structure, in the form of a cross, with aisles on each side, and an octagonal spire in the middle. The church yard is the most commodious in England, 300 feet long, and has been rendered extremely pleasant and agreeable by being shaded with double rows of lime trees; from thence a fine gravel walk conducts to the church mead, and after crossing the draw-bridge over the river Chelt, there is a magnificent promenade, shaded by venerable elms, whose embowering tops and verdant foliage exclude the fierce rays of the sun. This conducts the visiter to the pump, or spa, which is covered by a dome supported by four arches, and has a commodious room near it for the reception of company. On the left is the breakfasting room, 40 feet by 20, with an orchestra; this is occasionally converted into a ball-room. Around the buildings is a shrubbery upon a gentle ascent, with a walk round it, and seats, having a very extensive view

To the old church have been added, within a few years, five others, respectively dedicated to the Trinity, St. John, St. Paul, St. James, and Christ Church. The waters here first drew the attention of the public in 1740; they are impregnated with salts, sulphur, steel, and calcareous earth, and operate both as a purgative and restorative. The season for drinking them is from May to November, and the waters are strongest and most pure in dry weather. Here are also hot and cold baths, replete with convenience, together with very handsome assembly-rooms and good hotels, where every accommodation may be obtained; besides various circulating libraries, billiard-rooms, and, in short, every source of amusement and recreation generally to be found in similar places of fashionable resort.

Two miles further east of the town is Cleeve Hill, already noticed, on the top of which are still to be seen the remains of a Roman camp, and where also is Cheltenham race-course. Here are several places of worship for dissenters, various charity schools, an hospital founded in 1578, and other charitable institutions.

A number of the poorer classes are employed in spinning wool for the clothiers at Stroud. It has a commodious market-house, and a plentiful market on Thursday.

CHELTENHAM TO GLOUCESTER.

Quitting the Cheltenham Station, the Railway is carried forward with a gradual sweep in a south-west direction, through deep cutting for a ¼ of a mile, on a descent of 1 in 320, emerging from which, it enters on an embankment of about the same length, that carries it to the Grovefield excavation 1 mile long, passing in the first half of it the grounds of Grovefield House, that lie on right excluded from the view; to this excavation a short embankment succeeds, by which, in ¼ of a mile, it reaches the Badgemore road, here carried over the line, Badgemore lying 1 mile distant on left. A little beyond the Badgemore road it enters an excavation of ¼ of a mile in length, that, succeeded by an embankment, carries it in ¾ of a mile to the Churchdown excavation, in some places 30 feet deep, through which it arrives in ¼ of a mile at the Churchdown road, there thrown over the line. From the embankment between the Badgemore and Churchdown road is beheld, on left, the lofty range of the Cotswold Hills, already noticed; these, in the vicinity of Leckhampton, form a mountainous tract, that includes some of the boldest and most lofty of the Cotswold chain, where, as Bigland observes, "they are broken more precipitously, and exhibit a greater extent of bare granulated stone than any other." One of these scars, from its craggy and gigantic form, is termed the Devil's

Chimney. Near the precipice, on a very grand terrace, are vestiges of a vallation, or deep trench, across the point, which, as the sides were defended by nature, must, in the rude state of war, have been an impregnable fortress. A little beyond the Churchdown road the Railway arrives at the end of the excavation, and enters on an embankment that carries it, in a distance of rather less than 2 miles, in a direct line to the London road, through Cirencester to Gloucester at Barnwood. From the embankment, a little before reaching Barnwood on left, are seen winding up the beautifully wooded sides of Crickly and Birdlip Hills, the turnpike roads to Stow and Cirencester. Birdlip Hill is celebrated among travellers for the extent and beauty of the prospect displayed beneath. Here, from the summit of an immense declivity, the fertile vale of Gloucester lies expanded to the view, rich with woods, and gay with villages, seats, and pastures. The back ground is formed by " the blue mountains of Malvern, which relieve the flatness of the other parts, and give a sublimely beautiful effect to the whole." The most striking feature in the landscape, perhaps because the most singular, is the Roman road, which leads from the base of the hill to Gloucester, in an uninterrupted right line, nearly 6 miles in length. On left of Barnwood is Barnwood Court; about 3 miles distant is Whitcomb Park, and 4 miles distant Prinknash Park. From Barnwood the Railway is carried with a gradual bend westward, in a distance of rather less than $1\frac{1}{4}$ mile, to the tram road from Gloucester to Cheltenham, the first $\frac{3}{4}$ mile of which, an embankment, is on a descent of 1 in 330, which then changes to 1 in 180, an embankment, continued on which it is carried to the

GLOUCESTER STATION,

A PRINCIPAL ONE, DISTANT FROM CHELTENHAM $6\frac{3}{4}$ MILES, FROM BIRMINGHAM $52\frac{1}{2}$ MILES.

CHURCHDOWN,

From its singularly situated church, occupying the summit of a lofty eminence, forms a prominent feature in the landscape seen from the Railway in the approach to Gloucester. This hill, which commands a delightful prospect, and is about 3 miles in circumference at the base, rises suddenly from the plain. The only means of communication between the hamlet of Hucclecot, which forms part of the parish on the south, and Churchdown on the north, is the road over this hill, the top of which is attained by a toilsome walk of about $\frac{3}{4}$ of a mile. The larger portion of the elevation is clearly artificial; the whole exhibits evident signs of a dilapidated encampment; the double fosse, the projecting mounds at the extremities, and figures of the ramparts remaining very perfect. The church, which is about 80 feet long by 35 wide, consists of two aisles and a chancel, with a tower at its west end, which was originally much higher, but being considered dangerous, the upper part was some years since taken down. The erection of the church in a situation so inconvenient of access, is conjectured to have arisen from a desire to avoid an appearance of partiality, the hill forming the centre of the parish, the principal parts of which are at about equal distances on the north and south.

GLOUCESTER,

A city, and metropolis of the county, is situated on the east bank of the river Severn; it is rather a large but not populous place, consisting principally of four spacious streets, meeting each other at right angles nearly in the centre of the town. The city, from its elevated situation, with a gradual descent on every side, presents a remarkably clean appearance, is well paved and lighted, and contains, besides the cathedral, five parish churches, to which have been recently added a chapel of ease to the Church of St. Mary de Grace, on right of the Bristol road; and a chapel of ease to the Church of St. Michael, on right of the Painswick road; here are also places of worship for dissenters and quakers, a Jews' synagogue, two grammar-schools, a county infirmary, and several charitable institutions; here is also a magnificent shire-hall, in which are two admirably formed courts of law and justice, wherein are held the assizes and sessions for the city and county; two commodious market-houses, an elegant theatre, a custom-house, and a county gaol, erected after the plan of Howard, upon the site of the ancient castle. The inhabitants are chiefly employed in wool-stapling, rope-making, malting, and the manufacture of pins, of which latter article, the annual trade to the metropolis alone is said to amount to 20,000*l*. This city, which is situated above 30 miles from the junction of the Severn with the Bristol Channel, possesses many natural as well as artificial advantages for commercial purposes; by means of its connection with the great system of canal navigation in the north, and the Thames and Severn canal, which unites the two rivers, whence is derived its name, an extensive communication is opened with every part of the kingdom. Here is an elegant and commodious assembly-room, an excellent pump-room, with hot, cold, and vapour baths, and in its vicinity many handsome houses for the accommodation of visiters; the mineral springs are chalybeate. The cathedral is a splendid specimen of Gothic architecture; it was begun about the year 1407; in 1551, Abbot Horton built the north aisle and great hall, now used as a library, and succeeding abbots have enlarged and decorated the venerable pile; this magnificent fabric is 420 feet long, and 144 wide; from its centre rises a majestic tower 198 feet high, surmounted by four beautifully pierced pinnacles; the interior bears a very solemn and impressive aspect; the choir is extremely elegant, and its richly carved stalls are little inferior to those at Windsor; besides the various beautiful appendages to this edifice, its numerous monuments deserve attention, the most conspicuous of which are those of Edward II., the Earl of Hereford, and the Duke of Normandy. The corporation of Gloucester consists of a recorder, mayor, twelve aldermen, town-clerk, chamberlain, sword-bearer, forty common councilmen, four sergeants at mace, &c., besides twelve incorporated companies for trades, whose masters attend the mayor on all public occasions. It has sent two members to parliament ever since the 23d of Edward I. Market on Wednesday and Saturday. The Gloucester and Berkeley canal commences at a place called Berkeley Pill, upon the east bank of the Severn, nearly opposite Berkeley, and is capable of admitting ships of 200 tons burden; it falls into a basin on the south side of the city, sufficiently large to contain 100 vessels.

CHESTER AND CREWE RAILWAY.

The Chester and Crewe Railway branches forth from the Grand Junction line about a $\frac{1}{4}$ of a mile beyond the Crewe Station of the Grand Junction Company, distant by Railway from London 166 miles, from Birmingham $53\frac{3}{4}$ miles; and, carried by successive embankment and excavation, upon a descent of 1 in 1153, with an easy sweep round Oak Farm, reaches in that way the first mile from Crewe Station; when, commencing a descent of 1 in 480, carried chiefly through cutting, it extends in $1\frac{1}{4}$ mile to Coppenhall Heyes; in $\frac{1}{3}$ a mile more the road from Nantwich to Church Coppenhall; and in rather more than $2\frac{1}{4}$ miles the turnpike road from Nantwich to Middlewich; $3\frac{1}{2}$ miles on left of this is Nantwich; 7 miles on right is Middlewich. From the Nantwich and Middlewich road, continued on the descent of 1 in 480, chiefly through cutting, it reaches the viaduct over the river Weaver. One mile distant on left of this is Pool Hall. From the river Weaver, carried forward by embankment, on a rise of 1 in 480 in a direct line, it arrives in rather more than $\frac{1}{3}$ a mile at the Nantwich and Church Minshull road, and

THE NANTWICH STATION,

AN INTERMEDIATE ONE, DISTANT FROM CREWE $3\frac{1}{2}$ MILES, FROM CHESTER $17\frac{1}{4}$ MILES, FROM BIRMINGHAM $57\frac{1}{4}$ MILES, FROM LONDON $169\frac{1}{2}$ MILES.

From the Nantwich Station carried through cutting, in $\frac{1}{4}$ of a mile farther the road to Aston Hall runs over the line, which i little more than a mile extends to the Middlewich and Wardle Canal. Here the Railway commences a descent of 1 in 4200, upon which, in a curvilinear line, principally through cutting for 4 miles, it is continued; in $1\frac{1}{2}$ mile from the canal, it extends to Wardle Bank, 1 mile distant on right of which is Calveley Hall, when it crosses the road from Nantwich to Calveley, and, pursuing a course nearly parallel with the turnpike road from Nantwich to Tarporley, in $1\frac{1}{4}$ mile further reaches that thoroughfare and

THE CALVELEY STATION,

AN INTERMEDIATE ONE, DISTANT FROM CREWE $7\frac{3}{4}$ MILES, FROM CHESTER 13 MILES, FROM BIRMINGHAM $61\frac{1}{2}$ MILES, FROM LONDON $173\frac{3}{4}$ MILES.

From the Calveley Station ($5\frac{1}{4}$ miles distant from Nantwich on left, and Tarporley $4\frac{3}{4}$ miles distant on right) the Railway carried with an easy sweep, with the canal on its southern side, in another mile gains the road from Bunbury to Highwayside and the Ellesmere Canal, at a distance of $8\frac{3}{4}$ miles from Crewe, $11\frac{3}{4}$ miles from Chester. A quarter of a mile beyond the Ellesmere Canal the inclination changes to a descent of 1 in 480, upon which it continues for rather more than 3 miles. Three-quarters of a mile beyond the canal, to which point it is carried through excavation, the Railway enters on an embankment that carries it to Tilstone Fernall, at Tilstone Mill, 1 mile on right of which is Tilstone Lodge. At this point it crosses the Tilstone and Bunbury road, from whence it reaches, by a line nearly direct, Beeston Mill; in rather more than 1 mile beyond which the train arrives at the turnpike road from Whitchurch to Tarporley, and

THE BEESTON STATION,

AN INTERMEDIATE ONE, DISTANT FROM CREWE $10\frac{1}{2}$ MILES, FROM CHESTER $10\frac{1}{4}$ MILES, FROM BIRMINGHAM $64\frac{1}{4}$ MILES, FROM LONDON $176\frac{1}{2}$ MILES.

Two and a half miles distant on right is Tarporley, $12\frac{1}{2}$ miles distant on left is Whitchurch.

From the Beeston Station the Railway is carried for a short distance on an embankment, it then enters a cutting of considerable depth, through which, continued for rather less than $\frac{1}{2}$ a mile, it reaches an embankment of 2 miles in length; carried on this with an easy sweep it arrives at Warton's Mill, the rock and castle of Beeston rising on the left, in rather more than $\frac{1}{4}$ of a mile beyond which it crosses the road from Huxley to Beeston and Bunbury. Continued upon the last-named embankment, carried forward with an easy sweep in rather less than $\frac{1}{2}$ a mile, the inclination, a descent of 1 in 480, then changes to that of 1 in 1508, upon which it continues for 4 miles. One mile beyond the Huxley and Bunbury road, carried with an easy curve, the Railway crosses Crimes Lane and the Crimes Brook; and in $1\frac{1}{4}$ mile more, passing between those two villages, crosses the road from Newton to Huxley. From this point, the Railway, taking a N. W. direction, in another mile reaches the road from Huxley to Tattenhall, and

THE CROW NEST STATION,

AN INTERMEDIATE ONE, DISTANT FROM CREWE 14 MILES, FROM CHESTER $6\frac{3}{4}$ MILES, FROM BIRMINGHAM $67\frac{3}{4}$ MILES, FROM LONDON 180 MILES.

Three miles distant on right of the Crow Nest Station is Bolesworth Castle, 4 miles distant is Aldersey Hall, and 5 miles distant Carden Hall. From the Crow Nest Station, the Railway, in rather more than $\frac{1}{4}$ of a mile passes close to the Ellesmere and Chester Canal, and in $1\frac{1}{4}$ mile further crosses the Foole Stapleford and Halton road, two small villages that lie, the former on right, the latter on left of the line. From the last named road, carried forward in a direct line by embankment, till within $\frac{3}{4}$ of a mile before its arrival there, which is by excavation, it reaches in a further distance of 2 miles the turnpike road from Chester to Whitchurch, near the village of Waverton, on right of the line, Seighton being 1 mile distant on left; the last mile being carried on a declivity, that at its commencement changes from 1 in 1508 to 1 in 400. From the Chester and Whitchurch road, which runs over the line, the Railway is carried forward through excavation with an easy sweep in a N. W. direction, and inclination of 1 in 2555, in a distance of rather less than $\frac{1}{2}$ a mile to

THE BLACK DOG STATION

AN INTERMEDIATE ONE, DISTANT FROM CREWE $17\frac{1}{2}$ MILES, FROM CHESTER $3\frac{1}{4}$ MILES, FROM BIRMINGHAM $83\frac{1}{2}$ MILES, FROM LONDON $183\frac{1}{2}$ MILES.

In less than $\frac{1}{2}$ a mile from the Black Dog Station the Railway arrives by embankment at Rowton, from whence it bends gradually to the N. E. and commences a descent of 1 in 400, upon which it is continued to Chester; it is carried by embankment for about $\frac{3}{4}$ of a mile, when it enters an excavation, through which, in rather more than $\frac{1}{2}$ a mile, it extends to the Chester and Whitchurch road, here thrown over the line. From this last point it proceeds in a direction nearly due west, being crossed in a short distance by the Aqueduct of the Ellesmere canal; in another $\frac{1}{2}$ mile the turnpike road from Tarvin to Chester, and shortly after entering the city of Chester, reaches the Chester Station, the last $\frac{1}{2}$ mile upon the level, at a distance of rather more than $20\frac{1}{2}$ miles from Crewe, from Birmingham $74\frac{1}{4}$ miles, from London $186\frac{1}{2}$ miles.

BEESTON CASTLE.

This fortress was erected by Randle Blundeville, earl of Chester, in 1220, one side of its area is defended by a vast ditch, and the other by the abrupt precipice that overhangs the vale of Cheshire: in the time of the civil wars it partook of the changeable fate that attended so many fortresses, and was soon afterwards dismantled by the orders of parliament; the ruins, however, still exhibit strong features of its original strength and beauty. Beeston Castle was formerly proverbial for its immense strength, and forms a conspicuous object for many miles, owing to its situation on the summit of the insulated rock of Beeston, which is composed of sand-stone, very precipitous on one side, but on the other gradually sloping to the general level of the country. The perpendicular side of the rock (the height of which, taken from the level of the sea, and including the castle top, is 566 feet,) has a tremendous appearance, and is haunted by a kind of hawk which builds in its clefts: hence the prospect is very extensive on every side, except where interrupted by the near approach of the Peckforton hills; the city of Chester, the estuaries of the Dee, and Mersey, the town of Liverpool, and all the level country of Cheshire, are distinctly seen from it.

EATON HALL.

This superb mansion, with the exception of the vaulted basement story, and part of the original hall, was erected, from the designs of Mr. W. Porden: it is built with a light-coloured stone, and has two fronts, both of which consist of a spacious centre of three stories, finished with octagonal turrets, buttresses and pinnacles, placed between large wings finished in a similar manner; the entrance to the western front is under a lofty vaulted portico, that admits a carriage; on the eastern side there is a magnificent flight of steps, terminating in three rich and airy arches, that form the middle of an exquisitely beautiful vaulted cloister, which spreads along the whole centre, and connects the wings with each other. The entrance to the grand saloon is through these arches; this very noble apartment looks down upon a terrace, upwards of 350 feet long, from whence is seen one of the richest landscapes that the river Dee presents during its course through this highly interesting county. The prevailing style of the edifice is the pointed Gothic, but the plan of the house is not formed upon that of any kind of either castellated or religious building, or upon that of the domestic architecture of a later date; neither has the style of any particular period been exclusively attended to, in the form of the arches; for though the architect proposed to himself generally that of the reign of Edward III., yet he did not scruple to depart from it for the sake of producing what he deemed a better effect. A noble flight of steps leads from the vaulted portico, in the western front, to the great hall, which is a spacious and lofty room, rising to the height of two stories, and having a vaulted ceiling, ornamented with family devices, at the intersection of the ribs; it is paved with variegated marbles, arranged in Gothic compartments; and has on each side four niches with pedestals and canopies, over ornamented chimney-pieces, between which there are beautiful paintings by the celebrated West, of the dissolution of the long parliament by Cromwell, and the landing of Charles II. The saloon contains three large windows, the upper parts of which are decorated with the most brilliant specimens of painted glass, executed by Collins, from designs by Tresham. The dining and drawing rooms are of noble dimensions; they are magnificently furnished, and also contain an abundance of stained glass; besides which, their ceilings are decorated with all the ramifications of fan-shaped tracery. The library adjoins the drawing-room; this is very tastefully fitted up with elaborately carved Gothic book-cases of English oak, abounding with ancient and valuable manuscripts, besides an exquisite collection of the most esteemed authors. The grounds, enlivened by an artificial inlet of the Dee, have also received the more congenial features of modern gardening, under the superintendence of the present noble proprietor, whose superior taste is here rendered evident. A venerable avenue, situated westward, has been spared, and continued in that direction to a Gothic lodge in the hamlet of Belgrave, about 2 miles distant from the mansion. There is another lodge, similar in design to the former, approached by a road, that diverges from the avenue in the direction of Chester, and crossing the park, winds amidst the plantations, affording occasional views of the Broxton and Welch hills, which, with the addition of so rich a foreground, are seen to singular advantage. The approach from Chester near Grosvenor Bridge is by a lodge that, erected in 1838, is a perfect facsimile of Canterbury Gateway. The most favourable views of Eaton are from the Aldford road, and from the bank of the Dee, where the great quadrangle of the stables is seen in perspective beyond the mansion, and assists in forming a picture of unusual architectural grandeur, aided by the disposition of the pleasure grounds in front, and the stately elms of the avenue, which close up the distance.

CHESTER

Is a city, and the county town of Cheshire, in the hundred of Broxton, 183 miles from London by Coventry and Newport, and 188 by Lichfield. It is very ancient and extensive, approached on its southern side by Grosvenor Bridge (opened in 1834), a noble structure, that, consisting of a single arch of 200 feet span, and esteemed the largest stone arch in the world (being 80 feet wider than those of Waterloo Bridge at London), crosses the river Dee, which is navigable here, and falls into the Irish Channel, at the distance of 18 miles below the city. It was anciently called Caer Leon. It contains 9 parishes (exclusive of the precinct of the cathedral). The city consists of four principal streets, running to the four cardinal points, called East-gate, Water-gate, North-gate, and Bridge-street. The houses, in general, are ancient, and mostly built of timber, with piazzas before them. The streets are hollowed out of a rock, to the depth of one story beneath the level of the ground. The most modern street is Queen-street. At the entrance from the suburbs, called Boughton, formerly stood a postern gate, called the bars or limits of the city; Water-gate is on the opposite point of the city, to the west. In this district is the Linen Hall, built by the Irish merchants, in 1778, containing 111 shops. Passing through the gate on the left, is the Roodee, one of the most convenient race-courses in England. On the west side of the Roodee stands the House of Industry; and adjoining is the New River, cut through a large space of white sand, in 1785, which is navigable for vessels of 350 tons. Here are excellent conveniences for ship-building, and ten or twelve vessels are frequently seen on the stocks at a time. It has two inland canals, one of which goes to Nantwich, and from thence into Shropshire and Montgomeryshire; the other extends from Chester to Liverpool, and connects the rivers Dee and Mersey. From the Nantwich canal also are extensions to Middlewich and Birmingham. The chief manufactures consist of tobacco, snuff, patent-shot, white lead, iron, tobacco-pipes, and leather. The trades of the city consist of 25 corporations. The North-gate street has been much improved of late years, by the removal of the projecting shops. On the right of this street is the Theatre Royal, built out of the ruins of St. Nicholas chapel. The Exchange is a handsome pile, supported by five columns, and is 126 feet long: it was erected in 1698. On the west side is a row of shops. The Union Hall is a quadrangular edifice, built by subscription, in 1809, for the accommodation of the Yorkshire and Manchester merchants, who attend the two great fairs, in July and October, with their goods. The Commercial Hall, for the like purpose, was built in 1815. Here also the quarter sessions are held, and the city officers elected. On the west side, in St. Martins-in-the-Fields, in a most salubrious situation, is a spacious and elegant infirmary, erected in 1761. On the east side is the entrance into the abbey-court, over the gateway of which is the register office for wills. The abbey-court is a pleasant square, and the houses are regular and handsome; here also is the bishop's palace, erected in 1753. The old castle has been taken down, and a city gaol erected, after the design of Mr. Harrison, the architect of Lancaster castle. The grand entrance is built upon the model of the Acropolis at Athens. Opposite to this is the Shire Hall, a fine edifice, the portico of which is supported by 12 pillars, each 22 feet high, and about 37 inches in diameter. The hall itself, where the assizes are held, is of a semicircular form, 80 feet in diameter, 50 feet wide, and 44 in height; the roof is supported by 12 columns of the Ionic order. In the construction of the prison, a due attention has been given to a proper classification of the prisoners. In the castle yard are barracks for 120 men, and on the south west side is an arsenal for 27,000 stand of arms. This castle is a royal fortress. It has a governor, a lieutenant governor, and a constable. In a field adjoining is a figure of Minerva, cut on a rock, said to be the spot where king Edgar's palace stood. The centre of the city, where the four streets meet, is called the Peutice, whence there is a pleasant view of the whole. There stands a cross in the market-place, which is supposed to have been the site of the Roman Prætorium. At this cross an annual bull-bait was once held, which was attended by the mayor and corporation in their official habiliments. The cathedral church, dedicated to St. Werburgh, stands on the east side of North-gate; it was a nunnery, founded more than 1,100 years by Walpherus, king of the Mercians, for his daughter, St. Werburgh, who took the veil three years after she had been married. It afterwards became the abbey church of a monastery of Benedictines, founded by Hugh Lupus, earl of Chester. Henry VIII. dissolved the monastery, and endowed the cathedral with the revenues of the abbey, for the maintenance of a dean, six prebendaries, six minor canons, and other officers. The tower is 127 feet high, and springs from four beautiful pillars. The choir is very neat, and the bishop's throne, the ancient shrine of St. Werburgh, is superbly decorated. It is encircled by a group, representing saints and supposed Mercian kings. These were much defaced by the military, under Cromwell, but they have been repaired and greatly improved of late years. Here are several good monuments, and behind the choir is St. Mary's chapel, in which prayers are read every morning at 6 o'clock. Adjoining its entrance is the tomb of Henry IV., emperor of Germany, who lived here ten years as a hermit. The south part of the choir is spacious, and forms the parish church of St. Oswald, which has a chapel of ease standing more than 4 miles from Chester. The cloisters are in the north aisle, and contain that beautiful edifice, the Chapter-house, where lie the remains of several earls and abbots. It was built in 1128, by Randle Machine, earl of Chester, and is 50 feet long and 26 wide. The church of St. John, without the walls, was formerly collegiate, but there are now only the ruins of this once magnificent pile. It was founded 689, by king Ethelred, on being exhorted by a vision to build it on a spot where he should find a white hind. This legend is represented on the west side of the steeple. St. Peter's church is in the centre of the city. Trinity church stands in Water-gate street, having a handsome spire steeple. St. Bridget's, on the west side of Bridge-street, is also neat and convenient, opposite to which is St. Michael's. St. Mary's stands in the south-west part of the city, and has several very handsome monuments. St. Olave's stands in the lower part of Bridge-street. St. Martin's at a place called the Ash; and Christ church, a small neat structure, opened in 1839, in Newtown. In the town are several meeting-houses for Methodists, Independents, Baptists, Unitarians, Roman Catholics, and Quakers. The new Wesleyan Methodists, about 1834, erected a beautiful chapel in the Corinthian style of architecture; and the Independent chapel, with its adjoining room and school, a beautiful freestone edifice in the Doric style, in 1839, is considered quite an ornament to the city. The public charities of the town are numerous. Here are also two public libraries and a commercial news-room, which is a highly finished building in the Ionic order. The ancient walls that surround the city are in a state of preservation, being 1¾ miles and 101 yards round, and broad enough at the top to admit several persons walking abreast. The walks on them are kept up by a murage duty of 2d. on every 100 yards of linen imported. The walls were formerly defended by several strong towers; but only one, the Phœnix tower, now remains, from which Charles I. viewed the defeat of his army at Rowton-moor. The corporation consists of a mayor, who holds a court for trying all offences except treason, a recorder, 2 sheriffs, 24 aldermen, and 40 common councilmen, besides other inferior officers. This city sends two members to Parliament. The markets on Wednesday and Saturday are well supplied.

CHESTER AND BIRKENHEAD RAILWAY.

THE Chester and Birkenhead Railway commences at the terminus of the Chester and Crewe line, in Brook Street, Chester, one station being common to both. Quitting Chester, the Railway, carried forward upon an embankment 1½ mile in length, on a gradual ascent of 1 in 1367, reaches in rather less than a mile the Bache and Upton road (on left of which is Bache Hall); and in ¼ mile farther passes under a well-constructed oblique bridge, upon which the Chester and Birkenhead road is borne over the line.

Clearing this bridge, the Railway enters a deep cutting, through which it arrives at the Moston embankment, in the centre of which it crosses, by a viaduct, the Ellesmere canal, the Moston Brook, and valley. On left of the viaduct is Mollington Hall; on right of it, Moston Hall. From the Moston embankment on left, is obtained a view of the Welsh mountains, the most conspicuous amongst which is Moel Flamma, the loftiest of the Clwydian hills, bearing on its crest the Jubilee Monument, erected to commemorate the event of his majesty King George III. having completed the fiftieth year of his reign. In rather less than 3 miles from Chester, the Moston embankment terminates, when the Railway (which from the Ellesmere viaduct is carried forward on a rise of 1 in 330) enters an excavation, passing immediately under the Mollington and Backford road, in ¼ mile more the road to Lea Hall, in 1½ mile two roads to Backford Cross on right, and in a distance of rather more than 5 miles from Chester, the road to Capenhurst on left, near which is Capenhurst Hall. At the Capenhurst road the Railway, changing its inclination, commences a descent of 1 in 686, and, carried forward in a line nearly direct, still continued through cutting, in rather less than 2 miles extends to the road from Sutton to Great Neston and Parkgate. Sutton, a small village, lies 1 mile distant on right of the line: Great Neston, a small market-town, 5½ miles distant on left. One mile beyond Great Neston, on left, occupying a beautiful situation on the margin of the Dee (here of a width exceeding 3½ miles, and opposite to Flint Castle, on the Flintshire side of the river) is Parkgate, a watering-place of some celebrity, and formerly the principal station of the Irish post-office packets, long since removed to Liverpool. From the Sutton and Parkgate road, rather less than 7 miles from Chester, the Railway, still continued through cutting, constructed with an easy sweep, arrives in rather more than a mile at the turnpike-road from Hooton to Great Neston and Parkgate, and commencement of the Plimyard embankment, 8 miles from Chester. The Plimyard embankment, $2\frac{1}{2}$ miles in length, intersects the estate of Sir Thomas Massey Stanley, Bart., whose beautiful seat, Hooton Hall, lies $1\frac{1}{2}$ mile distant on right of the Hooton and Parkgate road. Hooton Hall is a magnificent mansion, its situation is singularly beautiful, being seated on the southern side of the Mersey, and commanding a fine view of that noble river (here 3 miles wide) and all the contiguous country to Liverpool. From the Hooton and Parkgate road, the Railway carried with an easy sweep on a descent of 1 in 7566 across the Plimyard valley, reaches in rather more than $\frac{1}{4}$ mile the road to Eastham, a village lying 1 mile distant on right of the line, of which and of its church, from the embankment, a passing glance is obtained; in a short distance further it crosses the Plimyard Brook, in rather less than $\frac{1}{2}$ mile beyond which it enters an excavation, through which it is carried in a direct line, chiefly on the increased descent of 1 in 600, to the Bromborough embankment and Bromborough Pool, $10\frac{3}{4}$ miles from Chester. On left of Bromborough Pool is Poulton Hall; $\frac{1}{4}$ mile distant on right, occupying a beautiful situation on the southern bank of the Mersey, of which and of the adjacent country it commands a fine view, stands Bromborough Hall. Just before reaching Bromborough Pool, the Railway, quitting the excavation, enters on a short embankment, which, carried at an elevation of 50 feet above the Bromborough valley, affords a good but transient glance of that delightful dell, which in the summer season presents a very beautiful appearance; rich-foliaged trees adorn the verdant banks; here the modest primrose and retiring violet vie with each other in beauty; a silvery stream pursues its silent course, and the eye leaves one charm but to alight on another. Shortly after quitting the Bromborough embankment, the Railway, carried forward in a direct line upon a descent of 1 in 600, enters an excavation that in less than $\frac{1}{4}$ of a mile is crossed by Spital Lane; $\frac{1}{4}$ a mile beyond which, passing under the Chester and Birkenhead road, it approaches the village of Bebbington, that lies on the left, of which, with its church, a good view is obtained. Three quarters of a mile beyond the Chester and Birkenhead road, continued in a direct line by embankment, the Railway crosses the turnpike road from Parkgate and Great Neston to New Ferry, and shortly after the old road to Woodside; a little beyond this it enters an excavation, carried through which, in rather less than 13 miles from Liverpool, it runs under the road to Rock Ferry, near which is Derby House, and in ¼ of a mile arrives at the Tranmere embankment. To prevent any misapprehension on the subject of the accommodation to be met with at Rock Ferry, it is proper to state that it contains numerous handsome buildings, a large hotel and public baths, with a beautiful esplanade facing the river; this during the summer evenings is enlivened by a band of music, that with occasional regattas attract numerous visitors, who, in addition to the pleasures of this delightful promenade, inhale the health-invigorating breeze. The Tranmere embankment, which crosses the valley at an average height of about 20 feet above its surface, presents a striking contrast to the confines of the gloomy cutting from which the tourist has just escaped, and the eye is regaled with a rich and varied landscape. One mile from Birkinhead on left, a most diversified prospect of hill and dale, wood and water, presents itself. The gently rising ground crowned with a picturesque church, a mill, and numerous villas, and intersected by verdant hedgerows, is a part of Holt Hill village, beyond which the eye reposes on the richly wooded hills of Oxton. On right is seen the town of Liverpool, its noble buildings, docks, and shipping bordering the river Mersey, whose bosom, proudly conscious of the wealth it bears, completes as interesting a coup-d'œil as can well be imagined; contemplating these combined beauties, the traveller reaches the termination of the Tranmere embankment, and shortly after

THE BIRKENHEAD STATION,

A PRINCIPAL ONE, DISTANT FROM CHESTER 15 MILES, FROM BIRMINGHAM 89½ MILES, FROM LONDON 201¼ MILES.

BIRKENHEAD.

The establishment of a regular ferry from hence to Liverpool has been productive of a great advantage to this place, which in a few years has rapidly increased in size and importance from an insignificant village to a large, handsome, and flourishing town. To this, in conjunction with the ferry, the amenity of the place, its proximity to Liverpool, and delightful situation, may safely be pronounced the supervening causes. In proof of this position, it needs only to remark, that the number of houses here in 1820 was only 19, with a population of about 70; in a word, it has increased within the last 9 years from 2,500 to 10,000 inhabitants. Among the lately erected buildings are a town-hall and market-house, two churches of the established religion, chapels for the different denominations of dissenters, a square that may be classed with the Eatons and Belgraves of London, some very excellent hotels, and streets of well-built private residences and shops. Many of the merchants of Liverpool, glad to escape from the noise, bustle, and smoke of that great commercial mart, have taken up their permanent residence here, and Birkinhead in consequence boasts a large population, not of mere artisans, but chiefly consisting of families of the higher classes and merchants of first-rate respectability; the society here is of the best description, and the walks and rides in the vicinity very beautiful. A well-attended fair is held here three times a year, viz. in the months of April, July, and October. The antiquary and admirer of the picturesque will be amply gratified by a visit to the ivy-mantled ruins of Birkinhead Priory. It was founded in the year 1190, by Haman Massie, third baron of Durham, for 16 monks and a prior of the Benedictine order; at the dissolution, its revenues were valued, according to Dugdale, at 90*l*. 13*s*. 0*d*. per annum, and were then granted to Ralph Worsley, from whom it has descended to the present lord of the manor, F. R. Price, Esq.

THE

NORTH MIDLAND RAILWAY.

THE North Midland Railway, a stupendous work, adds another link to the chain of railway communication in a northern direction, and may with truth be deemed a valuable acquisition to the already existing lines of transitory travelling. By its agency, in conjunction with the Midland Counties Railway, that commences at Rugby on the Birmingham line, and of which it is in fact a continuation, the manufacturing and mining districts of Yorkshire, the capital of that county and many of its principal towns will be reached in about 9 hours, thus conferring advantages of equal importance to the trade and commerce of the metropolis, the Midland and the Northern counties. Nor are these the only advantages the public will derive from the formation of this great effort of human ingenuity, the intervention of obstacles to the accomplishment of which, apparently unconquerable, must strike the mind of the mere ordinary observer with astonishment, but beheld by all who are in any way acquainted with the engineering difficulties that have here been surmounted, it can be viewed in no other light than a vast and prodigious work, the result of profound judgment, skill, and ability, and possessed of attraction sufficient of itself alone to be deemed worthy of a visit. To the tourist it will be the means of placing within easy reach the wonders of the Peak, the waterfalls and wolds of Yorkshire, its lofty mountains, expansive valleys, and delightful dales, which to have accomplished, time past, to all unpossessed of wealth, was altogether an impossibility. Time and space thus annihilated, these scenes will henceforth be the resort of admiring thousands, which to the larger portion would have remained unseen but for the introduction of steam travelling, and a ride to Richmond in Yorkshire be accomplished in little more than twice the time it would have taken some few years since to reach Richmond in Surrey. Its importance in a national point of view, and advantage to travellers, having by the foregoing remarks been rendered fully apparent, we shall now enter on a description of the line, pointing out to the tourist the objects of chief interest passed in the progress of the journey; with this single deviation from the plan adopted in the preceding pages of this work, viz. that, in the general description, the names of the proprietors of seats are, with some few exceptions, omitted, —a plan rendered necessary to condensation; the whole, however, will be found in the Itinerary line at the end of the book, where this road is given in that form, and upon reference to which the reader will find the required information.

General Description of the Line.

DERBY TO CHESTERFIELD.

The North Midland Railway commences at the terminus of the Midland Counties and Birmingham and Derby Railways, on the south-west side of the town, near Siddal Lane, the entrance from London, in the vicinity of the race course and upon the margin of the Derwent, crossing which it is carried forward upon an embankment with a gradual sweep to the Sandiacre and Nottingham Canal, and the Nottingham road, which it crosses by a viaduct of seven arches and openings. This affords a good view of the town, as does the embankment that succeeds it of the fine open valley of the Derwent, till the arrival of the train at Milford Tunnel. From the Nottingham road it is constructed with a curvilinear sweep through the valley of the Derwent to Duffield, the river Derwent running on its western, the Little Eaton canal upon its eastern side, as far as Little Eaton; ¾ of a mile beyond Derby it crosses the Mansfield road, which branches off to the right; in 1¼ mile the Alfreton road, running in the same direction through the village of Breadsall, ⅜ of a mile distant on right; the Allestry road at 2⅝, which conducts to the village of Allestry and Allestry Park, 1½ mile distant on left, reaching the village of Little Eaton in a distance of 3 miles. Half mile distant on left of the Nottingham road is Darley Hall, adjoining which is Darley Abbey. Two miles distant from the Allestry road on left lies Kedleston, the magnificent seat of Lord Scarsdale; 1 mile distant from Little Eaton, on right, is the Priory, formerly the residence of Dr. Darwin, author of the Botanic Garden, who for many years resided in Derby. From Little Eaton, carried between the banks of the Derwent river on the eastern, and the Little Eaton canal on the western side of the valley, the Railway, in ¼ of a mile, crosses the Derwent by a long timber bridge, and in 1 mile more arrives at the large, pleasant, and populous village of Duffield, its church being immediately on right of the Railway. Two miles distant on left of Duffield is Farnagh Hall. At Duffield the Railway runs under the road to Alfreton, which here branches out of the Derby and Chesterfield road, that to this point has been the companion of the line upon the left. From Duffield, carried forward with a graceful bend, crossing ¾ of a mile beyond it the Belper road, in another ¼ of a mile the line enters the Milford Tunnel, distant from Derby 5½ miles. On right of Milford Tunnel is Milford House, and 1 mile distant Holbrook. Emerging from the Milford Tunnel it soon reaches the Belper road, and crossing the Derwent arrives at

THE BELPER STATION,

AN INTERMEDIATE ONE, DISTANT FROM DERBY 7¼ MILES, FROM LEEDS 65¾ MILES, FROM LONDON 139¾ MILES. Journey resumed at next page.

BELPER

Has, from an inconsiderable village, become one of the most flourishing towns in the county, for which it is indebted to the cotton mills belonging to Messrs. Strutt; these were three in number, and the first of them was erected in the year 1776, but one was unfortunately destroyed by fire in 1803. The principal of these mills is considered as fire-proof, the floors being constructed on brick arches, and paved with brick. Its water wheels deserve notice, not only on account of their size, but for the manner of their construction; and the shuttles, near the top of which the water falls upon the wheels to work them, are likewise formed in a different manner from those used in similar works. About 1200 or 1300 persons are constantly employed in these mills, for whose accommodation the proprietors have erected a number of neat houses, a chapel, and a Sunday school for the instruction of the children. Lower down the river, near a mile and a half distant, there are two other cotton-mills, one of them like that described above, a bleaching mill, an iron forge, and a good stone bridge of two arches, all belonging to the same individuals, and erected by them; between 500 and 600 people are regularly occupied at these mills, and here, as well as at Belper, there is a Sunday school for the education of children. Market on Saturday.

From the Belper Station, carried through the town, crossing in its way the Chesterfield road, the Railway reaches in another $\frac{1}{2}$ mile the Matlock road and viaduct over the river Derwent, of which it affords a good view; quitting which, and in the course of another mile, twice crossing the Derwent, it arrives in $\frac{1}{2}$ mile from the last viaduct at the Belper Tunnel, 110 yards long; $\frac{1}{4}$ of a mile beyond which it crosses the viaduct over the river Derwent and Matlock road, and passing through Bull Bridge Tunnel, 120 yards long, in another $\frac{1}{4}$ of a mile it crosses the Chesterfield road and river Amber; in $\frac{1}{4}$ of a mile more it again bestrides that stream, and in another $\frac{1}{4}$ of a mile arrives at the

BULL BRIDGE OR AMBER GATE STATION,

A PRINCIPAL ONE, DISTANT FROM DERBY 10$\frac{1}{2}$ MILES, FROM WIRKSWORTH, 6$\frac{1}{4}$ MILES; FROM MATLOCK, 8$\frac{1}{2}$ MILES; FROM LEEDS, 62 MILES; FROM LONDON, 143 MILES. Journey resumed at next page.

A little before the Milford Tunnel, the valley of the Derwent, hitherto placid and expansive, now beautifully wooded, becomes bold and contracted, and the Railway from thence reaches Bull Bridge Station, as already observed, through deep cuttings, tunnels, and intervening embankments, from whence occasional glances are obtained of the striking and extraordinary scenery with which this district abounds. At Bull Bridge Station, tourists bent on exploring the wonders of the Peak quit the trains for Wirksworth, the most convenient spot for temporary sojourners; the town itself lying in the immediate neighbourhood of its most attractive scenery. Bull Bridge Station is seated in a beautifully romantic and richly wooded country, abounding with eminences, that exhibit prospects of the most enchanting character. It is in the vicinity of the Low Peak of Derby, a visit to which will amply repay every admirer of the picturesque. Alderwasly Park, the fine seat of F. Hurt, Esq., 2 miles distant, is remarkable for its delightful situation, its intermixture of rock and rich woods that, rising amphitheatrically from the margin of the Derwent, present from the Matlock road an appearance that captivates all beholders. 3½ miles from Bull Bridge on the right is Butterly Hall, Swanwick Hall, and the celebrated Butterly Iron Works, at which was cast the iron work for the arches of Vauxhall Bridge across the Thames.

WIRKSWORTH

Is a town of considerable antiquity, situated near the southern extremity of the mining district, in a low valley almost surrounded by hills. Here the features of the country begin to assume a less bold and prominent appearance; the lands are mostly in cultivation, and the inclosures, instead of being fenced with stone walls, are chiefly encompassed by hedges. At the time of the Norman survey, here were three lead mines: the manor was then the property of the Conqueror, and was given by King John to the Ferrers family at the same time with Ashbourn; it was afterwards annexed to the earldom and duchy of Lancaster, of which the manor and wapentake of Wirksworth are still members. The church is a Gothic building, apparently of the 14th century; it consists of a nave and side aisles, a north and south transept, a chancel, and a square tower, supported on four large pillars in the centre, and contains several curious monuments. In the churchyard is a grammar school, founded by Anthony Gell, of Hopton, in the time of Queen Elizabeth. The lands provided for the maintenance of the school produce a rental equal to the support of a better establishment than it at present possesses. The same Anthony Gell founded an hospital at Wirksworth for six poor men, and endowed it with 20*l*. per annum. The Moot Hall is a handsome brick structure, erected in the year 1773. In this building all causes respecting the lead mines within the wapentake are tried; and here is deposited the ancient brass dish which is the standard that others are made from to measure the lead ore. The weekly market held on Tuesday, was obtained in the year 1307, by Thomas, earl of Lancaster, grandson to Henry III. The inhabitants derive their chief support from the working of the lead mines, but between 200 and 300 hands are employed in the manufacture of cotton.

A quarter of a mile beyond Bull Bridge Station the train reaches Bull Bridge, where the Railway crosses by a viaduct the river Amber, the Cromford Canal, and the Nottingham and Matlock Road, of all which it affords a momentary glance, whence, carried through a deep cutting, it reaches in 1 mile from Bull Bridge Station the Lodge Hill Tunnel (260 yards long), 1 mile beyond which it again crosses the river Amber, and in ¾ of a mile more gains the Matlock, Wirksworth, Alfreton and Mansfield road, ¾ of a mile beyond which the train, crossing the river Amber at Dale Bridge on the Matlock road, arrives in ¼ of a mile more at Amber Mill and the

SOUTH WINGFIELD STATION,

DISTANT FROM DERBY 14 MILES, FROM LEEDS 58½ MILES, FROM LONDON 146½ MILES. Journey resumed at next page.

One mile before the Matlock and Alfreton road, on left, is Wingfield Manor; 1 mile distant on right of it is Alfreton Hall.

MATLOCK

Must be understood to include both the village and bath, the former of which is of considerable antiquity, and is chiefly inhabited by persons employed in the neighbouring lead mines, and in the manufacture of cotton; the latter is nearly a 1½ mile distant, and is much celebrated for the invigorating quality of its medicinal waters, which, though of undoubted efficacy in many disorders, did not begin to attract general notice till the end of the 17th century. The buildings of the baths and the adjacent lodging-houses are particularly well adapted to the comfortable accommodation of invalids: and the romantic beauties which adorn and enrich this sequestered spot will endear it to the man of taste, who may here survey nature in her wildest and most picturesque attire; the philosopher will also find a source of considerable interest and gratification in those objects which only amuse the eye of uninformed ignorance. The extraordinary beauty of many of the Derbyshire vales is universally acknowledged; but the unparalleled grandeur of the scenery round this place renders every attempt to delineate its varied characteristics by words, at least, hopeless, if not absolutely impossible. The bold and romantic steeps, skirted by a gorgeous covering of wood, and rising from the margin of the Derwent, whose waters sometimes glide majestically along, and sometimes flow in a rapid stream over ledges and broken masses of stone; the frequent changes of scene, occasioned by the winding of the dale which at every step varies the prospect, by introducing new objects; the huge rocks, in some places bare of vegetation, in others covered with luxuriant foliage; here heaped upon each other in immense piles, there displaying their enormous fronts in one unbroken perpendicular mass; and the sublimity and picturesque beauty exhibited by the manifold combinations of the interesting forms congregated near this enchanting spot, can never be adequately depicted by the powers of language. The creations of the pencil alone are commensurate to the excitation in the mind of corresponding images.

A little before the South Wingfield Station, the Railway emerges from the excavation and enters on an embankment. Here, quitting the valley of the Derwent, it enters the Amber valley, which though much less imposing in appearance is exceedingly rich, and presents many objects of interest. From the South Wingfield Station it is carried by embankment with a gradual sweep through the valley, with the Amber on its left; in $\frac{3}{4}$ of a mile to the Wessington and Shirley road and river Amber, which it crosses at Bump Mill; in $\frac{1}{4}$ of a mile more recrosses that river, and shortly after, entering an excavation, reaches the road to Ogstone Hall and Higham Street, here thrown over the line; still continued through cutting it arrives in another $1\frac{1}{4}$ mile at the Matlock and Mansfield road, under which it passes, and in $\frac{1}{2}$ a mile further arrives at Clay Cross, the summit of the Railway (360 feet above the level of the sea); $\frac{1}{4}$ of a mile beyond this it enters the Clay Cross Tunnel, one mile in length, that terminates in an excavation through which the line is carried to the North Wingfield and Tupton road, whence, twice crossing the river Rother in its way, the train arrives in $\frac{3}{4}$ of a mile at the

NORTH WINGFIELD STATION,

AN INTERMEDIATE ONE, DISTANT FROM DERBY $20\frac{1}{4}$ MILES, FROM LEEDS $52\frac{1}{4}$ MILES, FROM LONDON $152\frac{3}{4}$ MILES.—Journey resumed at next page.

On left of the North Wingfield and Tupton road is Tupton Hall, and the Tupton Iron Works; 1 mile distant is Wingerworth Hall, the fine old seat of Sir H. H. Hunloke, Bart.; 3 miles distant on right is Sutton Hall, and 4 miles distant Hardwicke Hall, a fine old seat of the Duke of Devonshire.

HARDWICKE HALL.

This far-famed and very interesting mansion stands in a fine park, well stocked with majestic timber; it is of stone, with a lofty tower at each corner, and a spacious court in front, surrounded by a high wall. The building was erected in the latter part of the 16th century, and forms an excellent specimen of the Elizabethan style: the apartments are lofty and of vast size, but defective in point of elegance of proportion; many of them are hung with arras, and the majority of the chimneys are sufficiently spacious for a hall or kitchen: the great gallery, chiefly remarkable for its extent, ranges along the whole of the east front, and is 195 feet long. In this mansion the beautiful Mary, Queen of Scots, passed several year of her captivity, and many of the apartments derive great interest from the furniture and other articles preserved in remembrance of that unfortunate princess; those occupied by her are situated on the second floor, and remain almost exactly as she left them; and the bed and chairs in one of the rooms were embroidered by her own fair hand. This venerable seat is enriched with a valuable collection of paintings, one of which is a portrait of the above Queen, taken in the tenth year of her imprisonment.

The Amber Valley is separated from that of the Rother, by the Clay Cross ridge of hills, through which the Clay Cross tunnel, 1 mile in length, a work of immense labour, has been formed. The valley of the Rother, from the commencement of that river till its junction with the Dun, is characterised throughout by enchanting scenery, upon which the limited space to which our observations are necessarily confined leave no room for enlargement; and the editor is thence of necessity constrained to direct particular attention to its numerous attractions, that noticed only in general terms, and enfeebled by brevity of style, would convey a very faint idea of the beauties observable in the journey through this delightful dale.

At the Clay Cross Summit the Railway commences a descent upon which it is for some time continued. From the North Wingfield Station the Railway, carried forward in a line nearly direct, by embankment, (crossing in its course three times the river Rother,) arrives in $\frac{1}{2}$ a mile at Wingerworth Mill. From Wingerworth Mill carried with a slight curve, by embankment through the valley of the Rother, the river running on the right, in $\frac{3}{4}$ of a mile it again crosses it, and carried through a short cutting, the Rother running on the left, in $\frac{3}{4}$ of a mile more, the Hasland and Chesterfield road. From this last point, carried forward with a gradual sweep, it soon enters a short but deep excavation, quitting which it is continued by embankment, in a distance of $\frac{1}{2}$ a mile from the last named road to the Rother, which it again crosses; in $\frac{1}{4}$ of a mile more the road from Mansfield to Chesterfield; in $\frac{1}{4}$ of a mile farther it crosses the Duckmanton and Chesterfield road, a short distance beyond which the train arrives at

THE CHESTERFIELD STATION,

A PRINCIPAL ONE, DISTANT FROM DERBY 24 MILES, FROM LEEDS $48\frac{1}{2}$ MILES, FROM LONDON $156\frac{1}{2}$ miles. — Journey resumed next page.

The Chesterfield Station is a handsome building in the Elizabethan style. $1\frac{1}{2}$ mile distant from Chesterfield; on right is Tapton Grove and Tapton House; 1 mile distant on right of the Mansfield and Chesterfield road is Hasland House.

CHESTERFIELD.

Chesterfield is a town of considerable antiquity, and is particularly distinguished in our national annals as the scene of a severe battle, which was fought in the reign of Henry III., between the forces of Henry, the king's nephew, and those of Robert de Ferrers, Earl of Derby, in which the former were victorious. Here likewise a severe conflict took place in the time of the civil wars, when the parliamentarian troops were defeated by the earl of Newcastle. It occupies an elevated position on the margin of the Rother, into which, upon its western side, flows a considerable tributary of that river. Chesterfield, by no means large, and irregularly built, is nevertheless esteemed, after Derby, the most considerable trading town in the county, and formerly belonged to the crown. King John made it a free borough, and granted it the same privileges as Nottingham and Derby. This town gives title of earl to the family of Stanhope. The corporation consists of a mayor, six aldermen, six brethren, and twelve burgesses. The old church, a spacious and handsome fabric, is by no means destitute of architectural beauty, but is more particularly remarkable for the curious construction of its spire, which is 230 feet high, and is so twisted and distorted that it appears to lean in whatever direction it is approached. In addition to this, Trinity church was opened in 1839. Here is a silk-mill and a cotton-mill, that give employment to the inhabitants, who are also engaged in the manufacture of stockings and carpets; and several potteries have been established in the vicinity. The neighbourhood abounds in coal, iron, and lead, which are worked to great advantage, and sent hence by the Chesterfield canal, that, in conjunction with others, affords the means of water communication to all parts of the kingdom. The carrying trade of this town, from its situation on the great north road, was, till recently, considerable, and the stage coach and posting establishments gave great employment; the whole of which has been carried off by the introduction of Railway travelling, that here, as in many similar instances, has inflicted a serious injury. Chesterfield contains a neat town-hall, a good free-school, founded by Queen Elizabeth, and several charitable institutions: it has a market on Saturday.

CHESTERFIELD TO ROTHERHAM.

Quitting the Chesterfield Station, the Railway, crossing the river Rother, is carried in a direct line in a short distance to the Worksop Road, from which point, the river Rother and Chesterfield canal running on its left side, in ½ mile further it crosses that navigation, and the Rother, and in ¼ mile more gains the Dronfield, Sheffield, and Worksop road, on left of which is Chesterfield Race Course, with its grand stand. From this last point it is carried by embankment, with a bold sweep (crossing four times in its course the tortuous Rother,) in a distance of rather less than 1¼ mile to an old tram road, when it enters a short cutting, clearing which, it reaches by a straight embankment and viaduct, over Stavely Pool, in rather less than 3¾ mile from Chesterfield, the Stavely Iron Works. From the Stavely Iron Works it is carried, through a cutting of great depth, in a distance of rather more than ½ a mile, to the Stavely and Handley Road, immediately on left of Stavely, a considerable village; a little beyond which, carried with a gradual sweep, it reaches an embankment, that conducts it in rather more than ¼ mile to another bridge over the Rother. Here it enters an excavation of great depth, and nearly ¼ a mile in length, at the end of which it gains an embankment, that carries it in ¾ of a mile from the last bridge to a viaduct of 5 arches, one of the longest on the line near the entrance to Renishaw Park, (the beautiful seat of Sir G. Sitwell, on left); that, affording a good view, carries it over the Staveley and Eckington road and river Rother, from whence, continued with an easy sweep, it is carried in ¾ of a mile by embankment to another bridge over the Rother, ¼ of a mile beyond which it arrives at the Mansfield, Worksop, and Sheffield road; Sheffield lying 8 miles on left, Worksop 10, and Mansfield 14½ miles on right of the line; and in less than ½ a mile more reaches

THE ECKINGTON STATION,

AN INTERMEDIATE ONE, DISTANT FROM DERBY 30¼ MILES, FROM LEEDS 42¼ MILES, FROM LONDON 162¾ MILES.

Two miles on right of the Stavely and Eckington road is Barlborough Hall. The Renishaw viaduct, which is of brick faced with stone, and is a handsome structure, presents, from the singularity of its construction, (viz. 3 straight arches in the centre and an oblique one at each end) a somewhat curious appearance; viewed from either extremity, it seems to consist of 7 arches instead of 5, the actual number. This departure from the usual plan was rendered necessary by the Eckington road and river Rother crossing each other at right angles. From the Eckington Station, carried with a curvilinear sweep by alternate excavation and embankment through the valley of the Rother, that here pursues a tortuous course, and is seven times crossed in a distance of 2 miles, the Railway gains the Sheffield and Worksop road, ¾ of a mile beyond which it reaches, chiefly through excavation, the Aston and Beighton road; in rather more than ¾ of a mile beyond which, two thirds through excavation, it crosses the river Rother and enters Yorkshire, and in another ¼ of a mile arrives by embankment at the Beighton and Rotherham road, from whence, carried with an easy sweep through the valley of the Rother, chiefly by excavation, in rather more than a mile it gains the Sheffield and Worksop road, near Woodhouse Mill.

From Woodhouse Mill the Railway, carried first with a curve and then in a course nearly direct, by an embankment for rather more than $\frac{3}{4}$ of a mile, (in the course of which it twice crosses the Rother) it then enters an excavation, through which, in $\frac{1}{4}$ of a mile, it reaches the lane leading to Treeton, and, in $\frac{1}{4}$ of a mile more, that village; a little beyond which, emerging from the excavation, and entering on an embankment, it soon crosses the Rother, and in $\frac{1}{4}$ of a mile further the road to Howorth Farm, where it enters a short excavation, clearing which, it is carried by embankment with an easy sweep to the Catcliff and Canklow road, near Canklow Mill, and in $\frac{1}{4}$ of a mile more arrives at the Sheffield and Tickhill road, at a distance of 5 miles from the former, and 11 miles from the latter town. From Canklow Mill, where it enters a deep cutting of nearly $\frac{1}{2}$ a mile in length, the Railway is carried almost in a direct line the remainder of the distance by embankment, the total being a mile, to a viaduct of 30 arches, varying from 25 to 30 feet span; that succeeded by a bridge of 2 arches, each of 70 feet span, carries it over the Sheffield and Rotherham road, the river Dun, the Ickles Cut, and low grounds in the vicinity, and finally over the Sheffield and Rotherham Railway, where the train arrives at the

MASBOROUGH OR ROTHERHAM STATION,

A PRINCIPAL ONE, DISTANT FROM DERBY $39\frac{3}{4}$ MILES, FROM LEEDS $32\frac{3}{4}$ MILES, FROM LONDON $172\frac{1}{4}$ MILES. — Journey resumed at next page.

The Masborough or Rotherham Station is situated at the road to Penistone, $14\frac{1}{2}$ miles distant on left, Rotherham being $\frac{1}{2}$ a mile distant on right of the line.

ROTHERHAM

Is pleasantly situated in a valley near the conflux of the rivers Rother and Dun; it is by no means a handsome town, but contains a spacious and rather elegant parish church, of Gothic architecture, that was erected in the reign of Edward IV. Here is likewise a meeting-house for dissenters, and another for methodists. This town is in a very thriving condition: its inhabitants carry on a considerable trade in coals and other articles by the river Dun, and have the benefit of a very excellent weekly market on Monday. On the other side of the bridge is the village of

Masborough, where the extensive and far-famed iron-works belonging to Messrs. Walker are carried on; these were begun in 1746, by that worthy, enlightened, and enterprising character, Mr. Samuel Walker, in conjunction with his brothers Aaron and Jonathan, and almost every kind of cast-iron articles are now manufactured at them, besides cannon of the largest calibre; the bridges of Sunderland and Yarm were also cast at the founderies of Masborough, as was the Southwark bridge over the Thames at London. On left of the Masborough Station is the Grange; ¼ of a mile distant on right is Clifton House. The Masborough Station of the North Midland is also the station of the Sheffield and Rotherham Railway, a short line of about 6 miles in length, from which the trains for Sheffield start several times a day.

ROTHERHAM TO WAKEFIELD.

The tourist has now quitted the valley of the Rother and entered that of the Dun, that, though less exuberant in scenery, is by no means destitute of beauty, but enlivened by the intervention of an occasional mill, exhibits, from many points, views that strongly participate of the picturesque. On leaving the Masborough or Rotherham Station the Railway is carried with a bold sweep, first through a cutting of ½ a mile in length, then by embankment to the Rotherham and Barnsley road, and thence by a direct line to the Greasborough Canal, a little beyond which it crosses the Rotherham and Rawmarsh road; 1¼ mile from the Masborough Station it reaches the Rawmarsh and Aldwark road, a little beyond which it enters an excavation of ½ a mile in length, through which it is continued in a right line, when it enters on an embankment, on which it is carried with a gradual sweep to the Rawmarsh and Hooton Roberts road, in another ½ of a mile again to the Hooton Roberts road, from whence, carried by embankment, it crosses Collier Brook, and shortly after reaches through an excavation the

KILNHURST STATION,

AN INTERMEDIATE ONE, DISTANT FROM DERBY 43¾ MILES, FROM LEEDS 28¼ MILES, FROM LONDON 176¼ MILES.

Three miles and a half distant, on left of Kilnhurst Station, is Wentworth House, the magnificent seat of Earl Fitzwilliam. From the Kilnhurst Station it is carried through cutting in a ¼ of a mile to the Swinton road, over which it is borne, and soon entering a short excavation, on quitting it, arrives in a direct line by embankment at the Swinton and Mexborough road, and in ½ a mile more attains

THE SWINTON STATION,

AN INTERMEDIATE ONE, DISTANT FROM DERBY 45 MILES, FROM LEEDS 27¼ MILES, FROM LONDON 177½ MILES.—Journey resumed below.

Half a mile distant on left of the Rotherham and Barnsley road is Clough; on right is Eastwood; 1¼ mile distant on right of the Greasborough and Aldwark road, on right, is Thribergh Hall, and 3 miles distant, Ravenfield. 3 miles distant, on right of the Swinton Station, is Melton Hall, and at Conisborough the ruins of Conisborough Cast.

WENTWORTH HOUSE

Is the superb seat of Earl Fitzwilliam. This magnificent mansion consists of a centre and two wings, and extends upwards of 600 feet in length; it contains several apartments of noble dimensions, which are furnished with extreme elegance; of these the hall and gallery are particularly admired; the ceiling of the latter is supported by beautiful Ionic columns, and the intervening niches are occupied by fine marble statues. The works of art contained in this princely residence are both numerous and valuable; the museum is stored with several fine antiques, and the various apartments decorated with the most exquisite paintings, by the best ancient masters, but of these no individual performance has attracted more attention than the celebrated picture of Lord Strafford and his secretary, by Vandyke. The park comprises upwards of 1500 acres of beautifully variegated ground, richly clothed with majestic timber, and ornamented with spacious sheets of water; in different parts of these extensive grounds there are a number of decorative buildings, well designed, and placed with particular attention to propriety of effect; the most conspicuous of them is an august mausoleum, 90 feet high, and consisting of three divisions, erected by the present earl, in honour of his late uncle, the Marquis of Rockingham: the first division is a square Doric basement; the second is of the same form, but of the Ionic order, each of its four sides opening into an arch, and disclosing a very elegant sarcophagus, which stands in the centre, and the whole is surmounted by a cupola supported by 12 columns of the same order. The interior of the lower story contains a marble statue of the marquis in his robes, executed by Nollekens, and on the pedestal are inscribed eulogiums to his memory, both in prose and verse.

From the Rotherham and Rawmarsh road to the Kilnhurst Station and Swinton and Mexborough road, the river Dun and Dun Navigation, called Mexborough Cut, accompany the Railway at no great distance on the right. Crossing the Dearne and Dove canal, the Railway carried forward from the Swinton and Mexborough road, upon an embankment, with an easy sweep, in ½ a mile farther, the latter part deep cutting arrives (as before observed) at the Swinton Station. From this, on left of which is a tunnel of the Dearne and Dove canal, the Railway in another ¼ of a mile reaches the Swinton and Ardwick road, here thrown over the line. Emerging a little beyond the latter from the deep cutting, it is carried with an easy sweep by embankment, in rather more than ¾ of a mile from Swinton Station, to the Rotherham and Ferry Bridge road. From this point it is carried forward in a straight line for rather more than 2 miles, twice crossing in its way the Wath and Bolton road, and river Dearne, to the river Dearne and road to Marlsbridge, from whence it passes with an easy sweep, still by embankment, to the Rotherham and Doncaster road, when it enters a cutting of considerable depth, through which, and the Cat Hill tunnel, 140 yards long, it is carried in ½ a mile to the Darfield Viaduct, at the Barnsley and Doncaster road, and river Dearne at

THE DARFIELD STATION,

AN INTERMEDIATE ONE, DISTANT FROM DERBY 49 MILES, FROM LEEDS 23½ MILES, FROM LONDON 181½ MILES.

On left of the Darfield Station is Middlewood Hall; 4 miles distant on right is Hickleton Hall.

At the Darfield Station the course of the Dearne has been diverted and made to run parallel with the Railway. A stone weir has been built here, and the original stream converted into a mill dam. This is crossed by a stone bridge; and the Barnsley and Doncaster road by a beam bridge, that succeeds it.

From the Darfield Station, 5 miles from Barnsley, 10 miles from Doncaster, the Railway, carried forward by embankment, sweeps through the valley of the Dearne, and crossing that river, reaches in rather more than ½ a mile the road to Houghton Mill, upon the left; here it passes through a short cutting, that, succeeded by an embankment, carries it in another mile (in the course of which it twice crosses that river) to an excavation, at the end of which it again crosses the Dearne, and arrives at Storr's Mill, from whence, continued by embankment in another mile, in which it twice crosses the Dearne, it arrives at Lund Wood, through which it passes in another ½ mile through a short excavation to

THE CUDWORTH BRIDGE OR BARNSLEY STATION,

A PRINCIPAL ONE, DISTANT FROM DERBY 53 MILES, FROM LEEDS 19½ MILES, FROM LONDON 183½ MILES.—Journey resumed below.

The Cudworth Bridge or Barnsley Station is distant 3 miles from Barnsley, that lies on left of the line. 1¾ mile distant on left of Barnsley is Wentworth Castle.

BARNSLEY.

This town is seated on the side of a hill, and the houses are mostly built of stone; it is frequently called Black Barnsley, very possibly from the number of forges which are continually at work here in the manufacture of wire, nails, hardware, &c., and which causes the houses to have a smoky and dirty appearance. The mother church, dedicated to St. Mary, a spacious and elegant structure, was rebuilt in 1820. An additional church, a beautiful building in the Gothic style, was opened in 1821, and a very handsome Roman Catholic chapel in 1829. Here is a good free grammar-school. Barnsley has likewise some extensive manufactories of linen cloth, check, and glass bottles; and coal being here in great plenty, the trade and population of the town have considerably increased since the completion of the Barnsley canal, that in conjunction with the Dearne and Dove canal, and Aire and Calder navigation, give it the benefit of an extensive water communication. Market on Wednesday.

From the Cudworth Bridge Station the Railway is taken by an embankment with a gradual sweep, in rather more than ¼ of a mile, to the turnpike-road from Doncaster and Pontefract to Barnsley and Penistone, and, carried forward in a direct line, reaches in another mile the road from Carlton to Shafton. The Railway now approaches the Barnsley canal, on right of which it is carried; in ¼ of a mile more, arrives at the Royston and Havercroft road, with the Barnsley canal now upon the left; in rather more than ½ mile beyond this it enters an excavation, through which it is carried in a tolerably direct line to the Barnsley canal, over which it is borne to the Yorkshire summit, 202 feet above the level of the sea, and Notton and Havercroft road, near Notton Bridge; 4 miles on right of which is Hemsworth Hall. From the Notton and Havercroft road it is carried forward in a direct line through an excavation of ½ a mile, at the end of which it enters on an embankment that carries it, in ⅜ of a mile more, to the Chevet viaduct, a noble stone structure of 13 arches, thrown over the Felkirk and Wakefield road, ¼ of a mile beyond which it enters an excavation, and passing Haw Park Wood on right, arrives at the Chevet tunnel, 600 yards long, on left of which is Chevet Hall. The Chevet viaduct, 110 yards long, is the property of Sir W. Pilkington, Bart. A short distance beyond the Chevet tunnel it enters on an embankment, by which it reaches the Chevet and Walton road, from whence, carried with a sweep, it gains, by alternation of excavation and embankment, in rather more than ¼ a mile, the village of Lower Walton, on right of which is Walton Hall; here it crosses the road from Millthorpe to Crofton, from whence it is carried, in a distance of about ½ of a mile, by embankment, with an easy sweep to the Oakenshaw viaduct, that, consisting of five arches, each of 60 feet span, is thrown over the Barnsley canal, and a tributary stream of the river Calder, ¼ a mile beyond which it arrives at

THE OAKENSHAW OR WAKE-FIELD STATION,

A PRINCIPAL ONE, DISTANT FROM DERBY 59¼ MILES, FROM LEEDS 12¾ MILES, FROM LONDON 190 MILES. — Journey resumed at next page.

On left of the Oakenshaw Station is Heath Hall, ¼ mile distant; on right of it is Crofton Hall, and 3 miles distant Nosel Priory. The Oakenshaw Station is situated near the road from Wakefield (2 miles distant on left) to Pontefract and Doncaster, the former being 6¾ miles on left, the latter 10¼ miles distant on right.

Wakefield is a large well-built town, pleasantly situated on the side of a hill, that slopes gently to the river Calder; it is one of the most handsome and opulent in the west riding of Yorkshire, the streets being, in general, regular and spacious, and many of the houses large, lofty, and elegant. The old church, dedicated to All Saints, is a spacious Gothic structure in the pointed style, having a spire that is generally said to be the loftiest in Yorkshire. A very elegant new church, dedicated to St. John the Baptist, was erected, in 1795, in an eligible part of the town, and is, as well as the domestic buildings by which it is surrounded, universally admired for beauty of site and excellence of plan. In addition to the above, a new church, dedicated to the Holy Trinity, has been recently erected in George Street. It was built by subscription. Wakefield likewise contains places of public worship belonging to the different classes of dissenters, a large and handsome house of correction, an excellent free grammar school, a neat theatre, and numerous charitable institutions. The neighbourhood of the town is rich in natural fertility, and beauty, and at its south entrance there is a handsome stone bridge over the Calder, a little above which is a dam that forms an admirable cascade. This place has long been noted for its manufacture of woollen cloths and stuffs, and, of late years, the increased prosperity of its trade has largely contributed to the improvement of the town, the whole of which is well paved and lighted. The numerous manufactories here and in the neighbouring villages principally supply the markets at Leeds and Huddersfield; it has also a considerable traffic in corn and coals. Wakefield is, from its locality, admirably situated for trade, the town forming, as it were, the centre of the manufacturing and mining district of Yorkshire, and to this may be added the advantage of canal navigation, whereby it is enabled to maintain communication with the rivers Humber, Trent, Mersey, Severn, and Thames. The market, at which there is considerable trade in wool and grain, is held on Friday.

WAKEFIELD TO LEEDS.

From the Oakenshaw Station (just before reaching which it enters an excavation) the Railway, thrown over the Wakefield and Doncaster road, is carried forward with a fine sweep, through deep cutting, to another mile (crossing Hell Lane in its way), to the Heath and Warmfield road, and in rather less than 1 mile beyond it arrives at an embankment upon Goose Hill Common, where it joins the Manchester and Leeds Railway, 1 mile beyond which, carried with a very gradual sweep through deep cutting, it arrives at the road to Altofts and Normanton, the former lying ½ a mile distant on left, the latter ¼ of a mile on right of the line. On left of Goose Hill Common is Newland Hall. Three quarters of a mile beyond the Altofts and Normanton Road, the Railway, carried on an embankment in a straight line, joins the south branch of the York and North Midland Railway, and arrives at

THE NORMANTON STATION,

A PRINCIPAL ONE, DISTANT FROM DERBY 63¾ MILES, FROM LEEDS 8¾ MILES, FROM LONDON 196¾ MILES.

Here commences the York and North Midland Railway, which connects this line with York and Selby. It will be found described at page 95. From the last Station the Railway in ¼ of a mile more gains the Altofts and Whitwood road, ¼ of a mile beyond which it crosses (by a bridge consisting of a noble arch of 90 feet span, with two side arches, each of 25 feet span,) the Aire and Calder canal, that succeeded by a viaduct of five arches, each of 60 feet span, over the river Calder, brings it to an embankment, whence is obtained a beautiful view, on which it is carried with a bold sweep, in rather more than ¼ of a mile, to a deep cutting of rather less than ½ a mile, through which it arrives at the Methley, Wakefield, and Pontefract road, and junction with the north branch of the York and North Midland Railway, that goes to York, Selby, and Hull. From this point the Railway in ¾ of a mile, carried with a gradual bend, reaches Methley, and passing Methley Church on the left, in rather less than ½ a mile crosses the road from Methley to Mickleton. On left of Methley see Methley Park, the noble seat of the Earl of Mexborough, 2 miles distant on right is Kippax Park, and 3 miles distant Ledstone Hall. From the Methley and Mickleton road the Railway, carried forward by embankment in a direct line, arrives in rather more than ¼ of a mile at Woodrow, in ¾ of a mile farther passes Fleet Farm on left, ¾ of a mile beyond it crosses the Wakefield and Abberford road, at Oulton, and carried through an excavation, in less than ¼ of a mile arrives at

THE WOODLESFORD STATION,

AN INTERMEDIATE ONE, DISTANT FROM DERBY 67½ MILES, FROM LEEDS 5 MILES, FROM LONDON 200 MILES.

One mile distant on right of Woodlesford is Swillington Hall. Carried through a cutting for about ½ a mile beyond Woodlesford, the Railway then enters on an embankment, that carries it with an easy sweep (the Aire and Calder navigation continuing on its left) in about 1¼ mile to the plantation near Rothwell Haigh Staith, in another ½ mile crosses the Wakefield road, on right of which is Haigh Park, ½ a mile beyond which it crosses the London road, and is thence carried with a gradual sweep to

THE LEEDS STATION,

A PRINCIPAL ONE, DISTANT FROM DERBY 72½ MILES, FROM LONDON 205 MILES.

Gradients of the Line.

The frequent changes in the gradients of this noble work, rendered necessary by the nature of the ground, for the sake of avoiding repeated interruption by a reference thereto, have been consolidated, and a brief summary of them here substituted. From Derby to the Clay Cross summit, a distance of 17½ miles, it is, with the intervention of a short level, a series of ascents, the steepest of which in no case exceeds 1 in 330, or 5⅓ yards in a mile. From thence it is constructed with a descent to Eckington, a distance of 12 miles, for the most part on an inclination of 1 in

332. From Eckington to Masborough, a distance of 9½ miles, it is carried, with the exception of a short rise, on a moderate descent. From the Masborough Station to the Rotherham and Ferry Bridge road, a distance of 9¼ miles, it proceeds by alternate rise and fall. It is thence carried, with the exception of a level of about 1¾ mile, on a continued rise, the steepest of which is 1 in 318, to the Barnsley canal and Yorkshire summit, a distance of about 10 miles. From the Yorkshire summit it is carried, on a descent of 1 in 358, to near Wakefield, a distance of about 4 miles, from whence to Leeds, a distance of 12½ miles, it is constructed by alternate rise and fall.

LEEDS,

The largest, richest, and most flourishing town of Yorkshire, is situated on the slope and summit of a hill, that rises from the north bank of the river Aire, over which is a beautiful free-stone bridge, that forms an ornament and fine entrance to the town from the south, and an additional bridge of stone, of one arch of 100 feet span, completed from a design by Rennie; this is 1 mile west of the other, and is universally admired. The streets in the upper part of the town are narrow, but in other parts they are broad, spacious, and well paved; and many of the houses are not only uniform, but elegant, and well suited to the taste and splendour of the inhabitants. Here are seven churches, to which in 1838 was added the new church of St. George, and an elegant Roman Catholic chapel. Here also are places of worship for different dissenting congregations, a free-school, and infirmary, hospital, and numerous charitable institutions. The chief articles of manufacture here are superfine cloths, kerseymeres, swans-downs, shalloons, carpets, blankets, camlets, and calimancoes; and here is a plate glass manufactory, and a pottery, that furnishes large quantities of earthenware, not only for home consumption, but likewise for exportation. The business transacted at Leeds is indeed immense; its trade in woollen cloth alone is perhaps the greatest in the world; and for the accommodation of the clothiers, here are two spacious cloth halls, comprising 3000 stands. The cloth halls are the most remarkable buildings in Leeds. It is here that all the great sales of woollen cloth take place. This forms the greatest mart for these goods in the kingdom; and the arrangements of the market are well adapted for the dispatch of business, and exhibit an interesting view of the trade of the town. The mixed cloth hall was erected in 1758, at the expense of the manufacturers; it is a quadrangular building, enclosing an open area. The building is 127½ yards long, and 66 broad. The white or undyed cloth hall is upon the same plan with the other. It was built in 1775. The quadrangle here is 90 yards long and 70 broad. The regulations are similar in both, and tend greatly to promote regularity and expedition. The market opens with the ringing of a bell; in a few minutes the hall is filled with merchants; each manufacturer appears behind his own stand, and the sales immediately begin. At the end of an hour, a warning bell announces the approaching close of the market; and the sound of the third bell, in 20 minutes more, terminates all the proceedings. No merchant can remain longer in the hall under a penalty of 5s., and of 5s. more for every five minutes he continues in it; and thus, in an hour and a quarter, transactions are completed, often to the amount of 15,000l. or 20,000l., and frequently to a still greater extent. Leeds is advantageously situated on the great line of river and canal navigation, which extends to Hull and the eastern sea on one hand, and to Liverpool and the western sea on the other; it communicates with the Yorkshire collieries, and with every great manufacturing and trading district in the kingdom, and also with the metropolis. The town is governed by a mayor, twelve aldermen, and twenty-four common councilmen. Here are a magnificent set of assembly-rooms, a commodious theatre, and a philosophical and literary hall, which latter is a neat stone edifice of the Grecian order, containing a museum, lecture-room, and library. Very extensive horse barracks have been erected here, and the markets are held on Tuesday and Saturday.

LANCASTER AND PRESTON RAILWAY.

The Lancaster and Preston Railway forms another link in the main line of communication between London, Birmingham, Liverpool, and Manchester, on the one hand, and Scotland on the other.

It commences at Dock-Street, Preston, where it joins the North Union Railway, being carried with a gradual sweep, in a western direction, on arches and retaining walls, through the town, passing close to several mills and factories, to the junction of the Preston and Wyre Railway, a distance of ¼ a mile. From this point, the town of Preston being cleared, a beautiful view is obtained down the river Ribble, almost to the sea. Penwortham Church, standing on a finely wooded eminence, overhanging the river, beheld from hence, forms also a fine feature of the landscape. A little beyond this, the line crosses the Lancaster canal by a handsome stone bridge, and carried in a direct line, chiefly through cutting, crossing in its way Cadely Mill dam, Lightforth and

Blunden brook, reaches in a distance of 4¼ miles the Barton embankment, that, in conjunction with a lofty viaduct of three arches, carries it across the Barton valley and Barton brook. The inclination of the Railway with the exception of the first ¼ of a mile, as far as Lightforth, a distance of about 3 miles, is a rise of 1 in 500. On left of Barton brook see Newsham Hall, on right seated on an eminence Barton Lodge. The owner of this property received as a compensation for the injury to his view (represented as very trifling) from the formation of the embankment, 1500l. Barton brook is crossed by a bridge consisting of three lofty arches, from whence, continued with a gradual sweep, the Railway reaches in a distance of 1¼ mile the tunnel (126 feet long) under the turnpike road from Preston to Lancaster. Emerging from the tunnel, to which, from Lightforth, it is constructed on a descent of 1 in 1060, the Railway, carried for a short distance with a gradual bend, is then continued in a direct line, almost entirely through cutting to the Bilsborrow road. A little beyond the Bilsborrow road, the Railway, quitting the excavation, enters on an embankment of ¾ of a mile in length, upon which, continued in a direct line, crossing at 7¼ miles from Preston the river Brock, reaches in a further distance of ¼ of a mile, by a descent of 1 in 640, the Myerscough and Chipping road, and in ¼ of a mile more, carried with an easy sweep, by embankment, on an ascent of 1 in 825, arrives at the Brockholes Arms. A little before Brook Bridge on left, is Brook House; immediately on left of it, Myerscough Hall; and on left of the Myerscough and Chipping road, Myerscough House. On left of the Brockholes Arms is the Lancaster canal, and on right Claughton Park, the seat of T. F. Brockholes, Esq. (whose ancestors have resided here from the time of Henry VII.) Of this a good view is obtained. From the Brockholes Arms, continued on embankment with an easy sweep, the Railway carried forward on a rise of 1 in 825, reaches in 1 mile,

THE GARSTANG STATION,

A PRINCIPAL ONE, DISTANT FROM PRESTON, 10¼ MILES, FROM LANCASTER 10¼ MILES, FROM LONDON 228¼ MILES.—Journey resumed at next page.

GARSTANG,

A market town of Lancaster, is very irregularly and meanly built; it was incorporated by Charles II., and is governed by a bailiff and seven burgesses. The old church is a stately Gothic structure, in addition to which, a new one, dedicated to St. Michael, has been erected. Within a small distance of the town runs the river Wyre, which supplies the inhabitants with excellent water.

and abounds with trout, chub, gudgeons, &c. Garstang, by means of the Lancaster and other canals, has communication with the rivers Mersey, Dee, Ribble, Ouse, Trent, Derwent, Severn, Humber, Thames, and Avon. There is no manufactory immediately in the town, except flax-dressing, and the weaving of sacks and other coarse articles; but there are considerable cotton-works in the adjacent townships. It has a small market on Thursday.

Half a mile beyond Garstang Station, the Railway enters an excavation through which it is constructed on the ascent of 1 in 825 to Higher Lingart; on left of which are seen the picturesque ruins of Greenhalg Castle; 1½ mile distant on left of the Myerscough and Chipping road is Catterall Hall. ¾ mile beyond Higher Lingart, continued on the rise of 1 in 825, in a direct line the Railway passes close to Woodacre Hall on the left. From Woodacre Hall, crossing Grisdale Beck, in rather more than ⅜ miles, it is carried, first in a direct line through Woodacre Wood, and on emerging from it, passes with an easy sweep, with the exception of the last ¼ mile, through cutting, some of considerable depth, to the Scorton road, constructed from a little before Grisdale Beck, nearly to the Scorton road, on a rise of 1 in 1320. The village of Scorton, a small one, containing a Roman Catholic chapel, school, and a cotton-mill, stands ¼ of a mile distant on right of the line. From the Scorton road, a little before which it commences a rise of 1 in 1060, the Railway enters on an embankment of a mile in length, that carries it with a curvilinear sweep across the valley of the Wyre, at the farther extremity of which it crosses that river by a bridge of 10 arches of the following dimensions— 20 feet span, 28 feet long, and 20 feet high. From this embankment is obtained a beautiful view of the river, the rich vale of Wyersdale, and Wyreside, the latter visible at between 2 and 3 miles distant: among the trees is the seat of Robert Garnett, Esq., said to be the largest Railway proprietor in the kingdom. Shortly after crossing the Wyre, the Railway enters a cutting of considerable depth, through which it is continued with an easy sweep on the rise of 1 in 1060 to the Cleveley road, here thrown over the line, which has now arrived at Hollins Lane on the old turnpike road from Preston to Lancaster, the village of Cleveley lying on the right. Here the Railway enters on a level of 3½ miles in length, and, carried with a slight curve, is crossed in a short distance by another road that leads also to Cleveley. Its course from the Cleveley road is through a deep cutting, for about ¼ a mile in a line nearly parallel with the old turnpike-road from Preston to Lancaster, when it enters on an embankment, that carries it over that once great thoroughfare, and in a distance of rather more than 1 mile from the Cleveley road reaches Foxholes. About ¼ mile beyond Foxholes, the Railway passes over the old turnpike-road from Preston to Lancaster, and the road to Quernmore, and crossing the river Cocker reaches the Hole of Ellel, on left of which is Hay Carr, and in another ½ mile, carried through deep cutting, arrives at Hampson Green, on left of which is Ellel Grange. ¾ mile beyond Hampson Green, the Railway carried by successive embankment and excavation, upon clearing the last cutting, arrives at the oblique bridge, 25 feet high, by which it is borne over the turnpike-road from Preston to Lancaster at Galgate, 16¾ miles from Preston, 5¾ miles from Lancaster, 235 miles from London. About 200 yards beyond this, it reaches the noble viaduct of six arches, each of thirty feet span, that carries it over the river Conder, the Lancaster road, and part of the village of Galgate. From the viaduct at Galgate, the Railway is carried forward in a gently waving line, between the old and new turnpike-roads from Preston to Lancaster, for rather more than ⅛ mile, when it enters a short but deep cutting, emerging from which ¾ mile beyond Galgate, it reaches Leach House; in the last excavation it enters on a rise of 1 in 660, in a short distance beyond Leach House, crosses the Ou Beck streamlet, soon enters a deep cutting through which it arrives at Ou Beck, where it crosses the road from that place to Five Ashes, in rather less than ⅛ mile, beyond which it passes under the old turnpike-road from Preston to Lancaster, and soon reaches Burrow Beck. Soon after crossing the Burrow Beck stream, the Railway entering upon a short level, and cutting of great depth, reaches in a distance of 19¼ miles from Preston the village of Scotforth, where two roads within a short distance of each other cross the line, and where terminates the last-named level. From Scotforth carried forward, through deep cutting, on a descent of 1 in 550, the Railway in less than ¾ of a mile emerging from the excavation, reaches the Greaves, and Ashton Lane, which it crosses, and carried with a rather sudden sweep through the grounds of West Bank, passing Springfield Hall, upon the left arrives at

THE LANCASTER STATION,

A PRINCIPAL ONE, DISTANT FROM PRESTON 20¼ MILES, FROM MANCHESTER 56½ MILES, FROM LIVERPOOL 59 MILES, FROM BIRMINGHAM 126 MILES, FROM LONDON 239 MILES.

Before taking leave of the Lancaster and Preston Railway, it becomes our duty to direct the tourist's attention to the following scene visible from the vicinity of the Lancaster Station. On emerging from the deep cutting, where the line turns somewhat suddenly, a burst of matchless beauty, one of the finest views in the kingdom, greets the eye; in front is beheld Lancaster Castle (of John of Gaunt memory) and the church, both being magnificently situated on an eminence, towering high above the town; behind them is seen the beautiful bay of Morecambe, called by Lady Morgan and others who have visited both, "The English Bay of Naples," the distance being terminated by the mountains of Westmoreland and Cumberland (the seat of the Lakes, the Switzerland of England), that rising in lofty majesty rear their heads among the clouds.

LANCASTER,

A seaport, and the county town of Lancashire, is 22 miles N. from Preston, and 240 N. W. from London. It is situate on a gentle ascent, on the southern bank of the river Lune, which forms a harbour of moderate size, but the shoals in the river prevent vessels of more than 250 tons coming up to the quay, larger ones being obliged to unload 5 miles below the town. The merchants' shipping is chiefly employed in the West India, American, and Baltic trades. It has a long fine quay, on which are a suite of noble warehouses. The houses are neat, many of them being handsome and well-built with free-stone, and covered with slate: it has one spacious square, and the streets, the principal ones in particular, wear an appearance strongly indicative of wealth and respectability. The old church is a handsome Gothic structure, at the west end of which is a square tower, containing eight bells. It stands on the crown of an eminence below the castle, from which it is separated by a moat, and both beheld in conjunction present a very imposing aspect. A new church dedicated to St. Thomas, has been recently erected. Here are also two neat and commodious chapels of ease, one of which has an elegant steeple, which has been rebuilt; and places of worship for Roman Catholics, Presbyterians, Quakers, Methodists, and Independents. The town-hall and exchange, in the centre of the town, is a good building, and has a noble portico. Here is also a neat theatre, a free-school, and a public library. The custom-house is a small building, having a portico, supported by 4 Ionic pillars, each $15\frac{1}{2}$ feet high, consisting of a single stone. The charitable institutions are a dispensary, many almshouses, some of them well endowed, and several charity and Sunday schools. The castle is said, by some, to have been originally built in the time of Adrian, but the present structure was erected in the reign of Edward III. It includes within its walls an area of about 380 feet square. The round towers were about 26 paces distant from each other, joined by a wall and open gallery; two towers on the western side remain entire, and the remains of 5 others may be traced. One of these towers is called Adrian's. On the top is a large square tower, called John of Gaunt's Chair, whence is a most extensive prospect. In this castle are the shire hall and the county courts, in which the assizes are held, and in it is now the county gaol. The whole area is supposed to be capable of containing 5000 men within its walls. Here was formerly an hospital for lepers, and a house for Dominican friars. The town is incorporated under a mayor, recorder, aldermen, bailiffs, &c. and sends two members to parliament. The Lancaster canal passes close to the town, by means of which it has a communication with the Mersey, Dee, Ribble, Ouse, Trent, Derwent, Severn, Humber, Thames, Avon, &c. The aqueduct bridge by which this canal is carried over the Lune is an elegant structure, consisting of five arches erected at an expense of 45,000*l*. The principal exports are hardware, woollen goods, cabinet ware, &c. the cabinet-makers of Lancaster being celebrated for their ingenuity, and its billiard tables in particular are much esteemed. It has a manufactory of sail-cloth, and the cotton-trade was successfully introduced some twenty years since. Here are also rope and twine walks, a sugar-house, two breweries, tobacco and snuff manufactories, a pipe, hat, and two coach manufactories. Ship-building is also carried on to a considerable extent, and several vessels of 500 tons have been launched here. In the vicinity is an excellent salt-marsh. The new bridge, a handsome building of five equal arches, is 549 feet long, and cost 12,000*l*. It was erected at the expense of the county. A sojourn of a day or two in Lancaster will be amply repaid by an excursion to its environs, an examination of its surrounding scenery and ancient castle, the view from the summit of which is magnificent beyond description. Hence is beheld to great advantage its noble aqueduct, that carries the canal across the river Lune; the distant view embracing the fells of Yorkshire, the mountains of Westmoreland and Cumberland, Piel Castle, and other islands in Morecambe Bay, that on a calm day resembles a lake of molten silver, and more to the eastward it is said the Isle of Man may be distinguished.

YORK AND NORTH MIDLAND RAILWAY.

The York and North Midland Railway commences near Altofts in Yorkshire, at the

NORMANTON STATION

OF THE NORTH MIDLAND RAILWAY,

A PRINCIPAL ONE,

Where it branches forth from the North Midland Railway at a point, distant from Derby 63¾ miles, from London 196¼ miles, from whence it is carried on a lofty embankment that commands some beautiful scenery, in a waving line, and distance of 1¾ mile to the Leeds and Pontefract Road, which it crosses, and thence with a gradual sweep to the

CASTLEFORD STATION,

AN INTERMEDIATE ONE, DISTANT FROM NORMANTON 3 MILES, FROM YORK 20¾ MILES, FROM DERBY 66¾ MILES, FROM LONDON 199¼ MILES.

One mile and a half distant from the Castleford Station, on left, see Kippax Park*, and 2 miles distant Ledstone Hall.†

From Castleford Station its course is that of a direct line to the east bank of the Aire and Calder canal, and thence with a gradual sweep to a bend of that navigation, which it crosses, and arrives in little more than ¼ of a mile at the tunnel under Ferrybridge and Abberford road, in rather more than ¼ of a mile, beyond which it reaches, by a direct line, the Ferrybridge and Tadcaster road (the great London road) at the

BURTON SALMON STATION,

AN INTERMEDIATE ONE, DISTANT FROM NORMANTON 6½ MILES, FROM YORK 17¼ MILES, FROM DERBY 70½ MILES, FROM LONDON 202¾ MILES.

The Burton Salmon Station is distant from Ferrybridge 2 miles, from Tadcaster 10½ miles; on right of it is Byram.‡

The Aire, that rises in the mountains of Craven, pursues its tortuous course through a valley, that little more than a mile in breadth, extends about 35 miles in length, to Leeds, where, after affording the benefit of its navigation, now considerably improved, to that great manufacturing town, it falls into the river Calder at Castleford, from whence, characterised as the Aire and Calder Navigation, it extends to Goole, where it unites with the Humber. The scenery of this valley is highly esteemed, and from the embankment beyond Castleford, previous to crossing these united streams, a fine view is obtained of that portion of it through which they here pursue their silent course. The country in this vicinity is beautifully wooded; and hence, embosomed in trees,

---

* T. Bland, Esq.   † C. Wilson, Esq.
‡ Sir J. Ramsden, Bart.

beheld, on right, Fryston Hall, the beautiful seat of R. M. Milnes, Esq.

From the Burton Salmon Station the Railway is carried with a sweep in 1½ mile to the Leeds and Selby road, and thence in a distance of 1¼ mile, by a direct line, to

THE MILFORD STATION,
OF THE LEEDS AND SELBY RAILWAY,

A PRINCIPAL ONE, DISTANT FROM LEEDS 12 MILES, FROM SELBY 8 MILES, FROM DERBY 73½ MILES, FROM LONDON 206 MILES.

From South Milford, the site of the Milford Station, the towers of York Minster are, on a fine day, clearly discernible.

From the Leeds and Selby Railway, that runs over the York and North Midland Railway, the latter reaches by a direct line and distance of 1¼ mile

THE SHERBURN STATION,

AN INTERMEDIATE ONE, DISTANT FROM NORMANTON 10¾ MILES, FROM YORK 13 MILES, FROM DERBY 74½ MILES, FROM LONDON 207 MILES.

Half a mile distant on left of Sherburn Station, is the small market town of Sherburn. Its venerable church, standing on an elevation, forms a prominent feature in the landscape for many miles, and hence may be seen the churches of Selby, Brayton, Fenton, and others.

From the Sherburn Station it is carried, in a distance of about 2 miles, by a line nearly direct to Church Fenton, on left of which see Scarthingwell Hall, and from thence, with the exception of a slight curve at its farther extremity, by a direct line to

THE ULLESKELFE STATION,

AN INTERMEDIATE ONE, DISTANT FROM NORMANTON 14¾ MILES, FROM YORK 9 MILES, FROM DERBY 78½ MILES, FROM LONDON 211 MILES.

One mile distant on left of the Ulleskelfe Station see Grimstone House, Lord Howden, 2 miles distant the village of Towton, rendered memorable by the battle of Towton Field, of which an account will be found in the Itinerary line; 3 miles distant is the town of Tadcaster and Haslewood Hall, and 5 miles distant Bramham Park. Quitting the Ulleskelfe Station the Railway is carried over the river Wharfe, of which and its valley the viaduct and embankment afford a most beautiful view; in this the church of Kirkby Wharfe, peeping forth from among the trees, forms a prominent and picturesque object. ¾ of a mile beyond the Wharfe viaduct the train arrives at

THE BOLTON PERCY STATION,

AN INTERMEDIATE ONE, DISTANT FROM NORMANTON 16 MILES, FROM YORK 7¾ MILES, FROM DERBY 79¾ MILES, FROM LONDON 212¼ MILES.

On right of Bolton Percy Station is Bolton Lodge, and 1¼ mile distant Nun Appleton, the seat of Sir W. M. Milner, Bart. The parish church of Bolton Percy is one of the neatest in this part of the country, and the rectory, the richest living in the gift of the archbishop of York, is supposed to be of the value of from 1500*l.* to 1600*l.* per annum. From the Bolton Percy Station the Railway is carried forward in a direct line, crossing in its way, at a distance of 1 mile from Bolton Percy, the Steeton road, and shortly after the Colton road extends in a total distance of 3¾ miles to

THE COPMANTHORPE STATION,

AN INTERMEDIATE ONE, DISTANT FROM NORMANTON 19¾ MILES, FROM YORK 4 MILES, FROM DERBY 83¾ MILES, FROM LONDON 216 MILES.

From the Copmanthorpe Station the line is carried with an easy sweep, in 1¼ mile, to the York and Tadcaster road, under which it passes. Emerging thence, the city of York rises into view: in ¾ of a mile more it extends to the Askham road, on right of which is Dring Houses, in the rear of which, strikingly conspicuous, stands Middlethorpe Lodge, and on left the village of Acombe, seated on an eminence, with its pretty church and lofty spire, forms a pleasing feature of the landscape. From the Askham road, constructed with a gradual sweep, it reaches, in rather less than a mile, the Wetherby road, and thence, in ¾ of a mile, a total of nearly 4 miles, to

THE YORK STATION,

A PRINCIPAL ONE, DISTANT FROM NORMANTON 23¾ MILES, FROM DERBY 87½ MILES, FROM LONDON 220 MILES.

One mile and a half distant on right of the Tadcaster road at Bishopthorpe is the palace of the Archbishop of York, and just before the Wetherby road, on right, Knavesmire, the site of the York race-course, which, with its grand stand, is visible from the line.

Gradients of the Line.

The gradients of the York and North Midland Railway are as follows:— For the first ¼ of a mile it is carried on a descent of 1 in 330, which then changes to one of increased steepness, 1 in 264, which continues for 1 mile: the next mile and a quarter is divided nearly into two equal parts, the first a rise of 1 in 1320, the other a descent of the same ratio. It is then continued for nearly 1½ mile, on a rise of 1 in 1885¾. Here it enters on a descent of 1 in 660, upon which continued for 3 miles, it is carried across the river Aire and Boroughbridge road to the Burton Salmon Station: to this succeeds a level of rather less than ¾ of a mile in length, at the end of which it commences a descent of 1 in 504, upon which it continues for 2 miles, that brings it almost to the Leeds and Selby Railway. At the termination of the last descent it enters on a level of rather less than 1½ mile, upon which it is carried to the Sherburn Station; to this succeeds a descent of 1 in 5280, upon which it is constructed for rather less than 1½ mile; it then enters on a rise of 1 in 961¾, upon which it continues for 1¼ mile, which, followed by a descent of 1 in 1320 for ¾ of a mile, carries it to a level of rather more than a mile in length. The next ½ mile, a descent of 1 in 1320, carries it almost to the Copmanthorpe Station, a little before arriving at which it enters on a level of ½ mile in length, at the end of which it commences a rise of 1 in 1320; upon this it is continued for a mile. Here it attains a level of 1¾ mile in length, at the end of which it is carried on a descent of 1 in 1320 for ¾ of a mile, that succeeded by a level of about the same length takes it to York.

YORK.

York, the capital of Yorkshire, inhabited successively by Hadrian, Severus, and other Roman emperors, is pleasantly situated on the rivers Foss and Ouse, and, in point of rank, classes as the second city in the kingdom; but it is far surpassed in wealth and population by many of the more modern trading towns. It is distant from London by road 196 miles, and is entered by four principal gates or bars, viz. that of Meiklegate bar, Bootham bar, Monk bar, and Walmgate bar. Of the six bridges of York, one alone crosses the river Ouse. This, which was begun in 1810, was finished in the succeeding 10 years. But the cathedral is justly esteemed the glory not only of York, but of Great Britain. Some of its principal dimensions are as follows: — The whole length from east to west is 524½ feet; breadth of the eastern end, 105; breadth of the western end, 109; length of the cross aisles, from north to south, 222; height of the grand lantern tower, 213; height of the two western towers, 196; height of the nave, or body of the church, 99; height of the eastern window, 75; breadth of the eastern window, 32. Of this magnificent structure, the west tern front is particularly superb. The eastern end being of somewhat later date, displays a more florid style of architecture, crowned with elegant niches and airy pinnacles. With the splendid exterior, the interior perfectly corresponds. The screen, which separates the nave from the choir, is a very curious piece of workmanship; but its history is unknown. Its extremely florid style of decoration, however, marks an age later than that in which the chief part of the choir was completed, and may with great probability be referred to the reign of Henry VI. The chapter-house is a magnificent structure, and singular in its kind. Its form is an octagon of 63 feet in diameter, and nearly 68 feet in height, estimated to the centre knot in the roof. Of this vast area, the roof is supported by a single pillar, geometrically placed in the centre.

Besides the cathedral, York contains 20 parish churches within the walls, and three (St. Olave, St. Maurice, and St. Lawrence) in the suburbs. The castle of York is of great antiquity. The present site was selected, according to some writers, in the time of William the Conqueror; but the fabric of that date falling to decay, it was repaired or rebuilt under Richard III. Dismantled of its garrison, it was converted into a county prison for felons and debtors, till again becoming ruinous, it was wholly taken down, and the existing structure erected in 1701. The Basilica, or new county hall, was opened at the summer assizes in 1777. It is of the Ionic order, 150 feet in length, and 45 in breadth. Great improvements throughout the castle have recently taken place, and more are still meditated. The mansion-house is an elegant building, erected in 1725, as a suitable residence for the chief magistrate of the city. Behind it on the bank of the river, stands the guildhall, erected in 1446, and regarded as one of the finest Gothic halls in the kingdom. Although the foreign commerce of York is totally annihilated, it still retains a considerable river trade; and vessels of 120 tons burden come up the Ouse as high as the bridge, near which there is a convenient quay. Some business is also transacted in gloves, linens, livery, lace, glass, and drugs; and printing and bookselling are conducted on a large scale. It derives its principal support from its assizes, music meetings, races, and fairs, and from being the winter residence of many of the provincial gentry, by whom it is regarded as a kind of northern metropolis. Its carrying trade, and maintenance of stage-coach and posting establishments, heretofore considerable and extremely advantageous, has, by the introduction of railway travelling, been utterly ruined. The race-ground (expressively called Knavesmire) is, by its horse-shoe form, admirably adapted for displaying the competition of the horses throughout the whole of the course. The assembly-room in Blake Street was built in 1730, on a plan designed by the celebrated Earl of Burlington: near this is the theatre, a neat building, erected in 1770.

Besides these public buildings, here are two receptacles for lunatics, a county hospital, a city dispensary, a blue-coat boys' and grey-coat girls' charity school, extensive national schools, almshouses, and other charitable institutions. In this city are two public banks, a subscription library, news room, Yorkshire philosophical society, and a museum of natural and artificial curiosities; also a gaol and a house of correction; with various chapels for quakers, Roman Catholics, and the different classes of dissenters. At a short distance from the town are extensive cavalry barracks, erected in 1796, at an expense of nearly 30,000l. The new walk along the banks of the Ouse is an agreeable promenade, well shaded with lofty trees. York received its charter of incorporation from Richard II., and is the only city in England, except London, whose chief magistrate is honoured with the title of lord. Its jurisdiction extends over a considerable district, besides the sole conservancy of the rivers Ouse, Wharfe, Derwent, Ayre, Dun, and some parts of the Humber. It sends two members to parliament. The government of the city is vested in the lord mayor, recorder, 12 aldermen, 2 sheriffs, 8 chamberlains, 24 common-council-men, 22 assistants, a town-clerk, and other inferior officers. The market-places, of which there are two, called the Pavement and Thursday Market, are spacious and convenient. Markets on Thursday and Saturday.

YORK TO SCARBOROUGH.

Of this line the following are the particulars: — From York to Haxby $4\frac{1}{2}$ miles; Strensall $6\frac{3}{4}$ miles; Flaxton $9\frac{1}{4}$ miles; Barton $11\frac{3}{4}$ miles; Kirkham $15\frac{1}{4}$; Hutton $18\frac{1}{4}$ miles; New Malton $21\frac{1}{4}$ miles; Rillington $25\frac{3}{4}$ miles; Knapton $27\frac{3}{4}$ miles; Heslerton $29\frac{1}{2}$ miles; Sherburn 33 miles; Ganton $34\frac{1}{2}$ miles; Seamer $38\frac{3}{4}$ miles; Scarborough $42\frac{1}{4}$ miles. Rather less than 3 miles beyond Malton the branch to Pickering commences, by which the distance to that town is accomplished in a total of $31\frac{3}{4}$ miles from York. Three miles distant from Barton, on left, is Castle Howard, the magnificent seat of the Earl of Carlisle.

⁎ For an account of the Whitby and Pickering Railway the reader is

BRISTOL AND GLOUCESTER RAILWAY.

The Bristol and Gloucester Railway commences in the vicinity of Stonehouse, a village on the road from Bath to Gloucester, at a distance of $9\frac{1}{4}$ miles from the latter city, from whence it is taken, on the Cheltenham and Great Western Union Railway, as follows. Shortly after quitting Gloucester, it is carried with a somewhat sudden turn to the Painswick road, which it crosses, and, in about another mile, carried with a gradual sweep in a south-west direction, gains the road to Stroud, from a little beyond which it is continued nearly in a direct line to the village of Haresfield and vicinity of Haresfield Court*, about 2 miles distant on right of which is Hardwick Court.† From Haresfield it is continued, in a course nearly direct, passing the foot of Broad Ridge, or Broad Barrow Green, an eminence that, rising suddenly on the left, is the site of a very singular camp, thought to have been a British camp, subsequent to the Roman invasion. The surrounding prospects from this spot are uncommonly fine, and include the windings of the Severn, that in front of it expands to an amplitude of breadth, Berkeley Castle, the Berkeley and Gloucester ship canal, the city of Gloucester, with its noble cathedral, and a large proportion of that part of the country. Continued in a direct line, the Railway, in about 2 miles beyond Haresfield, gains the Stroud and Gloucester Road, which it crosses $\frac{1}{2}$ a mile from Standish, a village on the road from Bath to Gloucester, about 1 mile from which, carried with a gently waving line, it unites with the Bristol and Gloucester Railway. 1 mile distant, on left of the Standish road, is Standish House, the beautiful seat of ‡. Carried with a gradual sweep, and western inclination, the Bristol and Gloucester Railway, in about 1 mile beyond its junction with the Cheltenham and Great Western Union Railway, arrives at the Stroud and Gloucester road, in the vicinity of Stonehouse, a considerable village, about 3 miles from Rodborough and Stroud, the chief seat of the woollen manufacture. The Stroud and Gloucester road is the site of

THE STONEHOUSE STATION,

AN INTERMEDIATE ONE, DISTANT FROM GLOUCESTER 9 MILES, FROM BIRMINGHAM $61\frac{1}{2}$ MILES, FROM STROUD $3\frac{1}{4}$ MILES, FROM BRISTOL $28\frac{1}{2}$ MILES, FROM EXETER 104 MILES.

One mile and a half distant, on left of Stonehouse Station, is Stanley Park §, and $1\frac{1}{2}$ mile distant, on right, The Leaze. ‖

* J. Niblett, Esq.   † B. Baker, Esq.
‡ Lord Sherborne.   § J. Wathen, Esq.

Quitting the Stonehouse Station, the Railway crosses the Stroudwater canal. This, which forms a part of the Thames and Severn canal, is a navigation of 8 miles in length, that commencing at Stroud, and falling into the Severn at Framilade, there unites the two noblest rivers of England. Continued with a gradual sweep, in a south-west direction, the Railway, in a further distance of $1\frac{3}{4}$ miles, reaches the

FROCESTER STATION,

AN INTERMEDIATE ONE, DISTANT FROM GLOUCESTER $10\frac{3}{4}$ MILES, FROM BIRMINGHAM $63\frac{1}{4}$ MILES, FROM BRISTOL $26\frac{3}{4}$ MILES, FROM EXETER $102\frac{1}{4}$ MILES.

Frocester is a small village situate on the road from Bath to Hereford, at a distance of $26\frac{1}{2}$ miles from the former, and 33 miles from the latter, city. Frocester occupies a position at the foot of an eminence which screens it from the east, and from its summit commands a very beautiful prospect. On left is Camley Pike, and the bold projecting head of Stinchcombe Hill, the intermediate space between the Forest Hills, the blue mountains of Malvern, and the turrets of Gloucester, being filled up with cultivated fields, village churches, and buildings of various descriptions, amongst which, the castle, the church, and tower of Berkeley, with their lofty battlements, stand forth boldly conspicuous. 2 miles distant from Frocester, on left, is Woodchester Park, the noble domain of Earl Ducie. This seat has obtained a considerable degree of celebrity, from the remains of antiquity that have been discovered here; the most splendid of these are the remains of a Roman villa, of very considerable extent and beauty of decoration; and, as a magnificent relic of Roman ingenuity, deemed the most extensive and costly ever discovered in this country. Continued with an easy sweep, in a south-west direction, the Railway, in $1\frac{1}{2}$ mile from Frocester, reaches Coaley, and, in another mile, the Dursley and Gloucester road, about 2 miles on left of which lies Dursley. In the vicinity of Dursley are the following seats: — Ferney Hill*, Bencomb House†, Kingshill House‡, Peers Court§, and Stancombe Park.|| Continued, with a bold sweep, the Railway, in a total distance of $4\frac{3}{4}$ miles, gains the Bristol, Gloucester, and Berkeley road, the site of

* H. Vizard, Esq.   † ———   ‡ R. B. Purnell, Esq.
     § F. Wilson, Esq. || P. B. Purnell, Esq.

THE BERKELEY ROAD STATION,

A PRINCIPAL ONE, DISTANT FROM GLOUCESTER $15\frac{1}{4}$ MILES, FROM BIRMINGHAM $68\frac{3}{4}$ MILES, FROM BRISTOL $22\frac{1}{4}$ MILES, FROM EXETER $97\frac{3}{4}$ MILES, FROM BERKELEY $1\frac{1}{2}$ MILE. JOURNEY RESUMED BELOW.

$1\frac{1}{2}$ m. distant from the Berkeley Road Station is Berkeley Castle, the fine old seat of Earl Fitzharding. This ancient pile appears to have been founded soon after the Conquest, but has at different times since received important additions: its present form approaches to a circle, and the buildings are inclosed by an irregular court, surrounded by a moat. The entrance to the keep is through an elegant sculptured arched doorway, leading to a flight of steps; over which an apartment, called the Dungeon Room, is shown as the place where Edward II. was barbarously murdered: this building is flanked by 3 semi-circular towers, and a square one of later construction. The various apartments contain a good collection of portraits, many of them executed in a very superior style.

The Railway from Frocester to the last Station is bordered, on left, by the finely-wooded eminences of Woodchester, Crawley Hill, and Uley Bury Camp; the latter, about 4 m. from Coaley, is clearly evinced to be Roman, from the various coins that have been found there, chiefly of the Emperors Antoninus and Constantine. It occupies the whole summit of the hill, including between 30 and 40 acres, and is defended by a double entrenchment, running round the edge. Its form is oblong, and its natural strength very great; the declivity being very abrupt on all sides but the entrance. In Uley parish, also, is Stouts Hill, the seat of *. The latter part of the above-mentioned ride is also enlivened by the finely-wooded eminences of Stinchcombe Hill, Nibley Knoll, and Westridge Wood, that, bordering the line, form a boundary at once bold and beautiful.

Quitting the Berkeley Road Station, the Railway, continued with a bold sweep, in a south-west direction, arrives, in rather more than a mile, at the Wotton-under-Edge and Berkeley Road, and, in $\frac{3}{4}$ m. more, gains Hogsdown, from whence its course is that of a direct line for $1\frac{3}{4}$ m., in one of which it reaches Lower Wick Green, and, skirting Michaelswood Chase, in less than $\frac{3}{4}$ m. more, arrives at Huntingford Mill, on left of which is Tortworth Court †; in less than a mile beyond which, it gains

* Col. Browne. † Earl Ducie.

THE CHARFIELD STATION,

AN INTERMEDIATE ONE, DISTANT FROM GLOUCESTER $20\frac{1}{4}$ MILES, FROM BIRMINGHAM 73 MILES, FROM BRISTOL 17 MILES, FROM EXETER $92\frac{1}{2}$ MILES.

Two miles and a half distant from Charfield Station, on left, is Wotton-under-Edge; in the vicinity of which are the following seats:— The Warren *, Bradley House †, Newark House §, at Alderley, the seat of ‖, Alderley House ¶, Kingscote Park.**

Quitting the Charfield Station, the Railway, continued with a bold sweep and south-west direction, arrives, in about 2 miles farther, at

THE WICKWAR STATION,

AN INTERMEDIATE ONE, DISTANT FROM GLOUCESTER $22\frac{1}{2}$ MILES, FROM BIRMINGHAM 75 MILES, FROM BRISTOL 15 MILES, FROM EXETER 90 MILES.

On leaving the Wickwar Station, the Railway, pursuing a serpentine course, in a further distance of about $4\frac{1}{4}$ miles, gains

THE YATE STATION,

AN INTERMEDIATE ONE, DISTANT FROM GLOUCESTER 27 MILES, FROM BIRMINGHAM $79\frac{1}{4}$ MILES, FROM BRISTOL $10\frac{1}{2}$ MILES, FROM EXETER 86 MILES.

One mile and a half from the Yate Station, on left, lies the town of Chipping Sodbury, $2\frac{1}{4}$ m. distant from which is Doddington Park, the fine seat of ††; and, 5 m. distant, Badminton, the splendid domain of §§. From the last station, the Railway, pursuing a serpentine course, arrives, in about $2\frac{1}{4}$ m., at the Bristol and Iron Acton Road, near Westerleigh, which it crosses, and, carried forward with a gradual sweep and southward direction, a little before its arrival at the next stage, bends suddenly to the east, and arrives at

THE MANGOTSFIELD STATION,

AN INTERMEDIATE ONE, DISTANT FROM GLOUCESTER $31\frac{1}{2}$ MILES, FROM BIRMINGHAM 84 MILES, FROM BRISTOL 6 MILES, FROM EXETER $81\frac{1}{2}$ MILES.

One mile distant, on left of the station, is Siston Court.

* L. S. Austin, Esq. † J. B. H. Burland, Esq.
§ L. Clutterbuck, Esq. ‖ R. B. Hale, Esq.
¶ Miss Burlton. ** Col. F. Kingscote.
†† Sir W. R. Codrington, Bart. §§ The Duke of Beaufort.

From Mangotsfield Station, it is continued with a curve round the base of Rodway Hill, crosses, in about ½ m., the road from Bath to Downend, near Rodway Bridge; 1 m. distant, on right of which, is Hill House *, 2 m. distant, Cleeve Hill †, and, beyond it, Cleeve Wood. ‡ From Rodway Bridge, the Railway, taking a north-west direction, approaches the Bristol and Mangotsfield roads, and pursues for a short distance a course nearly parallel with that thoroughfare, till it approaches the vicinity of the Ridgway, on right of which is Oldbury Court. § On right of the Ridgway, also, at Stapleton, are the following seats:— Heath House, The Grove ||, and Stoke Park. ¶ From the Ridgway, its course, after making a gradual bend to the southward, is that of a direct line to

THE BRISTOL STATION,

A PRINCIPAL ONE, DISTANT FROM GLOUCESTER 37½ MILES, FROM BIRMINGHAM 90 MILES, FROM EXETER 75½ MILES.

THE MANCHESTER AND BOLTON RAILWAY.

The Manchester and Bolton Railway is chiefly an inclined plane: it commences in New Bailey Street, Manchester, and is continued with a curve along the Salford Viaduct, that, carried upon arches, with a gradual sweep, affords a view of the Manchester and Liverpool Railway, which is seen upon the left: about ¾ of a mile from Manchester, carried with a sharp curve to the Manchester and Bolton road, it gains

THE WINDSOR BRIDGE STATION,

AN INTERMEDIATE ONE, DISTANT FROM MANCHESTER 1 MILE, FROM BOLTON 9 MILES.

Three quarters of a mile beyond this, continued with a gently waving line, in a north-eastern direction, and, pursuing a course nearly parallel with the Manchester, Bolton, and Bury Canal, it arrives at

THE PENDLETON BRIDGE STATION,

AN INTERMEDIATE ONE, DISTANT FROM MANCHESTER 1¾ MILE, FROM BOLTON 8¼ MILES.

On left lies the village of Pendleton, of which, with its new church, a good view is obtained. About ¼ of a mile farther, see, across the canal, on right, the Grand Stand on Kersal Moor Race

---

* J. Bayley, Esq. † D. Cave, Esq. ‡ Mr. Sergeant Stephens.
§ Mrs. Jones. || T. Castle, Esq. ¶ E. Hobson, Esq.

Course, whereon are annually run Heaton Park races, that derive their name from Heaton Park, a beautiful seat of the Earl of Wilton, about 2 m. distant on right: between the Race Course and Heaton Park is Sedgley.[a] In ½ mile beyond this last point, the Railway gains

THE AGECROFT STATION,

AN INTERMEDIATE ONE, DISTANT FROM MANCHESTER 3 MILES, FROM BOLTON 7 MILES.

On left of Agecroft Bridge is Agecroft Hall[b], ½ m. on left of it is Springfield[c], and Pendlebury House[d], 1 m. distant, Swinton House[e], and Irwell House.[f] Upon leaving Agecroft Bridge, the Railway enters on an embankment, of from 40 to 50 ft. high, that affords a fine view of the valley of the Irwell and of that river, with the Manchester and Bolton Canal, both of which border its base. Hence is beheld, on right, Prestwich Church, the tower of which stands forth strikingly conspicuous. At the foot of the embankment is Clifton Hall[g], the grounds of which were destroyed by the Railway. To this embankment, the Pepper Hill excavation succeeds; it is about 100 ft. in depth, and conducts to

THE DIXON'S FOLD BRIDGE STATION,

AN INTERMEDIATE ONE, DISTANT FROM MANCHESTER 5¼ MILES, FROM BOLTON 4¼ MILES.

1¼ m. beyond this, the Railway enters on an embankment, that conducts to

THE STONECLOUGH BRIDGE STATION,

AN INTERMEDIATE ONE, DISTANT FROM MANCHESTER 6½ MILES, FROM BOLTON 3½ MILES.

Half a mile beyond this, the Railway reaches an excavation, through which it arrives at the Halshaw Moor Tunnel, 290 yards in length; at the end of which is

THE TUNNEL STATION,

AN INTERMEDIATE ONE, DISTANT FROM MANCHESTER 7¾ MILES, FROM BOLTON 2¼ MILES.

A little beyond this, on left, is Birch House[h], and, on right, Darley Hall.[i] In ½ a mile farther, the train arrives at

[a] J. W. Stewart, Esq.
[b] Rev. J. Buck.
[c] T. Entwistle, Esq.
[d] J. A. Turner, Esq.
[e] A. Leibert, Esq.
[f] T. Drinkwater, Esq.
[g] J. Fletcher, Esq.
[h] G. Lomas, Esq.
[i] J.R. Barnes, Esq.

THE MOSES GATE STATION,

AN INTERMEDIATE ONE, DISTANT FROM MANCHESTER $8\frac{1}{4}$ MILES, FROM BOLTON $1\frac{3}{4}$ MILE.

Crossing the Priestcroft Valley, the train shortly after reaches

THE BOLTON STATION,

A PRINCIPAL ONE, DISTANT FROM MANCHESTER 10 MILES.

One mile before Bolton, on right, is Bradford House[a]; near which is Hollin's Hall[b], Lever Hall[c], and Mayfield House[d], Worsley Hall[e], and New Brook House[f]; 3 m. distant from Bolton, on left, is Hulton Hall.[g]

BOLTON AND PRESTON RAILWAY.

The Bolton and Preston Railway, on quitting the former town, is carried through a dull uninteresting country, in a distance of $11\frac{1}{2}$ miles, passing in its way the Blackrod and Adlington Stations to Chorley; in a distance of $5\frac{1}{2}$ m. beyond which it gains Euxton, on the North Union Railway, from whence its course is that of nearly a direct line to Preston, which it reaches in a total of $20\frac{1}{4}$ m. from Bolton. On left of Adlington is Adlington Hall[h], and, $\frac{1}{4}$ m. beyond it, Ellerbeck Hall[i]: 2 m. before Chorley, on left, is Duxbury Park[k]; and, on left of that town is Astley Hall[l], and Gillibrand Hall[m]. On left of Euxton is Euxton Hall[n]: 1 m. distant, on right, is Worden Hall[o], and Shaw Hill.[p]

[a] J. Walker, Esq.
[b] Mrs. Fletcher.
[c] J. Smith, Esq.
[d] J. Hargreaves, Esq.
[e] Lord Francis Egerton.
[f] W. F. Hulton, Esq.
[g] W. Hulton, Esq.
[h] B. Clayton, Esq.
[i] J. Cardwell, Esq.
[k] W. Standish Standish, Esq.
[l] Lady Hoghton.
[m] H. H. Fazakerly, Esq.
[n] W. S. Anderton, Esq.
[o] J. N. Farrington, Esq.
[p] T. B. Crosse, Esq.

THE MANCHESTER AND BIR-
MINGHAM RAILWAY.

The Manchester and Birmingham Railway branches forth from the Grand Junction at the Crewe Station of that line, distant from Birmingham 53¾ miles; from London 166 miles. Emerging from the Crewe excavation, and carried forward in a direct line, with the exception of a short embankment upon the surface of the earth rendered regular, it reaches in a distance of 2½ miles, partly on a level, but principally on a descent of 1 in 528, Brooke Farm, near which it enters on an embankment, and rise of 1 in 264, that carries it, in conjunction with a viaduct over the river Wheelock and valley, in half a mile more, to Rookery Bridge on the Grand Trunk canal, 1¼ mile beyond which it gains

THE SANDBACH STATION,

A PRINCIPAL ONE, DISTANT FROM BIRMINGHAM 58 MILES, FROM LONDON 170¼ MILES, FROM MANCHESTER 26½ MILES, FROM SANDBACH 1¼ MILE, FROM MIDDLEWICH 3¾ MILES.

¾ mile distant from Sandbach Station, on right, is Abbeyfield. *

From the Sandbach Station it reaches in 1¼ mile, on a rise of 1 in 528, principally by embankment, the Bradwall Hall and Mid-

---

* C. I. Ford, Esq.

dlewich Road, on right of which is Bradwall Hall, the seat of *. From the Bradwall Hall and Middlewich Road, a little before which it crosses Wood Lane, it arrives, in a further distance of 1¼ mile, partly by level and descent of 1 in 660, with the exception of two short embankments, on the surface of the earth equalised, at Back Lane, from whence it is continued by embankment chiefly on the rise of 1 in 264 to the Middlewich and Newcastle Road, on which in ¼ mile more it arrives at

THE HOLMES CHAPEL STATION,

A PRINCIPAL ONE, DISTANT FROM BIRMINGHAM 61¾ MILES, FROM LONDON 174 MILES, FROM MANCHESTER 22½ MILES, FROM MIDDLEWICH 4¼ MILES, FROM CONGLETON 6¾ MILES.

1 mile distant, on left of Holmes Chapel Station, is The Hermitage†; 1½ mile distant, Cranage Hall‡; 2½ miles distant, on right, is Brereton Hall§, Davenport Hall ||, and Somerford Park¶.

Quitting the Holmes Chapel Station, the Railway, continued by embankment, in a distance of rather more than a quarter of a mile crosses the Middlewich and Macclesfield road, here carried over the line, and soon after reaches the Dane Viaduct, that carries the railway across the Dane river and valley. It consists of 23 semicircular arches, each of 63 feet span, its total length being 573 yards, its mean height 88 feet 3 inches, and its width 31 feet. On leaving the Dane Viaduct the Railway regains the level of the land, that, succeeded by an embankment, carries it on the rise of 1 in 330, crossing Twemlow Lane in its way, to Goostrey Bridge, from whence it is continued by embankment with a gradual bend, passing Blackden and Edens Bridge in its way in a distance of 1½ mile to Bomish House. About 10¼ miles from Crewe the inclination changes from a rise of 1 in 330 to 1 in 528, which about ½ mile before Bomish House again alters to a rise of 1 in 660. ½ mile distant from Edens Bridge, on right, is Jodrell Hall**, 1½ mile distant from Bomish House, on left, is Over Peover Park.†† From Bomish House, about ½ mile beyond which it enters on a level, the Railway, carried with a gradual bend to the north-east, chiefly by embankment, arrives in a further distance of 2¼ miles at

* J. Latham, Esq. M.D.
† Rev. I. Armitstead.
‡ L. Armitstead, Esq.
§ J. Howard, Esq.
|| T. Tipping, Esq.
¶ Sir C. P. Shakerley, Bart.
** Egerton Leigh, Esq.
†† H. Mainwaring, Esq.

THE CHELFORD STATION,

A PRINCIPAL ONE, DISTANT FROM BIRMINGHAM $67\frac{1}{4}$ MILES, FROM LONDON $179\frac{1}{2}$ MILES, FROM MANCHESTER 17 MILES, FROM KNUTSFORD $4\frac{1}{2}$ MILES, FROM MACCLESFIELD $6\frac{1}{2}$ MILES.

$\frac{1}{2}$ mile distant from Chelford Station, on right, is Astle Park*; 1 mile distant, Withington Hall†; $2\frac{1}{2}$ miles distant, Capesthorne Hall‡, Alderley Park§, and Henbury Hall.‖

Alderley Park is the seat of Lord Stanley. The adjacent scenery is finely diversified by a natural sheet of water, called Radnor Mere, and the vicinity of that abrupt and elevated ridge, called Alderly Edge, which was formerly the site of a beacon, and appears to have been detached from the range of the Macclesfield hills by some great convulsion of nature; its sides are beautifully varied with wood, rock, and cultivated land, and presents as an entire mass a striking object to all the surrounding districts, over which it enjoys a most extensive prospect.

On leaving the Chelford Station, the Railway, bending eastward, is carried partly on a rise of 1 in 1320 and partly on a level to Sossmoss Hall, which it passes on the right, and shortly after Alderley Park, when taking a north-east direction it is then continued by embankment chiefly on a rise of 1 in 337 with a gradual bend to

THE ALDERLEY STATION,

AN INTERMEDIATE ONE, DISTANT FROM BIRMINGHAM $70\frac{1}{4}$ MILES, FROM LONDON $182\frac{1}{2}$ MILES, FROM MANCHESTER 14 MILES.

Previous to reaching the Alderley Station it enters on a short level, to which succeeds a descent of 1 in 880, and upon leaving it the Railway, with the exception of a short cutting, is continued by embankment on the same inclination in a direct line to

THE WILMSLOW STATION,

AN INTERMEDIATE ONE, DISTANT FROM BIRMINGHAM $71\frac{3}{4}$ MILES, FROM LONDON 184 MILES, FROM MANCHESTER 12 MILES.

On quitting the Wilmslow Station the Railway crosses by a viaduct the river and valley of the Bollin. This structure, which was erected at a cost of 14,360l., is built upon a curve, and will vie with any for the beauty of its outline, and the unpretending

---

* Capt. Dixon. † J. B. Glegg, Esq.
‡ E. D. Davenport, Esq. § Lord Stanley.
‖ Major Marsland.

yet striking simplicity of its details. It consists of 11 semicircular arches, each of 49 feet span, built principally of brick, its length being 630 feet, mean height 73 feet, and width 31 feet. The Bollin Viaduct passed, the Railway is carried forward in a direct line on a level, upon the surface of the earth rendered regular, to the viaduct over the river Dean, in less than ½ mile, beyond which it gains

THE HANDFORTH STATION,

AN INTERMEDIATE ONE, DISTANT FROM BIRMINGHAM 73¼ MILES, FROM LONDON 185½ MILES, FROM MANCHESTER 11¼ MILES.

From the Handforth Station, a little beyond which it commences a descent of 1 in 440, it is continued with a gradual bend by embankment to

THE CHEADLE STATION,

AN INTERMEDIATE ONE, DISTANT FROM BIRMINGHAM 74¾ MILES, FROM LONDON 187 MILES, FROM MANCHESTER 9 MILES.

1 mile distant from Cheadle Station on right is Bramhall Hall.* From the Cheadle Station the Railway is carried forward in a direct line, chiefly by embankment, for a distance of about 2 miles, gaining in the first ¾ of a mile Lady Bridge, where it crosses a tributary of the Mersey, where the inclination changes to a descent of 1 in 880, and from about 1 mile beyond which it is taken with a sweep to the Stockport Viaduct, that spans the town, the river, and valley of the Mersey, crossing which it arrives at

THE STOCKPORT STATION,

A PRINCIPAL ONE, DISTANT FROM BIRMINGHAM 78¼ MILES, FROM LONDON 190½ MILES, FROM MANCHESTER 6 MILES.

2 miles distant from Stockport, on left, is Heath Bank †, and 1 mile distant on right is Wood Bank.‡

THE STOCKPORT VIADUCT.

The Stockport Viaduct has been described, and with truth, as one of the most daring and stupendous works of art to which the railway system has given birth. This splendid structure was designed by and erected under the superintendence of G. W.

---

* Sir S. Davenport.   † H. Harrison, Esq.
‡ H. Marsland, Esq.

Buck, Esq., the talented engineer of this line, and invariably excites the admiration of all beholders. It is 1780 feet in length, and is carried on 26 arches, 22 of which are of 63 feet span. Its length, however, is its least remarkable feature, the height at which the traveller is carried securely and rapidly across the valley below being that which chiefly surprises; the elevation of the parapet above the river being 111 feet, and the rails about 120 feet above the foundation of the arches.

The summit affords one of the best views of a manufacturing town in England. Far below are beheld streets stretching out on either hand; mills and factories rise out of the dense mass of houses; while around them a forest of chimneys shoot into the air. The chief part of the town lying to the east of the Viaduct, appears in bold irregularity, the fine old church of St. Mary crowning the summit; westward the prospect is enlivened by the windings of the Mersey and more direct course of the Duke of Bridgewater's canal. Beheld from the valley, the Viaduct appears in all the grandeur of its vast proportions, stretching with giant strides over streets and houses, and affording a series of vistas that add materially to the interest of this very singular scene. The foundation stone of this gigantic undertaking was laid on the 10th of March, 1839, and the whole was completed in December 1840. The cost of its erection was 70,000*l*.

From the Stockport Station the course of the Railway is that of a direct line, nearly parallel with the turnpike road, by embankment chiefly on the descent of 1 in 337 for a mile and a quarter, that carries it to Heaton Norris, where it regains the earth's surface; to which, shortly after, succeeds an embankment, upon which it is carried with a gradual bend to Levenshulme, $\frac{3}{4}$ of a mile beyond which the descent diminishes to 1 in 557, on which it is taken to Rushford, and upon that inclination continues for $1\frac{1}{2}$ mile beyond it. The last mile and a quarter is divided into the different descents of 1 in 480 and 1 in 337, which last brings it to a level, upon which it enters

THE MANCHESTER STATION,

A PRINCIPAL ONE, DISTANT FROM BIRMINGHAM $84\frac{1}{4}$ MILES, FROM LONDON BY THE LINE OF THE BIRMINGHAM AND BIRMINGHAM AND MANCHESTER RAILWAY, $196\frac{1}{2}$ MILES.

CHELTENHAM AND GREAT WESTERN UNION RAILWAY.

SWINDON TO GLOUCESTER AND CHELTENHAM.

For the particulars of the line from London to Swindon, the reader is referred to page 25 of the Great Western Railway, where the details of that great work will be found. The continuation of the line from Swindon, which is 77 miles from London, to Gloucester, being as follows:—to Purton, $81\frac{1}{4}$ miles; Minety, $85\frac{1}{4}$ miles; Kemble $89\frac{3}{4}$ miles; where the Branch Railway to Cirencester commences, accomplishing the distance to that town in a total of 95 miles from London. (From Cirencester to Cheltenham, a distance of $15\frac{1}{4}$ miles, a new road was made not many years since.) The continuation of the Railway to Cheltenham from the last point named is as follows:—to the Tetbury Road, 91 miles; Brimscomb, near Chalford, $98\frac{1}{2}$ miles (from whence to Minchinhampton is only 2 miles); Stroud, $101\frac{1}{2}$ miles; Stonehouse, $103\frac{3}{4}$ miles; Gloucester, 114 miles; Cheltenham, $120\frac{3}{4}$ miles.

SOUTH WESTERN or LONDON and SOUTHAMPTON RAILWAY.

LONDON to SOUTHAMPTON

From *Nine Elms to the Road to Battersea	2
To Battersea ¾ m.—R.	
L.—To Tooting 3 m.	
Wandsworth Road	2¼
*Wandsworth Station......	2¾
To Wandsworth ¾ m.—R.	
L.—To Clapham 1½ m.	
Tooting and Wandsworth Road	3
Garrett Lane	4
River Wandle.............	4¼
Merton and Wandsworth Road	4¾
L.—To Merton 1¼ m.	
To Wandsworth 1½ m.—R.	
Garrett and Wimbledon Road	5
*Wimbledon Station	5¾
L.—To Merton 1 m.	
To Wimbledon ½ m.—R.	
Coombe Lane Viaduct	7
Malden and Richmond Park Road	8¼
L.—To Malden 1½ m.	
To Richmond Park 2 m.—R.	
Malden and Kingston Road	8¾
L.—To Malden 1½ m.	
To Kingston 1½ m.—R.	
Hogs' Mill River Bridge ..	9
*KINGSTON STATION at the Kingston and Ewell Road	10
L. {To Ewell 4 m. / To Epsom 5½ m.	
To Kingston 1 m.—R.	
Kingston and Leatherhead Road	10½
L.—To Leatherhead 6½ m.	
To Kingston 1½ m.—R.	

WIMBLEDON STATION, on right, at Wimbledon, is Wimbledon House, *Mrs. Marryat*, Woodhays, *W. Brown*, Esq., a seat of *T. Hankey*, Esq., Copse Hill, *Lord Cottenham*, The Priory, *Rev. W. Edelman*, Mount Arrarat, *W. Leake*, Esq., Carrol Lodge, *C. Manning*, Esq., and Wimbledon Park, *Duke of Somerset*, on left, Cannon Hill, *R. Thornton*, Esq., and 1½ m. distant, Morden Park, *G. C. Ridye*, Esq.

MALDEN and RICHMOND PARK ROAD, see on right, Combe House, *Rev. Dr. Biber*.

KINGSTON STATION, on right, at Kingston, Elmers, *Mrs. Disney*, and Woodbines, *W. Tart*, Esq.

Ditton and Ewell Road	11¼
Portsmouth Road Viaduct	12¼
L. { To Esher 1½ m.	
{ To Portsmouth 58 m.	
To Kingston 2½ m.—R.	
*Ditton Marsh Station at the Hampton Court and Esher Road............	12¾
L.—To Esher 1¼ m.	
To Hampton Court 2 m.—R.	
River Mole Viaduct over ..	13¾
Broad Lane	14¼
Hersham and Walton Road	15
L.—To Cobham 4½ m.	
To Walton 1 m.—R.	
*Walton Station	15½
L.—To Cobham 3½ m.	
To Walton 1 m.—R.	
Walton and Weybridge Road................	16¾
*Weybridge Station	17¼
L.—To Cobham 3 m.	
To Weybridge ¾ m.—R.	
Old River Wey Viaduct ..	18
Chertsey and Byfleet Road	18¾
L. { To Byfleet ½ m.	
{ To Cobham 3 m.	
To Chertsey 3½ m —R.	
River Wey Navigation....	19
Chertsey and Woking Road	21¾
L.—To Woking 1¾ m.	
To Chertsey 5½ m.—R.	
*Woking Station	22½
L. { To Woking 1¾ m.	
{ To Ripley 4¼ m.	
{ To Guildford 6 m.	
To Chertsey 6¼ m.—R.	
Chobham and Guildford Road	23½
L.—To Guildford 5½ m.	
To Chobham 3½ m. } R.	
To Windsor 13½ m. }	
Bagshot and Guildford Road	26
L.—To Guildford 5½ m.	
To Bagshot 5½ m.—R.	
Cowshot and Pirbright Road	27¼

DITTON MARSH STATION, ½ m. distant, on right, Ember Court, *Sir C. Sullivan*, Bart., and 1 m. distant, at Thames Ditton, Boyle Farm, *Sir Edward Sugden*, Bart., 2 m. distant, across the Thames, Hampton Court Palace, *The Queen*, and Bushy Park, *The Queen Dowager*.

RIVER MOLE VIADUCT, see on left, Esher Place, *J. W. Spicer*, Esq., beyond which, at Esher, is Esher Lodge, *R. Addison*, Esq., Claremont, *The King of Belgium*, and Melbourne Lodge, *Sir Robert Gardiner*, Bart.

WALTON STATION, on left, Burwood Park, *Sir R. Frederick*, Bart., on right, Oatlands, the noble seat of *Lord Francis Egerton*, and Ashley Park, *Sir H. Fletcher*, Bart., 1 m. distant, on left is Burhill, *Col. Tynte*, 2 m. distant, Burwood House, *Sir J. Williams*, and 3 m. distant at Cobham, Pains Hill Park, *W. H. Cooper*, Esq., Cobham Park, *H. C. Combe*, Esq., Cobham Lodge, *Lady Molesworth*, and Pointers, *J. Paye*, Esq.

WEYBRIDGE STATION, 2 m. distant, on right, Woburn Park, *Hon. P. J. Locke King*.

WOKING STATION, 1 m. distant, on left, Hoebridge Place, *A. Robertson*, Esq., 3 m. distant, Send Grove, *F. Norton Balmaine*, Esq., 4¼ m. distant, at Ripley, Dunsborough House, *Rev. G. W. Onslow*, and Ockham Park, *Earl of Lovelace*, 2¼ m. distant, on right, Ottershaw Park, *Lady Wood*, and 4 m. distant, Botleys, *R. Gosling*, Esq., 1 m. beyond Woking Station, on right, The Hermitage, *J. Gates*, Esq.

COWSHOT and PIRBRIGHT ROAD, 2¼ m. distant, on left, Henly Park, *H. Halsey*, Esq.

London and Southampton Railway.

Frimley Hill Deep Cut Bridge	29¼
Basingstoke Canal Aqueduct	30
Frimley and Guildford Road Viaduct over	30
Frimley and Ash Road	30¼
Blackwater River and Farnborough and Guildford Road Viaduct over	30¾

Enter Hampshire

*FARNBOROUGH STATION, at the Viaduct over the Southampton and Gosport Road	31½

To London 31½ m.—R.
L. { To Farnham 6¾ m.
{ To Southampton 45½ m.

Cove and Blackwater Road	32
Farnham and Blackwater Road	33¼
Fleet Pond Bridge	34¾
Farnham and Hartford Bridge Road	36
Lord Calthorpe's occupation Bridge	36½
Pale Lane Bridge	36¾
Water Lane Bridge	37¼
Winchfield and Hartley Row Road	37¾
*WINCHFIELD STATION	38
Shapley Heath Tunnel, under the London and Odiham Road	38½
Murrell Green Lane Viaduct	39
Whitewater River Viaduct	39½
Holt Lane	39¾
Hook Common, Reading and Odiham Road	40½

L.—To Odiham 2¾ m.
To Reading. 10 m.—R.

Hook Common, London and Basingstoke Road Viaduct	40¾

L.—To Basingstoke 5¼ m.
To London 40 m.—R.

FARNBOROUGH STATION, on left, Farnborough Place, *G. Morant*, Esq., on right, Windmill Hill, *Lady Palmer*, 1½ m. distant, at Frimley, Frimley House, *J. Jeckell*, Esq., 2½ m. distant, Hawley House, *H. Dumbleton*, Esq., and 2¾ m. distant, at Sandhurst, The Royal Military College.

FLEET POND BRIDGE, ¾ m. distant, on right, Brook Farm, a firme orneé.

LORD CALTHORPE'S OCCUPATION ROAD, leads to Elvetham, his lordship's seat.

WINCHFIELD STATION, on right, Winchfield House, *T. Bainbridge*, Esq., 3½ m. distant, Bramshill Park, *Sir J. Cope*, Bart., and 5½ m. distant, Strathfield Saye, *The Duke of Wellington*, on left, Dogmersfield Park, *Lady Mildmay*.

NEWNHAM and NATELY SCURES ROAD. 1 m. distant, on left, Graywell House, *Lord Dorchester*.

OLD BASING, on right, Basing House, *R. Booth*, Esq.

BASINGSTOKE, 1 m. distant, on left, Haskwood Park, *Lord Bolton*, 3¼ m. distant, Herriard Park, *G. P. Jervoise*, Esq. On right of the Station, are the ruins of the Holy Ghost Chapel, and 3½ m distant, The Vine, *Mrs. Chute*, 1 m. beyond Basingstoke, on left, is West Ham, *C. E. Lefroy*, Esq., and 1 m. distant, Down Grange, *Mrs. R. Terry*.

Newnham and Odiham Road	41¼
Newnham and Nately Scures Road	42
Loddon Stream	42¼
London and Basingstoke Old Road Viaduct over	43
Old Basing	44¼
Loddon River Viaduct	44½
Chinham and Old Basing Road	44¾
Basingstoke and Reading Road	45¾
*BASINGSTOKE STATION	46
L.—To Alton 10¼ m.	
To Reading 14¼ m. } R.	
To Newbury 17½ m.	
Worting	48
L.—To London through Basingstoke 47½ m.	
To Whitchurch 9 m. }	
To Andover 18 m. } R.	
To Salisbury 34 m. }	
East Oakley	49¾
Dean and Kempshot Road	51
Steventon	51½
Overton and North Waltham Road	52½
Litchfield Tunnel	53½
Overton and Stratton Road	54½
Popham Tunnels	55
*ANDOVER AND MITCHELDEVER STATION	55
Sheep House Farm	57
Weston	58
Lunways Inn Tunnel	60
Hook Pit Farm	61½
Headbourne Worthy	62¾
*WINCHESTER STATION	64½
Southampton Road near St. Cross	66
*Twyford Station	67¾
Brambridge Lane	68¾
Albrook	69¾

WORTING, on right, Worting House, *Mrs. Pelham Warren*, 1 m. distant, Manydown, *Sir R. Rycroft*, Bart., Tangier, *Rev. L. Bigge Wither*, and Malshanger, *D. T. Cunynghame*, Esq., 2 m. distant, on left, Kempshot Park, *E. W. Blunt*, Esq.

EAST OAKLEY, 1 m. distant, on right, Oakley Park, *W. Hicks Beach*, Esq.

STEVENTON, 1 m. distant, on right, Ash Park, *Rev. E. St. John*, and beyond it, Dean House, *Rev. J. Harwood*.

ANDOVER and MITCHELDEVER STATION, 2 m. distant, on left, Stratton Park, *Sir T. Baring*, Bart., and 4 m. distant, The Grange, *Lord Ashburton*.

LITCHFIELD TUNNEL, is 200 yards in length.

POPHAM TUNNELS, are each 200 yards in length.

HEADBOURNE WORTHY, on left, at Abbots Worthy, Worthy Park, *Col. Wall*, and 2½ m. distant, Avington Park, *Duke of Buckingham*.

TWYFORD STATION, on left, Shawford Lodge, *T. Waddington*, Esq., Twyford Lodge, *R. Waddington*, Esq., and Twyford House, *J. Clutterbuck*, Esq., and 4 m. distant Rose Hill Park, *Earl of Northesk*.

BRAMBRIDGE LANE, ½ m. distant, on left, Brambridge House, *Hon. Mrs. Craven*, and 2½ m. distant, Marwell Hall, *Mrs Long*, 1½ m. distant on right, Cranbury Park, *T. Chamberlayne*, Esq., and 4 m. distant Hursley Park, *Sir William Heathcote*, Bart.

Bishopstoke Road.........	71	SWATHLING, on left, South Stoneham House, *Col. Bouchier*, and 1½ m. distant, on right, North Stoneham Park, *J. Fleming*, Esq.
Gosport **Branch Railway**..	71¾	
To Gosport 15½ *m.*—R.		
Southampton and Winchester Road through Twyford	72½	PORTSWOOD HOUSE, is the seat of *G. Jones*, Esq.
Swathling.................	73¼	SOUTHAMPTON. In the immediate vicinity of Southampton, are the following seats, Middenbury House, *J. B. Hoy*, Esq., Bittern Lodge, *H. Burgh*, Esq., Chissel House, *Lord Ashtown*, Chilworth House, *Hon. R. Quin*, Bannister Lodge, *W. Fitzhugh*, Esq., and Bevis Mount, *Mrs. Hulton*.
L.—*To Romsey* 7¼ *m.*		
To Gosport 16 *m.*—R.		
Portswood.................	74½	
Itchen Bridge	75	
Portsmouth Road	75¾	
SOUTHAMPTON STATION	76½	

MIDLAND COUNTIES RAILWAY.

RUGBY to DERBY

From *Rugby Warwickshire to the Oxford Canal	1
Gill's Corner Tunnel under the Lutterworth and Coventry Road...........	4¾
L.—*To Coventry* 12 *m.* *To Lutterworth* 2 *m.*—R.	
Coalpit Lane.............	5¾
Willey....................	6
*Ullesthorpe Station at the Lutterworth and Hinckley Road	7¾
L.—*To Hinckley* 7 *m.* *To Lutterworth* 3 *m.*—R.	
Leer	9½
*Broughton Astley Station	11
Lutterworth and Leicester Road	13¼
L.—*To Leicester* 7¼ *m.* *To Lutterworth* 6 *m.*—R.	
Whetstone Brook..........	13¾
Union Canal Viaduct	16
*Wigston Station	16½
Knighton Tunnel..........	19
Leicester and Welford Road	19¼
**LEICESTER STATION*	20
L. { *To Hinckley* 12 *m.* *To Ashby de la Zouch* 17 *m.*	
To Uppingham 21 *m.* *To Melton Mowbray* 14 *m.* } R.	
Uppingham Road	20¾
*Syston Station and Melton Mowbray Road	24½
To Melton Mowbray 11½ *m.*—R	
River Wreak	25¾
**SILEBY or MOUNT SORREL STATION*..	27¾
L.—*To Mount Sorrel* 1¼ *m.*	
*Barrow upon Soar Station	30
River Soar Viaduct	30¾

OXFORD CANAL, 1 m. distant, on right. Brownsover House, *J. W. Boughton Leigh*, Esq., 1½ m. farther, and 1½ m. distant, on right, Coton House, *Marchioness of Queensberry.*

GILL'S CORNER TUNNEL, is 300 feet long, 1 m. distant, on left, Newnham Paddox, the beautiful seat of the *Earl of Denbigh.*

ULLESTHORPE STATION, on left, Claybrook Hall, *T. E. Dicey*, Esq.

LUTTERWORTH and LEICESTER ROAD, 2½ m. distant, on left, Narborough Hall, *T. I. T. Pares*, Esq.

KNIGHTON TUNNEL, is 300 feet long.

LEICESTER, 2 m. distant, on left, Braunston Hall, *C. Winstanley*, Esq., Leicester Frith Hall, *Mrs. Oldham*; 3½ m. distant, is Enderby Hall, *R. Mitchell*, Esq., 3 m. distant, on right, is Stoughton Grange, *G. A. Leigh Keck*, Esq., 3 m. beyond, Leicester, on left, and 1½ m. distant, Birstall House, *T. Smith*, Esq.

SYSTON STATION, 1¼ m. distant, on left, Wanlip Hall, *Sir G. I. Palmer*, Bart., and 3½ m. distant, Swithland Hall, *J. G. Danvers Butler Danvers*, Esq., 1½ m. distant, on right, Barkby Hall, *Mrs. Pochin.*

SILEBY STATION, 1¼ m. before, and 1½ m. distant, Rothley Temple, *T. G. Babington*, Esq.

BARROW UPON SOAR, on left, Quorndon Hall, *T. B. Oliver*, Esq., Quorndon House, *E. B. Farnham*, Esq., and 3 m distant, Beaumanor Park, *W. Herrick*, Esq.

*LOUGHBOROUGH STATION .... $32\frac{1}{4}$	LOUGHBOROUGH, at The Elms, T. Warner, Esq., $2\frac{1}{2}$ m. distant, on left, Garendon Park, C. M. Phillips, Esq., and Burleigh Hall, Miss Tuke, 3 m. distant, on right, Prestwould Hall, the fine seat of C. W. Packe, Esq., and Burton Hall, Lord Archibald Seymour, $3\frac{1}{4}$ m. distant, Stanford Hall, Rev. S. Vere Dashwood, near which, is Rempstone, John Smith Wright, Esq.
L.—To Ashby de la Zouch 12 m. To Nottingham 15 m.—R.	
River Soar Viaduct 34	
Cross the River Soar and enter Nottinghamshire	
Normanton Nottinghamshire................. $34\frac{3}{4}$	
Ashby de la Zouch and Nottingham Road .... $35\frac{1}{4}$	
L.—To Ashby de la Zouch $11\frac{1}{2}$ m.	SUTTON BONNINGTON, $1\frac{1}{2}$ m. distant, on left, Whatton House, E. Dawson, Esq.
To Nottingham 14 m.—R.	
Sutton Bonnington........ 36	
*Kegworth Station........ $37\frac{1}{4}$	KEGWORTH STATION, 2 m. distant, on left, Lockington Hall, J. B. Story, Esq., and 5 m. distant, Donington Park, Marquis of Hastings.
L.—To Kegworth 1 m.	
Red Hill Tunnel.......... $39\frac{3}{4}$	
Cross the River Trent and Cranfleet Cut and enter Derbyshire	
Nottingham Branch ...... $40\frac{1}{8}$	NOTTINGHAM BRANCH, 1 m. distant, on right, Thrumpton Hall, Mrs. Wescombe.
To Nottingham by Railway 6 m.—R.	
Erewash Canal .... $40\frac{3}{4}$	SAWLEY STATION, $2\frac{1}{2}$ m. distant, on left, Shardlow House, J. Sutton, Esq. and 2 m. distant, on right, Risley Hall, Mrs. Moore, 1 m. beyond Sawley Station, and 1 m. distant, on right, Draycott House, Capt. Scott, near which, is Hopwell Hall, T. Pares, Esq.
Junction of the Railway from Nottingham to Derby, and Ashby de la Zouch and Nottingham Road .... $41\frac{1}{2}$	
L. { To Castle Donington 4 m. To Ashby de la Zouch $10\frac{3}{4}$ m.	
To Nottingham $8\frac{3}{4}$ m.—R.	BORROWASH STATION, 1 m. distant, on left, Elvaston Hall, Earl of Harrington.
*Sawley Station .... $42\frac{1}{2}$	
*Borrowash Station ...... $45\frac{1}{2}$	
*Spondon Station .... $46\frac{3}{4}$	SPONDON STATION, on right, Spondon Hall, R. Cox, Esq., and $1\frac{1}{2}$ m. distant, Locko Park, Mrs. Drury Lowe.
Chaddesden Mill.......... $48\frac{1}{2}$	
*DERBY STATION .... $49\frac{1}{4}$	
	CHADDESDEN MILL, on right, Chaddesden Hall, Sir Robert Wilmot, Bart.

RUGBY TO NOTTINGHAM.

To the Nottingham Branch as page 7	40⅛
*Long Eaton Station, Junction with the Derby Line	41
River Erewash	42
Attenborough	42½
*Beeston Station	44½
Beeston Cut	45¾
*NOTTINGHAM STATION	47½

LONG EATON STATION, 2½ m. distant, on left, Stapleford Hall.

ATTENBOROUGH, 1 m. distant, on left, Chilwell Hall, *J. B. Charlton*, Esq., 1 m. beyond Attenborough, on right, rising from the margin of the Trent, see the woods of Clifton Hall, the beautiful seat of *Sir J. G. J. Clifton*, Bart.

BEESTON STATION, on left, Lenton Grove, *Mrs. Markham*, Highfield House, *A. Lowe*, Esq., Lenton House, *F. Wright*, Esq., Lenton Firs, *J. Wright*, Esq., and 1 m. distant, Wollaton Hall, the beautiful seat of *Lord Middleton*.

DERBY TO NOTTINGHAM.

From *DERBY STATION*, Derbyshire, to Chaddesden Mill	1
*Spondon Station	2½
*Borrowash Station	3¾
*Sawley Station	6¾
Ashby de la Zouch and Nottingham Road	8¼
L.—*To Nottingham* 8¾ m. *To Castle Donington* 4 m. *To Ashby de la Zouch* 10¾ m. } R.	
Erewash Canal	8¼
*Long Eaton Station	9
River Erewash............	10
Cross the River and enter Nottinghamshire	
Attenborough, Nottinghamshire	10¾
*Beeston Station	12½
Beeston Cut	13¾
*NOTTINGHAM STATION..................	15½

CHADDESDEN MILL, on left, Chaddesden Hall, *Sir R. Wilmot*, Bart.

SPONDON STATION, on left, Spondon Hall, *R. Cox*, Esq.

BORROWASH STATION, 1 m. distant, on right, Elvaston Hall, *Earl of Harrington*.

SAWLEY STATION, 1 m. before, and 1 m. distant, on left, Draycott House, *Capt. Scott*, near which is Hopwell Hall, *T. Pares*, Esq. 1 m. distant, on left of Sawley Station, is Risley Hall.

LONG EATON STATION, 2½ m. distant, on left, Stapleford Hall, 1 m. distant, on right, is Thrumpton Hall, *Mrs. Wescombe.*

ATTENBOROUGH, 1 m. distant, on left, Chilwell Hall, *J. B. Charlton*, Esq., and 1 m. distant, on right, Clifton Hall, *Sir J. G. J. Clifton*, Bart.

BEESTON STATION. For the seats in the vicinity of Beeston Station, the reader is referred to the preceding page.

NORTH MIDLAND RAILWAY.

DERBY TO LEEDS.

From *DERBY STATION, Derbyshire, to the Derby and Sandiacre Canal, and Nottingham Road Viaduct	¼
To Nottingham 15 m.—R.	
Derby and Mansfield Road	¾
To Mansfield 21¼ m.—R.	
Alfreton Road...........	1½
To Alfreton 11¾ m.—R.	
Allestry Road	2⅜
Little Eaton.............	3
River Derwent Bridge....	3¼
Duffield, Alfreton Road....	4¼
To Alfreton 10½ m.—R.	
Belper Road	5
Milford Tunnel	5½
Belper Road and River Derwent Viaduct	6½
*BELPER STATION ..	7¼
Matlock Road and River Derwent Viaduct over ..	7¾
To Matlock 10 m.—R.	
River Derwent Viaduct ..	8¼
River Derwent Viaduct ..	8¾
Belper Tunnel............	9¼
River Derwent and Matlock Road Viaduct over	9½
Bull Bridge Tunnel	9¾
Chesterfield and Matlock Road, and River Amber Viaduct................	10
L.—To Matlock 6¼ m.	
*BULL BRIDGE, or AMBER GATE STATION, at the Viaduct over the River Amber, the Cromford Canal Aqueduct, and Nottingham and Matlock Road......	10½
L.—To Matlock 6 m.	
To Nottingham 16¾ m.—R.	
Lodge Hill Tunnel	11¼

DERBY and NOTTINGHAM ROAD, ½ m. beyond, on left, Darley Hall, *The Misses Evans*, and Darley Abbey, *S. Evans*, Esq.

ALLESTREY ROAD, ½ m. distant, on left, Allestrey Park, *W. Evans*, Esq., 2 m. distant, Kedleston, the magnificent seat of *Lord Scarsdale*, and Langley Park, *G. Meynell*, Esq.

LITTLE EATON, 1 m. distant, on right, The Priory, *Sir. F. Darwin*.

DUFFIELD, 2 m. distant, on left, Farnah Hall, *Lord Scarsdale*, on right, Duffield Banks, *F. Hurt*, Jun. Esq.

MILFORD TUNNEL is 836 yards in length, on right of it is Milford House, *J. B. Crompton*, Esq. and 1 m. distant, Holbrook, *Rev. W. Leeke*.

BELPER, 1 m. distant, on left, Bridge Hill, *G. B. Strutt*, Esq.

BULL BRIDGE TUNNEL, is 120 yards in length.

BULL BRIDGE STATION, on left, Alderwasley Hall, the charming seat of *F. Hurt*, Esq., 3½ m. distant, on right, is Butterly Hall, *W. Jessop*, Esq., and the celebrated Butterly Iron Works. Here was cast the iron work that forms the arches of Vauxhall Bridge, across the river Thames. Near the Butterly Iron Works is Swanwick Hall, *Rev. J. Wood*.

Arrived at Bull Bridge Station, the tourist has reached the locality of the Low Peak of Derbyshire; a district, that encircling Wirksworth, is exuberant in scenery of the most grand and romantic character; it abounds

River Amber Viaduct	12¾
Matlock, Wirksworth, Alfreton and Mansfield Road	13¼
L. { To Matlock 6 m. To Wirksworth 7 m. To Alfreton 2 m. } R. To Mansfield 11 m.	
River Amber at Dale Bridge, on the Matlock and Alfreton Road.....	13½
L.—To Matlock 6½ m. To Alfreton 2 m.—R.	
*South Wingfield Station at the River Amber, near Amber Mill, on the Matlock and Chesterfield Road	14
L.—To Matlock 5 m. To Chesterfield 8 m.—R.	
River Amber at Bump Mill, on the Wessington and Shirland Road.........	14¾
River Amber	15⅛
Ogston Hall and Higham Street Road	15¾
Smithy Brook............	16¼
Matlock and Mansfield Road	17
L.—To Matlock 5½ m. To Mansfield 10½ m.—R.	
Clay Cross, Summit of the Railway...............	17½
Clay Cross Tunnel........	17¾
Wingfield and Tupton Road	19¼
River Rother	19¾
Bakewell and Mansfield Road..................	20
L.—To Bakewell 13½ m. To Mansfield 10½ m.—R.	
Cross the River Rother three times to the	
*North Wingfield Station, at the Grassmoor and Chesterfield Road	20¼
Wingerworth Mill........	20¾
River Rother	21½

with eminences of various heights and extent; interspersed among which are rock-bound vallies, and delightful dales, that, vieing with each other in beauty, present to the admirer of nature, scenes, of which the painter in his happiest mood, may, by possibility, give some idea; but to do justice to which, the powers of the pen are altogether inadequate. Of the hills in this vicinity, Aldwark, near Wirksworth, and Crich Cliff, are the most elevated, and command very extensive prospects. From Allport Heights, distant about 3 miles from Bull Bridge Station, on a clear day, the Wrekin, in Shropshire, is distinguishable at the distance of 50 miles.

LODGE HILL TUNNEL is 260 yards in length.

MATLOCK and ALFRETON ROAD, 1 m. before, on left, Wingfield Manor, *Rev. J. Halton*, 1 m. distant, on right, is Alfreton Hall, *W. P. Morewood*, Esq.

OGSTONE HALL ROAD, on left, is Ogstone Hall, *Mrs. Turbutt*, and Ford House, *Mrs. Holland*.

CLAY CROSS SUMMIT. This is the most elevated part of the Railway, which, carried by a succession of ascents from Derby, here attains a height of 360 feet above the level of the sea.

CLAY CROSS TUNNEL, is 1 mile in length.

NORTH WINGFIELD STATION, on left, Tupton Hall, *C. Binns*, Esq., and the Tupton Iron

Hasland and Chesterfield Road	22¼
River Rother, and Chesterfield and Mansfield Road	22⅞
L.—*To Chesterfield* ½ *m.* *To Mansfield* 12 *m.*—R.	
Duckmanton and Chesterfield Road..............	23⅛
Cross the River Rother to Chesterfield, at the Worksop Road..............	23½
To Worksop 15 *m.*—R.	
*CHESTERFIELD STATION	24
L.—*To Bakewell* 13 *m.*	
Chesterfield Canal and River Rother	24½
Dronfield, Sheffield and Worksop Road	24¾
L. { *To Dronfield* 5¼ *m.* *To Sheffield* 11 *m.*	
To Worksop 12¾ *m.*—R.	
Cross the River Rother four times, and Staveley Pool to Staveley Iron Works	27
Staveley and Handley Road	27¾
River Rother	28
Staveley and Eckington Road, and Renishaw Viaduct, at the entrance to Renishaw Park	28¾
River Rother	29½
*Eckington Station, at the Worksop, Mansfield and Sheffield Road..........	30¼
L.—*To Sheffield* 8 *m.* *To Worksop* 10 *m.* *To Mansfield* 14½ *m.* } R.	
Cross the River Rother seven times to the Sheffield and Worksop Road................	31¾
L.—*To Sheffield* 7½ *m.* *To Worksop* 11 *m.*—R.	
Cross the River Rother twice, to the Beighton and Aston Road.......	32½

Works; 1 m. distant, Wingerworth Hall, the fine old seat of *Sir H. I. J. Hunloke*, Bart., and farther to the left, Stubbing Court, *Lord Dunfermline*, 3 m. distant, on right, is Sutton Hall, *R. Arkwright*, Esq., and 4 m. distant, Hardwicke Hall, a fine old seat of *The Duke of Devonshire.* In this mansion, Mary Queen of Scots passed several years of her captivity, and many of the apartments derive great interest from the furniture and other articles preserved in remembrance of that unfortunate princess.

HASLAND and CHESTERFIELD ROAD, 1 m. distant, on right, Hasland House, *Mrs. Claughton*, and Hasland Hall, *B. Lucas*, Esq.

CHESTERFIELD STATION, ½ m. distant, on right, Tapton House, *J. Meynell*, Esq., 1½ m. distant, Tapton Grove, *George Stephenson*, Esq., 2 m. distant, Ringwood Hall, *J. G. Barrow*, Esq., and Brimington Hall, *E. T. Coke*, Esq.

DRONFIELD, SHEFFIELD and WORKSOP ROAD, 2 m. distant, on left, Whittington Hall, *H. Dixon*, Esq.

STAVELEY and ECKINGTON ROAD, on left, Renishaw Park, the beautiful seat of *Sir G. Sitwell*, Bart., 2 m. distant, on right, Barlborough Hall, *Rev. C. H. R. Rhodes*.

The River Rother	33¼
Cross the River Rother, and enter Yorkshire	
Beighton and Rotherham Road................	33¾
Sheffield and Worksop Road................	34¾
L.—*To Sheffield* 6½ *m.*	
To Worksop 11½ *m.*—R.	
Cross the River Rother twice to Treeton	36
River Rother	36½
Howorth Lodge..........	37
Catcliff and Canklow Road	37¾
Canklow Mill at the Sheffield and Tickhill Road..	38
L.—*To Sheffield* 5 *m.*	
To Tickhill 11 *m.*—R.	
Viaduct over the Sheffield and Rotherham Road, the River Dun and Ickles Cut..................	39
L.—*To Sheffield* 5 *m.*	
To Rotherham 1 *m.*—R.	
Viaduct over the New Cut and Sheffield and Rotherham Railway..........	39¼
*MASBOROUGH or ROTHERHAM STATION, at the Rotherham and Penistone Road	39¾
L.—*To Penistone* 14 *m.*	
To Rotherham ½ *m.*—R.	
Rotherham and Barnsley Road................	40¼
L.—*To Barnsley* 11¾ *m.*	
To Rotherham ¼ *m.*—R.	
Greasborough Canal......	40¾
Rotherham and Rawmarsh Road................	40⅞
Aldwark and Greasborough Road................	41½
Rawmarsh and Hooton Roberts Road	42⅞
Rawmarsh and Hooton Roberts Road..........	43⅛
Cross Collier Brook to the	

MASBOROUGH STATION, on left, The Grange, *Earl of Effingham*, ¾ m. distant, on right, Clifton House, *H. Walker*, Esq.

ROTHERHAM and BARNSLEY ROAD, on left, Clough, *G. W. Chambers*, Esq., on right, Eastwood, *J. Sothern*, Esq.

ALDWARK and GREASBOROUGH ROAD, 2 m. distant, on left, Wentworth House, the noble seat of *Earl Fitzwilliam*; on right, Aldwark Hall, *G. S. Foljambe*, Esq., 1 m. distant, Thribergh Hall, *I. Fullerton*, Esq., and 3 m. distant, Ravenfield Park, *T. Walker*, Esq.

North Midland Railway. 13

*Kilnhurst Station	43¾	
Hooton Roberts and Swinton Road	43⅝	SWINTON STATION, 3 m. distant, on right, Melton Hall, *R. F. Wilson*, Esq., and at Conisborough, the ruins of Conisborough Castle.
Swinton and Mexborough Road	44½	
Dearne and Dove Canal *Swinton Station, at the Swinton and Mexborough Road	45	
Swinton and Adwick Road	45¼	
Rotherham and Ferry Bridge Road	45¾	
L.—*To Rotherham* 5 m. To *Ferry Bridge* 15½ m.—R.		
Wath and Bolton Road	46¼	
Wath and Bolton Road	46½	
River Dearne	47	DARFIELD STATION, on left, Middlewood Hall, ——— 4 miles distant, on right, Hickleton Hall, *Sir F. L. Wood*, Bart.
River Dearne	47⅝	
River Dearne, and Road to Marls Bridge	47¾	
Rotherham and Darfield Road	48¼	
Cat Hill Tunnel	48½	
*Darfield Station, at the Barnsley and Doncaster Road and River Dearne	49	
L.—*To Barnsley* 5 m. To *Doncaster* 10 m.—R.		
River Dearne	49¼	
Darfield and Little Houghton Road	49½	BARNSLEY, 2½ m. distant, on left of, is Wentworth Castle, the beautiful seat of *F. Vernon Wentworth*, Esq.
Cross the River Dearne twice to the River Dearne at Storrs Mill	51	
Cross the River Dearne twice to Lund Wood	52	
*CUDWORTH BRIDGE, or BARNSLEY STATION, at the Barnsley, Penistone, Doncaster and Pontefract Road	53	
L. { *To Barnsley* 3 m. *To Penistone* 10 m. *To Doncaster* 12¾ m. *To Pontefract* 9½ m. } R.		
Carleton and Shafton Road	53⅞	CAT HILL TUNNEL is 149 yards in length.
Roystone and Havercroft Road	54⅛	

Barnesley Canal..........	$55\frac{5}{8}$
Notton and Havercroft Road.................	$55\frac{7}{8}$
Chevet Viaduct over the Felkirk and Wakefield Road.................	$56\frac{3}{4}$
Chevet Tunnel	$57\frac{3}{8}$
Chevet and Walton Road	58
Lower Walton	$58\frac{1}{2}$
Barnsley Canal..........	$59\frac{1}{4}$
Oakenshaw Viaduct, near the Wakefield, Pontefract and Doncaster Road....	$59\frac{1}{2}$
L.—*To Wakefield* 2 *m.*	
To Pontefract $6\frac{1}{2}$ *m.* / *To Doncaster* $10\frac{1}{2}$ *m.* } R.	
**OAKENSHAW* or *WAKEFIELD STATION*................	60
Hell Lane	$60\frac{1}{2}$
Heath and Warmfield Road	$60\frac{3}{4}$
Wakefield and Warmfield Road................	$61\frac{1}{4}$
* Manchester and Leeds Railway Station on Goose Hill Common	62
L.—*To Manchester by Railway* 50 *m.*	
Altofts and Normanton Road..................	$62\frac{3}{4}$
**NORMANTON STATION*, and commencement of the York and North Midland Railway	$63\frac{3}{4}$
To York by Railway $23\frac{3}{4}$ *m.* / *To Selby by Railway* 15 *m.* / *To Hull by Railway* 66 *m.* } R.	
Calder Canal and River Calder Viaducts........	64
*York and North Midland Railway Station, North Branch................	65
L.—*To Wakefield* $5\frac{3}{4}$ *m.*	
To Pontefract 5 *m.*—R.	
To York by Railway $23\frac{3}{4}$ *m.* / *To Selby by Railway* $15\frac{1}{2}$ *m.* / *To Hull by Railway* $66\frac{1}{2}$ *m.* } R.	

NOTTON and HAVERCROFT ROAD, 4 m. distant, Hemsworth Hall, *Mrs. Tempest.*

CHEVET TUNNEL is 688 yards in length; on left of it is Chevet Hall, *Sir W. Pilkington,* Bart., to whom also belongs the Chevet Viaduct.

LOWER WALTON, on right Walton Hall, *C. Waterton,* Esq.

OAKENSHAW STATION, on left, Heath Hall, *J. G. Smyth,* Esq., 1 m. distant, on right, Crofton Hall, — *Heniker,* Esq., and 3 m. distant, Nostel Priory, *C. Winn.*

GOOSE HILL COMMON, on left, Newland Hall, *Sir E. Dodsworth,* Bart.

METHLEY, see on left, Methley Park, the noble seat of the *Earl of Mexborough;* 2 m. distant, on right, Kippax Park, *T. D. Bland,* Esq. and 3 m. distant, Ledstone Hall, *T. Broadhead,* Esq.

North Midland Railway. 15

Methley Leeds and Pontefract Road	65⅛
Wood Row	65½
Oulton, Wakefield and Abberford Road	67¼
L.—To Wakefield 5½ m. To Abberford 7 m.—R.	
*Woodlesford Station	67½
Leeds, Wakefield and London Road	69¼
L. { To Wakefield 8 m. To London 194¼ m. To Leeds 1 m.—R.	
*LEEDS STATION	72½

WOODLESFORD, 1 m. distant, on right, Swillington Hall, *Sir J. Lowther*, Bart., and 3 m. distant, Temple Newsham, *Lady William Gordon*.

LEEDS and WAKEFIELD ROAD, on right, Stourton Lodge, *H. Teal*, Esq.

YORK AND NORTH MIDLAND RAILWAY.

NORMANTON TO YORK.

From *NORMANTON STATION, Yorkshire, at the Junction with the North Midland Railway, to the Leeds and Pontefract Road	1¾
L.—To Leeds by the North Midland Railway 9 m. To Pontefract 3 m.—R.	
*Castleford Station, at the Pontefract and Leeds Road	3
L.—To Leeds 10 m. To Pontefract 3 m.—R.	
River Aire Viaduct	5⅞
Fairburne, at the London, Ferrybridge, Abberford and Pontefract Road	6
L.—To Abberford 7 m. To Pontefract 3¾ m. To London through Ferrybridge 179¾ m. } R.	
*Burton Salmon Station at the London and Tadcaster Road	6½
L.—To Tadcaster 10½ m.	

CASTLEFORD STATION, 2 m. distant, on left, see Kippax Park, *T. D. Bland*, Esq., and Ledstone Hall, *T. Broadhead*, Esq., 1 m. beyond Castleford Station, on right, see Fryston Hall, *R. M. Milnes*, Esq.

BURTON SALMON STATION, on right, Byrom Park, *Lady Ramsden*.

CHURCH FENTON, 1 m. distant, on left, Scarthingwell Hall, — *Kendil*, Esq., Towton Hall, *J. Kendal*, Esq., and 2 m. distant, Towton Field, the scene of the sanguinary Battle of Towton, of which the following account may to the tourist prove not altogether unacceptable:

This memorable battle was fought on Palm Sunday, the 29th of March, 1461, between the armies of York and Lancaster, the former, consisting of 48,660 men, was commanded by Edward IV. and the latter, amounting to 60,000, was led on by the Duke of Somerset; this dreadful conflict lasted from morning till night, and the victory was contended for by both parties with the greatest obstinacy; but at length the Lancastrians were put to flight, and then a most dreadful slaughter ensued, for Edward had made proclamation before the battle, that no quarter should be given, notwithstanding which, however, one prisoner was taken, Thomas Courtenay, Earl of Devonshire, but only

To London 179¼ *m.*—R.
Monk Fryston, at the Leeds and Selby Road, and South Branch of the Leeds and Selby Railway 8¼
L.—*To Leeds by Road* 13¼ *m.*
To Selby by Road 7 *m.*—R.
**MILFORD STATION* of the Leeds and Selby Railway, Main Line, that runs over the York and North Midland Railway 9¾
L.—*To Leeds by Railway* 12 *m.*
To Selby by Railway 8 *m.*—R.
*Sherburne Station, and North Branch of Leeds and Selby Railway at the Sherburne and Cawood Road.................. 10¾
L.—*To Sherburne* ½ *m.*
To Cawood 5 *m.*—R.
Church Fenton 12¾
*Ulleskelfe Station 14¾
River Wharfe Viaduct.... 15¼
*Bolton Percy Station 16
Streeton Road 16½
Colton and Nun Appleton Road.................. 17⅝
*Copmanthorpe Station .. 19¾
Tadcaster Road.......... 21
L.—*To Tadcaster* 6¼ *m.*
To York 2⅝ *m.*—R.
Askham Bryan Road 21⅜
York and Wetherby Road 23⅛
L.—*To Wetherby* 13½ *m.*
To York 1 *m.*—R.
**YORK STATION* 23¾

spared to put him to a more inglorious death on the scaffold. The carnage on that dreadful day is said to have been so great, that the waters of the Wharfe were dyed with blood, and indeed this cannot be thought strange, since it is affirmed that no less than 36,776 men were killed in the battle, and such was also the hurry and confusion attending the flight, that vast numbers, in endeavouring to pass the Cock, a small river running into the Wharfe, were drowned, and in their misfortune, formed a bridge for some of their companions. The place where this dreadful battle was fought, is a ridge of high ground between the villages of Towton and Saxton, from whence there is an extensive and beautiful prospect; and it is supposed that the two wings of the Lancastrian army extended to those places, having its centre posted on the heights about midway between them.

ULLESKELFE STATION, 1½ m. distant, on left, see Grimstone House, *Lord Howden*, 3 m. distant, is Haslewood Hall, *Sir E. M. Vavasour*, Bart., and 5 m. distant, Bramham Park, *G. Lane Fox*, Esq.

BOLTON PERCY STATION, on right, Bolton Lodge, *Col. Thompson*, and Bolton Percy Rectory, *Rev. W. V. Harcourt*, and 2½ m. distant, Nun Appleton, *Sir W. M. Milner*, Bart.

TADCASTER ROAD, 1½ m. distant, on right, Bishopthorpe, the Palace of the *Archbishop of York*, near which, see Middlethorpe Lodge, *J. Meek*, Esq.

ASKHAM BRYAN ROAD, ½ m. beyond, on right, see York Race Course.

CHESTER AND CREWE RAILWAY.

*Crewe, Cheshire, to Oak Farm	½
Coppenhall Heyes	1¼
Nantwich and Church Coppenhall Road	1¾
Nantwich and Middlewich Road	2¼
L.—To Nantwich 3½ m.	
To Middlewich 7 m.—R.	
River Weaver Viaduct	2⅞
*Nantwich Station, at the Nantwich and Church Minshull Road	3½
L.—To Nantwich 3½ m.	
Aston Hall	3¾
Middlewich and Wardle Canal Viaduct	5
Wardle Bank	6½
*Calveley Station, at the Nantwich and Tarporley Road	7¾
L.—To Nantwich 5½ m.	
To Tarporley 4¾ m.—R.	
Ellesmere Canal Viaduct	8¾
Tilstone Fernall	9¼
*Beeston Station, at the Whitchurch and Tarporley Road	10½
L.—To Whitchurch 12½ m.	
To Tarporley 2 m.—R.	
Huxley and Bunbury Road	11½
Crimes Lane	12½
*Crow Nest Station, at the Huxley and Tattenhall Road	14
Golden Nook Road	15¼
Chester and Whitchurch Road	16¾
L.—To Chester 4 m.	
To Whitchurch 16 m.—R.	
*Black Dog Station, at Seighton Lane	17½

RIVER WEAVER VIADUCT, on left, The Rookery, *Major Pollock*, and 1 m. distant, Pool Hall, *Mrs. Massey*.

WARDLE BANK, 1 m. distant, on right, Calveley Hall, *Edward Davies Davenport*, Esq.

CALVELEY STATION, 4 m. distant, on right, Oulton Park, *Sir Philip de Malpas Grey Egerton*, Bart.

TILSTONE FERNALL, 1 m. distant, on right, Tilstone Lodge, *John Jervis Tollemache*, Esq., who, for the accommodation of the inhabitants in this vicinity, and promotion of Protestantism, has recently erected an Episcopal Chapel here. 1¼ m. beyond Tilstone Fernall, on left, the Rock and Castle of Beeston.

HUXLEY and TATTENHALL ROAD. 3 m. distant, on left, Bolesworth Castle. *T. Crallan*, Esq., 4 m. distant, Aldersey Hall, *S. Aldersey*, Esq., and 5 m. distant, Carden Hall, *J. H. Leeche*, Esq.

Chester and Whitchurch Road..................	19
L.—*To Chester* 1½ *m.*	
To Whitchurch 18½ *m.*—R.	
Ellesmere Canal Aqueduct	19¼
Chester and Tarvin Road	19¾
L.—*To Chester* ½ *m.*	
To Tarvin 5½ *m.*—R.	
*CHESTER STATION	20¾

CHESTER, 3½ m. distant, on left, Eaton Hall, the magnificent seat of *The Marquis of Westminster*, 1 m. distant, on right, Hoole Hall, *Mrs. Yates*, Hoole House, *Lady Broughton*, Hoole Lodge, *Rev. P. Hamilton*, and Hoole Bank, *R. Brittain*, Esq.

CHESTER AND BIRKENHEAD RAILWAY.

From *CHESTER*, Cheshire, to the

Bache and Upton Road..	¾
Chester and Birkenhead Road	1¼
Ellesmere Canal Viaduct..	2½
Mollington and Backford Road	2¾
Road to Lea Hall	3¼
Backford Cross, second Road..................	4¼
Capenhurst Road	5
Sutton and Parkgate Road	6⅞
Hooton and Great Neston and Parkgate Road	8
Eastham Road	8¾
Plimyard Brook..........	8⅞
Bromborough Pool Viaduct, farthest end............	10¾
Spittle Lane	11
Old Road, Chester to Birkenhead	12¼
Woodside, old road to	12⅝
Rock Ferry Road........	13
Upper Tranmere Road ..	14
Tranmere Ferry Road....	14⅛
Birkenhead Pool	14¼
*BIRKENHEAD STATION	15

BACHE and UPTON ROAD, on left, Bache Hall, — *Garnett*, Esq.

CHESTER and BIRKENHEAD ROAD, on right, Moston Hall, *R. Massey*, Esq.

ELLESMERE CANAL VIADUCT, on left, Mollington Hall, *I. Fielden*, Esq., and see, hence, the Welsh Hills, and Jubilee monument on Moel Flamma.

CAPENHURST ROAD, on left, Capenhurst Hall, *R. Richardson*, Esq.

HOOTON and PARKGATE ROAD, 1½ m. distant, on right, Hooton Hall, the beautiful seat of *Sir T. M. Stanley*, Bart.

PLIMYARD BROOK, see on right, the church and village of Eastham, the residence of *Archdeacon Clarke*.

BROMBOROUGH POOL VIADUCT, on left, Poulton Hall, *R. Green*, Esq., on right, Bromborough Hall, *Rev. I. Mainwaring*.

ROCK FERRY ROAD, on right, Derby House, *R. M. Barton*, Esq.

UPPER TRANMERE, see on left, *G. Orred*, Esq.

CROYDON RAILWAY.

LONDON to CROYDON.

From *Duke Street Station, London Bridge, by the Greenwich Railway to the commencement of the Croydon Railway at Corbetts Lane	$1\frac{3}{4}$
L.—*To Greenwich by the Greenwich Railway* 2 m.	
Grand Surrey Canal Viaduct	$2\frac{1}{4}$
Cold Blow Farm Bridge ..	$2\frac{1}{2}$
*New Cross Station, at the London and Dartford Road................	3
L.—*To Dartford* $11\frac{1}{2}$ m. *To London* $3\frac{1}{2}$ m.—R.	
*Dartmouth Arms Station, at the London, Dulwich, and Bromley Road	$5\frac{5}{8}$
To Dulwich $1\frac{1}{2}$ m. *To Charing Cross, London* $6\frac{3}{4}$ m. } R.	
*Sydenham Station at the Dulwich, Norwood, Beckenham, and Bromley Road	$6\frac{1}{2}$
To Dulwich 2 m. *To Norwood, The Crown* $2\frac{5}{8}$ m. } R.	
L. { *To Beckenham* $2\frac{1}{4}$ m. *To Bromley* 4 m.	
*Penge Station, at the Dulwich and Norwood, and Bromley and Beckenham Road	$7\frac{1}{8}$
To Dulwich $2\frac{1}{4}$ m. *To Norwood, The Crown* $2\frac{1}{4}$ m. } R.	
L. { *To Beckenham* 2 m. *To Bromley* $3\frac{3}{4}$ m.	
*Anerley Station, at the Norwood and Bromley Road	$7\frac{5}{8}$

The arched causeway from Corbetts Lane to the New Cross Station, being elevated considerably above the level of the land, affords a good view of the country on either side. Arrived there, the train toils up a steep ascent through deep cutting, to the Dartmouth Arms Station, from whence, and the succeeding embankments, on left, is beheld a beautiful view of the richly wooded country, in the vicinity of Chislehurst, Bromley, and Beckenham, in which the church of the latter stands forth conspicuously in the foreground, and forms an interesting feature; the distance being terminated by an extensive stretch of the county of Kent, which this eminence commands. The country bordering the Railway, on right, including the village of Norwood and the Beulah Spa, is highly interesting: but the great attraction and object of chief interest on this line is Dulwich.

DULWICH, delightful for its rural simplicity, and unquestionably one of the most beautiful villages in England, is thus celebrated by Akenside:

Or lose the world amid the sylvan wilds
Of Dulwich, yet by barbarous arts unspoil'd.

Dulwich, from its proximity to the metropolis, is too well known to render necessary its description here. It is chiefly celebrated for its college and picture gallery, the latter of which is well deserving of a visit; it is open to the public by tickets only, obtainable gratis, of the Editor, E. Mogg, Great Russell Street, Covent Garden.

L.—*To Bromley* 4 m.	
To Norwood 2 m.—R.	
Jolly Sailor Bridge 8⅜	
*Jolly Sailor Station, at the Norwood and Woodside Road................ 8½	
To Beulah Spa 1¼ m. ⎫ *To Norwood, the* ⎬R. *Crown* 2 m. ⎭	ANERLEY STATION, ½ m. distant, on left, see the Watermen's and Lightermen's Almshouses, recently erected by public subscription.
Brighton Railway Junction 8¾	
Croydon and Norwood Road Viaduct.......... 9¾	
Croydon and Norwood Road Viaduct.......... 9⅞	
Addiscombe and Broad Green Road Viaduct .. 10¼	
*CROYDON STATION 10½	

LANCASTER AND PRESTON RAILWAY.

PRESTON to LANCASTER.

From *PRESTON STATION* to	BARTON BROOK, on right, see Barton Lodge, *G. Jacson*, Esq., on left, Newsham Hall. ——.
The Preston and Wyre Railway .... ½	
Lancaster Canal.......... ¾	BILSBORROW ROAD, on left, Myerscough Hall, *J. Greenalgh*, Esq.
Cadely Mill Dam and River Savock 1½	RIVER BROCK, before, on left, Brook House.
Lightforth 2¾	
Broughton and Wood Plumpton Road 3¼	MYERSCOUGH and CHIPPING ROAD, on left, Myerscough House, *J. Cunliffe*, Esq.
Barton Brook 4¼	
Preston and Lancaster Road.................. 5¾	BROCKHOLES ARMS, see, on right, Claughton Park, *W. F. Brockholes*, Esq.
L.—*To Lancaster* 16½ m.	
To Preston 6 m.—R.	
Bilsborrow Road 6¾	
River Brock Viaduct 7¼	GARSTANG STATION, 2 m. distant, on right, Bleasdale Tower, *W. Garnett*, Esq.
Myerscough and Chipping Road.................. 8	
Brockholes Arms 8¾	
River Calder Viaduct 9⅛	RIVER CALDER VIADUCT, see, on left, the picturesque ruins of Greenhalgh Castle; 1½ m. distant, is Kirkland Hall, *T. B. Cole*, Esq.
GARSTANG STATION, at the Garstang and Chipping Road 9¼	
L.—*To Garstang* 1½ m.	

Lancaster and Preston Railway.

Higher Lingart	10½
Woodacre Hall	11¼
Scorton Road	12¼
River Wyre Viaduct	12¾
Hollins Lane, Clevely Road	13¾
Foxholes, Lancaster and Preston Old Turnpike Road	14½
Quernmore Road, at the Preston and Lancaster Old Road	15
Hole of Ellel, River Cocker	15¼
Hampson Green	16
Galgate Viaduct over the Lancaster and Preston Road, and the River Conder	16¾
Leach House	17½
Burrow Beck, Lancaster and Preston Old Turnpike Road	18½
The Greaves	20
Scotforth	19¼
*LANCASTER STATION	20½

RIVER WYRE VIADUCT. This and the embankment near Scorton affords a charming view of the river and rich valley of Wyersdale, on right, in which direction, in a beautifully romantic situation, visible between the trees, is beheld, at 3 m. distance, Wyreside, the seat of *Robert Garnett*, Esq., said to be the largest Railway proprietor in the kingdom.

HOLE OF ELLEL, on left, Hay Carr, *W. Lamb*, Esq.

HAMPSON GREEN, on left. Ellel Grange, *R. Atkinson*, Esq.

GALGATE, on left, Ellel Hall, *A. R. Ford*, Esq., and 1½ m. distant, Thurnham Hall, *Miss Dalton*.

SCOTFORTH, 2 m. distant, on left, on the margin of the Loyne, Ashton Hall, ———.

LANCASTER, 2½ m. distant, on right, Quernmore Park, *Lady Dallas*.

HULL AND SELBY RAILWAY.

From *HULL STATION, Yorkshire, to	
*Hessle Station	4
Road to Hessle Viaduct	4½
Hessle Cliff	5
Hessle Wood House	5¼
*Ferriby Station	7
Leaves Wood	7½
Road to Melton Landing	7¾
Cross Enters Wood to the Melton Road Viaduct	8
Road to Eastdale House	8¼
Road to Welton House	8¾
Road to Welton	9¼
*Brough Station	10
Brough	10½
Cave Sands Farm	12¼

HESSLE STATION, 1½ m. distant, on right, Anlaby House, *R. Tottie*, Esq., Tranby Cottage, *Miss La Marche*, and 2 m. distant, South Ella, *J. Beadle*, Esq.

HESSLEWOOD HOUSE is the seat of *J. R. Pease*, Esq. on right of it, is Tranby House, *J. Barkworth*, Esq., Tranby Park, *J. Todd*, Esq., and Hessle Mount, *T. B. Locke*, Esq., N.B. These and the preceding command delightful views, more or less extensive, of the Humber, that about the time of high water presents a beautiful panorama; and of the opposite coast of Lincolnshire.

FERRIBY STATION, 1½ m. distant, Swanland Hall, *J. Todd*, Esq.

LEAVES WOOD, ½ m. distant, on right, Melton Hill, *C. Whittaker*, Esq.

ROAD to EASTDALE HOUSE, ½ m. distant, on right, is Eastdale House, *R. Raikes*, Esq.

Crabley Creek............	13
Bromfleet and Providence Farm Road............	$13\frac{1}{2}$
Lane to Bromfleet	$14\frac{1}{4}$
Lane to Yokefleet Grange .	$14\frac{3}{4}$
Market Weighton Canal..	15
Mar House...............	$15\frac{1}{4}$
Scalby and Faxfleet Road	16
Warping Drain..........	$16\frac{1}{4}$
*Staddlethorpe Broad Lane Station.................	16
Blacktoft and Gilberdike Road..................	$16\frac{3}{4}$
Bennetland................	$17\frac{1}{4}$
Howden and South Cave Road..................	$17\frac{3}{4}$
L.—*To Howden* $4\frac{3}{4}$ *m.* *To South Cave* $7\frac{1}{2}$ *m.*—R.	
*Eastrington Station......	19
Green Lane.............	20
Eastrington and Howden Road..................	$20\frac{1}{8}$
Caville and Eastrington Road..................	$20\frac{1}{4}$
Caville and Eastrington Road..................	$20\frac{1}{2}$
Bishops Soil Drain........	21
Howden and Market Weighton Road.............	$21\frac{1}{8}$
L.—*To Howden* $1\frac{1}{2}$ *m.* *To Market Weighton* $10\frac{1}{2}$ *m.*—R.	
Road to Thorpe Hall......	$21\frac{3}{8}$
*Howden Station, at the York and Howden Road ..	22
L.—*To Howden* $1\frac{1}{4}$ *m.* *To York* 18 *m.*—R.	
Brind....................	23
Rowland Hall............	$23\frac{3}{4}$
Loftsome Bridge and Holme Road..................	$24\frac{3}{8}$
Wressel and Loftsome Bridge Road	$24\frac{3}{4}$
Wressel	$24\frac{7}{8}$
River Derwent Viaduct ..	25
Road to Woodhall House..	$25\frac{1}{2}$
Woodhall and Loftsome Bridge Road	$25\frac{3}{4}$
Green Lane..............	$26\frac{1}{4}$

WELTON HOUSE ROAD, $\frac{1}{2}$ m. distant, on right, Welton House, *Mrs. Ann Raikes*, Welton Garth, *J. C. Smith*, Esq., Spring Hall, *T. Raikes*, Esq., and $3\frac{1}{2}$ m. distant, Raywell, *Mrs. Daniel Sykes.*

CAVE SANDS FARM, $2\frac{1}{2}$ m. distant, on right, South Cave Castle, the beautiful seat of *H. G. Barnard*, Esq., rises into view, and from its elevated position, constitutes a chief feature of the landscape beheld from the Railway.

BROUGH STATION, 2 m. distant, on right, Brantingham Thorpe Hall, *R. F. Shaw*, Esq.

BLACKTOFT and GILBERDIKE ROAD, 3 m. distant, on left, see the new church at Blacktoft, 2 m. distant, on right, Blacktoft Grange, *A. Empson*, Esq.

EASTRINGTON, 4 m. distant, on left, Saltmarsh Hall, *P. Saltmarsh*, Esq., $5\frac{1}{2}$ m. distant, on right, see the Church of Holme, on Spalding Moor, that, seated on an eminence, stands forth strikingly conspicuous, forming a landmark, and chief feature of the landscape in the extensive level by which it is surrounded. The adjoining cemetery commands a complete view of this vast flat for some miles, in which Howden Church and the Cathedral of York are prominent objects; the view towards the east being terminated by the Wolds, stretching in a long line from north to south.

HOWDEN STATION, see, on left, the Town and Church of Howden, the former is of considerable antiquity, but contains nothing remarkable except its venerable, and formerly Collegiate Church, well worthy of a visit, that, despite the ravages of time and destruction of the barbarian, still retains the chief features of its former magnificence. The west front, bold in feature, is a fine composition, and the east one, now in ruins, was one of the richest specimens of decorated style in the kingdom. The whole, notwithstanding its present dilapidated state, excites universal

South Duffield and Hemmingbrough Road	26¾
*Cliffe Station, at the Selby and Howden Road ..	28
L.—*To Selby* 4 *m.*	
To Howden 6½ *m.*—R.	
Lund	28⅜
River Ouse Viaduct........	30½
*SELBY STATION	30¾

in opinion to which the claim of superiority belongs. The antiquarian and man of taste will rejoice to hear that the venerable ruins of this magnificent structure will probably be preserved from further destruction; directions having been given for a series of repairs, that, at present in progress, are conducted with equal good taste, energy, and skill, under the superintendence of Mr. Sharp, an architect of great eminence at York.

WRESSEL, on right, the ruins of Wressel Castle. The remains of this superb structure are considerable, and form one of the most striking and interesting objects beheld from the Railway between Hull and Selby. It was originally built by Thomas Percy, Earl of Worcester, but subsequently became the residence of the Earls of Northumberland, who here displayed a magnificence resembling, and scarcely inferior to that of the royal court. The civil war in the reign of Charles 1. proved fatal to this magnificent castle, the destruction of which was commenced by a detachment of soldiers, sent from Hull by Cromwell for that purpose, after which, it was dismantled by order of parliament. Its remains were afterwards occupied as a farm house, till the year 1796, when an accidental fire, that broke out on the 19th of February, completed its destruction, and the naked walls are now the only remains of this noble monument of feudal grandeur.

admiration. The Chapter House, erected by Walter Skirlaw, Bishop of Durham, and of which the sky is now the only covering, was a superb octagonal edifice, it contained thirty canopied stalls, richly ornamented with tabernacle work, after the manner of York Minster; the style of both being sumptuous in the extreme, architects and antiquaries are divided

SOUTH DUFFIELD and HEMINGBROUGH ROAD, see, on left, Hemingbrough Church, with its beautiful steeple, one of the finest in Yorkshire, that rising 126 feet above the battlements, from the flatness of this part of the country, forms a conspicuous object for many miles.

In passing along the line, the principal objects as they occur are distinctly pointed out, and an additional remark is alone necessary to render the account complete. From the Hull to the Hessle Station, the Railway affords a fine view of the Humber, that about the time of high water, presents an animated and busy scene, and of the opposite coast of Lincolnshire. On reaching Hessle, a cutting there temporarily excludes all objects from the view, but upon emerging from it, about 1 m. beyond Hessle, the ride from thence to Crabley Creek, a distance of about 6 m. is very delightful, and the scenery of surpassing excellence, most interesting. Hence is beheld one of the best views in the kingdom. On left, the Humber, apparently without an outlet, and of a width exceeding 2 m. assumes the appearance of a magnificent lake, backed by the beautifully swelling eminences of Lincolnshire; on right, rise the Wolds of Yorkshire, that, crowned with seats and villages, at once indicative of wealth and prosperity, and altogether dissimilar in feature, present, though less striking, an agreeable contrast.

MANCHESTER AND LEEDS RAILWAY.

From **MANCHESTER STATION*, Lancashire, to Ryders Mill	$\frac{3}{4}$
Lamb Lane	1
Mansell Lane	$1\frac{3}{8}$
Newton Vale Lane	$2\frac{1}{8}$
Dean Lane	$2\frac{1}{4}$
Moston Mill, and Moston Road	$2\frac{3}{8}$
Bear Green	3
Great Nuthurst	$3\frac{1}{4}$
Broad Lane	$3\frac{3}{4}$
Mough Lane	4
Slacks Brook, and Chadderton and Middleton Road	$4\frac{1}{2}$
Tram Road to Alkrington Colliery	$4\frac{3}{8}$
Lane End, at Linnels Inn, Hollinwood and Middleton Road	$4\frac{3}{4}$
Joshua Lane	5
Bawtry Lane	$5\frac{1}{4}$
*Mills Hill Station, at the Middleton and Oldham Road	$5\frac{1}{2}$
L.—*To Middleton* 1 *m.* *To Oldham* $2\frac{1}{4}$ *m.*—R.	
River Irk	$5\frac{3}{8}$
Rochdale Canal Viaduct	$5\frac{3}{4}$
Boarshaw Lane Viaduct	$6\frac{1}{8}$
Touchet Hole Brook	$6\frac{1}{2}$
Rochdale Canal Viaduct	$6\frac{5}{8}$
Jack Lane	$6\frac{3}{4}$
Slattocks, Middleton and Rochdale Road	$6\frac{7}{8}$
L.—*To Middleton* $1\frac{1}{2}$ *m.* *To Rochdale* 4 *m.*—R.	
Heywood Branch Canal Viaduct	$7\frac{3}{4}$
*Heywood Station	10
L.—*To Bury* $5\frac{1}{2}$ *m.*	

ALKRINGTON TRAM ROAD. From hence to Joshua Lane, the embankment affords a good view of the town of Oldham, the Slacks Valley, finely wooded, and Chemical Works of *E. H. Becker*, Esq., whose seat, Foxdenton Hall, is a short distance from the Rochdale Canal, that here closely approaches the line.

MILLS HILL STATION, see, on left, the town of Middleton, the chief seat of the silk trade, 2 m. distant, on left of the Station, is Gorsey Lea Cottage, *E. G. Hopwood*, Esq., and 2 m. distant from Middleton, Heaton House, *Earl of Wilton*. The Mills Hill Embankment, nearly 65 feet in height, where it crosses the Irk, affords at Boarshaw Lane Viaduct, a lengthened view of the Railway southward to Mough Lane, and northward nearly to the Heywood Branch Canal, a total of nearly 4 miles, and on right, a prospect of the beautifully wooded country, that from Mills Hill to Slattocks, borders the line.

SLATTOCKS, on left, Hopwood Hall, *R. G. Hopwood*, Esq., 1 m. distant, on right, at Thurnham, is Tandle Hill, an isolated eminence, that tufted with trees, and rising suddenly from the land, commands a fine prospect, and forms, in its turn, a striking object in the landscape for many miles.

HEYWOOD BRANCH CANAL, see, on right, the village of Trub Smithy, on the Manchester and Rochdale Road.

CASTLETON BROOK, see, on left, Castleton Hall, *W. Blakemore*, Esq.

ROCHDALE, on left, are the following seats, Crossfield, *R. W. Vasasour*, Esq., Green Hill, *C. Royds*, Esq., Mount Falinge, *G. Royds*, Esq., West Hill, *A. Brierly*, Esq., Foxholes, *J. S. Entwisle*, Esq., Orchard House, *J. Dearden*, Esq., and Brown Hill, *A. H. Royds*, Esq.

* *ROCHDALE STATION*	11
River Roche Viaduct	$13\frac{1}{2}$
*Littleborough Station, and Halifax and Rochdale Road	14
L.—*To Rochdale* $3\frac{1}{4}$ *m.*	
To Halifax $13\frac{1}{4}$ *m.*—R.	
The Summit Tunnel	$15\frac{1}{2}$
Fairclough Lane Tunnel	$18\frac{1}{4}$
Gauxholme	$19\frac{1}{4}$
*Todmorden Station	20
L.—*To Burnley* $9\frac{1}{2}$ *m.*	
*Eastwood Station, and end of Eastwood Tunnel	21
Charlestown Tunnel	23
*Hebden Bridge Station	24
Mytholmroyd	$24\frac{1}{2}$
*Luddenden Foot Station	26
Sowerby Bridge Tunnel	$27\frac{1}{2}$
*Sowerby Bridge Station	28
L.—*To Halifax* $2\frac{1}{2}$ *m.*	
Cross the River Calder three times, to Elland Tunnel, and *the Elland Station	31
To Huddersfield 5 *m.*—R.	
*Brighouse Station	34
L.—*To Halifax* 4 *m.*	
To Huddersfield 4 *m.* / *To Bradford* 7 *m.* } R.	
River Calder Viaduct	$35\frac{1}{2}$
*Cooper Bridge Station	36
L.—*To Leeds* 12 *m.*	
To Huddersfield $3\frac{1}{2}$ *m.*—R.	
Cross the River Calder twice to **DEWSBURY STATION*	41
L.—*To Dewsbury* $1\frac{1}{2}$ *m.*	
Calder and Hebble Navigation Viaduct	$41\frac{1}{2}$
River Calder Viaduct	$42\frac{1}{4}$
*Horbury Station	44
Thornes	47
* *WAKEFIED STATION*	48
Junction with the North Midland Railway at *Normanton Station	50

LITTLEBOROUGH. ¾ m. distant, on left, Town House, *Mrs. Newhall*, on right, Pike House, *J. H. Beswicke*, Esq.

THE SUMMIT TUNNEL, extends 2,860 yards, being 660 yards short of 2 miles in length.

SOWERBY BRIDGE on right, Haugh End, *H. Ingram*, Esq. Shay. *W. Huish*, Esq. Thorpe, *J. Priestley*, Esq. and Mill House, *W. H. Rawson*, Esq.

ELLAND STATION, on right, Whitwell Hall, — *Ramsden*, Esq.

BRIGHOUSE STATION, 2½ m. distant, on right, Fixby Hall, *G. Thornhill*, Esq.

COOPER BRIDGE STATION, on left, Kirklees Hall, *Sir G. Armitage*, Bart., and 3 m. beyond Cooper Bridge Station, on right, Whitley Hall, *R. H. Beaumont*, Esq.

DEWSBURY STATION, on left, Crow Nest, *J. Haigh*, Esq.

THORNES, on left, Thornes House, *J. M. Gaskell*, Esq. and Lupset Hall, *D. Gaskell*, Esq.

The MANCHESTER and LEEDS RAILWAY, from its entrance into Yorkshire, is carried in its course through the valley of the Calder to Wakefield, and is accompanied as far as Sowerby Bridge, by the Rochdale Canal, a navigation of 31½ m. in length, that commencing near Halifax, connects it with Manchester. From Todmorden, the Railway is continued through a succession of valleys, many of which are highly romantic and present specimens of the most enchanting scenery. These varying in extent, vie with each other in picturesque beauty, and the greater part of them being enclosed, well wooded, and thickly spread with almost continuous villages, present when viewed from the neighbouring eminences a terrestrial paradise. The views from the Viaducts over the Calder and Canal, perhaps enlivened by some passing sail, vary the scene, and render the ride from Todmorden to Wakefield, one of the most beautiful that can well be imagined.

‡ For the remaining distance to Leeds, see page 96, Appendix, where from the Altofts Station, now called the Normanton Station, it is continued.

EASTERN COUNTIES RAILWAY.

LONDON to CHELMSFORD.

From *Shoreditch Station to Dog Row, Mile End....	7/8
Regent's Canal Viaduct....	1½
Coborn Road	2
Old Ford Lane	2¼
River Lea Viaduct........	2⅝
Branch of the River Lea Viaduct, and commencement of the Northern and Eastern Counties Railway................	3½
*Stratford Station, at Angel Lane..............	3¾
Epping Road, Maryland Point	4
L.—To Epping 12¾ m.	
To London 4 m.—R.	
Epping Forest, Eagle and Child	4⅞
Wanstead Road	6⅛
L.—To Wanstead 1½ m.	
Aldersbrook River Viaduct	6½
River Roding Viaduct	6¾
*Ilford Station............	6⅞
To Barking 1¼ m.—R.	
Romford Road	8⅛
L.—To London 8¼ m.	
To Romford 3½ m.—R.	
Barking Road, Seven Kings Watering Place........	8½
To Barking 2½ m.—R.	
Rippleside and Forest Road	8¾
Chadwell	9⅛
Chadwell Green	9⅝
Rainham Road	10¼
To Rainham 5 m.—R.	
Cap Hall	11
*ROMFORD STATION.	11⅞
To Grays Thurrock 12¼ m.—R.	
Hare Street and Hornchurch Road.................	12
Hare Hall	12¼

ILFORD, on left, Ilford Lodge, *Mrs. Hall*, Ilford Cottage, *J. Graves*, Esq., Valentines, *C. Holcombe*, Esq., and Cranbrook House, *Mrs. Hall Dare.*

ROMFORD, on left, Priests, *O. Mashiter*, Esq., Marshalls, *H. Mackintosh*, Esq. 1½ m. distant, Bedfords, *J. Rogers*, Esq., at Haveringate Bower, Bower House, *E. Robinson*, Esq.

HARE HALL is the seat of *J. Braithwaite*, Esq., on left of it, is Gidea Hall, *Mrs. Black*, and 2½ m. distant, Pergo Park, *R. Field*, Esq.

GREAT GUBBINS, 1 m. distant, on left, Dagnam Park, the beautiful seat of *Sir T. Neave*, Bart.

Upminster Road..........	13¾
Great Gubbins	14¼
Nag's Head Lane	16¼
Warley Lane, Brook Street	16⅝
**BRENTWOOD STATION*................	17⅜
Lord Petre's Avenue......	18¼
Tilbury Fort Road	18⅜
To Tilbury Fort 11 *m.*—R.	
Mountnessing Road	21
Mountnessing Street......	21½
*Ingatestone Station	23¼
Margaretting	24¾
Margaretting Street Road.	25½
To Maldon, 12¼ *m.*—R.	
Stock and Writtle Road ..	26¼
Widford, London, and Chelmsford Road	27¾
L.—*To London* 27½ *m.*	
To Chelmsford, 1½ *m.*—R.	
River Cann Viaduct	28⅝
**CHELMSFORD STATION*	29
To Maldon, 9¾ *m.*—R.	
L.—*To Braintree*, 11½ *m.*	
River Chelmer Viaduct ..	29½
Springfield	30⅛
Boreham House, Road to	31¾
Hatfieldbury	35
**WITHAM STATION*	37
Rivenhall End	39
*Kelvedon Station	40¾
Blackwater River Viaduct	41½
Feering and Coggeshall Road..................	42½
Long Green	45
Marks Tey, Coggeshall, and Colchester Road	45⅜
L.—*Coggeshall* 4 *m.*	
To Colchester 5 *m.*—R.	
Halstead & Colchester Rd.	46⅞
L.—*To Halstead*, 11 *m.*	
To Colchester, 3 *m.*—R.	
Lexden and Nayland Road	48½
L.—*To Nayland*, 11½ *m.*	
River Colne Viaduct	48⅞
**COLCHESTER STATION*	50¾

NAG'S HEAD LANE, 1 m. distant on left, Weald Hall, *C. T. Tower*, Esq. near which is How Hatch, *Rev. W. Tower*, and Rockets, *Mrs. Mills*.

BRENTWOOD, 2 m. distant on right, Thorndon Hall, the magnificent seat of *Lord Petre*.

MARGARETTING, on left, the Hyde, *J. Disney*, Esq.

MARGARETTING STREET, 1 m. distant, on left, Copfold Hall, *J. A. Hardcastle*, Esq. and 2½ m. distant Writtle Lodge, *J. F. Fortescue*, Esq.

WIDFORD, ½ m. before, on left, High Elms, *J. Perkins*, Esq.

SPRINGFIELD, on left, Springfield Place, *C. G. Parker*, Esq.

BOREHAM HOUSE, is the seat of *Sir I. T. Tyrrell*, Bart.

HATFIELDBURY, 2 m. distant, on left, Terling Place, *Lord Rayleigh*; on right is Crix, *S. Shaen*, Esq.; and 1 m. distant, at Hatfield Peverell, a seat of *P. Wright*, Esq.

WITHAM, on left, Witham Place, *G. Edwards*, Esq.; and Witham Lodge, *W. W. Luard*, Esq.; and 1 m. distant, Faulkborne Hall, *J. Bullock*, Esq. on right is Witham Grove, *Rev. H. Ducane*.

RIVENHALL END, 2 m. distant, on left, Rivenhall Place, *P. R. Smith*, Esq. and 1 m. distant on right, Braxted Lodge, *Captain R. Ducane*.

KELVEDON, 1 m. distant, on left, Felix Hall, *Lord Western*.

MARKS TEY, 1½ m. beyond, and 1½ m. distant, on right, Copford Hall, *F. Harrison*, Esq.

RIVER COLNE VIADUCT, ½ m. distant, on right, Lexden House, *S. G. Cooke*, Esq.; Lexden Park, *Mrs. J. F. Mills;* and Villa Franca, *Mrs. Smithies*.

COLCHESTER, 2 m. distant, on right, Bere Church Hall, *Sir G. H. Smyth*, Bart.; and Wivenhoe Park, *Gen. Rebow;* 2½ m. distant is Wivenhoe Hall, *S. Brown*, Esq.; East Donyland Hall, *P. Havens*, Esq.; and Olivers, *J. T. Turner*, Esq. and 3 m. distant, Birch Hall, *C. G. Round*, Esq

NORTHERN AND EASTERN RAILWAY.

LONDON to CAMBRIDGE, NORWICH, and YARMOUTH.

From *Shoreditch Station, along the Eastern Counties Railway, to

The Regent's Canal Viaduct	1½
Coborn Road	2
Old Ford Lane	2½
River Lea Viaduct	2⅝
Enter Essex.	
Branch of the River Lea Viaduct, and commencement of the Northern and Eastern Railway	3½
To Romford, by the Eastern Counties Railway 8¼ *m.*—R.	
Road from Temple Mills to Stratford	4½
Road from Temple Mills to Leytonstone	5
*Lea Bridge Station, at the London and Epping Road .	6¼
L.—*To London* 4 *m.* *To Epping* 12¾ *m.*—R.	
Copper Mills Stream Viaduct	7⅛
River Lea Viaduct	7¾
*Tottenham Station, *Middlesex*	8
Lower Edmonton, Marsh Lane	9
*Edmonton Station, at Water Lane	9¾
Delano's Farm	11
Upper Edmonton, Road to	11¼
*Ponders End Station	11⅞
Enfield New Cut	13¾
Green Street	14
Enfield Wash, Road to Turkey Street	14½

TOTTENHAM STATION, 2 m. distant, on left, Bruce Castle, *E. Hill*, Esq., Mount Pleasant, *J. Lawford*, Esq., and Tottenham Park, *J. Rawlings*, Esq.

UPPER EDMONTON ROAD, 1 m. distant, on left, Grove House, *Mrs. Ray*, and Milfield House, *Mrs. Mushett.*

PONDERS END STATION, 1 m. distant, on left, Bush Hill, *J. Currie*, Esq., and Bush Hill Park, *L. Raphael*, Esq., 1½ m. distant, on right, Gilwell House,

ENFIELD WASH, 1½ m. distant on left, Forty Hall, *J. Meyer*, Esq. on right, Capel House, *B. Hooker*, Esq.

Boundary of the Counties of Middlesex and Herts	$14\frac{3}{4}$
*Waltham Cross Station, *Hertfordshire*	$14\frac{7}{8}$
L.—*To Waltham Cross* ½ *m.* *To Waltham Abbey* ½ *m.*—R.	
Waltham Cross, Marsh Street	$15\frac{1}{4}$
Windmill Lane	$16\frac{1}{8}$
Old Mill River Viaduct	$16\frac{5}{8}$
New Mill River Viaduct	$16\frac{3}{4}$
Cheshunt Nunnery	17
*Broxbourne Station	$18\frac{7}{8}$
Hoddesdon Mill Stream	20
River Lea Viaduct	$20\frac{3}{4}$
Old River Stort Viaduct, division of the counties of Essex and Herts	$21\frac{1}{4}$
River Stort Navigation Viaduct, *Essex*	$21\frac{1}{2}$
*Roydon Station	$22\frac{1}{4}$
Roydon Lee Farm	$23\frac{1}{2}$
Little Parndon	$24\frac{1}{4}$
Burnt Mill	$24\frac{7}{8}$
Latton Mill	$25\frac{3}{4}$
*Harlow Station, at the Harlow and Bishop's Stortford Road	$26\frac{1}{2}$
L.—*To Bishop's Stortford* 6 *m.* *To Harlow* ¾ *m.*—R.	
Road to Harlow	$26\frac{3}{4}$
River Stort, opposite Pishiobury Park	$27\frac{1}{4}$
Shearing Mill	$28\frac{1}{4}$
*Sawbridgeworth Station, *Hertfordshire*	$28\frac{1}{2}$
Old River Stort Viaduct	$28\frac{3}{4}$
River Stort Navigation Viaduct	29
Tednam Farm	$29\frac{3}{4}$
Spelbrook	30
Thorley Street	$30\frac{3}{4}$
River Stort Navigation Viaduct	$31\frac{3}{4}$
*Hockerill, or *BISHOP'S STORTFORD STATION*	$32\frac{1}{2}$
L.—*To Bishop's Stortford* ½ *m.*	

WALTHAM CROSS STATION, on left, Theobalds Square, *Mrs. Chauncy*, Theobalds Park, *Sir H. Meux*, Bart., and Theobalds, *J. Hans Busk*, Esq., at Cheshunt, is Cheshunt Park, *T. A. Russell*, Esq., Pengelly House, *Hon. C. L. Butler*, and Claramont House, *C. Johnston*, Esq.

BROXBOURNE STATION, 1 m before, on right, Broxbourne Bury, *G. J. Bosanquet*, Esq., and on left of Broxbourne, Wormley Bury, *Hon. Capt. Cust.*

ROYDON STATION, 1 m. distant, on left, Netherfield House, *C. Booth*, Esq., Stort Lodge, *Mrs. Booth*, Stanstead Bury, *W. F. Dick*, Esq., and Briggens Park, *C. Phelips*, Esq., 1½ m. distant, Hunsdon House, *N. Calvert*, Esq., and 2 m. distant, Bennington Park, *W. Wigram*, Esq.

LITTLE PARNDON, ½ m. distant, on left, Gilston Park, *R. Plumer Ward*, Esq.

LATTON MILL, ½ m. distant, on right, Mark Hall, *Rev. J. Arkwright.*

HARLOW STATION, 1 m. distant, on left, Pishiobury, *R. Alston*, Esq., 1 m. distant, on right, Durrington House, *Mrs. Glyn*, and 2 m. distant, Moor Hall, *J. Perry*, Esq.

SAWBRIDGEWORTH STATION, on right, Great Hyde Hall, *Earl of Roden.*

SPELBROOK, on right, Walbury Hall, *Mrs. Johnson*, and 2 m. distant, Hallingbury Place, *J. A. Houblon*, Esq.

THORLEY STREET, on right, Twyford House, *G. Frere*, Esq.

*Stanstead Station, Essex 35¼
*Elsenham Station 37
*Newport Station 41¾
1 m. farther to Saffron Walden 2 m.—R.
*Wenden Station 43½
To Saffron Walden 2 m. —R.
*Chesterford Station 47½
To Newmarket 6 *m.*—R.
*Whittlesford Station 50¾
*Shelford Station 54
**CAMBRIDGE STATION* 57¼
To Newmarket 13 *m.*—R.
L.—*To St. Neats* 15 *m.*
*Waterbeach Station 62¾
*ELY STATION 72
L.—*To St. Ives* 17 *m.*
*Mildenhall Road 79
R.—*To Mildenhall* 7½ *m.*
*Lakenheath Station 84¼
To Mildenhall 7 *m.*—R.
**BRANDON STATION* 88¼
L.—*To Stoke Ferry* 10 *m.*
To Swaffham 15 *m.*
**THETFORD STATION* 95¼
*Harling Road Station ... 103¼
*Eccles Station 106¼
**ATTLEBOROUGH STATION* 110
*Spooner Row Station ... 113
**WYMONDHAM STATION* 115½
*Hethersett Station 119½
*Trowse Station 125
***NORWICH STATION** 126
*Brundall Station 132
*Buckenham Station 134
*Cantley Station 136
*Reedham Station 138
*Berney Arms Station ... 142
**YARMOUTH STATION* 146

NEWPORT, 1½ m. before, on left, Quendon Hall, *Mrs. Cranmer*, 1½ m. distant, on right, Debden Hall, *Sir F. Vincent*, Bart.

WENDEN, on right, Shortgrove, *W. C. Smith*, Esq. and 1½ m. beyond Wenden, Audley End, the beautiful seat of *Lord Braybrook.*

WHITTLESFORD, 2½ m. distant, on right, Abington, — *Mortlock*, Esq. Babraham Hall, *H. J. Adeane*, Esq. and 2½ m. distant, Hildersham Hall, *A. Cotton*, Esq.

SHELFORD, 2 m. distant, on right, Gogmagog Hills, *Lord Godolphin.*

CAMBRIDGE, 5 m. distant, on right, Quy Hall, *I. T. Martin*, Esq. and, beyond it, Bottisham Hall, *Rev. G. L. Jenyns*, and Bottisham Vicarage, *Rev. — Hailstone.*

BRANDON, on right, Brandon Park, the fine seat of *Henry Bliss*, Esq. and 2 m. beyond Brandon, on right, Santon Downham Hall, *Lord W. Powlett.* 4 m. distant, on left, Lyndford Hall, *Sir R. Sutton*, Bart. near which is Buckenham House, *Hon. F. Baring.*

THETFORD STATION, on left, King's House, *J. Cole*, Esq. on right, Euston Park, *Duke of Grafton*, and Kilverston Hall, *J. Wright*, Esq. beyond which is Shadwell Lodge, *Lady Buxton*, and Riddlesworth Hall, *T. Thornhill*, Esq.

ECCLES, on right, Eccles Hall, *Lady Flower*, and 2 m. distant, on right, Quiddenham Hall, *Earl of Albemarle.* 1 m. beyond Eccles, on left, Hargham Hall, *Sir Thomas Beevor*, Bart.

WYMONDHAM, 2½ m. distant, on left, Kimberley Park, the magnificent seat of *Lord Wodehouse;* and 2 m. distant, on right, Stanfield Hall, *Isaac Jermy*, Esq.

HETHERSETT, 2½ m. distant, on left, Melton Hall, *E. Lombe*, Esq. and Earlham Hall, *I. J. Gurney*, Esq.; 1 m. distant, on right, Ketteringham Hall, *Sir I. P. Boileau*, Bart. 2 m.

beyond Hethersett, on right, Intwood Hall, *J. S. Muskett*, Esq. Keswick Hall, *H. Birkbeck*, Esq. and Keswick House, *H. Gurney*, Esq.

TROWSE STATION, on right, Crown Point, *Col. Money*.

NORWICH, 2 m. distant, on left, Catton Hall, *G. Morse*, Esq. Catton Lodge, *M. Redgrave*, Esq.

BRUNDALL STATION, 2 m. distant, on left, Plumstead Hall, *Admiral Stephens*.

CAMBRIDGE is generally considered to have been the Roman Granta; it has long been celebrated for its university, which maintains, on the different foundations, more than 1100 persons, and consists of 17 colleges or halls; most of them contain a number of portraits, and the principal buildings of each are the apartments for the students and fellows, the master's lodge, the chapel, the library, the hall, and the combination-room. Of all these foundations the most magnificent is King's College, indebted for its origin to Henry VI. and which would have rivalled the most splendid palaces of Europe, or perhaps the world, had it been completed according to the plan of the royal founder: the chapel, however, has been alone considered as sufficient to ennoble any age; it is a perfect specimen of Gothic or English ecclesiastical architecture, and exhibits an exterior of uncommon solidity, that, together with the height and magnitude of the building, and its numerous ornaments, will inevitably create the sensations that naturally emanate from the contemplation of works of sublimity and grandeur. The interior view is still more impressive, and the vast arched stone roof, of elegant workmanship, unsustained by a single pillar, at once astonishes and confounds the spectator. The interior of the senate-house, a magnificent building of Portland-stone, forms one spacious apartment, and contains four elegant statues: the schools surround a small court, and the university library, abundantly stored with the most choice books, curious and valuable MSS. &c. occupies the whole quadrangle of apartments over them: the botanic garden is arranged according to the Linnæan system; it is richly stored with curious exotics, and also contains a number of rare trees and plants. Cambridge consists of 14 parishes, and each of them, except one, is possessed of a church, but those only of Great St. Mary, and St. Sepulchre, require notice: in the first, the members of the university attend divine service; the second is of a singular form, but has been much altered since its original erection, and now appears to great disadvantage; its more ancient part is, however, completely circular, and seems to have been erected in imitation of the church of the Resurrection, or Holy Sepulchre, in Jerusalem, of which it is thought to be the best copy in England. The market-place nearly resembles in form the letter L, at the bottom of which stands the shire-hall, divided into two courts, where the civil and criminal causes are tried; and behind this is the town-hall, a building that, from its situation, is hardly ever seen, except by those who transact business in it: the conduit is in front of the shire-hall, and is surrounded by an iron railing. Cambridge contains several charitable institutions; it extends nearly a mile from north to south, and half that distance from east to west; but the streets are in general narrow and winding, and the houses ill built and closely crowded together. Many improvements have been made here of late years, and it is now well paved and lighted. The town, and the university, each sends two members to Parliament, and here is a market on Wednesday and Saturday.

BIRMINGHAM AND GLOUCESTER RAILWAY.

BIRMINGHAM to GLOUCESTER.

From *BIRMINGHAM STATION, Warwickshire, to	
The Coventry Road	¾
Birmingham and Warwick Canal	1
*Camphill Station, at the Stratford upon Avon Road	1¼
L.—To Stratford upon Avon 21¾ m.	
Moseley, Worcestershire	2¾
*Kingsheath Station, at the Alcester and Birmingham Road	3¼
L.—To Alcester 17¼ m. To Birmingham 2¾ m.—R.	
Kings Norton Road	4½
Bredon Cross, Worcester and Birmingham Canal	5
Birmingham and Redditch Road	5¾
L.—To Redditch 8½ m. To Birmingham 5 m.—R.	
Northfield, at the Birmingham and Redditch Road	7
L.—To Redditch 8½ m. To Birmingham 6 m.—R.	
Grovely Lane Tunnel	9
Cofton Hall	10
Barnt Green	10½
The Lickey	11¼
Blackwell Farm	12
Summit of the Incline	12¼
Burcott, Hales Owen, and Alcester Road	12¾
L.—To Alcester 11½ m. To Hales Owen 8¼ m.—R.	
Bromsgrove and Alcester Road	13½
L.—To Alcester 12 m. To Bromsgrove 1¼ m.—R.	
Rigby	14

MOSELEY, on right, Moseley Hall, *J. Taylor*, Esq.

KINGSHEATH STATION, 1 m. distant, on right, Selby Hall, *R. Dolphin*, Esq., and ½ m. beyond Kingsheath Station, on left, Kingsheath House, *W. Congreve Russell*, Esq.

KINGS NORTON ROAD, on left, at Kings Norton, *Rev. Joseph Amphlett*.

BARNT GREEN, 2½ m. distant on left, Bordesley Hall, *D. Guest*, Esq.

SUMMIT OF THE INCLINE. Arrived here, a burst of matchless beauty meets the traveller's eye, and he experiences regret, that of the magnificent prospect hence beheld, he obtains little more than a momentary glance. If for the purpose, however, of enjoying at more leisure the delightful scenery of this vast expanse, he should for that purpose at a future period revisit the spot, its features fully detailed will be found at p. 47 of this Appendix.

BURCOT, 1¼ m. distant, on left, Hewell Grange, *Hon. R. H. Clive*.

BROMSGROVE STATION, 1¼ m. before, on left, is Finstall House, *R. Brettell*, Esq., 1¼ m. distant, on left of the Station, is Bowling Green House, *G. Rufford*, Esq., and Grafton House *B. Collett*, Esq.

•*BROMSGROVE STATION*	14¼
To Bromsgrove 1½ *m.*—R.	
Newton Farm	14¾
Sugar Brook	15⅝
Stoke Prior, Bromsgrove, and Alcester Road	16
L.—*To Alcester* 12½ *m.*	
To Bromsgrove 2½ *m.*—R.	
•Stoke Prior Station	16¾
Red House	17¼
Astwood	17¾
Worcester and Birmingham Canal	18¾
•*DROITWICH STATION*, at the Droitwich and Alcester Road	19¼
L.—*To Alcester* 1½ *m.*	
To Droitwich 11¼ *m.*—R.	
Huntingtrap Farm	19½
Dean Farm	20½
Dunhamstead	21⅛
Trench Lane	21⅜
Oddingley	21¾
Evelench	22¾
Ravenshill, Worcester, and Crowle Road	23½
L.—*To Crowle* 1¼ *m.*	
To Worcester 4 *m.*—R.	
Bredicot	24½
•Spetchley Station, at the Junction of the Evesham, Alcester, and Worcester Roads	25¼
L. { *To Evesham* 12 *m.* / *To Alcester* 14 *m.*	
To Worcester 3½ *m.*—R.	
Pitchmoor Hill	26⅛
Worcester and Pershore Road	27
L.—*To Pershore* 5 *m.*	
To Worcester 3½ *m.*—R.	
Abbots Wood	28⅛
Narrow Wood Lane	29
Pirton Road	29½
Perry Wood	30

STOKE PRIOR STATION, 1½m. distant, on the hill upon the left, see Hanbury Church, which standing on an isolated hill, to which there is an ascent of 180 steps from the Parsonage House, forms a prominent feature in the prospect, and is visible in different directions for many miles.

DROITWICH STATION, 1½ m. distant, on left, Hanbury Hall, *P. Chalmers*, Esq. At the N.E. cornef of the Park, stands the village or Hanbury and Church above mentioned, 2 m. distant, on left of the Station, is Mere Hall, *E. Shelton*, Esq., 1 m. distant, on right of the Station, is Hadsor House, *J. H. Galton*. Esq. Eastward of Droitwich, 1 m. distant, is Westwood Park, the fine old seat of *J. S. Pakington*, Esq., 1¼ m. distant, High Park, *Rev. E. Wakeman*, and 3½ m. distant, Ombersley Court, *Lord Sandys*.

ODDINGLEY, 2 m. distant, on right, Hindlip Hall, *Lord Southwell*.

SPETCHLEY STATION, on right Spetchley Park, *R. Berkeley*, Esq.

WORCESTER, 1¼ m. distant from, is Perdiswell Park, *Sir O. P. Wakeman*, Bart., and 2 m. distant, Spring Bank, *Col. Taylor*.

DEFFORD COMMON, on right, Croome Court, *Earl of Coventry*.

Pershore and Severn Stoke Road	30½

L.—*To Pershore* 3¼ *m.*
To Severn Stoke 3¾ *m.*—R.

Defford Common, at the Pershore and Croome Road	31½
*Defford Station, at the Upton and Pershore Road	32½

L.—*To Pershore* 3½ *m.*
To Upton 5 *m.*—R.

*Eckington Station	33½
Bredons Norton Road	34¾
*Bredon Station, at the Tewkesbury and Pershore Road	36¼

L.—*To Pershore* 7 *m.*
To Tewkesbury 3¼ *m.*—R.

Carant Brook	37⅜
Northway, *Gloucestershire*	38⅝
*Ashchurch Station, at the Tewkesbury and Stow Road, and Tewkesbury Branch	38½

L. { *To Evesham* 11 *m.*
    { *To Stow on the Wold* 17 *m.*
To Tewkesbury 2 *m.*—R.

Tirle Brook	38¾
Piddington	40
Treddington Lane	40½
Stoke Orchard, and Bishops Cleeve Road	41¾
Brockhampton	43
Swindon, and Bishops Cleeve Road	43¾
*CHELTENHAM Station	45¾
Badgworth Road	47¾
Churchdown Road	49¼
Barnwood, at the Cirencester and Gloucester Road	51

L.—*To Cirencester* 15½ *m.*
To Gloucester 1½ *m.*—R.

*GLOUCESTER STATION	52½

ECKINGTON STATION, 1½ m. distant, on left, Wollashill, the beautiful seat of *C. Hanford*, Esq., and the Tower on Bredon Hill, 1134 feet above the level of the sea. Bredon Hill forms a fine feature in the landscape for many miles round, and the Tower, a pleasure house on its summit, commands a very delightful prospect. 1 m. distant from Eckington, on right, is Strensham, chiefly remarkable as being the birthplace of the celebrated Samuel Butler, the author of Hudibras, and here also is Strensham Court, *J. Taylor*, Esq.

BREDON STATION, 1½ m. distant, on right, Twyning House, *Miss Maxwell*.

TEWKESBURY, on left, Tewkesbury Lodge, *Miss Shapland*, across the Severn, on left, Forthampton Court, *J. Yorke*, Esq., on right, The Mythe, *J. Longmore*, Esq., and Pull Court, *W. Dowdeswell*, Esq.

ASHCHURCH STATION, 1 m. beyond, on right, see Oxenton Hill, and on right of the Stoke Orchard and Bishops Cleeve Road, the lofty range of the Cotswold Hills, that extend from Broadway Hill to near Tetbury, a distance of nearly 30 miles, and from Birdlip Hill to near Burford, about 20 miles; the area they include has been calculated to contain 200,000 acres, the portion lying on right of Bishops Cleeve, and denominated Cleeve Down, rises to the height of 1134 feet above the level of the sea.

BROCKHAMPTON, 2 m. distant, on left, Southam House, *Lord Ellenborough*.

CHELTENHAM, on left, Charlton Park, *Lady Russell*, 2 m. distant, Hewletts, *J. Agg*, Esq., 4 m. distant, Sandywell Park, *W. L. Lawrence*, Esq., and Dowdeswell House, *E. C. Rodgers*, Esq., 1 m. beyond Cheltenham, on right, Grovefield House, *R. Roy*, Esq.

BARNWOOD, on left, Barnwood Court, *Mrs. Hardwick*, 4 m. distant, Whitcombe Park, *Lady Hicks*, and Prinknash Park, *J. H. Howell*, Esq.

GREAT NORTH OF ENGLAND RAILWAY.

YORK to DARLINGTON.

From *YORK STATION Yorkshire, to the River Ouse Viaduct............	3¼
Overton and Skelton Road	3½
*Shipton Station	5¾
Tollerton and York Road..	6⅜
Tollerton and Easingwold Road....................	9¾
*Alne Station	11¼
To *Easingwold* 2½ *m.*—R.	
Spring House	12⅞
Lees Barn	14
Boroughbridge and Easingwold Road.............	14¾
L.—To *Boroughbridge* 6½ *m.* To *Easingwold* 3¾ *m.*—R.	
Helperby and Sessay Road	15¾
Sessay	18
Dalton and Thirkleby Road	19⅛
Sowerby Park, and Cod Beck Viaduct............	19⅞
Thirsk and Boroughbridge Road	21
L.—To *Boroughbridge* 10 *m.* To *Thirsk* 1 *m.*—R.	
*THIRSK STATION, at the Thirsk and Ripon Road	22¼
L.—To *Ripon* 11½ *m.* To *Thirsk* 1¼ *m.*—R.	
Woodhill Field	23½
Thirske and Kirby Wiske Road....................	24¼
Wood End	25¼
Thornton le Moor and Otterington Road.........	26¾
*NORTHALLERTON STATION..............	30
L.—To *Boroughbridge* 19 *m.*	
Northallerton and Richmond Road.............	31
L.—To *Richmond* 14 *m.* To *Northallerton* ½ *m.*—R.	

SHIPTON STATION, 1½ m. distant, on left, Benningborough Hall, *Viscount Downe*, and across the Ouse, Nun Monckton, *Hon. H. Butler*, and 1½ m. distant, on right, Skelton Hall, *W. Duesbury*, Esq.

ALNE STATION, on left, Alne House, *E. Strangeways*, Esq. 4 m. distant, Myton Hall, *M. Stapylton*, Esq. 4½ m. distant, on right, Sutton Hall, *W. C. Harland*, Esq., and 5 m. distant, Stillington Hall, *Col. Croft*. In this direction, also, overlooking the small town of Easingwold, is beheld Crake Castle, which in the time of the Saxon Kings was a royal palace; it is seated on a promontory on the south side of the Hambledon Hills, commands a prospect over great part of the vale of York, and is visible to the surrounding country for many miles.

SESSAY, 4 m. distant, on left, is Newby Park, *Earl de Grey*, on right of Sessay, is Sessay Hall, *Viscount Downe*, and 3½ m. distant, Thirkleby Hall, the elegant seat of *Sir Robert Frankland Russell*, Bart.

THIRSK, is a pleasant well-built town, situated on a plain nearly surrounded by hills, on the banks of the little river Codbeck, which divides the old town from the new, and is crossed by two small but substantial bridges. The Church, a handsome Gothic structure, is said to have been built with the ruins of the ancient castle that stood at the south western extremity of the town, and was destroyed in the reign of Henry II.; it contains a few monumental erections. Here are some dissenting chapels, and a few charitable institutions. It is a borough by prescription, sends one member to parliament, and has a market on Monday.

THIRSK STATION, 2 m. distant, on left, Sand Hutton Hall, *J. Walker* Esq.

WOODEND, is the seat of *Sir Samuel Crompton*, Bart.

Danby Wiske............	34
Hutton Bonville Hall......	34½
River Wiske Viaduct.....	35¾
Birkby and Est.Cowton Road	36
*East Cowton Station	37¼
Yarm and Richmond Road	38¾
L.—*To Richmond* 9¾ *m*.	
To Yarm 11¼ *m*.—R.	
Cooper House	39
Catterick Bridge and Darlington Road............	40
L.—*To Catterick Bridge* 7 *m*.	
To Darlington 5¼ *m*.—R.	
Pepper House............	40¼
Darlington and Northallerton Road and River Tees Viaduct	41
L.—*To Darlington* 5½ *m*.	
To Northallerton 9½ *m*.—R.	
*Croft Station, *Durham* ..	41¾
* DARLINGTON STATION	45

DARLINGTON is a borough and market town of Durham, distant from London by road, 241 mles, by Railway, 265 miles, and from York 45 miles. The inhabitants are principally employed in the manufactures of linen and woollen, in the former of which it is said to exceed any town in England. Here are mills for spinning wool, grinding glass for optical purposes, and spinning flax, and also two iron founderies. It has a stone bridge of three arches over the River Skern, which runs into the Tees. The church which has a high and elegant spire, was built by Hugh Pudsey, Bishop of Durham, about the year 1160; it was formerly collegiate and had a dean and four prebendaries. Here are also the remains of an episcopal palace The market-place, which is very spacious, forms the principal part of Darlington, and the market on Monday, is well supplied. Darlington sends two members to parliament.

THORNTON LE MOOR AND OTTRINGTON ROAD, 1 m. distant, on left, Newby Wiske, *W. Rutson*, Esq.

HUTTON BONVILLE HALL, is unoccupied.

EAST COWTON STATION, 1 m. distant, on left, Pepper Hall, *Hon. Col. Arden*, 2 m. distant, on right, is the village of Great Smeaton, remarkable for the beauty of the prospects thence beheld.

NORTHALLERTON, a small but genteel market town of Yorkshire, distant from London by Railway 250 miles, from York 30 miles; is surrounded by an exceedingly rich and fertile tract of country. It principally consists of one long street, about half a mile in length, is seated on a small stream called the Wiske, a branch of the Swale, and the houses, chiefly of brick, are situated on rising ground gently sloping towards the east, with a large market-place. The church, a spacious Gothic structure, built in the form of a cross, contains several handsome monuments. Here is a prison upon Mr. Howard's plan. It returns one member to parliament, and has a market on Wednesday. There is a good race course on the south side of the town, with a grand stand, and the races held in October, are generally well attended. Near Northallerton was fought in 1138, the celebrated battle of the Standard, in which the Scots, though superior in numbers, were totally routed with the loss of 10,000 men, notwithstanding David, King of Scotland, and his son, Henry, gave on that occasion, the most astonishing proofs of valour and intrepidity.

CROFT STATION, 2½ m. distant, on left, Halnaby Hail, *Miss Milbank*.

DARLINGTON, 1 m. before on left, Blackwell Grange Hall, *W. Allan*, Esq., and Blackwell Hall, *J. Allan*, Esq.; 1 m. distant, on right is Polam, *Jonathan Backhouse*, Esq., and Beechwood Villa, *J. Backhouse*, Esq.; at Darlington is Southend, *Joseph Pease*, Esq., and Woodlands, *J. Wood*, Esq.

The continuation of the Great North of England Railway is as follows:— From Darlington to Durham 17½ miles, Newcastle 21 miles, making a total of 39½ miles.

BRANCH RAILWAYS FROM DURHAM.

From Durham to Sunderland a branch Railway has been constructed; it is 13¾ miles in length, and is worked by stationary engines, at an average speed of 12 miles an hour.

Of the branches from Durham to Hartlepool there are two, but neither of them direct. One from Durham, from whence there is an omnibus to the two termini. The distance of the line by Sherburn, Murton and Haswell, to Hartlepool, being 19¾ miles; by the other 22 miles.

TAFF VALE RAILWAY.

The following are the distances on this line:— From Cardiff to Llandaff is 4¼ miles; from Cardiff to Merthyr Tidvill 20¼ miles; and from Merthyr Tidvill to Llandaff 20¼ miles.

GREAT WESTERN RAILWAY.
LONDON TO SLOUGH.

The Great Western Railway commences at Paddington, on the western side of the Paddington canal, from whence it is carried forward, through excavation, with a curvilinear sweep, on a rise of 3 feet in a mile, in a distance of $2\frac{1}{4}$ miles, to the Birmingham, Bristol, and Thames Junction Railway, which, carried under the Paddington Canal, branches forth from the Birmingham Railway (both these great works lying a short distance on right of the line) to the Great Western at Wormwood Scrubs; a little before arriving at which, on the northern bank of the canal, is the General Cemetery. From Wormwood Scrubs, carried forward in a south-west direction, it soon emerges from the excavation, and, entering on an embankment that affords a transient glance at the country, crosses Old Oak Common, from whence, taken through deep cutting, a short embankment intervening near Acton, it arrives at

THE EALING STATION.

AN INTERMEDIATE ONE, DISTANT FROM LONDON $5\frac{1}{2}$ MILES, FROM BATH $100\frac{3}{4}$ MILES, FROM BRISTOL $112\frac{1}{2}$ MILES.

On right of Ealing is Castle Bear Hill, long the residence of H. R. H. the late Duke of Kent: $1\frac{1}{2}$ mile distant is Twyford Abbey, the small but elegant domain of the late John Willan, Esq., the celebrated stage coach proprietor, now of his successor. Shortly before arriving at the Ealing Station, the Railway, increased in steepness to 4 feet in a mile, approaches very closely the Uxbridge road, from whence, carried forward in a direct line, through cutting, in rather less than a mile, it gains the Hanwell embankment, and soon reaches

THE HANWELL STATION.

AN INTERMEDIATE ONE, DISTANT FROM LONDON 7 MILES, FROM BATH $99\frac{1}{4}$ MILES, FROM BRISTOL 111 MILES.

The Hanwell embankment, in conjunction with the Wharncliffe viaduct, a beautiful structure *, constructed with a gradual sweep, carries the Railway over the Brent river and valley, to the Metropolis Bridge, a massive structure of brick, by which the line is borne over the Uxbridge road. The Hanwell embankment affords a good view of the country on either side, first of Hanwell Park upon the right; but, upon reaching the Viaduct, the prospect, particularly on the left, expands. In this direction is beheld one of the British " palaces for poverty," the far-famed Hanwell Lunatic Asylum, which, with its delightful grounds, is solely de-

* Of 8 arches, its entire length being 895 feet.

voted to the reception of pauper lunatics of the county of Middlesex. Beyond the Asylum lies Osterley Park, the beautiful seat of the Earl of Jersey: the view being terminated by the richly-wooded eminences of Richmond Park and the Surrey Hills. About a mile beyond the Wharncliffe Viaduct is

THE SOUTHALL STATION.

AN INTERMEDIATE ONE, DISTANT FROM LONDON $8\frac{3}{4}$ MILES, FROM BATH $97\frac{1}{2}$ MILES, FROM BRISTOL $109\frac{1}{4}$ MILES.

Southall, a mere village, ranks as a market town, from the market for cattle, held here weekly, and which, for its extent of business, is second only to Smithfield. Here also is Southall Park, some time the private lunatic asylum of the late Sir W. Ellis, till lately the resident physician and manager of the county establishment at Hanwell. Continued with a gradual sweep from Southall, the Railway in $1\frac{1}{2}$ mile reaches the Paddington Canal, and shortly after the Grand Junction Canal, both of which it crosses on a level. At the Grand Junction Canal ($\frac{1}{2}$ mile distant on left of which is Cranford Park, the seat of the Berkeley family), the Railway commences a descent of 4 feet in a mile, and carried with a gradual sweep, by alternate excavation and embankment, passing in its way Dawley, once the seat of the celebrated Lord Bolingbroke (on right), arrives in about $1\frac{1}{2}$ mile farther at

THE WEST DRAYTON STATION.

AN INTERMEDIATE ONE, DISTANT FROM LONDON 13 MILES, FROM BATH $93\frac{1}{4}$ MILES, FROM BRISTOL 105 MILES. — Journey resumed below.

West Drayton, distant from Uxbridge 3 miles, from Colnbrook 4 miles, from its confluence of waters, has long been the resort of the lovers of the angle, who, in the Colne and Crane, and their tributary streams, find ample room for the indulgence of their favourite sport. From the West Drayton station, the Railway, carried forward upon a level, with a gradual bend to the southward, soon crosses the Colne river (entering Buckinghamshire), and in a short distance further, carried through deep cutting, the Iver road. 1 mile distant on left of the Iver road is Richings Lodge, and about the same distance on right Delaford Park. $\frac{3}{4}$ mile beyond the Iver road, the Railway enters on an embankment by which it is carried to the 16 milestone and Langley Marsh road, 1 mile distant on left of which is Ditton Park, the seat of Lord Montague, and about the same distance on right Langley Park, R. Harvey, Esq. The house, a noble stone structure, the grounds of which are beautifully disposed, having at their northern extremity an enclosure denominated the Black

Park, from its appropriation to alpine scenery, of which it presents a very beautiful specimen, being wholly planted with firs and ornamented with a fine sheet of water.

From the Langley Marsh road, a little before reaching which it commences a descent of 4 feet in a mile, the Railway, carried forward with a curvilinear sweep, chiefly through excavation, in a distance of $1\frac{1}{2}$ mile from Langley Marsh, crosses the Upton and Stoke road, when it commences a rise of 2 feet in a mile, and continued, principally through cutting, in $\frac{3}{4}$ mile more, arrives at

THE SLOUGH STATION.

A PRINCIPAL ONE, DISTANT FROM LONDON 18 MILES, FROM WINDSOR $2\frac{1}{2}$ MILES, FROM ASCOT RACE COURSE $8\frac{1}{4}$ MILES, FROM BATH $88\frac{1}{4}$ MILES, FROM BRISTOL 100 MILES. — Journey resumed page 7.

SLOUGH.

A considerable village, and once great thoroughfare, on the Bath road, is chiefly remarkable as the residence of the late Dr. Herschel, who, during the reign of George III., assisted by a royal pension, here pursued his astronomical researches; a branch of science to which his son has greatly contributed, and here continues his labours. His telescope, a prodigious instrument, 39 feet 4 inches in length and 4 feet in diameter, presents a singular appearance as seen from the road. A description of this vast magnifier and its apparatus occupies 65 pages in the second part of the Philosophical Transactions for 1795, its parts being illustrated by 19 plates. It is altogether a most curious piece of mechanism, and the discoveries made by means of its magnetic power constitute some of the leading features of modern astronomy.

ETON.*

Eton, a considerable village, principally consisting of one long street, at the end of which a bridge over the Thames connects it with Windsor, is chiefly celebrated for its College. This college was founded by the unfortunate Henry VI., and is advantageously situated in a healthy and fertile valley near the river Thames, that greatly contributes to the beauty of this interesting scene. The institution supports 70 scholars, with officers and assistants; besides which, there are seldom less than 300 gentlemen, sons of the nobility and gentry, who board with the masters, and receive their education at this seminary. The college consists of two quadrangles, one appropriated to the school, and the lodging of the masters and scholars; the other containing the apartments of the

* The Eton Montem, triennially celebrated, consists of a procession of the pupils to Salt Hill, when a collection is made that, sometimes amounting to 800*l*., is given to the captain of the school for his support at the University.

provost and fellows, and also the library, which is considered one of the finest in Europe; some very valuable drawings, paintings, and Oriental manuscripts, are among its curiosities. The chapel is a fine structure, ornamented with large abutments, pinnacles, and embrasures; and is similar, in the disposition of its parts, to that of King's College, Cambridge.

WINDSOR.

Windsor is situated on the river Thames, and is connected with Eton by a neat bridge; it contains six principal streets, and several inferior ones; the houses in the former are chiefly built of brick, and the town is well paved and lighted. The Guildhall is a stately building. The Church, a modern Gothic structure, contains some handsome monuments, and a good organ. The town also contains an elegant little theatre, commodious barracks, and a good free-school: it returns two members to parliament. The corporation consists of a mayor, two bailiffs, and twenty-eight burgesses, thirteen of whom are called fellows, or benchers of the Guildhall; of these, ten, besides the mayor and bailiffs, are styled aldermen. The market is on Saturday. The inns are, the Castle, White Hart, Star and Garter, and Swan.

Windsor and its vicinity — both of extreme interest — have more than ordinary claims on the attention of the intelligent tourist. At Charter Island, near Runny Mead, the Egham race course, Magna Charta (the original of which may be inspected at the British Museum) was signed by King John, an event that Akenside, the poet of liberty, proposed to record by a column, to be erected on the spot, and for which he wrote an inscription. Cooper's Hill forms the subject of a poem by Denham, that Pope has eulogised in his "Windsor Forest," a work too well known to need encomium here. The town itself has been immortalised by Shakespear, in his Merry Wives of Windsor; while every reader of poetry will remember with pleasure Gray's Elegy, and Ode to Eton College.

WINDSOR CASTLE.

Windsor Castle, the most delightful and splendid palace of our sovereigns, was built by William the Conqueror, on account of its elevated and pleasant situation, as a place of security. It was enlarged by Henry I. Our succeeding monarchs resided in it till Edward IV., who was born in it, caused the ancient building to be taken down, with the exception of three towers at the west end of the lower ward, erected the present stately castle, and St. George's Chapel, enclosed the whole with a rampart of stone, and instituted the Order of the Garter. The rebuilding of the castle was principally under the direction of William of Wykeham, afterwards Bishop of Winchester. Great additions were made to it by Edward IV., Henry VII., Henry VIII., Elizabeth, and Charles II. The last entirely changed the face of the upper court, enlarged the windows, and made them regular; richly furnished the royal apartments, decorated them with paintings, and formed a magazine of arms: he likewise enlarged the terrace walk made by Queen Elizabeth, on the north side of the castle, and carried another terrace round the east and south-east sides of the upper court. In short, Charles II. left little to be done, except some additional paintings in the principal apartments, which were added by his successors, James II. and William III., in whose reign the whole was completed. Many improvements were made here during the reign of George III. Its complete reparation, with many improvements and additions of great magnificence, were, however, carried into effect during the reign of George IV., whose fine taste is strikingly exemplified throughout, and at whose suggestion it was completed, in its present state, by Sir Jeffery Wyatville, at an expense of 300,000*l.* The castle is divided into two courts or wards, with a large round tower between them, called the middle ward, the whole containing about twelve acres, with many towers and batteries. It is situated on a high hill, which rises by a sudden ascent, and has its base laved by the waters of the Thames. On the declivity of this hill is the fine terrace, faced with a rampart of freestone; and, for strength, grandeur of effect, and beautiful prospects, is universally allowed to be the noblest walk in Europe. St. George's Chapel, or the Collegiate Church of Windsor, is situated in the centre of the lower court: it is a beautiful structure, in the purest style of pointed architecture, and was founded by Edward III. in 1377; it was much improved and enlarged by Edward IV., and completed by Henry VII., who finished the body of it, and whose prime minister, Sir Reginald Bray, assisted in the construction of the roof, which is of stone, is decorated with an infinite number of devices, and, for the beauty and excellence of its workmanship, is universally considered a masterpiece of art. The whole was repaired and beautified, the choir in particular, about 1790, under the direction of Mr. Emlyn, by order of George III., who contributed, from his privy purse, 15,000*l.* towards the expense. The organ, built by Green, is esteemed one of the finest in England. Taste and convenience have been consulted in the various alterations and improvements, a light and airy style pervades the whole, and the general effect of the stone-work, with the neatness of the finishing, strikes the spectator with wonder. The *tout ensemble* is one of the most magnificent ever seen in a place of divine worship. The *Royal Vault* is a freestone edifice, built by

Henry VII., as a place of sepulture for himself and his successors; but, altering his purpose, he began the more noble structure at Westminster; and this remained neglected, till Cardinal Wolsey began a sumptuous monument for himself, whence the building obtained the name of Wolsey's Tomb House. The Cardinal, dying soon after his disgrace, was buried in the abbey at Leicester, and the building remained unfinished. James II. converted it into a Popish Chapel; but it afterwards fell to decay, and remained so till the reign of George III., when it was formed into a *Royal Mausoleum*, under the direction of Mr. Wyatt. Here are deposited the remains of George III. and his Queen, his daughter, the Princess Amelia; his sons, the Duke of Kent, the Duke of York, George IV., and William IV.; his granddaughter, the Princess Charlotte, and her infant son; and his nephew, the Duke of Gloucester. The remains of the infant Princes Alfred and Octavius, children of George III., were, during the life of that monarch, removed hither from Westminster Abbey. To do justice to Windsor Castle in the pages of this work is impossible: a volume might well be devoted to its description: to be appreciated it must be seen: it is deemed, by all who have visited it, as one of the most delightful spots in the world. When beheld from a distance, it at all times presents itself with superior dignity: but its majestic grandeur is best seen towards the close of day, when the broad effulgence of the setting sun illumines its walls and towers with vivid radiance.

From the Langley embankment, and occasional openings through the succeeding excavations, a good view is obtained of the surrounding country. Clearing the woods of Ditton Park, on left, rising in majestic grandeur, are beheld the stately towers of Windsor Castle. Enjoying an elevated and commanding situation, and occupying a position on the margin of the Thames, that here forms a sort of peninsula, from which it rises boldly, and surrounded by a richly wooded country, that may literally be said to revel in a luxuriance of rural beauties, it would appear to have been a spot pointed out by nature as worthy to be the abode of monarchs. Beneath the battlements of Windsor Castle, but somewhat in advance of that building, the tapering spires of Eton College, or, rather, its chapel, are seen to great advantage. Beheld in this direction, Eton College will forcibly remind the reader of Gray's Ode to that justly celebrated seat of learning, at which he is known to have pursued his studies. On right of the Upton and Stoke road is Stoke Place * On right of the Salt Hill and Stoke road is Stoke Park, the seat of Grenville Penn, Esq., a descendant of the Penns of Pennsylvania. The mansion, which consists of a

* The seat of Col. Vyse.

large square centre and two wings, standing in a park of considerable size, is seen to great advantage from the Railway, and forms a prominent feature in the landscape, viewed from the windows of Windsor Castle. Northward of Stoke Park, the church of Stoke Poges rears its "heaven-directed spire" among the trees; the surrounding cemetery forms the subject of Gray's Elegy. Here the poet passed his early days, and here also, together with his mother and aunt, he was buried. A monument to his memory, erected by the late Mr. Penn, stands in a field adjoining the churchyard, and forms the terminus of one of the views from Stoke House. Nearly adjoining Stoke Poges is Farnham Royal, a small village, the manor of which was held by its possessors on condition of finding the king a glove for his right hand on his coronation-day, and supporting his right arm while he held the royal sceptre. When the ancestors of the Earl of Shrewsbury exchanged this property with Henry VIII., they reserved the privilege to themselves and their posterity.

SLOUGH TO MAIDENHEAD.

From the Upton and Stoke road, the Railway is carried forward, with a curvilinear sweep, in a north-west direction, for a distance of $2\frac{1}{2}$ miles, crossing, in $\frac{3}{4}$ of a mile beyond Slough, the Salt Hill and Stoke road, from whence, carried principally through excavation, it arrives at the 20 mile stone. From this point the Railway proceeds with a gradual bend towards the Bath road, that runs on left of the line, and, carried by embankment, crosses near the 21 mile stone the road to Burnham and the 2 mile brook, on left of which is Ash Mill, in $\frac{3}{4}$ of a mile more the road to Hitcham, and, carried over the Bath road by a lofty brick bridge of 2 arches, reaches

THE MAIDENHEAD STATION.

A PRINCIPAL ONE, DISTANT FROM LONDON $22\frac{1}{2}$ MILES, FROM BATH $83\frac{3}{4}$ MILES, FROM BRISTOL $95\frac{1}{2}$ MILES. — Journey resumed page 9.

The Maidenhead station, which is a principal one and of some extent, is situate near the Dumb Bell Inn on the Bath road, at a distance of about $1\frac{1}{2}$ miles east from the centre of the town.

MAIDENHEAD.

Maidenhead, a market town of Berkshire, is situated on the borders of the Thames, in the parishes of Bray and Cookham, and is distant from London by road 26 miles, by Railway $22\frac{1}{2}$ miles.

It consists principally of one long paved street, the south side of which is in the former parish. Its present consequence may be attributed to the building of the bridge about the time of

Edward III., by which means the great western road was carried through the town. Previous to this, travellers usually crossed the river at a ferry, called Babham's End, at Cookham (where a bridge has recently been built), about 2 miles northward. The first bridge was of wood, towards the repairs of which the corporation were allowed a tree annually out of Windsor Forest. The present bridge consists of seven large semicircular arches, built with stone, and three smaller ones of brick at each end. The approach to this structure is grand and spacious, the ends being formed with a noble curve outwards. Along the sides is a broad pavement, fenced with a handsome balustrade. The view from the centre of the bridge northward is particularly pleasing. The hills of Cliefden and Taplow, with their elegant mansions, and fine hanging woods, form a very diversified and beautiful prospect. The principal trade of this town is in malt, meal, and timber; independent of this, from its favourable position on the Bath road, of which it was a principal stage, and being situate on the great thoroughfare from London to Oxford, Cheltenham, Gloucester, Birmingham, South Wales, and the West of England, prior to the introduction of the railway system, it enjoyed from its extensive connexion with mail-coach contractors, and stage-coach and posting establishments, that employed very many hands, a large share of the carrying trade; and this, in conjunction with the expenditure of travellers, proved a fruitful source of revenue to the town: the appearance of which, from the constant traffic passing through it, was that of a bustling, busy place.

Maidenhead, like many others in the kingdom, however, similarly circumstanced, has been doomed to experience a sad reverse; its business in these branches has all been carried off by the completion of the Great Western Railway, and suffering severely therefrom, save on the arrival of the trains, it now wears an appearance varying little from village tranquillity. This town was originally incorporated under the name of the Guild or Fraternity of the Brothers and Sisters of Maidenhithe, in the 26th year of the reign of Edward III. After the Reformation, it was governed by a warden and burgesses; but the charter of James II. vests the authority in a mayor and alderman, who are empowered to choose a high steward and other officers. The mayor, his predecessor, and the steward, act as justices. The corporation have the power of making bye-laws, and there is a jail for debtors and felons. The corporation revenues consist chiefly of the tolls of the market and the bridge. Market on Wednesday.

From the Burnham road, particularly to the right, the country assumes a better aspect, becomes more picturesque as we approach Maidenhead, and the woody hills of Taplow present themselves to view. On right, finely elevated above the Thames, that flows upon its western side, stands Taplow, distinguished by its noble woodlands and picturesque appearance, and adorned with many handsome houses, the residences of persons of rank and fashion: of these Taplow Court, standing on the summit of the hill, embosomed in wood, and, at no great distance from it, Taplow House, are two of the principal; but the chief feature of Taplow is Cliefden, which, together with Hedsor Lodge and Dropmore, form a complete cluster of seats. The stately mansion first erected at Cliefden was built by George Villiers, second duke of Buckingham, and was, with its costly furniture, fine pictures, and rich tapestry hangings, (the latter representing the victories of the great duke of Marlborough), totally destroyed by fire on the 20th of May, 1795. The Cliefden estate, and remains of its once splendid mansion, lay for some years a melancholy memorial of its former grandeur; and the property, divided into lots, was sold by auction on the 15th of June 1819. The chief part of the estate eventually became the property of Sir G. Warrender, Bart., who has erected an elegant mansion here. The grounds rise boldly from the banks of the Thames, and command (particularly from the terrace and adjoining parterre), in addition to an extensive reach of that noble river, some of the finest prospects in this part of the country. The home scenery is very picturesque, and the grounds (ornamented with a cascade), greatly improved, are also finely wooded, and possess so much diversity of surface, that the views assume a grandeur of character but seldom seen.

MAIDENHEAD TO READING.

From the Maidenhead Station, the Railway, carried forward by embankment in a direct line, soon crosses, by a bridge of 10 arches*, the river Thames, of which the fleeting glance the traveller obtains occasions a temporary regret at his now rapid rate of procedure, that deprives him of the enjoyment of one of the best, if not most beautiful, prospects on the line. Of these, supposing him to terminate his journey here, we shall proceed to point out the chief features. The view southward is, from the erection of the viaduct, no longer visible from Maidenhead Bridge, and can be seen only from the embankment; viewed in this direction, the river, continuing a direct course, pursues its way through a country which, though flat, is not unpleasant. Houses and villages are scattered amidst delightful meadows; the scene is closed in the horizon by a very distant country—Windsor Castle and the royal forest appearing on the left. The view northward from Maidenhead Bridge, though not so extensive, is greatly ad-

* Of these, 2 are water and 8 are land arches.

mired. In this direction the rising grounds of Taplow are beheld upon the right: the beautiful scenery of Cliefden and its neighbourhood present a picturesque landscape, backed by the beautifully wooded hills of Buckinghamshire, that terminate the view. Resuming the journey, the viaduct crossed, the embankment affords a good view of the town of Maidenhead, at the end of which the Railway crosses the road to Windsor, 9 miles distant on left. From the Windsor road, it proceeds, with a gradual bend, to the southward, and, carried through cutting of considerable depth, crosses, a mile beyond it, Shoppenhanger Lane, at $26\frac{3}{4}$ miles, the White Waltham road, reaching, in $1\frac{1}{4}$ mile more, the Waltham St. Lawrence road, 1 mile beyond which, crossing the Waltham St. Lawrence and Hare Hatch roads, it enters on an embankment that carries it in rather less than a mile to Ruscombe, $\frac{1}{2}$ mile beyond which, carried through deep cutting, it arrives at

THE TWYFORD STATION,

AN INTERMEDIATE ONE, DISTANT FROM LONDON $30\frac{1}{4}$ MILES, FROM BATH 76 MILES, FROM BRISTOL $87\frac{3}{4}$ MILES. — Journey resumed page 11.

One mile on left of Maidenhead lies Bray, celebrated in song for its vicar, Simon Symmonds, who, according to Fuller, changed his religion four times in the reign of Henry VIII. and his successors, adhering to one principle only, that of living and dying vicar of Bray. The story is told with some variations; but the fact is not doubted. The excavation through which the Railway is continued, from about a mile beyond the Windsor road for 5 miles, excludes all objects from the view, and the ride is for that distance by no means pleasant, the beautiful country through which it is carried being completely barred out by the monotonous mounds of earth that line its sides: the roads now crossed, are consequently carried over the line and conduct to the seats hereinafter named. $\frac{1}{2}$ mile distant on left of Shoppenhanger Lane is Heywood Lodge, 1 mile distant on right of it Stubbings, and 2 miles distant Hall Place. $\frac{1}{4}$ mile distant on left of the White Waltham road is Shottesbrook Park, a beautifully wooded domain that surrounds a stately mansion, the seat of the Vansittart family. 1 mile distant on right of the Waltham St. Lawrence road is Bear Place. This is an elegant mansion, with wings, pleasantly situated on an elevated spot, in a fine woodland country: the grounds, tufted with trees, exhibit an agreeable diversity of surface, and the views, particularly towards the south and east, are extensive and beautiful. At the Waltham St. Lawrence road, the Railway enters on the Waycock Field, an ancient Roman highway, passing immediately on left of Castle Hill, formerly a considerable fort. On right of the line, between the White Waltham and Waltham St. Lawrence roads, and north of the Bath road (that here runs at no great distance on right of the Railway), rise the finely wooded eminences known as the Ashley and Bowsey hills. They form a fine feature in the landscape of the beautiful country by which they are surrounded, and from their height, which is considerable, are visible for many miles, being clearly discernible, in fine weather, from Hampstead Heath, near London, at a distance of 36 miles: they are, however, altogether excluded from the view till the arrival of the train at the Ruscombe embankment, from whence, looking eastward, they suddenly present themselves. On left of Ruscombe is Ruscombe House, and 1 mile distant Stanlake House. 1 mile distant on right of Ruscombe, at Hare Hatch, is Scarletts, and 3½ miles distant on the Henly road, upon the right, Park Place, the seat of E. Fuller Maitland, Esq. The mansion is delightfully situated on an eminence, sheltered by extensive plantations from the severity of the winds. It is elegantly furnished. The grounds possess all the features characteristic of beauty: they consist of a fine intermixture of hill and dale, plentifully stocked with woods and ornamented by several buildings, one of which, a Druid's temple, brought from the Isle of Jersey, is a curious relic of antiquity. A subterraneous passage leads to a valley bordered with cypress, containing a grand representation of a Roman amphitheatre falling into decay. The prospects are delightfully varied and extensive, and the river Thames, seen in many parts to great advantage, considerably heightens the beauty of the scene.

From the Twyford station, situated in an isolated part of the county of Wilts, the Railway continued in a direct line, emerges from the excavation, and, carried forward by embankment, soon crosses the Slake stream and Loddon river, and re-enters Berkshire, when with a gentle bend to the Bath road, which is carried over the line, it arrives, through a cutting of tremendous depth, at Sonning, on right of which is Holme Park.* About a mile beyond the Bath road, the Railway enters on an embankment that affords a good view of the river Thames and the country on its Oxfordshire side; the land rising suddenly on left, excluding from the view the following, which here form, as it were, a complete cluster of villas: Early Court, Woodly Lodge, ½ mile distant; and Maiden Early, 1½ mile distant, near which is White Knights.

From 33 mile-stone in the Sonning excavation, the Railway, carried on a descent of 4 feet in a mile, soon crosses the Kennett, from whence, constructed on a level embankment, it is carried between the town and the Thames to

* The seat of R. Palmer, Esq.

THE READING STATION,

A PRINCIPAL ONE, DISTANT FROM LONDON 35½ MILES, FROM BATH 70¾ MILES, FROM BRISTOL 82½ MILES.—Journey resumed page 15.

2 miles distant on right of Reading is Caversham Park, and 2½ miles distant, Caversham Grove. 1 mile distant on left of Reading is Coley Park, 1½ mile distant Southcote House, and 7 miles distant Strathfieldsaye, Duke of Wellington.

READING.

Reading, a market and borough town of Berkshire, is the chief town of the county, and by much the largest and most considerable for trade and commerce. It is situate on the river Kennett, near its junction with the Thames, and stands on two small eminences, rising with a gentle acclivity from the vale of the Kennett. The surrounding country is also agreeably diversified with an intermixture of hill and dale, wood and water, and ornamented with a number of elegant seats. The town (which is situate at a distance from London of 39 miles by road, by railway, 35½ miles) is in the form of an equilateral triangle: it chiefly consists of four principal streets, crossed by various other smaller ones, with a moderate sized market-place in the centre: the approach from London has also been greatly improved, by the formation of a new road that leads directly into the heart of the town. The principal streets are spacious, and well paved and lighted, and the houses, chiefly of brick, which are of a mixed character, lay claim, the modern ones in particular, to great respectability, the London style being here generally adopted. The prospect from the Forbery, a beautiful outwork N. E. of the town, and now used as a public walk, is very extensive, commanding a fine view over a large portion of Oxfordshire. The ancient churches, three in number, are respectively dedicated to St. Mary, St. Lawrence, and St. Giles. St. Mary's is regarded as the most ancient, and is generally admired for its tessellated tower; to these a new church, dedicated to St. John, has recently been added by the Parliamentary commissioners. Here are also two episcopal chapels, a Roman catholic church, and places of worship for almost every class of dissenters; sectarianism, indeed, being said, and perhaps with truth, to prevail to a greater extent in Reading than in any other town in the kingdom. Of the public buildings of Reading, the town-hall was rebuilt in 1785, at an expense of 1800*l.*, and now forms a noble room 100 feet long: adjoining it is a spacious council-chamber, which contains portraits of Queen Elizabeth, considered as a good likeness, Archbishop Laud, and other benefactors to, or natives of, the town and neighbourhood. The County

Hospital was erected by subscription in 1838, and is entirely supported by voluntary contributions. The County Gaol is a spacious building, erected, on the site of the abbey, in 1793; it comprises a commodious house for the keeper, a room for the reception of the magistrates, a neat chapel, an infirmary, day-rooms, and airy yards for the prisoners, and a treadmill. The town gaol, in conjunction with the police office, was formerly a priory. The other public buildings are the new market-house, a theatre (rendered unsuccessful by the prevalence of sectarianism), and baths. Of the once celebrated abbey of Reading little now remains but fragments of massive walls, composed of flint and gravel. The walls, which are in some parts 8 feet thick, were formerly cased with stone, which has long since been removed for different purposes. The building appears to have occupied a circumference of nearly half a mile. It was a very magnificent structure, and was founded by Henry I., for the maintenance of Benedictines and refreshment of travellers. It was commenced in 1121, completed in 1125, and consecrated, in 1164, by St. Thomas à Beckett, in presence of the king and many of the nobility. This was one of the richest religious houses in the kingdom, and of the class called mitred abbeys, whose abbots sat in parliament. Among the important privileges conferred upon it by the founder were those of coining money, conferring knighthood, holding fairs, trying and punishing criminals, &c. Two councils are recorded to have been held here, the one in the reign of King John, the other in the time of Edward I. At the dissolution, in 1539, the revenues were valued at the sum of 1938*l.* The commissioners also found considerable quantities of plate, jewels, and other valuable articles. The last abbot was attainted for high treason, for refusing to deliver up the abbey, and, together with two monks, was hanged, drawn, and quartered. A noble gateway, and a portion of the hall, now used as a school-room, are nearly all that at present remain of this formerly magnificent fabric. Various charitable institutions have been founded at different times in Reading, of which the principal is a legacy of 7500*l.*, bequeathed, in 1624, by Mr. Kendrick, for erecting a building for the joint purpose of employing the poor, and introduction of the woollen trade; but this establishment, called the Oracle, did not fulfil the benevolent intentions of the founder; its success is said to have been defeated by the very means adopted, with a mistaken view, to its support; and the building is at present occupied by sacking manufacturers, sail-cloth weavers, pin-makers, &c.; the remaining portion being used as a lumber-room, and a receptacle for the broken looms employed in the woollen trade at its first introduction here. The royal grammar school was founded, in the reign of Henry VII., by one of the abbots, endowed by Queen Elizabeth, and further enriched by Archbishop Laud, who was a native of Reading, and a great benefactor to the town. He considerably enhanced the value of the living of St. Lawrence, and increased the salary of the master of the grammar school, that, under the superintendence of the late Dr. Valpy, attained great eminence. Two scholarships at Oxford were annexed to the school by Sir Thomas White. A bluecoat school, a handsome building, with a revenue of 1000*l.* a year, for the maintenance of forty-seven boys, was founded in 1646. Besides these there are national schools, a Lancastrian school, a school of industry, infant and Sunday schools, some almshouses, and numerous small donations for beneficial purposes. Reading is not a manufacturing town, but is advantageously situated for trade, the Thames affording the means of transport to the metropolis for articles of bulk, and the Kennett rendered navigable westward as far as Newbury, whence the Kennett and Avon canal, opening a communication with Bath, Bristol, and the Severn, afford great facilities to commercial pursuit. The trade is accordingly very considerable, and consists chiefly in the exportation of the rude produce of the surrounding country, that abounds in the finest wheat, in timber, oak bark, wool, corn, cheese, and malt, and in the import, for its supply, of all the articles of daily consumption. The flour-mills are chiefly situated on two streams, which branch off from the Kennett near the town, and are in constant work, as the reader will readily imagine, when informed that, independent of the flour necessary for a town containing a population of not less than 17,000, 20,000 sacks of that article are sent annually to the metropolis. Here are also iron founderies, extensive breweries, and yards for barge and boat building. Prior to the introduction of the Railway system, the carrying trade of Reading was considerable. The town being situate on the great line of road from London to Bath and Bristol, from its extensive connexion with mail, stage-coach, and posting establishments, all maintained on a great scale, added to the expenditure of travellers, is said to have derived no inconsiderable portion of its revenues, the loss of which, and it is irreparable, will long be felt. The inhabitants, on the whole, consist of tradesmen, farmers, corn-factors, a few manufacturers, and many genteel families. Reading has its literary institution and reading-room; a philosophical society, with a library of 300 volumes, and a small museum; a horticultural society and amateur musical society; and the races, held in August, on Bulmarsh Heath, are well attended. The corporation at present consists of a mayor, recorder, six aldermen, and twelve burgesses. The police is established upon the metropolitan plan. It sends two members to parliament, and has exercised this privilege from tne earliest period of parliamentary history. Reading is a place of great antiquity, though its origin is unknown. It was inhabited by the Saxons many years before the invasion of the Danes, and appears to have had two castles, one of which stood upon the spot where the abbey was founded. In the years 1263, 1440, 1451, and 1452, parliaments were held here, the last having been adjourned hither on account of the plague. The parliament was again adjourned from Westminster, on account of the plague, in 1466; and from the same cause Michaelmas term was kept here, by the temporary removal of the courts of law and equity to Reading. In 1642 the town was garrisoned by the troops of the Parliament, but their commander withdrew with precipitation on the approach of the king; and it was held by the royal party until the siege of 1643 by the Earl of Essex, when Sir Arthur Ashton being wounded, he surrendered on rather unfavourable terms, for which he was condemned to death by a court-martial, but pardoned on account of his former services; and in 1644 the king withdrew the garrison to defend Oxford. Reading, situate in a fine sporting country, at a distance of only 11 miles from Windsor, and within easy reach of the royal hunt, presents an ample field for amusement to the admirers of the horse, the dog, and gun; others, indisposed to these robust pursuits, however, may "the path of pleasure trace" in the many delightful walks with which the vicinity abounds: while lovers of the angle will find good fishing in the Thames. The market-days are Wednesday and Saturday; the first is chiefly for provisions, but the last, for corn, the sale of which is considerable, is of far more importance. The fairs of Reading are held on the 2d of February, 1st of May, 25th of July, and 21st and 22d of September; the July and September fairs, the former for horses, and the latter for horses and cheese, are the best frequented; of the latter article 40,000*l.* worth has occasionally been pitched. Inns. Bear, Crown.

Quitting Reading, the Railway, carried forward by a level embankment across the valley of the Thames, at no great distance from that river on the right, the Oxford road running on its left, for a distance of about 2 miles, the road and river there converging, form a narrow defile, through which the train proceeds to the Roebuck excavation, that, succeeded by an embankment, carries it to the cutting through Purley Park, of considerable depth, from which, emerging, it reaches by embankment

THE PANGBOURNE STATION.

AN INTERMEDIATE ONE, DISTANT FROM LONDON $40\frac{3}{4}$ MILES, FROM BATH, $65\frac{1}{2}$ MILES, FROM BRISTOL $77\frac{1}{4}$ MILES. — Journey resumed page 17.

The embankment upon which the Railway is carried along

the valley of the Thames to the Roebuck excavation affords a good view of the country on either side, but particularly upon the right on the Oxfordshire side of the river, where the Mapledurham hills, ranged in soft and beautiful variety, rise from the margin of the Thames. Through the thick woods that in some places crown the tops of these elevations, and, in others, beetle down to their base, are cut walks prolific of the most captivating prospects; indeed this part of Oxfordshire is admirably adapted to the taste of the pictorial traveller, being fertile in subjects for the employment of the pencil. At the foot of the Mapledurham hills lies Mapledurham House, an ancient mansion in the Elizabethan style. It is seated on an extensive lawn and approached by an avenue of elms. During the civil war, Mapledurham House was fortified by its proprietor, Sir Charles Blount, in aid of the royal cause, when the town of Reading apprehended a siege. It was courageously defended when attacked by the Parliamentarians, but was at length compelled to submit. The Purley Park excavation, as a matter of course, excludes from observation all sight of that delightful domain; but from the embankment beyond it, the richly-wooded eminences of Oxfordshire, skirting the Thames, again present themselves. At the foot of these, on the margin of the river, stands Hardwick House. Northward of Hardwick House is Collins End, in which is a small publichouse once honoured with the presence of King Charles, who, during his residence at Caversham, rode hither under the escort of a troop of horse. Bowls were then a fashionable amusement, and the village inn possessed a bowling green, occasionally the resort of the neighbouring gentry: here the king is said to have forgotten his sorrows for a time, and amused himself with the exercise of the place. About $\frac{1}{2}$ mile before the Pangbourne Station, on left, stands Purley Hall, a mansion in the heavy formal style, erected by Mr. Hawes, a gentleman deeply implicated in the South Sea scheme. 1 mile distant from Pangbourne, on left, is De la Bere, formerly a seat of the Abbots of Reading; and 3 miles distant is Englefield House, the seat of Richard Benyon de Beauvoir, Esq.

On right of Pangbourne, across the Thames, is Walliscote, long the residence of the late Sir John Simeon, and at no great distance from it Coombe Lodge, an elegant modern mansion. The grounds of Coombe Lodge, comparatively of modern creation, are indebted for their present picturesque and beautiful appearance to a former possessor, who here effected all that art could accomplish. The meander of the Thames, on the margin of which they are seated, here assumes the tranquil semblance of a lake, on the glassy bosom of which is reflected a weighty mass of foliage, from the Berkshire side of the river; beyond this is beheld a gay and countless succession of hills smiling in cultivation or abounding in wood and natural verdure.

FROM PANGBOURNE STATION TO THE GORING STATION.

From the Pangbourne Station, the Railway, carried forward in a north-west direction, pursuing a course parallel with the turnpike road to Wallingford, at no great distance from the Thames, and continued on a rise of 4 feet in a mile by alternate excavation and embankment, that occasionally affords good views of the river, in a distance of rather more than $1\frac{3}{4}$ mile, crosses the turnpike road, and passing Basildon Park upon the left, is thence borne over the valley by a level embankment, gradually approaching the river, passing the village of Basildon on the right to the viaduct over the Thames, $43\frac{1}{2}$ miles from London. Here the Railway, quitting Berkshire, enters the county of Oxford, and in $\frac{3}{4}$ mile further arrives at

THE GORING STATION.

AN INTERMEDIATE ONE, DISTANT FROM LONDON $44\frac{1}{4}$ MILES, FROM BATH 62 MILES, BRISTOL $73\frac{3}{4}$ MILES.—Journey resumed below.

Goring is an insignificant village, seated on the margin of the Thames, that, with Streatly, upon the Berkshire bank of the river, of no great importance, are much subject to inundation in the winter, when the river, overflowing its banks, lays waste the country in the vicinity. From the Goring Station, the vicinity of which is nowise remarkable, if we except the disjointed remains of an Augustine nunnery, founded here in the reign of Henry II., the Railway, carried forward in a northern direction, with a gradual sweep, chiefly through deep cutting for $1\frac{1}{4}$ mile, reaches an embankment that carries it across the valley to South Stoke, from whence, bending gradually towards the Thames, it crosses, for the last time, that noble river, and, in less than $\frac{1}{2}$ a mile, arrives at the turnpike road from Reading, through Wallingford to Oxford, and

THE WALLINGFORD ROAD, OR MOULSFORD STATION.

A PRINCIPAL ONE, DISTANT FROM LONDON $47\frac{1}{4}$ MILES, FROM BATH 59 MILES, FROM BRISTOL $70\frac{3}{4}$ MILES, FROM WALLINGFORD $2\frac{3}{4}$ MILES.—Journey resumed page 18.

On left of the Basildon embankment is Basildon Park, the seat of James Morrison, Esq. The mansion, a magnificent building, was erected from designs by Mr. Carr, of York, and is constructed on the principle of Wentworth House in that county. The walls of the grand saloon were painted in imitation of basso relievo by Monsieur de Bruin, and the ceiling, richly ornamented, is executed in a very beautiful manner. The apartments throughout are splendidly furnished. The park is enlivened by numerous herds of deer, and commands some rich prospects of the windings of the Thames, and of the surrounding country. The grounds are disposed with great taste, the gardens abound with aromatic shrubs, and the hot-houses teem with the choicest fruits of the warmer climates. On right of the Basildon embankment is beheld the Thames, backed by the finely wooded eminences of Oxfordshire, that, rising suddenly from the margin of that noble river, cast their dark shadows in the passing stream; 2 miles distant from the Wallingford Station, on right, upon the margin of the Thames (in Oxfordshire), but otherwise unfavourably situate, is Mongewell, long the seat of the Bishop of Durham. From the vicinity of Mongewell the Roman vallum, termed Grims Dike, runs in a south-east direction towards Nuffield.

WALLINGFORD.

Wallingford is an ancient town, pleasantly situated on the banks of the Thames, over which there is a stately stone bridge of 19 arches. Near the river side stands the remains of its ancient castle, which was formerly deemed impregnable, and in the reign of King Stephen sustained a considerable siege against that usurper. This place was also surrounded by walls, and is said to have possessed 12 churches, of which 3 only remain, St. Mary's, St. Leonard's, and St. Peters. The latter is a modern edifice, and has a very singular tower. Though the original consequence and magnificence of Wallingford have been greatly diminished by various circumstances, among which may be noticed the building of Culham and Dorchester bridges, still it is a place of importance, consisting of 2 principal streets, and has of late years much increased, both in population and extent. This town contains several dissenting meeting-houses, and has a convenient and well-built Town Hall, in which the assizes have been sometimes held, and the business of the quarter sessions for the borough is always executed. Wallingford sends one member to parliament, and has a market on Friday. Inn, the Lamb.

WALLINGFORD ROAD STATION TO STEVENTON STATION.

Quitting the Wallingford Road Station $\frac{1}{2}$ mile distant, on left of which lies the little village of Moulsford, the Railway, continued on a rise of 4 feet in a mile, and carried forward in a line tolerably direct, at first through cutting of great depth, reaches an embankment that carries it to Cholsey, a large and straggling village chiefly remarkable for a monastery, founded in 986 by Ethelred, in atonement for the murder of his brother King Edward the Martyr. From Cholsey, carried forward on a rise of 3 feet 6 inches in a mile, with a gradual bend, chiefly by embankment, in a distance of about 1½ mile, the Railway reaches South Moreton, a small village, North Moreton being ½ mile on right, and Aston Tyrrel 1½ mile distant on left of the line. The appearance of the country, from the Wallingford to the Steventon Station, is decidedly dissimilar to that bordering the Railway between the former and Reading, and the observant tourist will at once perceive the change; the Railway now pursues its course through a country purely agricultural, that consisting, till within a few years, in many instances, of open common-fields, have by successive enclosure acts been converted to the more beneficial purposes of cultivation, and the land chiefly divided into large farms, being indifferently wooded, presents, in consequence, a somewhat monotonous appearance. From South Moreton (2½ miles distant, on right of which rises Wittenham Hill, where are the traces of a Roman encampment,) carried forward, in a line nearly direct at first, through an excavation of a mile in length, the line then enters on an embankment, an agreeable contrast to the cutting just quitted, by which, carried across Hagbourne Marsh, and the Wantage and Wallingford road, it reaches, in a distance of about 1 mile more, nearly to Dudcot, distant from London 53 miles.* From Dudcot, where it commences a rise of 7 feet in a mile, the Railway enters an excavation of ¼ a mile in length: on its emerging thence, bending gradually to the westward, it is constructed by embankment to the 55 mile stone, when, entering an excavation, it is carried past Milton, ¼ mile beyond which the train arrives at

THE STEVENTON STATION.

A PRINCIPAL ONE, DISTANT FROM LONDON 56 MILES, FROM BATH 50¼ MILES, FROM BRISTOL 62 MILES, FROM ABINGDON 3 MILES, FROM OXFORD 10 MILES. — Journey resumed page 20.

1 mile distant, on left of Steventon, is Milton House and Milton Hill; 2 miles distant is Hendred House; 2 miles distant, on right of Steventon, at Sutton Courtney, is the Abbey Manor House.

* From this point it is proposed to carry a Branch Railway to Oxford, distance of about 10 miles.

ABINGDON.

Abingdon is said to derive its name from an abbey formerly existing here, and traditionally reported to have been of great magnificence, so much so that, at the time of the Conquest, its wealth and grandeur are said to have been equal to any similar foundation in England. The town (which stands at the confluence of the Ock with the Thames, at its junction with the Wilts and Berks canal,) consists of several streets, which centre in a spacious area, where the market is held. The Market House and Town Hall is a very remarkable structure, being built with Ashler or free-stone, rough as it comes from the quarry. It appears to have been erected about the commencement of the last century. The hall is supported by arches and lofty pillars. Here the summer assizes are held, the Lent assizes being held at Reading. The corporation consists of a mayor, two bailiffs, nine aldermen, and sixteen assistants. It sends one member to parliament. It has two churches; one, the church of the abbey, dedicated to St. Nicholas, the other dedicated to St. Helen. To the last is annexed the chapelry of Drayton. St. Helen's is adorned with an elegant spire. Here are two hospitals, one for 6, the other for 13 poor men, and as many poor women, a free-grammar and charity schools. Much business is done here in the malting line, greatly facilitated by means of the Thames, which is navigable to London. Here also is a manufactory of sail-cloth, sacking, &c. The markets are held on Monday and Friday, and are reckoned among the most considerable in England for grain. Inns, Crown and Thistle and Queen's Arms.

From the Steventon Station, where commences the Vale of White Horse, carried forward in a line tolerably direct upon the ascent (on which it entered at Dudcot), the Railway reaches in a distance of 2 miles, chiefly through excavation, West Hendred Wood, from whence, continued by embankment on a level, in $\frac{3}{4}$ mile more, it arrives at the Wilts and Berks canal, borne over over which it reaches by a rise of 7 feet in a mile, at $59\frac{3}{4}$ miles from London, the turnpike road from Abingdon to Wantage (the former being $7\frac{1}{4}$ miles distant on right, the latter 2 miles distant on left of the line); $\frac{1}{4}$ mile beyond this it crosses the river Ock. On left of the river Ock is the village of Grove, and 1 mile distant on right East and West Hanney. From the river Ock, the Railway, carried forward in a course nearly direct, reaches by alternate excavation and embankment, in a distance of rather more than $1\frac{1}{2}$ mile, the road to Denchworth, a village on right of the line, $1\frac{1}{4}$ mile beyond which it arrives at the Wantage and Farringdon road and

THE FARRINGDON ROAD STATION.

A PRINCIPAL ONE, DISTANT FROM LONDON 63 MILES, FROM BATH 43¼ MILES, FROM BRISTOL 55 MILES, FROM FARRINGDON 5¼ MILES, FROM WANTAGE 3¾ MILES.—Journey resumed page 23.

The country from the Steventon to the Farringdon road Station strongly resembles, particularly on right of the line, the approach to Steventon from the Wallingford Station, the Railway being bordered on that side by large tracts of arable land, not many years since converted to the purposes of cultivation, but still distinguished by the appellation of the villages in their vicinity, such as Steventon Field, Draycot Field, East and West Hanney Field, through which at a distance the Ock pursues its tortuous course to the Thames. In this direction the view is bounded by the high grounds about Kingston Bagpuze, westward of which the range of hills that, commencing in the vicinity of Oxford and extending thence to Farringdon, terminate the view, Farringdon High Trees, on Farringdon Hill, a well-known landmark to the surrounding country, forming the most prominent feature of the prospect. From the Steventon to the Farringdon Station, the view is bounded on the left by gently swelling eminences that descend in slopes to the valley through which the Railway is carried in its course. 2½ miles distant on left of West Hendred Wood, seated on an eminence, is Lockinge Park. 3 miles distant from Farringdon Station on left is East Challow, 3 miles distant on right Shellingford Castle and Hatford. 6 miles distant is Pusey House, 7 miles distant is Buckland House, and Wadley House, and at Farringdon, Farringdon House.

FARRINGDON.

This town is situate about 2 miles from the Thames, on the west side of Farringdon Hill. The church, which stands on the hill, is an ancient and spacious edifice, displaying specimens of different styles of architecture: it was built in the form of a cross, but with a double transept. In the organ gallery (formerly the rood-loft), are various niches and small recesses, some of which contain carved busts of heads of religious orders. Part of the spire was destroyed during the civil wars; the remainder is but very little higher than the body of the church, within which are several fine monuments; and, on the south side, that of the unknown founder. Robert, Earl of Gloucester, erected a castle here in the reign of King Stephen; but the monarch, after some resistance, reduced and levelled it with the ground. The site of it appears to have been granted by King John, in the year 1202, with all its appurtenances, to build an abbey of the Cistercian order. In the reign of Edward VI., the possessions of the abbey, with the manor of Farringdon, &c., were granted to Thomas, Lord Seymour; but reverting to the crown after his execution, were, in the second year of Queen Mary, bestowed on Sir Frederick Englefield. In the immediate vicinity of the town is Farringdon Hill, an eminence rising gradually from the vale of White Horse, and surmounted by a small grove which forms a kind of landmark for the surrounding counties, being seen at a great distance in every direction. This charming place commands a rich and extensive view over parts of Oxfordshire, Gloucestershire, and Wiltshire, in addition to the whole of the beautiful and interesting vale beneath. " But the muse of Mr. Pye, who on this spot strung her lyre with melody, has snatched the fruitful subject from the attempts of prose, and by interweaving the beauties it owes to nature, with the embellishments it receives from art, and the interest it derives from history, has precluded description from all but those who have been permitted to partake of the Heliconian stream." Near Farringdon is a camp of a circular form, 200 yards in diameter, with a ditch 20 yards wide. About 30 years ago, in levelling the north rampart, human bones and coals were found, and similar relics are frequently discovered in digging for peat, in the swampy ground about 1 mile south of the hill. This camp is supposed to be of Danish origin, and the neighbouring flat the theatre of battle on which Alfred won his 12th victory. Farringdon House is the seat of W. Bennet, Esq. This is an elegant edifice, standing in a small park, on the north side of the town, the view of which is judiciously excluded by lofty elms and plantations. The grounds are agreeable from their inequality of surface, and sufficiently covered with wood. During the civil wars, the ancient mansion was garrisoned for Charles I., and was one of the last places that surrendered, its defenders having repulsed a large party of the parliament forces but a short time before the reduction of Oxford. This attack was attended with a singular circumstance;—Sir Robert Pye, the owner of the house, who married Anne, the eldest daughter of Hampden, and was colonel in the parliament army, being himself the person who headed the assailants. It was in this action that the spire of Farringdon Church was beaten down by the artillery. Inns: Bell, Crown.

WANTAGE,

A market-town of Berkshire, is situate at the foot of a ridge of hills that borders the vale of White Horse on its southern side and shelters the town. It is very irregularly built, chiefly consisting of two principal streets, the houses of which, with a very few exceptions, are mean in character. It is watered by the Ock, a small stream, that in its course from hence to Abingdon, where it falls into the Thames, turns several mills. The church, a spacious and handsome cruciform structure in the Gothic style, stands near the centre of the town. This place is governed by a chief constable, and the petty sessions are held every Saturday. The inhabitants are chiefly employed in agriculture, the manufacture of coarse cloth, and in the flour and malt trade, Wantage being the centre of a large agricultural district. A branch of the Wilts and Berks Canal comes up to the town, by means of which coal is received, and flour, corn, and malt are sent to different parts of the kingdom, chiefly to Bath, Bristol, and London. The market, held on Saturday, principally for corn, is considerable; and here are four annual fairs. Wantage is celebrated in history as the birth-place of Alfred the Great. In this neighbourhood, that affords a fine field for the antiquary, the footsteps of various nations may be discovered, but they are all imperfect: Roman works have been demolished to make room for Saxon, and these again have been superseded by the devices of modern times. Wantage, always a dull country town, has been rendered more so by the introduction of Railway travelling, that, having swept off its carrying trade, has inflicted considerable injury, leaving it, except on market-days, a perfect picture of inactivity. Inn, the Bear.

FROM FARRINGDON ROAD STATION TO SHRIVENHAM STATION.

From the Farringdon Road station, the Railway, continued in a direct line on the ascent of 7 feet in a mile, arrives, in a distance of $2\frac{1}{2}$ miles, chiefly by embankment, at Baulking. A little before this it enters a short, but deep, cutting, emerging whence it reaches an embankment of rather more than 3 miles in length, on which it is taken very near the Wilts and Berks canal, with a gradual bend, to the Uffington road. From the Uffington road it is carried forward, with an easy sweep, upon an embankment, to the southward, for about $\frac{3}{4}$ mile, thence, in a course south-west, to the Wilts and Berks canal, which it crosses, and thence to the Compton Beauchamp road, 2 miles beyond which, passing Beckett Park on the right, the beautiful seat of Lord Barrington, it arrives at

THE SHRIVENHAM STATION.

AN INTERMEDIATE ONE, DISTANT FROM LONDON $70\frac{3}{4}$ MILES, FROM BATH $35\frac{1}{2}$ MILES, FROM BRISTOL $47\frac{1}{4}$ MILES. — Journey resumed at page 25.

From the Farringdon Road station the Railway traverses the

vale of White Horse, through which, bordered on the left by a lofty range of hills that descend in graceful slopes and sweeps to their base, it is carried to Shrivenham. The summit of this ridge, that here ascends to a height of 833 feet above the level of the sea, and is crossed by a very ancient track, not inaptly termed the Ridgeway, extends from near Letcombe into Wiltshire, affords a fine field for the antiquary, abounding as it does in the remains of Roman and British camps, the records of British valour and conquest, and re-establishment of liberty, while its sides, assuming every variety of form, from the towering cliff to the finely swelling eminence and hollow comb, constitute a boundary bold and beautiful in the extreme. $2\frac{1}{2}$ miles distant from Baulking, on left, is Kingston Lisle. Here is the celebrated Blowing Stone, deemed a great curiosity; it has several holes in it of various sizes, three of which are at the top; and by blowing into any one of these a very loud noise is produced, somewhat similar to the bellowing of a calf, or the first effort of a beginner on the French horn; and the effect produced is so powerful as to be heard at Farringdon-High Trees, a distance of nearly 6 miles in a right line. $\frac{3}{4}$ mile distant, on left of the Uffington road, is the village of Uffington; and $2\frac{1}{4}$ miles distant the celebrated White Horse, formed by order of Alfred, as a token of the signal victory which he obtained over the Danes at Ashdown, in this neighbourhood, in the year 871. A short remove from the White Horse, occupying a bold promontory, and in a commanding position, is Uffington Castle, the supposed site of the Danish encampment. About 2 miles distant, on left of the Compton-Beauchamp road, is Compton House; and upon the hill, overlooking that village, is Hardwell Camp, where King Ethelred is conjectured to have slept the night before the engagement. $2\frac{1}{2}$ miles southward of this is a roundish entrenchment called Ashbury Camp, or King Alfred's Castle. About 1 mile westward of Hardwell Camp, situate near the Ridgeway, are the remains of an ancient cromlech, called Wayland Smith's Forge, of whom, as noticed by Sir Walter Scott in his novel of Kenilworth, a singular tradition is still related by the peasantry of the neighbourhood, who maintain that this mysterious spot was formerly inhabited by an invisible blacksmith, who good naturedly shod any horse that was left there, provided a piece of money was deposited on a stone as a reward for his services; on the other hand, Mr. Wise, the antiquary, considers it a monument erected by the Danes to the memory of King Basseg, who, falling with other chiefs in the dreadful battle with Alfred, was buried here; but thinks the chiefs were interred in a spot termed the Seven Barrows, although more than twenty of those tumuli may still be counted. 2 miles distant, on right of Shrivenham station, is Warneford Place, long the seat of the family of Warneford, and Watchfield House. 3 miles distant Coleshill House, the seat of the Earl of Radnor; and 5 miles distant, occupying an elevated position, and overlooking the Thames, Buscot Park, the beautiful seat of Pryse Pryse, Esq.

From Shrivenham Station, through an excavation of about $\frac{3}{4}$ mile, the Railway reaches Bourton, from whence, by an embankment and viaduct of 2 miles in length, it is carried over the valley of the Cole, the river, and Wilts and Berks canal, to a cutting through which, in less than $1\frac{1}{2}$ mile, it arrives at Stratton Green, a considerable village, situate on the Roman road, that, commencing at Cirencester, passes through Cricklade, and continued to Wanborough, 2 miles south of Stratton, then separates into two branches, one continuing by Baydon to Speen, the other by Ogbourne, Tottenham, and Marton, through Chute Park, to Winchester. From Stratton Green, carried forward in a gently waving line, in less than $\frac{1}{4}$ mile, the Railway crosses the turnpike road from Highworth, $6\frac{1}{2}$ miles on right to Swindon, 2 miles on left, from whence it reaches, by alternate excavation and embankment, the Cricklade and Swindon road; $\frac{3}{4}$ miles beyond this, it arrives, by embankment, at the North Wilts canal, the junction of this line with the Cheltenham and Great Western Union Railway. the summit of the Great Western, 268 feet above the London depôt*, and

THE SWINDON STATION.

A PRINCIPAL ONE, DISTANT FROM LONDON 77 MILES, FROM BATH $29\frac{1}{4}$ MILES, FROM BRISTOL 41 MILES, FROM CHELTENHAM BY RAILWAY $42\frac{1}{4}$ MILES, FROM CIRENCESTER 18 MILES, FROM SWINDON $1\frac{1}{4}$ MILE, FROM CRICKLADE 7 MILES, FROM HIGHWORTH 6 MILES.—Journey resumed page 27.

2 miles distant, on right of Stratton Green, at Stanton Fitzwarren, is Stanton; 3 miles distant, on Blunsdon Castle Hill, is a large circular entrenched work, which is generally supposed to have been a Roman encampment, an opinion rendered extremely probable from its proximity to the Roman road that passes immediately under the hill. At Swindon is Swindon House, A. Goddard, Esq., $2\frac{1}{4}$ miles distant from Swindon, on left, is Burdrop Park. 4 miles distant is Liddington Castle, an extensive circular entrenchment, occupying the summit of Beacon Hill, which overlooks the village whence the fortification derives its name. This work, from its lofty position and simple construction, was most likely of British

---

* The rails at that point being 60 feet and 21 parts of an inch above the level of Trinity high water mark at London Bridge.

origin, and is considered by Whitaker to have been the "Mons Badonicus" described by the ancient writers as having been a British outpost of great strength. 4 miles westward of this, and immediately opposite, is Barbury Camp, or Castle, another very large British entrenchment, that, in some respects, resembles that at Liddington, and is said to have been the scene of a sanguinary battle between the West Saxons and the Britons, A. D. 556. The conflict, which is said to have lasted from break of day till night, terminated in the total rout of the Britons, and capture of their fortress, events which secured the annexation of Wiltshire to the West Saxon dominions.

HIGHWORTH.

Highworth is a market town and parish of Wiltshire, situated near the confines of Berkshire, at the distance of 76 miles from London. It comprehends about 10,000 square acres of ground, and, in spiritual matters, is subject to the Dean of Sarum. The town of Highworth occupies very elevated ground, and consequently commands fine views of the adjacent country. The houses are, for the most part, built of stone, and tiled. The church is an ancient building, and consists of a nave, two side aisles, a chancel, and two small monumental oratories, or chapels, with a tower at the west end, which is surmounted by an open balustrade, and four figures for angular pinnacles. It has a corporation, consisting of a mayor, alderman, and council; but their powers are very limited. As it gives name to the hundred in which it stands, some have supposed that it anciently was more important than at present. In Domesday-book it is mentioned under the appellation of "Wrde;" and is stated to have constituted part of the royal domains. Here are held the petty sessions for the Highworth division of the hundred. The market is on Wednesday, and there are three annual fairs. Inn, The King and Queen.

CRICKLADE

Is a market town of Wiltshire, $84\frac{1}{2}$ miles from London. Concerning the origin of this place much diversity of opinion has prevailed among antiquaries and historians; it is situated in a flat tract of country on the southern bank of the Isis or Thames, and consists principally of one long street, in the centre of which stands the town house, supported upon 10 pillars, which appears, from an inscription on the south east side, to have been erected in the year 1569, when the town was, probably, much more extensive than at present. The places of public worship here are the parish churches of St. Sampson and St. Mary, and a methodist chapel. St. Sampson's is a large ancient church, built in the form of a cross, with a handsome tower in the centre, resting upon four pointed arches, and open to a considerable height within; its summit is adorned by an open balustrade, and four angular pinnacles, with niches and pedestals. St. Mary's is an ancient building: the interior consists of a nave and two aisles with a chancel; in its cemetery stands a stone cross, as does also another in the middle of the street. Cricklade is a borough by prescription, and was formerly a populous and flourishing town, though it has shrunk now into a comparatively small one. It first sent members to parliament in the reign of Edward I., and continued to do so, with some intermissions, till the time of Henry VI., since which period the returns have been regular; but a change took place in 1784, confirmed by the reform bill, in the right of voting at elections, which was before confined to residents within the borough, but is now enjoyed by the freeholders of the hundreds of Cricklade, Highworth, Staple, Kingsbridge, and Malmesbury. Market on Saturday. Inns: Swan, White Horse.

SWINDON.

Swindon, a market town of Wiltshire, is agreeably situated on the summit of a considerable eminence, commanding a delightful prospect over parts of Berkshire and Gloucestershire. There is no particular trade carried on here; but, as a number of persons of independent fortune reside in the town, their constant intercourse gives a degree of life to this place, while, at the same time, their mansions contribute, in no small degree, to ornament it. The church stands at the south-east end of the town: this edifice is mean in its architecture, but is neatly fitted up in the interior, and contains several monumental erections. Here is a very respectable free-school. The market is held on Monday, weekly, for corn and other commodities; and on every alternate Monday for cattle, which last is called the Great Market. Here are, besides, five annual fairs; and the petty sessions for Swindon division of the hundred are held in the town. Some very extensive stone quarries are wrought in this neighbourhood, which, together with the pursuits of husbandry, afford sufficient employment for the mass of the inhabitants. Inns: Bell, Goddard Arms.

SWINDON STATION TO WOTTON BASSET STATION.

The line which, from its commencement at London, till its arrival at the summit, has been, with a few exceptions, an almost continued succession of ascents, now proceeds on the opposite principle, and, carried on a descent of 6 feet 6 inches in a mile, crossing the valley, and a tributary of the river Ray, reaches, in another mile, the Wotton Basset and Swindon road, from whence, continued on a level embankment of 1½ mile in length, in a southern direction, it arrives, in about 1½ mile, at the Lydiard Tregoze road, 1 mile distant on right of which is Lydiard Park, the fine seat of Lord Bolingbroke, whose family have resided here since the time of Henry VI. From the Lydiard Tregoze road, where it approaches very near the Wilts and Berks canal, its course is nearly a direct line for about another mile to that navigation, which it passes, and from thence, continued with a gradual bend, it extends in about 1¼ mile more to the Wotton Basset and Marlborough road, and

THE WOTTON BASSET STATION,

A PRINCIPAL ONE, DISTANT FROM LONDON 82¼ MILES, FROM BATH 24 MILES, FROM BRISTOL 35¾ MILES, FROM MALMESBURY 11 MILES, AND FROM WOTTON BASSET ½ MILE. — Journey resumed p. 29.

WOTTON BASSET.

This is an ancient borough, that regularly sent 2 members to parliament since the reign of Henry VI., till the passing of the Reform Bill, when it was disfranchised. It is governed by a mayor, two aldermen, and twelve burgesses, has a market on Tuesday, a monthly market for fat cattle, and 3 annual fairs. The houses are of brick, but covered with thatch; they are principally disposed into one street; in the centre stands the town-hall, market-house, and shambles. A considerable trade in the manufacture of broad cloth was formerly carried on here: though that is discontinued, the town has nevertheless increased in size and importance. The church is an old building, possessing nothing, either in external appearance or internal decoration, to render it worthy of particular notice. In the parish are two free schools for 12 boys, and an equal number of girls; and in the town-hall a curious machine, called a ducking-stool, formerly used for the punishment of female scolds, was for a long time preserved. Inn, Royal Oak.

MALMESBURY.

Malmesbury, a market town of Wiltshire, 96½ miles from London, is pleasantly situated on a peninsulated eminence formed by two streams; some remains of the wall by which it was formerly surrounded still exist at the entrance of the town from Cirencester, which furnish a sufficient specimen of its original strength; it was also defended by a castle, but no relic of the building now remains; yet, from the many hard struggles and bloody contentions, on several occasions, in its defence and capture, it must have been a fortress of considerable importance. Malmesbury consists of three parochial divisions, which include the borough and parish, comprised in four respectable streets. A small market for provisions.

&c. is held on Saturday, and a large and well attended cattle-market on the last Tuesday in every month; but the principal support of the inhabitants is derived from the woollen trade, which is here carried on to a considerable extent. The town appears, by the records, to have been much larger than it is at present, and to have had several churches, only one of which now remains: it has, undoubtedly, been the theatre of several important events connected with history, and the ruins of its once splendid abbey convey an idea of its former extent and grandeur: the abbey-house and market-cross are also objects well worthy the attention of those who have a taste for architectural antiquities. This is a very ancient borough, originally incorporated by Edward the Elder, as early as 916; it now returns one member to parliament, and is governed by a mayor and body corporate. Inn, White Lion.

WOTTON BASSET TO CHIPPENHAM.

From the Wotton Basset Station, continued with a gradual sweep, it is carried by embankment to the Wotton Basset and Calne Road, under which it passes, and is thence taken through a short cutting to an embankment of $1\frac{1}{4}$ miles in length, by which it reaches the margin of the Wilts and Berks canal, round which it bends; and, continued in a line tolerably direct, the embankment passed, enters an excavation that carries it to the 85 mile stone, and summit of the incline, $\frac{1}{4}$ mile beyond which it is crossed by Trow Lane.

The incline, constructed chiefly on an embankment, with a descent of rather more than 50 feet in a mile, affords a good view of the valley beneath, and of the Wilts and Berks Canal, that for some time continues the companion of the Railway. From the foot of the incline, continued through excavation, it is carried to the Calne and Malmesbury road here thrown over the line. $1\frac{1}{4}$ mile distant, on right, is Dantsey, or Dauntsey, House. 1 mile distant from the Calne and Malmesbury road, on left, occupying an elevated position overlooking the Railway, and an extensive tract of country, stands Bradenstoke Priory. This monastic institution was founded about the year 1142, by Walter Eureuse, or de Seresbuie (Salisbury), who dedicated it to the Virgin Mary, and filled it with monks of the Augustine order. After the death of his lady he abandoned the world, and, assuming the habit of a monk, lived there till his death, when he was buried in the priory church. In later times this monastery was united to the Duchy of Lancaster, and, as a part thereof, vested in the crown on the accession of Henry VII. to the throne. It subsequently passed into the hands of the Methuen family, by one of whom it was converted into a private residence, with offices, for a farm. The house, though somewhat modernized by alterations, still preserves the fashion of antiquity in its general features; the style of its architecture is Anglo-Norman, corresponding to the age in which it was erected. The cellars are supported by arches and columns. From the Malmesbury and Calne road the Railway is carried forward, through excavations, with a gradual bend, to the Wilts and Berks canal, a little beyond which it enters on an embankment, upon which, constructed in a direct line, passing, in its way, Thorn End and Christian Malford, a considerable village on right of the line; it is borne across the valley of the Avon to the viaduct over that river, in less than ½ mile beyond which it commences an ascent of 8 feet in a mile; that, continued in a gently waving line, carries it to the Langley Burrell road, 1¾ mile beyond which it extends, by alternate excavation and embankment, with a curvilinear sweep to

THE CHIPPENHAM STATION.

A PRINCIPAL ONE, DISTANT FROM LONDON 93½ MILES, FROM BATH 12¾ MILES, FROM BRISTOL 24½ MILES.—Journey resumed p. 31.

On left of Chippenham station are Monkton House and Ivy House, and 3 miles distant Bow Wood, the magnificent seat of the Marquis of Lansdowne. On right is Harden, Huish Park. 3½ miles distant, Draycot Park; and 6 miles distant, Grittleton House, Joseph Neeld, Esq.

CHIPPENHAM.

Chippenham, a large and ancient borough, is situated in a fine valley, upon the south bank of the river Avon, which makes a bold sweep round the town, and is here crossed by a handsome free-stone bridge. It consists, principally, of one street, above ½ mile in length, nearly in the centre of which stands the town-hall.* The church is a large and ancient edifice, and consists of a nave, south aisle, chancel, and chapel, with a tower and spire. The inhabitants are chiefly engaged in the woollen trade. Chippenham is governed by a mayor, four aldermen, and twelve councillors; sends two members to Parliament, and has a weekly market on Friday: Inn, The Angel.

CALNE.

Calne, seated on the river Marden, is a borough and market-town of Wiltshire, 87 miles from London. It is an ancient borough by prescription, and returned 2 members to Parliament from the 23d of Edward I. till the passing of the Reform Bill, when the number was reduced to 1. It is neat and well-built, and has a good town-hall. The church is an ancient building,

* A handsome modern structure, erected at the expense of Joseph Neeld, Esq.

with a handsome square tower, and a beautiful carved roof. There are three meeting houses for dissenters, and a free-school, recently rebuilt. The chief manufactures are broadcloths, kerseymeres, and serges; and there are several fulling and corn mills on the river. Its trade has been somewhat increased by a branch of the Wilts and Berks canal, that gives it the benefit of an extensive water communication. The neighbourhood has many curious fossils. Population about 5000. Inns, the Lansdowne Arms and White Hart. Market on Tuesday. Fairs, March 6th and July 22d. 3 miles south-east of Calne, the figure of a white horse, cut by direction of Dr. Alsop of Calne, about the year 1780, appears on the side of a chalk hill: it is 157 feet in length, and, from its elevated position, is visible for many miles.

A little beyond the Chippenham Station, the Railway enters on an embankment, that, constructed with a curvilinear sweep, with the exception of two short cuttings, carries it almost to Thingley. The embankment affords a good view of the valley it traverses, and of Notton and Lackham, two seats that lie on left of it. The Bath road through Chippenham is crossed by this embankment, about a mile beyond the latter town. A little before Thingley, ½ a mile beyond which it crosses the road from Corsham to Devizes, the former lying 1¼ mile on right, the latter 11½ miles distant on left of the line, the Railway enters an excavation that, in rather more than 1 mile, carries it to

THE CORSHAM STATION.

AN INTERMEDIATE ONE, DISTANT FROM LONDON 97½ MILES, FROM BATH 8¾ MILES, FROM BRISTOL 20½ MILES. — Journey resumed below.

Corsham is a considerable village on the Bath road. It was formerly a market town, but the market has long been discontinued. An unsuccessful attempt was made to revive it in 1784 by Mr. Methuen, who, with a view to its re-establishment, erected a market-house and town-hall, near the centre of the village. The situation of Corsham is airy and salubrious, and the houses, all built of stone, are principally ranged in one long street. The church is a handsome edifice, with a tower formerly surmounted by a spire, and, beheld from the Bath road, forms a striking object, as does the magnificent mansion of Lord Methuen, whose seat, Corsham House, enriched with a large and valuable collection of paintings (shown on application*), is the great attraction here.

CORSHAM TO BOX.

The excavation through which the Railway is carried past

* On Mondays only, when the family is at home.

Corsham, being of considerable depth, of course excludes it from the view. On right of Corsham is Pickwick, to which Dickens's novel of that name has given no small celebrity; and 1½ mile distant is Hartham Park, an elegant seat, long the residence of Lady James, the friend and correspondent of Sterne. From Corsham, continued upon the rise it commenced after crossing the Avon, 90 miles from London, viz. 8 feet in a mile, in rather less than 1¼ mile beyond Corsham, it gains a short level, at the end of which it enters the Box tunnel, distant from London 98½ miles.

BOX TUNNEL.

This is a stupendous work, by far the greatest of its kind in this or any other country; the following are its dimensions. The entire length is 1 mile and ⅘, 3,168 yards, or 88 yards more than 1¾ of a mile. In width it is 30 feet; and its height, from the line of the rails to the crown of the arch, (which varies according to the nature of the ground excavated,) from 25 to nearly 40 feet. The quantity of material here excavated cannot amount to less than 450,000 cubic yards, and, considering that its course lies principally through lias limestone, Bath stone, and a hard dry quartz, it may unquestionably be pronounced the noblest and boldest specimen of tunnelling that engineering excellence has hitherto achieved. The passage through this elaborately formed gallery is an inclined plane, constructed with a fall of rather more than 50 feet in a mile, and is succeeded by an embankment that affords a good view, and conducts to

THE BOX STATION.

AN INTERMEDIATE ONE, DISTANT FROM LONDON 100½ MILES, FROM BATH 5¾ MILES, FROM BRISTOL 17½ MILES.

Quitting the Box Station, the Railway, continued on the incline, enters an excavation that carries it to Middle Hill Tunnel, 193 yards in length, on right of which is Middle Hill Spa, an unfrequented mineral spring. Quitting the confines of Middle Hill Tunnel, a beautiful view greets the eye, embracing the valley of the Avon and city of Bath, seated in an amphitheatre of hills. To Middle Hill Tunnel, a short embankment and excavation succeeds, the two filling up the space of a mile, when the Railway enters on an embankment, of nearly 2 miles in length, that carries it across the valley, the Box brook and river Avon, passing Bathford upon the right, very nearly to Bathampton. At the commencement of the last embankment on right lies Shockerwick, long the seat of the Wiltshire family, whose ancestor, Walter Wiltshire, from being the driver, became proprietor of the Bath and Bristol waggons, a portion of the carrying trade that owes its ruin to railway travelling. From Bathampton, where it reaches the 104 mile stone, the Railway, carried on a gradual descent, in a direct line, a little to the north of the Kennet and Avon canal, which it reaches by alternate cutting and embankment, then crosses that navigation, and, bending southward, reaches the

BATH STATION.

A PRINCIPAL ONE, DISTANT FROM LONDON $106\frac{1}{4}$ MILES, BRISTOL $11\frac{3}{4}$ MILES.—Journey resumed, page 37.

$1\frac{1}{2}$ mile distant, on left of Bath, lies Prior Park, formerly the seat of Ralph Allen, Esq. (the Allworthy of Fielding's "Tom Jones"), who was proprietor of the Bath stone quarries. The mansion, an elegant structure *, built of that material from designs by Mr. Wood, a gentleman to whose taste and judgment Bath is indebted for many of its embellishments, stands strikingly conspicuous on the declivity of an eminence that rises on the south of Bath, and slopes, in beautiful inequalities, to the Avon, affording charming prospects over the vale of Bath, that city forming the principal object in the centre, backed by the swelling summit of Lansdowne, of itself a magnificent feature. Lansdowne Hill is rendered famous in history by the battle fought there in the year 1643, between the royal army under the Marquis of Hertford and Prince Maurice, and the parliamentary forces, commanded by Sir William Waller. The action was warmly contested for several hours, the victory being finally gained by the king's troops. The number of gentlemen killed in that engagement far exceeded the private soldiers; among them was Sir Beville Grenville, a Cornish gentleman of great interest and reputation, to whose conduct the success of the royal party in Cornwall was chiefly owing. A superb monument of free-stone was erected to his memory on the north declivity of the hill, near the spot on which he fell. About 3 miles distant from Bath, on left, delightfully situated on the west bank of the Avon, at the foot of Claverton Down, stands the village of Claverton, celebrated as having been the rectory of the Rev. Richard Graves, M. A., author of the Spiritual Quixote, who purchased the advowson from the trustees of Ralph Allen, Esq. of Prior Park.

BATH.

Bath, justly esteemed the most elegant city in the kingdom, is situated in a delightful vale, and on the acclivity of a hill, facing the south and south-east, in the north-east extremity of the

* Now the residence of the Roman Catholic Vicar Apostolic of the western district.

county of Somerset, near the borders of Gloucester and Wilts; 12 miles from Bristol, 87½ from Exeter, 19 from Wells, 38 from Salisbury, 42 from Gloucester, 60 from Oxford, and 106¼ by Railway from London. It is surrounded by an amphitheatre of hills, of considerable elevation, intersected only by the river Avon, which is here of considerable magnitude, and encircles or passes through a great portion of the city and its suburbs, being navigable hence to Bristol; the Kennet and Avon canal, which here falls into the Avon, completes the inland communication by water from London, through the counties of Middlesex, Bucks, Berks, Hants, Wilts, Somerset, and Gloucester, to this city and Bristol.

The antiquity of Bath is beyond the reach of research; but all its ancient names, as handed down to us, were derived from its waters, that, though known to the Britons, were not greatly in repute till the arrival of the Romans in this country under Julius Cæsar, 44 years before Christ.

To this enlightened people the praise is due of fully appreciating their value and properties, of which the relics of magnificent baths and other public buildings erected by them in this place bear ample testimony. Amongst these, preserved and classed in a building erected for the purpose, are the remains and fragments of columns, cornices, and capitals of a magnificent temple dedicated to Minerva by Julius Agricola, on the present site of the great pump-room. In 444, when the Romans left this country, the city extended 12,000 feet in length and 1150 in breadth, and was surrounded by a wall 9 feet thick and 20 feet high, some remains of which are still visible. The several gates have been taken down at various times to open and improve the avenues to the city.

This beautiful place, which has long been considered as the fountain of health, and seat of elegance and fashion, is singularly favoured both by nature and art, and is worthy of the distinguished pre-eminence it has acquired as the finest city in Europe. Most of the new buildings, and by far the largest and finest part of the city, are without the ancient walls, particularly Queen Square, The Royal Crescent, St. James's Square, Lansdowne Crescent, Somerset Place, Camden Place, Portland Place, Catherine Place, Mount Zion, a large extent of buildings on the summit of Beacon Hill, and Cavendish Crescent and Place, Lansdowne Grove, Lansdowne Place, and Belle Vue, commanding all the advantages of prospect, air, and scenery. Besides these there are Belvidere, Belmont, and Paragon Buildings, Marlborough Buildings, Burlington Place, and many other intervening streets and buildings, alike healthy and delightful. Nothing, indeed, can be more picturesque than the appearance of this part of the city, where houses rise above houses in progressive order, while the most elevated look down with proud superiority on the no less elegant and extensive structures below.

On the eastern side of the city, across the Avon, stands Pulteney Bridge, an elegant structure of three arches, and leading immediately from High Street, in the centre of the city, to Bathwick, where Laura Place, built in the form of a lozenge, is peculiarly beautiful; and passing through the centre of this place diagonally, in a direct line from the bridge, is Great Pulteney Street, of considerable length, beautifully spacious, elegantly and uniformly built in a superior style of architecture. At the distant extremity of this street, in front, is Sydney Gardens, or Vauxhall, which range and expand up the side of Claverton Hill, and are tastefully laid out: through these run the Kennet and Avon Canal, and the Great Western Railway. Around Sydney Gardens extends Sydney Place, in one of the wings of which her late Majesty, Queen Charlotte, resided during her illness in 1817; and near it stands the elegant church of Bathwick. In the south-east part of the town is Orange Grove, a spacious area, having an obelisk in its centre; adjoining to this are the walks, where the North Parade Bridge is situated, and near to which are the North and South Parades, elevated on arches, and uniformly built, whence are extensive and enchanting views of Prior Park, Beechen Cliff, with its hanging woods, and Claverton Hill, richly diversified with villas and enclosures, and crowned with an ornamental castellated structure, which is surrounded with a plantation of firs to a considerable extent. In the gardens below the South Parade, on the banks of the Avon, is the Great Western Railway Station, which, with new streets, and a spacious esplanade next the water, occupies the space of ground formerly vacant between the city and river on that side. On the lower side of the town are many ranges of buildings, which, in other places, would be deemed fine: amongst these are St. James's Parade and Westgate Buildings; and adjacent to Kingsmead Square are New King Street, Green Park Place, east and west, forming two sides of a triangle, the base or hypothenuse of which opens to the river, and Brunswick Terrace and Kingsmead Terrace, pleasantly overlooking the meadows, and commanding views of the surrounding country. On the north-eastern extremity of the city, at the entrance from the London road, are ranges of magnificent buildings with paved terraces, called Kensington, Piccadilly, Grosvenor Place, and Walcot Terrace. The fashionable amusements of Bath are under the superintendence of a master of the ceremonies, who is elected to that office by the subscribers to the Rooms. The lodging houses are numerous and commodious, and adapted to all ranks, from families of the first distinction, down to the more humble classes, who may be induced to seek benefit from these salutary waters. Here are also hackney coaches, chariots, and sedan chairs. Besides the Assembly Rooms and Pump Room, which are the usual promenades for persons of fashion, in wet or unfavourable weather, and the riding schools, which are the resort of equestrians on similar occasions, the neighbourhood of Bath abounds with beautiful walks and rides, and particularly Claverton Downs and Lansdown for the latter, affording the most salubrious air, and the most extensive prospects. The Old Bridge over the Avon should be rebuilt. The Guildhall, situate on the east side of High Street, is worthy of such a city and such a public spirited body. Behind this elegant structure is the Marketplace, which is exceedingly commodious, spacious, well paved, and under cover. The markets are held daily for all kinds of provision, and, in point of supply and regulation, are equalled by few and excelled by none in England. The new prison is a handsome edifice, built of free-stone, near the river, in Bathwick. The several public baths next claim attention: these are the King's, the Queen's, the Cross, and the Hot Baths, which are the property of, and under the superintendence of, the corporation, besides which there are the Kingston Baths. The taste of the waters is pleasant, impregnated with a vitriolic principle, which yields, upon evaporation, a small portion of neutral salt, with a calcareous earth and iron. They prove highly serviceable in bilious complaints, as well as in nervous, paralytic, rheumatic, and gouty disorders. The seasons for bathing are the spring and fall. The other public buildings in Bath for the accommodation of its visiters are numerous. The assembly rooms, spacious, commodious, and elegant, are in the vicinity of the Circus, and with tea and coffee rooms, ball and billiard rooms, together with a library and other appropriate apartments, form perhaps, the most superb suite of rooms dedicated to pleasure in the kingdom; they are also very elegantly fitted up, and are appropriated chiefly to public meetings, promenades, balls, concerts, cards, and other amusements during the winter and spring seasons. The theatre, on the south side of Beaufort Square, opened in 1805, in point of size, elegance of structure, and magnificence of decoration, is superior to any provincial theatre, and the company have long been esteemed the best out of the metropolis. The two riding-schools, the many public libraries, the Bath and West of England Agricultural Society, the Literary and Scientific Institution, the Philosophical, Harmonic, and other societies, are among the many useful and elegant establishments which this city affords. The charitable institutions are, the General Hospital, or Bath Infirmary, which dispenses its benefits to persons from all parts of the country. Bellot's Hospital and the Black Alms; the Stranger's Friend Society; the Eye Infirmary; and the Puerperal or Child-Bed Society, are benevolent establishments, whose names explain their objects. Besides the Free Grammar School, of high reputation, where the sons of citizens are educated for the university, and the Blue School for poor boys and girls, Bath may justly boast her numerous Sunday and other schools for the education of poor children, and various institutions for the promotion of industry and the improvement of morals. The four parishes of Bath, properly so called, are the Abbey, or St. Peter and St. Paul's, St. Michael's, St. James's, and Walcot, to which the vicarage of Widcombe and Lyncombe is annexed. The cathedral, or abbey church, is a magnificent building, being the last and purest specimen of ecclesiastical Gothic architecture in the kingdom; it is in the form of a cross, from the centre of which rises a fine tower 162 feet high, in which is a beautiful set of twelve bells. Each of the other churches above mentioned possesses peculiar and appropriate architectural beauties; and to these have been added Christ Church in Walcot parish, and St. Mary at Bathwick. Besides several chapels of ease for the established religion, there is a Roman catholic chapel, and places of worship for the various sects of dissenters. The government of the city is vested in a mayor, recorder, fourteen aldermen, and forty-two town council. It sends two members to parliament. This city, united with Wells, forms a bishopric, called the diocese of Bath and Wells, which comprehends the whole county of Somerset, except a few churches in the city of Bristol. The Bishop's Palace is at Wells. Bath races are usually held in September on Lansdown, one of the highest hills near the city, about 3 miles in extent, and commanding the richest and most extensive prospects. On this down is also held an annual fair, on the 10th of August, for cheese, cattle, horses, and all kinds of merchandize; and a fair is also held in Holloway, on the other side of the city, May 14.: two other fairs are held in the city, but they are inconsiderable. Inns: Castle, Greyhound, White Lion, White Hart, York Hotel.

BATH TO BRISTOL.

From the Bath station, carried in a line nearly direct, at no great distance from that once great, but now neglected, thoroughfare, the Bath and Bristol road, the Railway, carried at first on a viaduct, is continued, by embankment and excavation, to Twiverton Valley, where it crosses, by an embankment and a suspension bridge, the Bath road, the village, and an arm of the Avon, to the

TWIVERTON, OR TWERTON, STATION.

AN INTERMEDIATE ONE, DISTANT FROM LONDON 107¾ MILES, FROM BRISTOL 10¼ MILES.

Quitting the Twiverton station and embankment, a short cutting conducts to the Twiverton tunnel, 227 yards in length, emerging from which, an embankment and excavation, that, combined, occupy rather less than ½ a mile, carry it to the Bath and Bristol road, here thrown over the line.

In the last-named excavation, which is 30 feet deep, were found, in January, 1838, the remains of a Roman villa of considerable magnitude. At the Bath and Bristol road (on left of which is the village of Newton St. Loe and Newton Park, the seat of Colonel Gore Langton) commences the Corston embankment, nearly 1¾ mile in length, constructed on which, in conjunction with a viaduct, the Railway crosses the Corston brook and valley, affording a good view of the village on left, and of the Avon, that for some time continues its companion, on the right. The scenery here is as pleasing, and as beautiful, as can well be imagined; on left the vale is edged by the villages of Newton and Corston, with a high range of cultivated hills rising behind them; while from the margin of the Avon, on right, belted by its beautiful wood, rise the grounds of Kelston House, the mansion embosomed in trees occupying the summit. This was originally the seat of the Harrington family, of whom Sir John Harrington, the translator of Orlando Furioso, and a godson of Queen Elizabeth, and celebrated scholar of that day, was the original proprietor. The present manor-house, an elegant structure, was built by the late Sir Cæsar Hawkins, some sixty years since, and is now the seat of Joseph Neeld, Esq. The Corston embankment carries the Railway to the road to Saltford Mills, and

THE SALTFORD STATION.

AN INTERMEDIATE ONE, DISTANT FROM LONDON 111 MILES, FROM BRISTOL 7 MILES.— Journey resumed below.

The Saltford station, an establishment of minor importance, was formed principally with a view to facilitate the transport of articles manufactured at the brass mills established there, on the banks of the Avon.

Quitting the Saltford station, the Railway enters the Saltford excavation of, in some instances, 60 feet deep and about 1¼ mile in length, that, in rather more than ¼ of a mile, conducts to the Saltford tunnel, 154 feet long, faced with a Gothic archway. The train here reaches the 111 mile-stone, and, clearing the tunnel, continues its course through the remainder of the cutting, at the termination of which it comes out at the natural level of the land, where it is crossed by a handsome bridge. From this bridge, the Railway, carried with a sweep, crosses the valley of the Avon by an embankment of about ¾ of a mile in length, that again brings it to the level of the land, from whence a viaduct carries it over the little river Chew to an excavation, through which, crossed by the turnpike road to Bitton, it arrives at

THE KEYNSHAM STATION.

AN INTERMEDIATE ONE, DISTANT FROM LONDON 113 MILES, FROM BATH 6¾ MILES, FROM BRISTOL 5 MILES. — Journey resumed below.

KEYNSHAM.

Keynsham, a small market town, is situated on the south side of the river Avon, where it receives the Chew, and nearly intermediate between the towns of Bath and Bristol. It consists chiefly of one street, about a mile long. The rock on which it is built abounds with animal remains, chiefly the cornua ammonis, the fossils of which have the appearance of serpents coiled up. Near the centre of the town is the church, a large and handsome building, dedicated to St. John the Baptist. It belonged to an abbey of Black Canons, which was formerly here. Over the Avon to Gloucester there is a stone bridge of 15 arches, and another across the Chew. The inhabitants are principally employed in malting. Woad for dying is raised in great quantities in the neighbourhood.

Situate on the road from Bath to Bristol, an immense thoroughfare, that, independent of the coaches perpetually passing between these cities, was travelled by the stages to and from London to Bristol, Exeter, Plymouth, and Falmouth, Keynsham consequently presented, prior to the introduction of railway travelling, a very lively aspect; its appearance, however, is now changed to that of a dull country town, and its loss of trade, from the abstraction of business it has occasioned, has been very detrimental to the place.

Quitting the Keynsham Station, and passing under a bridge that carries the road from Keynsham to Bitton and Gloucester, the Railway, constructed on an embankment of about ¾ of a mile in length, crosses the valley of Keynsham Hams, and the road to Lodge Farm. This embankment, which is 30 feet high, commands a beautiful view of the winding Avon and its finely wooded shores. A little beyond the Lodge Farm road, where it terminates, the line enters an excavation of great depth, in some instances 70 feet, that conducts to the Keynsham Tunnels, the first being

39, the second 51 yards long. Emerging from the latter, the line soon enters on an embankment, a scene of seclusion of about half a mile in length, that carries it, with the intervention of a cutting, to the mouth of the first Brislington Tunnel, 132 yards long, from which, separated by a short excavation, it arrives at the second Brislington Tunnel, 149 yards long, to which almost immediately succeeds the third Brislington Tunnel, 330 yards long, that terminates in a short perpendicular cutting of considerable depth. These tunnels, formed through the solid rock, present, from the variety of stratification they exhibit, independent of the striking proofs of engineering ability evinced in their construction, one of the most interesting portions of the line. The last named cutting conducts to an elegant bridge of three arches, erected in the pointed style, here thrown over the Avon, by which the Railway reaches the St. Philip's embankment, that, succeeded by a viaduct across the feeder and canal, then enters on another formed across the harbour, continued on which, it arrives at

THE BRISTOL STATION

118 MILES FROM LONDON, FROM BATH, $11\frac{3}{4}$ MILES.

BRISTOL.

Bristol was known at a very early period, being mentioned by Gildas, about the year 430, among the fortified cities of Britain, and also by Nemmius about 620. In the latter part of the 11th century, a market is said to have been held here for slaves, and in the beginning of the succeeding one it was encompassed with a strong wall by Robert, the illegitimate son of Henry I., who also rebuilt and improved the castle, then a spacious structure. This was long an object of contention, and, at last, ordered by Oliver Cromwell to be demolished. In the reign of Henry II., Bristol was a rich and flourishing place. It is a city and county of England, locally situate between the counties of Gloucester and Somerset, is seated on the river Avon, which here receives the Frome, and is navigable for ships of great burden down to the Severn, at King's Road, where commences the Bristol channel. The Avon is crossed by a stone bridge of three arches, erected in 1768, and one of cast-iron, that conducts to Bedminster, which is thus connected with the city. St. Giles's bridge, of two arches, crosses the Frome, which is also spanned by many others of minor importance, as is the harbour by several of cast-iron. The river here is deep and very rapid, and flows to the height of 40 feet, so as to bring a vessel of 1000 tons up to the bridge. The total surface occupied by the city is computed at 16,000 acres, over which its buildings are irregularly dispersed in about 600 streets and lanes. Many of the houses in the older part of the city are built of wood and plaster, and are crowded together in narrow streets, which are high and irregular; but those of more recent erection are disposed in spacious streets and squares, the whole being well paved and lighted with gas. The city is supplied with excellent water, both from pumps and conduits. The common sewers that run through the city render it remarkably clean. Carts are not admitted into the streets for fear of damaging the arches of the vaults and gutters that are made under ground for conveying the soil into the rivers; on this account, everything is conveyed by sledges, to the no small danger of the foot passengers. Bristol, recently united with Gloucester, was constituted a bishop's see by Henry VIII., and part of a monastery, founded by Stephen, in 1140, has been converted into a cathedral. This venerable structure is 175 feet long, the tower being 130 feet high, square, and ornamented with four pinnacles. The church, though not large, has many Gothic beauties within, and a good organ; it is adorned with painted windows, and several handsome monuments, particularly that of Mrs. Draper, the celebrated Eliza of Sterne. Behind the church is a cloister, in which are the entrances to the library and bishop's palace. To the west of the church is a most beautiful Gothic gateway, ornamented with statues. The church of St. Mark, opposite the cathedral, was formerly collegiate; it is now the mayor's chapel. All the churches, 19 in number, are neat, some are beautifully decorated, and most of them have handsome monuments; that of St. Mary's Redcliffe is one of the finest in the kingdom, containing two beautiful monumental statues of its founder, William Canninge, who had been five times mayor of the city; in the one he appears habited as a magistrate, and in the other as a priest, he having in his latter days taken holy orders; there is also another of Sir William Penn, father of the famous quaker. Here are places of worship for almost every class of dissenters, two Roman catholic churches, and a Jews' synagogue. This city has long been celebrated for its well-conducted and extensive charities, many of which are at once an ornament and honour to the city. Among the principal are the Bristol General Hospital, the Bristol Infirmary, the Bristol Dispensary, an Institution for Diseases of the Eye, the Blind Asylum, and various others. The Exchange, in Corn Street, is a fine edifice of Grecian architecture, 110 feet in front and 148 deep; and the part designed for the reception of the merchants is capable of containing 1440 persons. The Commercial Rooms, in Corn Street, upon the plan of Lloyd's Coffeehouse in London, were erected in 1809. An elegant and convenient Theatre was built, in King Street, in 1766; and in Princes Street is an Assembly Room with a fine front. Its other remarkable public buildings are the Merchants' Hall, Council House, and Guildhall. Its Custom House is large and convenient, as is the Gaol, which is capable of containing 200 prisoners, has a house for the governor, a chapel, and treadmill.

There are thirteen city companies, several of whom have elegant halls, particularly the Merchants' hall in Princes Street, and the Coopers' hall in King Street, which has a superb front. Of metals, its manufactories are of great importance; its brass works are the largest in England; and here cotton works have recently been established, which, with the manufacture of copper, lead, iron, patent shot, pins, pottery, glass, soap, tobacco, snuff, hats, and floorcloth, furnish the chief employment of the labouring classes. Here are also distilleries and sugar refineries. Bristol has long enjoyed a very extensive foreign trade; and though many other ports, and particularly its great rival Liverpool, have made far more rapid advances, the increase of its commerce has been considerable and progressive, its merchants being engaged in the East and West India trade, the South American trade, the trade to Spain and Portugal, and the United States of America; the communication between the latter and the mother country being maintained by steam-ships, that, fitted up with great elegance, and propelled by engines of extraordinary power, regularly traverse the great Atlantic every fortnight, during which period the voyage is generally performed. Its commercial connections with Ireland are also very extensive. The internal commerce of this city is said to have decreased since the prevalence of canal navigation in England, goods being distributed from one place to another without the intervention of the port. Bristol returns two members to parliament. It is governed by a mayor, 12 aldermen, 2 sheriffs, and 28 common councilmen, with inferior officers, and has a police upon the metropolitan plan. It is divided into 12 wards, an alderman presiding over each. The city was erected into an independent county, in 1372, by Edward III., and has since been endowed with various privileges and immunities. All persons are free to trade here, and the freedom of the city can be purchased at a very moderate sum. The market days are Wednesday and Saturday. The city gives the title of earl to the family of Harvey. Here the unfortunate Thomas Chatterton was born, his father being sexton of St. Mary's, Redcliffe. About a mile west of Bristol, close to the river, stands the village of the Hot Wells, " where pale eyed suppliants drink, and soon flies pain." It is celebrated for a tepid spring, which has been found a powerful specific in various maladies. It rises near the bottom of the cliff, above 26 feet below high water mark, and 10 feet above low water mark. forcibly gushing from an aperture in the solid rock, and is so copious as to discharge 60 gallons a minute. This spring was once much frequented by invalids, but at present the Hot Wells, as well as the village of Clifton, most beautifully situated on the hill above, are the resort of the fashionable rather than the valetudinarian. Both have assembly rooms and hotels upon a large scale. The views from Clifton Down are beautiful in the extreme, as are the cliffs called the St. Vincent's Rocks, that, 250 feet in height, evidently appear, from their configurations, to have once joined, having, probably, been separated by some great convulsion of nature. Through this chasm flows the river Avon. Bristol is a great commercial city. It has a noble harbour, upwards of 3 miles in length, that, connected with the river by two entrance basins, is rendered accessible at every tide. It is the third city in England as regards trade, has a population of 64,266, and may, with truth, be termed the metropolis of the west.

Steam Packets start weekly for the following places, the distances by water being here given:— Dublin, 253 miles; Cork, 264 miles; Waterford, 210 miles; and daily, for Chepstow, 20 miles; Newport, 31 miles; Cardiff, 30 miles; Swansea, 73 miles; Tenby, 100 miles; and Ilfracombe, 71 miles. The principal Hotels and Inns are the Bush, Full Moon, Talbot, White Hart, White Lion, and Victoria; in addition to which, it may be observed, that Bristol, like London, abounds in houses of entertainment, suited to the taste of travellers of every class.

In the year 1831, Bristol was the scene of dreadful riots, which continued for 3 days, in the course of which the city suffered severely. The public entry of Sir Charles Wetherell into the city, in his capacity of recorder, to whose political opinions the lower classes were opposed, was the signal for its commencement; and the leaders, encountering little opposition, their numbers swelled into an immense mob, that soon became masters of the town, which was consequently sacked. During this period, owing to the pusillanimous conduct of Brereton, the commanding officer of the regiment, to whom the civil authorities were compelled to resort for assistance, the Bishop's Palace, the Mansion House, the Custom House, the Excise Office, the New Gaol, Gloucester Prison, and Queen Square, with many private houses and warehouses, were destroyed. For his misconduct on this occasion, Brereton was afterwards tried by a court-martial, the proceedings of which abruptly terminated, in consequence of his committing suicide.

BRISTOL AND EXETER RAILWAY.

The Bristol and Exeter Railway commences at Temple Meads, Bristol, at the terminus of the Great Western Railway, one station being common to both companies. Carried in a gently waving line, with the intervention of a short but deep cutting by embankment, it arrives in two miles at the turnpike road to Wells and Bridgewater, under which it is taken, and is thence continued, by an alternation of embankment and excavation, to the 3 milestone, where it reaches another embankment, from whence is beheld a beautiful view. On left, rising in lofty grandeur, is seen Dundry Beacon, the summit of which, 700 feet above the level of the sea, commands one of the most beautiful and extensive prospects in the West of England. On right rises Leigh Down, the eastern extremity of which, called Ashton Hill, also commands a fine view. Here the rocks are nearly perpendicular and extremely craggy, and being hollowed out into caverns by the hand of nature, and shaded with a variety of shrubs, exhibit a scene alike romantic, wild, and beautiful. At the foot of Ashton Hill lies the village of Long Ashton, much resorted to in the summer season by visiters from Bristol, for the enjoyment of the enchanting scenery in its vicinity. Above Long Ashton are also seen the grounds of Ashton Court, the fine old seat of Sir John Smith, Bart.

At $3\frac{3}{4}$ miles from Bristol, the Railway enters an excavation, carried through which it passes, at $4\frac{1}{2}$ miles from that city, unseen, upon the right, Ashton Watering, a little beyond which terminates the rise of 1 in 440 upon which it has to that point been constructed. Here the Bristol and Bridgewater Road crosses the line. It now commences a descent of 1 in 374 feet, and, carried through deep cutting to an archway of 300 feet in length, it arrives at Flax Bourton, 6 miles from Bristol. From Flax Bourton $\frac{1}{4}$ mile beyond which it crosses the road to Wraxhall, and in rather more than half a mile the road from Farley to Nailsea, it is constructed with a gradual bend, chiefly through cutting, to very near the 7 milestone, when it enters on an embankment that carries it to

THE BACKWELL STATION

AN INTERMEDIATE ONE, DISTANT FROM BRISTOL 8 MILES, FROM EXETER $67\frac{1}{2}$ MILES, FROM LONDON 126 MILES. — Journey resumed page 45.

The Backwell Station is situate at the Backwell and Nailsea road, the former a considerable village, about 1 mile distant on left, the latter a large village, about 1 mile distant on right. Nailsea is situate in the centre of the great coal field to which gives name, and, extending in various directions to a great distance, proves a fruitful source of revenue to its proprietors. The Bedminster coal field, it may here also be remarked, is traversed for some time after quitting the Wells road, from which point the tourist travels for several miles over a successive continuation of inexhaustible coal mines that may, with truth, be termed the gold mines of England. From the Backwell Station, continued by embankment, in another mile, it reaches Chelvey, ¼ mile beyond which it passes Nailsea Court upon the right, and in ¼ mile more, where it enters on a level course, carried forward in a direct line through alternate excavation and embankment, it arrives at

THE YATTON STATION.

AN INTERMEDIATE ONE, DISTANT FROM BRISTOL 11½ MILES, FROM EXETER 64 MILES, FROM LONDON 129¼ MILES.—Journey resumed below.

Four miles on right of Yatton station is

CLEVEDON.

Clevedon, a small village, situated upon the margin of the Bristol Channel, is chiefly remarkable for the beauty of its scenery. The rocks in the vicinity of this place rise, with great boldness and grandeur, to an immense height; and the scenery around, wildly scarred with craggy cliffs intermixed with herbage, is beautifully romantic. One of these rocks, which commands a fine prospect, particularly down the Channel, was formerly the site of a tower, long since demolished, called Wakes Tower, from the family of that name, who erected it as a place of observation. The church stands near the edge of a rugged rock overhanging the shore, at the west end of the village. Its elevation alone defends it from the fury of the sea, which, in stormy weather, beats here with great violence, and, with a rising tide and a westerly wind, is tremendous. The ride over the hill, from Leigh Down to this place is justly considered one of the finest in the county of Somerset.

From about a mile before Chelvey to Yatton, on left, are seen the villages of Backwell and Brockley, distinguished by their churches, while Clevedon, situate on rising ground that, broken into knolls of variegated form, beheld upon the right, presents a beautiful appearance. Yatton is a considerable village, as is Congresbury, 1½ mile distant on right. 1 mile beyond Yatton station the Railway crosses the river Yeo; in 1¼ mile, passing Wick St. Lawrence, on the left, gains West Huish; in another mile St. George; and in 1¼ mile more the road from Banwell to Worle and Weston-super-Mare.* ½ mile beyond the Banwell and Worle road it gains the Lockinge and Worle road, and in ¾ mile more the Lockinge and Weston-super-Mare road. ¾ mile beyond this is

---

* Where is the Banwell Station

THE WESTON BRANCH STATION.

DISTANT FROM BRISTOL 18¼ MILES, FROM WHICH TO WESTON A BRANCH LINE OF 1¼ MILE IN LENGTH IS CONTINUED; FROM AXBRIDGE 5¼ MILES, FROM EXETER 57¼ MILES, FROM LONDON 136¼ MILES.—Journey resumed below.

AXBRIDGE.

Axbridge consists principally of one street about ⅓ mile in length, and running in a winding direction from east to west. The church is a large handsome structure, in the Gothic style, standing on an eminence, and built in the form of a cross; from its west end rises a very fine tower: the interior contains a nave, chancel, north and south transept, two aisles, and two chapels, one on each side of the chancel. Near the church stands the market-house and shambles. The market is held on Saturday, and affords a plentiful supply of corn, sheep, and pigs. Knit hose is the chief or rather the only manufacture. Here was formerly a hunting-chase belonging to the kings of England. The village of Cheddar lies about 2 miles to the S. E. of Axbridge, at the foot of the Mendip Hills. It is situated in a parish of the same name, which extends from the middle summit of the hills a considerable way into the moors. The soil and surface are as various as can well be imagined. The lofty Mendip raises his rugged brow on the one hand, and forms a fine contrast with the rich extensive level on the other. The slopes of the hills are every where diversified. Here immense caverns, enormous chasms, and bold protuberances, are mixed together in awful variety; indeed, nothing can exceed the grandeur of the scenery which this parish displays. The chasm called Cheddar Cliffs is certainly one of the most striking objects of its kind in England.

The course of the Railway, which from Chelvey to this point, a distance of 8 miles, has been that of a nearly direct line, now changes, and continues, with a gradual bend, to Uphill, 19¼ miles from Bristol. 1 mile distant, on left of Uphill, is Bleadon, backed by Bleadon Hill; a little beyond which commence the Mendip Hills, that, at 5¼ miles from the Western Branch Station, overhang the town of Axbridge and village of Cheddar, the latter celebrated for its cliffs, its rocky and romantic scenery, and also for its cheese.

From Uphill the Railway is continued, with a gradual bend, to the viaduct over the river Axe; from whence, passing in ¾ mile Cripps Farm, upon the left, it is continued, in a direct line, to South Brent; on left of which Brent Knoll, a conical eminence, rising to the height of nearly 1000 feet above the level of the sea, presents a singular appearance. 1½ mile beyond South Brent the

Railway reaches the Burnham road, ¾ mile beyond which it crosses the Bristol and Bridgewater road, and in less than ½ a mile further arrives at

THE HIGH BRIDGE STATION.

AN INTERMEDIATE ONE, DISTANT FROM BRISTOL 26¼ MILES, FROM EXETER 49¼ MILES, FROM LONDON 144¼ MILES.

From High Bridge station, that on left affords a glance at Glastonbury Tor, 13 miles distant, in a right line, the Railway crosses the river Brue (that falls into the Bristol channel, 1½ mile distant on right), reaching, in rather more than ½ a mile, the road to Huntspill. At 29¼ miles from Bristol it enters a short cutting that carries it, in ¼ mile more, under the old Bristol road, near Puriton; shortly after which, emerging from the excavation, it again enters on a level embankment, that carries it to the 32 mile-stone; ¼ mile beyond which, again crossing the old Bristol road, it soon arrives at

THE BRIDGEWATER STATION;

A PRINCIPAL ONE, DISTANT FROM BRISTOL 33 MILES, EXETER 42½ MILES, FROM LONDON 151 MILES.—Journey resumed, page 48.

Bridgewater, a market town of Somersetshire, is seated on the river Parret, over which is an iron bridge; here the tide rises at high water six fathoms, and sometimes flows in with such impetuosity, that it rises near two fathoms deep at a time, which often occasions considerable damage to the shipping, driving them foul of each other, and oversetting the small craft. It is termed the *boar*, and is frequent in the rivers of the channel, particularly the Severn. The church is a handsome spacious structure, containing a fine altar-piece of our Saviour taken from the cross, by Guido, and the spire is the loftiest in the county. Near the church is a handsome free-school built of stone; the town-hall is a large building, beneath which is a cistern whence the inhabitants are supplied with water. It was first incorporated as a borough by King John, who built a castle here; and it was one of the first towns seized by the barons in the reign of Henry III., being then considered of great importance. The Duke of Monmouth was here proclaimed king, and lodged some time in the castle; but being betrayed by Lord Gray, and his army consisting chiefly of raw countrymen, he was defeated by the royal army on a moor near Weston, 3 miles distant, when 1000 were killed and 1500 taken prisoners; and here Judge Jefferies and Colonel Kirk had most of the survivors executed. The houses in general are irregular, but the streets are wide and well paved. It sends two members to parliament, and has a market on Tuesday and Saturday; at the former, cattle of all kinds are sold, and cheese in great quantities; and provisions of all sorts are plentiful. The midsummer county sessions are held here, and the assizes every other year. Through the convenience of its navigation, it has also a very good coasting trade; and a number of coal ships are constantly employed.

Inns: Royal Clarence Hotel, and George Hotel, both of them posting-houses. The commercial inns are, The Globe, Bristol Arms, Albion, and White Hart.

Bridgewater: 2½ miles before on left is Knoll Hall*; 3½ miles distant from Bridgewater on the right is Halswell House†; 4 miles distant Enmore House‡; Brymore§; and Barford.||

Continued by embankment, the railway, in ¾ mile, carried with a gradual sweep, crosses the river Parrett, 1 mile beyond which, pursuing a course parellel with the Bridgewater and Taunton Canal upon its right, the Parrett running at no great distance on the left, it arrives at the North Petherton road at a distance from that village, a considerable one, formerly a market town, of 2 miles. At North Petherton is North Petherton House¶, 1 mile south of which is Mansell House.** In another mile it arrives at the Newton and Burrowbridge road, Newton being 1 mile distant on the right. Two miles beyond this it is continued by embankment, with the exception of the last mile to the Taunton and Glastonbury road, 38½ miles from Bristol. From this point, soon quitting the cutting, carried with a very gradual sweep at a short distance from the Bridgewater and Taunton Canal on its right, it arrives in 1¼ mile at Chillerton, where terminates the level upon which it has been continued from Bridgewater, when it enters the valley of the Tone, passing between that river on the left, and the Bridgewater and Taunton Canal upon the right, the two being about ¼ mile apart. The valley of the Tone, denominated Taunton Dean, proverbial for its beauty, presents an unparalleled picture of fertility, and is thus described by Drayton:—

"What ear so empty is that hath not heard the sound
Of Taunton's fruitful Dean not matched by any ground?"

Through this luxuriant vale the railway pursues its course as far as Wellington. Approaching Taunton, the Quantock Hills, that rise on right of it, assume a mountainous aspect; while on the opposite side the valley, gradually increasing in elevation from the margin of the river, is, at no great distance, backed by the bold

* B. C. Grunhill, Esq.   † C. R. K. Tynte, Esq.
‡ H. Broadmead, Esq. || Hon. P. P. Bouverie.
§ G. Evered, Esq.   ¶ H. Ansty, Esq.
** Lieut. Gen. Sir John Slade, Bart.

eminences known as Black Down Hills. These, suddenly rising to a height of 800 feet above the level of the sea, assume a grandeur of character that has not inaptly been compared to mountains torn piecemeal by the raging elements. An ideal line on the summit of this lofty region divides the counties of Dorset and Somerset; and on Beacon Hill, the point of greatest elevation, boldly conspicuous, is beheld the Wellington pillar, erected in honour of the hero of Waterloo. From Chillerton, ¼ mile beyond which the railway commences a rise of 1 in 880, it is continued with an easy bend between the last named canal and river to Creech St. Michael, a considerable village, where both the Bridgewater and Taunton Canal and river Tone approach within an ⅛ of a mile of each other, the intervening space being filled with the village and railway, the latter running between both. From hence it is carried in a course, nearly direct, between the river and canal, in a distance of 1½ mile to Bath Pool, where it twice crosses the river and the road from Bridgewater to Taunton. From hence, pursuing a serpentine course on the border of the Tone, it reaches, in rather less than a mile, the Bridgewater and Taunton Canal, and shortly after enters an excavation, through which it is carried with an easy sweep to

THE TAUNTON STATION,

A principal one, distant from Bristol 44 miles, from Exeter 31¾ miles, from London 162 miles.

At Taunton, roads branch on left to Ilminster, 12¾ miles, and Honiton 18 miles: and on right to Milverton 7½ miles; to Watchet, 19½ miles; to Dunster, 21 miles; and to Minehead 23 miles.

Taunton, 1 mile distant, on left is Batts*; 2 miles distant, Amberd House†; 2½ miles distant is Poundisford Park‡, and Poundisford Lodge§; and 3 miles distant Barton Grange ‖; 1¼ mile distant, on right, is Pyrland Hall¶; and 2½ miles distant Hestercombe House.**

TAUNTON.

Taunton, a market-town of Somersetshire of great antiquity, is esteemed one of the principal in the county. It is well built, and consists of wide airy streets, that extend over a considerable portion of ground, most of the houses having small gardens in front, which add greatly to their beauty, as well as to the health

---

* Unoccupied. † J. Gould, Esq.
‡ T. Thompson, Esq. § C. J. Hellyar, Esq.
‖ Lady Cooper. ¶ R. M. King, Esq.
** Miss Warre.

and convenience of the inhabitants; and the whole, which is about a mile in length, is well paved and lighted. The surrounding country is particularly delightful, and the temperature of its climate and fertility of its soil form the continual boast of the natives. Here are three churches dedicated to St. James, St. Mary Magdalen, and the Holy Trinity; the former, a strong plain building with a tower, appears to have been erected in the 13th century, but is far inferior in point of beauty to St. Mary Magdalen, which stands near the centre of the town, and is a very elegant and splendid edifice in the florid Gothic style of architecture. It is extremely capacious, and has a lofty tower at one end of truly magnificent workmanship. The height of the whole is 153 feet; and from the balustrade of it is beheld a most delightful and extensive view of the adjacent country. The interior of this church also deserves notice on account of its very curious roof, and beautifully carved desk and pulpit. There are no less than forty-four windows in this church, some of which still retain traces of ancient painting on the glass; it is likewise richly decorated, has a screen of elegant fret-work, and one of the finest organs in the county. Trinity Church, a modern structure, is situate near the eastern entrance of the town. Taunton contains a Roman Catholic chapel, meeting-houses for Dissenters of different denominations, and various charitable institutions. Of late years it has undergone great alteration and improvement; and has a very handsome market-house, with several apartments in it for different purposes. In the lower part is the town-hall and coffee-room; on the first floor an elegant assembly room; on the upper floor a handsome billiard-room; and on each side of the house is a large wing or arcade for the use of the farmers and tradesmen, besides an extensive area in front, where temporary butchers' shambles are erected, in the middle of which, towards the north, is a noble pavement, upwards of 200 feet in length, called the parade. Taunton has a considerable trade in silk; and its ale, the excellence of which is proverbial, forms an article of exportation. Among the more recent improvements which this place has experienced must be mentioned the Taunton and Bridgewater Canal, with the success of which, however, it is not improbable the Bristol and Exeter Railway will in some measure interfere. This place sends two members to Parliament. Ina, a king of the West Saxons, erected a castle here in the year 700, which, being destroyed, was again rebuilt about the time of the conquest. Its existing remains are considerable, and appropriated to various uses; and the west wing, still tolerably entire, is thought to have belonged, to the original building of King Ina.

Inns: The Castle, Fackrell's Hotel, London Inn, the George, and White Hart.

From the Taunton Station the Railway is carried forward in a direct line for $1\frac{1}{4}$ mile through cutting, a short distance on left of the Bridgewater and Taunton Canal, to the Milverton road, on right of which is the Lunatic Asylum, and thence to the Bishops Hull and Norton Fitzwarren road; the former $\frac{1}{2}$ mile distant on right, the latter $\frac{1}{2}$ mile on left of the line. Here the gradual rise of 1 in 880 terminates, and commencing an ascent of 1 in 356 it enters on an embankment, and passing close to the former village, crossing in its way a tributary stream of the Tone, continued with a gradual bend reaches Allerford, where it approaches very close to the Grand Western Canal, $1\frac{1}{4}$ mile beyond Allerford; crossing two tributaries of the Tone, the Railway arrives at the Bradford and Milverton road, the last $\frac{1}{4}$ mile through cutting. At $48\frac{1}{2}$ miles from Bristol the Bradford and Nynehead road is carried over the line, which in $\frac{1}{4}$ mile more entering on an embankment gains the Grand Western Canal, which it crosses, in less than another $\frac{1}{4}$ mile the viaduct over the Tone, and very shortly after Ham Bridge. A little beyond Ham Bridge it enters an excavation, and pursuing a serpentine course, crossing in its way the Wellington and Nynehead road, it arrives in $1\frac{3}{4}$ mile more, partly by excavation, but principally by embankment, at the Milverton road and

THE WELLINGTON STATION,

A PRINCIPAL ONE, DISTANT FROM BRISTOL $51\frac{1}{4}$ MILES; FROM EXETER $24\frac{3}{4}$ MILES; FROM LONDON $169\frac{1}{4}$ MILES. — Journey resumed page 52.

At Wellington a road branches off on right, through Milverton, $4\frac{1}{4}$ miles distant, to Wiveliscombe, 8 miles distant.

Wellington gives title of Duke to the illustrious hero of Waterloo, and is a large and populous town, consisting of four streets, the principal of which is very spacious. The Old Church, dedicated to St. John the Baptist, stands near the entrance of the town from London. It is a large and very handsome Gothic structure, with an elegant embattled tower at its west end 100 feet high. In its south chapel is a magnificent tomb to the memory of Sir John Popham, who was a very munificent patron of this town, and erected an hospital for twelve infirm persons, which is still in existence and the charity applied. The New Church, dedicated to the Holy Trinity, stands at the west end of the town. The market is held on Thursday, and is well supplied with provisions.

Inns: The White Hart and Squirrel.

Near the Bradford and Nynehead road, on right of which is

Nynehead Court*, and 1½ m. distant on left Heatherton Park†, the rise of 1 in 336 terminates, and the Railway, increased in steepness to a rise of 1 in 126, is so continued for 4 miles. Quitting the Wellington Station, it shortly after crosses the little Tone river, and is carried on an embankment with a gradual bend to Westford, where it again crosses that stream, and thence in a line tolerably direct to the Wellington and Exeter road; carried over which it arrives at

THE BEAM BRIDGE STATION,

AN INTERMEDIATE ONE, DISTANT FROM BRISTOL 53¼ MILES; FROM EXETER 22¼ MILES; FROM LONDON 171¼ MILES.

From Beam Bridge, carried forward with a gradual sweep, it enters an excavation near the 53½ milestone, and in less than half a mile more reaches the White Ball Tunnel, ⅝ of a mile in length. Near the centre of this tunnel, that derives its name from a small but well-remembered village-inn about half a mile distant on right, the traveller gains the summit of the Railway. The Wellington and Exeter road runs over this tunnel, from whence, emerging near the 55 milestone from Bristol, and commencing a descent of 1 in 220, it enters Devonshire, and an excavation through which it is continued to the 55½ milestone, near which the road to Burliscombe, a small village on the left, is borne over the line. 2 miles distant on rt. of this is Holcombe Court.‡ In rather more than ¼ m. beyond this the Railway, quitting the confines of the cutting, enters on an embankment, that in rather less than ½ a mile carries it with a gradual sweep to the Grand Western Canal, immediately on right, and thence to the river Culm, near Pugham Mill, about 1 m. beyond which it crosses the Tiverton Road, and in another arrives at

THE TIVERTON ROAD STATION,

A PRINCIPAL ONE, DISTANT FROM BRISTOL 60 MILES; FROM EXETER 15½ MILES; FROM LONDON 178 MILES; FROM TIVERTON 5 MILES.—Journey resumed, page 53.

1½ m. distant on left of the Tiverton Road is Bridwell. §

TIVERTON.

Tiverton, a large handsome town of Devonshire, of considerable antiquity, is pleasantly situate on the slope of a hill and

---

* E. A. Sandford, Esq.   † A. Adair, Esq.
‡ P. C. Bluett, Esq.   § Mrs. Clarke.

banks of the Exe, at its junction with the Lowman, over each of which is a stone bridge. It is nearly a mile in length, and the same in breadth, and chiefly consists of four principal streets, disposed in the form of a quadrangle, in the centre of which is a handsome market-place. The principal buildings here, are the castle, the old church, and the free grammar school; the former stands in the north-west part of the town, and from its remains appears to have been a fortress of considerable strength; the old church is situate on an eminence at the N. W. end of the town, and is a more respectable gothic pile than any in Devonshire, except St. Peter's at Exeter; the view from the churchyard is strikingly picturesque, and attracts the attention of most strangers; the tower contiguous to the church, a short remove from the west wall of the churchyard, likewise merits attention, the summit affords a beautifully diversified view, that amply rewards the labour of ascending it. In addition to this a new church, or chapel of ease, a regular stone structure of the Doric order, has been erected on the south-west side of Fore Street. The Free Grammar School, a fine building, was erected at the sole cost of Peter Blundell, a rich clothier, and a native of the town. This gentleman also left lands for the maintenance and support of three scholars in each of the universities, to be chosen out of the above school. There are also a free English school, an extensive hospital, several alms-houses, and other charitable bequests. The Town House, in which the corporation hold their meetings, is a spacious structure, and there is a good market-house. By a charter granted by James I. the town was incorporated, under a mayor, twelve capital burgesses, and twelve assistants, who elect a recorder. The inhabitants are principally employed in the lace trade. It sends two members to Parliament. Market-days, Tuesday and Saturday. Population 10,770. Inns: Three Tuns; Angel.

From the Tiverton Road Station the Railway, continued by embankment, with a gradual sweep, on a descent of diminished steepness, viz. 1 in 459, enters a cutting, carried through which it reaches in another mile the Exeter Road at Stones' Hill, $1\frac{1}{2}$ m. distant on left of which is Bradfield *, about $\frac{1}{2}$ m. beyond Willand; shortly after which it enters on an embankment that carries it by a direct line in about a mile to the river Culm, and entrance of Cullompton at the Honiton Road, the site of

* W. H. Walrond, Esq.

THE CULLOMPTON STATION,

A PRINCIPAL ONE, DISTANT FROM BRISTOL $62\frac{1}{2}$ MILES; FROM EXETER 13 MILES; FROM HONITON $10\frac{1}{2}$ MILES; FROM TIVERTON $5\frac{1}{3}$ MILES; FROM LONDON $180\frac{1}{2}$ MILES.—Journey resumed, below.

The situation of Cullompton is singularly agreeable; the town, seated on the river Culm, being surrounded by luxuriant scenery and cultivation. The main street of this place, that suffered some few years since from a dreadful conflagration, having been rebuilt of considerable width, now wears in consequence an appearance of great respectability; and, being enlivened by a stream of water constantly running on each side, presents a pleasing and cheerful aspect: it is situated on a gravelly soil, upon a small elevation gradually declining for half a mile to the river, that abounds with remarkably fine trout and eels, and is crossed by three bridges. The church, an ancient and venerable structure, dedicated to the Virgin Mary, greatly improved and enlarged, with a lofty tower, 100 feet, has an elegant roof of gilt carved work. In addition to this, the Wesleyans, Baptists, Independents, and Presbyterians have chapels here. The inhabitants are chiefly employed in the woollen trade. Market on Saturday; in addition to which there is a great cattle-market on the first Saturday in every month, except May and November, being fair months. Population, 3,909. Inns: White Hart; Half Moon.

From the Cullompton Station the Railway, crossing the river, is carried forward in a gently waving line through the valley of the Culm, a little to the left of it, chiefly by embankment, to Water Slade, about $\frac{3}{4}$ m. on right of which is the town of Bradninch, and thence with a bold sweep to

THE HELE STATION,

AN INTERMEDIATE ONE, DISTANT FROM BRISTOL $66\frac{1}{2}$ MILES; FROM EXETER 9 MILES; FROM SIDMOUTH 16 MILES; FROM LONDON $184\frac{1}{2}$ MILES.

Quitting the Hele Station[*], the Railway, crossing the river Culm, arrives in about $\frac{1}{2}$ m. farther at the Bristol and Exeter road, that lies in a short excavation. Carried with a curvilinear sweep from this last point, twice crossing the Culm in its way, and passing the confines of Killerton Park[†], $\frac{1}{2}$ m. distant on left

---

[*] From whence a new road is to be made to Sidmouth.
[†] The seat of Sir T. D. Acland, Bart.

of which is Spraydown House; in 1¾ m. more it arrives, through the valley of the Culm, at Pound Mill. Shortly after which, crossing the Culm, and in ½ m. further again bestriding that stream, it reaches Rew, a village on the road from Exeter to Silverton, 2 m. distant on left of which is Poltimore House.*

From the Silverton road, ½ m. beyond which it crosses the Stoke Canon road, carried with a curvilinear sweep crossing the Exe in its way, entering a little before the 72 milestone a short excavation, from which it soon emerges, it reaches in 72¾ miles Pynes Mill, a little to the northward of which rise the grounds of Pynes, the beautiful seat of †; ½ m. beyond this it arrives at Cowley Bridge, whence, bending suddenly to the south, it is carried in a course tolerably direct, first through a short cutting, and then by embankment, between the river Exe and London and Exeter road, to

THE EXETER STATION,

A PRINCIPAL ONE, DISTANT FROM BRISTOL 75½ MILES; FROM PLYMOUTH 43 MILES; FROM DEVONPORT 45 MILES; FROM LONDON 193½ MILES.

EXETER.

This is a city of great antiquity, and has been for many centuries a place of considerable importance in the West of England. It is pleasantly situated on the aclivity of an eminence, on the banks of the river Exe, over which is a stone bridge. The city is about 3 miles in circumference, intersected by four principal streets, well paved, that unite near the centre, which is thence denominated Carfax. The mildness of the climate, proverbial for its salubrity, the beauty of the surrounding country, and cheapness of provisions, have latterly induced many families to resort to Exeter for health and the education of their children, for whose accommodation a handsome quarter, called Southernhay, was erected about the year 1816; and at a still later period Mount Radford Park, formerly belonging to the Baring family, about ¼ of a mile from the city, has been let for building, and now contains probably 100 genteel residences: a literary institution and small museum have also been established; and the society of this city is now little inferior to that of Bath and Bristol. The streets and buildings have most of them an appearance of antiquity. In 1697 a canal was constructed, which, by means of floodgates, &c., admits vessels of 150 tons to the quay

---

* Lord Poltimore.   † Sir Stafford H. Northcote, Bart.

near the city walls, having within the last twenty years undergone great improvement and extension, at a cost of not less than 100,000*l*. The city of Exeter is a county of itself, enjoying an extensive jurisdiction, privileges, and charters, and was one of the first cities which sent members to parliament: it is governed by a mayor, twelve aldermen, thirty-six town councillors, a recorder, sheriff, and town clerk. It has also 13 companies of incorporated trades, and two spacious handsome markets. The principal employment of the inhabitants was in the woollen trade; but this is now almost extinct. In the north-east part of the city were situated the ruins of the castle of Rougemont, which appears to have been a very strong fortress, and of considerable extent: it was formerly the residence of the West Saxon kings. On the ancient site of Rougemont a building of comparatively modern date has been erected, called the Castle, where the assizes, quarter sessions, elections, and county meetings are held. The ruins above referred to are only interesting on account of their antiquity, and presenting from the ramparts a most advantageous view of the surrounding country. Among the numerous public buildings within the city of Exeter, its ancient and venerable cathedral, with its noble organ, claims particular notice. The extent, beauty, uniformity, and grandeur of the design, together with the propriety, taste, and richness displayed in the decorative ornaments, render it a truly interesting specimen of ancient English architecture. Besides this magnificent monument of ecclesiastical splendour and national piety, there are 15 parish churches within the walls, and 4 in the suburbs, several chapels, a Jew's synagogue, numerous charitable institutions, and a neat theatre. It sends two members to parliament. Market-days, Tuesday and Friday. Population, 37,431. Inns: Old London Inn; New London Inn; Clarence Hotel.

BRIGHTON RAILWAY.

The Brighton Railway, literally speaking, commences at Croydon, whither it is taken upon two other lines of railway, of which we now proceed to give the details. Leaving the London terminus, it is carried on arches through the Borough, the buildings of which, the neighbourhood being crowded, present a singular appearance; the principal feature here being Queen Elizabeth's Grammar School, in Bermondsey Street, recently rebuilt. In a mile and a quarter it arrives at Corbet's Lane, where, quitting the Greenwich, it enters on the Croydon Railway; here a lengthened causeway, affording a good, though not extensive, view, carries it, in conjunction with a viaduct, over the Grand Surrey Canal* to

THE NEW-CROSS STATION,

AN INTERMEDIATE ONE, DISTANT FROM LONDON $2\frac{3}{4}$ MILES, FROM BRIGHTON $47\frac{3}{4}$ MILES.

Arrived here, the train toils up a steep ascent (a rise of 1 in 100, rather more than 52 feet in a mile), through deep cutting, to

THE DARTMOUTH ARMS STATION,

AN INTERMEDIATE ONE, DISTANT FROM LONDON $5\frac{1}{4}$ MILES, FROM BRIGHTON $45\frac{1}{4}$ MILES.—Journey resumed.

From this station (in front of which passed the Croydon Canal), and from the succeeding embankments on the left, is beheld a beautiful view of the richly-wooded country in the vicinity of Chislehurst, Bromley, and Beckenham; in which the church of the latter stands forth conspicuously in the foreground, and forms an interesting feature; the distance being terminated by an extensive stretch of the county of Kent, which this eminence commands.

The country bordering the Railway on the right, beautifully wooded, including the village of Norwood and the Beulah Spa, is highly interesting; but the great attraction, and object of chief interest in this vicinity, is Dulwich.

Dulwich, delightful for its rural simplicity, and unquestionably one of the most beautiful villages in England, is thus celebrated by Akenside:

> Or lose the world amid the sylvan wilds
> Of Dulwich, yet by barbarous arts unspoiled.

Dulwich, from its proximity to the metropolis, is too well known to render necessary its description here. It is chiefly celebrated for its College and Picture Gallery; the former founded, in 1614, by Mr. Edward Alleyne, an actor in the reign of Queen Elizabeth, and the principal performer in many of Shakspeare's plays; the latter, containing a fine collection of paintings, the

* From whence a Branch to the Bricklayer's Arms Station, a distance of not quite $1\frac{3}{4}$m., has been made, with a view to avoiding the confusion hitherto prevalent at the London Bridge terminus.

P

bequest of the late Sir Francis Bourgeois, is well worthy of a visit; it is open to the public by tickets only, obtainable gratis of the Editor.*

At the Dartmouth Arms Station, the Railway reaches a level embankment of rather less than ½ a mile in length; from whence it is carried, with a gently waving line, principally through excavation, on a descent of 2 feet in a mile, to

THE SYDENHAM STATION,

AN INTERMEDIATE ONE, DISTANT FROM LONDON 6¼ MILES, FROM BRIGHTON 44¼ MILES.

From the Sydenham Station, where the road from Dulwich and Norwood to Bromley crosses over the line, the Railway, carried with an easy sweep on a rise of 8 feet in a mile, principally through excavation, gains the Norwood and Beckenham road, that at Penge Common (previously to arriving at which it enters on an embankment) runs under the line where is

THE PENGE STATION,

AN INTERMEDIATE ONE, DISTANT FROM LONDON 7 MILES, FROM BRIGHTON 43½ MILES.

From the Penge Station, carried through excavation, in a line nearly direct, the Railway crossing Penge Common, where still exist some remains of the Croydon Canal, one of the bubbles of 1801, arrives at an embankment that carries it, still on the rise of 8 feet in a mile, almost to

THE ANNERLY STATION,

AN INTERMEDIATE ONE, DISTANT FROM LONDON 7½ MILES, FROM BRIGHTON 43 MILES.

A little before reaching the Annerly Station, the line enters an excavation, over which runs a road from Norwood to Bromley; and from this point it is carried in a line nearly direct, partly by excavation and partly by embankment, to

THE JOLLY SAILOR STATION,

AN INTERMEDIATE ONE, DISTANT FROM LONDON 8¼ MILES, FROM BRIGHTON 42¼ MILES.

Shortly after quitting the Jolly Sailor Station, the Railway reaches an embankment, that on left affords a good view of the country, the prospect on right, from the elevation of the ground, being circumscribed; in this direction the spire of Norwood Church stands forth conspicuous. A little before the 9¼ milestone, where terminates the descent of 2 feet in a mile, the Rail-

---

* E. Mogg, Great Russell Street, Covent Garden.

way enters an excavation, through which, constructed first on a rise of rather more than 6 feet in a mile, it attains a level, on which it reaches

THE LOWER CROYDON STATION,

A PRINCIPAL ONE, DISTANT FROM LONDON 9¼ MILES, FROM BRIGHTON 41¼ MILES.

We now enter on a description of the Brighton Railway, that actually commences ⅜ of a mile beyond the Jolly Sailor Station, where the Railway divides into two lines; that on right, above described, conducting to the lower Croydon Station, that on left being carried nearly on the surface of the earth to the Croydon and Addiscombe road, where is

THE CROYDON STATION OF THE BRIGHTON RAILWAY,

A PRINCIPAL ONE, DISTANT FROM LONDON 10¼ MILES, FROM BRIGHTON 40¼ MILES. — Journey resumed page 5.

CROYDON.

On left of Croydon is Shirley House, the seat of *; at Addiscombe is the military College of the East India Company, and a seat of †, at the entrance of the town; 1½ m. distant, on right, is Beddington Park ‡, and at the end of the town Hailing Park. §

Croydon, a market-town of Surrey, on the edge of Banstead Downs, 9½ miles south from London, consists of two parts, namely, the old and new towns; each of which is about 1 mile in length. The old town is situate in a bottom, where numerous springs arise, forming the source of the river Wandle; in this division are the ancient archiepiscopal Palace of the Province of Canterbury, the Church, and the Vicarage. The new town, called the High Street, was originally nothing more than a bridle-way over the fields; but in consequence of leading over higher ground, and in a more direct course than the old road, it was at length built on, and became the principal road to Brighton, and other southern parts. The Court-house, a handsome building, in which the summer assizes are held alternately with Guildford, the Butter Market, and Whitgift's Hospital, are situated in this part. The parish is 36 miles in circumference, and includes several hamlets: its population in 1831 was 2447; in the town of Croydon are about 900 houses, and about 7000 inhabitants. The manor has belonged to the See of Canterbury ever since the Conquest, and probably much earlier. The first prelate that can be traced, as residing in the old palace, was Archbishop Kilwardley, in 1273;

* M. T. Smith, Esq. † Lord Ashburton.
‡ Captain Carew. § R. Fenwick, Esq.

the last was Archbishop Hutton, in 1757. The palace was afterwards neglected, and fell into decay, which, in 1780, led to the passing of an act of parliament, by which certain trustees, named in the act, were empowered to sell the premises, and erect a new palace at Park-Hill Farm, about half a mile from Croydon, the leasehold interest of which had been purchased by Archbishop Cornwallis. The old palace was accordingly sold; and, together with the grounds, is now occupied by persons engaged in printing linens, and in bleaching. Such are the vicissitudes attending on works of earthly grandeur. In this palace, in July, 1573, Queen Elizabeth, and her whole court, were entertained by Archbishop Parker, for seven days, when commencing her progress through Kent. The Hospital, built by Archbishop Whitgift, is chiefly of brick, and was erected and endowed between the years 1596 and 1599. Here are schools for general education, on the system of Lancaster and Dr. Bell. The Church, which is one of the finest in Surrey, and contains a noble organ, is dedicated to St. John the Baptist. It is in the pointed style of architecture, and very capacious; the length of the nave and chancel being 130 feet, and the breadth 74 feet. At the west end is a lofty and well-proportioned tower of flints and stones, embattled, and surmounted by pinnacles. The remains of the Archbishops Grindall, Whitgift, Sheldon, Wake, Potter, and Herring, lie buried here, and have monuments; but that of Archbishop Sheldon far exceeds all the others, and is, indeed, a most exquisite specimen of the sculptor's art: the figure of the Archbishop is of white marble, and represents him in his episcopal robes, leaning on his left hand, and holding a crosier in his right.

The inhabitants are chiefly employed in bleaching, dyeing, and calico-printing; and large quantities of charcoal are also made here, the produce of wood procured from the neighbouring hills: here, also, is a very extensive brewery. The town has sustained severe injury in the loss of its carrying trade, of which, prior to the formation of the Brighton Railway, it enjoyed a large share; its connexion with stage coach, and maintenance of posting establishments, both on an extensive scale, proved, for many years, a fruitful source of revenue to the town, the loss of which, and it is irreparable, will long be felt. The market, on Saturday, is well supplied with all kinds of provision. It has two fairs, on the 5th of June and the 2d of October; and the latter, called the Walnut fair, attracts a large number of visiters from London.

The Public intending to stop at any of the intermediate stations between London and Croydon, must take their places by the Croydon trains, that stop at all the stations on the Croydon railway, while the Brighton trains stop at no place between London and Croydon.

Leaving the Croydon station, where the railway commences a rise of 1 in 264, or 20 feet in a mile, it then passes under the Addiscombe road bridge, and enters a cutting, through which it arrives at the Coombe Lane, or Addington road bridge, and the 11 milestone. 1½ m. distant, on left of Coombe Lane, in a beautiful situation, is Addington Palace*. From Coombe Lane, on left of which is Coombe House †, a short embankment and succeeding excavation conduct to a long embankment, a terrace of 2 m. in length, that, affording a good view of Smitham Bottom and the Brighton road, on right, carries it almost to

THE GODSTONE STATION,

AN INTERMEDIATE ONE, DISTANT FROM LONDON 13¼ MILES, FROM BRIGHTON 37¼ MILES.—Journey resumed below.

The Godstone Station is situate in a cutting, previous to arriving at which, a ¼ of a mile beyond Coombe Lane, the Railway crosses the road to Selsden, 1½ mile distant on left, where, seated amid luxuriant plantation, is an elegant mansion, the seat of ‡.

From the Selsden road, carried with a bend on the border of Smitham Bottom, it crosses, near the 12 milestone, the Sanderstead road, 1¼ mile distant, on left of which is Sanderstead Court, the seat of §.

The Sanderstead Hills command a delightful prospect extending westward over Banstead Downs to Berkshire, and into Hampshire, and north-west to Harrow on the Hill and Buckinghamshire. In about ¾ m. more, the Railway arrives at Purley House, just beyond which it crosses the old Godstone road, gaining, in rather more than ½ m., the end of the embankment, and new Godstone road (the road to Lewes), a little beyond which it enters a cutting, where, in the immediate vicinity of Foxley Hatch Turnpike, that lies unseen upon the right, is the Godstone Station.

Purley House, the seat of ||, was formerly the residence of John Horne Tooke, Esq., whence an ingenious philological work, written by that gentleman, derived the singular title of the Diversions of Purley. This house was the seat of Bradshaw, president of the court at the trial of Charles I., a circumstance to which Mr. Tooke humorously alludes, in his preface to the above-mentioned work. 2½ miles distant from Godstone Station, on right, is The Oaks ¶, long the seat of the late Earl of Derby, who, in a style that did honour to the spirit of that distinguished nobleman, entertained, during the race week, the frequenters of Epsom, the patrons of the turf; and in the hunting season, the

* Archbishop of Canterbury. † John Currie, Esq.
‡ G. R. Smith, Esq. § Colonel Houston.
|| E. B. Kemble, Esq. ¶ Unoccupied.

heroes of the chace, for whose amusement a pack of fox-hounds and other appurtenances of a hunting establishment, were here maintained. This celebrated villa, which contains 50 sleeping rooms for visitors, is seated in a park of more than 2 miles in circumference, the grounds of which are beautifully planted. Here was given a grand *fête champêtre*, in celebration of the late earl's first marriage, which furnished General Burgoyne with the subject of a musical entertainment, entitled the Maid of the Oaks. The Oaks Stakes, for 3 year old fillies only, was first made at this place, then the seat of the Earl of Derby, by a party of noblemen and gentlemen that, in the year 1777, were partaking his lordship's hospitality, and thence derive their name. The Derby Stakes, for horses 3 years old, also originated here in the following year, and were so named in compliment to that nobleman. Epsom Races, of which the above stakes form the grand attraction, are always run for on Wednesday and Friday immediately preceding Whitsun week, except when Easter falls in March; when, agreeable to a regulation of the Jockey Club, they take place a fortnight later.

Quitting the Godstone Station, the Railway, continued in a line nearly direct, by alternate excavation and embankment, on the margin of Smitham Bottom, soon crosses the Caterham Road, about half a mile beyond which, passing Foxley Wood on left, it arrives at

THE STOAT'S NEST STATION,

AN INTERMEDIATE ONE, DISTANT FROM LONDON 14½ MILES, FROM BRIGHTON 36 MILES. — Journey resumed below.

The Stoat's Nest station is situate a short remove from the Brighton road, running through Smitham Bottom, and about ¾ m. north of the Red Lion, a house well known to all frequenters of the Surrey hunt; and from whence, or from the Stoat's Nest station, over the Downs, or by the road through Woodmansterne and Banstead to Epsom race-course, a distance of about 6½ m. is a delightful ride.

From the Stoat's Nest station, the railway is continued, on the rise of 1 in 264, or 20 feet in a mile, through excavation, with the exception of a short embankment near the 15¼ milestone, to the mouth of the Merstham Tunnel (17¼ miles from London) crossing in its way, at 15⅜ miles, the Hooley House bridge, about ¾ mile before which another road, to Caterham, crosses the line. The Merstham Tunnel is approached through a cutting of considerable depth, in some places nearly 100 feet, forming a sort of mountain pass, whose lofty sides exclude all objects from the view. The Brighton Railway directors, in whitewashing and partially illuminating the Merstham and other tunnels with gas have set an example well worthy of imitation by other companies; as, independently of divesting these subterraneous passages of the darkness in which they are enveloped, the light, of no mean advantage to the driver, inspires confidence in the traveller; and, in the event of an accident happening therein, would prove of inestimable value; in proof of which let any one contemplate the consequence of a collision or disaster of any kind in a tunnel of a mile in length, and imagine what, in such a situation, would be the feelings of persons suffering therefrom, increased by being shrouded in impenetrable gloom!

The Merstham Tunnel, about 1820 yards, rather more than a mile in length, is constructed, from the entrance to its centre, on a rise of 1 in 1034, or 5 feet in a mile; and from thence to its termination, on a descent of 1 in 1089, or $4\frac{8}{10}$ feet in a mile: it terminates in a cutting of great depth, and $\frac{3}{4}$ of a mile in length— emerging whence, it is carried on an embankment, and descent of 1 in 264, or 20 feet in a mile, crossed in its way at $18\frac{7}{8}$ miles by the Nutfield road, to

THE MERSTHAM STATION,

AN INTERMEDIATE ONE, DISTANT FROM LONDON $19\frac{1}{2}$ MILES, FROM BRIGHTON 31 MILES. — Journey resumed page 8.

At Merstham is Merstham House, the seat of *. The Merstham Embankment affords a fine view of Gatton Park, the effect of which is considerably heightened from its succeeding the Merstham Tunnel and excavation, clearing which it suddenly bursts upon the sight.

GATTON AND GATTON PARK.

Gatton, a mean village, was long remarkable as being one of the most rotten boroughs in England, having sent two members to parliament from the time of Henry VI. till the passing of the Reform Bill, when it was disfranchised.

Gatton Park, or Lower Gatton House, is a noble modern structure, that carries with it the entire property of the borough, and was purchased by S. Petrie, Esq., of Robert Ladbroke, Esq., for 110,000*l.*, and by him sold to Sir Mark Wood, Bart.; of whose representative it was purchased by the late Lord Monson, at the price, it is said, of 100,000*l.*, a few years prior to its disfranchisement. The approach to this house† is thought to equal any thing of the kind in the kingdom. From the lodge, which is on the summit of the hill leading to Reigate, the road winds beautifully

---

* Sir W. G. H. Jolliffe, Bart.
† Now the property of the Countess of Warwick.

down the park for a mile, amid woods and groves of fir, presenting here and there, through breaks, some enchanting views of the country below. From the south front of the house the prospects are rich, various, and extensive. At the foot of the sloping eminence on which it is situated is a fine lake of 40 acres, enriched with two beautiful well-planted islands, the haunts of swans, and other aquatic fowls. The adjacent country is finely broken, and diversified by wood-crowned hills, and luxuriant vales.

Northward of this noble domain is Upper Gatton House.*

From the Merstham Station the Railway, continued by successive excavation and embankment reaches, near the $20\frac{3}{4}$ milestone, the junction of the South Eastern with the Brighton Railway, and arrives at

THE REIGATE STATION

OF THE SOUTH EASTERN RAILWAY, A PRINCIPAL ONE, DISTANT FROM LONDON 21 MILES, FROM DOVER $65\frac{3}{4}$ MILES, FROM REIGATE $1\frac{1}{4}$ MILE.

Leaving the Reigate Station, the Railway, constructed with a sweep, on a rise of 1 in 274, arrives in about $\frac{1}{2}$ m., principally through the Redstone Hill cutting, at the road leading from Reigate to Godstone, over which it is carried, and commencing a descent of the same ratio, enters the Robert's Hole excavation, taken through which it reaches, in about $\frac{3}{4}$ of a mile from the Reigate Station, Robert's Hole Farm; $\frac{1}{4}$ m. beyond this it enters on the Nutfield enbankment, of about 2 miles in length, constructed on which it crosses, near the $22\frac{3}{4}$ milestone, the road to Midge Street, and at $23\frac{1}{2}$ m. Nutfield Lane, the village of Nutfield, remarkable for its fullers' earth pits, lying about $1\frac{1}{4}$ m. on left. In rather more than $\frac{3}{4}$ of a mile beyond Nutfield Lane, the Railway gains the $23\frac{3}{4}$ milestone, and end of this long embankment, that, from a little beyond the 22 milestone, constructed nearly on a level, and then on a rise of 1 in 660, affords a good view of the country on either side; the one on left somewhat circumscribed, being bounded by the beautiful slopes of the Nutfield and Bletchingley hills, whose summits, crowned by the road from Godstone to Reigate, afford some of the finest views in the county of Surrey. Near the $23\frac{3}{4}$ milestone the Railway enters the Bletchingley excavation, through which it gains the 24 milestone, and road from Pound Hill to Bletchingley, a village that, with a population of about 2000, was one of the rotten boroughs of Surrey, having from the time of the 21st of Edward I. to the passing of the Reform Bill, sent two members to Parliament. From the Pound Hill and Bletchingley

* Unoccupied.

Road, here carried over the line, the Railway arrives, in rather less than ½ a mile, at the mouth of the Bletchingley Tunnel (1324 yards in length), where it commences a descent of 1 in 1760, and on clearing it is continued through cutting to the 25½ milestone, and an embankment by which, in rather more than ¼ of a mile, it reaches the old road from London to Lewes, through Godstone, and in less than ½ a mile, carried on a level, the new road from Godstone to East Grinstead, where is

THE GODSTONE STATION,

A PRINCIPAL ONE, DISTANT FROM LONDON 26½ MILES, FROM DOVER 60¼ MILES, FROM GODSTONE 2 MILES, FROM EAST GRINSTEAD 6½ MILES.

Two miles and a half distant, on left of the Godstone Station, is Flower House *, Rooksnest †, and 3 miles distant, Marden Park.‡ From the Godstone Station the Railway is continued in a direct line, with the intervention of a short level on a descent of 1 in 264, to the Tanridge and Blindley Heath Road, at Tanridge Lane, a little beyond which the embankment terminates, and the Railway, continued through shallow cutting, arrives at the 27 mile-stone; a little beyond which it commences a descent of 1 in 880, on which it reaches the Tanridge excavation and 28 milestone, from whence the next ½ mile is a descent of 1 in 264. At the 28¼ milestone, the railway clears the Crowhurst excavation, and a little before the 28½ milestone enters on a level embankment that carries it to the road from Crowhurst to Stafford's Wood, the Stafford's Wood cutting, and 29 milestone. At the Crowhurst excavation, which is of considerable depth, the railway is constructed for a short distance on the rise of 1 in 660, when it changes to a descent of 1 in 264, on which inclination it gains the end of the cutting, the 30 milestone, a short embankment, and Kent Brook. Crossing this, it quits Surrey, and enters the county of Kent. To the last embankment the Little Brown's cutting succeeds; that, terminating near the 30¾ milestone, carries it on a descent of 1 in 264, near the 31 milestone to Marlpit Hill, where is

THE EDENBRIDGE STATION,

A PRINCIPAL ONE, DISTANT FROM LONDON 31¼ MILES, FROM DOVER 55⅓ MILES, FROM EDENBRIDGE 1 MILE, FROM WESTERHAM 4½ MILES.

A little before arriving at the Edenbridge Station, the line enters, on a level, the Edenbridge embankment, of rather more

---

* Hon. G. F. Neville. † C. Turner, Esq. ‡ Mrs. Ricardo.

than ¼ a mile in length, that carries it to the Edenbridge and Four Elms Road; from whence, still continued by embankment, it is constructed on a descent of 1 in 264 to the 32¼ milestone, a short excavation, and the vicinity of Medhurst Row. From this point, continued on a level, the Four Elms embankment, of ¼ a mile in length, it arrives at the Crispin cutting, that takes it, on a descent of 1 in 264, to the 33¼ milestone, about ¼ m. before which the road from Four Elms Green to Hever crosses the line. A little beyond this, the excavation terminates, when a short cutting and succeeding embankment carry it to the 33¾ milestone, where the road from Four Elms Green to Leigh crosses the line, 1¼ mile distant, on right of which are the venerable remains of Hever Castle, in her youthful days the happy home of Anne Bullen. At the Four Elms Green and Leigh Road, the Railway enters the Bough Beach cutting, through which it gains the 34¼ milestone. At Bough Beach Green the road from Four Elms to Leigh crosses over the valley at the commencement of the Bough Beach embankment, under which, near the 34½ milestone, the same road re-crosses the line. On right of this embankment is beheld Chiddingstone Castle, the seat of the Streatfeilds from the time of James I. This is an elegant modern mansion, that, with its beautiful grounds, is now the property of *. In this direction, also, is seen the tower of Chiddingstone Church. From a little beyond the 34¼ milestone, where terminates the descent of 1 in 264, the Railway is continued on the descent of 1 in 1056 to the 35 milestone and Summerden cutting; taken through which, it enters on a level (the Chiddingstone) embankment, that in less than ⅛ a mile carries it to

THE PENSHURST STATION,

AN INTERMEDIATE ONE, DISTANT FROM LONDON 36 MILES, FROM DOVER 50¾ MILES. —Journey resumed page 13.

HEVER CASTLE.

Hever Castle was erected in the reign of Edward III. by William de Hever, and became in the reign of Henry VI. the property of Sir Geoffrey Bullen, whose grandson was the father of the unfortunate Anne Bullen, who, in consequence of Henry VIII.'s attachment to his daughter, was created Viscount Rochefort, Earl of Wiltshire and Ormond, and Knight of the Garter. The greater part of it still remains in good preservation, solid but heavy, and is used as a dwelling house by a farmer; in its perfect state it was a good house, substantially built, and, as at present, was surrounded by a moat, which is supplied by the river Eden,

* H. Streatfeild, Esq.

and approached by a bridge through a gateway embattled and machicolated, in which the portcullis still remains. The inner buildings form a quadrangle, inclosing a court. The hall still retains vestiges of its ancient festive splendour. The great staircase communicates with various chambers, wainscotted with small oaken panels, and a long gallery having a curious ornamented ceiling in stucco. The windows of the staircase display several shields in painted glass, collected from different parts of the castle, charged with the arms and alliances of the Bullens, &c. A small recess or apartment opening from the gallery is said to have been occasionally used by Henry as a council chamber. At the upper end of the gallery is a part of the floor which lifts up, and discovers a narrow and gloomy descent, said to lead as far as the moat, and called the dungeon. Few places can be viewed with greater interest than Hever Castle. Who can enter its walls without calling to mind the fate of Anne Bullen? Who will enter the great hall, and there see probably the identical oak table at which the royal Henry has sat, a suitor and a guest, and not allow his imagination some stretch of fancy towards those extraordinary scenes, and heave the mingled sigh of pity and indignation at the fatal termination of events to which they were the delusive preludes? Here, then, we may fancy the fierce and arbitrary tyrant soothed into mildness by the fascinating charms of Anne Bullen, playing the lover, submitting to the inconveniences of a contracted situation, and sharing in the charms of private life. Three years' possession, and the rise of another meteor, to engage his fancy and excite his lust, alienated his affections from his amiable queen. On the decline of her favour, fell also the family, which had, through her influence, been raised to the first order in the state, and which appears to have borne its honours with a becoming moderation. With them also this place fell into neglect. Having served as a portion for another repudiated queen, it afterwards passed into a family who disparked it, and allowed it gradually to sink into its present forlorn state; wherein it only remains a monument of the amorous tyranny of an unprincipled monarch, and of the instability of fortune attended by the caprices of passion.

Hever Castle, an object of great interest, and in a state of good preservation, is the property of *

PENSHURST. †

Penshurst, the ancient seat of the Sidneys, endeared by the recollections of Sir Philip Sidney and of Waller, and still occupied by one of the original family, has frequently been the theme of

* F. Mead Waldo, Esq.
† The public are permitted to view on Saturdays and Mondays from 10 to 6.

the poet's lay; the remembrance of the illustrious persons who have resided here, and the venerable character of the place, having a strong tendency to excite those vivid emotions of melancholy feeling and awakened sensibility, to scenes long past, which form no inconsiderable portion of the imagery of the poet's day-dream.

The lyre of Waller was strung by love; yet even the pathos of his warblings has been equalled by the airy harp of the late Mrs. Charlotte Smith, who, whilst wandering amidst the groves of Penshurst, in the autumn of 1788, composed the following very beautiful

"SONNET.

"Ye towers sublime, deserted now and drear,
Ye woods, deep-sighing to the hollow blast,
The musing wanderer loves to linger near,
While History points to all your glories past ;
And, startling from their haunts the timid deer,
To trace the walks obscur'd by matted fern,
Which Waller's soothing notes were wont to hear ;
But where now clamours the discordant her'n.*
The spoiling hand of Time may overturn
These lofty battlements, and quite deface
The fading canvass, whence we love to learn
Sydney's keen look, and Sacharissa's grace ;
But fame and beauty still defy decay,
Sav'd by th' historic page, the poet's tender lay."

The park, though much lessened since the decease of the last Earl of Leicester of the Sidney family, still includes more than 400 acres of ground, finely diversified by gentle eminences, lawns, and woods. On the south-east side it is nearly approached by the united streams of the Eden and the Medway, and within it is a fine piece of water called Lancup well; above the latter, and at a short distance from it, stood the famous oak, said to have been planted at the birth of Sir Philip Sidney. Ben Jonson and Waller have both celebrated this tree; and in the poem called "Penshurst," by E. Coventry, are these elegant lines in reference to its connection with the natal day of Sidney :—

"What genius points to yonder oak !
What rapture does my soul provoke !
There let me hang a garland high,
There let my muse her accents try.
Be there my earliest homage paid,
Be there my latest vigils made ;
For thou wast planted in the earth
The day that shone on Sidney's birth."

The oak, beech, and chesnut trees are mostly of luxuriant growth and fine character. The mansion, which stands near the south-west angle of the park, is a very extensive pile; it is one of those castellated dwellings which immediately succeeded the

---

* In the park is a heronry.

more gloomy residences of the 13th and 14th centuries: some few parts, however, are of a later period. The principal buildings form a quadrangle, inclosing a spacious court, and comprehending a great hall, chapel, and numerous apartments. The state rooms are splendid; but the most noble ornaments are the portraits of the Sidneys and Dudleys, with the monarchs who favoured them, some of which are by Holbein. Besides these, here are also some other very curious and rare pictures, finely painted, both historical and portrait. Too many of these now, however, only show what might once have been their pretensions, scarcely any of them having escaped the effect of the damps, to which they have been lamentably exposed.

Quitting the Penshurst Station, the Railway reaches the White Post cutting, entering which it soon gains the 36¼ milestone, and the White Post Tunnel, 64 yards long. Clearing this, and continuing its course through the Leigh cutting, which is of considerable depth, the Railway near the 36¾ milestone commences a descent of 1 in 264, upon which it continues for rather more than 3 miles. The White Post and Leigh excavations, about 1½ mile in length, completely exclude all view of the beautiful country, the most luxuriant perhaps in the county of Kent, that here borders the line; of which Penshurst Place*, on right, forms the great feature; nearly adjoining this is Redleaf†, that contains a fine collection of pictures; and southward of Penshurst Place, South Park, the seat of. ‡ The house, built in 1789 by R. Allnutt, Esq., and enlarged by his son, is admirably placed on rising ground, forming a pleasing object to the whole of the adjacent country, and commanding a view over the village and grounds of Penshurst, and extensive prospects in all directions. In the valley before the house, a branch of the river Medway holds its winding course; it is not navigable here, but flowing with a tolerable body of water, that, chancing at this point to fall over a shallow bed of stones, forms a natural cascade, that adds materially to the beauty of the place. The turnpike road from Penshurst to Tunbridge, near the 37¼ milestone, crosses the Leigh excavation, which terminates in little more than a ¼ of a mile beyond it. Here the Railway enters on the Medway valley embankment that in conjunction with three viaducts carry it across the river and valley of the Medway, of which a good view is obtained, and of the high grounds about Bidborough, that, beautifully wooded, are beheld to great advantage on right, to the 39½ milestone, when the descent diminishes to 1 in 854. From the Medway Valley embankment,

* The magnificent seat of Lord De Lisle and Dudley.
† W. Wells, Esq. ‡ Sir Henry Hardinge, Bart.

near the 37¾ milestone, Hall Place*, and the village of Leigh, are beheld on left. Near the 40 milestone the embankment terminates, when the train enters a slight cutting at Barden, taken through which it arrives at

THE TUNBRIDGE STATION, *⁎*

A PRINCIPAL ONE, DISTANT FROM LONDON 40¼ MILES, FROM DOVER 46¼ MILES, FROM TUNBRIDGE WELLS 5¾ MILES, FROM SEVENOAKS 6½ MILES, FROM MAIDSTONE 13¾ MILES, FROM HASTINGS 33¾ MILES.—Journey resumed, p. 21.

At Tunbridge is Tunbridge Castle†; 5 miles distant from Tunbridge, on left, is Oxonheath‡; and 5½ miles distant, Knowle Park §; 1 mile distant, on right, is Mabledon‖; 1½ mile distant, visible from the Railway, Somerhill ¶; and 2 miles distant, Bounds.** The admirer of nature, and traveller of taste, cannot fail to be struck with the appearance of the range of hills, some of them of great eminence; that from the Limpsfield Road, near the 28 milestone, to the Tunbridge Station, bordering the valley of the Eden on left, here the course of the Railway, and assuming every variety of form, constitute a boundary bold and beautiful in the extreme.

KNOWLE PARK. ††

The magnificent and immense pile which graces the demesne of Knowle, and forms a noble and conspicuous object from the London road, exhibits specimens of the styles of different ages: the most ancient is probably coeval with the Marechels and Bigods, who formerly possessed this seat; the most modern is of the erection of Thomas first Earl of Dorset, in the reign of James I.: many subsequent improvements have however been made; and the building is now of a quadrangular shape, chiefly in the castellated style, with square towers, and two large embattled gateways. This edifice covers a space of upwards of 5 acres in extent; the magnificent and feudal manner of the mansion conveys most forcibly to the mind the idea of days long past, when baronial pomp and romantic chivalry shone in their meridian splendour; nor is the charm broken on entering the hall, still ornamented with all the paraphernalia of its original decorations. The apartments are splendidly fitted up, but their most attractive ornaments will be found in the invaluable collection of pictures they contain. Among the portraits

* The beautiful seat of W. Smith, Esq. † J. E. West, Esq.
‡ Sir William Geary, Bart. § Lord Amherst.
‖ J. Deacon, Esq. ¶ J. Alexander, Esq.
** Rev. Sir Charles Hardinge, Bart.
†† Knowle Park is shown every day except Sunday from 12 to 4.
⁎ From this Station a branch Railway is now made to Tunbridge Wells.

are many of the principal nobility and statesmen who lived in the reign of Henry VIII. and his children; some of them are by Holbein; the collection also contains the finest productions of Titian, Correggio, Vandyck, Rembrandt, and Sir Joshua Reynolds. Here is likewise a collection of antique busts, mostly purchased in Italy by the late Duke of Dorset. The park, between 5 and 6 miles in circumference, presents a richly diversified surface, abounds with fine timber and woods, and contains numerous herds of deer. At no great distance from Knowle Park is the Wilderness, Marquis Camden.

TUNBRIDGE,

DISTANT FROM LONDON, BY ROAD, 30 MILES; BY RAILWAY, 40¼ MILES.

A market town*, in the county of Kent, is situate on the river Tun, or Tone, which forms one of the five branches into which the Medway here divides itself, and over each of which there is a stone bridge. The town consists chiefly of one long wide street. At the entrance from London is a stone causeway, the gift of John Wilford, of London, in 1528. The principal bridge was erected in 1775, from a design by Mr. Milne, at an expense of 1100*l*. Near it is a wharf for the reception of timber, brought hither from the Weald, and afterwards sent down the Medway. The Church is a large and handsome fabric, dedicated to St. Peter and St. Paul. It was new pewed and ornamented, from a bequest of 500*l*. made by the late John Hooker, Esq. It contains some good monuments. The Free Grammar School, a capacious structure, is situate at the north end of the town, and was founded and endowed by Sir Andrew Judde, a native of this place, and Lord Mayor of London in the reign of Edward VI. The Skinners Company of London, who are the governors of the school, pay a visit to it every year in May, and attended, as the statutes direct, by some eminent clergyman, to examine the school, and distribute premiums to the scholars. The masters have, in general, been men eminent for abilities. Many other charitable bequests have been made to the town by different persons. The remains of Tunbridge Castle stand on the south-west side of the town; they consist principally of an entrance gateway, flanked by round towers, and tolerably perfect; and the artificial mount on which the keep stood. It was surrounded by three moats, within the compass of the outermost of which the then ancient town was principally confined. The ruins are picturesque, though much of the venerable remains were dilapidated by a late proprietor, Mr. Hooker, to build a residence, attached to the entrance, in a style by no means corresponding to the original; the grounds are

* The population of which is 23,184.

pleasant. This castle, the outer walls of which inclosed an extent of 6 acres, was built by Richard de Tunbridge, otherwise Fitzgilbert, and afterwards Earl of Clare, a kinsman of William the Conqueror, who, for his services at the battle of Hastings, had numerous lordships granted to him, and became one of the most puissant barons in England. It afterwards became a place of great importance, and under its protection the town arose. At a short distance from the castle was a priory of Austin canons, founded by Richard de Clare, in the reign of Henry I., of which some small remains still exist. Inns: Rose and Crown Royal Hotel, Castle Inn, Angel Inn, Bull Inn; the two latter being commercial houses.

The environs of Tunbridge are very beautiful, the town being seated in the centre of a well-wooded country, and nearly surrounded by hills, the summits of which command some very extensive prospects. The walks and rides, pleasant in every direction, and fertile in subjects for the pencil, conduct to points of great interest, among which may be named Hever Castle, Penshurst Place, Chiddingstone, and South Park. On approaching the latter by the Bidborough Road, that commands some good views, the church of Penshurst, with its pinnacled tower, forms a prominent feature. The ride to Frant through the Wells is greatly admired, terminating as it does in an eminence that 600 feet above the level of the sea is crowned by Eridge Castle, the noble seat of the Earl of Abergavenny, well worthy of a visit. From Frant Steeple, the following objects, in fine weather, are clearly discernible:— The tower in Heathfield Park; Fairlight Down, near Hastings; the principal part of Pevensey Level; and it is also said the cliffs above Dover may be distinguished hence. But among the most favourite excursions from Tunbridge and the Wells, is the ride to the ruins of Bayham Abbey, that, at a short distance beyond Frant, takes its course through a country deeply wooded, and of exquisite beauty. The monks to whom Bayham Abbey was allotted, the remains of which are considerable, belonged to the canons regular of the Præmonstratensian order. It is said to have been founded about the year 1120, and continued in their possession till the dissolution of monasteries in the reign of Henry VIII., when its revenue amounted to 152*l.* 9*s.* 4*d.* per annum.* The ride to East Grinstead through Groombridge and Wythiam, though somewhat circuitous, if not deemed too distant (it is 21 miles from Tunbridge, from the Wells 15¼ miles), conducts, through a richly wooded country, to places of great celebrity, among which may be named Buck-

* Bayham Abbey is the property of Marquis Camden, whose second title of Viscount Bayham is derived therefrom.

hurst, formerly Stoneland Park, the fine seat of Earl Delawarr, the grounds of which were greatly improved by Repton; the remains of Bolebroke, an ancient seat of the Sackvilles; Kidbrook, the residence and property of Lord Colchester; and at no great distance from it the ruins of Bramble Tye House, the subject of a novel from the pen of the late Horace Smith. Finally, the ride from Tunbridge to Maidstone, a distance of $13\frac{3}{4}$ miles, over one of the best roads in the county, through Hadlow, Mereworth, Wateringbury, and Teston, which may with truth be termed the hop garden of Kent, is an excursion to which a day may well be devoted.

TUNBRIDGE WELLS,

A favourite resort of the fashionable world, is the appellation given to a series of scattered villages or dwellings within 5 or 6 miles of the town of Tunbridge, immediately bordering on Sussex, and which owe their origin and importance to the celebrated mineral waters in the vicinity. They are situated in the three parishes of Tunbridge, Frant, and Speldhurst, and consist of four divisions; Mount Ephraim, Mount Pleasant, Mount Sion, and the Wells properly so called. The distance of the latter from London is $35\frac{3}{4}$ miles by road, $40\frac{3}{4}$ miles by railway. The prevailing ingredient in the soil, and that which forms the characteristic feature of the country, is a sandstone of considerable hardness. Where this lies near the surface, as the light soil is washed away, various considerable prominences are presented to the eye, which tend to vary the scene; and when mixed with the verdure of intervening trees and shrubs, and enlivened with moving objects, present scenes highly fascinating to the admirers of the wild beauties of nature. In some places where the inequality of the ground has favoured more extensive failures of the adjacent soil, these protuberances are of considerable magnitude, and the external surface of the stone having, from exposure, acquired hardness and a darker hue, they assume the majestic character of rocks. Within a short distance from the Wells there are three principal aggregations of them, which are objects of attraction and curiosity. The nearest are distinguished by the appellation of the High Rocks; the others, being named from the proprietors of the adjacent lands, are called Harrison's and Penn's Rocks: the former about 5 miles from the Wells, the latter about a mile further in the same direction. At a considerable depth below the surface the sand becomes white and of a delicate fineness, and is in such request for household purposes that it forms a tolerably profitable pursuit with poor persons to collect it for sale. The excavations for this purpose in some are so considerable as to give them the character of caverns; and cottages having been erected among the rocks above, not only is the general effect interesting, but between the increased pressure from above and the encroachments on the substratum, the idea of danger to the parties occupying either station is so heightened as to make it a scene to be viewed with no inconsiderable apprehension. The Rocks, in a valley adjoining Rust Hall Common, are not indeed so large as those already noticed, but are no less remarkable for the singular shapes which many of them present. Here, with the aid of a little imagination, many counterparts of art or nature have been traced; and the walk through the valley is amongst the most agreeable in the immediate vicinity.

These rocks afford a principal source of amusement to the frequenters of Tunbridge Wells. The walk to the High Rocks is exceeded, in point of beauty, by nothing in the country, whilst the greater distance of the others affords a pleasing variety to the riders. Adjoining nearly to the High Rocks, but nearer to Rust Hall, is an excellent cold bath. It is situated in a beautiful romantic dell; and for the coldness and transparency of the water, may be pronounced as exceeded by none in the kingdom. When Rust Hall was the principal rendezvous of the company, this was a place of much public resort; but on the failure of that, it has declined in its celebrity. At a still later period, accommodations for entertainment were provided at the High Rocks, which induced many pleasant meetings under a rustic shed, at one termination of them, where romantic scenery, combining with the wish to please and to be pleased, tended to create an agreeable relief to that tedium, which will frequently encroach on a place of fashionable resort. Of late years, these seem to have yielded to the superior attractions of Harrison's Rocks, where, by the side of a lake of considerable extent, the proprietor has erected some rooms for the accommodation of the public on their occasional visits.

The naturalist will amongst these rocks find a source of much botanical amusement. Heaths of great variety and beauty, forest shrubs, and rock plants abound; and that which is peculiarly appropriate, being denominated, from the spot, the Trichomanes Tunbridgiensis, is here found in great perfection.

The air of this district is very pure and salubrious, and aid powerfully the medicinal qualities of the waters. The general appearance of the country is inviting, and the aspect of the villages picturesque; the whole appearing like a large town in a wood, interspersed with rich meadows, and inclosing a large common, including walks, rides, handsome rows of trees, an other objects of variety. The village is nearly 2 miles in length, by 1 in breadth, and of late years the buildings have been rapidly increasing, many persons of rank and respectability having houses here for occasional or constant residence. The accommodations for visitants have been much improved, and the population is decidedly on the increase. During the last two reigns, this place was frequently visited by different branches of the Royal Family, among the latest of whom may be named the Duchess of Kent, and, during her minority, Her present Majesty. That part, by way of distinction, called the Wells, is the centre of business and amusement, as it is here that all the public places are situated : the springs, public parades, assembly-rooms, the chapel, and the market-place. The Parades, usually called the Upper and Lower Walks, run parallel to each other, and are much frequented; the former by the better classes, the latter being chiefly used by servants and the country people. A portico, supported by Tuscan pillars, runs the entire length of the principal walk, and affords an agreeable shelter from the sun and rain. A row of luxuriant limes contributes also to the amenity of the place, and under their shade the company meet together during the hours of general resort. On the right stands one set of the Public Rooms, opposite to which is an orchestra, in which a band of music plays three times a day during the season; here are also the Libraries, and a number of neat little shops for the sale of millinery, perfumery, jewellery, and Tunbridge ware. On the left is the Theatre, one of the best conducted out of London, the lower set of Assembly Rooms, and several lodging-houses. The Bath-house, which contains baths of all kinds, is a handsome building at the end of the Parade. Amidst the buildings in the vicinity of Mount Sion, is a very fine clump of trees, called the Grove, that forms a prominent and very important feature, around which are disposed villas, lodging-houses, and gardens, and on the brow of an eminence called Grove Hill (a gift of 4 acres, in 1707, of John, Duke of Buckingham) are some large and respectable houses, that command delightful views over Calverly Park, and an extended range of country, including Frant, Crowborough, and many other places. The chief feature of improvement Tunbridge Wells has experienced, in modern times, is Calverly Park, which, in style and manner, somewhat resembles the Regent's Park, near London, but devoid of the range of terraces, that, by their continuity, destroy the simplicity of that once delightful spot; or perhaps resembles, but upon a more extended scale, Park village, in its vicinity. The Park, a beautiful inclosure, pleasingly disposed by nature and adorned by art, is studded with villas that command views over an extensive tract of wild and cultivated country. The Chapel of Ease, a fine venerable building, was erected, in 1684 and 1696, at an expense of 2300*l*. The New Church, erected from designs by Decimus Burton, Esq., a handsome edifice with a square tower, forms a conspicuous object from different parts of the Wells, and is beheld at some distance in the country on the south and west. The discovery of the springs is generally ascribed to Dudley Lord North, a distinguished courtier in the reign of James I., who, on returning to London from the country, whither he had retired for the recovery of his health, happened to notice a peculiarity in their taste, and having examined them and consulted with his physieians, resorted to the wells to try their effect, which soon restoring him to health, they shortly after rose into notice. The waters are considered to be of great use in removing complaints arising from sedentary occupations, weak digestion, and nervous and chronical disorders; and their utility in cases of barrenness is also stated to be very great. The springs are of the chalybeate kind; the water at the fountain head is extremely clear and pellucid; it has little smell, but the taste is strongly impregnated with iron. Its component parts are steely particles, marine salts, an oily matter, an ochreous substance, a volatile vitriolic spirit, too subtle for analysis, and a simple fluid. Nash, whose history is more immediately involved in the annals of Bath than those of Tunbridge Wells, was, for a series of years, the *Arbiter Elegantiarum* at the latter. It was also a favourite resort of Richardson, and was visited by Dr. Johnson and other eminent wits of the last century. One of its most distinguished settled inhabitants was Cumberland,

"The Terence of England, the mender of hearts,"

who laboured sedulously to infuse into his dramatic compositions as strong a bias to the interests of virtue and innocence as the nature of the subject would admit. The plays he published whilst living are well known; but it is greatly to be lamented that he was not in easy circumstances in the latter part of his life.

The trade of Tunbridge Wells is similar to that of the Spa in Germany, and chiefly consists of turnery and toys in wood of different kinds, that, under the denomination of Tunbridge ware, comprise tea-chests, dressing-boxes of different kinds, punch-ladles, snuff-boxes, and other trifling articles. The principal hotels are the following: Calverly Hotel, Royal Kentish Hotel, Royal Sussex Hotel, and Mount Ephraim Hotel. The commercial inns are the Castle and ———— the Swan.

From the Tunbridge Station, the Railway, carried forward in a direct line, commences a rise of 1 in 264, entering near the 41 milestone, the Walter's Farm cutting, clearing which, it crosses, by an embankment and bridge, the Marl Bourn Brook and Valley, entering near the 41½ milestone, the Postern cutting a short one of considerable depth. Clearing the Postern, cutting at the 42 milestone, and commencing a descent of 1 in 264, the Railway reaches an embankment and bridge that carries it across the Tudely brook to the Tudely cutting, through which the train arrives at Tudely. The Tudely cutting terminates a little before the 42¾ milestone, from whence the line, carried on an embankment that affords a view of Capel on right, gains the footpath from Tatlingbury to Moat Farm, a little beyond which stands the 43¾ milestone; half a mile beyond this, carried on the diminished descent of 1 in 320, it arrives at the road from Five Oak Green to Moat Farm, at 44¼ miles, the road from Five Oak Green to Brandbridges, a little beyond which the descent diminishes to 1 in 1396, upon which inclination it is continued to the 44¾ milestone, crossing a little beyond the 45 milestone, the Badshill Mill Brook, when the descent increases to 1 in 330, upon which inclination it passes through Paddock Wood to the turnpike road from Brenchley to Brandbridges, the site of

THE PADDOCK WOOD, OR BRENCHLEY STATION. *˟*

AN INTERMEDIATE ONE, DISTANT FROM LONDON 45½ MILES, FROM DOVER 41¼ MILES, FROM BRENCHLEY 3 MILES.—Journey resumed below.

Four miles distant from Brenchley Station on left, see Roydon Hall* and the church of East Peckham; near which is Mereworth Place† and Yote's Place. ‡

A little beyond the 45¾ milestone, the inclination changes to a rise of 1 in 330, which soon alters to a descent of the same ratio; upon which inclination the railway reaches the road from Mile Oak to Fowl Hill, and the 46½ milestone, from whence it is continued on a rise of 1 in 520 to the road from Brenchley to Yalding, and the 46¾ milestone, in less than ½ a mile beyond which it crosses the Teise, where the inclination changes to a descent of 1 in 528, and upon this it is taken to the turnpike road from Horsemonden to Yadling. The line, which, from a little beyond Tudely to the Horsemonden and Yalding road, runs upon the surface of the land rendered regular by gradation,

* — Cooke, Esq.   † Lady le Despencer.
‡ Lord Torrington.
˟ From whence a branch is now made to Maidstone 10 miles.

affords a good view on right, of the richly wooded eminences that overhang Brenchley, and on left of the valley of the Teise and Beult rivers, backed by the high grounds about Yalding, Hunton, and East Peckham, that in that direction terminate the view. At the Horsemonden and Yalding road, 2½ m. distant, on left of which, occupying a beautiful situation, is beheld Hunton Rectory *, the Railway commences a rise of 1 in 440, upon which it continues for half a mile, from whence it is taken on an ascent over the Beult river, about a mile beyond which, carried on an embankment, it gains the 50 milestone, and

THE MARDEN STATION,

AN INTERMEDIATE ONE, DISTANT FROM LONDON 50 MILES, FROM DOVER 36¾ MILES, FROM MAIDSTONE 7½ MILES.

Three and a half miles distant, on left of Marden Station, see Linton Place†, Boughton Place‡, and Wierton Pier.§ Quitting the Marden Station, the railway enters the Marden cutting, which, at 50¼ miles from London, is crossed by the turnpike road from Marden to Maidstone, at a distance of 7½ miles from the latter. Here it enters on a short level, and, crossing a streamlet, commences a descent of 1 in 264, on which it is carried to the 51¼ milestone; from whence it reaches, by a level embankment that carries it over the river Beult to the 51½ milestone, ½ mile beyond which, taken on an ascent of 1 in 1223, it gains Duck Pits, a little beyond which, carried through cutting on a descent of 1 in 338, it arrives at the Maidstone and Cranbrook road, and

THE STAPLEHURST STATION,

A PRINCIPAL ONE, DISTANT FROM LONDON 52¾ MILES, FROM DOVER 34 MILES, FROM MAIDSTONE 9 MILES, FROM CRANBROOKE 4 MILES, FROM HAWKHURST 9 MILES, FROM BATTLE 19¼ MILES, FROM HASTINGS 27 MILES, FROM RYE 25½ MILES. ‖

Staplehurst is a small village, whose church and windmill stand forth conspicuous on right of the line. Here the Railway enters on the surface of the land again rendered regular by gradation, and, carried forward in a direct line, is so continued for about miles, crossing, in about ¾ of a mile, the road from Staplehurst to Sutton Valence, to which it proceeds on a descent of 1 in 876, when the inclination alters to a rise of 1 in 1702, upon which reaches, in rather less than ¼ m. from the Sutton Valence road, the

---

* Rev. Robert Moore. † Earl Cornwallis.
‡ T. Rider, Esq. § T. F. Best, Esq.
‖ A new road now making from Hawkhurst to Cripps Corner, in Sussex, will considerably shorten the distance to Hastings.

bridge over the Beult river, gaining, a little beyond the 55 milestone, the road from Frittenden to Headcorn, the Frittenden stream at $55\frac{1}{2}$ miles, the river Beult, and in $\frac{3}{4}$ m. more the Franks Bridge stream and turnpike road from Biddenden to Headcorn, and Maidstone, the site of

THE HEADCORN STATION.

AN INTERMEDIATE ONE, DISTANT FROM LONDON $56\frac{1}{4}$ MILES, FROM DOVER $30\frac{1}{2}$ MILES, FROM MAIDSTONE $10\frac{1}{2}$ MILES, FROM TENTERDEN $8\frac{1}{2}$ MILES. — Journey resumed below.

$3\frac{1}{2}$ m. distant on left of Headcorn, see the picturesque ruins of Sutton Castle and East Sutton Place, the seat of the Filmer family from the eighth of James I., of whom the present baronet * is the representative. About 4 m. distant from Headcorn station is Boughton Malherbe, celebrated as the birthplace of the accomplished Sir Henry Wotton, whose ancestors were first seated here in the reign of Richard II. Of Boughton Hall, the family seat of the Wottons, the major part of which has long been pulled down, the remains † are occupied by a farmer, and are remarkable as still retaining the drawing room, of which a good view is given in "Nash's Mansions of the Olden Time," where it is represented in the style in which it was refitted for the reception of Queen Elizabeth in 1573; and the waggon-roofed ceiling, with its Moorish decorations, is deemed one of the most beautiful specimens of interior embellishment in the kingdom, and is indeed unique of its kind. About $\frac{3}{4}$ m. east of this is Chilson, the seat of ‡

A little beyond the Headcorn Station the inclination of the Railway changes to a rise of 1 in 264, on which it continues for about $1\frac{1}{4}$ mile, when it again alters to one of diminished steepness, 1 in 483. Near the 57 milestone the Railway enters on an embankment that carries it to the 58 milestone and Hegg Hill cutting, over which runs the road from Cranbrook to Charing, $\frac{1}{4}$ m. beyond which it reaches the end of the cutting and $58\frac{3}{4}$ milestone. Here the Railway commences a rise of 1 in 370, and passing the road to Biddenden Green, and shortly after Hedgerden, enters the Valentine's Green excavation, in which lies the 60 milestone, and a little beyond it the turnpike road from Smarden to Charing crosses over the line. At the 60 milestone the Railway commences a descent of 1 in 330, and clearing

---

* Sir Edmund Filmer.   † The property of Earl Cornwallis.
‡ J. S. Douglas, Esq.

the excavation at 60½ miles, enters on the Valentine's Green embankment, that carries it (with the intervention of a short level) to the road from Bethersden to Pluckley and Charing, where is

THE PLUCKLEY STATION,

AN INTERMEDIATE ONE, DISTANT FROM LONDON 61 MILES, FROM DOVER 25¾ MILES, FROM CHARING 4¾ MILES, FROM FAVERSHAM 14¼ MILES. — Journey resumed below.

One mile distant from Pluckley Station on left is Surrenden, that for three centuries has been the seat of the very ancient family of Dering, one of whom is mentioned in the Textus Roffensis, and in Doomsday Book, as holding lands at Farningham in this county in the Saxon times, and of whom the present baronet* is the representative. 2 m. distant from Pluckley Station is Cale Hill, that from the time of Henry IV. has been the family seat of the Darells.†

The village of Pluckley, seated on an eminence, commands views of great extent and beauty: hence the eye ranges over a large portion of the Weald of Kent and adjoining county of Sussex, extending westward into Surrey. Of the Weald of Kent, traversed by the Railway from Tunbridge to Pluckley, Harris, the historian of Kent, says, " It affords one of the finest prospects imaginable, to look down from the tops of the hills into the Weald in summer time; for the whole being composed of inclosures, the corn-fields and meadows of different colours, adorned with all manner of flowers, the green woods" (he might have added the hop grounds, unquestionably one of its most beautiful features) "and hedge-rows, and the towns and villages here and there interspersed, do afford so very great and agreeable a view, that I never saw any thing any where more delightful and charming." No part of Kent presents, perhaps, a more delightful panorama, not the least enlivening feature of which may be named the Railway trains, that in their progress to and from this place to Tunbridge, and even beyond it, may be traced by occasional evaporations of smoke and steam for very many miles. The church, which contains several sepulchral memorials of the Dering family, stands forth a striking object, and is beheld at a great distance in every direction.

From the Pluckley Station, a little beyond which it commences a rise of 1 in 264, the Railway carried on the surface of the land rendered regular, reaches on a rise of 1 in 264 the 61¾ milestone,

---

* Sir Edward Cholmeley Dering. † Now of Edward Darell, Esq.

and the Surrenden Hill excavation, carried through which it arrives, on a rise of 1 in 330, at the 62 milestone. A little beyond this the road from Bethersden to Charing crosses the line, and the Railway carried forward on an ascent of diminished steepness, viz. 1 in 528, gains the $62\frac{3}{4}$ milestone and the Hothfield Road excavation, that constructed chiefly on a level, and crossed by the Bethersden and Hothfield Road, carries it to the 63 milestone. One mile distant from the Bethersden and Hothfield Road on left is Hothfield, the hereditary seat of the Tuftons, Earls of Thanet and Godington.* At the 63 milestone the Railway enters on the Chart embankment, $\frac{3}{4}$ of a mile in length, that constructed upon a rise of 1 in 264, carries it to the Chart Hill cutting, soon after entering which it gains the 64 milestone and road from Etchden and Bethersden to Swinford Mill, that here crosses the line. From hence it is continued through the Chart Hill cutting to the $64\frac{1}{4}$ milestone, where the inclination changes to a rise of 1 in 330; and a little beyond it the road from Great Chart to Swinford Mill crosses the line. Soon after crossing the last road the Railway enters on a short level, at the end of which it crosses a small stream, and continued through cutting on a descent of 1 in 330, gains the end of the excavation and 65 milestone; near this the coach road to Godington crosses the line. Near the 65 milestone it gains a short embankment that carries it on the descent of 1 in 660 across the river Stour to the $65\frac{1}{4}$ milestone and a shallow cutting, in which stands the $65\frac{1}{2}$ milestone, where the turnpike road from Tenterden to Ashford crosses over the Railway, a little before which the descent increases to 1 in 330, and so continues to the end of the cutting. In rather less than $65\frac{3}{4}$ miles from London, the Railway reaches a level embankment that takes it to the $66\frac{1}{4}$ milestone, from whence it arrives by shallow cutting, on a descent of 1 in 330, and a short level at the

ASHFORD STATION, *⁎*

A PRINCIPAL ONE, DISTANT FROM LONDON $66\frac{3}{4}$ MILES, FROM DOVER 20 MILES, FROM CANTERBURY $14\frac{1}{2}$ MILES, FROM RYE $12\frac{1}{2}$ MILES, FROM NEW ROMNEY 16 MILES, FROM TENTERDEN $12\frac{1}{4}$ MILES, FROM FAVERSHAM $12\frac{3}{4}$ MILES, FROM LENHAM $10\frac{1}{2}$ MILES. — Journey resumed page 27.

Three miles distant from Ashford, on left, is Eastwell Park†; 5 m. distant, Ollantigh‡; 6 m. distant, Godmersham Park §; and $7\frac{1}{2}$ m. distant, Chilham Castle. ‖

* Rev. Nicholas Toke. † Earl of Winchelsea.
‡ S. E. Sawbridge, Esq. § E. Knight, Esq.
‖ J. B. Wildman, Esq.

⁎ From whence a branch is now made to Canterbury 15 miles, and Ramsgate $30\frac{1}{2}$ miles.

EASTWELL PARK.

The family mansion of Eastwell is a large edifice, situated in an extensive park; the grounds are boldly irregular, and are enlivened by numerous herds of deer. Some of the eminences are well clothed with wood, particularly a high hill in the northwest part, which is embellished with eight avenues, diverging from an octangular plain on the top of the hill: these are called the Star Walks, and command some fine views; in particular, the sea may be seen hence in two different directions, viz. that at the Buoy of the Nore at the junction of the Thames and Medway towards the north, and the other to the south, over Romney Marsh, towards the coast of France.

ASHFORD

is a respectable market town situated on a gentle eminence near the confluence of the upper branches of the river Stour. The church is a spacious and handsome fabric, consisting of a nave, aisles, and three chancels, with a lofty tower arising from the intersection of the nave and principal chancel; it is of very remote origin, but was renovated in the reign of Edward IV. by Sir John Fogge, who also founded a college here, with a small ecclesiastical establishment. In a chapel adjoining to the south transept, formerly appropriated to the Smyths, Lords of Westerhanger, and owners of this manor, are three sumptuous monuments of that family, composed of various coloured marbles: these were repaired by the late chief baron Smyth, a descendant, and whose great-grandmother was the Lady Dorothy Sydney, celebrated by Waller as Sacharissa. Adjoining the church is a free grammar-school, built and endowed by Sir Norton Knatchbull, in the time of Charles I., and the master is appointed by that family. Ashford contains many large and well-built houses, and the High Street is of considerable width, near the middle of which stands the market house, a good modern edifice, and at the east end of the town is a stone bridge of four arches crossing the river Stour. Inns: — the Saracen's Head; the Castle.

Leaving the Ashford Station, the Railway, continued through a beautiful country, first on a level of rather more than ½ a mile, soon reaches an embankment, that carries it, with a gradual sweep, to the viaduct over the Upper and Lower Stour rivers; a little beyond which it crosses a tributary stream of the latter, and soon enters a small excavation, through which it arrives at the Willesborough embankment, the Aylesford stream, and 67½ milestone, where it commences a rise of 1 in 264; 1½ mile beyond which, passing in its way the villages of Sevington and Willesborough on left, it arrives, by an alternation of embankment and excavation, at the Mersham embankment, that constructed partly on a level and a rise of 1 in 330, carries it to the Mersham excavation, and 70 milestone, ¼ m. before which the road at Mersham runs over the line; 1 m. distant on left of this is Mersham Hatch, an elegant domain, excluded from the view, that for three centuries has been the seat of the Knatchbull's, now of Sir Edward Knatchbull, Bart. From the Mersham excavation the Railway, continued on the rise of 1 in 330, enters on the surface rendered uniform, that takes it to the Smeeth cutting, of considerable depth, carried through which, and Park Wood, it gains the road from Smeeth to Aldington and Romney Marsh, that near the 71 milestone, is carried over the line. A little beyond the 71 milestone, ¼ m. before which it commences a descent of 1 in 350, and so continues for ¼ a mile, the Railway enters on the Smeeth and Aldington embankment; that, in conjunction with bridges, carries it, on the rise of 1 in 264, across the Stour river and valley, to the Sellinge and Aldington road; this, near the 72 milestone, runs under the line. At the end of the Smeeth and Aldington valley the Railway passes through Sellinge Wood, leaving the village of that name ½ a mile to the left, and is then continued through a shallow cutting to Grove Bridge, which carries the Railway over the turnpike road from Ashford to Hythe. At Grove Bridge, where the ascent diminishes from 1 in 264 to 1 in 379, the Railway enters on the Grove Bridge embankment; that takes it across the valley, to the 74 milestone and Standford excavation, through which, passing Westenhanger Farm* on right, it arrives at the site of the intended

---

* The ancient grandeur of Westenhanger, originally a fine seat, is still apparent through the devastation its remains exhibit; it is the property of Lord Strangford.

HYTHE STATION,

A PRINCIPAL ONE, DISTANT FROM LONDON 74 MILES, FROM HYTHE 2½ MILES, FROM DOVER 13 MILES.—Journey resumed below.

HYTHE.

That this place was formerly of far greater importance, as a maritime town, than at present, is demonstrated by its being one of the principal cinque ports. The houses are chiefly situated in one long street, running parallel with the sea, but having two or three lesser ones branching off at right angles; near the middle of the principal street is the court hall and market place, and in one of the streets leading towards the beach, on the opposite side, is a small theatre. The church, dedicated to St. Leonard, occupies a very elevated situation on the acclivity of the hill above the town, and the church-yard commands a fine view of the sea and coast of France. Market days, Thursday and Saturday; Inns, the Swan, White Hart, and Red Lion. Population, 2265.

The little village of Standford is so called from its situation on the ancient Via Strata, a Roman road called Stone Street; that, with very little variation from a straight line, extends from Duvernum or Canterbury to Lympne, a distance of 14 miles.

From the Standford or Hythe Station the Railway, continued on the rise of 1 in 379, passes under the Stone Street Road, and along an excavation, across which several private-road bridges are erected, till it reaches Sandling Park*, just before entering which it passes under an oblique bridge of rather singular construction, called Honeywoods Bridge, from its proximity to a farm of that name; this carries the road from New Inn Green to Postling. A little before Honeywoods Bridge, the Railway commences a descent of 1 in 264. Crossing the park close to the mansion, an elegant structure, erected from designs by Bonomi, and of which a good view is obtained, the Railway enters the Saltwood excavation, through which it arrives at the Saltwood tunnel. This, which is 964 yards long, and is excavated at a depth of 100 feet from the surface of the land above, terminates in a short, but deep cutting, as does the descent of 1 in 264; emerging whence, it crosses a beautiful valley by an embankment 80 feet high, from which, looking to the right, the first view of the sea is obtained; the ruins of Saltwood Castle† also rise into view, and in the bottom of the valley near the sea lies the town of Hythe.

* The seat of William Deedes, Esq.
† The Archdeacon of Canterbury occupies the Manor House of Saltwood.

The last embankment passed, on left is beheld the singular building, situate on an isolated conical hill, known as Beachborough Summer House; and beyond it, but unseen, seated among most romantic grounds, lies Beachborough.* In about another mile the tourist gains the village of Newington, that lies invisible on the left, and the 78 milestone. The Railway now, carried through the Cheriton excavation, of considerable depth, and a continued descent from the west end of Saltwood tunnel, varying between the inclinations of 1 in 264 and 1 in 444, in that way reaches the commencement of the Ford valley; this, which is $1\frac{1}{2}$ mile in length, and at its deepest part 93 feet in height, above the surface of the Mill-stream, is crossed by a viaduct of good design, but devoid of ornament, that consists of 20 semicircular arches, of 30 feet span each, by which, carried with a sweep, in conjunction with an embankment, to the opposite side of the valley, it crosses a double-arch oblique bridge over the Folkstone and Dover, and Folkstone and Canterbury roads, to

THE FOLKSTONE STATION,

A PRINCIPAL ONE, DISTANT FROM LONDON $81\frac{1}{2}$ MILES, FROM DOVER $5\frac{1}{2}$ MILES, FROM CANTERBURY $17\frac{1}{4}$ MILES, FROM BOULOGNE 30 MILES. — Journey resumed, p. 30.

FOLKSTONE,

A market town and member of the port of Dover, was once a much larger and more flourishing place; but from the encroachments of the sea, four of its churches, out of five, which it formerly had, have been destroyed, together with many other buildings, &c. The town is situated on irregular ground, and the streets are narrow and not well paved; but some parts of them command distinct views of the French coast, this being the nearest point of England to France; and from the Signal House, about a mile and a half from Folkstone, on the Dover road, on a clear day the harbour of Boulogne, with the flag on the pier-head, and vessels entering and leaving that port may be distinctly seen. The construction of a safe and spacious harbour capable of containing 100 vessels from 100 to 300 tons burden, with piers that extending a considerable distance into the sea encircle a space of about 19 acres, has greatly increased the importance of the place. The church, a plain structure with a square tower, having a beacon turret, with a clock, and set of eight bells, stands at the west end of the town, and on the margin

* The seat of William Brockman, Esq.

of the cliff that overhangs the sea. Market day, Thursday; Inns, the Folkstone Arms, the South Eastern Pavilion. Popula. 4,413.

From the Folkstone Station, half a mile before its arrival at which the descent of 1 in 264 diminishes to 1 in 541, which soon changes to 1 in 264, and upon that inclination after reaching Folkstone; it is thence continued through the Warren cutting, of great depth, to the Martello tunnel; that, 150 feet below the surface of the earth at its highest point, is about 616 yards in length. It terminates in the Warren cutting, through which the Railway reaches, at 83¾ miles, the Abbot's Cliff tunnel. This stupendous work, which is 1895 yards in length, perforates the cliff at a depth of nearly 400 feet from its surface, and conducts to the sea wall*, on the top of which, between the parapet and the cliffs, it is taken to the Shakspere tunnel, 1331 yards in length; emerging whence, it is carried, on the descent of 1 in 177, by an embankment and a timber viaduct, to a short tunnel, 70 yards long, under Archcliff Fort, and thence on a level into

THE DOVER STATION,

A PRINCIPAL ONE, IN THE VICINITY OF THE HARBOUR, DISTANT FROM LONDON 87 MILES, FROM CANTERBURY 15¾ MILES, FROM DEAL 8½ MILES, FROM RAMSGATE 22½ MILES, FROM MARGATE, 24½ MILES, FROM CALAIS 25 MILES, FROM BOULOGNE 30 MILES.

We cannot conclude our account of this stupendous work without remarking that its talented engineer, Mr. Cubitt, in erecting this imperishable monument to his fame, has succeeded in overcoming difficulties, which to a less-gifted individual would have appeared insurmountable; in proof of which it is only necessary to point attention to the fact, that for the purpose of forming the sea wall and works in its vicinity, with a view to avoid precipitations of the soil, by sloping them back, the elevation known as Round Down Cliff, and other eminences, had to be removed. For this purpose mining operations were the means employed: and we have Mr. Cubitt's authority for the assertion, that the result of successive blasts of gunpowder, fired by the agency of the galvanic battery, in conjunction with manual labour, was the removal of 2,000,000 tons of chalk, as, even at the Round Down alone, the materials blown down in a minute covered a space of 15 acres of surface, the average depth of which was full 50 feet; and upon a second explosion, Mr. Wright remarks, that the extent of surface acted upon and removed was about 300

* 1511 yards long, from 25 to 30 feet thick at its base, and from 50 to 70 feet high.

feet in length, 200 in height*, and averaging rather more than 20 feet in thickness; the whole quantity of powder employed, and fired in different charges, being on this occasion 97 barrels, and the quantity of earth removed about 40,000 cubic yards.

DOVER.

Dover, a sea-port town of England in the county of Kent, is situated on a small stream, the Dour or Idle river, that rising in the parish of Ewell about three miles north of the town, and turning some few mills in its way, on its arrival near the sea, bends suddenly to the west, and following in the rear of Snargate Street, where it has been further enlarged, forms Dover harbour, and finally falls into the sea at the Pier-head. Dover lies in a valley almost surrounded by chalky cliffs, from the precipitations of which serious accidents have occasionally ensued. It consists chiefly of three long streets converging to one point; the upper part called the town, and the other the Pier, with a spacious Market-place at its eastern extremity, in which vicinity it has experienced considerable enlargement by the erection of many new buildings; among others, Waterloo Crescent, and the Marine Parade. For some years past, but more particularly in the bathing season, when it always experiences a great influx of visitors, it has become the favourite summer residence of many respectable families; its situation being singularly beautiful, its attractions numerous, and the prospects particularly interesting. The broad beach lying at the embouchure of the valley, the romantic view of the cliffs and castle, the singular situation of the buildings, the entrance of the harbour constantly enlivened by the arrival and departure of the steam packets, backed by an extensive sea prospect, with the French coast in the distance, and the many vessels, from the introduction of steam, now more numerous than ever, combine from various points a series of views, which for imposing grandeur and impressive effect are not to be equalled by any on the shores of Britain. The town is divided into two parishes, and has three churches, one dedicated to St. James the Apostle, the patron of mariners, and another to St. Mary the Virgin.† The former, a spacious edifice consisting of a nave and aisles, is supposed to have been erected about the year 1216, and the latter is considered of Norman origin. It contains numerous monuments, among which is one to the memory of Churchill the satirist, and another to the English Aristophanes

---

* The height of the Monument in London.
† This is shortly to be rebuilt.

Samuel Foote.* The third church, a modern structure, dedicated to the Holy Trinity, has been erected in Strond Street. The Methodists, Quakers, Baptists, and other dissenters from the established religion have also places of worship here. The Town Hall stands in the Market Place; the interior is ornamented with several good portraits, and a curious print of the embarkation of Henry VIII. for France. It has also a small theatre, a good assembly-room, where balls and concerts are occasionally held, two libraries, hot and cold baths of various kinds, and all the appurtenances of a regular watering-place, a character it has long since assumed. Dover is defended by a strong and spacious castle, that, though venerable in appearance, still seems to frown defiance to the power of France; it includes an area of 35 acres, and during the late war this, as well as the western heights, were strongly fortified. The castle occupies a lofty eminence, steep and rugged towards the town and harbour, and on its southern side presents a precipitous cliff of 320 feet above the level of the sea. Some antiquaries have ascribed its origin to Julius Cæsar, but according to tradition, Arviragus the British chief fortified himself here, when he refused to pay the tribute imposed by Cæsar, and that afterwards King Arthur also held his residence here. It is certain however that a Roman pharos or watchtower, whose site exhibits a modern redoubt, stood in the neighbourhood. Altogether it consists of numerous edifices, among which are many towers, erected at different times, and all designated by particular names. The keep, which stands in the upper court, is 92 feet high; it is in good preservation and now used as a magazine. Water is drawn from wells 370 feet deep to supply the garrison. The castle makes a distinguished figure in history, and was once deemed impregnable; but was surprised and taken by a small party of the parliamentary forces in the reign of Charles I. Near the edge of the cliff is a piece of brass ordnance, 24 feet long, cast at Utrecht in 1544, called Queen Anne's pocket pistol; it was a present from the States of Holland to the Queen. Among the improvements and fortifications resulting from the apprehension of invasion by the French during the late war, are subterraneous works with casemates, capable of containing 2000 men. Dover is one of the cinque ports, and a borough returning two members to Parliament. The harbour, which will admit vessels of from 400 to 500 tons, is well defended. It is the principal place of embarkation for France, which, by the introduction of Railway travelling and steam navi-

* Who died at the Ship Inn, in this town, and was buried in London.

gation, may now be reached in the short space of 6 or 7 hours from London; and between which and Dover the intercourse by steam packets may almost be pronounced perpetual. The bold and lofty cliff that breasts the surge on the south-east side of the harbour, in front of the heights, bears the name of the immortal Shakspere, from the following faithful description of it in the tragedy of King Lear:—

> There is a cliff, whose high and bending head
> Looks fearfully on the confined deep:——
>   Here's the place;—— How fearful
> And dizzy 'tis, to cast one's eyes so low!
> The crows, and choughs, that wing the midway air,
> Seem scarce so gross as beetles. Half way down
> Hangs one that gathers samphire; dreadful trade!
> Methinks, he seems no bigger than his head:
> The fishermen, that walk upon the beach,
> Appear like mice; and yon' tall anchoring bark,
> Diminish'd to her cock; her cock, a buoy
> Almost too small for sight. The murmuring surge,
> That on the unnumber'd idle pebbles chafes,
> Cannot be heard so high:— I'll look no more;
> Lest my brain turn, and the deficient sight
> Topple down headlong.   *King Lear*, Act IV.

Samphire, that makes a fine-flavoured pickle, is still gathered, as in the days of Shakspere. The poor people who gather it, fix a rope to an iron crow driven into the ground at the top of the cliff, and then descending by its aid, over the precipice, in a basket, gather the samphire; an employment that makes the spectator shudder. The market days are Wednesday and Saturday, the last being the principal. Population, 13,872.

The Custom House, where all baggage destined for France must be sent for examination previous to its shipment*, is in Stroud Street; and passports for France may be obtained of Mr. Henry Morris, French Consul, at his office, Custom House Quay. The Ship Inn and York Hotel are the principal houses, and supply post horses; but for those who can dispense with wax lights at dinner, there are many others where every accommodation may be obtained, at charges varying with the style of the establishment, such as the London Hotel, near the Custom House and Alien Office, the Shakspere, in Bench Street, near the Market Place, whose windows command a view of the sea, with Calais and Boulogne on the opposite coast.

* This regulation is now no longer enforced.

down the park for a mile, amid woods and groves of fir, presenting here and there, through breaks, some enchanting views of the country below. From the south front of the house the prospects are rich, various, and extensive. At the foot of the sloping eminence on which it is situated is a fine lake of 40 acres, enriched with two beautiful well-planted islands, the haunts of swans, and other aquatic fowls. The adjacent country is finely broken, and diversified by wood-crowned hills, and luxuriant vales.

Northward of this noble domain is Upper Gatton House*.

From the Merstham station the Railway, continued by successive excavation and embankment, passes near the $20\frac{3}{4}$ milestone, the intended junction with the South-Eastern, or London and Dover Railway; about $\frac{1}{2}$ m. beyond which the train arrives at an excavation, in which lies

THE RED HILL STATION,

A PRINCIPAL ONE, DISTANT FROM LONDON $21\frac{1}{4}$ MILES, FROM BRIGHTON $29\frac{1}{4}$ MILES.— Journey resumed page 9.

In the vicinity of Reigate, about 2 miles distant on right, are the following seats: the Priory, the beautiful seat of †, Rose Bank ‡, and Beech Lodge §.

REIGATE.

Reigate is situated at the foot of the ridge of chalky downs that cross the county, and consists of two streets; the principal, or the High Street, running nearly east and west, and the other, called Bell Street, from north to south. It is supplied with excellent water from wells dug in the rock, which is composed of a beautiful white sand, said not to be equalled for colour by any in the kingdom. The Church stands at the eastern extremity of the town, and contains several costly monuments; it has two aisles, extending through the chancel nearly to the east end of the nave, and an embattled tower. The Market-House was erected about the year 1708: it is a small brick building, with piazzas below, and a room above for the purposes of a town-hall; and contiguous to it is a place called the Clock-House, that was designed as a prison for felons, and others who are brought to the Easter Sessions, held at Reigate. Behind the principal street on the north side of the town stood the Castle, but no part of the building now remains. Reigate sends one member to parliament, and has a weekly market on Tuesday: it is a place of some trade, and the neighbourhood of the first respectability; the chace is also here kept up with great spirit. The route to Brighton through Reigate is certainly not the least interesting, and lays claim to a very

* Unoccupied. † Lord Eastnor.
‡ Miss Collingwood. § H. Lainson, Esq.

superior accommodation; indeed the White Hart Inn in this town was, by a late writer, not inaptly styled "The Clarendon of the Brighton road." It is scarcely necessary to remark, that the carrying trade of Reigate, that gave employment to many hands, and, in conjunction with the expenditure of travellers, formed a fruitful source of revenue to the town, has all been swept off by the Brighton Railway. Inns:— White Hart, Swan.

A little beyond the Red Hill Station, the Railway, continued on the descent of 1 in 264, or 20 feet in a mile, and carried with a sweep, reaches, near the 21¾ milestone, the Earl's Wood embankment, that, from its height, 45 feet, commands a very extensive view: hence the eye ranges, unconfined, over a beautiful tract of country, the most prominent features of which are Cockham Windmills, on the margin of the Brighton road, leaving Reigate, and Leith Hill Tower, that, at a distance of 9 miles, in a right line, here rises into view. From the Earl's Wood embankment the railway, carried with a gradual bend, on the border of the Brighton road, through Balcombe, reaches the river Mole, which, near the 23 milestone, it crosses, and shortly after enters another excavation that conducts to the Horley embankment; this crossing the river Mole, near Bonehurst Bridge, and the 23¼ milestone, brings it to the earth's surface, the Brighton road, and

THE HORLEY STATION*,

A PRINCIPAL ONE, DISTANT FROM LONDON 25½ MILES, FROM BRIGHTON 25 MILES.—Journey resumed page 10.

The Horley station standing nearly on the level of the land, gates for the protection of the public have been erected, that are closed against carriages during the passing of the trains.

LEITH HILL.

This beautiful, picturesque eminence, which is the highest ground in this part of the kingdom, rising to an elevation of 993 feet above the level of the sea, crowned with its isolated tower, is visible from various points of the surrounding country to an immense extent; hence the eye ranges over a boundless and truly enchanting scene, displaying the rich and highly cultivated country, by which it is surrounded, to singular advantage; the whole, enlivened by the ever-varying tints of nature, and animated with lively villages, appearing to the enraptured eye of the spectator like a map. To the south, through an opening in the Downs, called Beding Gap, the blue water of the ocean is distinctly visible at a distance of 50 miles; to the north, over Box Hill, the cupola of St. Paul's is seen at 26 miles

---

* Where is intended to be formed a dépôt for the manufacture and repair of the Company's engines.

distance; and towards the east, the tower in Heathfield Park forms an interesting object in the landscape. Nettlebed in Oxfordshire, portions of Hants, Berks, Bucks, Herts, Kent, and Essex, are also distinctly visible; and, with the assistance of a glass, part of Wilts is likewise included in the view. Leith Hill Tower was built in 1766, by R. Hull, Esq., who then resided at Leith Hill Place, in its vicinity. On the demise of this gentleman, according to an injunction contained in his will, his remains were deposited under the tower, which was subsequently repaired, heightened, and the entrance bricked up; it is now, however, in such a sad state of decay, as must at no distant period terminate in its total demolition, unless rescued by the public spirit of the surrounding nobility and gentry, from whose estates it forms so fine an object in the view, not to mention its general utility to mariners as a sea mark.

From the Horley Station, where it commences a rise of 1 in 460, or $11\frac{1}{2}$ feet in a mile, the Railway is carried on the surface of the ground in a direct line to Horley Land Farm, which it passes on the left; from whence, continued in the same way, it arrives a little beyond the $27\frac{1}{2}$ milestone at Oakland Farm, where, quitting the county of Surrey, it enters Sussex. From this point, crossing the river Mole, at Hazlick Mill, near the $28\frac{1}{2}$ milestone, it is carried by embankment on an ascent of increased steepness, 1 in 264, or 20 feet in a mile, to

THE THREE BRIDGES' STATION,

A PRINCIPAL ONE, DISTANT FROM LONDON $29\frac{1}{4}$ MILES, FROM BRIGHTON $21\frac{1}{4}$ MILES, FROM CRAWLEY $1\frac{1}{4}$ MILE, FROM HORSHAM 9 MILES. — Journey resumed page 11.

On the left of Three Bridges' Station are the following seats, at Crabbet *, at Worth, Worth Park †, Worth Hall ‡, and farther to the left, Rowfant §.

CRAWLEY.

Crawley, a small but well-known village on the Brighton and Reigate road, was chiefly celebrated for its inns; of which the Rising Sun, at the entrance from Reigate, and the George, in the centre, were the principal, and between these was the business shared. In the by-gone days of stage-coach and posting prosperity, the traffick here was, during the Brighton season, brisk, and the profits derived from the expenditure of travellers considerable, Brighton being, particularly during the reign of George IV., the most favourite watering-place and chief resort of the fashionable world. It is scarcely necessary to remark, that to all this the Brighton Railway has given a death-blow, and the loss

* Is a seat of F. S. Blunt, Esq.   † Mrs. Montefiore.
‡ E. Graham, Esq.   § C. G. Bethune, Esq.

it has sustained from the abstraction of business is one it is by no means likely to recover. — Inn, the George.

The Three Bridges' Station is situate near a branch of the Mole that has its source in this vicinity; from whence pursuing a tortuous course, and passing in its way Dorking, Leatherhead, and Cobham, it finally falls into the Thames near East Moulsey, in Surrey. Quitting the Three Bridges' Station, the Railway, continued on the last-named rise, crosses, near the $29\frac{3}{4}$ milestone, Maiden Bower Lane; a little beyond this it enters Tilgate Forest, the rich scenery of which is of surpassing excellence. Near the $31\frac{1}{4}$ milestone it gains the road to Pease Pottage Gate, upon the Brighton Road, when it bends eastward, reaching, by an alternation of embankment and excavation, the last of great depth, the $31\frac{3}{4}$ milestone, and mouth of the Balcombe Tunnel (1120 yards in length), where it commences a descent of 1 in 264, or 20 feet in a mile. The Tunnel cleared, the Railway is continued by successive embankment and excavation to

THE BALCOMBE STATION,

AN INTERMEDIATE ONE, DISTANT FROM LONDON $33\frac{1}{2}$ MILES, FROM BRIGHTON 17 MILES.

From the Balcombe Station*, continued with a sweep, by a succession of deep excavation and lofty embankment, carried on the descent of 1 in 264, it reaches, near the Ryeland Bridge and the $35\frac{3}{4}$ milestone, the noble viaduct over the Ouse valley and river, of which it affords a good view. From the viaduct over the Ouse, the Railway is continued for some time on an embankment, at the end of which it is carried through deep cutting to another embankment, where the descent diminishes to 1 in 317, or $16\frac{6}{10}$ feet in a mile. Crossing in its way, a little before its arrival there, the Cuckfield and Lindfield road, it gains

THE HAYWARD'S HEATH STATION,

A PRINCIPAL ONE, DISTANT FROM LONDON $37\frac{3}{4}$ MILES; FROM BRIGHTON $12\frac{3}{4}$; FROM CUCKFIELD 2 MILES. — Journey resumed page 12.

2 miles distant, on right of Hayward's Heath Station, is Cuckfield Place † and Ockenden ‡.

The Viaduct over the Ouse river and valley, a handsome structure of brick, with a stone parapet, consists of 37 arches of 30 feet span, the height of the centre arch between the water and the rail being 100 feet; its total length, including the abutments, 1437 feet.

---

* On left of which is Balcombe House, Mrs. Chatfield; and $2\frac{1}{2}$ miles distant, Wakehurst Place, J. Peyton, Esq.

† Rev. R. Sergison. ‡ Rev. H. Fearon.

CUCKFIELD.

Cuckfield, a small but pleasant town of Sussex, situate nearly in the centre of the county, at a distance of 37 miles from London, by the Balcombe road, chiefly consists of one small street. The Church, a spacious and handsome building, with a lofty spire, contains numerous monuments of several distinguished families, especially of the Burrells, of whom there are memorials from the time of Dr. Gerard Burrell, who was Archdeacon of Chichester, and vicar of this parish; among which is a marble tablet, by Flaxman, to the memory of Sir William Burrell, Bart., author of the Burrell manuscripts illustrative of the history, antiquities, and topography of this county; that including nine portfolios, containing views, extends to forty-two volumes, many of them thick folios; which noble work, a monument of his industry and public spirit, he bequeathed at his death to the British Museum. Here are also monuments to the Sergisons of Cuckfield Place. A Free Grammar School was founded here in the time of Elizabeth, by the munificence of private individuals. The market, held on Friday, is but indifferently attended. Inn, the King's Head. Fairs, Whit Tuesday and September 16th.

THE OUSE RIVER.

The Ouse derives its origin from two branches, one of which rises in the forest of Worth, and the other in that of St. Leonard, near the source of the Adur. These streams form a junction not far from Cuckfield; and their united current running southward to Lewes discharges itself into the sea at Newhaven. This river was formerly navigable only as far as Lewes, for small barges at particular times of the tide, but having been widened, deepened, and otherwise improved, it is now navigable for boats of larger burden, as high as five miles eastward of Cuckfield.

The Hayward's Heath Station is situate on an embankment; to this succeeds an excavation, of great depth, carried through which the Railway reaches the 38 milestone, and mouth of the Hayward's Heath Tunnel, 227 yards long; over it runs the road from Cuckfield to Lewes. Clearing the Hayward's Heath Tunnel, the Railway, continued through deep cutting, gains an embankment that carries it in a direct line to the Vale Bridge Viaduct, over the valley of the Adur and that river, at which at $39\frac{1}{2}$ miles from London it arrives. The Vale Bridge Viaduct crossed, the Railway in $\frac{1}{3}$ mile more enters on a rise of 1 in 264, or 20 feet in a mile, upon which it is continued by embankment and excavation for 1 mile, in about half of which it gains St. John's Common. From the 41 milestone, which lies in deep cutting, and near which it commences an ascent of diminished steepness, 1 in 320, or $16\frac{1}{2}$ feet in a mile, for $1\frac{1}{2}$ mile, it is carried, with the intervention of a short embankment, crossing in its way, at 41⅛ miles, the Burgess Hill Road, through deep cutting to the 42 milestone, and an embankment, that, affording a good view of the country bordering the line, and of the range of hills extending from Bramber to Lewes, carries it to

THE HASSOCKS GATE STATION,

AN INTERMEDIATE ONE, DISTANT FROM LONDON 43½ MILES, FROM BRIGHTON 7 MILES. — Journey resumed below.

The Adur river, sometimes called the Beeding, rises in St. Leonard's Forest, whence, directing its course southward, it passes Steyning and Bramber; but, on reaching Shoreham, turns suddenly to the east, and, after forming a narrow peninsula, about three miles in length, falls into the sea, a little to the westward of Brighton.

The Hassocks Gate Station* is situate at the cross turnpike road from Ditchling to Henfield, on the Keymer embankment, that commences near the 42½ milestone, at which point the inclination changes to a rise of 1 in 264, or 20 feet in a mile, on which it is carried from Hassocks Gate Station through cutting to the Brighton Road and mouth of the Clayton Tunnel, 44¾ miles from London; this stupendous work is 2240 yards, or rather more than 1¼ mile in length; emerging whence into a deep cutting it gains a short level, at the end of which it commences a descent of 1 in 264, or 20 feet in a mile; carried through which, and passing near the 46 milestone the village of Pangdean, that lies unseen upon the left, it reaches a short embankment, on which it arrives, near the 47¾ milestone, at the Patcham Tunnel, 480 yards long. From the Patcham Tunnel † the Railway continues its downward inclination of 1 in 264 by successive excavations and embankments, some of them works of great labour, and passing Withdean at 48 miles, and Preston at 49¼ miles, reaches, a little beyond the 50 milestone, a short level, that, crossing at 50⅝ the New England Farm Viaduct, thrown over the Montpelier Road, carries it to

THE BRIGHTON STATION,

A PRINCIPAL ONE, DISTANT FROM LONDON 50½ MILES, FROM LEWES 8¼ MILES, FROM SHOREHAM BY RAILWAY 6 MILES, FROM WHENCE TO WORTHING BY ROAD IS 4½ MILES.

Three miles distant from Brighton, on the Lewes Road, is Stanmer Park, the fine seat of the Earl of Chichester.

The Brighton Station, which is also that of the Shoreham Branch, is erected in a style worthy of the great work of which it is the terminus. It is situate in Trafalgar Street, and is remarkable as being formed on an embankment on one side and a cutting

---

* Two miles distant on right of which is Danny, W. J. Campion, Esq.
† On left of which is Patcham Place, J. Payne, Esq.

on the other. The passenger sheds here are covered with three spacious roofs, two of 52 feet span for the London, and one of 62 feet span for the Shoreham business, and altogether affords the most ample accommodation.

BRIGHTON.

Brighthelmston, or Brighton, a sea-port and market-town of Sussex, derives its celebrity partly from its proximity to London, but principally from being the fashionable resort of persons of distinction for the purpose of sea-bathing. It is situate on an eminence that declines gently to the south-east, with a regular slope to the Steyne, from whence it again stretches with a moderate ascent along the cliffs to a considerable distance. The amphitheatrical range of hills by which it is protected from the north and north-easterly winds are of easy access, and covered with an agreeable verdure, their summits commanding a good view of the Isle of Wight, and also of the Weald of Sussex. The air is particularly salubrious, and the soil naturally dry; which united advantages, together with the now ready means of access afforded by the Railway, and numerous amusements provided by the inhabitants, have latterly caused an influx of visitors unparalleled in the annals of watering places. This observation is borne out by the well-known fact, that since the year 1811 its population, which in 1801 was 7,399, had increased in 1821 to 24,429, and in 1831 to 40,634; and still Brighton, like the metropolis, is on the increase. In one instance only it experienced the addition of four hundred houses, all of noble dimensions, in the erection of Kemp Town, which stands at the extremity of the East Cliff. Its general appearance is as follows:—The line of houses facing the sea extends from the eastern extremity of Kemp Town to Adelaide Terrace, beyond the western esplanade, a distance of 2½ miles, forming an almost uninterrupted range of beautiful buildings, that, chiefly consisting of noble mansions disposed in stately terraces and squares, presents an appearance unequalled in England, and probably unparalleled in Europe, if we except the city of St. Petersburgh. Nearly in the centre, but rather inclining towards the west, is the opening of the Steyne, from whence a fine level extends northwards to the fields, flanked about the centre of the Steyne on the west by the Pavilion, and terminated by the elegant pinnacled tower of the new church, backed by a prospect of the Downs that at no great distance rise behind it. This fine expanse is equally conducive to health and pleasure. A little before reaching the Pavilion, North Street, one of its oldest erections, which is in fact the High Street of Brighton, runs westward up a hill of somewhat inconvenient steepness, eventually attaining the height of 150 feet, on the summit of which stands the old church; and on the east side of the Steyne, St. James's Street, the Regent Street of Brighton, issues forth, and is thence carried with an easy ascent to Kemp Town.

The original buildings are chiefly composed of flint stones and mortar, with brick-work for the door and window cases; but the majority of the more recent erections are extremely elegant and commodious, particularly those in Kemp Town, in Adelaide Crescent, Brunswick, Bedford, and Regency Squares, the Royal Crescent, the Old and New Steyne, Marine Parade, and numerous detached residences. The town is of a quadrangular form, the streets intersecting each other at right angles.

Brighton is not incorporated, its government being vested in 36 commissioners, who, becoming ex-officio magistrates, hold their sittings at the Town-hall, and are empowered by a late act that, supplementary to some preceding ones, provided for the paving, lighting, and improvement of the town, the erection of a new town-hall and market house, appointment of a chief clerk and constables, and redress of grievances; and who, availing themselves of the powers of the Rural Police Act, have introduced that useful force into Brighton, where, as in London, they constantly patrol the town, and preserve the peace. The principal public buildings, exclusive of the churches above mentioned and the Pavilion, hereafter to be noticed, are, the New Town-hall, the County Hospital, the Market-house, and Theatre. The Town-hall, erected at an expense of 30,000*l.*, is a spacious building, with a handsome exterior. In the lower story are various offices for the magistrates, commissioners, directors of the poor, &c. On the second story is a capacious room, wherein are held the petty sessions; with some smaller rooms for the magistrates' private sittings, handsomely fitted up. The third story contains a handsome assembly-room, with tea, coffee, and card rooms. From the balcony at the east end is a view of the town, in a striking and novel light, which will alone repay the labour of a visit. The New Market-house, erected in 1830, is a neat but spacious building, bearing some resemblance to Farringdon Market in London. The County Hospital is a neat edifice, standing on an elevated spot near Kemp Town, the ground being given, with a donation of 1000*l.*, by T. R. Kemp, Esq.; to which was added, by Brighton's great patron, the late Earl of Egremont, the sum of 2000*l.* The Theatre, in the New Road, is, externally, an unornamented building, with a portico, but the interior is considered to be one of the best out of London. The audience part, chastely decorated, consists of two tiers of boxes, a pit, and gallery. Concerts, balls, and assemblies are held at the Old Ship, which contains a noble suite of rooms; and at the New Concert and Ball Room, in Cannon Place. This has been pronounced, by various artists and musicians, one of the best adapted to its purpose in the kingdom; and, with its elegant chandeliers, expensive ornaments, and beautiful coved ceiling, quite eclipses the assembly-room at the Town-hall, which is also occasionally appropriated to these entertainments.

Here are various hot, cold, and air-pump water baths, of the latest construction, combining all the luxuries of the baths of the East, and highly salutary in many diseases; and numerous machines on the beach, for the use of those who prefer the rough embraces of Neptune to the more insipid attractions of artificial places of immersion. Here are likewise libraries, supplied with all the newspapers and periodical publications; two banks; and a club, consisting of 200 members, all peers, members of parliament, or members of clubs in London. One of the greatest improvements that Brighton has experienced consists of a magnificent suspension chain pier, which cost 30,000*l*.; it was erected under the superintendence of Capt. Browne, and opened to the public in the summer of 1823, since which it has become a very fashionable lounge. It is founded on four clusters of piers; has a neat iron railing on each side; is supported on eight chains, the end ones being made fast to the cliff; and is approached from the Steyne by an esplanade of considerable length. On each side of the pier are three cast-iron buttresses or towers, fitted up as shops for the sale of trifling articles; and at the end is a platform, furnished with seats for the accommodation of the company, who can sit there and enjoy the salutary and refreshing sea breezes, a band of music, stationed in its centre, occasionally adding to their amusement. The Steyne, an agreeable lawn, dividing the old from the modern town, is the favourite promenade for the visitors of Brighton every evening during the season; the Esplanade, the approach to the chain pier, the Marine Parade, above it, and Western Esplanades, in front of the King's Road, being the resort of the morning lounger. In the enclosure of the Steyne nearest the Palace is a bronze statue of George IV., by Chantrey, on a pedestal 9 feet in height, erected in 1828, by a subscription of 3,000*l*., in commemoration of the prince to whom Brighton is principally indebted for its prosperity.

The Old Church, dedicated to St Nicholas, mean in character, with a low square tower, is situated on rising ground at the west end of North Street; and from its elevated position, 150 feet above the level of the sea, is in that direction visible for many miles; and in the churchyard, which commands some delightful prospects, are monuments to the memory of well-known and somewhat celebrated individuals. The New Church, dedicated to St. Peter, stands at the entrance of the town from London, where it forms an agreeable object, and was much wanted, as, previous to its erection, but few of the inhabitants belonging to the established religion could attend public worship, the old church being totally inadequate to their accommodation. To these may be added the Chapel Royal, and the following Episcopal chapels, respectively dedicated to St. James, the Trinity, St. Mary, St. George, St. Margaret, and St. Andrew: there also are places of religious worship for various sects of Dissenters. About half a mile west of the old church is a chalybeate spring: the waters are strongly impregnated with iron, and considered beneficial in all diseases where tonic remedies are required. The race-ground, about 1 mile from the town, furnishes a very pleasant airy ride or walk; and from the stand on it, which is capable of containing a considerable number of spectators, the Isle of Wight, with many other beautiful objects, may be distinctly seen; and among the various delightful rides in the neighbourhood, the road to the Devil's Dyke, which is by an ascent of nearly 5 miles to the north-west, chiefly over the finest turf, is one of the most agreeable: the Dyke itself is well worthy of observation, but will probably not long detain the attention of the visitor, as from the summit of Dyke Hill nature in her grandest form lies before him, and he may here survey great part of Sussex, with portions of Hampshire, Surrey, and Kent, the whole interspersed with woods and villages, highly cultivated fields, and distant hills. At this place Charles II. embarked for France, after the battle of Worcester in 1651. The only manufacture here (if it can be termed one) is the making of part of the nets for the use of the fishery, the materials of which come from Bridport. The fishery employs about a hundred boats, carrying three, four, or five men each. The mackerel season commences in April, and the herring fishery in October; besides these, almost every kind of fish are found in plenty, of which the new market makes a great display: the wholesale fish-market is on the beach. To the fishery, and the numerous visitants during the bathing season, the stationary inhabitants look for support. It is much benefitted by the many travellers to France, embarking from hence by the steam-packets to Dieppe, and through Rouen to Paris*, it being a much shorter route by land than from Calais. The principal market is on Saturday; but it is open every day except Sunday, and is well supplied with every kind of provision. The mutton of this place, being chiefly fed on the South Downs, is particularly admired for its fine flavour. The Race-ground, which is fenced in and properly attended to, is justly admired; and the Races, which last four or five days, are usually held in the

* Between which cities a Railway is now constructing, under the superintendence of Mr. Locke.

first week in August, which is esteemed the fullest part of the season. This place sends two members to parliament. Brighton is by no means deficient in accommodation, as the following list of Inns and Hotels will testify, and at the under-mentioned the first families will, comparatively speaking, find themselves at home:— Old Ship, Ship Street; New Ship, Ship Street; New Steyne Hotel, St. James's Street; Royal York Hotel, Steyne Place; Marine Parade Hotel, Marine Parade; Norfolk Arms Hotel, Norfolk Street; Regent Hotel, Church Street; Sea House Hotel, East Cliff; Gloucester Arms Hotel, Gloucester Place; and Albion Hotel, on the Steyne. The following also furnish excellent accommodation: — New Inn, North Street; White Lion, North Street; the Gun, East Cliff; Richmond Arms, Richmond Place; The Waterloo, Waterloo Street; King and Queen, Marlborough Place; Golden Cross, Princess Street. For those who, upon a temporary sojourn at Brighton, may be desirous of meeting with society, the Boarding Houses, of which there are many, will afford the opportunity. The charges at these vary according to the style in which each establishment is maintained.

THE PAVILION.

A description of this splendid palace of the Queen of England, — to describe which a volume might well be devoted, — cannot, as a matter of course, be expected here. We shall endeavour, however, to compensate for the absence of detail, by a general notice of this magnificent pile, deduced from the work of a modern writer, whose account of it, the result of a close examination, and remarks thereon, are alike creditable to his taste and judgment. "We know, for we have personally met with as well as read of it, that an idea has been not unsparingly disseminated of the Pavilion's being characterised by frivolity or gaudiness, — 'a Fancy or a Folly,' in which costliness is more eminent than taste or beauty.* We do not dissemble this circumstance; on the contrary, we draw it boldly forward, for the purpose of giving it the most decided contradiction : and if the reader will believe us to speak candidly, we assure him, in simple terms, that it is no such thing. The Pavilion is enriched with the most magnificent ornaments and the gayest and most splendid colours, yet all is in good keeping and well relieved. There is positively nothing glaring or gaudy; and the person who would quarrel with its richness might as reasonably do so with the flowers of the parterre,—the lively carnation, or the painted tulip. We do not see why the Monarch of England should not have her *Oriental*

* The injustice of this remark would, upon visiting it, instantly vanish.

Marine Pavilion, the more particularly as it recalls to us one branch of that mighty continental influence which we wield, it may be hoped and trusted, for the general happiness and benefit. The Queen of England is almost 'de facto' *Queen of India;* and therefore may we not say, without fanciful exaggeration, that an eastern palace, placed on the shore of that element by the ancient and continued sovereignty of which England wields such a powerful sceptre, presents an idea to the mind fully interesting and effective? The whole of this magnificent pile, the interior of which contains numerous rooms of noble proportions, in the decorations of which throughout the first artists were employed, presents a coup d'œil of a most imposing and enchanting character, and is altogether strikingly indicative of the master mind in which originated the idea of its erection. The Palace Chapel is a very spacious and handsome apartment, eighty feet by forty. The royal seat is splendidly adorned with ormolu ornaments and crimson velvet; the organ is a very fine one, and the communion plate is of gold. The stables and riding-house form a large and imposing pile. The interior of the stables, whose outward appearance is octagonal, is a magnificent circular area of 250 feet, with a dome in the centre 88 feet in diameter, and, after St. Paul's, one of the largest in England. Into this area the suite of stables, which will accommodate seventy horses, open. There are also other projecting buildings, and a large square court-yard for carriages. The riding-house and tennis-court are each 250 feet by 50. The spacious dome is a handsome object in every view of the town. Moresque is the term usually conferred on the architecture of this edifice; but we imagine it possesses some features exhibited in the buildings of Hindostan. We should be guilty of great injustice to the royal founder if we omitted to mention, what is deserving of remembrance, that almost all the ornaments and furniture of the Pavilion, excepting some oriental rarities, are of English manufacture, an object by no means neglected by his Majesty; a circumstance that, considered, should be viewed in an extenuating light by those who complain of George the Fourth's profusion. If the fountain of regal munificence burst forth with rather too heedless impetuosity, its waters, on reaching the level, branched out, through various meandering and fertilizing streams, into the quiet retirements of labour and industry, and the resources of many a poor family have been kindly supplied by the expense bestowed on the decorations of a palace. Great and severe economy on the part of a monarch, as well as his more wealthy nobles, would almost amount to a crime: they have freely received, and should freely give. The editor cannot conclude his remarks on this magnificent palace without alluding to an opinion expressed by Mr. Jesse in his work on Windsor Castle, and in which he fully coincides. 'The time will probably come when Windsor * will derive not the least interesting of its associations from having been the residence of a monarch,' who, if he had lived in a remoter period, would have been deemed *George the Magnificent*. When we call to mind how his taste and splendour have been displayed, not only in this ancient seat of monarchy, but also in the metropolis, which (as was related of Augustus with regard to Rome) he may be said to have found of brick and to have left of marble, and when we remember the glorious victories which were achieved during his administration of affairs, we shall surely confess that he may, with justice, be ranked high among those monarchs who have raised the glory of England by their talents, and immortalized Windsor by having made it their residence.'"

THE SHOREHAM BRANCH RAILWAY.

The Shoreham Branch Railway commences at the Brighton Station in Trafalgar Street, leaving which it is carried with a sweep, on a descent of 1 in 264, or 20 feet in a mile, through a deep cutting in chalk, and a short tunnel of 200 yards in length, under Windmill Hill (over which runs the old road to London through Henfield) to the Hove Station, 1¾ mile from Brighton. Here it enters on an embankment that (with the exception of one cutting, affords on left a fine view of the sea, and on right of the adjacent country) carries it to the Portslade Station, 3 miles from Brighton. The village of Portslade lies on right; it contains some good houses, of which, with its antique church, situate on a hill and surrounded by foliage, a good view is obtained. At 4⅜ miles from Brighton the Railway reaches the Southwick Station. Southwick is a pretty and somewhat extensive village, finely situated, and beautifully interspersed with trees. Continuing its downward inclination, the Railway gains the five-milestone and the Kingston Station. The village of Kingston-on-Sea, an auxiliary to Shoreham, exhibits an appearance of considerable naval traffic. On approaching this point the scene is of a cheerful and active character, indicating no small portion of business; there is no port, perhaps, on the southern coast, the public arsenals excepted, that, its size considered, displays this feature in a higher degree. Between the town and Southwick is an observatory overlooking the harbour; and the solid central tower of its collegiate-looking church adds its full effect to the appearance of the town.

Quitting the Southwick Station, the Railway reaches by a level of a mile in length

* And the Pavilion at Brighton of his creation.

THE SHOREHAM STATION,

A PRINCIPAL ONE, DISTANT FROM BRIGHTON 6 MILES.

NEW SHOREHAM.

New Shoreham, a sea port, borough, and market town of Sussex, 6 miles east of Brighton; lies about a mile within the haven; and is singularly built, having a market house, standing on Doric pillars, erected in the centre. This is a place of considerable trade, and has an elegant and commodious Custom-house (erected in 1830, from designs by Mr. Sydney Smirke), with a collector, comptroller, and other inferior officers. The church, dedicated to St. Mary, is very ancient, being the remains of the former collegiate one; it was repaired and beautified about the year 1822. The tower, about 80 feet high, bears a strong resemblance to that of St. Alban's Abbey; the interior is both graceful and elegant, and is considered to be, in the excellent proportions and correct disposition of its mouldings, and beauty of its arches and pillars, inferior to few on the Continent. Shoreham Harbour is what is called a tide-harbour, and, though shallow, the best on this line of coast. Vessels of considerable burden come into it, Brighton being within the port of Shoreham; where, when the weather will not permit their lying alongside the chain pier, the steam-packets land and embark their passengers. The inhabitants are principally engaged in the building of ships, some of which are as large as 700 tons burthen. An elegant suspension bridge across the Adur, that forms a striking feature on approaching the town from Worthing, the distance between which place and Shoreham is thus diminished 1 mile, is a great ornament to the town, and was erected at the expense of the Duke of Norfolk, from designs by —— Clarke, Esq.; it was opened in 1834, and in appearance resembles Hammersmith Bridge. Ella is supposed to have landed here with his three sons in 477, when he defeated the Britons, and founded the kingdom of the South Saxons. Shoreham, in conjunction with the rape of Bramber, sends two members to parliament, and has a market on Saturday. Inns:— Fountain and Star.

WORTHING.

Worthing, under the title of Ordings, is mentioned in Domesday Book, where it is valued at 117 shillings. From an obscure town Worthing has risen, within the last forty years, to its present height of popularity; for which it is partly indebted to a visit of the late Princess Amelia in 1798. The town is irregularly built; but does not suffer in appearance from that circumstance, as every turn presents a new object. Like

Brighton, it follows the line of the sea; but has many openings in an opposite direction, the principal of which is the Steyne, a very neat oblong enclosure of about four acres, bordered on three sides by handsome houses, of which Warwick House is the principal. About the centre of the Esplanade, a short but well-built street opens into a large space or square, forming the body of the town, with several neat shops, offices, and a bazaar on right and left. At the end is the Chapel of Ease, Worthing being a hamlet of Broadwater. At the south extremity are the Market, the Theatre, and the back of the Steyne. At the south-west angle is the approach to Park Crescent, the most recent and finest pile of buildings in Worthing. It is beautifully situate, and commands a pleasing prospect, of which Cisebury Hill, overlooking Finden, the spire of West Tarring Church, and well-wooded summit of Highdown Hill, the site of Oliver's tomb, are the principal features. The Esplanade, a neat gravelled terrace, of about three quarters of a mile in length, is of sufficient elevation to afford protection from the waves that flow upon its southern side. Here is a small but neat Theatre, and the general market-place, of quadrangular form, the wholesale fish-market being held upon the beach. The Baths here are of a very superior character; the bathing machines are ranged immediately below the Esplanade, upon the beach, which is one of the finest, smoothest, and most regular expanses of firm sand upon the English coast, affording the readiest facilities for bathing at all seasons, and for riding and driving, that are to be met with in this part of the kingdom. Inns:— The Sea House Hotel, Marine Hotel, Steyne Hotel, and New Inn.

LEWES.

This town stands on the border of the South Downs. Its situation on a declivity washed by the Ouse, surrounded by an amphitheatre of higher hills, is more than commonly beautiful, and highly favourable to commerce. It is a borough by prescription, having returned two members to parliament ever since the 23d of Edward I. That Lewes is a place of high antiquity, the numerous relics discovered in the town and neighbourhood, as well as its architectural remains, sufficiently attest. The great gateway of the castle, said to have been built by the Earl of Surrey, in the reign of William the Conqueror, is still entire: many vestiges of the walls, &c. also remain, sufficient to justify the idea of its having been a fortress of considerable strength and magnitude. Some small remains of an ancient religious establishment of a very extensive nature are also visible. Before the Reformation, this town, including the suburbs of Southover and Cliffe, comprehended twelve parish churches, which have since been reduced to half that number. There are, however, besides these, several religious edifices for Dissenters. Among the public buildings to be found in Lewes, the Shire-hall claims pre-eminence. This building is situated in the High Street, and is planned with equal attention to elegance and convenience: here the summer assizes for the county, and the quarter sessions for its eastern division, are regularly held. The House of Correction, built about 1794, on the plan of Howard, contains thirty-two cells, a chapel, and other accommodations for the prisoners, besides the apartments of the keeper. Here is also a free grammar-school, established in 1512, a neat theatre, and assembly-rooms at the Star Inn. A library society was established here in 1786: from a small beginning it has gradually acquired a considerable degree of importance, and now possesses an excellent collection of books. The meetings of the Sussex Agricultural Society, instituted in 1796, are held at Lewes. The show of cattle for the premiums offered by the Society generally takes place in the beginning of August, and is numerously attended by the gentlemen and farmers of this and the neighbouring counties. The market is daily supplied with necessaries for the table, but Tuesday and Saturday are the market-days for corn; and every other Tuesday for cattle also. There are two fairs for black cattle, and one for sheep annually; this last is very extensive, not less than eighty thousand sheep being generally drawn together on the occasion. The air of Lewes is considered very salubrious, the town, from its declivity of site, being remarkably clean; the streets are in general spacious, and well lighted. The river Ouse, which runs through the town under a handsome bridge, is navigable for barges 5 miles to the east of Cuckfield, and affords a ready communication with the harbour of Newhaven at its mouth. The increase of its trade of late years has been proportionate to that of its population; and two respectable banks facilitate the transaction of business. On a hill about a mile from the town is the Race Course, accounted one of the best in England; and a commodious stand, commanding a view of nearly the whole course. The Races, generally held in the first week in August, continue three days, on the first of which the Queen's Plate of 100 guineas is run for. This hill was the scene of an obstinate battle, fought on the 14th of May, 1264, between Henry III. and the army of the Barons, under Simon de Montfort, Earl of Leicester; in which the latter was victorious. Lewes is not incorporated, but is governed by two constables, who are chosen annually at the court leet. The rural police have been introduced here. Inns. White Hart, Star.

ARUNDEL CASTLE.

This was a place of great fame and strength in the earliest periods of English history; it became alternately the property of different individuals, and underwent two sieges during the civil wars of the 17th century; from which period it continued little better than a mass of ruins, till the late Duke of Norfolk undertook to restore it to its ancient magnificence. Arundel Castle occupies an elevated situation, and commands a fine view over the sea as far as the Isle of Wight; it is embsomed in a luxuriant grove, and presents a singularly beautiful, imposing, and majestic appearance. The building is in the Gothic style, of freestone, that was carefully selected so as to assimilate in colour with the remains of the ancient fabric. The internal arrangements and decorations of this superb residence are eminently calculated to exhibit the talent and taste of the late noble proprietor; and among the many specimens of the arts with which it is adorned, are several curious paintings of the Howard family, and a large window of painted glass executed by Egginton, in the dining room, representing the late Duke and Duchess in the characters of King Solomon and Queen Sheba at a banquet. Arundel Castle enjoys the peculiar privilege of conferring the dignity of Earl on the possessor, without any patent or creation from the crown,— a privilege not enjoyed by any other place in the kingdom.

GOODWOOD.

Goodwood, the magnificent seat of the Duke of Richmond, independent of its great celebrity, from its attraction in the racing season, when it has many visitors from Brighton, it would be unpardonable to pass unnoticed here. The mansion, with a handsome and imposing front, has a singular outline, tending to the semi-octagonal, or oriel form; it consists of a centre of 166 feet long, and two wings each 106 feet long, forming a total of 378 feet. The wings recede in an angle of 45 degrees, and at all the corners are very bold and handsome circular towers. In the centre is a light and very graceful portico and loggia of six Doric columns below, and six Ionic above; with a good entablature, and a surmounting balustrade. The wings are differently ornamented. Prior to the year 1800. the south wing was the principal front, as erected by Sir William Chambers. The extensive additions were erected under the direction of Wyatt. The material of the walls is squared flint, cut very small, and of a light colour; which, contrasted with the Portland-stone composing all the architectural ornaments, has a cheerful and pleasing effect. The interior, which consists of numerous suites of rooms, many of noble proportions, is splendidly decorated; with smaller ones, that, simply elegant, are appropriated to domestic comfort. It contains a rare and valuable collection of paintings, and a choice library of upwards of 10,000 volumes. In the hall, not the least valuable of its contents, are some armour and trophies won by the present duke, when Earl of March, at Waterloo, when the combined armies under the Duke of Wellington rescued Europe from the indomitable power of the tyrant Bonaparte. Of this splendid victory, attained June 18th, 1815, a day never to be forgotten, a modern writer observes—

"——— Agincourt may be forgot,
And Cressy be an unknown spot,
  And Blenheim's name be new;
But still in story and in song,
For many an age remember'd long,
Shall live the towers of Hougomont,
  And field of Waterloo!"

In another room is a small standard, also captured at the battle of Waterloo.

Speaking of this splendid seat of English hospitality, it may be remarked, that of the many noblemen's seats which this kingdom contains, some of which boast of antiquity, others of magnificence, or classic and elaborate architectural decorations, from the harmony which prevails throughout, and in the keeping of its various parts, no seat in England is more entitled to the epithet *Elegant* than the mansion at Goodwood.

The stables and offices, somewhat too near the mansion, erected by Sir William Chambers, form a neat quadrangular structure, containing 54 stalls. On an eminence further removed, and forming a handsome object, are the dog kennels, erected from a design by Wyatt, at an expense of 6000*l.*; they are considered to exceed in magnificence and convenience of every kind, even to luxury, any structure perhaps ever raised before for the reception of such tenants. The gardens, at some distance from the house, are laid out with great taste, and are very extensive; adjoining them is a magnificent tennis-court.

The Park, nearly six miles in circumference, contains upwards of 1214 acres, and is beautifully planted, embracing almost every kind of forest tree, including 1000 cedars of Lebanon, planted by the Duke in 1762, being then of four years' growth; and here are two cork trees in a very flourishing condition.

Cairney Seat, an originally splendid summer erection, is seated on an eminence; and near it is a curious grotto of shell-work, executed by the second Duchess of Richmond and her daughters. The former commands a magnificent view, embracing the whole tract of plain beneath, the spire of Chichester Cathedral, and projections and recesses of the coast from Brighton to the harbours of Portsmouth and Southampton, and a considerable extent of country northward of the Downs. The Park, also, contains an excellent Race Course, whereon are annually run the celebrated Goodwood Races, on which occasion the *élite* of fashion congregate here, and are sumptuously entertained by the noble owner; who, to his honour be it recorded, is a great benefactor to the poor, and to whom, as was observed of Howard the philanthropist, may be applied the following lines:—

"Who, friend to nature, by no blood confined,
Is the glad relative of all mankind."

BRIGHTON RAILWAY, CHICHESTER BRANCH.

Of the Chichester branch of the Brighton Railway, the first portion, viz. the particulars of the line from Brighton to Shoreham, they will be found fully detailed at page 20 of that line; to which it is only necessary to add, that 2 m. before Shoreham on right is Portslade House[1]; at Kingston, Kingston House[2]; on right of Shoreham is Buckingham House[3]. After crossing the Adur River at Shoreham by a timber Viaduct 320 yards long, consisting of 30 openings each 30 ft., in conjunction with 12 brick arches; the tourist enters on a singularly wild and uncultivated country, to which it would be difficult to assign the proper appellation, being too dreary for pastoral effect, yet having some herbage it can hardly be termed a desert, but is nevertheless very desert-like, short thin grass with a sandy soil. Over this the Railway is continued in a line nearly direct to Lower Lancing 2½ m. beyond which it gains

THE WORTHING STATION.

A PRINCIPAL ONE, DISTANT FROM BRIGHTON 11 MILES, FROM LONDON 61½ MILES, FROM CHICHESTER 18 MILES. Journey resumed.

For an account of Worthing the reader is referred to page 21 of the Brighton Railway. The following seats are in its vicinity; 1½ m. distant on right is Offington House[4], an ancient seat of the De la Warrs; 3½ m. distant Findon House[5]; and Muntham[6]. About a mile beyond Worthing the Railway continued with an

---

[1] E. Hall, Esq.   [2] W. P. Goring, Esq.   [3] H. Bridger, Esq.
[4] J. B. Daubuz, Esq.   [5] W. Richardson, Esq.
[6] T. Fitzgerald, Esq.

easy sweep arrives at West Tarring, now a mere village, but anciently a place of much importance, the manor having been given by King Athelstan to Christchurch, Canterbury, between the years 941 and 944, and continued in the possession of the Archbishop of Canterbury till it was usurped by the crown about the time of Cranmer; the impropriate rectory, however, is still possessed by the archbishop. About 2 m. beyond West Tarring the Railway gains

THE GORING STATION,
AN INTERMEDIATE ONE, DISTANT FROM BRIGHTON 14 MILES, FROM LONDON $64\frac{1}{2}$ MILES, FROM CHICHESTER 15 MILES.

One mile distant from Goring Station, on right is Castle Goring[1]; and 3 m. distant Mitchel Grove[2]. Long before reaching Goring Station Highdown Hill, a conical eminence crowned with a windmill, the site of Oliver's tomb, an eccentric miller, and former tenant of that far-seen object rises into view, and between Worthing and Goring glances are occasionally caught of Cisbury Hill and Chanctonbury Ring, that in the palmy days of coaching prosperity formed prominent features, beheld on west of the Brighton road. $2\frac{1}{2}$ m. beyond the Goring Station the Railway carried in a course nearly due west, and passing the foot of High-down Hill reaches

THE ANGMERING STATION,
AN INTERMEDIATE ONE, DISTANT FROM BRIGHTON $16\frac{1}{2}$ MILES, FROM CHICHESTER $12\frac{1}{2}$ MILES.

From this last point the Railway, carried with a gradual bend in a north-west direction, in another mile and a half gains

THE LITTLE HAMPTON STATION,
AN INTERMEDIATE ONE, DISTANT FROM BRIGHTON 18 MILES, FROM LONDON $68\frac{1}{2}$ MILES, FROM CHICHESTER 11 MILES.

Little Hampton is a retired and pretty watering-place on the Sussex coast. Two miles beyond Little Hampton Station the Railway, continued with a sweep, and crossing the river Arun in its way by a drawbridge of 60 feet clear opening, arrives at

THE ARUNDEL STATION,
A PRINCIPAL ONE, DISTANT FROM BRIGHTON 20 MILES, FROM LONDON $70\frac{1}{2}$ MILES, FROM CHICHESTER 9 MILES.

Arundel is pleasantly situated on the declivity of a commanding hill, on the north-west bank of the river Arun, and consists

[1] G. R. Pechell, Esq.   [2] W. Wyatt, Esq.

of two principal streets, one of them running north and south, and the other westward from their common centre; the houses in general are of a respectable character, and many of those belonging to the Duke of Norfolk have been rebuilt in the Gothic castellated style. The church, dedicated to St. Nicholas, stands at the northern extremity of the town; it is a handsome Gothic edifice, with transepts, from the centre of which rises a low square tower, surmounted by a small wooden spire, and contains several beautiful monuments of the Earls of Arundel; but the chapel, which has for ages served as the burial place of the noble owners of the castle, is in a ruinous state. Arundel has a stone bridge of three arches over the Arun; it is not a place of much trade, but sends two members to parliament, and has a weekly market on Thursday. Hotels:— Norfolk Arms and Bridge Hotel. Population, 2,628.

The great attraction here is Arundel Castle, the noble seat of the Duke of Norfolk, upon which a late munificent proprietor is said to have expended the vast sum of 600,000*l.*: it is consequently well worthy of a visit: a brief account of it will be found at page 24. of the Brighton Railway.

One mile beyond the Arundel Station the Railway reaches

THE YAPTON STATION,

AN INTERMEDIATE ONE, DISTANT FROM BRIGHTON 21 MILES, FROM CHICHESTER 8 MILES.

One mile distant, on right of Yapton Station, is Walberton House[1]; 1½ m. distant Avisford House[2]; 2½ distant, Slindon House[3]; 3 m. distant, Dale Park[4]; and 3½ m. distant, Madehurst Lodge.[5]

Two miles and a half beyond the Yapton Station the Railway continued in a course nearly direct arrives at

THE WOODGATE STATION,

AN INTERMEDIATE ONE, DISTANT FROM BRIGHTON 23½ MILES; FROM CHICHESTER 5½ MILES.

One mile distant from Woodgate Station; on right is Knighton Park[6], and Aldingbourne House.[7]

Woodgate Station is the point of departure for the retired village and watering place of Bognor, from which it is distant about

[1] R. Prime, Esq.
[2] Sir T. Reynell, Bart.
[3] Countess of Newburgh.
[4] John Abel Smith, Esq.
[5] Lord Charles Fitzroy.
[6] C. Smith Peckham, Esq.
[7] R. Hasler, Esq.

4½ miles on left; 2½ miles distant, on right, is Boxgrove Priory[1]; and 3 miles distant, Halnaker House[2]; at Bognor is Arran Lodge.[3]

Bognor is a very retired watering-place, situated on a dry healthy spot, remarkable for the purity of its air, and comprising an assemblage of brick and stone buildings, without any regular plan: it is full a mile long, owing to the houses being mostly detached, but this separation gives them the appearance of gentlemen's villas. It is tolerably frequented in the summer season, and the company is uniformly select, and of the first respectability. The crescent, a princely habitation, contains many superb and capacious apartments, and is crowned by a handsome dome, from whence the Isle of Wight is seen majestically rising from the ocean: thence also the eye ranges over a vast extent of country, including a part of Hampshire, Chichester Cathedral, the beautiful grounds of West Dean, the Duke of Richmond, the Countess of Newburgh, and the delightful country surrounding the Duke of Norfolk's venerable castle of Arundel.

Continued in a direct line, nearly due east, in a farther distance of 3½ miles, the Railway gains

THE DRAYTON STATION,

AN INTERMEDIATE ONE, DISTANT FROM BRIGHTON 27 MILES, FROM CHICHESTER 2 MILES.—Journey resumed below.

This is the point of departure for Goodwood, the noble seat and splendid domain of the Duke of Richmond, situate 3 m. distant on right, and of which an account will be found at page 24. of the Brighton Railway.

Continued in a direct line the Railway, in a farther distance of two miles, arrives at

THE CHICHESTER STATION,

A PRINCIPAL ONE, DISTANT FROM BRIGHTON 29 MILES, FROM LONDON 79½ MILES, FROM HASTINGS 61½ MILES.

1¼ m. distant from Chichester on right is Salt Hill[4]; 2 m. distant, Northlands[5]; 2½ m. distant, Oakwood, the very beautiful seat of[6]; 3 m. distant, Stoke House[7]; and 6 m. distant, West Dean House.[8]

[1] Rev. Archdeacon C. Webber.
[2] W. M. Bridger, Esq.
[3] Lord George Lennox.
[4] Zadik Levin, Esq.
[5] C. Crosbie, Esq.
[6] John Baring, Esq.
[7] Sir H. B. Seymour, Bart.
[8] Rev. —— Vernon Harcourt.

CHICHESTER.—The city of Chichester, situated near an arm of the sea, on a gentle eminence, nearly surrounded by the little river Lavant, is a place of great antiquity, dating its origin before the Roman invasion, when it became an important station of those conquerors. The city principally consists of four spacious and well-paved streets, meeting in a centre, and named from their situation after the four cardinal points of the compass. At the end of each street was formerly a gate; and the city is surrounded with a stone wall, supposed, with the exception of the bastions, to be the work of the Romans. Chichester has six parish churches within the walls; it had also two without, but the inhabitants demolished them, to prevent their being occupied by the parliament forces, who besieged the city in the reign of Charles I. One of the churches is within the cathedral, which is the most conspicuous building in the city, the spire being 297 feet high, built of stone, and adorned with pinnacles at its base. This beautiful structure suffered considerably from the fanatics, under the command of Cromwell's generals, who destroyed every thing that was not proof against their fury. At the west end of the middle south aisle of the nave is a fine whole length statue of the late Mr. Huskisson. The council chamber is an edifice raised on arcades, built by subscription in 1738, contiguous to which is the assembly-room, built also by subscription, where assemblies are held during the winter season. Here is likewise a theatre, situated at the lower end of South Street; and the cross in the centre of the city is considered one of the best buildings of the kind in England. Chichester is a county in itself, a bishop's see, and sends two members to parliament. Population 8,512. Inns:— Dolphin Hotel, Anchor Inn, Wheatsheaf Inn, White Horse Inn, and the Fleece Inn; at which, when sojourning, the editor experienced good accommodation at moderate charges.

BRIGHTON RAILWAY, HASTINGS BRANCH.

Quitting the station, and continued for a short distance on the London line, the Hastings branch turns off to the east, and crossing over the London road and the valley by a brick viaduct 330 yards long, 67 feet high, and 30 feet span, the remaining arches, each 30 feet, being 26 in number, pursuing a meandering course, and passing under the Ditchling turnpike road by a tunnel 150 yards long; a tunnel under Palmer Hill about 500 yards long; and a tunnel at Kingstone about 100 yards long; in that way reaches

THE LEWES STATION.

A PRINCIPAL ONE, DISTANT FROM BRIGHTON, 8 MILES; FROM HASTINGS, 24½ MILES.

For an account of Lewes the reader is referred to page 22 of the Brighton Railway.

About 1½ m. before Lewes, on left, near Ashcomb turnpike, is Lewes race-course and a seat of [1]. On left of Lewes is Malling House [2] and Malling Deanery [3], 1½ m. distant from Lewes, on left, is Combe Place [4], and Hamsey Place [5], and 2½ miles distant, Wellingham.[6] On leaving Lewes the railway winds round the base of the Cliffe Hill*, an eminence that rises on left of the line, and taken through a short cutting of about 40 feet deep, and crossing the river Ouze by a drawbridge, in a further distance of about 2¾ miles reaches

THE GLYNDE STATION.

A PRINCIPAL ONE, DISTANT FROM BRIGHTON, 10½ MILES; FROM HASTINGS, 22 MILES.

On left of Glynde Station is Glynde Place. This was formerly the property of the Viscounts Hampden, and bequeathed by John, the last lord, to the Hon. Henry Brand, younger brother of Lord Dacre, of the Hoo, in Hertfordshire, from whom it descended to the present proprietor [7]; 1½ m. distant Glyndbourne [8]; 2 miles distant Middleham.[9]

Glyndbourne was, for about two centuries, the seat of the family of Hay, that produced in the last generation a poet of some celebrity, well known for the deformity of his body, and the elegance of his mind. Wm. Hay, Esq., entered into public life, was a member of parliament, wrote an ingenious essay on Deformity, and celebrated in a poem, after the manner of Cooper's Hill, Mount Caburn, a noble hill in this parish, which commands magnificent views, and afforded him an opportunity of introducing the principal features of this part of the county in verses very often extremely beautiful. The mansion is partly ancient, and partly modern; the lawn, water, and surrounding hills, are very bold and beautiful.

One mile distant on right of Glynde Station is Firle Place,

1, F. Barchard, Esq.   2, Rev. P. G. Crofts.   3, A. S. Green, Esq.
4, Sir H. Shiffner, Bart.   5, Mrs. Guy.   6, John Rickman, Esq.
* The highest summit of this eminence is the southernmost, crowned by a Saxon earthwork, having double trenches: it is denominated Mount Caburn, and affords one of the finest views in the kingdom, of which a long line of the Brighton and Hastings Railway forms a very interesting feature.
7 General the Hon. Henry Trevor.   8, Sir James Langham, Bart.
9, Rev. J. Constable.

the beautiful seat of¹. Firle Place came into the possession of the Gage family by marriage with the heiress of St. Clair, in the reign of Henry VII.

Leaving the Glynde Station the railway continued with a bold sweep, and south-east direction, in a further distance of 5¼ miles arrives at

THE BERWICK STATION.

AN INTERMEDIATE ONE, DISTANT FROM BRIGHTON, 15¼ MILES; FROM HASTINGS, 17¾ MILES. — Journey resumed below.

The railway from the Glynde to the Berwick Station traverses a tract of country, that naked and bare, on the left, is totally devoid of interest, but on right of it is beheld Firle Place, backed by the fine eminence of Firle Hill, the site of a signal station, and Firle beacon, that descending in slopes and sweeps to the valley beneath, forms a very beautiful boundary. Firle Hill rises to a height of 820 feet above the level of the sea, above double the height of St. Paul's Cathedral. Quitting the Berwick Station the railway soon crosses the little river Cuckmere by a drawbridge, and in a further distance of 3¾ miles continued with a gradual sweep, gains

POLEGATE GREEN STATION.

A PRINCIPAL ONE, DISTANT FROM BRIGHTON, 19 MILES; FROM HASTINGS, 13½ MILES; FROM EASTBOURNE, 3½ MILES; FROM HAILSHAM, 3½ MILES.

Passengers are conveyed from Polegate Station to Eastbourne, by a stage coach that regularly attends for that purpose.

Two miles distant from Polegate Green Station on right is Ratton Park.²

The following seats are in the vicinity of Eastbourne: Compton Place³; The Grays⁴; South Field Lodge⁵; The Gore⁶; Larkfield Villa⁷; Chapel House⁸; The Elms⁹; Sea Beach House¹⁰; Rose Cottage.¹¹

Eastbourne is a fashionable sea-bathing place, situated in a valley almost surrounded by hills, which command some very extensive prospects of this part of Sussex. It consists of 4 parts,

---

1. Viscount Gage. 2. Inigo Thomas, Esq. 3. The Honourable Mrs. Cavendish; 4. Nicholas Willard, Esq.; 5. Sir William Domville, Bart; 6. Mrs. Brodie; 7. C. W. Rawdon, Esq.; 8. Henry Mason, Esq.; 9. John Graham, Esq.; 10. Mrs. Henry Ogle; 11. Mrs. Johnson; and a seat of Mrs. Willard.

& of which, near the sea, at the eastern and western extremities of the parish, are denominated Sea Houses and Meades; the others are Southbourne, and Eastbourne, about 1¼ mile from the sea. The bathing here is remarkably good, and it has also the advantage of a chalybeate spring, the water of which is recommended in the same cases as the Bristol waters. A subscription ball-room and library may be reckoned among the amusements of Eastbourne, which is fashionably attended in the summer season. The church, one of the best in the county, is a handsome edifice. At Langley Point, about 1¼ mile eastward of the village, are 2 forts; about 1 mile behind them, on an eminence, is a battery; and from this place eastward the coast is defended by Martello towers. To the west of Eastbourne is Beachy Head, the most stupendous cliff on this coast, being 564 feet perpendicular height, in which are a number of caverns. Population 3,015.

The following are the hotels at Eastbourne: Albion Hotel, Hope and Anchor Hotel, New Inn Hotel, Lamb Inn Hotel.

From Polegate Green Station the railway carried in a direction eastward, and continued in a course resembling Hogarth's line of beauty, reaches in a further distance of 3½ miles

THE WEST HAM AND PEVENSEY STATION.

AN INTERMEDIATE ONE, DISTANT FROM BRIGHTON, 22½ MILES: FROM HASTINGS, 10 MILES.— Journey resumed.

Three and a half miles distant from Pevensey on left is Herstmonceux Park, and the ruins of Herstmonceux Castle, well worthy of a visit by the antiquary, and adjoining it is Windmill Hill, the seat of.*

Pevensey, though now of little note, yet deserves the first place among the villages of the Rape to which it gives name, on account of its ancient importance. From this circumstance we may naturally infer that it was formerly accounted its capital. There can be little doubt that Pevensey owed its ancient prosperity to its favourable situation for commerce as a port; and its subsequent decline to the gradual receding of the sea, from which it now stands at a considerable distance. That it was a place of high antiquity is undeniable. Pevensey is reckoned among the seaports ravaged by Godwin, Earl of Kent, in the time of Edward the Confessor. It is also celebrated in history as the place where William the Conqueror landed with his invading army. The

* Herbert Curteis, Esq., to whom also belong the before-mentioned park and castle.

only relic of the ancient consequence of Pevensey is the castle, on the east side of the town; the name of the builder and the date of its erection are alike unknown; but from the quantity of Roman bricks employed in the work, there is every reason to believe that it was constructed out of some Roman fortress. The external walls, which, with the towers, are pretty entire, to the height of 20 or 25 feet, are circular, and enclose an area of seven acres. The principal entrance is on the west or land side, between two round towers, in which are considerable layers of Roman brick, some single, others double, about 20 feet from the ground, and 4 or 5 asunder.

From Pevensey Station the railway continued across the Pevensey level, and in rear of the line of Martello Towers, seen in front, has a pretty gain of 7 miles to

THE BEXHILL STATION,

AN INTERMEDIATE ONE, DISTANT FROM BRIGHTON 27½ MILES, FROM HASTINGS 5 MILES.

Three miles beyond Bexhill Station the train arrives at

THE ST. LEONARD'S STATION,

A PRINCIPAL ONE, DISTANT FROM BRIGHTON 32½ MILES; FROM HASTINGS 1 MILE.

ST. LEONARD'S.

The entrance to St. Leonard's astonishes and detains the eye of a stranger with the spectacle of a new creation, brought almost simultaneously to perfection, and presenting long and splendid facades, excelling the architecture of Brighton, and nearly equalling the most splendid suburb of the metropolis, the Regent's Park in London. The Marina is the appellation given to the whole sea line of buildings. The architecture of the various piles is very fine, being decorated with Corinthian and Ionic columns, and with long and low piazzas in front of the basements, with occasional breaks also forming squares; and another street of handsome architecture at the back. The style is different from either Kemp Town or Brunswick Terrace at Brighton, and for its especial purpose nothing could have been better conceived. The Esplanade is, we suppose, one of the finest in Europe. Its close contiguity to the sea renders it superior to the western one at

Brighton; to which, its length, however, as a whole is not equal. It is well faced with stone, and not only varied with a grass-plot, but also with flower-beds — a most happy addition. It reminds us more of the esplanade at Weymouth than any other we have seen. The assembly-rooms, in which frequent balls are held, form a grand and elegant structure of the Doric order, consisting of a centre and two wings of considerable length, with an elegant portico at the entrance, and a pediment at the other extremity. One wing is used as a billiard-room, the other as a card-room. The ball-room is spacious and very handsome, with a receding gallery for music, and a coved ceiling.

The slender belfry of the new church has a tolerable appearance in perspective, aided by a commanding situation; but, when seen in front, has a paltry and toy-like appearance. Passing through the very elliptical Doric arch, at the east extremity, we enter upon the sheltered road, under bold cliffs, gradually increasing in grandeur, which leads into the lower town of Hastings, and passing the Priory bridge, and the Pelham sweep of architecture, arrive at the centre beyond the Parade, where the old and narrow streets rise to the extremity on the London road.

Inns: — Victoria Hotel, South Saxon Hotel.

In the vicinity of Hastings are the following seats: — Beauport, Ore Place, Ridge Cottage, Vale Brook.

HASTINGS.

The old part of Hastings, but little altered in its predominant features since it has become a place of resort, although individually many of the houses have been rebuilt, consists of two long streets, called High and All Saints Streets. Between the backs of the houses a small unnoticed brook of clear water, which is an advantage to its vicinity, flows down to the sea. Beyond the opening which leads to the sea, the line of coast immediately rises into lofty cliffs; so that between the Castle Hill, at the entrance under which the Pelham New Buildings and the Parade lie closely sheltered, the body of the town is completely in a hollow, and the height of the two hills is not very dissimilar. The Castle Hill takes a sweep inward at the end of the Parade, forming the valley up which the old streets ascend. The sea-line lies under the hill in a singularly commanded style; the houses seem almost built into the rock, in fact, in one place it has been cut away to receive them; it frowns over them, at a great elevation, with either a despotic or

protecting aid, as the fancy of the spectator chooses to invest it.
The entrance to Hastings by the London Road from Fairlight
Down, is extremely beautiful. It opens on a smooth terrace,
whence is an extensive prospect of Pevensey Bay, Beachy Head,
Bourne Hills, and a wide range of ocean. Advancing farther,
the valley of Hastings is displayed; and at the bottom of the hill
you enter a pleasant shady lane, which leads to the town, consisting of two parallel streets of considerable length, running
nearly north and south, with an opening to the sea; these are
intersected by some lanes intermixed with gardens, while a
suburb extends along the beach. Between the two main streets
runs a small stream of water called the Bourne. The present rage
for building has extended itself to Hastings, which is now rapidly
increasing both in size and population. The town is well paved
and lighted, and from its inclination toward the sea, is very neat
and clean. Here are two churches, St. Clements, and All Saints,
which, within the last half-century, have been united into one
rectory. The town-hall, or court-house, under which is the
market-house, was erected in 1700. This place, the principal
of the cinque ports, once enjoyed the advantage of a good
harbour, formed by a wooden pier, which projected in a south-
east direction, below the site of the present fort. About the
beginning of Queen Elizabeth's reign, this pier was destroyed
by a violent tempest; large pieces of timber, of which it was
composed, and vast stones that formed the foundations, are still
to be seen at low water. The only method of securing vessels
from the fury of the waves at present, is by drawing them up on
the beach, which is here called the Stade; at the west end of this
is a fort mounting 11 twelve pounders, that serves to defend the
town not only against an enemy, but also against the encroachments of the sea in boisterous weather; which nevertheless sometimes occasions considerable damage: the defence of the town,
however, and indeed the whole of this coast, has been still farther
provided for by the erection in appropriate situations of different
batteries, and construction of a range of martello towers that
extend from hence to Eastbourne. The trade of Hastings is
altogether inconsiderable compared with that which it formerly
possessed. The inhabitants are principally engaged in the
fisheries, and a little coasting trade. The former, independent of
an abundance furnished to the town, supplies the London market
with soles, scait, mackerel, and herrings, of which latter, fish to
the amount of 900*l*. have been caught here in a single day. Boat-
building also employs a considerable number of hands, and the
people of this place have gained as high reputation for their skill

in constructing the vessels as for their courage and dexterity in managing them. Hastings, however, derives no inconsiderable emolument from the very great influx of fashionable visitors with which during the bathing season the town is invariably honoured. The promenade, erected by subscription near the sea, is a very great improvement, and its interest is increased by very respectable libraries, furnished with billiard-rooms: they front the sea, and are well supplied with newspapers, magazines, pamphlets, and every literary accommodation. The bathing-machines stand to the westward of the town, close to the promenade, on which is a small building called the bathing room. At low-water a fine level sand extends for a great distance, and the shore has such a gentle ascent, that bathing is rendered safe at any time of the tide; the beach is particularly fine, and the water no where more pure. Convenient warm baths have also been constructed here. The assemblies are held once a week during the season, at the Swan Inn. The romantic walks and rides, and the variety of interesting objects with which the vicinity of Hastings abounds, together with the grandeur of its sea views, and general beauty of the surrounding country, all concur to render it certainly one of the most beautiful watering places in the kingdom.

On a lofty rocky cliff westward of the town, are the remains of a very ancient castle, which approached in shape to two sides of an oblique spherical triangle, with the points rounded off. The area of the castle is about 1¼ acre; and the walls, which are no where entire, are in some places 8 feet thick. History, however, is wholly silent as to the time when this ruined pile was first erected; it is, however, undoubtedly very ancient, perhaps coeval with the time when Arviragus threw off the Roman yoke. Hastings received charters from Edward the Confessor, William the Conqueror, and several subsequent monarchs down to James II.; but it was that of his predecessor which gave the corporation its present form. It is composed of a mayor, jurats, and freemen; is exempted from toll, and is empowered to hold courts of judicature in capital cases. This place sends 2 members to parliament, and has 2 weekly markets on Wednesday and Saturday. Inns.—Albion Hotel, Castle Hotel, Marine Hotel, Royal Oak Hotel, Swan Hotel. Population 11,607.

LONDON:
Printed by A. SPOTTISWOODE,
New-Street-Square.

www.ingramcontent.com/pod-product-compliance
Lightning Source LLC
Chambersburg PA
CBHW062123160426
43191CB00013B/2183